THE U.S.
INTELLIGENCE COMMUNITY

FOURTH EDITION

THE U.S. INTELLIGENCE COMMUNITY

Jeffrey T. Richelson

Westview Press
A Member of the Perseus Books Group

Copyright © 1999 by Jeffrey T. Richelson

Published in 1999 in the United States of America by Westview Press, 5500 Central Avenue, Boulder,
Colorado 80301-2877, and in the United Kingdom by Westview Press, 12 Hid's Copse Road, Cumnor
Hill, Oxford OX2 9JJ

Library of Congress Cataloging-in-Publication Data
Richelson, Jeffrey T.
   The U.S. intelligence community / Jeffrey T. Richelson. — 4th ed.
      p.   cm.
   Includes bibliographical references and index.
   ISBN 0-8133-6893-6 (pbk.)
1. Intelligence service—United States.   I. Title.   II. Title: US
intelligence community.   III. Title: United States intelligence
community.
JK468.I6R53   1999
327.1273—dc21   98-52830
                                                                                          CIP

The paper used in this publication meets the requirements of the American National Standard for Per-
manence of Paper for Printed Library Materials Z39.48-1984.

10   9   8   7   6   5   4   3   2

CONTENTS

TABLES AND ILLUSTRATIONS

Photos

PREFACE

This book represents an attempt to accomplish in one volume what could better be done in several. It attempts to provide a comprehensive and detailed order of battle of the U.S. intelligence community—to describe its collection and analysis organizations, their activities, and the management structure that is responsible for directing and supervising those organizations and activities.

Given the purpose of the book, I do not seek to evaluate the community's effectiveness in performing its varied tasks or to comment on the acceptability, wisdom, or morality of all of its activities. Those are important topics and require far more space than would be available here. In the concluding chapter I do address some of the issues and challenges facing America's intelligence community in the coming century.

The data used in this book come from a variety of sources—interviews; official documents (many of which were obtained under the Freedom of Information Act); books written by former intelligence officers, journalists, and academics; trade and technical publications; newspapers and magazines. The public literature on intelligence is vast and of varying quality, and I have done my best to sort the wheat from the chaff. I have also sought to incorporate the most recent available information at each stage of the production process, to minimize the inevitable discrepancies between the situation as described when the book went to press and the situation when it is actually read. In addition, I have identified sources to the maximum extent possible, while protecting the identities of those individuals who wish to remain anonymous.

The book's structure is largely the same as that of the third edition, with a few exceptions. I have eliminated the "Ocean Surveillance, Space Surveillance, and Nuclear Monitoring" chapter that appeared in the previous three editions. Some of the subjects discussed in that chapter can now be found in the imagery and signals intelligence chapters, particularly the SIGINT chapter. That change reflects the fact that much of the effort of Navy SIGINT assets is directed at targets on shore as well as at sea. Two new chapters—one on MASINT and the other wholly dedicated to space surveillance—focus on the other topics previously discussed in the single chapter. In addition, the internal structure of the chapter on analysis and estimates is based on the types of intelligence rather than on the entities that produced it—reflecting the extent to which analytical products are read by varied consumers.

Two groups of individuals were instrumental in helping me write this book. The work of the freedom of information and public affairs officers who responded to my many hundreds of requests is greatly appreciated. A listing of specific individuals would include one or more from virtually every organization discussed in this book. Some may have been frustrated that supplying one set of requested documents only led to additional requests.

In addition, various journalists, researchers, and others have provided information, documents, suggestions, corrections, and assistance for various editions. Those who can be acknowledged publicly are: Steven Aftergood, Matthew Aid, William Arkin, Desmond Ball, Robert Bolin, William Burrows, Duncan Campbell, Dwayne Day, Seymour Hersh, David Morison, Jay Peterzell, John Pike, Joseph Pittera, John Prados, Owen Wilkes, Marshall Windmiller, Robert Windrem, and several members of the National Security Archive—Tom Blanton, Bill Burr, Kate Doyle, Michael Evans, and Peter Kornbluh.

I would also like to thank the National Security Archive for the multitude of ways in which it provided support and the Center for Defense Information for the use of its extensive library.

Jeffrey T. Richelson

THE U.S.
INTELLIGENCE COMMUNITY

1

INTELLIGENCE

The United States government includes a substantial number of officials—individuals who make policy as well as ones who implement it—who require foreign intelligence to perform their duties. Only if those individuals are sufficiently informed about the state of the world and the likely consequences of policies and actions can they be expected to make intelligent decisions.

The individuals and institutions with the most prominent need for foreign intelligence are those concerned with making and implementing national security policy. Hence, the president and his national security adviser, the National Security Council (NSC) and its staff, the Departments of State and Defense, the Joint Chiefs of Staff (JCS), and the military services are the most visible consumers of foreign intelligence. In 1995, the Under Secretary of State told the Senate Select Committee on Intelligence:

> Everyday I need to know about the military and political developments in all corners of the former Yugoslavia, about the stability of the regime in North Korea, about the origins of the latest terrorist bomb in France, about the possible outcome of elections in Haiti or Russia, about potential starvation in the Sudan, and about Iran or Iraq's latest attempts to circumvent sanctions.[1]

In addition, policymakers with responsibilities in the areas of international economics, trade and technology transfer, energy, the environment, and public health may also require foreign intelligence. In the 1970s it became evident that foreign actions with respect to oil could have a dramatic impact on the well-being of the United States. In his role as chairman of the House Permanent Select Committee on Intelligence, Edward Boland noted that "many believe . . . that energy and related economic problems can threaten us more deeply and affect our national security more rapidly than any change in the military picture short of war itself."[2]

Clearly, the availability of foreign energy resources as well as the stability of the dollar can be influenced by the actions of foreign governments and groups. Foreign actions concerning environmental matters are of importance to officials of the

Environmental Protection Agency (EPA). As a result, the EPA requires intelligence regarding environmental accidents, foreign government compliance with international environmental obligations, and the status of environmentally sensitive areas. With respect to compliance, the EPA is interested in the disposal of nuclear wastes, illegal ocean dumping, and the smuggling of prohibited animals and animal products. Environmentally sensitive topics of concern to the EPA include tropical rain forest destruction, antarctic pollution sources, and arctic ice conditions.[3]

The National Aeronautics and Space Administration (NASA) is interested in foreign technology developments and foreign space programs and is also concerned with space debris that might threaten its manned and unmanned spacecraft. The Department of Agriculture has been concerned with foreign government compliance with negotiated agricultural agreements, the development of global trading blocks, agricultural production and supply, and food requirements of countries with chronic food deficits.[4]

INTELLIGENCE

Intelligence can be defined as the "product resulting from the collection, processing, integration, analysis, evaluation and interpretation of available information concerning foreign countries or areas."[5] Collection can be defined as the purposeful acquisition of any information that might be desired by an analyst, consumer, or operator. Collection activity can take any of several overlapping forms: open source collection, clandestine collection, human source collection, and technical collection.

Open source collection includes the acquisition of material in the public domain: radio and television broadcasts, newspapers, magazines, technical and scholarly journals, books, government reports, documents and other material to be found on the Internet, and reports by foreign service officers and defense attachés concerning public activities. The extent to which open source collection yields valuable information will vary greatly with the nature of the targeted society and the subject involved. The information might be collected by human sources—individuals who buy books and journals or observe military parades—or by technical means—recording television and radio programs.

Clandestine collection involves the acquisition of data that are not publicly available. As with open source collection, both human and technical resources may be employed. The traditional human spy may be employed to provide sensitive political, military, or economic information. Alternatively, technical collection systems can be used to photograph military installations, intercept a wide variety of communications and electronic signals, or detect the infrared, acoustic, and other signatures of weapons systems or events.

Great secrecy and sensitivity characterize human source clandestine collection. Although much technical collection is also clandestine, secrecy is not always as vital in technical collection as it is in human collection. Foreign nations are well aware that the United States operates extensive space imagery and signals intelligence (SIGINT) programs. Even those nations capable of tracking the movements of U.S. spacecraft are limited in the denial and deception measures they can employ. As a result, the ability to effectively collect the required data does not always require secrecy with regard to the identity and location of the collection system. In contrast, a human asset whose identity becomes known to the foreign security service of the targeted nation will soon be arrested or become the channel for disinformation.

Analysis involves the integration of collected information—that is, raw intelligence from all sources—into finished intelligence. The finished intelligence product might be a simple statement of facts, an evaluation of the capabilities of another nation's military forces, or a projection of the likely course of political events in another nation.

Strictly speaking, intelligence activities involve only the collection and analysis of information and its transformation into intelligence; however, counterintelligence (CI) and covert action are intertwined with intelligence activity. Counterintelligence encompasses all information acquisition and activity designed to assess foreign intelligence and security services and neutralize hostile services. These activities involve clandestine and open source collection as well as analysis of information concerning the structure and operations of foreign services. Such collection and analysis, with respect to the technical collection activities of hostile services, can be employed to guide denial and deception operations. Counterintelligence may also involve the direct penetration and disruption of hostile intelligence activities.

Traditionally, covert action, also known as "special activities," includes any operation designed to influence foreign governments, persons, or events in support of the sponsoring government's foreign policy objectives, while keeping the sponsoring government's *support* of the operation secret. Whereas in clandestine collection the emphasis is on keeping the activity secret, in covert action it is on keeping the sponsorship secret.

There are several distinct types of covert action: black propaganda (propaganda that purports to emanate from a source other than the true one); gray propaganda (in which true sponsorship is not acknowledged); paramilitary or political actions designed to overthrow, undermine, or support a regime; paramilitary or political actions designed to counteract a regime's attempts to procure or develop advanced weaponry; support (aid, arms, training) of individuals or organizations (government components, political parties, labor unions, and publishing concerns); economic operations; disinformation; and assassination.

THE INTELLIGENCE CYCLE

It is important to put the collection and analysis activities conducted by various intelligence units into proper perspective—that is, to relate those activities to the requirements and needs of the decisionmakers and to the use made of the finished intelligence product. That objective is achieved through the concept of the "intelligence cycle." The intelligence cycle is the process by which information is acquired, converted into finished intelligence, and made available to policymakers. Generally, the cycle comprises five steps: planning and direction, collection, processing, analysis and production, and dissemination.[6]

The planning and direction process involves the management of the entire intelligence effort, from the identification of the need for data to the final delivery of an intelligence product to a consumer. The process may be initiated by requests or requirements for intelligence based on the needs of the president, the Departments of State, Defense, and Treasury, or other consumers. In some cases, the requests and requirements become institutionalized. Thus, the intelligence community need not be reminded to collect information on nuclear proliferation, Chinese nuclear forces, or developments in Mexico.

Collection, as indicated above, involves the gathering, by a variety of means, of raw data from which finished intelligence will be produced. Processing is concerned with the conversion of the vast amount of information coming into the system to a form suitable for the production of finished intelligence. It involves interpretation and measurement of images and signals, language translation, decryption, sorting by subject matter, and data reduction.

The analysis and production process entails the conversion of basic information into finished intelligence. It includes the integration, evaluation, and analysis of all available data and the preparation of various intelligence products. Because the "raw intelligence" that is collected is often fragmentary and at times contradictory, specialists are needed to give it meaning and significance. The final step in the cycle, dissemination, involves the distribution of the finished intelligence to the consumers—the policymakers (and operators) whose needs triggered the process.

Like any model, the outline of the intelligence cycle is a simplification of the real world. As noted above, certain requirements become standing requirements. Similarly, policymakers do not specify, except in rare cases, particular items of information to be collected. Rather, they indicate a desire for reports on, for example, Chinese strategic forces or the political situation in Israel. The collectors are given the responsibility of determining how to obtain the information necessary to prepare such reports. In addition, the collection agencies have certain internal needs to acquire information to provide for their continued operations—information related to counterintelligence and security and information that will be useful in potential future operations.

It should also be noted that decisionmakers, particularly in the midst of a crisis, may require only processed intelligence instead of fully analyzed intelligence. Thus, in the midst of the Cuban Missile Crisis, the most important intelligence was purely factual reporting concerning Soviet activities in Cuba and on the high seas.

TYPES OF INTELLIGENCE

One step in understanding how specific varieties of foreign intelligence can be useful to government officials is to consider the different varieties of intelligence—political, military, scientific and technical, economic, sociological, and environmental.

Political intelligence encompasses both foreign and domestic politics. Clearly, the foreign policies of other nations have an impact on the United States. A variety of issues might be involved: support or opposition to the expansion of the North Atlantic Treaty Organization (NATO), a nation's political and economic relations with North Korea or Iran, attitudes and policies concerning the Middle East, the support of revolutionary groups, and perceptions of U.S. leadership.

The domestic politics of other nations—whether friendly, neutral, or hostile—are also of significant concern to the United States. A recent study by the National Intelligence Council observed that "most conflicts today are internal, not between states. This trend will continue."[7] The resolution of such conflicts—whether by coup, election, or civil war—can affect the orientation of that nation in the world, the regional balance of power, the accessibility of critical resources to the United States, or the continued presence of U.S. military bases.

Thus, the outcome of elections in Russia or Israel can have a dramatic impact on U.S. relations with those nations. Likewise, the resolution of the internal conflict in Iran in 1979 deprived the United States of oil, a military ally, and critical intelligence facilities from which Soviet missile telemetry could be monitored. And developments within China, such as the repression of protesters at Tienanmen Square in June 1989, can have a major impact on the state of U.S.-Chinese relations.

Military intelligence is useful and required for a variety of reasons. In order to determine its own military requirements—whether nuclear, conventional, or special operations—the United States must know the capabilities of potential adversaries. In addition, military intelligence is also required to assess the need and impact of any military aid the United States may be asked to provide. Further, military intelligence is required to assess the balance of power between pairs of nations (e.g., India-Pakistan, North Korea–South Korea) whose interactions can affect U.S. interests.

Scientific and technical intelligence includes both civilian- and military-related scientific and technical developments. A nation's ability to employ modern agricultural methods or efficiently extract energy resources may affect that country's stability, which may, in turn, affect the United States. In many cases, technological developments that occur in the civilian sector have military applications. Examples include computer technology, biotechnology, mirrors and optical systems, and lasers. Hence, intelligence concerning a nation's progress in those areas or its ability to absorb foreign-produced technology in those areas is relevant to its potential military capability.

One aspect of scientific and technical intelligence that has been of constant concern for more than fifty years is atomic energy intelligence. Whether the announced purpose of a nation's atomic energy activities has been civilian or military, those activities have received a high intelligence priority. In addition to the obvious need to determine whether various foreign nations are developing nuclear weapons, there also has been a perceived need to acquire secret intelligence in support of decisionmaking concerning applications for nuclear technology exports. In 1947, the first Director of Central Intelligence (DCI) noted that the United States "cannot rely on information submitted by a licensee" and that it was necessary for the United States to "determine actual use, [to] endeavor to discover secondary diversions."[8]

Economic intelligence is also of great importance. One component is the strengths and vulnerabilities of national economies. Knowledge of the strengths may be important in understanding their capacity for conflict, whereas knowledge of their vulnerabilities may be important in assessing threats to stability as well as the likelihood that economic sanctions will produce a change in policy.

Another component is the availability and pricing of key resources, from oil to an assortment of metals and minerals. In addition, economic intelligence is concerned with the European Economic Community and other economic organizations, national fiscal monetary policy, and international payments mechanisms. Economic intelligence also concerns topics such as sanctions busting, money laundering, terrorist financing, bribery and corruption, and economic espionage.[9]

Sociological intelligence concerns group relations within a particular nation. The relations between groups, whether they be ethnic, religious, or political groups, can have a significant impact on a nation's stability as well as on the nature of its foreign policy—as has been demonstrated in recent years by events in the former Yugoslavia, in Africa, and in Russia.

TARGETS

Despite the collapse of the Soviet Union there remains an impressive array of intelligence targets for the U.S. intelligence community to monitor in the post–Cold War world. These targets can be grouped into three sometimes overlapping categories:

- transnational targets
- regional targets
- national targets

Transnational targets extend across regions and may require new approaches to the collection and analysis of relevant intelligence, as well as to the manner in which the intelligence effort is organized. Among the most prominent transnational targets are proliferation of weapons of mass destruction, international terrorism, illicit arms trafficking, and international crime and narcotics trafficking.[10]

Although attempts to develop or procure weapons of mass destruction are undertaken by individual governments, the efforts undertaken by Iraq, Iran, Pakistan, and Libya make use of indigenous capabilities as well as a significant international supplier network and the assistance of foreign governments. This contrasts sharply with the largely indigenous manner in which the Soviet Union and China developed their nuclear arsenals.

Iraq received key nuclear-related equipment from corporations in Britain (plutonium), Switzerland (metal casings), France (research reactors), Italy (plutonium separation utility), South America (uranium ore concentrate), Finland (copper coils), Japan (carbon fiber), Africa (uranium ore concentrate), and the United States (power supply units). Meanwhile, Pakistan has received considerable assistance in its nuclear program from the People's Republic of China.[11]

Terrorist groups, whether located in Middle East or Asia, have killed, maimed, and destroyed property far from their home nation or region. Further, such groups, unlike states, are capable of relocating when a host government decides their presence is too burdensome or their operations at a particular location become the target of retaliation. Likewise, the tentacles of South American or Asian drug cartels as well as the Russian Mafia extend far beyond the borders of their home territories.[12]

Other transnational concerns include developments in information warfare, the state of the environment (from the fear of global warming to the impact of toxic waste dumping in the oceans), uncontrolled refugee migrations, population growth, communications, the spread of diseases such as AIDS, and international economic activity.[13]

The concept of regional targets recognizes that developments in a particular area of the world may be produced not only by distinct choices of individual governments but as the result of interaction between governments. Clearly, a war in the Balkans, the Middle East, Southwest Asia, or on the Korean peninsula would represent the most violent of such regional targets. Regional targets, which increase the chance of war, include border clashes, arms races, and multi-nation movements of weapons and troops. Thus, the criteria for U.S. arms transfer policy include the requirement to take into account "consistency with U.S. regional stability interests, especially when considering transfers involving power projection capability or introduction of a system which may foster increased tension or contribute to an arms race."[14]

Regional activity of interest to the U.S. intelligence community may extend beyond governmental activities. The Asian financial crisis of 1997 was of concern to U.S. officials, for it had the potential to affect internal political developments, the foreign trade activities of a number of nations, and, ultimately, the U.S. economy.

National targets are the most traditional targets and still require a significant commitment of resources. All nations whose policies can have a significant impact on the United States, from the friendliest to the most hostile, represent "targets"— although the type of information required and the means employed to acquire it will vary considerably.

With respect to many countries the intelligence requirements may be substantial. Even after the collapse of the Soviet Union and the end of the Cold War, Russia is still a significant object of concern to U.S. national security officials—and hence a target of intelligence activities, ranging from open source collection to human intelligence to various forms of technical collection.

Topics of concern to U.S. officials concerning Russia include: Boris Yeltsin's health and behavior, the personalities and views of key Russians, the prospects for Russian democracy, the state of the economy, organized crime and corruption, the security of Russian nuclear weapons, the state of its armed forces, the status of its strategic weapons programs, its arms sales and technology transfer activities, its export control system, its compliance with arms control treaties, its policy toward Bosnia, NATO, China, and other entities, and its intelligence activities targeted on the United States.[15]

The above survey only represents a small sampling of the targets of U.S. intelligence collection. To further illustrate the target set, Table 1.1 lists some of the topics concerning foreign developments about which the Senate Select Committee on Intelligence queried the Director of Central Intelligence in 1997, topics that are also undoubtedly of concern to the president, the NSC, and the State and Defense Departments.

THE UTILITY OF INTELLIGENCE

The utility of intelligence activity, here narrowly construed to mean collection and analysis, depends on the extent to which it aids national, departmental, and military service decisionmakers. Two questions arise in this regard: In what ways does intelligence aid decisionmakers, and what attributes make intelligence useful? With respect to the first question, five distinct areas exist in which intelligence can be useful to national decisionmakers: policymaking, planning, conflict situations (ranging from negotiations to war), warning, and monitoring treaty compliance.

In their policymaking roles, national decisionmakers set the basic outlines of foreign, defense, and international economic policy, as well as decide specifics of key issues. Their need for intelligence in order to make sound decisions is summed up in the report of the Rockefeller Commission:

> Intelligence is information gathered for policymakers which illuminates the range of choices available to them and enables them to exercise judgment. Good intelligence will not necessarily lead to wise policy choices. But without sound intelligence, national policy decisions and actions cannot effectively respond to actual conditions and reflect the best national interests or adequately protect . . . national security.[16]

In addition to its value in policymaking, intelligence is vital to the specific decisions needed to implement policies and decisions that might be labeled planning decisions. Some planning decisions may be concerned with the development and deployment of new weapons systems. It has been noted that "timely, accurate, and detailed intelligence is a vital element in establishing requirements and priorities

TABLE 1.1   Foreign Topics of Interest to the SSCI, 1997

Russian military research and development
Russia's reliance on nuclear weapons
Russia's safeguarding of nuclear materials
Organized crime and the Russian election
Chinese proliferation
China's strategic modernization
Hong Kong's future
Chinese foreign policy
China's population
China and Taiwan
Risk of nuclear war between India and Pakistan
Stability of Indonesia
North Korea as a continuing threat
The North Korean Framework Agreement
North Korean military capabilities
The North Korean economy
The PLO and the Middle East peace process
Saddam's hold on power
Saddam's goal of dominating Kuwait
Saddam Hussein's family
The Dhahran bombing
Iranian involvement in international organized crime
Iran and Iraq
Iranian forces in Bosnia
Developments in Serbia
Future of the Iranian regime
Libya's chemical weapons program
Taliban militia in Afghanistan
The situation in Mexico
Fidel Castro's hold on power
Cuban nuclear reactor
Peace in Guatemala
Haiti and the Preval government
Haitian National Police's Special Investigative Unit
Former President Aristide's role in Haiti
Haitian human rights abuses
Political problems in Colombia
Terrorist situation in Peru
Shifting tactics in narcotics trafficking
Missile threats to the United States
Proliferation of ballistic missile systems
International organized crimes
Developments in international terrorism
Environmental threats to the United States
Smuggling components of weapons of mass destruction

SOURCE: U.S. Congress, Senate Select Committee on Intelligence, *Current and Projected National Security Threats to the United States* (Washington, D.C.: U.S. Government Printing Office, 1997), pp. 60–97.

for new systems. Intelligence provides much of the rationale for planning and initiating RDT&E (Research, Development, Test, and Evaluation) efforts and continues to impact these efforts throughout the development and system life cycle."[17]

One incident illustrating the role of intelligence in weapons development occurred in 1968, when the U.S. Navy monitored a member of the oldest class of Soviet nuclear submarines traveling faster than 34 miles per hour, with apparent power to spare. That speed exceeded previous Central Intelligence Agency estimates for the submarine and led the CIA to order a full-scale revision of speed estimates for Soviet submarines. The revised estimates also provoked one of the largest construction programs in the history of the U.S. Navy—the construction of the SSN 688-class attack submarine.[18]

At the same time, intelligence can help save substantial sums of money by avoiding unneeded research and development and deployment programs. Several of the CIA's Soviet human assets, including Peter Popov, Adolf G. Tolkachev, and Dmitri Polyakov, have provided information that cumulatively saved the United States billions of dollars in research and development costs. The first successful U.S. reconnaissance satellite system, code-named CORONA, produced information that eliminated fears of a missile gap—and thus permitted U.S. deployment of strategic missiles to be capped at a lower level than otherwise would have been possible.[19]

Another set of planning decisions involves the development of war plans. In the months between the Iraqi invasion of Kuwait (August 1990) and the beginning of Operation Desert Storm (January 1991), the United States collected a massive quantity of intelligence about Iraqi nuclear, chemical, and biological weapons programs, electrical power networks, ballistic missiles, air defense systems, ground forces, and air forces. The data collected allowed for development and implementation of a war plan based on the most up-to-date information that could be gathered.

Other decisions aided by intelligence include the suspension or resumption of foreign aid, the employment of trade sanctions and embargoes, and attempts to block the transfer of commodities related to nuclear or ballistic missile proliferation. Intelligence might be able to tell the decisionmaker(s) the likely effects of such actions, including the reactions of those nations targeted by the decision. The Carter administration went ahead with the planned sale of planes to Saudi Arabia in part as a result of intelligence indicating that if the United States backed out of the deal the Saudis would simply buy French planes.[20]

In 1992, the United States, based on intelligence indicating a "suspicious procurement pattern" by Iran, acted to prevent the sale of equipment that would have allowed that nation to begin manufacturing nuclear weapons. Argentina halted certain sales to Iran after the United States expressed concern that the equipment in question would have allowed Iran to convert natural uranium into precursor forms of highly enriched uranium. Similarly, the United States successfully lobbied the People's Republic of China to halt the sale of a large nuclear reactor that would have included a supply of enriched fuel and would have permitted Iran to conduct research related to the nuclear fuel cycle.[21]

In January 1998, National Security Agency intercepts of communications between a senior Iranian official and mid-level counterparts in Beijing indicated that Iran was negotiating to purchase "a lifelong supply" of a chemical that could be used to transform naturally occurring uranium to the highly enriched form required for nuclear weapons. Senior Chinese officials halted the sale after being contacted by U.S. officials.[22]

Intelligence is also useful in a variety of conflict situations, most prominently combat. Indeed, "support to military operations"—including combat operations as well as planning and exercise activities—has become a major priority of U.S. intelligence. Regardless of how well-developed a war plan is, combat forces require intelligence on the movements and actions of enemy forces as well as on the impact of air and other attacks against enemy facilities and troops. Thus, even after months of extensive collection prior to Operation Desert Storm, the United States still needed to conduct an intense intelligence collection campaign during the conflict.

Conflict situations in which intelligence is of value need not be exclusively of a military nature, however. Any situation where nations have at least partially conflicting interests—such as in arms control negotiations, trade negotiations, or international conferences—would qualify. Intelligence can indicate how far the other negotiator can be pushed and the extent to which a position must be modified to be adopted. In 1969 the United States intercepted Japanese communications concerning the negotiations between the United States and Tokyo over the reversion of Okinawa to Japanese control.[23]

Intelligence can also provide warning of upcoming hostile or unfavorable actions—which might include military, terrorist, or other action to be taken against the decisionmaker's nation or against another country that the decisionmaker is interested in protecting. Sufficient advance notice allows defenses to be prepared, responses to be considered and implemented, and preemptive actions (diplomatic or military) to be taken to forestall or negate the action. Thus, in 1980, on the basis of intelligence from a human source, President Jimmy Carter warned Soviet General Secretary Leonid Brezhnev of the danger of invading Poland. In March 1991, on the basis of communications intelligence indicating Iraqi intentions to use gas against rebel forces, the United States warned the Iraqis that such an action would not be tolerated.[24]

Intelligence is also necessary to assess whether other nations are in compliance with various international obligations. The United States is concerned, for example, with whether Russia and China are complying with arms control agreements currently in force. Intelligence is also vital in detecting violations of agreements and treaties limiting nuclear proliferation and nuclear testing. In 1993 it was reported that the United States was concerned with China's apparent violation of its pledge not sell M-11 missiles to Pakistan.[25]

The overall utility of intelligence in regard to military matters was concisely summarized by the Eisenhower administration's Technological Capabilities Panel:

If intelligence can uncover a new military threat, we may take steps to meet it. If intelligence can reveal an opponent's specific weakness, we may prepare to exploit it. With good intelligence we can avoid wasting our resources by arming for the wrong danger at the wrong time. Beyond this, in the broadest sense, intelligence underlies our estimate of the enemy and thus helps guide our political strategy.[26]

For maximum utility, the intelligence must not only address relevant subjects but also possess the attributes of quality and timeliness. Unless all relevant information is marshaled when assessing intelligence on a subject, the quality of the finished product may suffer. Covertly obtained intelligence should not be assessed in isolation from overtly obtained intelligence. As Professor H. Trevor-Roper observed:

Secret intelligence is the continuation of open intelligence by other means. So long as governments conceal a part of their activities, other governments, if they wish to base their policy on full and correct information, must seek to penetrate the veil. This inevitably entails varying methods. But, however the means may vary, the end must still be the same. It is to complement the results of what for convenience, we may call "public" intelligence: that is, the intelligence derived from the rational study of public or at least available sources. Intelligence is, in fact, indivisible.[27]

In addition to being based on all relevant information, the assessment process must be objective. As former Secretary of State Henry Kissinger told the U.S. Senate in 1973: "Anyone concerned with national policy must have a profound interest in making sure that intelligence guides, and does not follow, national policy."[28]

Further, intelligence must reach decisionmakers in good time for them to act decisively—either by warning a foreign government before it is irrevocably committed to a particular course of action (whether diplomatic or military) or by ordering actions to undermine or negate such actions.

THE INTELLIGENCE COMMUNITY

The U.S. intelligence community has been precisely, but not always identically, defined in a number of government publications, directives, and regulations—most of which do not reflect the recent changes in the intelligence community. However, based on the traditional definitions the following organizations would be considered part of today's intelligence community: the CIA, the National Security Agency, the National Reconnaissance Office, the National Imagery and Mapping Agency, the Defense Intelligence Agency, the Bureau of Intelligence and Research of the State Department, the intelligence elements of the military services, the FBI, the Drug Enforcement Administration, and the intelligence components of the Department of Energy and the Department of the Treasury.

Also important to consider are the intelligence components of the unified commands and the intelligence elements of the Department of Commerce. These intelligence elements, along with those mentioned directly above, can be grouped into five categories:

- national intelligence organizations
- Department of Defense intelligence organizations
- military service intelligence organizations
- the intelligence components of the unified commands
- civilian intelligence organizations

Notes

1. Statement of Under Secretary of State Peter Tarnoff to the Senate Select Committee on Intelligence, *Hearing on Intelligence in Support of Foreign and National Security Policy in a Post–Cold War World,* September 20, 1995, p. 3.

2. U.S. Congress, House Permanent Select Committee on Intelligence, *Intelligence on the World Energy Future* (Washington, D.C.: U.S. Government Printing Office, 1979), p. 2.

3. Environmental Protection Agency, "EPA NSR–29 Intelligence Requirements," May 14, 1992.

4. National Aeronautics and Space Administration, "NSR–29 Intelligence Requirements," January 17, 1992; "Space Surveillance Network NASA Support Requirements Matrix," attachment to Daniel S. Goldin, Administrator, NASA to General Howell M. Estes III, August 27, 1997; Department of Agriculture, "NSR–29 Intelligence Requirements," January 15, 1992.

5. Joint Chiefs of Staff, *U.S. Department of Defense Dictionary of Military Terms* (New York: Arco Publishing, 1988), p. 183.

6. Central Intelligence Agency, *Intelligence: The Acme of Skill,* n.d., pp. 6–7; Central Intelligence Agency, *Fact Book on Intelligence,*1993, pp. 10–11.

7. National Intelligence Council, *Global Trends 2010* (Washington, D.C.: NIC, 1997), p. 1.

8. Sidney Souers, "Atomic Energy Intelligence," RG 218 (Joint Chiefs of Staff), File 131, July 1, 1947, Military Reference Branch, National Archives and Records Administration.

9. U.S. Congress, Senate Select Committee on Intelligence, *Current and Projected National Security Threats to the United States and Its Interests Abroad* (Washington, D.C.: U.S. Government Printing Office, 1997), p. 92.

10. For discussions of various transnational threats, see: Hans A. Binnendijk and Patrick L. Clawson, eds., *1997 Strategic Assessment: Flashpoints and Force Structure* (Washington, D.C.: National Defense University, 1997), pp. 185–228; Office of the Secretary of Defense, *Proliferation: Threat and Response* (Washington, D.C.: U.S. Government Printing Office, November 1997); U.S. Congress, Senate Select Committee on Intelligence, *Current and Projected National Security Threats to the United States,* pp. 7–11, 22–23.

11. R. Jeffrey Smith and Glenn Frankel, "Saddam's Nuclear-Weapons Dream," *Washington Post,* October 13, 1991, pp. A1, A44–A45; Michael Wines, "U.S. Is Building up a Picture of Vast Iraqi Atom Program," *New York Times,* September 22, 1991, p. A8; William E. Burrows and Robert Windrem, *Critical Mass: The Dangerous Race for Superweapons in a Fragmenting World* (New York: Simon & Schuster, 1994), pp. 378–402; 500th MI Brigade, U.S.

Army Intelligence and Security Command, "Pakistani Use of Chinese Nuclear Weapons Test Facilities," June 19, 1991.

12. See Department of State, *Patterns of Global Terrorism 1996* (Washington, D.C.: U.S. Government Printing Office, 1997); U.S. Congress, House Committee on International Relations, *The Threat from Russian Organized Crime* (Washington, D.C.: U.S. Government Printing Office, 1996); Roger Medd and Frank Goldstein, "International Terrorism on the Eve of a New Millennium," *Studies in Conflict and Terrorism* 20, no. 3 (July-September 1997): 281–316.

13. Binnendijk and Clawson, *1997 Strategic Assessment: Flashpoints and Force Structure*, pp. 209–228; Richard Smith, "The Intelligence Community and the Environment: Capabilities and Future Missions," *Environmental Change and Security Project Report* 2 (Spring 1996): 103–108.

14. The White House, Office of the Press Secretary, "Criteria for Decisionmaking on U.S. Arms Exports," February 17, 1995, p. 1.

15. Some of these concerns are mentioned in U.S. Congress, Senate Select Committee on Intelligence, *Current and Projected National Security Threats to the United States*, passim; and U.S. Congress, Senate Committee on Governmental Affairs, *Compilation of Hearings on National Security Issues* (Washington, D.C.: U.S. Government Printing Office, 1998), pp. 285–333.

16. Commission on CIA Activities within the United States, *Report to the President* (Washington, D.C.: U.S. Government Printing Office, 1975), p. 6.

17. HQ USAF, ACS, I INOI 80–1, "The Intelligence Role in Research, Development, Test and Evaluation (RDT&E)," January 18, 1985.

18. Patrick Tyler, "The Rise and Fall of the SSN 688," *Washington Post*, September 21, 1986, pp. A1, A18.

19. On Popov, Polyakov, and Tolkachev, see Jeffrey T. Richelson, *A Century of Spies: Intelligence in the Twentieth Century* (New York: Oxford University Press, 1995), pp. 257–258, 269, 272, 395; David Wise, *Nightmover: How Aldrich Ames Sold the CIA to the KGB for $4.6 Million* (New York: HarperCollins, 1995), pp. 59–66, 105–106, 124, 271, 327. On CORONA, see Dwayne A. Day, John Lodgson, and Brian Latell, eds., *Eye in the Sky: The Story of the CORONA Spy Satellites* (Washington, D.C.: Smithsonian Institution Press, 1998); Curtis Peebles, *The CORONA Project* (Annapolis, Md.: Naval Institute Press, 1997).

20. Zbigniew Brzezinski, *Power and Principle: Memoirs of the National Security Adviser, 1977–1981* (New York: Farrar, Straus, and Giroux, 1983), p. 248.

21. Steve Coll, "U.S. Halted Nuclear Bid by Iran," *Washington Post*, November 17, 1992, pp. A1, A30.

22. Barton Gellman and John Pomfret, "U.S. Action Stymied China Sale to Iran," *Washington Post*, March 13, 1998, pp. A1, A20.

23. Seymour Hersh, *The Price of Power: Kissinger in the Nixon White House* (New York: Summit, 1983), p. 103.

24. Benjamin Weiser, "A Question of Loyalty," *Washington Post Magazine*, December 13, 1992, pp. 9ff.; Patrick E. Tyler, "U.S. Said to Plan Bombing of Iraqis if They Gas Rebels," *New York Times*, March 10, 1991, pp. 1, 15.

25. Ann Devroy and R. Jeffrey Smith, "U.S. Evidence 'Suggests' China Breaks Arms Pact," *Washington Post*, May 18, 1993, p. A9; Douglas Jehl, "China Breaking Missile Pledge, U.S. Aides Say," *New York Times*, May 6, 1993, pp. A1, A6; John M. Goshko, "U.S. Warns China of Sanctions of Missile Exports to Pakistan," *Washington Post*, July 26, 1993, p. A10; "Psst!

Want to Buy a Missile?" *Newsweek*, September 6, 1993, p. 28; R. Jeffrey Smith, "Ukraine Begins to Dismantle Nuclear Missiles Aimed at U.S.," *Washington Post*, July 28, 1993, p. A13.

26. James J. Killian Jr., *Sputnik, Scientists, and Eisenhower: A Memoir of the First Special Assistant to the President for Science and Technology* (Cambridge, Mass.: MIT Press, 1977), p. 80.

27. Hugh Trevor-Roper, *The Philby Affair–Espionage, Treason and Secret Services* (London: Kimber, 1968), p. 66.

28. U.S. Congress, Senate Committee on Foreign Relations, *Nomination of Henry A. Kissinger* (Washington, D.C.: U.S. Government Printing Office, 1973). For evidence that Kissinger did not always follow his own advice, see Hersh, *The Price of Power*, pp. 529–560.

2

NATIONAL INTELLIGENCE ORGANIZATIONS

Over twenty years ago an internal National Security Council (NSC) study noted that "U.S. intelligence is unique in the world for its state of the art, the scope of its activities, and the extraordinary range and variety of organizations and activities that constitute its consumership."[1] That judgment remains just as valid today.

The United States collects information via reconnaissance satellites, aircraft, ships, signals intercept and seismic ground stations, radar, and undersea surveillance, as well as through the traditional overt and clandestine human sources. It processes and analyzes the information collected, using the most advanced computers and a variety of specially developed techniques for extracting a maximum of information from the data. The total cost of these activities is approximately $27 billion per year.[2]

Given this wide range of activity and the large number of intelligence consumers, it is not surprising that a plethora of organizations are involved in intelligence activities. Of these organizations, four are considered to be national intelligence organizations—in that they perform intelligence functions on behalf of the entire government (rather than just a department or military service). Their activities provide intelligence for national-level policymakers, and they are responsive to direction by supra-departmental authority. The four organizations are: the Central Intelligence Agency (CIA), the National Security Agency (NSA), the National Reconnaissance Office (NRO), and the National Imagery and Mapping Agency (NIMA).

CENTRAL INTELLIGENCE AGENCY

World War II resulted in the creation of America's first central intelligence organization—the Office of Strategic Services (OSS). OSS functions included traditional espionage, covert action (ranging from propaganda to sabotage), counterintelligence, and intelligence analysis. The OSS represented a revolution in United States intelligence, not only because of the varied functions performed by a single, national agency, but because of the breadth of its intelligence interests and its use of scholars to produce finished intelligence.[3]

In the aftermath of World War II, the Office of Strategic Services was disbanded—officially closing down on October 1, 1945, as ordered by President Harry S. Truman. The X-2 (counterintelligence) and secret intelligence branches were transferred to the War Department to compose the Strategic Services Unit, and the Research and Analysis Branch was relocated in the State Department.[4]

At virtually the same time that he ordered the termination of OSS, Truman authorized studies of the intelligence structure required by the United States in the post–World War II world. The result was the creation of the National Intelligence Authority (NIA) and its operational element, the Central Intelligence Group (CIG). In addition to its initial responsibility of coordinating and synthesizing the reports produced by the military service intelligence agencies and the FBI, the CIG was soon assigned the task of clandestine intelligence collection.[5]

As part of a general consideration of national security needs, the question of intelligence organization was addressed in the National Security Act of 1947. The act established the Central Intelligence Agency as an independent agency within the Executive Office of the President to replace the CIG. According to the act, the CIA was to have five functions:

1. to advise the National Security Council in matters concerning such intelligence activities of the government departments and agencies as relate to national security
2. to make recommendations to the National Security Council for the coordination of such intelligence activities of the departments and agencies of the government as relate to national security
3. to correlate and evaluate the intelligence relating to national security, and to provide for the appropriate dissemination of such intelligence within the Government, using, where appropriate, existing agencies and facilities
4. to perform for the benefit of existing intelligence agencies such additional services of common concern as the National Security Council determines can be more effectively accomplished centrally
5. to perform other such functions and duties related to intelligence affecting the national security as the National Security Council may from time to time direct[6]

The provisions of the act left considerable scope for interpretation. Thus, the fifth and final provision has been cited as authorization for covert action operations. In fact, the provision was intended only to authorize espionage.[7] The ultimate legal basis for covert action is presidential direction and congressional approval of funds for such programs.

Whatever the intentions of Congress in 1947, the CIA developed in accord with a maximal interpretation of the act. Thus, the CIA has become the primary U.S.

government intelligence agency for intelligence analysis, clandestine human intelligence collection, and covert action. It has also played a major role in the development of reconnaissance and other technical collection systems employed for gathering imagery, signals, and measurement and signature intelligence. In addition, as stipulated in the CIA's founding legislation, the Director of the CIA also serves as Director of Central Intelligence and is responsible for managing the activities of the entire national intelligence community. As a result, the Deputy DCI (DDCI) usually assumes the responsibility of day-to-day management of the CIA itself.

Under President Ronald Reagan's Executive Order 12333, which is still in effect, the CIA is permitted to secretly collect "significant" foreign intelligence within the United States if the collection effort is not aimed at the domestic activities of U.S. citizens and corporations. The order also gives the CIA authority to conduct, within the United States, "special activities" or covert actions approved by the president that are not intended to influence U.S. political processes, public opinion, or the media.[8]

CIA headquarters is in Langley, Virginia, just south of Washington, although the agency has a number of other offices scattered around the Washington area. As of 1991, the CIA had approximately 20,000 employees, but post–Cold War reductions and the transfer of the CIA's imagery analysts to the new National Imagery and Mapping Agency (NIMA) have probably reduced that number to about 16,000. Its budget remains in the vicinity of $3 billion.[9]

As indicated in Figure 2.1, in addition to the offices and staff elements that report to the DCI, the Deputy DCI (DDCI), and the Executive Director, there are four directorates—Administration, Intelligence, Science and Technology, and Operations—each headed by a deputy director.*

The Directorate of Administration consists of twelve elements that perform a wide variety of administrative services: the Office of Communications, the Office of Facilities and Security Services, the Office of Finance and Logistics, the Office of Information Technology, the Office of Medical Services, Human Resource Management, the Office of Personnel Security, the Office of Training and Education, the DCI Center for Security Evaluation, the Center for Support Coordination, the Human Resources Oversight Council Program Office, and the Office of Business Process Transformation.[10]

The Office of Communications maintains facilities for secret communications between CIA headquarters and overseas bases and agents. Presumably, this duty includes control over any CIA satellite communications systems. Its personnel

---

*A Directorate of Planning and Coordination was created in September 1989 to identify long-term priorities, determine the resources required to support those priorities, and monitor annual progress against the strategic plan. The directorate was abolished after a short and unhappy existence (William Webster, "Establishment of the Position of Deputy Director for Planning and Coordination," September 11, 1989; interview with former CIA official).

FIGURE 2.1   Organization of the Central Intelligence Agency

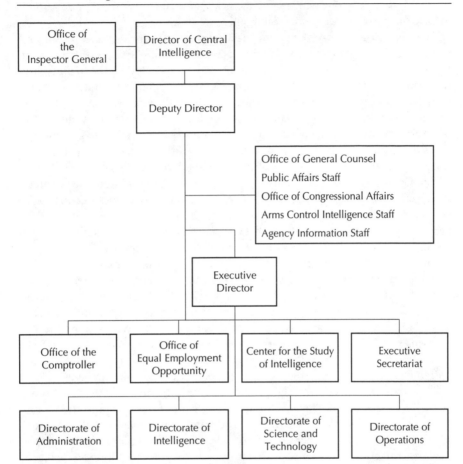

install and maintain communications and high-speed data transmission equipment. The Office of Facilities and Security Services oversees the installation of security systems in CIA facilities in the United States and abroad as well as provides protective services for the facilities and their employees.[11]

The Office of Finance and Logistics operates warehouses in the United States for weapons and other equipment and supplies office equipment. It also is responsible for the disbursement of funds for CIA activities, and maintains offices in cities, such as Geneva and Buenos Aires, with easy access to money markets. The Office of Medical Services plans and directs the CIA's medical programs. The office is responsible for medical examinations and immunizations for employees and dependents traveling overseas, health education and emergency health care, and psychiatric services. It also helps develop the Psychological Assessment Program—to determine which individuals are best suited for the agency—and is involved in psychiatric and medical intelligence production.[12]

The Human Resource Management element of the directorate is responsible for recruitment and maintenance of CIA personnel files. With the Office of Training and Education it operates CIA training facilities—including the main facility, the Armed Forces Experimental Training Facility at Camp Peary, Virginia. Along with the Office of Medical Services and the Office of Personnel Security it shares responsibility for screening agency applicants. In response to the statement of personnel needs from agency components, Human Resource Management prepares an Advanced Staffing Plan for the following fiscal year, listing the total personnel requirements by category of personnel and job titles.[13]

The Office of Training and Education conducts courses on operations, intelligence analysis, management, languages, information science, and executive leadership. One consequence of the arrest of Aldrich Ames was the separation of the personnel and security functions of the Office of Security, with personnel security becoming the responsibility of a new Office of Personnel Security.[14]

The Office of Information Technology operates the CIA's computer facilities. It is also responsible for the agency's domestic communications and computer security.[15]

The Directorate of Operations (formerly the Directorate of Plans) is responsible for clandestine collection and covert action (special activities). The directorate, with about 5,000 personnel, is organized into various staffs and divisions and also contains two DCI centers—a defector resettlement center, joint office with the Directorate of Science and Technology (DS&T), and the National HUMINT Requirements Tasking Center (discussed in Chapter 18)—as shown in Figure 2.2.

The staffs, which perform supervisory, planning, and evaluative functions, include the Foreign Intelligence Staff, the Covert Action Staff, and the Operations and Resource Management Staff. The Foreign Intelligence Staff is responsible for checking the authenticity of sources and information; screening clandestine collection requirements; and reviewing the area division projects, budget information, and operational cable traffic.[16] According to a former head of the staff:

> The Foreign Intelligence Staff had a continuing responsibility for monitoring intelligence-collection projects and programs carried out abroad. These operations and collection programs were of course controlled and directed by the area divisions concerned; the FI Staff simply read the progress charts on the various projects (or the lack of progress) and played the role of determining which intelligence-collection programs should be continued, changed, or terminated. With the exception of a few individual operations of special sensitivity, this FI Staff function was worldwide.[17]

The Covert Action Staff, in cooperation with the area divisions, develops plans for covert action operations, considers plans proposed by area divisions, and evaluates the implementation of the plans. The Operations and Resources

FIGURE 2.2   Organization of the Directorate of Operations

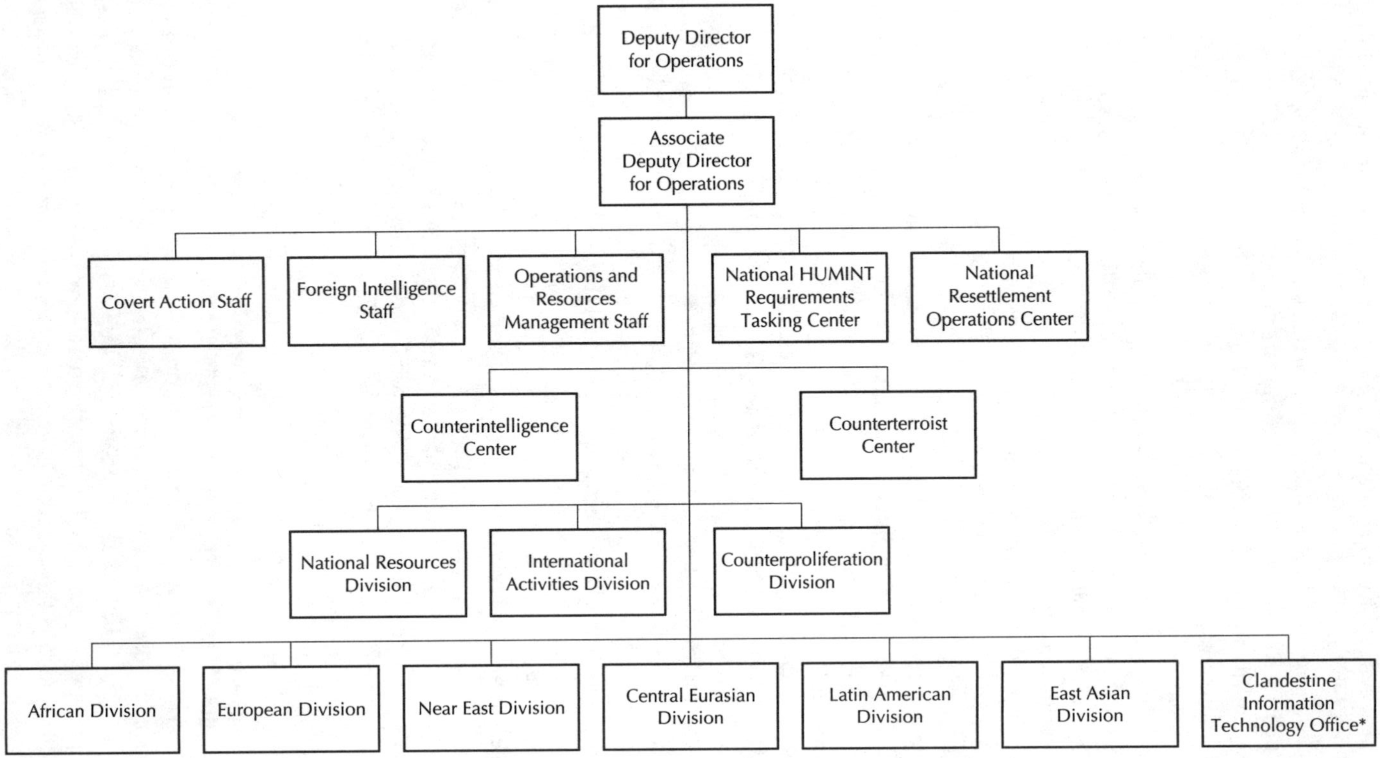

*Joint office with Directorate of Science and Technology.

Management Staff probably approves and reviews the allocation of funds and personnel to various projects.[18]

Actual implementation of staff-approved intelligence collection and covert action activities is the responsibility of the directorate's nine "area" divisions, its one office, and its two DCI centers. Six of those divisions—Central Eurasian, Latin American, European, East Asian, Near East, and African—correspond to foreign geographic areas.[19]

The National Resources Division (NRD) area of operations is the United States, having been established by the 1991 merger of the Foreign Resources Division (FRD) and National Collection Division (NCD), which became branches under the new division. It has offices in 36 U.S. cities. The FRD was created in 1963 as the Domestic Operations Division and given the responsibility for "clandestine operational activities of the Clandestine Services conducted within the United States against foreign targets."[20]

The present function of the Foreign Resources Branch (FRB) is to locate foreign nationals of special interest who reside in the United States and recruit them to serve as CIA assets when they return home (or to some other foreign location). As a means of identifying such individuals the FRB has relationships with scores of individuals in U.S. academic institutions, including faculty. These individuals do not attempt to recruit students, but assist by providing background information and occasionally by brokering introductions.[21]

According to one report, a key element in FRB operations (which composes nearly 30 percent of the NRD's activities) is the recruitment, while they are in the United States, of foreign scientists, engineers, and corporate officials to provide telecommunications intelligence or assist the U.S. intelligence community in acquiring such intelligence. The program involved is designated MXSCOPE, according to the report.[22]

The National Collection Branch (NCB), known previously as the Domestic Collection Division and Domestic Contact Service, openly collects intelligence from U.S. residents who have traveled abroad, including scientists, technologists, economists, and energy experts returning from foreign locations of interest. Among those interviewed are academics—in 1982 the Domestic Collection Division was in touch with approximately 900 individuals on 290 campuses in the United States.[23]

The chief of the NRD (and probably the chiefs of the NCB and FRB) can approve the use of individuals who are employees or invitees of an organization within the United States to collect significant foreign intelligence at fairs, workshops, symposia, and similar types of commercial or professional meetings that are open to those individuals in their overt roles but closed to the general public.[24]

Two divisions have worldwide responsibilities. The International Activities Division, previously known as the Special Operations Division, handles paramilitary activities—such as those directed against the Sandinista government in Nicaragua and the Soviet intervention in Afghanistan during the 1980s. The Counterproliferation Division was established in the mid-1990s, in recognition of the transnational character of the proliferation of weapons of mass destruction. Creation of the CPD allows the CIA to conduct operations to collect information regarding, or neutralize such activities that involve, multiple regions of the world without having to operate through several divisions.[25]

The two DCI centers contained within the operations directorate—the Counterterrorist Center (CTC) and the Counterintelligence Center (CIC)—were established during the tenures of William Casey and William Webster, respectively. The objective was to give heightened status to the counterintelligence and counterterrorism missions as well as to bring together representatives of different intelligence community components, including analysts, involved in these missions. In 1997, a Terrorism Warning Group was established within the CTC with the mission of alerting civilian and military leaders to specific terrorist threats.[26]

The CIC consolidated the Counterintelligence Staff, the Foreign Intelligence Capabilities Unit (established in 1983 to look for attempts by foreign intelligence agencies to influence the perceptions of U.S. intelligence), elements of the administration directorate's Office of Security, and other intelligence community elements. The director of the CIC was given the status of Associate Deputy Director for Operations for Counterintelligence.[27]

A third center within the directorate is the National Resettlement Operations Center (NROC), previously known as the Defector Resettlement Center. The center was established to eliminate CIA deficiencies in handling defectors, such as those that played a role in the redefection of Vitaly Yurchenko.[28]

The joint office with the Directorate of Science and Technology is the Clandestine Information Technology Office (CITO), established in 1996. The CITO is officially described as being responsible for addressing "collection capabilities within emerging information technologies." One possible problem the office may address is the interception of data transmitted by landline, particularly by fiberoptic cables—intercept operations that cannot be accomplished by remote sensing but, if possible at all, require placement of an intercept system in proximity to the cable.[29]

CITO is one of eight offices or elements of the Directorate of Science and Technology, which has about 5,000 employees. The DS&T was created in 1962 as the Directorate of Research and assumed responsibility for the CIA's efforts in developing and operating technical collection systems—particularly the U-2 and A-12 aerial reconnaissance and the CORONA space reconnaissance systems. In 1963, it became the Directorate of Science and Technology.[30]

The DS&T has undergone several reorganizations and has gained and lost responsibilities in the twenty years since it was created. Both the Directorate of Intelligence (DI) and the Directorate of Operations have at times disputed actual or planned DS&T control of various offices and divisions. In 1963, the DS&T assumed control of the Office of Scientific Intelligence, which had been in the Directorate of Intelligence. In 1976, all scientific and technical intelligence analysis functions were transferred back to the DI. In 1996, the National Photographic Intelligence Center (NPIC), which had been transferred to the DS&T in 1973, was merged into the newly created National Imagery and Mapping Agency (NIMA).[31]

In addition to CITO, the components of the DS&T, as shown in Figure 2.3, are: the Planning and Resources Staff, the Systems Analysis Staff, the Office of Development and Engineering, the Office of Technical Collection, the Office of Technical Services, the Foreign Broadcast Information Service, the Community Open Source Program Office, the Office of Advanced Projects, and the Office of Advanced Analytic Tools.[32]

The Office of Development and Engineering (OD&E), as it has been known since 1973, is the successor to several CIA components involved in overhead reconnaissance, including the Development Project Staff (established in 1954 to manage the U-2 program), the Office of Special Activities, and the Office of Special Projects. It has been involved in the development of major technical collection systems, such as the KH-11 imaging satellite. The office "provides total systems development for major systems—from requirements definition through design engineering, and testing and evaluation, to implementation, operation and even support logistics and maintenance." Specific areas of research in developing such systems include laser communications, digital imagery processing, real-time data collection and processing, electro-optics, advanced signal collection, and advanced antenna design.[33]

The Office of Technical Collection was created by merging the Office of SIGINT Operations (OSO) and the Office of Special Projects. OSO "develop[ed], operat[ed] and maintain[ed] sophisticated equipment required to perform collection and analysis tasks . . ." The OSO was heavily involved in the development and operation of the RHYOLITE/AQUACADE series of signals intelligence satellites. Through the Special Collection Service, operated in conjunction with the NSA, the OSO operated a large number of covert listening posts in U.S. embassies. It was involved in the construction of signals intelligence (SIGINT) facilities operated by foreign nations such as China and Norway, in the training of their personnel, and in the maintenance of equipment at the site.[34]*

The Office of Special Projects, in its last incarnation, was involved in the development and operational support of systems, probably emplaced sensor systems, that collected measurement and signatures intelligence, signals intelligence, and nuclear intelligence. According to a CIA document, the office "develop[ed] collection systems tailored to specific targets."[35]

---

*OSO itself was established in 1978, bringing together the Office of Electronic Intelligence (ELINT), the Special Collection Service, and Division D (formerly Staff D) of the Directorate of Operations, which was absorbed by the Special Collection Service. Staff D had originally been the funnel for COMINT into the CIA, had operated against foreign cipher personnel, and had conducted some COMINT activities.

FIGURE 2.3   Organization of the Directorate of Science and Technology

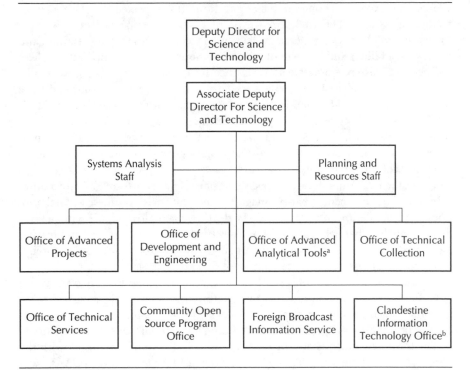

a Joint office with Directorate of Intelligence.

[a] Joint office with Directorate of Intelligence.
[b] Joint office with Directorate of Operations.

The Office of Research and Development (ORD), which was one of the original offices of the Directorate for Research, was disestablished in 1998. Upon its abolition, ORD personnel were assigned to other DS&T offices in order to make the research and development effort more responsive to the needs of those offices.

The Office of Technical Services (OTS) was previously the Technical Services Division (TSD) of the Directorate of Operations. The TSD was transferred to the DS&T in 1973, as part of a series of moves by DCI William Colby to break down barriers between the operations directorate and the rest of the agency. The technical services provided by OTS include secret writing methods, bugging equipment, hidden cameras, coding and decoding devices, video and image enhancement, and chemical imagery. Prior to the April 1980 attempted mission to rescue U.S. hostages in Iran, OTS devised battery-powered landing lights that could be emplaced easily and switched on remotely from the air.[36]

The Office of Advanced Projects is one of three new offices established by the DS&T in 1996, and the only one of the three that is solely the responsibility of the DS&T. Its mission will be to "address the insertion of technology into the

intelligence process [and] facilitate the transfer of technology from various sources and expedite its operational application." It is expected to look ahead for technologies that will be needed in the future for the collection and analysis of information, to identify commercially developed technologies that are relevant, and to seek to develop required technologies when none are commercially available.[37]

The DS&T also operates two services of common concern for the entire intelligence community. The Foreign Broadcast Information Service (FBIS) can trace its origin back to 1941, when the Federal Communications Commission (FCC) established, at the request of the State Department, the Foreign Broadcast Monitoring Service. From that point on the U.S. government had an organization to "record, translate, analyze and report to other agencies of the government on broadcasts of foreign origin."[38]

Today, the FBIS "monitors, selectively translates, and reports on . . . information from radio, television, newspapers, magazines and journals, commercial databases, books, and underground literature." To do this, it employs high-frequency receivers, satellite channels, subscriptions, news agencies, wire services, and foreign databases. The FBIS's collection effort brings in data from about 3,500 foreign broadcast and press outlets. It has employees who cover 82 languages.[39]

The directorate also administers the Community Open Source Program Office (COSPO), which is responsible for coordinating consumer needs, establishing requirement priorities, finding means of more effectively obtaining and handling open source information, and ensuring funding for critical open source activities.[40]

The third new office established within the DS&T is jointly managed with the Directorate of Intelligence. The Office of Advanced Analytic Tools (OAAT) will focus on alleviating the problems of information overload by developing analytical methodologies to assist in the processing and analysis of information. The OAAT has been described as having two missions—obtaining common access to knowledge that is available, and developing and applying automatic tools that will cull the relevant data to allow analysts to look at data more effectively while simultaneously looking at less data.[41]

The Office of Research and Development conducted research in the areas of communications, sensors, semiconductors, artificial intelligence, image recognition, process modeling, database management, and high-speed computing. The ORD also conducted research for all directorates of the CIA, attempting to go beyond the state of the art in order to anticipate and answer the future technology needs of the intelligence community. The office's Advanced Concepts Staff provided a place for experienced researchers to conduct individual research projects aimed at identifying future intelligence issues and problems.[42]

Of all the CIA directorates, the Directorate of Intelligence has undergone the most extensive reorganization in the post–Cold War years. A 1996 reorganization, the directorate's first major reorganization since 1981, reduced the number of directorate offices from nine to six (including the jointly managed Office of Advanced Analytic Tools). Additional directorate components include the President's

Analytical Support Staff, the Operations Center, the Council of Intelligence Occupations, the Collection Requirements and Evaluation Staff, the Balkans Task Force, and three DCI centers. Figure 2.4 shows the present structure.[43]

There are now three rather than five offices within the directorate that focus on regional issues—the Office of Russian and European Analysis, the Office of Near Eastern, South Asian, and African Analysis, and the Office of Asian Pacific and Latin American Analysis. The Russia/Europe office was formed by merging the Office of Russian and Eurasian Analysis and the Office of European Analysis. The remaining two regional offices represent the rearrangement of the responsibilities of three former offices—those for Near Eastern and South Asian Analysis, East Asian Analysis, and African and Latin American Analysis.[44]

FIGURE 2.4   Organization of the Directorate of Intelligence

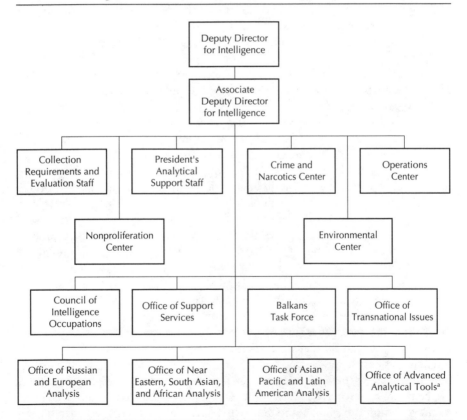

[a] Joint office with Directorate of Science and Technology.

A new Office of Transnational Issues (OTI) was formed from the merger of the Office of Weapons, Technology, and Proliferation (OWTP) and the Office of Transnational Security and Technology Issues (OTSTI). OWTP was the successor to the Office of Scientific and Weapons Research, which itself was formed from the late 1970s merger of the Office of Weapons Intelligence (OWI) and Office of Scientific Intelligence (OSI), both of which had been transferred to the Directorate of Intelligence from the Directorate of Science and Technology in 1976. OTSTI was first established in 1981 as the Office of Global Issues and designated the Office of Resources, Trade and Technology (ORTT) in 1990.[45]

The Office of Transnational Issues explores the technical characteristics of foreign weapons and missile delivery systems and the policy implications for regional stability and U.S. force posture. It also examines advanced technologies in telecommunications and information warfare. In addition, it analyzes developments in international energy, trade, and finance, as well as topics such as refuge flows, food security, and border tensions. Money laundering, illicit arms trafficking, and alien smuggling are also subjects of OTI analysis.[46]

The Office of Support Services (OSS) unites the responsibilities of the former Office of Information Resources (OIR) with the duties of the former Office of Current Production and Analytic Support (CPAS). Thus, the Support Services office provides library and reference support, computer-based applications development, and training and consulting in automated data processing; it also publishes DI reports, and produces CIA maps, charts, and specialized graphics for use in CIA reports and briefings.[47]

The President's Analytical Support Staff is responsible for preparing briefings and analytic products specifically for the president and for producing the *President's Daily Brief*. The Operations Center maintains watch over data flowing into the CIA from a variety of collection assets and can inform authorities if incoming intelligence indicates that a crisis situation is developing somewhere in the world.[48]

The Council of Intelligence Occupations is intended to help provide guidance to analysts throughout their careers and ensure that they receive the necessary training. The Collection Requirements and Evaluation Staff oversees the process by which requirements flow from the Directorate of Intelligence to the Directorate of Operations, the NRO, the NSA, and other collection activities; the staff also evaluates the response to those requirements. The DCI Balkans Task Force was established in response to growing U.S. concern over and involvement in events in the former Yugoslavia. It brings together analysts and collectors from throughout the intelligence community to support policymakers by providing intelligence support, including finished intelligence.[49]

The DCI's Crime and Narcotics Center (CNC) is staffed by analysts and operators from the CIA, the Federal Bureau of Investigation, the Defense Department, the National Security Agency, the State Department, and the Treasury Department, who monitor, analyze, and disseminate intelligence on narcotics trafficking and international organized crime. It was established in 1989 as the DCI Counternarcotics Center. Its mission and name were changed in 1994 to include international organized crime intelligence.[50]

Also housed in the Directorate of Intelligence is the DCI Nonproliferation Center (NPC), which was established in September 1991 after disclosures about Iraq's capabilities to produce nuclear and other weapons of mass destruction indicated that the intelligence community had underestimated both the diversity and progress of the program. The NPC consists of about 200 intelligence analysts and clandestine operators, about a quarter to a third of whom come from agencies other than the CIA. The center monitors the worldwide development and acquisition of production technology, designs, components, or entire military systems in the area of nuclear, chemical, and biological weapons, as well as advanced conventional weapons. The NPC's Transfer Network Groups analyze and identify international suppliers of technologies and the trade mechanisms used to transfer goods.[51]

The NPC has also developed strategic plans to help guide the U.S. government's response to the proliferation problem and provided support to collection and law-enforcement organizations. It also worked on collection platform development and produced a "gaps" study that identified deficiencies in proliferation-related collection activities. The NPC was also authorized to review the intelligence community's performance on proliferation activities and to make relevant budget recommendations.[52]

In its 1997 intelligence authorization report, the House Permanent Select Committee on Intelligence, although praising the NPC's accomplishments, noted that the "NPC has attempted to bring a Community focus to the proliferation issue, but has been thwarted in these efforts by internal (CIA) and external turf battles." The committee went on to note that "because of this, the NPC has not been able to position itself as the focal point for [intelligence community]-wide non-proliferation activities."[53]

A 1997 summer study by the President's Foreign Intelligence Advisory Board (PFIAB) concluded that the dangers associated with chemical and biological weapons warranted giving the center added powers to oversee intelligence spending and collection priorities. However, in the fall of 1997 it was reported that the NPC would be slashed in size and responsibility. Congressional reaction soon resulted in a reversal of plans, and it was announced that the NPC would expand from 100 to 200 analysts. The analysts would be primarily drawn from the Office of Transnational Issues, although the NSA, the DIA, and the NIMA would be requested to provide personnel. In addition, a new Director of Central Intelligence Directive was expected to expand the authority of the NPC.[54]

In 1997 a DCI Environmental Center was established to bring together analysts working on environmental intelligence issues such as environmental degradation in central Europe and the former Soviet Union, damage from sudden actions such as the destruction of Kuwait's oil wells during the Gulf War, and the environment's impact on the spread of infectious diseases. Analysts with the new center also provide support to U.S. officials who negotiate environmental treaties and help in assessing whether other nations are in compliance with such treaties.[55]

The center has three main components. The Environmental Issues Branch was established in the late 1980s to deal with policymakers' questions concerning global environmental issues—including treaty negotiations and compliance, environmental crime, and foreign environmental policy and performance. Established in the early 1990s, the Civil Applications Branch, along with a group of scientists now known as MEDEA, investigates the extent to which intelligence information and systems could enhance understanding of environmental issues. The Long-Term Assessment Branch "focuses on the impact of environmental change on national, regional, and international political, economic, and social dynamics."[56]

An analytic unit outside the Directorate of Intelligence is the Arms Control Intelligence Staff (ACIS), headed by the DCI's Special Assistant for Arms Control. The present ACIS can trace its origin to the creation in the mid-1970s of a four-person staff within the Directorate of Intelligence to coordinate CIA arms control-related activities and positions on pivotal verification and monitoring issues. The staff grew in the 1980s, in concert with negotiations on intermediate nuclear forces, strategic arms reduction, and the verification protocols of the Peaceful Nuclear Explosions Treaty and the Threshold Test Ban Treaty. In 1989 the ACIS was further expanded when it absorbed the DCI's Treaty Monitoring Center and the conventional forces component of the Office of Soviet Analysis. At that time the ACIS was transferred from the Directorate of Intelligence to the office of the DCI. Among its recent activities has been its participation in an assessment of the impact of the proposed Chemical Weapons Convention on U.S. forces abroad.[57]

NATIONAL SECURITY AGENCY

The National Security Agency (NSA) is one of the most secret (and secretive) members of the U.S. intelligence community. The predecessor of NSA, the Armed Forces Security Agency (AFSA), was established within the Department of Defense, under the command of the Joint Chiefs of Staff, on May 20, 1949, when Secretary of Defense Louis Johnson signed JCS Directive 2010. In theory, the AFSA was to direct the communications intelligence and electronic intelligence activities of the military service signals intelligence units (at the time consisting of the Army Security Agency, Naval Security Group, and Air Force Security Service). In practice, the AFSA had little power, its functions being defined in terms of activities not performed by the service units.[58]

On October 24, 1952, President Harry S. Truman sent a top-secret, eight-page memorandum (now declassified), entitled "Communications Intelligence Activities," to the Secretary of State and the Secretary of Defense; the memorandum abolished the AFSA and transferred its personnel to the newly created National Security Agency, which was established that day by draft National Security Council Intelligence Directive No. 9 (which was formally approved in December).[59]

The creation of NSA had its origins in a December 10, 1951, memo sent by Walter Bedell Smith to National Security Council Executive Secretary James B. Lay, stating that "control over, and coordination of, the collection and processing of Communications Intelligence had proved ineffective" and recommending a survey of communications intelligence activities. The proposal was approved on December 13, 1951, and the study authorized on December 28, 1951. The report was completed by June 13, 1952. Generally known as the "Brownell Committee Report," after committee chairman Herbert Brownell, it surveyed the history of U.S. communications intelligence activities and suggested the need for a much greater degree of coordination and direction at the national level. As the change in the security agency's name indicated, the role of the NSA was to extend beyond the armed forces. The NSA is considered to be "within but not part of DOD [Department of Defense]."[60]

Although the agency was created in 1952, it was not until 1957 that its existence was officially acknowledged in the *U.S. Government Organization Manual* as a "separately organized agency within the Department of Defense" that "performs highly specialized technical and coordinating functions relating to national security." Despite the lack of official acknowledgment, the NSA's existence was a matter of public knowledge from at least early 1954, when Washington newspapers ran several stories concerning the construction of the NSA's new headquarters at Fort George G. Meade, Maryland. In late 1954 the NSA was again in the news when an NSA employee was caught taking secret documents home.[61]

The charter for the NSA is National Security Council Intelligence Directive (NSCID) 6. In its most recently available version, which was in force at least as late as 1987, NSCID 6 ("Signals Intelligence") of January 17, 1972, directs the NSA to produce SIGINT "in accordance with the objectives, requirements and priorities established by the Director of Central Intelligence Board." The directive also authorizes the Director of NSA (DIRNSA) "to issue direct to any operating elements engaged in SIGINT operations such instructions and assignments as are required" and states that "all instructions issued by the Director under the authority provided in this paragraph shall be mandatory, subject only to appeal to the Secretary of Defense."[62]

NSCID 6 defines the scope of SIGINT activities—which can be divided into Communications Intelligence (COMINT) and Electronic Intelligence (ELINT)—as follows:

COMINT activities shall be construed to mean those activities which produce COMINT by interception and processing of foreign communications by radio, wire, or other electronic means, with specific exception stated below and by the processing of foreign encrypted communications, however transmitted. Interception comprises range estimation, transmitter operator identification, signal analysis, traffic analysis, cryptanalysis, decryption, study of plain text, the fusion of those processes, and the reporting of the results.

COMINT and COMINT activities as defined herein shall not include (a) any intercept and processing of unencrypted written communications, press and propaganda broadcasts, or (b) censorship.

ELINT activities are defined as the collection (observation and recording) and the processing for subsequent intelligence purposes, of information derived from foreign non-communications, electro-magnetic radiations emanating from other than atomic detonation or radioactive sources. ELINT is the technical and intelligence product of ELINT activities.[63]

Signals intercepted include diplomatic, military, scientific, and commercial communications, as well as the electronic emanations of radar systems and the signals sent by weapons systems while being tested. The intercepted signals may be transmitted by telephone, radio-telephone, radio, or cables.

The responsibilities of the NSA and its director are specified by DOD Directive S-5100.20, "The National Security Agency and the Central Security Service." According to the directive, the Director of NSA is to:

- Exercise SIGINT operational control over SIGINT activities of the U.S. Government to respond most effectively to military and other SIGINT requirements . . .
- Provide technical guidance to all SIGINT or SIGINT-related operations of the U.S. Government
- Produce and disseminate SIGINT in accordance with the objectives, requirements and priorities established by the Director of Central Intelligence . . .
- In relation to Department of Defense SIGINT activities, prepare and submit to the Secretary of Defense a consolidated program and budget, and requirements for military and civilian manpower, logistics and communications support, and research, development, test, and evaluation, together with his recommendations pertaining thereto
- Prescribe within his field of authorized operations requisite security regulations covering operating practices, including the transmission, handling, and distribution of SIGINT material within and among the elements under his control[64]

The NSA has a second major mission, originally known as Communications Security (COMSEC), which became Information Security (INFOSEC) in the 1980s. (In the 1990s, INFOSEC has become the defensive portion of Information Warfare). In its INFOSEC role NSA performs the same basic COMSEC functions as it did in the past. It creates, reviews, and authorizes the communications procedures and codes of a variety of government agencies—including the State Department, the DOD, the CIA, and the FBI. This role includes development of secure data and voice transmission links on such satellite systems as the Defense Satellite Communications System (DSCS). Likewise, for sensitive communications FBI agents use a special scrambler telephone that requires a different code from NSA each day. The NSA's COMSEC responsibilities also include ensuring communications security for strategic weapons systems, so as to prevent unauthorized intrusion, interference, or jamming. In addition, the NSA is responsible for developing the codes by which the president must identify himself in order to authorize the release of nuclear weapons.[65] As part of its INFOSEC mission the NSA is also responsible for protecting national security data banks and computers from unauthorized access by individuals or governments.

NSA headquarters at Fort George G. Meade, Maryland, houses somewhere between 20,000 and 24,000 employees in three buildings. The NSA budget is approximately $3.5 billion. As indicated in Figure 2.5, it is divided into several directorates, the three most important being the Directorate of Operations, the Directorate of Information Systems Security, and the Directorate of Technology and Systems (formerly known as the Directorate of Research and Engineering).

The Directorate of Operations, headed by the Deputy Director of Operations, traditionally had three groups responsible for regional operations and the analysis of data collected. The A Operations Analysis Group, commonly known as A Group, was responsible for the Soviet Union and Eastern European nations. B Group was responsible for China, North Korea, Vietnam, and the rest of Communist Asia, and G Group was responsible for all other nations, both Third World and allied. In the aftermath of the demise of the Soviet Union the three groups were reduced to two—one dealing with all European nations (A Group) and another focusing on all other nations (B Group).[66]

Two other Directorate of Operations components were W Group and the National SIGINT Operations Center (NSOC). W Group was responsible for space SIGINT—the interception and processing of all communications and signals emitted by foreign spacecraft and missiles. Subordinate to W Group were the Defense Special Missile and Astronautics Center (DEFSMAC) and the National Telemetry Processing Center (NTPC).[67]

A further reorganization, in 1997, eliminated A and B Groups and established two new or modified groups. M Group was established to assess potential threats to and vulnerabilities of technologies and infrastructures such as telecommunications systems. A new W Group was established to deal with transnational threats. According to a NSA official, the reorganization resulted from a "realization of [the] need to think differently about intelligence requirements," and the "requirement to get the most effective analytical tools to the work force." In addition, it was concluded that it was no longer efficient to think in terms of geographical regions and that intelligence requirements fell into two groups—transnational and geopolitical.[68]

FIGURE 2.5   Organization of the National Security Agency

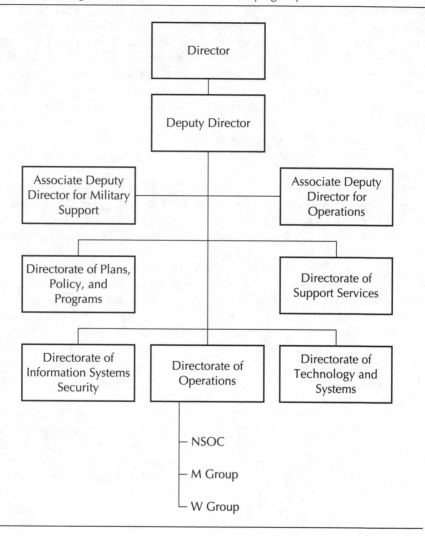

DEFSMAC, which continues in operation, was established as a joint operation of the NSA and Defense Intelligence Agency (DIA) by Department of Defense Directive S-5100.43, "Defense Special Missile and Astronautics Center," of April 27, 1964. According to DEFSMAC, it "is responsible for worldwide all-source intelligence data. It provides time-sensitive alerts, initial event assessments, and mission support to national agencies, national command authorities, unified commands, and deployed sensor platforms and stations."[69]

According to a former deputy director of the NSA, DEFSMAC:

is a combination of the DIA with its military components and the NSA. It has all the inputs from all the assets and is a warning activity. They probably have a better feel for any worldwide threat to this country from missiles, aircraft or overt military activities, better and more timely, at instant fingertip availability than any group in the United States. So DEFSMAC is an input to NSA, but it also [is] an input to DIA and the CIA and the White House Situation Room and everybody else.[70]

DEFSMAC receives data bearing on Russian, Chinese, and other nation's space and missile launches. In turn, it warns collection assets that a launch is imminent, so that they can prepare to monitor the event. The National Telemetry Processing Center (NTPC) processes the electronic signals radioed back to earth by Russian, Chinese, and other nation's missiles during their test flights.

The National SIGINT Operations Center's function was to oversee and direct the SIGINT coverage of any crisis event. It operated around the clock and was in instantaneous touch with every major NSA facility in the world. In the event that a facility intercepts signals that it believed to be significant, the facility personnel filed a CRITIC intelligence report with NSOC, which might immediately pass the message on to the Director of NSA. If NSOC authorities felt that the event was really not of sufficient importance they could revoke the report's CRITIC status.[71]

As a result of the increased emphasis on information warfare, NSOC has been given a new name—the National Security Operations Center. It continues to perform its previous missions but now operates a Information Protect Cell (IPC) and has a Defensive Information Operations Staff.[72]

The Directorate of Information Systems Security is responsible for INFOSEC with respect to the communications, signals, and databases discussed above. The Directorate of Technology and Systems (formed by the merger of the Directorate of Research and Engineering and the Directorate of Telecommunications and Computer Services) develops the techniques and equipment necessary for conducting intercept operations, breaking codes, and ensuring secure U.S. codes. The directorate explores code-breaking possibilities, develops the equipment required for the NSA's COMINT and ELINT intercept programs, and seeks to develop secure cipher machines.[73]

In addition to the three main directorates there are two additional directorates. The Directorate of Support Services (formerly the Directorate of Installations and Logistics) is responsible for overseas housing, the disposal of classified waste, the construction of facilities at Fort Meade, and the procurement of computers. The Directorate of Plans, Policy, and Programs is charged with the management and allocation of SIGINT/INFOSEC resources, including the preparation of the Consolidated Cryptologic Program (discussed in Chapter 17).[74]

In addition to directing the activities at NSA headquarters and NSA installations overseas, the Director of NSA is responsible for supervising the SIGINT activities of the Service Cryptologic Elements (SCEs). In this role, the director serves as the head of the Central Security Service (CSS). The CSS function of the NSA, with the DIRNSA serving simultaneously as Chief of the CSS, was established in 1971 in order "to provide a unified, more economical and more effective structure for executing cryptologic and related operations presently conducted under the Military Departments." There is, however, no separate CSS staff.[75]

NATIONAL RECONNAISSANCE OFFICE

In its May 2, 1946, report, *Preliminary Design for an Experimental World Circling Spaceship*, the Douglas Aircraft Corporation examined the potential value of satellites for scientific and military purposes. Possible military uses included missile guidance, weapons delivery, weather reconnaissance, communications, attack assessment, and "observation."[76]

A little less than nine years later, on March 16, 1955, the Air Force issued General Operational Requirement No. 80, officially establishing a high-level requirement for an advanced reconnaissance satellite. Over the next five years the U.S. reconnaissance satellite program evolved in a variety of ways. The Air Force program was first designated the Advanced Reconnaissance System (ARS), then SENTRY, and finally SAMOS. Management responsibility for SAMOS was transferred from the Air Force to the Advanced Research Projects Agency (ARPA), established on February 7, 1958, and then back to the Air Force in 1959.[77]

Concern about the length of time it would take to achieve the primary objective of the SAMOS program—a satellite that could return its imagery electronically—led to President Dwight Eisenhower's approval, in early February 1958, of a CIA program to develop a reconnaissance satellite. That program, designated CORONA, focused on development of a satellite that would physically return its images in a canister—an objective that had been a subsidiary portion of the SAMOS program.[78]

By June 1960 the continued problems with the SAMOS program led the president to order reviews of a various aspects of the program. The urgency of attaining an operational satellite reconnaissance program had increased with the Soviet shoot-down of Francis Gary Powers and his U-2 on May 1. The reviews culminated in a August 25, 1960, meeting with the president in which a streamlined form of management for the SAMOS program was recommended and accepted by Eisenhower. Under the new arrangement, there would be a direct line of authority from the Secretary of the Air Force to the SAMOS project director, eliminating intervening levels of bureaucracy, including the Air Staff.[79]

On August 31 Secretary of the Air Force Dudley C. Sharp signed Secretary of the Air Force Order 115.1, establishing the Office of Missile and Satellite Systems within his own office. The office's director was to assist the Secretary "in discharging his responsibility for the direction, supervision and control of the Samos project." He was also made responsible for "maintaining liaison with the Office, Secretary of Defense and other interested Governmental agencies on matters relative to his assigned responsibilities."[80]

With Order 116.1, Sharp designated Brig. Gen. Robert E. Greer, Assistant Chief of Staff for Guided Missiles, as director of the SAMOS project. Greer was to organize a project office at the California headquarters of the Air Force Ballistic Missile Division, as a field extension of the Office of the Secretary of the Air Force, and to carry out development of the satellite. The order very specifically stated that "The Director is responsible to and will report directly to the Secretary of the Air Force."[81]

The decisions of August and September 1960 gave a new structure to the Air Force program but did not affect the management arrangements for the CIA's secret CORONA program. However, a number of events and individuals would lead to the creation of a new office to manage overhead reconnaissance. Among them were James Killian and Edwin Land, two key presidential scientific advisers. Looking at the successful Air Force-CIA partnerships that had existed with respect to the U-2, OXCART, and CORONA programs, they pushed for permanent and institutionalized collaboration between the two organizations.[82]

Subsequent to John F. Kennedy's assumption of the presidency, Undersecretary of the Air Force Joseph Charyk drafted a proposal, at Killian and Land's request, for the establishment of a national coordinating agency for satellite reconnaissance. They were sufficiently persuasive, for sometime after the middle of July, Secretary of Defense Robert McNamara asked Charyk to draft the specific documents that would put the proposal into effect.[83]

On September 6, 1961, an agreement signed by the acting DCI, Gen. Charles Pearre Cabell, and Deputy Secretary of Defense Roswell Gilpatric established the National Reconnaissance Office (NRO) as a joint CIA-Air Force operation.[84] For the next thirty-one years the NRO's existence was classified SECRET. Outside of the Department of Defense directive that served as a charter, its name or initials could not be used in any government document that did not carry a special security classification.

From its inception the NRO's core responsibilities have included overseeing and funding the research and development of reconnaissance spacecraft and their sensors, procuring the space systems and their associated ground stations, determining launch vehicle requirements, operating spacecraft after they attain orbit, and disseminating the data collected.

The NRO has also performed a number of other missions. According to the 1964 Department of Defense directive on the NRO, the Director of the NRO "will establish the security procedures to be followed for all matters of the (TS) National Reconnaissance Program . . . to protect all elements of the (S) National Reconnaissance Office."[85]

Those security procedures—which constituted the BYEMAN Control System—concerned both the criteria for granting personnel access to information about NRO programs and the requirements concerning the physical security of documents relating to those programs.

NRO representatives also served on policy review committees and conducted studies dealing with topics related to satellite security and secrecy—such as the NSAM [National Security Action Memorandum] 156 committee, established in 1962 to review the political aspects of U.S. policy on space reconnaissance.[86] In the early 1980s, the NRO examined the question of how to maintain secrecy concerning NRO payloads launched on the space shuttle. More recently, it has been concerned with U.S. policy concerning commercial imagery satellites.

Undoubtedly, the NRO also has had a voice in decisions concerning the sharing of images, imagery-derived information, or space SIGINT data with other nations. Over the years, nations that have received access to such data have varied from close allies (Britain, Israel) to strategic partners of convenience (China) to nations such as Iraq.

The NRO's involvement in aerial reconnaissance issues has varied over the years. During the Cuban Missile Crisis it was involved in developing overflight plans for the U-2 and other aerial reconnaissance platforms. In 1974, it undertook a review of remotely piloted vehicles to "establish the evolution of present vehicles in the inventory, R&D that has been undertaken, and current requirements that exist for which they may be utilized."[87]

By 1989, the Director of the National Reconnaissance Office (DNRO) had assumed responsibility for managing the Airborne Reconnaissance Support Program (ARSP). It would seem likely that the NRO also was assigned responsibility for developing a highly secret, unmanned follow-on to the SR-71, the Advanced Airborne Reconnaissance System (AARS). (The AARS program was canceled in 1993 for budgetary reasons.)[88]

The NRO's structure, from shortly after its creation to 1992, reflected the fact that it was, rather than a unified organization, a federation of intelligence and military organizations that, in addition to maintaining their separate identities, were part of the NRO and conducted space reconnaissance programs.

There was a central headquarters; and the NRO staff used the already existing Office of Missile and Satellite Systems(renamed the Office of Space Systems at the time of NRO's creation) as a cover—with the director of this office, an Air Force general, serving as NRO staff director.[89]

However, rather than establishing an organization fully subordinate to its director and divided among different aerospace reconnaissance functions—imagery, signals intelligence, ocean surveillance—the new organization became an umbrella organization for the ongoing reconnaissance efforts of the Air Force, the CIA, and the Navy. The early years of the arrangement would see a number of fierce battles between the CIA and the director of the NRO over the extent of the director's control. Throughout the 1960s and 1970s, at the very least, the CIA and the Air Force would compete over which organization would be responsible for new collection systems.[90]

The Air Force Office of Special Projects, as the SAMOS project office had been renamed, retained that unclassified designation and its California headquarters but also became the NRO's Program A. The CIA effort—which included aspects of CORONA, the A-12 reconnaissance aircraft, and its U-2 fleet—became Program B. The Navy was also brought into the NRO on the basis of the signals intelligence satellite system it was operating, ostensibly as the Galactic Radiation and Background (GRAB) experiment. That effort, initially funded through the Naval Research Laboratory, became Program C. Although the Air Force and Navy elements were fully subordinate to the director of the NRO, the CIA element, coming from an organization outside the Defense Department, was not.[91]

In early 1963, a second Air Force element, Program D, was established. The program initially encompassed what was then designated the R-12, and which subsequently became known as the RF-12 and then the SR-71—the Air Force version of the CIA's A-12/OXCART. Program D also assumed responsibility for the TAG-BOARD/D-21 reconnaissance drone and a non-reconnaissance project—the interceptor version of the R-12, variously designated the AF-12, XF-12, and YF-12.[92]

Program D continued as a major component of the NRO until the responsibility for the SR-71 was turned over to the Strategic Air Command in 1969—although as early as the summer of 1963 elements of the Air Force were seeking to assume control of the programs it managed. Program D was formally dissolved in 1970 or 1971.[93]

The NRO operated through the 1960s, the 1970s, and the 1980s with the same basic structure, excluding Program D, with the cover arrangements that had been established in the 1961–1963 period. But the 1990s produced a wide-ranging restructuring of the NRO—prompted by congressional pressure, the recommendations of a review group, and post–Cold War budget constraints.

In April 1990 the position of Deputy Director for Military Support (DDMS) was established to facilitate the provision of NRO support to military commanders. In late 1996 the position of Deputy Director for National Support (DDNS) was established—to balance the DDMS position. According to the DDNS mission statement the new official is to "maintain close coordination with senior officials in all national-level departments and agencies who can represent their respective current and future space-based reconnaissance needs." The position was created for balance, given the concern that had been frequently expressed about the extent of focus on supporting military operations.[94]

In April 1992 DCI Robert Gates had announced before a joint public hearing of the Senate and House intelligence oversight committees that there would be "a far-reaching internal restructuring of the Intelligence Community organization responsible for designing, building, and operating our overhead reconnaissance assets."[95]

That restructuring, which replaced the Air Force, CIA, and Navy program offices with a functional structure, resulted in the creation of three major directorates: the IMINT Systems Acquisition and Operations Directorate, the SIGINT Systems Acquisition and Operations Directorate, and the Communications Systems Acquisition and Operations Directorate. Each directorate is responsible for both acquiring and supervising contractor research and development as well as purchasing and operating the relevant spacecraft and ground stations.[96]

In March 1997, in response to the recommendation of a review panel, the Office of Systems Applications (OSA), which was established to investigate the feasibility of small satellites for reconnaissance, was upgraded to become NRO's fourth directorate—the Advanced Systems and Technology Directorate. The directorate's mission is to investigate and conduct research and development for systems that would be significantly different from those operated by the acquisition and operations directorates at that time.[97]

Other elements of the NRO, as shown in Figure 2.6, are: Resource, Oversight, and Management; the Technical Director: the Management Services and Operations Office; the Operational Support Office; the Office of Space Launch; the Office of Plans and Analysis; Counterintelligence Staff; and a Director of Security. The latter two elements are among the elements of the NRO Staff—which report directly to the director and deputy director.

The Resource Oversight and Management Office was established in 1996, in the wake of the discovery that over a $1 billion (ultimately determined to be $3.8 billion) had accumulated in NRO accounts. Its mission was "to strengthen NRO resource management and budgetary controls and improve all aspects of the NRO's responsiveness to Congress." The Operational Support Office "orchestrates and delivers tailored support to DOD, national, and other approved users of NRO products and services in concert with appropriate agencies and offices." Its prime function has been to support military forces, both operationally and during exercises. In 1998 it inherited the similar responsibilities that had been assigned to the Defense Support Project Office (DSPO). The Office of Space Launch "manages . . . launch vehicle procurement, spacecraft/launch vehicle integration, launch related systems safety, and launch operations." The Office of Plans and Analysis is responsible for strategic planning; independent assessment of architectural, technical, and related fiscal issues; cost/product trade-offs; and development and operation of cross-program simulation capabilities.[98]

The Counterintelligence Staff was established in June 1992 to "increase the awareness of foreign intelligence threats to NRO programs, facilities and personnel, . . . communicating that information to NRO CI activities." Its primary functions include research and analysis, and coordination within the NRO, the CI community and investigative agencies, and operations support.[99]

NRO's budget is approximately $6.2 billion. As of late 1997 it had 2,753 government employees. As has always been the case NRO employees are assigned to the reconnaissance office from their parent organizations. Thus, the 2,753 employees consisted of representatives of the Air Force (1,456), the CIA (649), the NSA (412), the Navy (214), and other agencies such as DIA and the Army (22).[100]

NATIONAL IMAGERY AND MAPPING AGENCY

In his April 1992 testimony before the House and Senate intelligence committees, DCI Robert Gates noted that the Imagery Task Force he had established upon

FIGURE 2.6   Organization of the National Reconnaissance Office

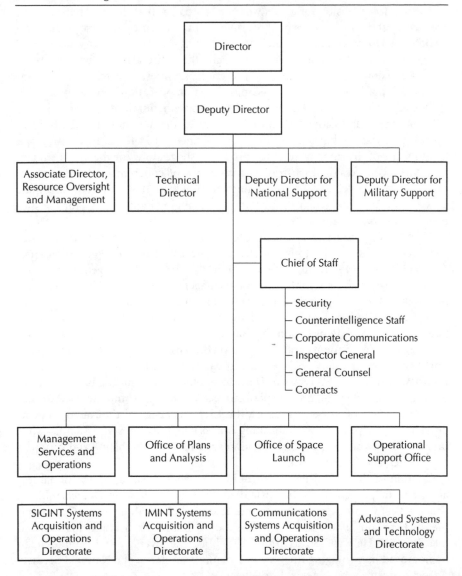

SOURCES: NRO, "NRO Organization," January 12, 1998; *Department of Defense Telephone Directory, December 1997* (Washington, D.C.: U.S. Government Printing Office, 1997), p. O-163.

becoming DCI had recommended the creation of a National Imagery Agency (NIA), which would absorb the CIA's National Photographic Interpretation Center as well as the Defense Mapping Agency (DMA).[101]

The task force's vision for a NIA was not as broad as that that had been recommended by some in congressional hearings and written into proposed legislation by both the House and Senate intelligence committees. The broader vision would have created an NIA responsible for virtually the entire range of imagery functions—decisions on spacecraft and aircraft capabilities, research and development to support those decisions, tasking, collection operations, and analysis.[102]

During his testimony Gates rejected the recommendations of both his task force and the congressional committees. However, the next month a Central Imagery Office was established within the Department of Defense. Its creation was due to some of the same factors that produced suggestions for the establishment of a NIA—congressional frustration with a lack of coherent imagery management, imagery collection and dissemination problems that surfaced during the Persian Gulf War, budgetary constraints, and changing requirements for the support of military operations.[103]

Thus, the Central Imagery Office (CIO) was established on May 6, 1992. It was chartered by both a Department of Defense Directive (5105.56) and a Director of Central Intelligence Directive (2/9) as a DOD Combat Support Agency.[104]

In contrast to the alternative national imagery agencies that had been proposed, the CIO was not designed to absorb existing agencies or take on their collection and analysis functions. Rather, the mission of the CIO included tasking of national imagery systems (assuming that mission in place of the DCI Committee on Imagery Requirements and Exploitation) to ensure responsive imagery support to the Department of Defense, combat commanders, the CIA, and other agencies; advising the Secretary of Defense and the DCI regarding future imagery requirements; and evaluating the performance of imagery components. Pursuant to the provision of imagery support, the CIO was assigned the role of systems development—specifically, establishing imagery architectures and standards for interoperability of imagery dissemination systems, and supporting and conducting research and development.[105]

Creation of the CIO delayed, but did not prevent, creation of a national imagery and mapping agency. In April 1995, DCI-designate John Deutch told the Senate Select Committee on Intelligence that, if confirmed, he would "move immediately to consolidate the management of all imagery collection, analysis, and distribution." He went on to argue that "both effectiveness and economy can be improved by managing imagery in a manner similar to the National Security Agency's organization for signals intelligence."[106]

After his confirmation, Deutch established a National Imagery Agency Steering Group, which in turn chartered an NIA Task Force. The Task Force produced eleven different options for a NIA, ranging from a strengthened CIO to a highly centralized NIA, with program, budget, and management authority for all aspects of imagery.[107]

In late November 1995 Deutch and Secretary of Defense William Perry sent a joint letter to congressional leaders and relevant committees on their joint plan to establish a National Imagery and Mapping Agency as a combat support agency within the Department of Defense on October 1, 1996. Their letter noted that the proposed agency would be formed by consolidating the Defense Mapping Agency, Central Imagery Office, National Photographic Interpretation Center, the imagery exploitation element of the Defense Intelligence Agency, and portions of the Defense Airborne Reconnaissance Office and National Reconnaissance Office that were involved in imagery exploitation and dissemination.[108] The planned agency would thus leave the acquisition and operation of space systems and their ground stations to the NRO, and it would also leave the imagery exploitation activities of the service intelligence organizations untouched.

According to the letter, the task force recommended the consolidation proposed for three basic reasons:

1. A single, streamlined and focused agency could best serve the imagery and mapping needs of a growing and diverse customer base across government;
2. the current dispersion of imagery and mapping responsibilities does not allow one agency to exploit the tremendous potential of enhanced collection systems, digital processing technology and the prospective expansion in commercial imagery; and
3. the revolution in information technology makes possible a symbiosis of imagery intelligence and mapping which can best realized through more central management.[109]

The wisdom of the plan was questioned by both former intelligence (particularly CIA) officials and many within Congress—particularly the vice-chairman of the Senate Select Committee on Intelligence, Robert Kerrey (D–Neb.), and the House Permanent Select Committee on Intelligence. The primary concern was that, as a result of the transfer of NPIC personnel from the CIA to the Defense Department, imagery support to national policymakers would suffer in order to support the requirements of military commanders. However, although the opposition was unable to block the creation of the new agency, the Senate Select Committee on Intelligence did persuade the Senate Armed Services Committee to amend the legislation creating NIMA. Thus, the final legislation stipulated that the DCI retained tasking authority over national imagery systems and that the Secretary of Defense must obtain the DCI's concurrence before appointing the NIMA director, or note the DCI's lack of concurrence before recommending a candidate to the president. In addition, the armed services committee agreed to the modification of the National Security Act, such that it explicitly stated NIMA's responsibility to provide intelligence for national policymakers.[110]

NIMA came into being as projected on October 1, 1996. It incorporated all the elements mentioned in the late November statement as well as the Office of Imagery Analysis of the CIA's Directorate of Intelligence and the Defense Dissemination Program Office. The consolidation thus created an agency with about 9,000 personnel—about 2,000 from the imagery interpretation activities, and about 7,000 from DMA.[111]

As with the CIO, NIMA is chartered by both a DOD directive—(5105.60 of October 11, 1996, "National Imagery and Mapping Agency (NIMA)"—and a DCI directive. The DOD directive specifies that NIMA is, inter alia, to:

2. Provide responsive imagery, imagery intelligence and geospatial information products, support, services, and information (to include the coordination of imagery collection requirements, national tasking, processing, exploitation, and dissemination) to the DOD Components, and, for national intelligence purposes, to the DCI, the non-DOD members of the Intelligence Community, and other Federal Government Departments and Agencies

3. Manage imagery and geospatial analysis and production

4. Manage the tasking of and task national collection operations . . . as follows:

   A. Developing and consolidating geospatial information requirements and national imagery collection requirements

   B. Supporting the imagery requirements of the Department of State and other non-DOD Agencies, in accordance with the requirements and priorities established by the DCI

   C. Tasking DOD imagery collection elements to meet national intelligence requirements and priorities, as established by the DCI . . .

   D. Advising DOD imagery collection elements on the collection of imagery to meet non-national intelligence requirements

5. Establish and/or consolidate DOD geographical information data collection requirements and collecting or tasking other DOD components to collect and provide necessary data . . .

6. Provide advisory tasking for theater and tactical assets, including advising imagery collection elements on collection of imagery to meet national intelligence requirements, when the collection elements are both assigned to or under the operational control of the Secretary of a Military Department or the Commander of a Combatant Command, and not allocated by the Secretary of Defense to meet national intelligence requirements

7. Disseminate or ensure the dissemination of imagery, imagery intelligence, and geospatial information by the most efficient and expeditious means consistent with DOD and DCI security requirements . . .

10. Develop and make recommendations on national and non-national policy for imagery, imagery intelligence, and geospatial information, including as it relates to international matters . . .

11. Prescribe and mandate standards and end-to-end technical architectures related to imagery, imagery intelligence, and geospatial information for the DOD Components and non-DOD elements of the Intelligence Community . . .

12. Perform . . . or direct . . . the research, design, development, deployment operation and maintenance of systems related to the processing, dissemination, and archiving of imagery . . . imagery intelligence, and geospatial information

13. Evaluate the performance of imagery, imagery intelligence, and geospatial information components of the Department of Defense in meeting national and military intelligence requirements . . .

15. Review and respond to the imagery, imagery intelligence, and geospatial information requirements and priorities for military operations, in support of the Chairman of the Joint Chiefs of Staff and the Combatant Commanders

16. Develop and submit to the Secretary of Defense a consolidated statement of the geospatial information production requirements and priorities in accordance with the National Military Strategy and the national security objectives of the United States

17. Review and validate the national reconnaissance imagery and imagery intelligence requirements and priorities for national customers, and develop and submit to the DCI a consolidated statement of these imagery and imagery intelligence requirements and priorities . . .

21. Develop policies and provide DOD participation in national and international imagery, imagery intelligence, and geospatial information activities, in coordination with appropriate DOD officials for geospatial information activities and with the DCI for imagery activities and activities which involve an intelligence or security service of a foreign country . . .

23. Advise the Secretary of Defense and DCI on future needs for imagery, imagery intelligence, and geospatial information capabilities and systems . . . [112]

The core of NIMA's organizational structure is composed of the three directorates shown in Figure 2.7. Directorate of Corporate Affairs components are responsible for human and financial resources, contacts with external organizations and the public, and plans, programs, and analysis. The Directorate of Systems and Technology is responsible for research and development activities relating to the processing, interpretation, and dissemination of imagery and mapping data.

The Directorate of Operations consolidates the actual tasking and processing/interpretation activities that were carried out by the organizations absorbed by NIMA. Thus, the Central Imagery Tasking Office is the successor to the CIO tasking function. The Imagery Analysis Office houses the imagery interpreters who formerly worked for NPIC, the DIA Office of Imagery Analysis, and the CIA Office of Imagery Analysis. The Geospatial Information and Services Office is the

FIGURE 2.7   Organization of the National Imagery and Mapping Agency

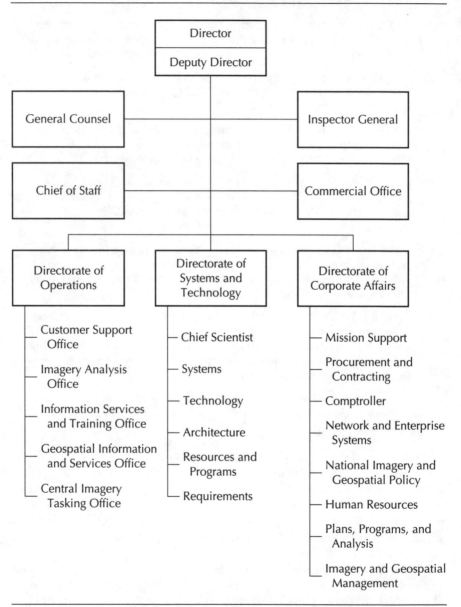

SOURCE: *Department of Defense Telephone Directory, December 1997* (Washington, D.C.: U.S. Government Printing Office, 1997), p. O-25; http://162.214.2.59/nimahome.html.

new home for the map and chart makers who worked for the Defense Mapping Agency.

Because of the geographical distribution between and within the agencies absorbed by NIMA, significant portions of NIMA are not located at its northern Virginia headquarters—but at the Washington Navy Yard (former NPIC); the DIA; Bethesda, Maryland (DMA hydrographic production); and St. Louis, Missouri (DMA aerospace production). It is expected that NIMA will complete a reduction of personnel from about 9,000 to 7,500 by late 2000.

Notes

1. National Security Council, *Report on Presidential Review Memorandum/NSC 11: Intelligence Structure and Mission*, 1977, p. 1.

2. Tim Weiner, "Voluntarily, C.I.A. Director Reveals Intelligence Budget," *New York Times*, March 21, 1998, p. A11.

3. See R. Harris Smith, *OSS: The Secret History of America's First Central Intelligence Agency* (Berkeley: University of California Press, 1981) and Bradley F. Smith, *The Shadow Warriors: O.S.S. and the Origins of the C.I.A.* (New York: Basic Books, 1983).

4. Harry S. Truman, "Executive Order 9621: Termination of the Office of Strategic Services and Disposition of its Functions," September 20, 1945, in *Emergence of the Intelligence Establishment*, ed. C. Thomas Thorne Jr. and David S. Patterson (Washington, D.C.: U.S. Government Printing Office, 1996), pp. 44–46.

5. Thomas F. Troy, *Donovan and the CIA: A History of the Establishment of the Central Intelligence Agency* (Frederick, Md.: University Publications of America, 1981), pp. 325–349.

6. U.S. Congress, House Permanent Select Committee on Intelligence, *Compilation of Intelligence Laws and Executive Orders* (Washington, D.C.: U.S. Government Printing Office, 1983), p. 7.

7. Lawrence Houston, "Memorandum for the Director, Subject: CIA Authority to Perform Propaganda and Commando Type Functions," September 25, 1947.

8. Ronald Reagan, "Executive Order 12333: United States Intelligence Activities," December 4, 1981, in *Federal Register* 46, no. 235 (December 8, 1981): 59941–54 at 59950.

9. Ronald Kessler, *Inside the CIA: Revealing the Secrets of the World's Most Powerful Spy Agency* (New York: Pocket Books, 1992), pp. xxvii, 144; Walter Pincus, "CIA Struggles to Find Identity in a New World," *Washington Post*, May 9, 1994, pp. A1, A9; U.S. Congress, House Committee on Appropriations, *Department of Defense Appropriations for 1995, Part 3* (Washington, D.C.: U.S. Government Printing Office, 1994), p. 784.

10. Central Intelligence Agency, *Fact Book on Intelligence, 50th Anniversary Edition*, 1997, p. 8.

11. Victor Marchetti and John Marks, *The CIA and the Cult of Intelligence* (New York: Knopf, 1974), p. 74; David Atlee Phillips, *Careers in Secret Operations: How to Be a Federal Intelligence Officer* (Frederick, Md.: University Publications of America, 1984), pp. 26, 28; Jeffrey Lenorovitz, "CIA Satellite Data Link Study Revealed," *Aviation Week and Space Technology*, May 2, 1997, pp. 25–26; Arnaud de Borchgrave, "Space-Age Spies," *Newsweek*, March 6, 1978, p. 37.

12. Marchetti and Marks, *The CIA and the Cult of Intelligence*, pp. 73–74; Commission on CIA Activities in the United States, *Report to the President* (Washington, D.C.: U.S. Government Printing Office, 1975), p. 91; *Directorate of Administration, Central Intelligence Agency* (Washington, D.C.: CIA, n.d.), unpaginated; Phillips, *Careers in Secret Operations*, p. 27.

13. Marchetti and Marks, *The CIA and the Cult of Intelligence*, p. 74; *Directorate of Administration, Central Intelligence Agency,* unpaginated; Phillips, *Careers in Secret Operations*, p. 27.

14. Commission on CIA Activities Within the United States, *Report to the President*, p. 92; R. James Woolsey "National Security and the Future Direction of the Central Intelligence Agency," address to the Center for Strategic and International Studies, Washington, D.C., July 18, 1994, p. 12.

15. *Directorate of Administration, Central Intelligence Agency*, unpaginated.

16. U.S. Congress, Senate Select Committee to Study Governmental Operations with Respect to Intelligence Activities, *Final Report, Book IV: Supplementary Detailed Staff Reports on Foreign and Military Intelligence* (Washington, D.C.: U.S. Government Printing Office, 1976), p. 46, n. 4.

17. Peer de Silva, *Sub Rosa: The CIA and the Uses of Intelligence* (New York: Times Books, 1978), p. 291.

18. The staff is mentioned in Commission on the Roles and Capabilities of the United States Intelligence Community, *Preparing for the 21st Century: An Appraisal of U.S. Intelligence* (Washington, D.C.: U.S. Government Printing Office, 1996), p. C–5.

19. "The CIA's Darkest Secrets," *U.S. News & World Report*, July 4, 1994, pp. 34–37; Duane R. Clarridge, *A Spy for All Seasons: My Life in the CIA* (New York: Scribner, 1997), pp. 8, 49, 180, 193; Walter Pincus, "Justice Asked to Investigate Leaks by CIA Ex-Officials," *Washington Post*, July 19, 1997, p. A16.

20. Kessler, *Inside the CIA*, p. 18; David Wise, *Nightmover: How Aldrich Ames Sold the CIA to the KGB for $4.6 Million* (New York: HarperCollins, 1995), p. 77 n; David Wise, *The American Police State* (New York: Vintage, 1976), p. 188; Robert Dreyfuss, "Left Out in the Cold," *Mother Jones*, January/February 1998, pp. 52–84.

21. U.S. Congress, Senate Select Committee to Study Governmental Operations with Respect to Intelligence Activities, *Final Report Book I: Foreign and Military Intelligence* (Washington, D.C.: U.S. Government Printing Office, 1976), p. 439; Ralph E. Cook, "The CIA and Academe," *Studies in Intelligence* (Winter 1983): 33–42 at 38–39; Kessler, *Inside the CIA*, p. 18.

22. Dreyfuss, "Left Out in the Cold."

23. U.S. Congress, Senate Select Committee to Study Governmental Operations with Respect to Intelligence Activities, *Final Report Book 1: Foreign and Military Intelligence*, p. 439; Cook, "The CIA and Academe," p. 38; Wise, *The American Police State*, p. 189.

24. Central Intelligence Agency, *Appendices to Guidance for CIA Activities Within the United States and Outside the United States*, November 30, 1982, p. 20.

25. Robert Parry, "CIA Manual Producers Say They're Scapegoats," *Washington Post*, November 15, 1984, p. A28; "Aides Disciplined by CIA Are Irked," *New York Times*, November 15, 1984, pp. A1, A8; Clarridge, *A Spy for All Seasons*, p. 190. The existence of the CPD was confirmed by the CIA Public Affairs Staff.

26. Loch Johnson, "Smart Intelligence," *Foreign Policy* (Winter 1992–1993): 53–69; Clarridge, *A Spy for All Seasons*, pp. 322–329; Roberto Suro, "2 Terrorist Groups Set Up U.S.

Cells, Senate Panel Is Told," *Washington Post*, May 14, 1997, p. A4; Vernon Loeb, "Where the CIA Wages Its New World War," *Washington Post*, September 9, 1998, p. A17.

27. Johnson, "Smart Intelligence"; David Wise, *Molehunt: The Secret Search for Traitors That Shattered the CIA* (New York: Random House, 1992), pp. 298–299; Angelo Codevilla, *Informing Statecraft: Intelligence for a New Century* (New York: Free Press, 1992), p. 155.

28. "The CIA's Darkest Secrets"; Barry G. Royden, "CIA and National HUMINT: Preparing for the 21st Century," *Defense Intelligence Journal* 6, no. 1 (Spring 1997): 15–22. On the CIA's handling of Yurchenko, see Ronald Kessler, *Escape from the CIA: How the CIA Won and Lost the Most Important KGB Spy Ever to Defect to the U.S.* (New York: Pocket Books, 1991).

29. Central Intelligence Agency, "Restructuring in the DS&T," June 1996; Jeffrey T. Richelson, "CIA's Science and Technology Gurus Get New Look, Roles," *Defense Week*, August 19, 1996, p. 6. In the early 1990s there was also, within the DO, a Technology Management Office (TMO), whose mission apparently involved foreign telecommunications. Whether that office has been absorbed by CITO or remains a separate organization is not clear. See Crime and Narcotics Center and Community Open Source Program Office, CIA, *1997 Open Source Conference for the Intelligence and Law Enforcement Communities*, September 16–18, 1997, McLean, Va., Biography of Dr. Joseph B. Markowitz. The TMO is described as a joint CIA-NSA operation in Dreyfuss, "Left Out in the Cold." A related element of the CIA Directorate of Operations that existed in 1995 and possibly still does is the Advanced Technology Acquisition Group, whose mission is to "exploit [deleted] information on the signal processing [deleted] . . . " See Office of Naval Intelligence, *Office of Naval Intelligence Command History, 1995*, n.d., p. 8.

30. See Jeffrey T. Richelson, "The Wizards of Langley: The CIA's Directorate of Science and Technology," *Intelligence and National Security* 12, no. 1 (January 1997): 82–103.

31. Ibid.

32. Central Intelligence Agency, *Fact Book on Intelligence, 50th Anniversary Edition*, p. 8; Crime and Narcotics Center and Community Open Source Program Office, *1997 Open Source Conference for the Intelligence and Law Enforcement Communities*, Biography of Russell E. Dressell.

33. U.S. Congress, House Select Committee on Intelligence, *U.S. Intelligence Agencies and Activities: Intelligence Costs and Fiscal Procedures* (Washington, D.C.: U.S. Government Printing Office, 1975), pp. 537–544; *Directorate of Science and Technology, Central Intelligence Agency* (Washington, D.C.: CIA, n.d.), unpaginated.

34. *Office of SIGINT Operations* (Washington, D.C.: CIA, n.d.), unpaginated; Desmond Ball, *A Suitable Piece of Real Estate: American Installations in Australia* (Sydney: Hale & Iremonger, 1980), p. 73; Bob Woodward, *Veil: The Secret Wars of the CIA, 1981–1987* (New York: Simon & Schuster, 1987), pp. 313–314.

35. CIA document fragment, released under the FOIA; Kessler, *Inside the CIA*, p. 168.

36. *Directorate of Science and Technology, Central Intelligence Agency*; Thomas Powers, *The Man Who Kept the Secrets: Richard Helms and the CIA* (New York: Knopf, 1979), p. 340 n. 38; U.S. Congress, Senate Select Committee to Study Governmental Operations with Respect to Intelligence Activities, *Final Report, Book IV*, p. 101; William Colby, with Peter Forbath, *Honorable Men: My Life in the CIA* (New York: Simon & Schuster, 1978), p. 336; Robert Gates, *From the Shadows: The Ultimate Insider's Story of Five Presidents and How They Won the Cold War* (New York: Simon & Schuster, 1996), p. 154.

37. Central Intelligence Agency, "Restructuring the DS&T;" Richelson, "CIA's Science and Technology Gurus."

38. Central Intelligence Agency, *Fact Book on Intelligence*, 1993, p. 9; Ray S. Cline, *Secrets, Spies, and Scholars* (Washington, D.C.: Acropolis, 1976), pp. 11–12; U.S. Congress, Senate Select Committee to Study Governmental Operations with Respect to Intelligence Activities, *Final Report, Book IV*, p. 236.

39. Central Intelligence Agency, *A Consumer's Guide to Intelligence*, 1995, p. 19; Kessler, *Inside the CIA*, p. 78; Central Intelligence Agency, *Fact Book on Intelligence* (1993), p. 9; CIA, *Foreign Broadcast Information Service*, n.d.; Stephen Barr, "Monitoring Service Spared in Latest Cuts," *Washington Post*, February 6, 1997, p. A21; Vice President Al Gore, *Accompanying Report of the National Performance Review, Intelligence Community* (Washington, D.C.: U.S. Government Printing Office, September 1993), p. 6.

40. Central Intelligence Agency, *A Consumer's Guide to Intelligence*, p. 19.

41. Central Intelligence Agency, "Restructuring the DS&T"; Richelson, "CIA's Science and Technology Gurus"; Barbara Starr, "CIA Looks to Web to Solve Data Overload," *Jane's Defence Weekly*, July 23, 1997, pp. 29–30.

42. *Office of Research and Development* (Washington, D.C.: CIA, n.d.), unpaginated; Private information.

43. Central Intelligence Agency, *Fact Book on Intelligence, 50th Anniversary Edition*, p. 8.

44. Ibid.; "Directorate of Intelligence Organizational Components," http://www.odci.gov/cia/di/mission/components.html.

45. Information provided by the CIA Public Affairs Staff; Richelson, "The Wizards of Langley"; CIA, *A Consumer's Guide to Intelligence*, p. 17; John J. Gentry, *Lost Promise: How CIA Analysis Misserves the Country* (Lanham, Md.: University Press of America, 1993), pp. 8, 10.

46. "Directorate of Intelligence Organizational Components."

47. *Directorate of Intelligence, Central Intelligence Agency* (Washington, D.C.: CIA, n.d.), pp. 4–5; Gentry, *Lost Promise*, p. 39.

48. "Directorate of Intelligence Organizational Components."

49. Information provided by CIA Public Affairs Staff.

50. Robin Wright and Ronald J. Ostrow, "Webster Unites Rival Agencies to Fight Drugs," *Los Angeles Times*, August 24, 1989, pp. 1, 27; Michael Isikoff, "CIA Creates Narcotics Unit to Help in Drug Fight," *Washington Post*, May 28, 1989, p. A12; Central Intelligence Agency, *A Consumer's Guide to Intelligence*, (1993), p. 18.

51. "Bush Approved Covert Action by CIA to Halt Spread of Arms," *Los Angeles Times*, June 21, 1992, p. A20; Bill Gertz, "CIA Creates Center to Monitor Arms," *Washington Times*, December 3, 1991, p. A5; "Intelligence Will Be Key Tool in Proliferation Battle," *Defense Week*, December 9, 1991, p. 3; Johnson, "Smart Intelligence"; Paula L. Scalingi, "Intelligence Community Cooperation: The Arms Control Model," *International Journal of Intelligence and Counterintelligence* 5, no. 4 (Winter 1991–1992): 402–403; Barbara Starr, "Woolsey Tackles Proliferation as the Problem Gets Worse," *Jane's Defence Weekly*, November 13, 1993, p. 23; Central Intelligence Agency, *A Consumer's Guide to Intelligence* (1995), p. 18.

52. U.S. Congress, House Permanent Select Committee on Intelligence, *Intelligence Authorization Act for Fiscal Year 1998*, Report 105–135, Part 1 (Washington, D.C.: U.S. Government Printing Office, 1997), p. 25.

53. Ibid.

54. Barbara Starr, "Non-Proliferation Centre Expands for Added Tasks," *Jane's Defence Weekly*, November 12, 1997, p. 17; R. Jeffrey Smith, "Top CIA Proliferation Aide, Facing

Budget Cuts, Quits," *Washington Post*, October 22, 1997, p. A19; R. Jeffrey Smith, "CIA to Enlarge Nonproliferation Center," *Washington Post*, November 4, 1997, p. A15.

55. Richard Smith, "The Intelligence Community and the Environment: Capabilities and Future Missions," *Environmental Change and Security Project Report* 2 (Spring 1996): 103–108.

56. "Governmental Activities," *Environmental Change and Security Project Report* 4 (Spring 1998): 125; Jeffrey T. Richelson, "Scientists in Black," *Scientific American*, February 1998, pp. 48–55.

57. Scalingi, "Intelligence Community Cooperation," pp. 405–406; Bill Gertz, "Report Demanded on Chemical Pact," *Washington Times*, March 17, 1997, p. A4.

58. *Report to the Secretary of State and the Secretary of Defense by a Special Committee Appointed Pursuant to Letter of 28 December 1951 to Survey Communications Intelligence Activities of the Government*, June 13, 1952, pp. 47–48, 119; RG 457, SR–123, Military Reference Branch, NARA; The National Cryptologic School, *On Watch: Profiles from the National Security Agency's Past 40 Years* (Ft. Meade, Md.: NCS, 1986), p. 17.

59. Harry S. Truman, Memorandum for: The Secretary of State and the Secretary of Defense, Subject: Communications Intelligence Activities, October 24, 1952; Center for Cryptologic History, *The Origins of NSA* (Ft. Meade, Md.: NSA, n.d.), p. 4.

60. Walter Bedell Smith, "Proposed Survey of Communications Intelligence Activities," December 10, 1951; *Report to the Secretary of State and the Secretary of Defense by a Special Committee*, p. 118; U.S. Congress, Senate Select Committee to Study Governmental Operations with Respect to Intelligence Activities, *Final Report, Book III: Foreign and Military Intelligence* (Washington, D.C.: U.S. Government Printing Office, 1976), p. 736; National Security Agency/Central Security Service, *NSA/CSS Manual 22–1* (Ft. Meade, Md.: NSA, 1986), p. 1.

61. *United States Government Organization Manual* (Washington D.C.: U.S. Government Printing Office, 1957), p. 137; "Washington Firm Will Install Ft. Meade Utilities," *Washington Post*, January 7, 1954, p. 7; "U.S. Security Aide Accused of Taking Secret Documents," *New York Times*, October 10, 1954, pp. 1, 33.

62. NSCID No. 6, "Signals Intelligence," February 17, 1972; Department of Justice, *Report on CIA-Related Electronic Surveillance Activities* (Washington, D.C.: Department of Justice, 1976), pp. 77–78.

63. NSCID No. 6, "Signals Intelligence."

64. Department of Defense Directive S-5100.20, "The National Security Agency and the Central Security Service," December 23, 1971.

65. U.S. Congress, Senate Select Committee to Study Governmental Activities with Respect to Intelligence Activities, *Final Report, Book I*, p. 354; U.S. Congress, House Committee on Appropriations, *Department of Defense Appropriations for 1983, Part 3* (Washington, D.C.: U.S. Government Printing Office, 1981), pp. 824–829; Leslie Maitland, "FBI Says New York Is a 'Hub' of Spying in U.S.," *New York Times*, November 14, 1981, p. 12; Patrick E. Tyler and Bob Woodward, "FBI Held War Code of Reagan," *Washington Post*, December 13, 1981, pp. 1, 27.

66. James Bamford, *The Puzzle Palace: A Report on NSA, America's Most Secret Agency* (Boston: Houghton Mifflin, 1982), p. 91; Bill Gertz, "Electronic Spying Reoriented at NSA," *Washington Times*, January 27, 1992, p. A4; Private information.

67. Private information.

68. Barbara Starr, "U.S. 'Puzzle Palace' Seeks New Clues to Combat Old Threats," *Jane's Defence Weekly*, September 3, 1997, pp. 35–36; Unattributable comments of NSA official, November 1997.

69. Department of Defense, *Defense Special Missile and Astronautics Center: Organization, Mission, and Concept of Operations*, September 27, 1982, p. 1; NSA, "FOIA J9347–98," June 15, 1998.

70. Raymond Tate, "Worldwide C3I and Telecommunications," Harvard University Center for Information Policy Resources, Seminar on C3I, 1980, p. 30.

71. Seymour Hersh, *"The Target Is Destroyed": What Really Happened to Flight 007 and What America Knew About It* (New York: Random House, 1986), pp. 52–53, 67–69.

72. "NSOC Opens New Information Protect Cell (IPC)," *NSA Newsletter*, July 1997, p. 7.

73. Bamford, *The Puzzle Palace*, pp. 96–97.

74. Ibid., pp. 97–113.

75. Ibid., p. 157; Melvin Laird, *National Security Strategy of Realistic Deterrence: Secretary of Defense Melvin Laird's Annual Defense Department Report, FY 1973* (Washington, D.C.: U.S. Government Printing Office, 1972), p. 135.

76. Douglas Aircraft Corporation, *Preliminary Design of an Experimental World-Circling Spaceship* (Santa Monica, Calif.: DAC, 1946).

77. Robert L. Perry, *Origins of the USAF Space Program, 1945-1956* (Washington, D.C.: Air Force Systems Command, June 1962), pp. 42–43; Jeffrey T. Richelson, *America's Secret Eyes in Space: The U.S. KEYHOLE Spy Satellite Program* (New York: Harper & Row, 1990), pp. 31–64.

78. Richelson, *America's Secret Eyes in Space*, p. 27; Richard M. Bissell Jr., with Jonathan E. Lewis and Frances T. Pudlo, *Reflections of a Cold Warrior* (New Haven, Conn.: Yale University Press, 1996), p. 135.

79. Jeffrey T. Richelson, "A Secret Journey: The Creation and Evolution of the National Reconnaissance Office," in preparation.

80. Carl Berger, *The Air Force in Space Fiscal Year 1961*, (Washington, D.C.: Air Force Historical Liaison Office, 1966), pp. 41–42; Secretary of the Air Force Order 115.1, "Organization and Functions of the Office of Missile and Satellite Systems," August 31, 1960.

81. Berger, *The Air Force in Space Fiscal Year 1961*, p. 42; Secretary of the Air Force Order 116.1, "The Director of the SAMOS Project," August 31, 1960.

82. Richard M. Bissell Jr. to Allen W. Dulles, August 8, 1961; Donald Welzenbach, "Science and Technology: Birth of a Directorate," *Studies in Intelligence* 30 (Summer 1986): 13–26; Albert Wheelon, "CORONA: A Triumph of American Technology," in *Eye in the Sky: The Story of the CORONA Reconnaissance Satellite*, ed. Dwayne Day, John S. Logsdon, and Brian Latell (Washington, D.C.: Smithsonian Institution Press, 1998), pp. 29–47.

83. Richelson, "A Secret Journey."

84. Frederic C. E. Oder, James C. Fitzpatrick, and Paul E. Worthman, *The CORONA Story* (Washington, D.C.: NRO, 1987), p. 69.

85. DOD Directive TS 5105.23, "(S) National Reconnaissance Office," March 27, 1964, p. 4.

86. Raymond Garthoff, "Banning the Bomb in Outer Space," *International Security* 5 (1980/1981), pp. 25–40.

87. John McCone, Memorandum of Mongoose Meeting Held on Thursday, October 4, 1962; Office of the Deputy Director, NRO Memorandum for Colonel [deleted] The Inspector General, USAF, Subject: RPVs, February 26, 1974.

88. Letter from William H. Webster, Director of Central Intelligence, and Richard B. Cheney, Secretary of Defense, to David L. Boren, Chairman, Select Committee on Intelligence,

U.S. Senate, February 26, 1990; U.S. Congress, Senate Armed Services Committee, *Department of Defense Authorization for Appropriations for Fiscal Year 1994 and the Future Years Defense Program* (Washington, D.C.: U.S. Government Printing Office, 1993), p. 477.

89. Secretary of the Air Force/Public Affairs, "Biography: Major General John L. Martin Jr.," November 1, 1969.

90. See Richelson, *America's Secret Eyes in Space*, pp. 87–143.

91. Interview; *GRAB: Galactic Radiation and Background, First Reconnaissance Satellite* (Washington, D.C. Naval Research Laboratory, 1998), p. 2.

92. "Procurement and Security Provisions for the R-12 Program," attachment to letter, Eugene Zuckert to General Schriever, April 5, 1963; NRO, "Analysis of 'A $1.5 Billion Secret in Sky,' *Washington Post*, December 9, 1973," n.d., p. 2.

93. Interview; B. A. Schriever, General USAF, Commander, AFSC, to Honorable Eugene M. Zuckert, July 11, 1963; Brockway MacMillan, Director, NRO, Memorandum for Deputy Chief of Staff, Research and Development, October 30, 1964; Headquarters, Air Force Systems Command, Andrews Air Force Base, Air Force Aeronautical Systems Operations, Operations Order No. __ (Draft), March 26, 1964.

94. NRO, "Deputy Director for National Support," 1996; Interview; U.S. Congress, Senate Armed Services Committee, *Department of Defense Authorization for Appropriations for Fiscal Year 1997 and the Future Years Defense Program, Part 7* (Washington, D.C.: U.S. Government Printing Office, 1997), p. 366.

95. U.S. Congress, Senate Select Committee on Intelligence and House Permanent Select Committee on Intelligence, *S. 2198 and S. 421 to Reorganize the United States Intelligence Community* (Washington, D.C.: U.S. Government Printing Office, 1993), p. 18.

96. NRO Home Page @ www.nro.odci.gov.

97. Admiral David Jeremiah et al., *Report to the Director, National Reconnaissance Office: Defining the Future of the NRO for the 21st Century, Executive Summary*, August 26, 1996, p. 24.

98. NRO Home Page @ www.nro.odci.gov; U.S. Congress, House Permanent Select Committee on Intelligence, *Intelligence Authorization Act for Fiscal Year 1999* (Washington, D.C.: U.S. Government Printing Office, 1998), pp. 27–28.

99. Mission Statement, NRO CI Home Page, June 14, 1996.

100. Commission on Roles and Capabilities of the United States Intelligence Community, *Preparing for the 21st Century: An Appraisal of U.S. Intelligence* (Washington, D.C.: U.S. Government Printing Office, 1996), p. 132; "NRO Organization," Briefing Slide for Presentation of Frank Strickland, NRO, to National Military Intelligence Association, November 19, 1997.

101. Robert M. Gates, Director of Central Intelligence, *Statement on Change in CIA and the Intelligence Community*, April 1, 1992, p. 28.

102. H.R. 4165, "National Security Act of 1992," 1992; S. 2198, "Intelligence Reorganization Act of 1992," 1992.

103. Central Imagery Office, *Briefing Slides*, 1992.

104. Department of Defense Directive 5105.26, "Central Imagery Office," May 6, 1992; Central Imagery Office, *Briefing Slides*, pp. 2–3; Director of Central Intelligence Directive 2/9, "Management of National Imagery Intelligence," June 1, 1992.

105. Central Imagery Office, *Briefing Slides*, p. 2.

106. Statement of John Deutch before Senate Select Committee on Intelligence, April 26, 1995, pp. 8–9.

107. "DCI Plans a National Imagery Agency," *Communiqué*, August 1995, pp. 1, 8.

108. Central Intelligence Agency, "National Imagery and Mapping Agency Proposed to Congress," November 28, 1995.

109. Ibid.

110. U.S. Congress, Senate Select Committee on Intelligence, *Special Report of the Senate Select Committee on Intelligence, United States Senate, January 4, 1995 to October 3, 1996* (Washington, D.C.: U.S. Government Printing Office, 1997), pp. 7–8. There was also some concern about the proposed merger from Defense Mapping Agency officials, who feared that their formal inclusion in the intelligence community might have a negative impact on the relationship with foreign nations who provide mapping information.

111. NIMA, "National Imagery and Mapping Agency Established," October 1, 1996.

112. DOD Directive 5105.60, "National Imagery and Mapping Agency (NIMA)," October 11, 1996.

3

DEFENSE DEPARTMENT
INTELLIGENCE ORGANIZATIONS

In addition to the national intelligence organizations within the Department of Defense—the National Security Agency (NSA), the National Reconnaissance Office (NRO), and the National Imagery and Mapping Agency (NIMA)—the department has its own agency, the Defense Intelligence Agency (DIA), which operates in support of the Secretary of Defense, the Joint Chiefs of Staff, and military commanders.

The DIA contains within it a service for the collection of human intelligence, as well as two intelligence production centers—one focuses on space and missile systems and the other on medical intelligence—that had previously been operated by the Army. DIA's human intelligence organization is treated in a separate section in this chapter.

DEFENSE INTELLIGENCE AGENCY

The Defense Intelligence Agency was one manifestation of the trend toward centralization that began in the Eisenhower administration and reached its peak in the Kennedy administration. The Eisenhower administration concluded in the late 1950s that a consolidation of the military services' general (that is, all non-SIGINT, non-overhead, nonorganic) intelligence activities was needed.[1] This belief was, according to one analyst, a by-product of the missile gap controversy of the time: "Faced with the disparate estimates of Soviet missile strength from each of the armed services which translated into what have been called self-serving budget requests for weapons of defense, the United States Intelligence Board created a Joint Study Group in 1959 to study the intelligence producing agencies."[2]

The Joint Study Group, chaired by the CIA's Lyman Kirkpatrick, concluded that there was a considerable overlap and duplication in defense intelligence activities and a resulting maldistribution of resources. The consequence was that the "overall direction and management of DOD's total intelligence effort becomes a very difficult if not impossible task. Indeed, the fragmentation of effort creates 'barriers' to the free and complete interchange of intelligence information among the several components of the Department of Defense."[3]

The study group thus recommended that the Secretary of Defense "bring the military intelligence organization within the Department of Defense into full consonance with the concept of the Defense Reorganization Act of 1958."[4] How to do this was a subject of controversy.

The study group's report noted that it had been suggested that a single intelligence service be established for the entire Defense Department, reporting directly to the Secretary of Defense. The study group concluded, however, that "on balance it would be unwise to attempt such an integration of intelligence activities so long as there are three military services having specialized skills and knowledge."[5]

Despite the study group's conclusions, in a February 8, 1961, memorandum to the Joint Chiefs of Staff, Defense Secretary Robert McNamara observed:

> It appears that the most effective means to accomplish the recommendations of the Joint Study Group would be the establishment of a Defense Intelligence Agency which may include the existing National Security Agency, the intelligence and counterintelligence functions now handled by the military departments, and the responsibilities of the Office of the Assistant Secretary, Special Operations.[6]

McNamara requested the JCS to provide, within thirty days, a concept for a defense intelligence agency, a draft DOD directive that would establish such an agency, and a time-phased implementation schedule. He also provided some preliminary guidelines for developing a plan that included the complete integration of all defense intelligence requirements and the elimination of duplication in intelligence collection and production.[7]

On February 9, the Joint Staff suggested that the JCS direct the staff to develop a concept for the DIA that would be consistent with McNamara's memo and would place the new agency under the control of the JCS.[8] On March 2, 1961, the Joint Chiefs sent McNamara recommendations, including an organizational concept for the establishment of a Military Intelligence Agency (MIA) under the JCS. On April 3, McNamara requested advice on several basic issues concerning the proposed agency, including its proposed placement under the JCS and its specific functions. Ten days later the JCS approved a Joint Staff draft memorandum for the Secretary of Defense. The memo justified placing a DIA/MIA under the JCS on the grounds that the DOD Reorganization Act of 1958 specifically assigned the Joint Chiefs the responsibility of strategic planning and operational direction of the armed forces, and the fulfillment of such responsibilities required control of appropriate intelligence assets. In contrast, placing the DIA/MIA in the Office of the Secretary of Defense (OSD) would "concentrate military intelligence assets at a level above, and isolated from, the organization charged with strategic planning and operational direction of the armed forces."[9]

The Joint Staff memo also suggested placing NSA under the authority of the JCS. In addition, it argued that total integration of all military intelligence activities might not be a sound concept, but if any intelligence activities were left with the services, the DIA/MIA director should be charged with closely monitoring them. Further, the director would be authorized to eliminate duplication, review all service intelligence programs and budgets, and assign priorities to military intelligence collection requirements.[10]

The agency that resulted was a compromise, but it was close to the JCS viewpoint. On July 5, 1961, McNamara decided to establish a DIA reporting to the Secretary of Defense through the JCS. On August 1, he did so via DOD Directive 5105.21, as a DOD agency, and made it responsible for: (1) organization, direction, management, and control over all DOD intelligence resources assigned to or included within the DIA; (2) review and coordination of those DOD intelligence functions retained by or assigned to the military departments; (3) supervision over the execution of all approved plans, programs, policies, and procedures for intelligence functions not assigned to the DIA; (4) exercise of maximum economy and efficiency in allocation and management of DOD intelligence resources; (5) response to priority requests by the United States Intelligence Board; and (6) fulfillment of intelligence requirements of major DOD components.[11] As a result of the DIA's creation, the Joint Staff Director for Intelligence (J-2) was abolished, as was the Office of Special Operations, the small intelligence arm of the Secretary of Defense.

On December 16, 1976, the Secretary of Defense issued a new charter for the DIA (i.e., a new version of DOD 5105.21), limiting the operational control of the JCS over the DIA to (1) obtaining the intelligence support required to perform their statutory function and assigned responsibilities and (2) assuring that adequate, timely, and reliable intelligence support was available to the unified and specified commands. In all other matters, the Director of the DIA would report to the Secretary of Defense through the Assistant Secretary of Defense for Intelligence (ASDI). The mission of the DIA was also stated more concisely as being "to satisfy, or to ensure the satisfaction of, the foreign intelligence requirements of the Secretary of Defense, the Joint Chiefs of Staff, DOD components and other authorized recipients, and to provide the military intelligence contribution to national intelligence.[12]

About five months later, on May 19, 1977, the Secretary of Defense signed a new version of DOD Directive 5105.21 that slightly altered the organization and administration of the agency. Under the revised charter the director would report to the Secretary of Defense and the chairman of the JCS. In addition, the Director of the DIA would be under the operational control of the JCS for purposes of: (1) obtaining intelligence support required to perform the statutory and assigned responsibilities of the JCS and (2) ensuring adequate, timely, and reliable intelligence support for the unified and specified commands. Staff supervision of the DIA would be exercised by the Assistant Secretary of Defense for Command, Control, Communications, and Intelligence (C³I) with respect to resources and by the ASD for International Security Affairs with respect to policy.[13]

In February 1990 the ASD (C^3I) established a steering group of senior officers in DOD intelligence organizations to review the readiness of the defense intelligence system in the face of the changing international security environment. The effort, which would be labeled "Defense Intelligence in the 1990s," was intended to identify the potential issues, risks, and opportunities expected to emerge in the 1990s.[14]

In June 1990 the group prepared a fairly brief TOP SECRET/CODEWORD draft interim executive summary of issues that had been raised by the participants in the effort and appended a listing of "issues" suggesting alternative ways of addressing individual topics.[15]

The draft summary was intended to be a forerunner of the final review. However, because of a shift in thinking at the senior level of the DOD, no final review study was completed—although the results of the study were presented to the Secretary of Defense, Deputy Secretary of Defense, and other senior defense officials in the September–December 1990 period. And on December 14, 1990, Undersecretary of Defense Donald J. Atwood issued a memorandum entitled "Strengthening Defense Intelligence Functions" that noted that senior-level DOD officials had reviewed the department's intelligence activities and requested from the memo's addressees detailed plans to achieve a variety of objectives, including strengthening "the role and performance of the Defense Intelligence Agency in the intelligence requirements, production, and management processes."[16]

The memo resulted in the March 15, 1991, ASD (C^3I) *Plan for Restructuring Defense Intelligence*. With respect to the DIA, the plan called for:

- strengthening the role of DIA as a Combat Support Agency

- improving the quality of the Defense Intelligence product through streamlining and reconfiguring DIA to improve its estimative capability with emphasis on quality analysis and reporting strategically important intelligence

- strengthening DIA's management of intelligence production and analysis

- assigning DIA responsibility to perform/oversee basic encyclopedic data production

- establishing within DIA a capability to validate threat information to ensure an independent intelligence input to the acquisition process

- establishing within DIA a Policy Issues Office to improve support to the Office of the Secretary of Defense[17]

Much of the effort to implement those and other aspects of the plan would take place in the administration of Lt. Gen. James R. Clapper, who became DIA director in November 1991. In part, the effort would be reflected in organizational changes.

It would not be until almost six years after the March 1991 plan was issued that a new DIA directive, reflecting many of the DIA's new responsibilities, would be issued. The directive itself was produced only after several years of effort. Thus, DOD Directive 5105.21, "Defense Intelligence Agency," of February 18, 1997, replaced the 1977 directive, which had been only slightly modified in 1978. The new directive specifies 31 responsibilities and functions for the Director of the DIA, including:

- Organize, direct, and manage the DIA and all assigned resources

- Provide peacetime, crisis, contingency, and combat intelligence support to the operational military forces

- Provide military intelligence support for the policy and planning activities of the DOD Components and, as appropriate, for similar activities of non-DOD national authorities

- Be responsible for planning, programming, and budgeting activities in furtherance of the Defense Department intelligence mission . . .

- Establish and operate a Joint Staff Intelligence Directorate (J2) that shall be responsible for responding to the direct intelligence support requirements of the Chairman of the Joint Chiefs of Staff . . .

- Manage and direct DOD human intelligence activities . . .

- Prepare intelligence assessments and estimates concerning transfers of technology, goods, services, munitions, and associated transfer mechanisms . . .

- Provide intelligence biography, reference library, and research services as appropriate, to facilitate accomplishment of the DOD Intelligence Components' mission

- Operate the National Military Joint Intelligence Center (NMJIC) in support of military planning and operations . . .

- Operate the Defense Intelligence Network as the principal DOD-wide current intelligence activity

- Support the DOD weapons system acquisition process by producing threat assessments within DIA, or validating assessments produced by other DOD Intelligence Components, for all major DOD acquisition programs . . .

- Operate the Defense Attaché System . . .

- Validate, register, and recommend priorities for military intelligence requirements; and assign collection responsibility, and monitor the application of DOD collection resources, other than signals intelligence (SIGINT) and imagery intelligence (IMINT) resources, to such requirements

- Provide central management of Measurement and Signature Intelligence . . .

- Implement National Intelligence Collection Tasking Authority after such has transferred from the DCI to the Secretary of Defense in crisis and/or conflict situations . . . [18]

In fulfilling his programming, planning, and budgeting responsibility the Director of the DIA serves as Program Manager for the General Defense Intelligence Program (GDIP) and as program coordinator of the General Defense Intelligence and Applications Program (GDIAP) of the Joint Military Intelligence Program (JMIP).[19]*

During the 1960s and 1970s the DIA underwent several extensive reorganizations. Although subsequent years were not without occasional organizational changes, they were not as frequent or as dramatic. However, between 1991 and 1993 the DIA underwent two extensive reorganizations designed to improve performance, deal with mandated personnel and budget reductions, adapt to changing international realities, and better coordinate military intelligence activities—as intended by the March 1991 *Plan for Restructuring Defense Intelligence*. The primary result of the latter reorganization was the creation of three DIA centers—the National Military Intelligence Collection Center, the National Military Intelligence Production Center, and the National Military Intelligence Systems Center. The centers were renamed after the retirement of DIA director Lt. Gen. James R. Clapper Jr., who had established them.

As shown in Figure 3.1, the elements subordinate to the Director of the DIA include three staffs—Director of Military Intelligence Staff; Plans, Programs, and Operations Staff; and General Defense Intelligence Program Staff—and six directorates—Policy Support; Intelligence, J2; Intelligence Production; Intelligence Operations; Information Systems and Services; Administration.

Policy Support and Intelligence

The Directorate for Policy Support provides direct intelligence support for the Office of the Secretary of Defense and other national-level policymakers, through the DIA's senior analysts: the Defense intelligence officers. It also manages selected special access programs.[20]

The Directorate for Intelligence, J2 serves as the Joint Chiefs of Staff intelligence directorate. Subordinate to its director are Deputy Directors for Crisis Management; Crisis Operations; Assessments, Doctrine, Requirements, and Capabilities; and Targets.[21]

The directorate provides current and warning intelligence to the Secretary of Defense, the chairman of the JCS, and other DOD officials. It also assesses, coordinates, produces, and integrates all-source current and indications and warning intelligence; provides daily briefings on current intelligence to the Secretary of Defense, the chairman of the JCS, and other DOD officials; produces a Morning Summary, daily *Defense Intelligence Notices*, and intelligence appraisals, and contributes to the *National Intelligence Daily*.[22]

The National Military Joint Intelligence Center, operated under the supervision of one of the J2 directorates, is an indications and warning center that "operates 24 hours a day and is responsible for providing time-sensitive intelligence to the

---

*The GDIP, GDIAP, and JMIP are discussed in chapter 17.

FIGURE 3.1   Organization of the Defense Intelligence Agency

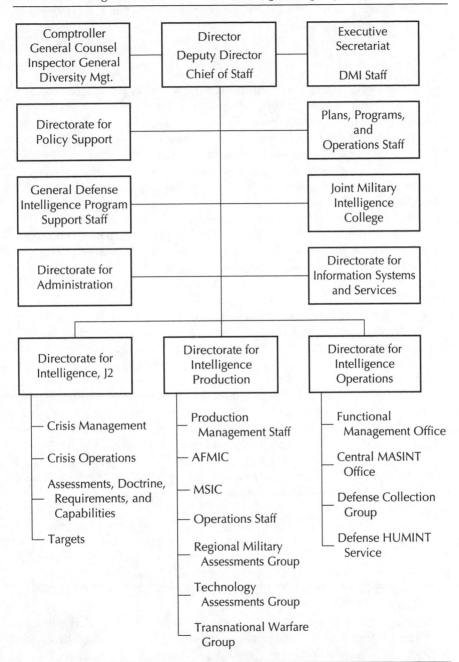

SOURCE: *Department of Defense Telephone Directory, December 1997* (Washington, D.C.: U.S. Government Printing Office, 1997), pp.O-21 to O-22.

National Military Command Center, the Secretary of Defense, Joint Chiefs of Staff, military commands, and military services.[23]

Intelligence Production

The Directorate of Intelligence Production includes five key production elements. The Regional Military Assessments Group consists of six offices—Asia, Europe, Infrastructure, Latin America, Middle East/Africa, Russia/NIS. The Technology Assessment Group produces assessments through six offices—Acquisition Threat Support, DODFIP (DOD Futures Intelligence Program), Advanced Conventional Weapons, Foreign Materiel Program, Advanced Technology/Technology Transfer, and Modeling and Simulation. The Transnational Warfare Group (TWG) has five offices—Counterterrorism Analysis, Counter-drug, Information Warfare Support, Joint Warfare Support, and Counterproliferation and NBC Assessment.[24]

The Information Warfare Support Office (and its Special Activities, Intelligence Preparation of the Battlespace, Threat Analysis and Foreign Denial and Deception divisions) produces studies on computer and cybernetic warfare, electronic warfare, psychological operations, deception, and physical destruction of information systems.[25]

The Office of Counterterrorism Analysis consists of two divisions—the Terrorism Analysis Division (TAD) and the Terrorism Warning Division (TWD). The TAD is the primary producer of terrorism assessments and studies for the Defense intelligence community. It produces and maintains the DOD terrorism database, which contains over 20,000 finished intelligence products on terrorist threats, groups, incidents, facilities, and personalities. It also reviews the terrorist threat to hundreds of Defense Department exercises and deployment operations each year. The TWD is responsible for terrorism-related indications and warning and crisis support and staffs the National Military Joint Intelligence Center (NMJIC) Terrorism Desk. In addition, the TWD produces the daily *Defense Intelligence Terrorism Summary* (DITSUM), which "serves as the primary source of terrorism-related analysis and threat information for senior policymakers as well as commanders, security officers, and planners."[26]

The Office for Counter-drug Analysis produces the *Interagency Assessment of Cocaine Movement*. Along with the FBI, in Project DOMINANT CHRONICLE, it has translated and exploited over 160,000 documents. It has also provided intelligence support to counternarcotics operations in Southeast and Southwest Asia.[27]

The Armed Forces Medical Intelligence Center (AFMIC) and the Missile and Space Intelligence Center (MSIC) were transferred to the DIA from the Army. In its 1991 report, *Intelligence Authorization Act, Fiscal Year 1992*, the House Permanent Select Committee on Intelligence strongly recommended that "the Armed Forces Medical Intelligence Center [and] the [Army] Missile and Space Intelligence Center . . . be transferred in their entirety to DIA and become designated

Field Production Activities of DIA." By early 1992 the DIA had developed a plan for transfer of the centers to its control, and the transfer orders were issued.[28]

AFMIC had been established in 1982, replacing the Army's Medical Intelligence and Information Agency (MIIA), which provided medical intelligence for the entire defense community. AFMIC's formation was possibly the result of unhappiness with the medical intelligence efforts of the MIIA. Discussions of Defense Audit Service personnel with the Director of the General Defense Intelligence Program Staff in 1981 indicated intelligence community concern about a lack of adequate medical intelligence in Southwest Asian and Third World countries, "where casualties from unusual diseases and environmental conditions could occur."[29]

Medical intelligence is particularly vital in planning for combat operations, particularly in areas significantly different from the United States in terms of environment and prevalence of disease. One aspect of AFMIC's activities consists of producing general medical intelligence on health and sanitation, epidemiology, environmental factors, and military and civilian medical care capabilities—as in AFMIC's "Medical Capabilities Study: Democratic People's Republic of Korea." A second aspect of its work involves the production of medical, scientific, and technical intelligence concerning all basic and applied biomedical phenomena of military importance, including biological, chemical, psychological, and biophysical. The AFMIC report entitled "Medical Effects of Non-Ionizing Electromagnetic Radiation-LASER" represents one example of the effort.[30]

AFMIC is also responsible for assessing foreign biomedical R&D and its impact on the physiological effectiveness of medical forces, as well as for assessing the exploitation of foreign medical materiel obtained under the DOD Foreign Materiel Exploitation Program (FMEP).[31]

Subordinate to the director, deputy director, and technical director of AFMIC are three divisions—Intelligence Production Integration, Epidemiology and Environmental Health, and Medical Capabilities—and two branches—Collection and Information Requirements and Programs and Security.[32] The organization of AFMIC is shown in Figure 3.2.

The Missile and Space Intelligence Center has several hundred employees and is located at Redstone Arsenal, Alabama. In June 1956 the Special Security Office of the Army Ballistic Missile Agency (ABMA) was established to procure missile and space intelligence data for the commander of the ABMA. To analyze the data, a Technical Intelligence Division (TID) was established. This division was subordinate to the ABMA's Assistant Chief of Staff for Research and Development. Subsequent to the March 1958 consolidation of all Army activities at Redstone Arsenal into the Army Ordnance Missile Command (AOMC), the fifty-person TID was redesignated the Office of the Assistant Chief of Staff for Missile Intelligence (OACSMI). When the AOMC was absorbed in 1962 by the Army Missile Command (itself subordinate to the U.S. Army Materiel Command), the

FIGURE 3.2   Organization of the Armed Forces Medical Intelligence Center

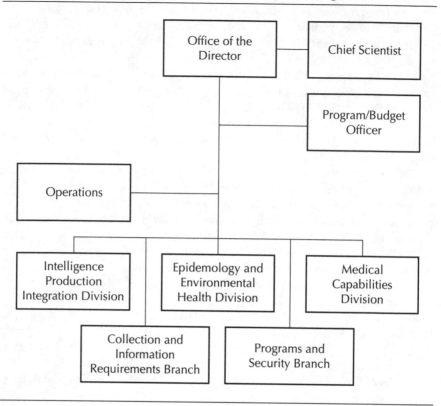

OACSMI was redesignated the Directorate of Missile Intelligence, and in September 1970 it became the Missile Intelligence Agency. On August 1, 1985, it was redesignated the U.S. Army Missile and Space Intelligence Center (AMSIC).[33]

The MSIC's mission is to "produce worldwide scientific and technical intelligence (S&TI) on surface-to-air missiles, ballistic missiles defense systems (both strategic and tactical), antitank guided missiles, antisatellite missiles, directed energy weapons, and relevant space programs/systems and command, control, communications, and computers."[34] The organization of the MSIC is shown in Figure 3.3.

Intelligence Operations and Administration

The Directorate for Intelligence Operations consists of four components: the Functional Management Office, the Central MASINT (Measurement and Signature Intelligence) Office, the Defense Collection Group, and the Defense HUMINT Service.

FIGURE 3.3   Organization of the Missile and Space Intelligence Center

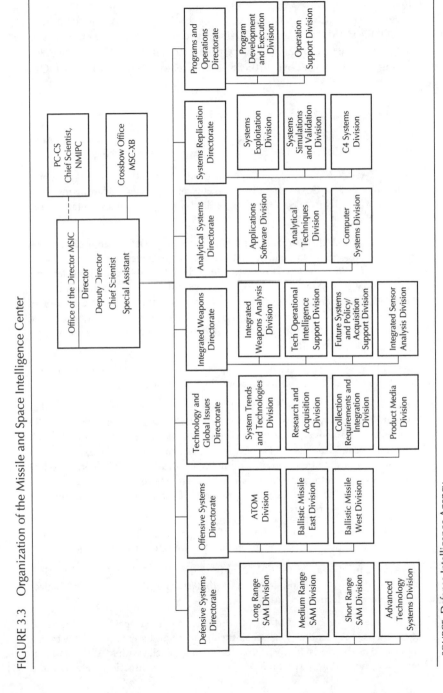

SOURCE: Defense Intelligence Agency.

The Central MASINT Office (CMO) was established in 1993 and today has about forty employees. It is a "joint combat support directorate, [which] serves a dual role as the Director of Central Intelligence's Executive Agent for MASINT and as the DOD MASINT Manager." Hence, its responsibilities are enumerated in both a DCI directive (DCID 2/11 of December 1992) and a DOD directive.[35]

According to DOD Directive 5105.58, the Director, Central MASINT Office, shall:

- Organize, direct, and manage the CMO and all assigned resources

- Manage the establishment of national MASINT collection requirements consistent with the guidance received from the Director of Central Intelligence . . .

- Provide MASINT support to the Department of Defense, the CIA, and as appropriate, other Federal Government Departments and Agencies, including the coordination of MASINT collection tasking, collection, processing, exploitation, and dissemination

- Task MASINT collection elements of the Department of Defense to meet national intelligence collection requirements established by the Director of Central Intelligence . . . except that the Director, CMO, shall advise MASINT collection elements on collection of MASINT to meet such national intelligence requirements when the collection element both (a) is assigned to, or under the operational control, of the Secretary of a Military Department or a commander of a unified or specified combatant command and (b) is not allocated by the Secretary of Defense to meet national intelligence requirements

- Advise MASINT collection elements of the Department of Defense on the collection of MASINT to meet non-national intelligence requirements

- Establish the architectures of MASINT tasking, collection, processing, and dissemination within the Department of Defense, in coordination with the DOD components and consistent to the maximum practicable extent with the overall functional architectures of the Department of Defense. Also, to the extent authorized by the heads of other Department or Agencies with MASINT tasking, collection, processing, exploitation, and dissemination functions, establish the architectures for MASINT tasking, collection, processing, exploitation, and dissemination in those other Departments and Agencies

- Serve as functional manager for the MASINT programs in the NFIP consistent with applicable guidance received from the Director of Central Intelligence . . .

- Serve as the functional manager, an advisor to the ASD (C³I) and the DOD components, for the MASINT programs in the budget aggregation known as "Tactical Intelligence and Related Activities"

- Evaluate the performance of MASINT components of the Department of Defense in meeting national and non-national intelligence requirements and, to the extent authorized by the heads of other Departments or Agencies with MASINT tasking, collection, processing, exploitation, and dissemination functions, evaluate the performance of the MASINT components of those other Departments or Agencies in meeting national and non-national intelligence requirements

- Develop and make recommendations on national and non-national MASINT policy, including relationships to international matters, for the approval of appropriate Federal Government officials

- In coordination with the appropriate DOD Components, support and conduct research, development, test, and evaluation activities related to MASINT tasking, collection, processing, exploitation, and dissemination, consistent with applicable law and DOD Directives[36]

The CMO produces or participates in the production of documents such as the *U.S. Spectral Plan, CMO MASINT Plan,* and *MASINT 2010—Planning the U.S. MASINT System for the 21st Century.*[37] The organization of the CMO is shown in Figure 3.4.

The Defense Collection Group, in support of military forces and policymakers, levies intelligence requirements on collection agencies and resources, monitors collection responses, and evaluates collection efforts in terms of reliability, efficiency, and cost. It operates the twenty-four-hour Defense Collection Coordination Center (DCCC). During the Persian Gulf War the DCCC acted as the executive agent for all national imagery in support of Desert Storm operations. All overhead imagery supporting the war effort was planned and developed at the coordination center.[38]

The Directorate for Administration contains the Counterintelligence and Security Activity (CISA), which serves as the focal point for counterintelligence issues and for assessments of the threat from foreign intelligence activities. The CISA provides counterintelligence staff support to the chairman of the JCS and the combatant commands. Other functions of the CISA include serving as the Defense Department counterintelligence collection requirements manager; providing staff support to the DOD HUMINT manager; conducting all-source analysis of foreign intelligence activity; producing counterintelligence assessments, studies, and estimates, and the coordination of the counterintelligence production programs of all Defense Department counterintelligence components.[39]

Main headquarters for the DIA is the Defense Intelligence Analysis Center (DIAC) at Bolling Air Force Base, Washington, D.C. It has about 7,100 personnel (including about 2,000 overseas) and a budget of approximately $900 million.

DEFENSE HUMINT SERVICE

Early in the Reagan administration, Deputy Undersecretary of Defense (Policy) Richard Stillwell sought to establish a DOD HUMINT agency. His effort, codenamed MONARCH EAGLE, partially resulted from DOD and military service

FIGURE 3.4   Organization of the Central MASINT Office

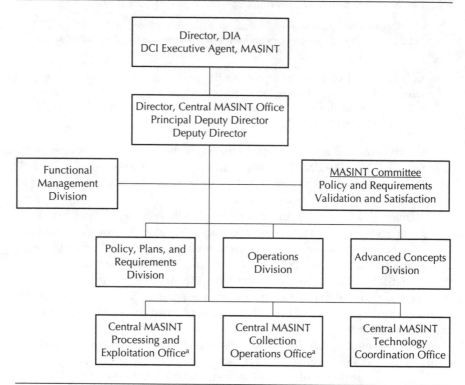

ª planned.

SOURCE: John L. Morris, Principal Deputy Director, CMO, *MASINT: Progress and Impact, Brief to NMIA,* November 19, 1996, slides 7, 15.

dissatisfaction with CIA collection priorities. The project was vetoed by Congress, however, on the grounds that it would overlap with CIA HUMINT collection efforts and make control of sensitive operations more difficult.[40]

In December 1992, DOD Directive 5200.37, "Centralized Management of DOD Human Intelligence (HUMINT) Operations," centralized HUMINT decisionmaking under a DOD HUMINT manager, established the concept of HUMINT support elements at combatant commands, and required consolidation of HUMINT support services.[41]

In June 1993, in response to discussions with DCI James Woolsey during the annual Joint Review of Intelligence Programs, Deputy Secretary of Defense William J. Perry requested that the ASD (C³I) develop a plan to consolidate the separate human intelligence components of the Defense Department into a single organization.[42]

That plan, *Plan for Consolidation of Defense HUMINT*, was approved by Perry in a November 2, 1993, memorandum. It specified that the ASD (C³I) effect the consolidation of the service HUMINT operations by fiscal year 1997 to establish a Defense HUMINT Service (DHS).[43] The plan also called for the Director of the DIA to activate the DHS as a provisional organization, "using existing DOD GDIP HUMINT resources and structures within FY 1994," and "to establish a headquarters structure . . . followed by support, clandestine, and overt elements in accordance with [a] time-phased schedule."[44]

Thus, the *Plan* made the Director of the DIA responsible for consolidating the DIA's human intelligence activities with those of the Army, Navy, and Air Force. The DIA's HUMINT operations included the activities of its over 100 openly acknowledged attaché offices throughout the world. The mission of the attachés is to observe and report military and politico-military information, represent the Department of Defense and the military services, administer military assistance programs and foreign military sales, and advise the U.S. ambassador on military and politico-military matters. The DIA also maintained a small contingent of clandestine case officers responsible for recruiting agents.[45]

Of the military services, the most significant contribution in forming the DHS came from the Army, specifically the Intelligence and Security Command's Foreign Intelligence Activity. The Army had maintained a significant clandestine HUMINT effort throughout the Cold War. Not surprisingly, significant opposition to creation of the DHS emanated from Army intelligence officials.[46]

In 1966 the Navy established an organization—first known as the Naval Field Operations Support Group and then as Task Force 157—to conduct clandestine and overt collection operations. That organization was disestablished in 1977. At the same time, Task Force 168 was assigned the task of overt collection. The Navy's contribution to the DHS came from the turnover of much of 168's assets, which were absorbed by the Office of Naval Intelligence in 1993, as well as the contingent of clandestine case officers (to reach a maximum of 100) that the Navy began recruiting around 1993.[47]

The Air Force contribution to the DHS came from the transfer of personnel from the former Air Force Intelligence Command's 696th Intelligence Group. The group, which conducted clandestine collection activities and debriefed defectors, was previously known as the Air Force Special Activities Center, the 7612th Air Intelligence Group, and the 1127th Field Activities Group. The 1127th was described as "an oddball unit, a composite of special intelligence groups who 'conducted worldwide operations to collect intelligence from human sources.' The men of the 1127th were con artists. Their job was to get people to talk—Russian defectors, North Vietnamese soldiers taken prisoner."[48]

The DHS headquarters organization that resulted from the consolidation is shown in Figure 3.5. The Office of Operations, with its Current Operations, Defense Central Cover, and Operations Analysis divisions, directs and evaluates DHS collection operations. The operations are carried out through six divisions—European,

FIGURE 3.5   Organization of the Defense HUMINT Service

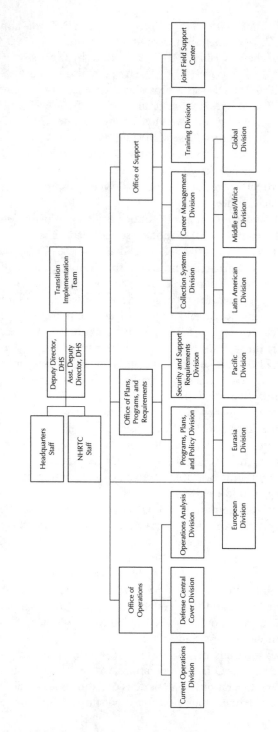

SOURCE: Defense Intelligence Agency.

Eurasia, Pacific, Latin America, Middle East/Africa, and Global. Cover support is provided by the Office of Support's Joint Field Support Center.

Outside of Washington a key component of the DHS's collection operations are the HUMINT Support Elements (HSE) at the headquarters of the commanders in chief of the Atlantic, Southern, Pacific, European, and Central Commands and at headquarters of the sub-unified commands, in order to "improve support to warfighters." The HSEs "help commands develop and process HUMINT collection requirements and facilitate planning and coordination of DOD HUMINT support to operational commands." The HSEs also "develop exercise scenarios and Command contingency plans to ensure HUMINT support is planned, practiced, and available for deployment."[49]

Other DHS elements overseas include a large number of operating bases. The largest of the bases outside the United States is Operations Base Stuttgart (OBST), which has fifteen separate operating locations and served as "the primary resource for DIA personnel deploying in support of Operations Joint Endeavor." Thus, by October 1995, when the DHS was declared to have achieved initial operating capability, it had "over 2,000 personnel stationed in over 100 locations including Washington, D.C."[50]

Notes

1. U.S. Congress, Senate Select Committee to Study Governmental Operations with Respect to Intelligence Activities, *Final Report, Book I: Foreign and Military Intelligence* (Washington, D.C.: U.S. Government Printing Office, 1976), p. 325.

2. U.S. Congress, Senate Select Committee to Study Governmental Operations with Respect to Intelligence Activities, *Final Report, Book VI: Supplementary Reports on Intelligence Activities* (Washington, D.C.: U.S. Government Printing Office, 1976), p. 266.

3. Secretary of Defense Robert S. McNamara, Memorandum for the President, Subject: The Establishment of a Defense Intelligence Agency, July 6, 1961, *DDRS* 1986–000085.

4. Joint Study Group, *The Joint Study Group Report on Foreign Intelligence Activities of the United States Government*, December 15, 1960, p. 31.

5. Ibid., p. 23.

6. Robert McNamara, Memorandum for the Chairman, Joint Chiefs of Staff, Subject: Establishment of a Defense Intelligence Agency, February 8, 1961, NA, MRB, RG 218, CCS 2010 (Collection of Intelligence), 1960 Box, Dec. 20, 1960 Folder, p. 1127.

7. Ibid., p. 1129.

8. Joint Staff, DJSM–156–61, Memorandum for General Lemnitzer et al., Subject: Establishment of a Defense Intelligence Agency, February 8, 1961, NA, MR, RG 218, CCS 2010 (Collection of Intelligence), 1960 Box, Dec. 20, 1960 Folder.

9. JCS 2031/166, Joint Chiefs of Staff Decision on JCS 2031/166, Memorandum by the Director, Joint Staff, on Establishment of a Defense Intelligence Agency, April 13, 1961; JCS 2031/166, Memorandum by the Director, Joint Staff for the Joint Chiefs of Staff on Establishment of a Defense Intelligence Agency, April 7, 1961, with Enclosure (Revised Draft Memorandum [April 12, 1961] for the Secretary of Defense, Subject: Establishment of a

Defense Intelligence Agency [DIA], both in NA, MRB, RG 218, CCS 2010 [Collection of Intelligence]), 1960 Box, Dec. 20, 1960 Folder.

10. Revised Draft Memorandum for the Secretary of Defense, Subject: Establishment of a Defense Intelligence Agency (DIA).

11. Historical Division, Joint Secretariat, Joint Chiefs of Staff, *Development of the Defense Agencies*, November 3, 1978, p. B-1.

12. Ibid., p. B-2, citing Department of Defense Directive 5105.21, "Defense Intelligence Agency," December 16, 1976.

13. Historical Division, Joint Secretariat, Joint Chiefs of Staff, *Development of Defense Agencies*, pp. B-2 to B-3.

14. William K. O'Donnell, Memorandum for W. M. MacDonald, Director, Freedom of Information and Security Review OASD (PA), Subject: Freedom of Information Act (FOIA) Appeal—Jeffrey T. Richelson, July 31, 1991.

15. Ibid.

16. Ibid., Assistant Secretary of Defense (Command, Control, Communications, and Intelligence), *Plan for Restructuring Defense Intelligence*, March 15, 1991, p. 1; Donald J. Atwood, Memorandum for Secretaries of the Military Departments et al., Subject: Strengthening Defense Intelligence Functions, December 14, 1990.

17. Assistant Secretary of Defense (Command, Control, Communications, and Intelligence), *Plan for Restructuring Defense Intelligence*, p. 3.

18. DOD Directive 5105.21, "Defense Intelligence Agency," February 18, 1997.

19. Ibid.

20. Defense Intelligence Agency, *Vector 21: A Strategic Plan for the Defense Intelligence Agency*, 1996, p. 13.

21. *Department of Defense Telephone Directory, December 1997* (Washington, D.C.: U.S. Government Printing Office, 1997), p. O-21.

22. Defense Intelligence Agency, *Organization, Mission, and Key Personnel*, 1984, pp. 43–46.

23. Central Intelligence Agency, *A Consumer's Guide to Intelligence*, 1993, p. 42.

24. *Department of Defense Telephone Directory, December 1997*, p. O-22; Defense Intelligence Agency, *Vector 21*, p. 13.

25. Dr. John J. Yurechko, "On Guard Against Information Warfare," *Communiqué*, April/May 1997, p. 37.

26. Maj. Chip Cutler and Jeff Rote, "Terrorism: Threat and Response," *Communiqué*, March 1997, pp. 15–17.

27. Rex Mills, "The Office of Counterdrug Analysis," *Communiqué*, June/July 1997: p. 17.

28. U.S. Congress, House Permanent Select Committee on Intelligence, *Report 102–65, Part 1 on Intelligence Authorization Act, Fiscal Year 1992* (Washington, D.C.: U.S. Government Printing Office, 1991), p. 8; Letter, John W. Shannon, Acting Secretary of the Army, to Lt. Gen. James R. Clapper Jr., Director, Defense Intelligence Agency, February 4, 1992; Defense Intelligence Agency, *Plan for the Transfer of the Armed Forces Medical Intelligence Center to the Defense Intelligence Agency*, n.d.

29. Defense Audit Service, *Semiannual Audit Plan, First Half, Fiscal Year 1982* (Washington, D.C.: DAS, 1981), p. 32.

30. Armed Forces Medical Intelligence Center, *Organization and Functions of the Armed Forces Medical Intelligence Center* (Ft. Detrick, Md.: AFMIC, April 1986), p. vi; Defense Audit Service, *Semiannual Audit Plan, First Half, Fiscal Year 1982*, p. 32.

31. Defense Audit Service, *Semiannual Audit Plan, First Half, Fiscal Year 1982*, p. 32.

32. Col. Gerard Schumeyer, "Medical Intelligence . . . Making a Difference," *American Intelligence Journal* 17, no. 1&2 (1996): pp. 11–15.

33. *Organization, Mission and Functions: U.S. Army Missile and Space Intelligence Center, Redstone Arsenal, Alabama* (Redstone Arsenal, Ala.: AMSIC, n.d.), pp. 4–6.

34. Missile and Space Intelligence Center, "Missile and Space Intelligence Center (MSC)," 1996.

35. Defense Intelligence Agency, "Mission Description" (Central MASINT Office), n.d.; CMO, "Script for CMO Brief to the 8th Annual Defense Intelligence Status Symposium," November 1996, p. 1.

36. Department of Defense Instruction Number 5105.58, *Management of Measurement and Signature Intelligence (MASINT)*, February 9, 1993.

37. CMO, "Script for CMO Brief . . . ," pp. 1–2.

38. William B. Huntington, "DIA's Collection Group," *Communiqué*, November/December 1996, p. 18.

39. Defense Intelligence Agency, *Vector 21*, p. 14.

40. Raymond Bonner, "Secret Pentagon Intelligence Unit Is Disclosed," *New York Times*, May 11, 1983, p. A13; Robert C. Toth, "U.S. Spying: Partnership Re-emerges," *Los Angeles Times*, November 14, 1983, pp. 1, 12; Robert M. Lisch, *Implementing the DHS: Views from the Leadership* (Washington, D.C.: Joint Military Intelligence College, 1995), p. 9.

41. Office of the Assistant Secretary of Defense (Command, Control, Communications, and Intelligence), *Plan for the Consolidation of Defense HUMINT*, 1993, p. 1.

42. Ibid.; For an account of the formation of the Defense HUMINT Service, see Jeffrey T. Richelson, "From MONARCH EAGLE to MODERN AGE: The Consolidation of U.S. Defense HUMINT," *International Journal of Intelligence and Counterintelligence* 10, no. 2 (Summer 1997): 131–164.

43. William J. Perry, Memorandum for Secretaries of the Military Departments et al., Subject: Consolidation of Defense HUMINT, November 2, 1993.

44. Office of the Assistant Secretary of Defense (Command, Control, Communications, and Intelligence), *Plan for the Consolidation of Defense HUMINT*, p. 7.

45. U.S. Congress, House Committee on Armed Services, *Hearings on H.R. 4181 to Authorize Certain Construction at Military Installations for Fiscal Year 1987, and Other Purposes* (Washington, D.C.: U.S. Government Printing Office, 1986), pp. 199–200; Defense Intelligence Agency, *Organization, Mission, and Key Personnel*, pp. 22–23; Joint Chiefs of Staff, *JCS Pub 1.1*, pp. III-10-14 to III-10-15; Private information.

46. Richelson, "From MONARCH EAGLE to MODERN AGE: The Consolidation of U.S. Defense HUMINT."

47. Jeffrey T. Richelson, "Task Force 157: The U.S. Navy's Secret Intelligence Service, 1966–1977," *Intelligence and National Security* 11, no. 1 (January 1996): 106–145; Office of Naval Intelligence, "ONI–65 Mission Statement," n.d.

48. Benjamin Schemmer, *The Raid* (New York: Harper & Row, 1975), pp. 26–27.

49. Barbara Starr, "Military Network Now Handles DOD HUMINT," *Jane's Defence Weekly*, March 11, 1995, p. 13; Les Aspin, *Secretary of Defense Annual Report to the President and the Congress* (Washington, D.C.: U.S. Government Printing Office, 1995), p. 240; Nick Eftimiades, "DHS Stands Up," *Communiqué*, October 1995, pp. 1, 10.

50. Starr, "Military Network Now Handles DOD HUMINT," p. 13; Aspin, *Secretary of Defense Annual Report to the President and the Congress*, p. 240; Eftimiades, "DHS Stands Up"; "Director Visits DHS Element," *Communiqué*, September 1996, p. 35.

4

MILITARY SERVICE
INTELLIGENCE ORGANIZATIONS

Unlike the United Kingdom and Canada, who abolished their military service intelligence organizations in favor of a unified defense intelligence organization, or Australia and France, whose service intelligence organizations are restricted to tactical intelligence production, the United States has maintained elaborate service intelligence organizations.

The continued major role of U.S. service intelligence organizations is partly a function of bureaucratic politics, partly a function of law, and partly the result of the structure and requirements of the U.S. military. A military force with large service components, and major combat commands distributed across the globe, may be better served in terms of intelligence support by organizations that are not too detached from the service components and the commands.

Until the early 1990s, it could be said that each of the major services maintained an intelligence community of its own—a number of distinct, often geographically separated, intelligence organizations directed by the service's intelligence chief. However, in 1991, a significant process of disestablishment and/or consolidation of formerly separate intelligence organizations began in each of the major services. The factors producing the changes included budget and personnel cuts taking place in the aftermath of the Cold War and pressure exerted by congressional oversight committees. In a 1990 report, the Senate Select Committee on Intelligence observed:

> While new requirements and the increasing cost of collection systems have driven a share of the increase in intelligence, the cost of maintaining large numbers of intelligence organizations internal to the Department of Defense has also contributed. Every echelon from the Office of the Secretary of Defense, to the Service Departments, to the CINCs [Commanders in Chief] and below have their own organic intelligence arms. For each organization, we need separate buildings, separate administration, separate security, separate communications, and separate support services.
>
> The existence of these multiple organizations raises other important concerns. Over the years, numerous individuals and reports . . . have criticized the Defense De-

partment for significant duplication of effort; insufficient integration and sharing of information; uneven security measures and regulations; pursuit of parochial service, CINC, [and] other interests rather than joint intelligence interests; and gaps in intelligence support and coverage, despite the number of intelligence organizations.[1]

As a result, the committee, along with the Senate Armed Services Committee, directed the Secretary of Defense to review all of the Defense Department's intelligence activities and "to the maximum degree possible, consolidate or begin consolidating all disparate or redundant functions, programs, and entities."[2]

The next year, on March 15, the Assistant Secretary of Defense (C³I) issued his *Plan for Restructuring Defense Intelligence*. The plan instructed each military service to "consolidate all existing intelligence commands, agencies, and elements into a single intelligence command within each Service."[3] Although that objective has not been completely met, each of the major services has undertaken significant consolidations of their intelligence activities.

ARMY INTELLIGENCE ORGANIZATIONS

U.S. Army intelligence collection and production operations are the responsibility of the Deputy Chief of Staff for Intelligence (DCSI). Those operations are carried out by the U.S. Army Intelligence and Security Command (INSCOM)—which conducts imagery, MASINT, and SIGINT operations—and the National Ground Intelligence Center (NGIC)—which produces scientific and technical, as well as general, military intelligence. NGIC is formally subordinate to INSCOM.

The Deputy Chief of Staff for Intelligence determines Army intelligence policy, supervises the activities of INSCOM and NGIC, and represents the Army in military and national intelligence fora. The DCSI's office consists of an Administrative Executive Office and seven directorates—Foreign Intelligence, Intelligence Futures, Intelligence Information Management, CI/HUMINT, Intelligence Policy, Intelligence Programs and Analysis, and Reserve Affairs—as shown in Figure 4.1.

The Foreign Intelligence Directorate is concerned with current intelligence, long-term assessment, and threat intelligence. The Intelligence Futures Directorate focuses on future intelligence requirements and architectures. The CI/HUMINT Directorate is responsible for overseeing Army counterintelligence operations as well as for defining Army human intelligence requirements. The Intelligence Policy Directorate and its two divisions (Battlespace Surveillance and Operations, and Integration) focuses on the collection of intelligence by space systems and signals intelligence platforms, particularly with respect to supporting combatant commanders.

On January 1, 1977, the U.S. Army Security Agency (ASA) was redesignated as the U.S. Army Intelligence and Security Command and absorbed the U.S. Army Intelligence Agency (AIA), the Forces Command Intelligence Group, the Intelligence Threat Analysis Detachment, and the Imagery Interpretation Center. The

FIGURE 4.1   Organization of the Office of the Deputy Chief of Staff for
Intelligence

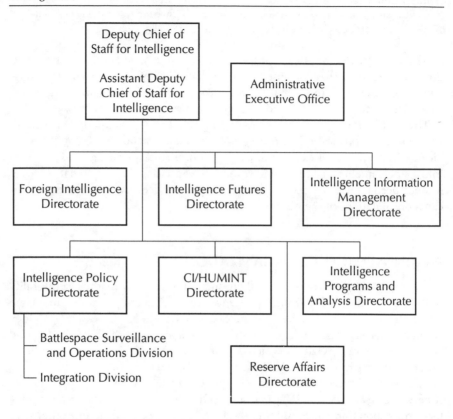

SOURCE: *Department of Defense Telephone Directory, December 1997* (Washington, D.C.:
U.S. Government Printing Office, 1997), pp. O-42 to O-43.

latter three organizations had been field operating activities of the Assistant Chief
of Staff for Intelligence.[4]

The commanding general of INSCOM is therefore responsible both to the Army's
DCSI and to the Chief of the Central Security Service (i.e., the Director of the NSA).
INSCOM personnel staff SIGINT collection facilities at numerous overseas bases. In
addition, INSCOM conducts MASINT and imagery collection operations as well as
offensive counterintelligence operations (OFCO). In 1992, it was assigned responsibility for supervising the intelligence production activities of the Foreign Science
and Technology Center (FSTC) and the Intelligence and Threat Analysis Center
(ITAC).[5] The two organizations were subsequently merged to form NGIC.

In INSCOM a number of Assistant Chiefs of Staff are responsible for different
areas of activity. Thus, as illustrated in Figure 4.2, there are ACSs for Personnel,

FIGURE 4.2   Organization of the U.S. Army Intelligence and Security Command

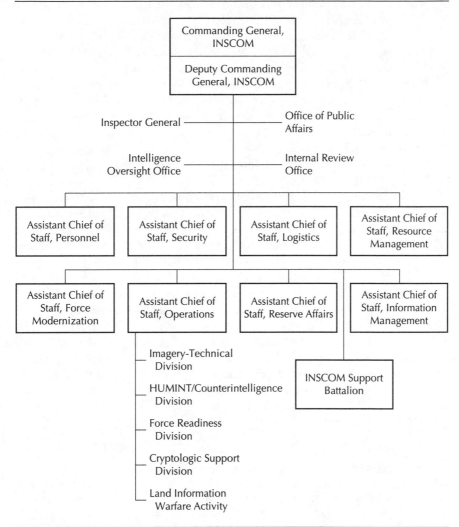

SOURCE: *Department of Defense Telephone Directory, December 1997* (Washington, D.C.: U.S. Government Printing Office, 1997), p. O-66.

Security, Logistics, Resource Management, Force Modernization, Operations, Reserve Affairs, and Information Management.

Subordinate to the ACS for Operations are four divisions—Imagery-Technical, HUMINT/Counterintelligence, Force Readiness, Cryptologic Support—and the Land Information Warfare Activity. The Imagery and Technical Division supervises the aerial imagery and assorted MASINT activities carried out by INSCOM field units. The division's imagery element administers and/or coordinates imagery collection, exploitation, processing, and dissemination in support of Army requirements at the Echelon Above Corps level.[6]

The HUMINT component of the HUMINT/Counterintelligence Division probably provides validation of Army HUMINT requirements and analysis of the extent to which the Defense HUMINT Service is satisfying those objectives. The CI component of the division develops and disseminates guidance to implement Army policy concerning technical surveillance countermeasures, Special Access Program support, offensive counterintelligence operations, and operations security support.[7]

The Cryptologic Support Division conducts liaison with the NSA, engages in long-range SIGINT planning, reviews and validates SIGINT architectures and concepts for future SIGINT operations, and serves as the point of contact for INSCOM SIGINT support to military operations.[8]

Units in the field include the SIGINT collection units, which operate under NSA/INSCOM tasking. Present INSCOM SIGINT units include those at Kunia, Hawaii; Misawa, Japan; San Antonio, Texas; Bad Aibling, Germany; and Menwith Hill, United Kingdom. Other field units, in both the United States and abroad, are those involved in counterintelligence, imagery, and MASINT collection. The 902nd MI Group handles Army counterintelligence investigations within the United States. One of the Group's elements is the Foreign Counterintelligence Activity, which conducts most of the Army's offensive counterintelligence operations.[9]

The National Ground Intelligence Center, located in Charlottesville, Virginia, was established in 1962 as the Foreign Science and Technology Center (FSTC) by consolidating the intelligence offices of the individual Army technical services—among them Signal, Ordnance, Quartermaster, Engineering, and Chemical services. It was redesignated as the NGIC during 1994 and absorbed the Intelligence and Threat Analysis Center in 1995.[10]

NGIC functions include:

- Developing and maintaining a data base of ground forces intelligence

- Producing ground intelligence in support of research, development, and acquisition programs of the Department of the Army, United States Marine Corps, warfighting commanders, the Army force modernization community, the Defense Intelligence Agency, Department of Defense and national policymakers

- Discovering S&T threats to the security of U.S. ground forces

- Forecasting foreign military trends and developments through study of worldwide S&T and GMI [General Military Intelligence] accomplishments

- Identifying significant foreign improvements that may be incorporated into U.S. weapon and equipment systems

- Pinpointing deficiencies in foreign developments to assist in evolving U.S. countermeasures for exploitation

FIGURE 4.3 Organization of the National Ground Intelligence Center

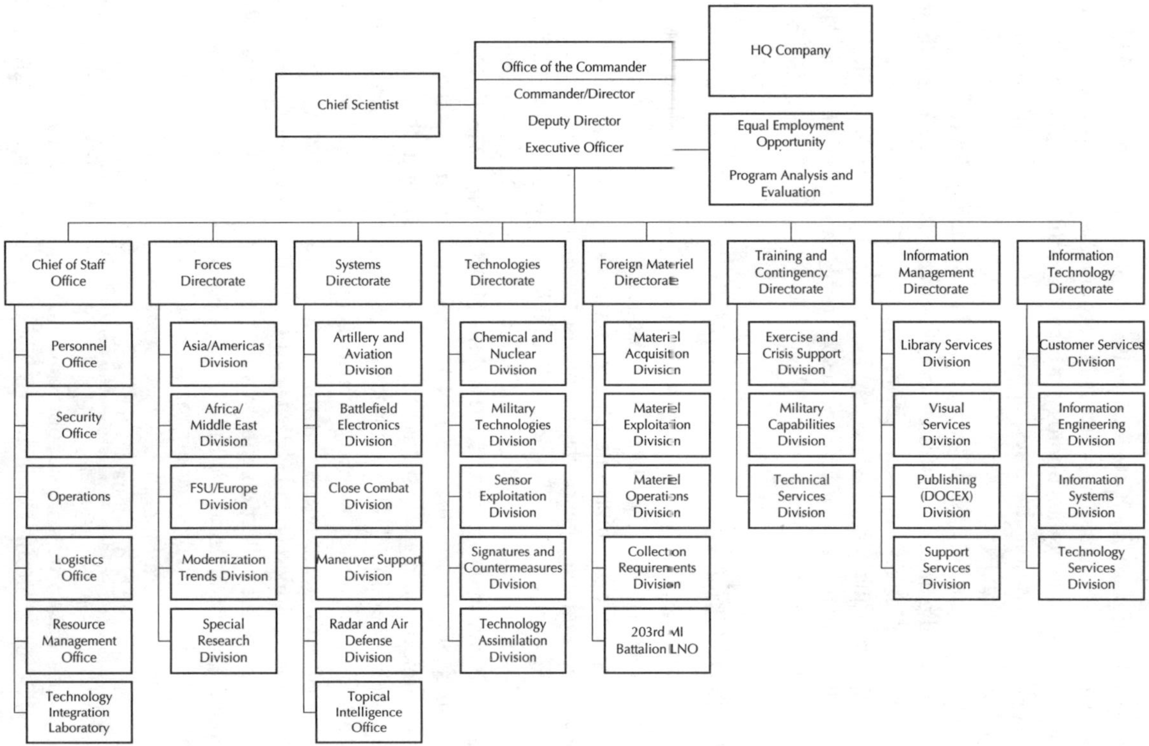

SOURCE: National Ground Intelligence Center.

- Managing the U.S. Army program for the acquisition and exploitation of foreign materiel

- Providing support to the U.S. Army S&T intelligence collection effort[11]

The specific areas that NGIC focuses on include: close combat, fire support, air combat, maneuver support, battlefield reconnaissance, battlefield electronics, chemical warfare and biotechnology, advanced military applications, military technologies, acquisition strategies, signatures, imagery exploitation, and foreign materiel exploitation.[12]

As shown in Figure 4.3, NGIC is composed of six major directorates, with production of intelligence concentrated in the Forces, Systems, Technologies, and Foreign Materiel directorates and their divisions. NGIC has approximately 800 employees, three-quarters of whom are located at the Charlottesville headquarters, with the remainder at NGIC facilities at Fort Meade, Maryland, the Aberdeen Proving Ground, and the Washington Navy Yard.[13]

NAVY INTELLIGENCE ORGANIZATIONS

Of all the military services, the Navy saw the most dramatic changes in its intelligence structure in the early 1990s. On September 30, 1991, the Navy had seven distinct intelligence organizations. On January 1, 1993, it had two.

The seven naval intelligence organizations that existed on September 30, 1991, were: the Office of Naval Intelligence, the Naval Intelligence Command, Task Force 168, the Naval Technical Intelligence Center, the Navy Operational Intelligence Center, the Naval Intelligence Activity, and the Naval Security Group Command.

The Office of Naval Intelligence (ONI) represented the apex of the naval intelligence community and was responsible for management and direction and some intelligence production. The Naval Intelligence Command (NIC), a second-echelon command, performed a variety of management functions. The remaining organizations, with the exception of the Naval Security Group Command, were third-echelon commands and reported to the NIC. Task Force 168 engaged in overt human source collection and provided support to fleet technical collection operations. The Naval Technical Intelligence Center (NTIC) was the Navy's scientific and technical intelligence organization, its primary focus being the Soviet navy. The Navy Operational Intelligence Center (NOIC) monitored naval movements, relying heavily on signals intelligence acquired by national and Navy collection systems. The Naval Intelligence Activity (NIA) was responsible for providing automatic data processing support to naval intelligence organizations. Finally, the Naval Security Group Command (NSGC) performed SIGINT and COMSEC missions.

On October 1, 1991, Task Force 168, NOIC, and NTIC were disestablished as separate organizations and their functions and personnel were assigned to a newly created Naval Maritime Intelligence Center (NAVMIC). Under the new arrangement the analytical functions previously performed by NTIC and NOIC were integrated into NAVMIC's Intelligence Directorate.[14]

The consolidation was designed to achieve several objectives, including satisfying congressional and OSD instructions to consolidate and reorganize the service intelligence structures, and adjusting "to current and anticipated future changes in the threat to maritime forces and to an expected redefinition of requirements levied upon naval intelligence."[15]

On January 1, 1993, an even more drastic consolidation took place. The Naval Intelligence Command, Naval Maritime Intelligence Center, and Naval Intelligence Activity were all disestablished and their functions and most of their personnel absorbed by the Office of Naval Intelligence.[16]

Although it was intended, as of Fall 1991, to merge the NSGC with the Naval Intelligence Command, no such merger took place.[17] Thus, the Navy remains the only major service that has not merged its Service Cryptologic Element (SCE) with one or more of its other intelligence components. However, the Navy consolidation still represents, overall, the most complete consolidation among the services—with all other intelligence functions being assigned to the new ONI, with no subordinate commands, and with the consolidation of all activities at a single location—the National Maritime Intelligence Center complex at Suitland, Maryland.

According to the ONI's *Strategic Planning for the Office of Naval Intelligence*, "ONI's ongoing intelligence role is now defined as providing basic and background maritime intelligence for the JICs [Joint Intelligence Centers]; providing support to Department of the Navy RDT&E, acquisition and training functions; providing maritime S&T and general military intelligence support to many branches of the Government; and support for certain unique national-level programs."[18]

In accordance with its absorption of the functions and personnel of the disestablished units, ONI was radically reorganized. The new ONI structure consists of the Director of Naval Intelligence (DNI), a Deputy DNI, a Chief of Staff, six special assistants, and eight directorates, as shown in Figure 4.4. The two key directorates are the Intelligence Directorate and the Collection Directorate.

The ONI Intelligence Directorate performs functions that were previously the responsibility of the NAVMIC Intelligence Directorate. The Intelligence Directorate—with its six departments, Joint Intelligence Research Office, Cryptologic Support Group, and Newport Detachment—conducts regional studies of relevance to the Navy, produces scientific and technical intelligence on foreign naval systems, and monitors military and civil maritime activities.

The directorate's Civil Maritime Analysis Department monitors the movements of merchant ships of all nations. It also maintains a technical characteristic database of the world's merchant and fishing ships. In addition, it reports on merchant ships possibly associated with arms deliveries, counternarcotics, or terrorism.

The Strike and Air Warfare Department establishes and directs scientific and technical analysis programs to determine the technical capabilities, performance,

FIGURE 4.4 Organization of the Office of Naval Intelligence

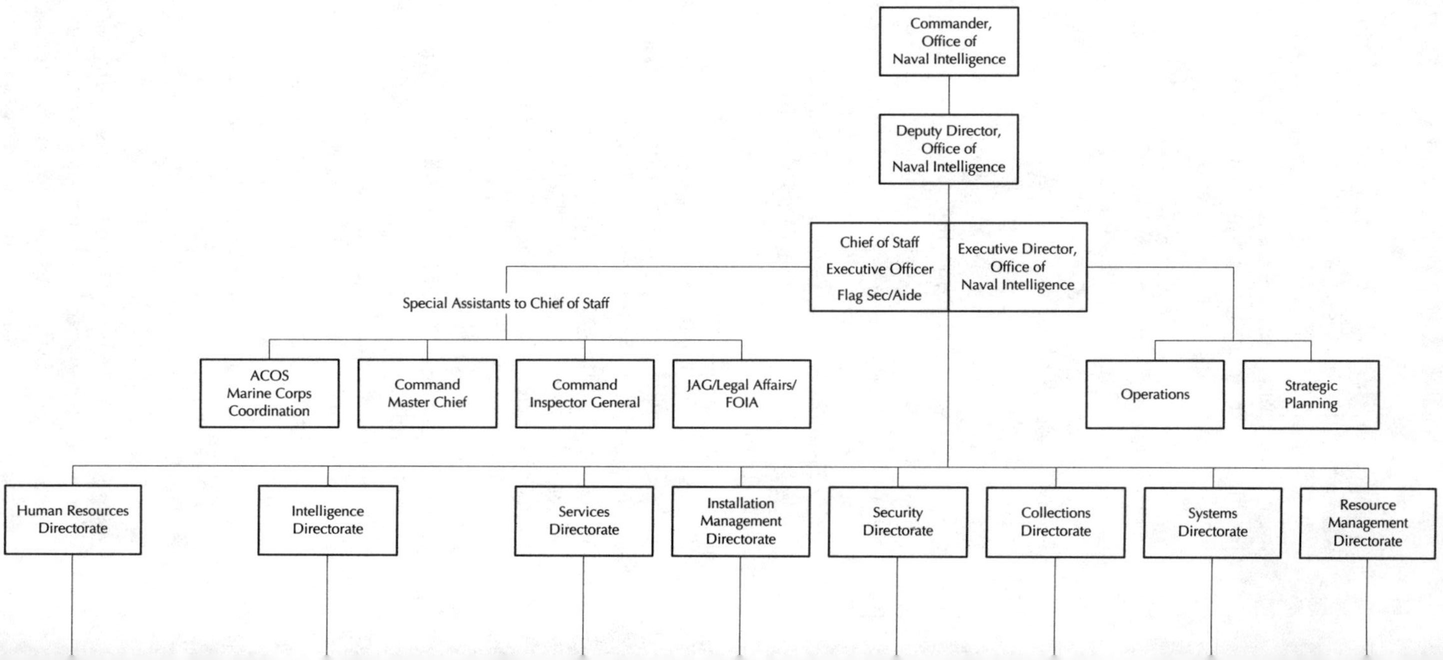

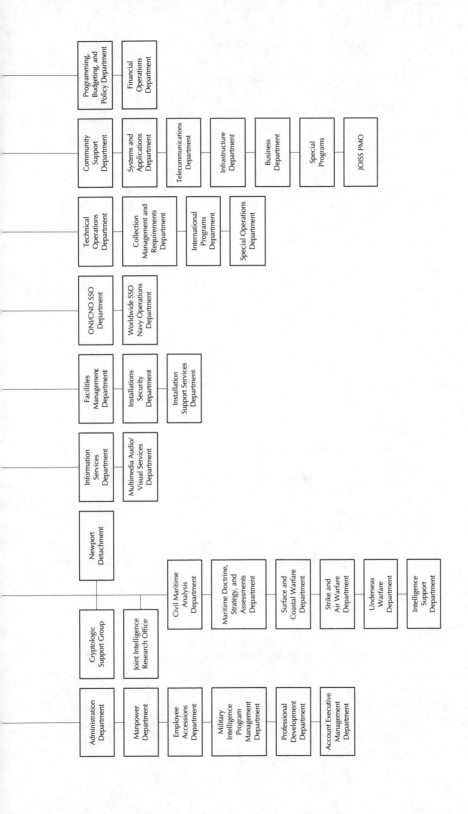

SOURCE: Office of Naval Intelligence.

and vulnerabilities of foreign, air, surface, and space warfare platforms and systems.[19]

The Underseas Warfare Department's functions include:

- assessing current and projected foreign acoustic and nonacoustic ASW [antisubmarine warfare] system capabilities;
- processing, exploiting, and reporting acoustic signals produced by foreign ships, submarines, underwater weapons, and detection systems;
- monitoring foreign submarine order-of-battle, readiness, production, and acquisition; and
- assessing foreign submarine operations and tactics.[20]

The ONI Collection Directorate, whose structure is shown in Figure 4.5, consolidated the collection units of NIC and NAVMIC. It consists of four departments: Technical Operations; Collection Management and Requirements; International Programs; and Special Programs.

The Collection Management and Requirements Department is responsible for identifying and prioritizing key intelligence collection issues and gaps, targeting priority Navy intelligence issues for collection emphasis, and presenting Navy collection requirements and priorities to the national intelligence community and tasking authorities.[21] The Special Operations Department is concerned with "Special Navy" submarine collection programs such as HOLYSTONE and IVY BELLS (discussed in Chapter 8).

The Naval Security Group Command (NSGC), headquartered at Fort Meade, Maryland, is the descendant of the Communications Security Group (OP-20-G) within the Office of Naval Communications, which was established in March 1935. After World War II it was renamed the Communications Supplementary Activities. In 1950 it adopted the title Naval Security Group, it and became the Naval Security Group Command in 1968.[22]

For over two decades the NSGC had two basic responsibilities—signals intelligence and communications security. As a result, NSGC personnel staff land-based HF-DF collection sites, run sea-based collection equipment, install SIGINT and COMSEC equipment on ships and submarines, man the downlinks for the Navy's CLASSIC WIZARD ocean surveillance satellite system, and conduct COMSEC monitoring operations. On April 1, 1994, the commander of NSGC was designated as the Executive Agent for Information Warfare and Command and Control Warfare, which is reflected in the current organizational structure of the NSGC.[23]

As shown in Figure 4.6, subordinate to the Commander of NSGC, are several special assistants and nine Assistant Chiefs of Staff—for Reserves; Security, Human Resource Management, and General Administration; Strategic Plans, Policy, and Readiness; Logistics and Material; Information Warfare/Command and Control Warfare Operations; Training; Resources, Planning, Programming, Budgeting, and Comptroller; Marine Corps Matters; and Technology.[24]

FIGURE 4.5   Organization of the ONI Collections Directorate

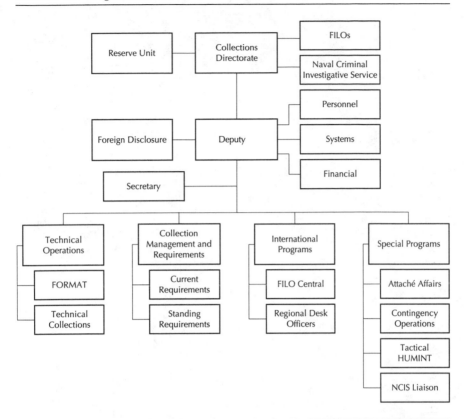

SOURCE: Office of Naval Intelligence.

SIGINT collection operations are conducted by the elements subordinate to the Assistant Chief of Staff for Information Warfare/C²W (Command and Control Warfare)Operations. SIGINT operations are handled by two of the directors under the Assistant Chief of Staff—for Command and Control Warfare Shore Operations, and Fleet Support.[25]

The most important NSGC units are the Naval Security Group Activities distributed across the world. The location of these units is listed in Table 4.1. The list reflects the closure of a number of NSGAs in recent years—including those at Keflavik, Iceland; Pyong Taek, South Korea; Augsburg, Germany; and Key West, Florida. The list also reflects the creation of new NSGAs—often the result of NSG participation in staffing the ground segment of SIGINT satellite systems or in the three Regional SIGINT Operation Centers (discussed in Chapter 8).

86

FIGURE 4.6   Organization of the Naval Security Group Command

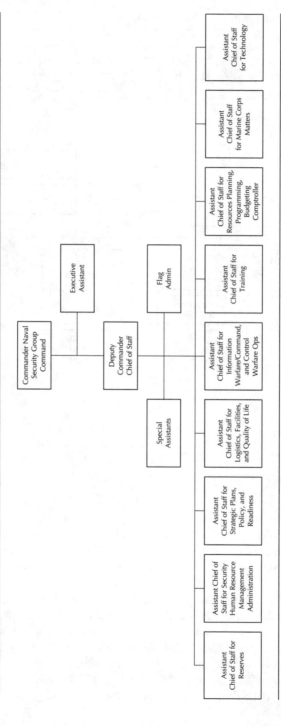

SOURCE: Naval Security Group Command Headquarters, *Naval Security Group Command Organizational Manual* (Washington, D.C.: NSGC, 1994), p. I-4; *Department of Defense Telephone Directory, December 1997*, p.O-121.

TABLE 4.1   Naval Security Group Command Activities

Anchorage, Alaska
Charleston, South Carolina
Denver, Colorado
Fort Gordon, Georgia
Fort Meade, Maryland
Groton, Connecticut
Kunia, Hawaii
Medina Annex, Lackland AFB, Texas
Norfolk, Virginia
Northwest, Virginia
Pearl Harbor, Hawaii
Pensacola, Florida
Sabana Seca, Puerto Rico
Sugar Grove, West Virginia
Washington, D.C.
Winter Harbor, Maine

Bad Aibling, Germany
Guantanamo Bay, Cuba
Menwith Hill, U.K.
Misawa, Japan
Naples, Italy
Yokosuka, Japan

SOURCE: NAVSECGRU Notice 5215, Checklist of Effective NAVSECGRU Instructions, June 19, 1996.

AIR FORCE INTELLIGENCE ORGANIZATIONS

Two Air Force organizations perform departmental intelligence functions: the Directorate of Intelligence, Surveillance, and Reconnaissance (DISR) and the Air Intelligence Agency (AIA). A third Air Force intelligence unit, the Air Force Technical Applications Center (AFTAC), serves the entire intelligence community.

In early 1997, the Air Force disbanded the Office of the Assistant Chief of Staff, Intelligence (OACSI) and assigned the tasks previously performed by the OACSI to the Directorate of Intelligence, Surveillance, and Reconnaissance within the office of the Deputy Chief of Staff for Air and Space Operations.[26] As a result, the Air Force is the sole military service where the senior intelligence position is not independent of the operations and plans organization.

In addition to supervising Air Force intelligence operations, the directorate is also responsible for information warfare activities. Creation of DISR represents both the increased integration of intelligence into operations (made possible by the development of real-time collection and dissemination systems) and the view that intelligence activities are closely related to information warfare.

The intelligence functions of the Director of Intelligence, Surveillance, and Reconnaissance include:

- participating in the preparation of Joint and National intelligence estimates
- preparing policies and provisions of Air Staff guidance for developing and operating USAF intelligence, collection, processing, production, and dissemination systems worldwide
- managing or coordinating programming and budgetary matters for Air Force intelligence, surveillance, and reconnaissance
- representing U.S., DOD, and Air Force intelligence interests on international, national, departmental, interagency, or command and Air Force committees, boards, panels, and study groups
- monitoring the development, procurement, and management of intelligence systems and equipment and the conduct of related research, development, and test and evaluation activities[27]

As shown in Figure 4.7, subordinate to the director are the Intelligence Community Affairs Group, the Associate Director for Intelligence, the Deputy Director for Surveillance and Reconnaissance Systems, and the Deputy Director for Information Operations.

The Intelligence Community Affairs Group is the Air Force focal point for intelligence matters related to the Joint Chiefs of Staff (JCS), Joint Requirements Oversight Council (JROC), National Foreign Intelligence Board (NFIB), and the Military Intelligence Board (MIB).

The Associate Director for Intelligence directs the activities of the Resources, Force Development and Plans, and Applications and Production divisions. Among the most important resource management functions of the first two divisions are intelligence resource programming with respect to the General Defense Intelligence Program (GDIP), the Consolidated Cryptologic Program (CCP), the Defense Airborne Reconnaissance Program (DARP), and the Tactical Intelligence and Related Activities (TIARA) program—as well as preparation of the Air Force Intelligence Strategic Plan and Air Force Intelligence Mission Support Plan. With regard to intelligence production, the Analysis and Production Division is responsible for policy with respect to Air Force intelligence production, Air Force participation in defense intelligence production, intelligence production support to weapons systems, and the foreign materiel program.[28]

The Deputy Director for Surveillance and Reconnaissance Systems, through the Surveillance, Reconnaissance, and Collections Division, manages Air Force manned and unmanned airborne reconnaissance systems as well as ground intelligence and space surveillance systems. Included are the U-2, RC-135 aircraft, COBRA JUDY and COBRA DANE radars, and the Defense Support Program (DSP), DSP-Augmentation (DSP-A), and forthcoming Spaced Based Infrared System (SBIRS) satellite systems.[29]

FIGURE 4.7   Organization of the Directorate for Intelligence, Surveillance, and Reconnaissance

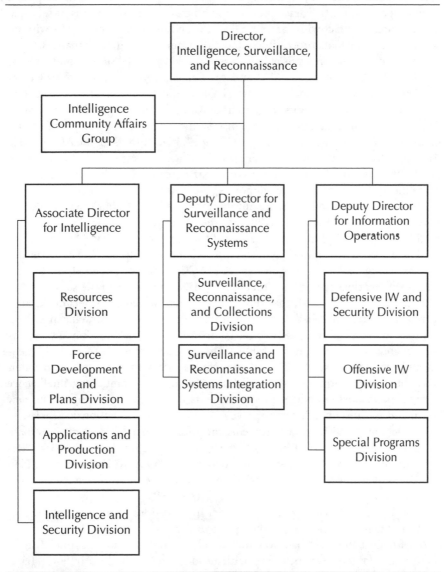

SOURCE: *Department of Defense Telephone Directory, December 1997* (Washington, D.C.: U.S. Government Printing Office, 1997), p. O-148.

Through the Surveillance and Reconnaissance Systems Integration Division, the deputy director "develops, coordinates and oversees policy for all intelligence collection systems," including imagery, signals intelligence, measurement and signature intelligence, and human intelligence systems. The division also develops and oversees policy for intelligence processing and dissemination systems. It serves as the Air Force's contact with the CIA, DIA, NSA, NRO, DARO, and NIMA with respect to collection, data processing, exploitation, and dissemination matters.[30]

The collection and analysis activities supervised by the DISR are conducted by the Air Intelligence Agency (AIA) and Air Force Technical Applications Center (AFTAC). AIA is the ultimate product of a 1971 directive issued by the Secretary of the Air Force mandating reassignment of Air Staff operating and support functions to other organizations. In response to the directive, the Air Force Intelligence Service (AFIS) was established on June 27, 1972.[31] In 1988, the AFIS's status was upgraded, and it became the Air Force Intelligence Agency (AFIA). On October 1, 1991, as part of a reorganization of Air Force intelligence activities, it became the Air Force Intelligence Support Agency (AFISA).

A second part of the 1991 reorganization involved the establishment of the Air Force Intelligence Command (AFIC) by merging the Electronic Security Command, the Foreign Technology Division of the Air Force Systems Command, the Air Force Special Activities Center, and other elements of the AFIA. The result was the creation of an Air Force equivalent of INSCOM that combined SIGINT operations with intelligence production and HUMINT functions in the same organization. And, like INSCOM, the AFIC had a center located a significant distance from headquarters that had its own identity and produced S&T intelligence.

In addition to fulfilling the ASD (C³I)'s mandate for consolidation and satisfying congressional oversight committees, the AFIC was intended to provide "enhanced intelligence support to theater commanders in the conduct of their warfighting responsibilities" by establishing a "single focal point across intelligence disciplines to satisfy intelligence requirements to support operations." The new command was also intended to improve Air Force support to national agencies.[32]

On October 1, 1993, yet another reorganization occurred. Under the new plan, mandated by the June 15, 1993, HQ USAF Program Action Directive 93–8, "Restructuring Air Force Intelligence," and detailed in HQ AFIC Programming Plan 93–01, *Establishment of the Air Force Intelligence Field Operating Agency*, the AFIC became the Air Intelligence Agency (AIA).[33] HUMINT operations were to be transferred to the Defense HUMINT Service. In addition, an internal restructuring of the remaining AFIC elements was undertaken.

As of August 1997 AIA had over 16,000 military and civilian personnel distributed among ninety-five locations, with headquarters at Kelly Air Force Base, Texas.[34] The present headquarters organization of the AIA is shown in Figure 4.8.

Two of AIA's key directorates are Operations and Plans and Requirements. Among the functions of Plans and Requirements is the orchestration of the acquisition process for intelligence systems. Thus, it performs management engi-

FIGURE 4.8   Organization of HQ, Air Intelligence Agency

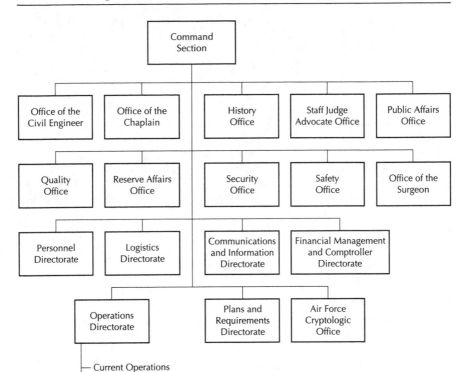

neering studies, approves manpower requirements, and disburses available resources. The Operations Directorate "oversees and directs" the integration of
SIGINT, MASINT, HUMINT, scientific and technical intelligence, and general
military intelligence collection and production activities "into products which directly support United States Air Force (USAF) operations and components commands." It also serves as AIA's manager for collection activities—including open
source, human source, and technical collection activities. The directorate's Tactical Information Broadcast Service (TIBS) Special Management Office (of the
Current Operations division) manages the worldwide TIBS network.[35]

AIA's various collection and analytical activities are distributed across the United
States, as indicated in Figure 4.9. The 67th Intelligence Wing (IW), headquartered at

FIGURE 4.9   Air Intelligence Agency Operational Components

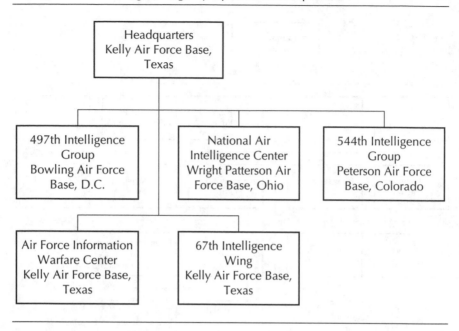

Kelly Air Force Base, manages the AIA's collection activities. It is the AIA's largest wing, with more than 9,500 individuals assigned to it. Directly subordinate to the 67th IW are the intelligence squadrons (IS) that operate SIGINT ground collection sites, help man satellite ground stations, operate unmanned aerial vehicles (UAVs), and install sensors on aerial reconnaissance platforms.[36]

The 67th Intelligence Wing largely consists of the units of the former Electronic Security Command (ESC), which was first established informally as the Air Force Security Group (AFSG) in May 1948 and then formally on July 1, 1948, under the same title. In October 1948 it became the Air Force Security Service (AFSS), headquartered at Arlington Hall Station, Arlington, Virginia. The AFSG of May 1948 consisted of eleven officers and some enlisted clerical personnel on loan from the Army Security Agency.[37] The components of the 67th IW are listed in Table 4.2. Squadrons directly involved in intelligence collection operations may either man ground-based collection systems, provide aircrews for airborne reconnaissance missions, or serve at ground stations for airborne (e.g., U-2) or satellite collection systems. (Their specific roles will be noted in subsequent chapters.)

The 544th Intelligence Group (IG), headquartered at Peterson Air Force Base, Colorado, was established on September 7, 1993, to conduct space SIGINT activities in support of the Air Force Space Command and other intelligence consumers. Subordinate to the 544th IG are the 16th IS at Denver, Colorado, and the 18th IS headquartered at Falcon Air Force Base, Colorado, with detachments at Holloman

TABLE 4.2   67th Intelligence Wing, Units and Locations

Unit	Location
10th Intelligence Squadron	Langley AFB, Texas
22nd Intelligence Squadron	Fort George G. Meade, Maryland
25th Intelligence Squadron	Hurlburt Field, Florida
26th Intelligence Group	Ramstein AB, Germany
26th Intelligence Squadron	Vogelweh, Germany
29th Intelligence Squadron	Fort George G. Meade, Maryland
31st Intelligence Squadron	Fort Gordon Army Installation, Georgia
32nd Intelligence Squadron	Fort George G. Meade, Maryland
39th Intelligence Squadron	Nellis AFB, Nevada
48th Intelligence Squadron	Beale AFB, California
67th Intelligence Group	Kelly AFB, Texas
67th Support Squadron	Kelly AFB, Texas
68th Intelligence Squadron	Brooks AFB, Texas
91st Intelligence Squadron	Fort George G. Meade, Maryland
93rd Intelligence Squadron	Medina Annex, Lackland AFB, Texas
94th Intelligence Squadron	Fort George G. Meade, Maryland
97th Intelligence Squadron	Offutt AFB, Nebraska
301st Intelligence Squadron	Misawa AB, Japan
303rd Intelligence Squadron	Osan AB, Korea
315th Intelligence Squadron	Yokota AB, Japan
324th Intelligence Squadron	Hickam AFB, Hawaii
381st Intelligence Squadron	Elmendorf AFB, Hawaii
390th Intelligence Squadron	Kadena AB, Japan
402nd Intelligence Squadron	Bad Aibling, Germany
426th Intelligence Support Squadron	Vogelweh, Germany
451st Intelligence Squadron	Menwith Hill, U.K.
485th Intelligence Squadron	Mainz-Kastel, Germany
488th Intelligence Squadron	RAF Mildenhall, U.K.
543rd Intelligence Group	Medina Annex, Lackland AFB, Texas
692nd Intelligence Group	Hickam AFB, Hawaii
692nd Intelligence Support Squadron	Hickam AFB, Hawaii
694th Intelligence Group	Fort George G. Meade, Maryland
694th Operations Support Group	Fort George G. Meade, Maryland
4416th Intelligence Squadron	Al Kharj, Saudi Arabia

SOURCE: "67th Intelligence Wing," *The Spokesman,* August 1997, pp. 43–53.

Air Force Base, New Mexico (Detachment 1); Osan, Korea (Detachment 2); Misawa, Japan (Detachment 3); and RAF Feltwell, U.K. (Detachment 4). The 544th IG's detachments are located at Sabana Seca, Puerto Rico (Detachment 2); Sugar Grove, West Virginia (Detachment 3), Yakima, Washington (Detachment 4); and Washington, D.C. (Detachment 5). The 18th IS provides SIGINT support to Air

Force Space Command space surveillance activities, whereas the detachments at Yakima, Sabana Seca, and Sugar Grove intercept the traffic emanating from a variety of communications satellites.[38]

AIA's two analytical components are the 497th Intelligence Group at Bolling Air Force Base, Washington, D.C., and the National Air Intelligence Center at Wright-Patterson Air Force Base, Ohio. The 497th's Operations Applications Division "provides targeting, threat assessments and forecasts, geospatial support and intelligence infrastructure to weapon system acquisitions." It also influences "moving map displays, mensurated coordinates, vertical obstruction/terrain elevation data, and databases in the realm of mapping, charting, geodesy and targeting."[39]

The National Air Intelligence Center (NAIC) has it headquarters at Wright-Patterson Air Force Base, Ohio, where about 1,600 of its 2,059 employees work. The NAIC is, in one sense, the latest version of what began in 1917 as the Foreign Data Section of the Airplane Engineering Department. Shortly after its creation it was transferred from Washington, D.C., to Dayton, Ohio. It was subsequently renamed the Technical Data Section (1927), the Technical Data Laboratory (1942), and T-2 (Intelligence) of the Air Technical Service Command (1945). In 1947 all non-intelligence functions were removed from T-2's mission statement. In 1951, T-2 became the Air Technical Intelligence Center and, in 1962, the Foreign Technology Division (FTD) of the Air Force Systems Command (AFSC).[40]

The FTD's intelligence activities were directed at avoiding technological surprise, advancing U.S. technology by use of foreign technology, identifying weaknesses in foreign weapons systems, and using certain design traits of foreign weapons systems as indicators of strategic intent. Under the October 1, 1991, restructuring of Air Force intelligence, the FTD was removed from control of the AFSC, renamed the Foreign Technology Center (FTC), and placed under the AFIC. In 1992, it was renamed again, becoming the Foreign Aerospace Science and Technology Center (FASTC).[41]

The NAIC was established on October 1, 1993, as part of the restructuring that produced the AIA, by the organizational (but not geographic) consolidation of FASTC with the 480th Intelligence Group—which prepares "cockpit oriented target material and mission planning intelligence." The 480th had been previously attached to the Air Combat Command as the 480th Air Intelligence Group. Prior to that it was the 480th Reconnaissance Technical Group. In July 1994, the 497th Intelligence Group's Directorate of Assessments, which produced a variety of general intelligence products, was integrated into the NAIC.[42]

With respect to air and space forces, the NAIC is the National and Department of Defense executive agent for the processing, exploitation, and dissemination of MASINT data collected from radar, electro-optical, and infrared sensors. It prepares spectral, spatial, and temporal signatures of potential targets; it is the sole organization involved in interpreting the imagery obtained under the Open Skies Treaty; and it also is responsible for the exploitation of signals collected during RC-135 RIVET JOINT and COMBAT SENT missions.[43]

Overall, the NAIC "acquires, processes, analyzes, and integrates intelligence data and information on foreign weapon systems, subsystems, technologies, and forces into products and services required to support the Technical Assessments and Global Threat Directorates and selected external intelligence community customers."[44]

As indicated in Figure 4.10, the main body of the NAIC consists of seven directorates and the 480th Intelligence Group. The Directorate of Data Exploitation (with Programs, Requirements, and Foreign Materiel, MASINT Exploitation, Imagery Exploitation, Information Exploitation, and Signals Exploitation divisions) "acquires, processes, analyzes, and integrates intelligence data on foreign weapon systems, subsystems, technologies, and forces into products and services required to support the Technical Assessments and Global Threat Directorates and selected external intelligence community customers."[45]

FIGURE 4.10   Organization of the National Air Intelligence Center

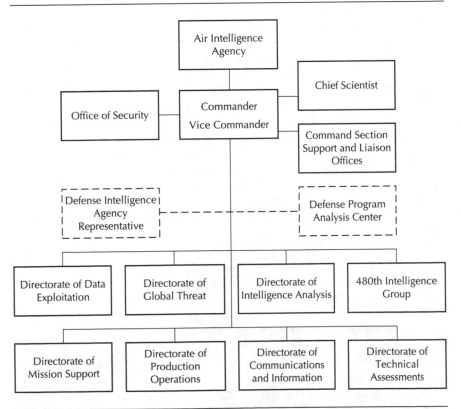

SOURCE: National Air Intelligence Center NAICP 38-101, NAIC: Mission and Organization Pamphlet (Wright Patterson AFB, Ohio: NAIC, March 1996), p. 1.

The Directorate of Global Threat has six divisions: Acquisition Integration, Integrated Air Defense Systems, National Policy Integration, Air Capabilities, Asia and Africa Issues, and Europe and Americas Issues. It "plans, directs and manages the production of integrated all source intelligence" that "present complete threat assessments for acquisition, operational, and national customers, merging all pertinent intelligence to present complete and tailored intelligence assessments."[46]

The Directorate of Technical Assessments (with Aerodynamic Systems, Ballistic Missile, C[4], Electronic Systems, Engineering, Advanced Programs, Space Systems, and Technology divisions) "plans, directs, and manages the production of intelligence on the characteristics, capabilities, employment, limitations, and vulnerabilities of foreign offensive aerospace systems, foreign space systems, foreign technology development, electromagnetic systems developments, and command, control, and communications."[47]

The Directorate of Intelligence Analysis (located in Washington, D.C., and consisting of five divisions—Forces Employment, Global Analysis, Operations, Special Projects, and Systems and Technology) is responsible for providing substantive military/political as well as scientific and technical intelligence support to the Secretary of the Air Force, the Chief of Staff of the Air Force, the Director of ISR, and HQ USAF. It participates in producing studies affecting weapons system acquisition and force structure and prepares and coordinates national and joint estimates on foreign force capabilities.[48]

The 480th Intelligence Group produces "geocoded and ortho-rectified imagery data for use by the mission and force planning systems." It also "performs target analysis, weaponeering, and weapons effectiveness assessments, and integrated intelligence and MCG&I [mapping, charting, geodetic, and imagery] requirements into the development of USAF weapons systems." Headquartered at Langley Air Force Base, Virginia, it has three subordinate squadrons: the 20th Intelligence Squadron at Offut Air Force Base, Nebraska, and the 27th and 36th Intelligence Squadrons at Langley Air Force Base.[49]

The Air Force Technical Applications Center (AFTAC) was first established in 1948 as the Special Weapons Squadron and subsequently became known as AFOAT-1 (Air Force Office of the Assistant Deputy Chief of Staff for Atomic Energy, Section 1). It received its present name in July 1959. Until the 1970s its mission was classified, and it was described in sanitized congressional hearings only as "Project CLEAR SKY."[50]

With a little more than 1,000 personnel, and headquartered at Patrick Air Force Base, Florida, the AFTAC operates the U.S. Atomic Energy Detection System (AEDS). AEDS is a worldwide system, which employs space-based, aerial, ground, and hydroacoustic sensors to detect indications of nuclear detonations and accidents, collect information relevant to the discrimination between earthquakes and nuclear detonations, and detect signs of nuclear weapons research and development and production. AFTAC's operations and the analysis, by AFTAC and other organizations, of the data collected is relevant to the monitoring of a variety of treaties—the Limited Test Ban Treaty, the Non-Proliferation Treaty, the Threshold Test Ban Treaty (which limits the yield of underground tests to 150 kilotons), the Peaceful Nuclear Explosions Treaty, the Intermediate Range Nuclear Forces (INF) Agreement, the Strategic Arms Reduction Treaty (START), and the Comprehensive Test Ban Treaty (CTBT). AFTAC was also responsible for tracking debris from the Chernobyl disaster of 1986. In addition, today's operations are particularly directed at collecting data on the nuclear activities of nations such as North Korea, Pakistan, India, Iran, and Iraq. Furthermore, AFTAC collection and analysis activities are also directed at monitoring chemical and biological warfare programs—both for intelligence and treaty verification purposes.[51]

AFTAC worldwide operations are managed through its headquarters organization, the structure of which is shown in Figure 4.11. (AFTAC's detachments are discussed in Chapter 9.) AFTAC's Directorate of Operations (with Mobile Sensors, Operations Center, and Current Operations divisions) is responsible for planning, coordinating, and operating the U.S. Atomic Energy Detection System

FIGURE 4.11   Organization of HQ, Air Force Technical Applications Center

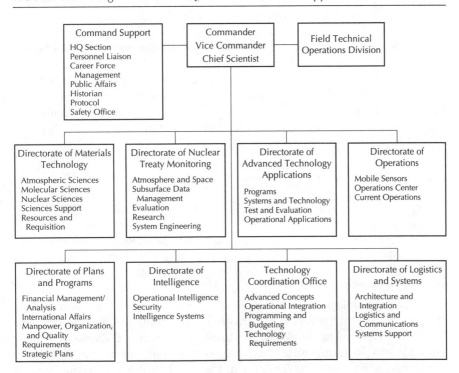

SOURCE: Air Force Technical Applications Center.

(USAEDS) data collection effort. The Directorate of Intelligence (with Operational Intelligence, Security, and Intelligence Systems divisions) provides all-source intelligence support to the AFTAC commander and staff, including current intelligence briefings.[52]

The Directorate of Materials Technology (with Nuclear Sciences, Atmospheric Sciences, Molecular Sciences, Sciences Support, and Resources and Requisition divisions) is responsible for laboratory analysis, evaluation, and reporting of the various materials obtained from collection operations. The Directorate of Nuclear Treaty Monitoring (with Research, Subsurface Data Management, Systems Engineering, Atmosphere and Space, and Evaluation divisions) plans, manages, and coordinates research and development for all components of the AEDS used in monitoring nuclear test ban treaties.[53]

The components of the Technical Operations Division include the McClellan Central Laboratory (MCL) at McClellan Air Force Base, California. The MCL consists of four laboratories:

- Applied Chemistry Laboratory: responsible for processing samples involving standard radiochemical and radionuclide measurement techniques. It also processes inert materials for quantitative analysis using atomic absorption, infrared, and X-ray techniques.
- Gas Analysis Laboratory: responsible for separation, purification, and radioassay of gases from air samples. Operates chromotographic, cryogenic, and measurement equipment.
- Organic Analysis Laboratory: responsible for evaluating technology for verification of chemical and biological warfare agreements.
- Applied Physics Laboratory: responsible for analysis of particulates using mass spectrometry, optical and electron microscopy, and other microanalytical techniques.[54]

MARINE CORPS INTELLIGENCE ORGANIZATIONS

Management of Marine Corps intelligence activities is the responsibility of the Assistant Chief of Staff for Command, Control, Communications, Computers, and Intelligence (C^{4}I). Subordinate to the ACSC^{4}I is the Intelligence Division. The division consists of four branches—Counterintelligence/HUMINT, Intelligence Plans and Estimates, Signals Intelligence and Electronic Warfare, and Intelligence Plans and Policy—and the Special Security Office.[55]

The Counterintelligence/HUMINT Branch is the focal point for coordination of counterintelligence and HUMINT matters with commands, agencies, and offices external to the Marine Corps. The Intelligence Plans and Estimates Branch participates in the formulation of JCS papers containing current and estimative intelligence. It also conducts liaison with the JCS, DIA, NSA, CIA, the Department of State, and other intelligence organizations in matters pertaining to intelligence estimates. The Signals Intelligence and Electronic Warfare Branch is the focal point for coordination of cryptologic/signals intelligence matters with commands, agencies, and offices outside the Marine Corps.[56]

Analysis for the Marine Corps is conducted by the Marine Corps Intelligence Activity (MCIA), located at the National Maritime Intelligence Center (NMIC) complex at Suitland, Maryland, and the Marine Corps facility at Quantico, Virginia. The activity was created as the Marine Corps Intelligence Center (MCIC), as the result of a 1987 study on Marine Corps intelligence requirements. On January 1, 1993, the center was redesignated as the MCIA. As of mid-1995 it had a staff of eighty-two analysts. Its overall workforce in early 1997 was 130.[57] Figure 4.12 shows the MCIA organization structure.

The Expeditionary Warfare Support Division provides intelligence support to Fleet Marine Forces and supporting establishments for predeployment planning,

FIGURE 4.12   Organization of the Marine Corps Intelligence Activity

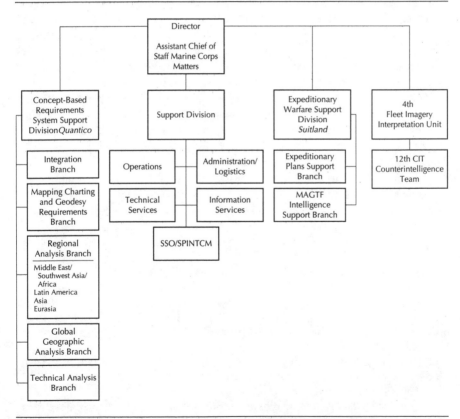

SOURCE: Robert W. Livingston, "Marine Corps Intelligence Activity: Excellence in Expeditionary Intelligence," *American Intelligence Journal* 17, nos. 1 and 2 (1996).

training, and exercises. The division's Expeditionary Plans Support Branch conducts predeployment analysis, related to specific missions, of the environment, threat forces, and capabilities. The *Expeditionary Warfare Intelligence Support Product* provides missions planners with intelligence on the politics, culture, environment, and conventional/unconventional threats capable of affecting expeditionary operations.[58]

The Concept-Based Requirements System (CBRS) Support Division at Quantico contains the majority of MCIA analytical personnel and consists of five branches—Integration; Mapping, Charting, and Geodesy (MC&G) Requirements; Regional Analysis; Global Geographic Analysis; and Technical Analysis.[59]

The Integration and Regional branches provide general military intelligence threat analysis and assessments, including the *Mid-Range Threat Assessment*. The assessment is an estimate of the threat to Marine Corps expeditionary forces over the next ten years, including regional threat analysis, description of possible expeditionary environments, and possible international instabilities. The Technical Analysis Branch provides scientific and technical intelligence support to Marine Corps research and development, testing, and evaluation activities. It produces the *Integrated Anti-Amphibious Assault Study*, which provides a description of mines, obstacles, and other obstructions to a landing force in likely areas of deployment. It also produces *Systems Threat Assessment Reports* (STARs) on major Marine Corps ground acquisition items as well as the bimonthly, unclassified, *Scientific and Technical Intelligence Review*. The Global Geographic Analysis Branch employs standard and multispectral imagery to conduct terrain analysis in support of the Marine Corps Combat Development Command (MCCDC) and reserve forces. The Mapping, Charting, and Geodesy Requirements Branch validates Marine Corps MC&G requirements.[60]

The Marine Support Battalion, headquartered at Fort Meade, Maryland, provides for Marine Corps participation in Naval Security Group Command activities, with lettered companies assigned to NSGC field sites throughout the world.[61]

Notes

1. U.S. Congress, Senate Select Committee on Intelligence, *Report 101–358: Authorizing Appropriations for Fiscal Year 1991 for the Intelligence Activities of the U.S. Government, the Intelligence Community Staff, the Central Intelligence Agency Retirement and Disability System, and for Other Purposes* (Washington, D.C.: U.S. Government Printing Office, 1990), pp. 4–5.

2. Ibid., p. 5.

3. Assistant Secretary of Defense (Command, Control, Communications, and Intelligence), *Plan for Restructuring Defense Intelligence*, March 15, 1991, p. 7.

4. Memorandum to Correspondents, n.d.

5. Letter, Paul D. Sutton, INSCOM to the author, November 20, 1992; INSCOM Permanent Order 41–1, "United States Army Intelligence and Security Command, Intelligence

Production Management Activity (Provisional), Falls Church, Virginia, 22041," April 9, 1992; INSCOM Permanent Order 41–2, "United States Army Foreign Science and Technology Center (WOKPAA), Charlottesville, Virginia, 22901, United States Intelligence and Threat Analysis Center (W3YDAA), Washington, D.C. 20370," April 9, 1992.

6. *Department of Defense Telephone Directory, December 1997* (Washington, D.C.: U.S. Government Printing Office), p. O-66; USAINSCOM Regulation 10–2, "Organization and Functions, United States Army Intelligence and Security Command," May 5, 1995, pp. 11-1 to 11-25; USAINSCOM Regulation 10–2, "Organization and Functions, United States Army Intelligence and Security Command," June 25, 1989, pp. 2-7-1 to 2-7-9.

7. *Department of Defense Telephone Directory, December 1997*, p. O-66; USAINSCOM Regulation 10–2, "Organization and Functions, United States Army Intelligence and Security Command," June 25, 1989, pp. 2-7-23 to 2-7-30, 2-7-34 to 2-7-38; USAINSCOM Regulation 10–2, "Organization and Functions, United States Army Intelligence and Security Command," May 5, 1995, p. 11–2.

8. USAINSCOM Regulation 10–2, "Organization and Functions, United States Army Intelligence and Security Command," June 25, 1989, pp. 2–7–14 to 2–7–21; *Department of Defense Telephone Directory, December 1997*, p. O–66.

9. Capt. Kristyn Jones, "One Echelon Can't Do It All," *INSCOM Journal* (May-June 1997): 14–17, 39.

10. *U.S. Army Foreign Science and Technology Center Unit History, FY 63–77* (Charlottesville, Va.: FSTC, n.d.), p. 3; Paul E. Menoher, "INSCOM Thrives Despite Changes," *INSCOM Journal* (September 1994): 1.

11. NGIC, ". . . About the National Ground Intelligence Center," 1998.

12. Ibid.

13. "Army Intelligence Site Lifts Secrecy Veil," *Washington Post,* January 5, 1997, p. A10.

14. R. M. Walsh, Assistant Vice Chief of Naval Operations, Memorandum for the Secretary of the Navy, Subject: Disestablishment and Establishment of Certain Naval Intelligence Command Shore Activities, July 31, 1991; OPNAV Notice 5450, Subject: Disestablishment and Establishment of Commander, Naval Intelligence Command Shore Activities, and Modification of Detachments, September 13, 1991; Naval Intelligence Command, *Organization, Mission, and Key Personnel: Naval Intelligence Command, HQ, Naval Maritime Intelligence Center, Naval Intelligence Activity,* October 1991, pp. 59–80.

15. "Fact and Justification Sheet: COMNAVINTCOM Claimancy Reorganization," attachment to R. M. Walsh, Assistant Vice Chief of Naval Operations, Memorandum for the Secretary of the Navy.

16. Memorandum for the Secretary of the Navy, Subject: Disestablishment of Three Shore Activities and Establishment of One Consolidated Shore Command, December 1, 1992; Office of Naval Intelligence, *Consolidating the Naval Intelligence Command, Naval Maritime Intelligence Center, Naval Intelligence Activity* (Suitland, Md.: ONI, January 7, 1993).

17. Maj. Herbert M. Strauss, *Status Report: Strengthening Defense Intelligence* (Washington, D.C.: OASD [C³I], 1991), p. 4.

18. Office of Naval Intelligence, *Strategic Planning for the Office of Naval Intelligence: Vision and Direction for the Future,* July 1992, p. 2.

19. Naval Intelligence Command, *Organization, Mission, and Key Personnel,* pp. 60, 62, 68.

20. Ibid. p. 68.

21. Ibid., p. 90.

22. HQNSGINST 5450.2G CH–1, *Headquarters, Naval Security Group Command Organizational Manual*, August 17, 1995, pp. I-1 to I-2.

23. Ibid.

24. Ibid., pp. O-1 to O-2; *Department of Defense Telephone Directory, December 1997*, p. O-121.

25. HQH5GINST 5450.2G CH-1, *Headquarters, Naval Security Group Command Organizational Manual*; Ibid., pp. N6-6 to N6-9.

26. Jeffrey Richelson, "New Look for Air Force Intelligence," *Defense Week*, March 31, 1997, p. 6.

27. "Director, Intelligence, Surveillance, and Reconnaissance (AF/XOI)," p. 20. Provided by Air Force.

28. Ibid., pp. 21–25.

29. Ibid., p. 26.

30. Ibid., pp. 26–27.

31. "Air Force Intelligence Service," *Air Force Magazine*, May 1982, p. 126.

32. Department of the Air Force, "Air Force Creates New Intelligence Command," June 6, 1991.

33. HQ USAF, "Basic Plan to HQ USAF Program Action Directive (PAD) 93–8, Restructuring Air Force Intelligence," June 15, 1993; Headquarters, Air Force Intelligence Command, HQ AFIC Programming Plan 93–01, *Establishment of the Air Force Intelligence Field Operating Agency*, August 17, 1993.

34. United States Air Force Office of Public Affairs, "Air Intelligence Agency," Fact Sheet 95–10, September 1995, p. 1; "About the Agency," *Air Intelligence Agency Almanac*, August 1997, pp. 12–13.

35. HQ Air Intelligence Agency, Air Intelligence Agency Mission Directive 1501, *HQ AIA Organization and Functions Chart Book*, August 1, 1996, pp. 5–6, 21.

36. United States Air Force Office of Public Affairs, Fact Sheet 95–10, "Air Intelligence Agency," p. 2; "About the Agency."

37. Gabriell Marshall, "FOA Becomes Fact," *Spokesman*, November 1993, p. 8; *Electronic Security Command: Master of the Electronic Battlefield* (San Antonio, Tex.: ESC, n.d.), p. 1.

38. United States Air Force Office of Public Affairs, Fact Sheet 95–10, "Air Intelligence Agency"; untitled, undated Mission Briefing; "Bullet Background Paper on the 544th Intelligence Group," June 2, 1994; Doug Karas, "AIA's 18th Intelligence Squadron," *Spokesman*, February 1997, p. 6; "544th Intelligence Group," *Air Intelligence Agency Almanac*, August 1997, pp. 30–32.

39. "497th Intelligence Group," *Air Intelligence Agency Almanac*, August 1997, pp. 28–29.

40. *FTD 1917–1967* (Dayton, Ohio: FTD, 1967), pp. 8, 10, 12, 22, 26; Col. Robert B. Kalisch, "Air Technical Intelligence," *Air University Review* 12 (July-August 1971): 2–11 at 7, 9; "National Air Intelligence Center," *Air Intelligence Agency Almanac*, August 1997, pp. 14–15.

41. Kalisch, "Air Technical Intelligence"; Bruce Ashcroft, "National Air Intelligence Center Emerges from FASTC, 480th IG," *Spokesman*, November 1993, p. 12; Rob Young, "National Air Intelligence Center," *Spokesman*, September 1996, pp. 4–5.

42. United States Air Force Office of Public Affairs, Fact Sheet 95–10, "Air Intelligence Agency," p.1; Ashcroft, "National Air Intelligence Center Emerges from FASTC, 480th IG."

43. "National Air Intelligence Center."

44. National Air Intelligence Center, NAICP 38–101, *NAIC: Mission and Organization Pamphlet*, (Wright Patterson AFB, Ohio: NAIC, March 1996), p. 5.

45. Ibid., p. 4.

46. Ibid., p. 11.

47. Ibid., p. 35.

48. Ibid., p. 18.

49. Ibid., p. 46; "480th Intelligence Group," *Air Intelligence Agency Almanac*, August 1997, pp. 16–17.

50. U.S. Congress, Senate Committee on Appropriations, *Department of Defense Appropriations, FY 1973, Part 4* (Washington, D.C.: U.S. Government Printing Office, 1972), pp. 364–365; "Air Force Technical Applications Center," *Air Force Magazine*, May 1987, pp. 165–166; Mary Welch, "AFTAC Celebrates 50 Years of Long Range Detection," *AFTAC Monitor*, October 1997, pp. 8–32; Science Applications International Corp., *Fifty Year Commemorative History of Long Range Detection: The Creation, Development, and Operation of the United States Atomic Energy Detection System* (Patrick AFB, Fla.: AFTAC, 1997), pp. 4–5.

51. "Air Force Technical Applications Center," *Air Force Magazine*, May 1997, p. 126; Air Force Technical Applications Center, Center Instruction 38–101, *Organization and Functions Chart Book*, April 21, 1997, p. 27.

52. Air Force Technical Applications Center, Center Instruction 38–101, *Organization and Functions Chart Book*, pp. 9–12.

53. Ibid., pp. 16, 19.

54. Ibid., p. 27.

55. *Department of Defense Telephone Directory, December 1997*, p. O-91.

56. MCO P5400.45, *Headquarters Marine Corps Organization Manual* (HQMCORGMAN), May 15, 1989, p. 7-47, 7-51 to 7-55.

57. Neil Munro, "Center Will Spearhead Marines' Data Analysis," *Defense News*, January 20, 1992, p. 12; "Director Visits MCIA," *Communiqué*, January/February 1997, p. 30; Robert W. Livingston, "Marine Corps Intelligence Activity—Excellence in Expeditionary Intelligence," *American Intelligence Journal* 17, nos. 1 and 2 (1996): 29–33.

58. Livingston, "Marine Corps Intelligence Activity."

59. Ibid.

60. Ibid.

61. "Marine Corps Intelligence," *Military Intelligence*, July-September 1983, pp. 121ff.

5

UNIFIED COMMAND
INTELLIGENCE ORGANIZATIONS

In addition to the intelligence functions performed by organizations reporting to the headquarters of the Department of Defense and the military services, a substantial intelligence capability is maintained within the unified military commands. The missions, functions, forces, and geographic areas of responsibilities of those commands are detailed in the Unified Command Plan (UCP), drawn up by the Joint Chiefs of Staff and approved by the Secretary of Defense.[1]

The unified commands consist of forces drawn from all the military services. Five unified commands focus on specific regions of the world—the Atlantic Command, Central Command, European Command, Pacific Command, and Southern Command. Four additional commands have worldwide responsibilities—U.S. Space Command, U.S. Special Operations Command, U.S. Strategic Command, and U.S. Transportation Command. The geographic responsibilities of the relevant unified commands are shown in Figure 5.1.

The intelligence responsibilities of the unified commands have included intelligence analysis—for both the command and higher authorities—as well as supervision of national reconnaissance and other sensitive collection operations conducted within the command's theater. Until 1991, intelligence analytical functions were often distributed across several unified and component command organizations.*

However, as part of the overall streamlining mandated by the *Plan for Restructuring Defense Intelligence*, the ASD (C³I) specifically required that the analysis centers of the Atlantic, Pacific, and European commands and their components be consolidated into joint intelligence centers that would be under the control of the unified command's commander in chief. That other commands would be expected to follow this lead was clear. It was believed that such action would "not

---

*A component command of a unified command is a particular service command. Thus, the Pacific Fleet is a component command of the Pacific Command.

FIGURE 5.1 Unified Commands: Areas of Responsibility

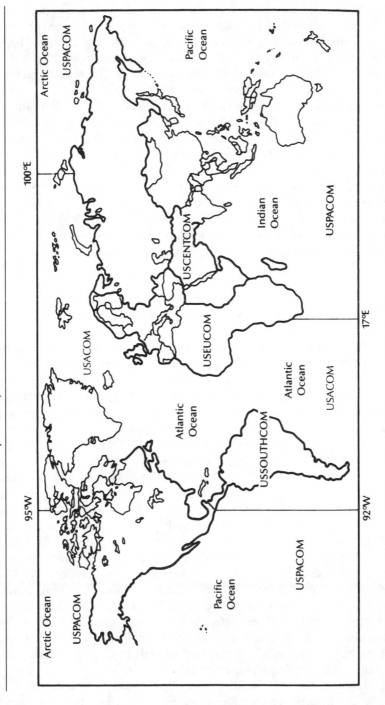

NOTE: Alaska, Antarctica, Canada, Conus, and Mexico are not assigned for normal operations; JCS has cognizance over Russia.

only yield resource savings through elimination of duplicative efforts but . . . strengthen support to the CINC and components through improved efficiency."[2]

The plan allowed for the retention of intelligence staffs in the form of J-2/Intelligence Directorates at both the unified and component command levels in order to "support planning for and conduct of current military operations and to provide focused intelligence requirements statements."[3]

The formation of the joint intelligence centers meant the disestablishment of organizations such as the Fleet Intelligence Center, Pacific (FICPAC), the European Defense Analysis Center (EUDAC) and the Fleet Intelligence Center, Europe and Atlantic (FICEURLANT) as well as the assignment of their responsibilities and personnel to new joint intelligence organizations.[4] The unified command operations directorates were unaffected by the changes and are still responsible for reconnaissance activities in their specific geographic areas.

As of November 1997, there were approximately 4,000 individuals working in the various joint intelligence centers, at which time it was announced that there would be a 10 percent reduction in personnel.[5]

ATLANTIC COMMAND

The present U.S. Atlantic Command (USACOM) is the successor to the Atlantic Command (LANTCOM), established in 1947, and the U.S. Atlantic Command (USLANTCOM), established in 1983. USLANTCOM had geographic responsibility for the Atlantic Ocean, the Caribbean, and other areas. In 1993, the Unified Command Plan was revised to further expand the responsibilities of USLANTCOM, transforming it into USACOM. USACOM was assigned the responsibility of conducting joint training of most U.S.-based forces and staffs assigned to joint task forces and of providing joint trained and ready forces for worldwide employment. As a result of a 1995 review, a part of USACOM's responsibilities were transferred to the U.S. Southern Command, as discussed below. USACOM's component commands include the Air Combat Command, Forces Command, Marine Forces Atlantic, and the Atlantic Fleet.[6]

The restructuring that produced the present USACOM intelligence arrangements took place on August 9, 1990, when the Atlantic Joint Intelligence Center (LANTJIC) was renamed the Atlantic Intelligence Command (AIC). The command absorbed the responsibilities of the Fleet Intelligence Center, Europe and Atlantic (FICEURLANT); the Atlantic Defense Analysis Center (LANTDAC); the Fleet Ocean Surveillance Information Center (FOSIC) Detachment, Norfolk; the Atlantic Forward Area Support Team (LANTFAST); and components of the LANTCOM Intelligence Directorate. Those organizations produced intelligence assessments on nations of concern—particularly their military forces—monitored maritime movements, and provided support to the fleet in installing and operating technical collection systems on ships.

The present structure of the Atlantic Intelligence Command is shown in Figure 5.2. The AIC Intelligence Directorate consists of four key divisions: Targeting,

FIGURE 5.2 Organization of the Atlantic Intelligence Command

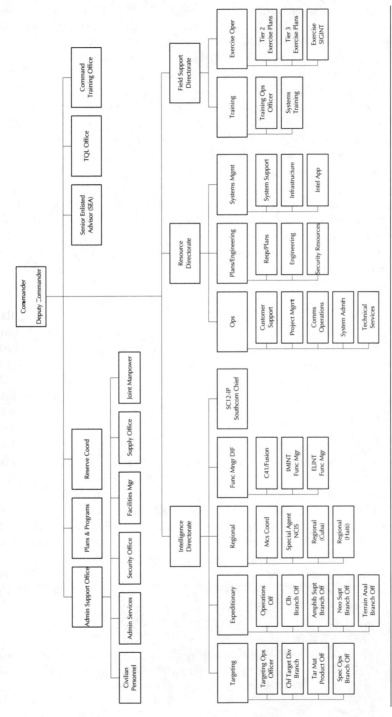

SOURCE: U.S. Atlantic Command.

Expeditionary, Regional, and Functional. The Targeting Division produces intelligence that can be employed in the destruction of assorted facilities where command forces may operate—whether by aircraft, missiles, ships, or special forces.[7]

The Expeditionary Division (with its CLB, Amphibious Support, NEO Support, and Terrain Analysis branches) prepares intelligence that could be used by naval and marine forces in the event of deployment—including intelligence on beach and port conditions as well as intelligence on the terrain.[8]

The Regional Division focuses on political and military forces in various countries—particularly Haiti and Cuba. The Functional Division handles imagery interpretation in support of the three other branches of the directorate. It also analyzes electronic intelligence and is particularly employed to monitor foreign maritime activity.[9]

The AIC is subordinate to the J-2/Intelligence Directorate of USACOM, whose director serves as the principal intelligence advisor to the Atlantic Command's commander in chief. It is responsible for "ensuring that all-source intelligence is disseminated to subordinate operational commands," and it "manages intelligence collection, processing, production and dissemination within the Atlantic Command intelligence organization." The Directorate's Deputy Director of Intelligence for Products and Services also serves as commander of the AIC.[10]

The USACOM's Operations Directorate is responsible for active intelligence collection operations employing submarines, surface ships, fixed arrays, and aircraft. The directorate's Joint Reconnaissance Branch supervises, controls, coordinates, and monitors U.S. military reconnaissance operations conducted within USACOM's area of responsibility.[11]

CENTRAL COMMAND

The U.S. Central Command (CENTCOM) was formed on January 1, 1983, as a successor to the Rapid Deployment Force. It assumed responsibility for the nations of the Middle East and the Persian Gulf area (including Iran, Iraq, Jordan, Saudi Arabia, and Kuwait), Northeast Africa (Egypt, Somalia, Kenya, Ethiopia, and Sudan), and Southwest Asia (Pakistan and Afghanistan).[12]

The Intelligence Directorate (J-2) of the Central Command "conducts intelligence collection, targeting, planning systems development, and international exchanges to support combined exercises, contingencies, and the command's warfighting mission."[13]

The organization of the Joint Intelligence Center, Central (JICCENT), which grew out of Operation DESERT STORM, is shown in Figure 5.3. The JIC's mission is to:

- provide a deployable, all-source intelligence and warning, operational intelligence, and assessments capability to [the Commander in Chief, CENTCOM], to meet wartime and peacetime needs

FIGURE 5.3   Organization of the Joint Intelligence Center, Central

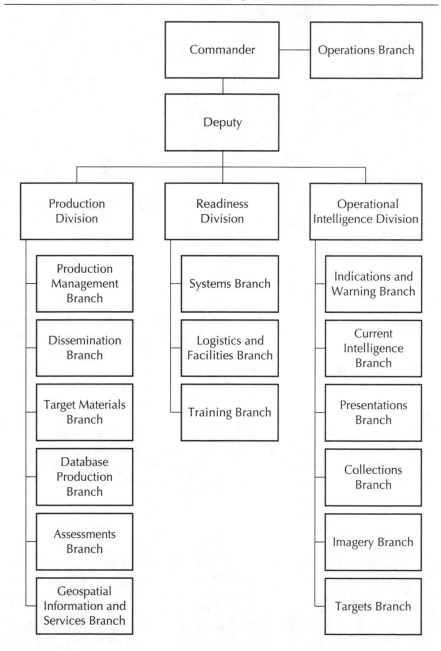

SOURCE: U.S. Central Command, "Joint Intelligence Center, Central," 1997.

- provide mission-oriented intelligence support to component commanders
- serve as the theater collection manager
- produce finished intelligence[14]

The Production Division produces intelligence assessments concerning a variety of regional issues (oil, water, arms shipments, weapons proliferation, and technology transfer) as well as of particular countries—including Iran, Iraq, Saudi Arabia, Yemen, Kuwait, and Afghanistan. It maintains and produces order of battle documents concerning ground, naval, air, and defensive missile forces. It also provides target folders and maps, charts, and geodetic products.[15]

The Operational Intelligence Division monitors incoming intelligence to provide indications and warning reports, produces current intelligence, conducts bomb damage assessment, and interprets imagery obtained by national and command assets.[16]

In the event of a war in which CENTCOM is a participant, several additional components would be established under the JIC: a Joint Intelligence Production Complex, a Joint Interrogation Facility, a Joint Debriefing Center, and a Joint Captured Material Exploitation Center.[17]

EUROPEAN COMMAND

The European Command (EUCOM) geographic area of responsibility includes eighty-three countries. In addition to the nations of Europe, EUCOM's responsibility extends to most of Africa (minus only those nations assigned to CENT-COM), Turkey, Syria, Lebanon, and Israel.[18]

The European Command's Intelligence Directorate, whose structure is shown in Figure 5.4, is responsible for:

- providing intelligence support to European Command headquarters, component commands, and Allied Command Europe (ACE)
- coordinating intelligence planning, collection analysis, targeting, and dissemination activities throughout the European theater in support of U.S. and allied requirements
- planning, programming, and budgeting for resources necessary to conduct the European Command's peacetime and wartime missions[19]

The directorate's Intelligence Operations Division is responsible for twenty-four-hour Indications and Warning, including near-real-time warning of terrorist attack, as well as for policy and planning direction for theater intelligence support to the detection and monitoring of illicit drug trafficking.[20]

The Collections Division is the EUCOM authority responsible for receiving, reviewing, validating, prioritizing, assigning, and/or forwarding European Command

FIGURE 5.4 Organization of the EUCOM Intelligence Directorate

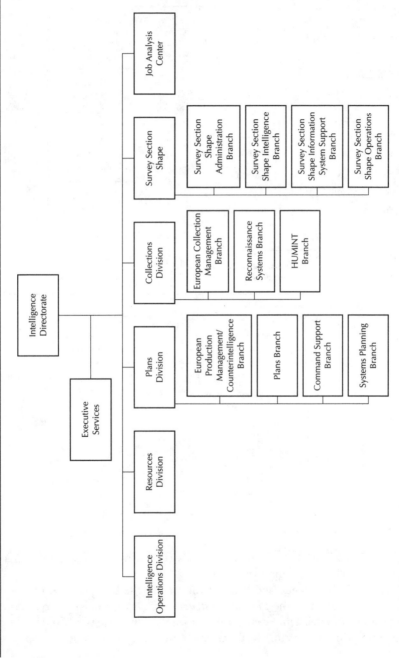

SOURCE: ED20-1, *Headquarters United States European Command Organization and Functions*, February 8, 1993, p. O-2.

FIGURE 5.5   Organization of the Joint Analysis Center

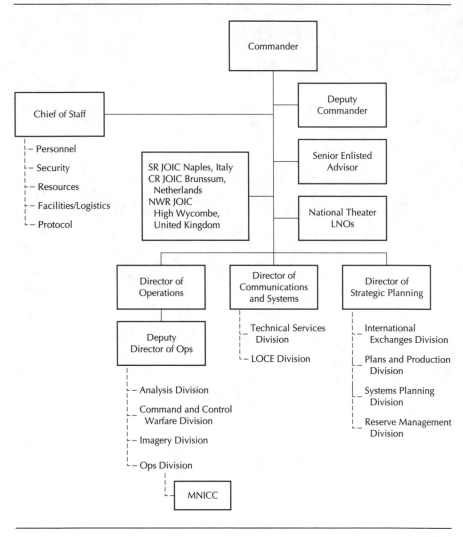

imagery, signals intelligence, human intelligence, and measurement and signature intelligence collection requirements.[21]

Along with the Atlantic and Pacific Commands, the European Command was specifically required by the *Plan for Restructuring Defense Intelligence* to develop plans for a joint intelligence center, called a Joint Analysis Center (JAC) in the case of the European Command. The functions of the JAC, located at RAF Molesworth, include:

- theater-wide, all-source analyses and assessments
- collection management
- multisource processing/exploitation/dissemination
- indications and warning (I&W) support
- target intelligence support
- support to NATO multinational forces and U.S. joint task forces
- distributed production[22]

The Joint Analysis Center's products include theater current intelligence summaries; theater regional assessments; theater threat assessments; electronic, air, defensive missile, and ground orders of battle; topical reports; I&W reports; counterterrorism, counterintelligence, and counternarcotics events reports; and exercise analyses and support.[23]

JAC intelligence operations, as shown in Figure 5.5, fall under the direct control of the Director of Operations. The directorate consists of four divisions. The Imagery Division oversees the JAC imagery intelligence process and the production of imagery intelligence to satisfy consumer requirements. The Analysis Division is the "primary all-source intelligence analysis and production division for JAC." The division's Terrorism Analysis Branch provides assessments of terrorist activities and capabilities through estimates and through daily current intelligence products. The C^{2}W (Command and Control Warfare) Division is a point of contact with the NSA and the U.S. SIGINT System (USSS), both with respect to SIGINT operations as well as information warfare operations.[24] The Operations Division is responsible for indications and warning, particularly of terrorist attack, and is simultaneously a component of the EUCOM Intelligence Directorate.

Under the JAC are a set of Joint Operational Intelligence Centers (JOICs) that are responsible for intelligence support to NATO's Allied Command Europe (ACE). The subordinate JOICs are located at Brunssum, Netherlands (Central Region); Naples, Italy (Southern Region); and High Wycombe, U.K. (Northwest Region).[25]

PACIFIC COMMAND

The geographic area of responsibility for the Pacific Command (PACOM) includes the Indian and Pacific Oceans; Japan, China, and the rest of East Asia; parts of Russia, Guam, and Hawaii.

Directly subordinate to the Commander in Chief, PACOM (CINCPAC) are the Director for Intelligence (head of the Intelligence Directorate) and the Director for Operations. In addition to managing the Intelligence Directorate, the Director for Intelligence serves as head of the Joint Intelligence Center, Pacific (JICPAC).

Reconnaissance operations are carried out under the cognizance of the Current Operations Division of the Directorate of Operations. Thus, the division's Reconnaissance Operations Branch manages the PACOM element of the Peacetime Aerial Reconnaissance Program (PARPRO), PONY EXPRESS, and space reconnaissance operations. It also conducts coordination and liaison activities with components of PACOM, as well as with other commands (U.S. and allied) and national agencies on PARPRO and related matters.[26]

As noted above, PACOM was one of three commands specifically commanded to establish a joint intelligence center. On July 3, 1991, the JICPAC was commissioned. It absorbed the Intelligence Center, Pacific (IPAC), the 548th Reconnaissance Technical Group, Task Force 168's Forward Area Support Team, Pacific (PACFAST), the Fleet Intelligence Center, Pacific (FICPAC), and the Fleet Ocean Surveillance Information Center (FOSIC)—creating a single organization with more than 1,200 personnel.[27]

Those organizations had been responsible for intelligence concerning the nations within PACOM's area of responsibility (IPAC), imagery interpretation (the 548th), technical support to fleet collection operations (PACFAST), intelligence on foreign naval capabilities and issues (FICPAC), and the monitoring of maritime movements (FOSIC).

The organizational structure of the JICPAC is shown in Figure 5.6, which indicates that the intelligence production functions of the center are concentrated in the six departments of the JICPAC Directorate of Operations.

The responsibilities of the Combat Application Department include production of port directories, employment of multispectral imagery in support of amphibious and special operations, production of target materials in support of conventional and special operations actions, analysis of target systems, and battle damage assessment.[28]

The Customer Support Department is responsible for foreign disclosure, tasking for the Directorate of Operations, and managing the production efforts of the other directorate departments. The Operational Intelligence Department is responsible for indications and warning, operational intelligence concerning maritime movements, first phase imagery analysis, Special Navy programs, and production of the *Daily Intelligence Bulletin*, the *Morning Brief*, and other current intelligence products.[29]

The North Asia Department produces political and military analysis, general military intelligence, and order of battle products for the Russian Far East, both Koreas, as well as China, Taiwan, Japan, Mongolia, Macau, and Hong Kong. The South Asia Department performs similar tasks for over twenty nations—from Indonesia, Vietnam, and India to the Bhutan, the Comoros, and La Reunion.[30]

The responsibilities of the Transregional Department are rather varied. Its Counterterrorism and Counterintelligence Division produces force protection analytical products, provides counterintelligence and counterterrorism support to operations, and assesses terrorist threat reporting against U.S. interests. Its Air Defense Division produces intelligence on air defense systems throughout the North and South Asia regions, conducts penetration and attrition analysis, and provides current intelligence support. The Collection Requirements Division is

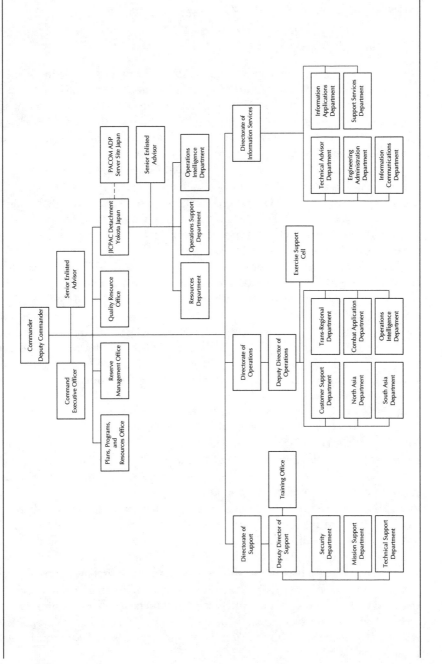

FIGURE 5.6 Organization of the Joint Intelligence Center, Pacific

responsible for collection requirements management, evaluation of intelligence information reports as well as tracking assessments.[31]

SOUTHERN COMMAND

The U.S. Southern Command (SOUTHCOM) has been responsible for U.S. military activities in Central and South America since 1946, when it was established as the Caribbean Command (CARIBCOM). As a result of a 1995 review of the unified command structure the USACOM's responsibility for the Gulf of Mexico, the Caribbean Sea and the nations within it, and adjoining waters around Central and South America were transferred to SOUTHCOM.[32]

The SOUTHCOM Intelligence Directorate consists of four components—a Directorate Administration Office, the Special Assistant to J2 (in Washington, D.C.), the Deputy Directorate for Operations (with Operations, Reserve Affairs, and Security divisions and an MDCI [Multidisciplinary Counterintelligence] Branch), and the Deputy Directorate for Plans and Programs (with Programs and Strategy, Resources, and Systems divisions).[33]

The director of the Intelligence Directorate is responsible for all aspects of intelligence for SOUTHCOM headquarters and components commands. He or she is also responsible for the operations of the SOUTHCOM Joint Intelligence Center. The Operations Division of the Deputy Directorate for Operations coordinates intelligence operations with the SOUTHCOM Staff, the Joint Chiefs of Staff, the CIA and other national intelligence agencies, and other unified commands. The MDCI Branch produces analytical studies, advisories, and assessments that cover espionage, foreign intelligence collection operations, terrorism, deception, and sabotage.[34]

As shown in Figure 5.7, the SOUTHCOM Joint Intelligence Center consists of six divisions—Requirements, Collection Management, Imagery, Indications and Warning, Analysis, and Production. The center is responsible for providing intelligence support to the Commander in Chief SOUTHCOM, SOUTHCOM, and its components. It also produces finished intelligence to support national decisionmakers under the Shared Production Program.[35]

The Collection Management Division is responsible for validating and presenting SOUTHCOM requirements with respect to human, signals, and imagery intelligence assets. The Imagery Division focuses on providing imagery support for contingency and operations plans requirements. The Indications and Warning Division maintains a twenty-four-hour-a-day watch and prepares current intelligence briefings for the CINCSOUTH and his staff. The Analysis Division "produces all-source general military intelligence products in support of national, theater and component requirements." It produces target analyses, daily updates to the *USSOUTHCOM Intelligence Summary*, and provides bibliographical intelligence products.[36]

FIGURE 5.7   Organization of the SOUTHCOM Joint Intelligence Center

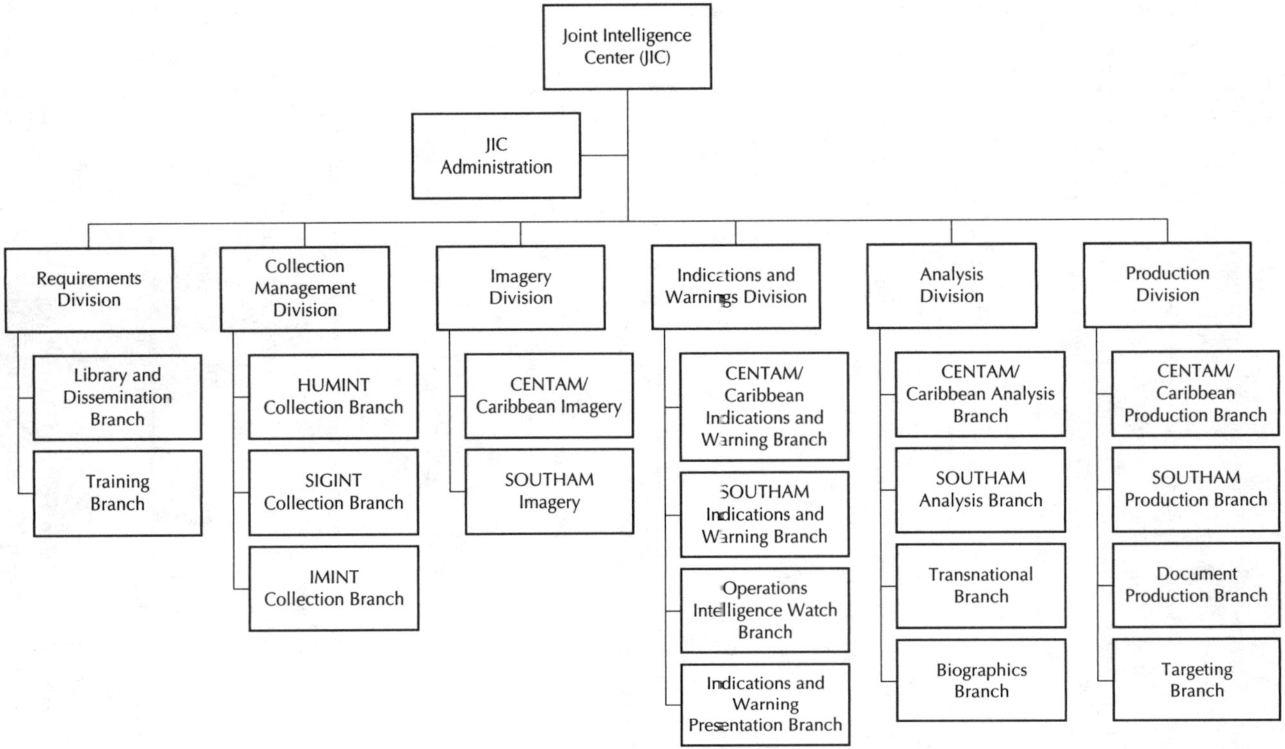

SOURCE: U.S. Southern Command.

U.S. SPACE COMMAND

The Air Force Space Command was established on September 1, 1982, to bring responsibilities for the Air Force's space-related operations as well as research and development activities under one managerial roof. The deputy commander of the Space Command is the head of the Air Force's Space and Missile Systems Center—the research, development, and acquisition organization at El Segundo, California.[37] The Navy followed suit by establishing a Naval Space Command, whereas the Army established an Army Space Command, which has become part of the Army Space and Strategic Defense Command. To provide overall direction of U.S. and military service space activities, a U.S. Space Command (USSPACECOM) was established in 1985. The Commander in Chief of USSPACECOM also serves as commander of the Air Force Space Command.

The Unified Command Plan of 1992 enumerated the functions of the USSPACECOM, which include:

- Providing missile warning and space surveillance . . .
- Exercising combat command over assigned U.S. forces that provide warning and assessment of strategic space and missile attack on the Continental United States and Alaska
- Planning for and developing requirements for strategic ballistic missile defense and space-based tactical ballistic missile defense[38]

The USPACECOM Directorate of Intelligence is responsible for providing:

- strategic and tactical indications and warning
- missile, space, command and control, atmospheric and operational intelligence and analysis to support threat assessment, force planning, development, posturing, and employment[39]

Subordinate to the Director of Intelligence are three divisions, the Special Security Office, and the Combined Intelligence Center, as shown in Figure 5.8. The Intelligence Operations Division is responsible for estimates, intelligence requirements, providing intelligence to senior decisionmakers, and liaison with external organizations. The Intelligence Policy, Plans, and Programs Division also is responsible for estimates as well as planning and requirements and exercise support. The Intelligence Systems Division is responsible for both systems acquisition and management.[40]

The Combined Intelligence Center (CIC), with five branches (Current Intelligence, Production, Space Forces, CMAS Intelligence Watch, Exercise) and the Missile Analysis Center in Omaha, produces a large variety of current and estimative intelligence, as well as indications and warning reports. It produces the Defense Intelligence Space Order of Battle (DISOB), issues foreign ASAT threat

FIGURE 5.8   Organization of the USSPACECOM Directorate of Intelligence and Combined Intelligence Center

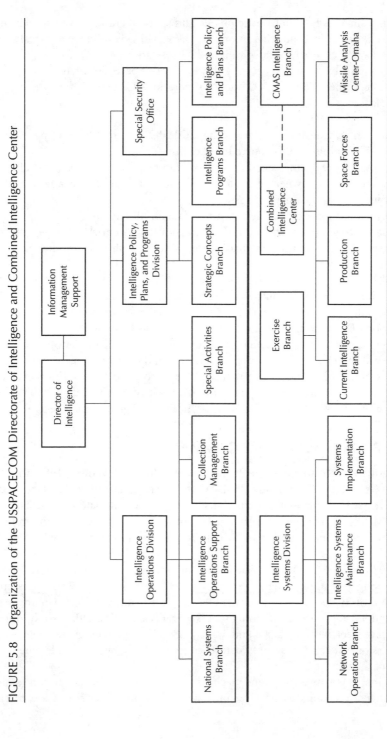

SOURCE: U.S. Space Command, *HQ United States Space Command Organization and Functions*, December 8, 1995, p. 17.

warnings, analyzes foreign ballistic missile and space operations, assesses new foreign missile and space launches, monitors the worldwide military/political situation, and analyzes foreign strategic air and C^3 operations.[41]

The ground-based sensors run by the Air Force Space Command provide information to the USSPACECOM Space Operations Center (SOC), which is responsible for:

- detecting, tracking, and providing COMBO information for space objects by employing all-source input data
- providing real-time coordination for status and alert of U.S. and allied space assets to owners, operators, and users of interference, attack, malfunctions, and damage assessment
- providing space object identification data for all satellites
- generating alert, warning, and verification of potentially hostile space-related events that affect space systems' survivability by employing all-source data[42]

Real-time operational control of the Space Surveillance Center (SSC), which was integrated into the SOC in December 1985, is the responsibility of the Current Operations Division, USSPACECOM. The SSC also tasks and alerts sensors for tracking support of routine catalog maintenance, space object identification support, space launches and maneuvers, and decays and deorbits. Finally, it maintains a catalog of orbital characteristics that can be used to predict the position of all observable, human-made space objects. This activity involves more than 20,000 space observations daily to monitor the status of more than 5,400 space objects.[43]

U.S. SPECIAL OPERATIONS COMMAND

On April 16, 1987, pursuant to Public Law 99-661 of November 1986, the U.S. Special Operations Command (USSOCOM) was established by Secretary of Defense Caspar Weinberger on instructions from President Ronald Reagan. The US-SOCOM was established to exert supervision over the activities of the military services special operations units, which became component commands of the USSOCOM.[44]

In 1997 the USSOCOM consisted of the organizations shown in Figure 5.9 and had a budget of approximately $3 billion. Its approximately 47,000 personnel consisted of 30,000 on active duty, 14,000 reservists and National Guard members, and 3,000 civilians. According to a General Accounting Office study, during an average week between 2,000 and 3,000 USSOCOM personnel are deployed on 150 missions in sixty to seventy countries (where they operate under the command of the theater CINC).[45]

Originally, ten missions were specified for USSOCOM: direct action (small-scale offensive actions), special reconnaissance, unconventional warfare, foreign

FIGURE 5.9   Organization of the U.S. Special Operations Command

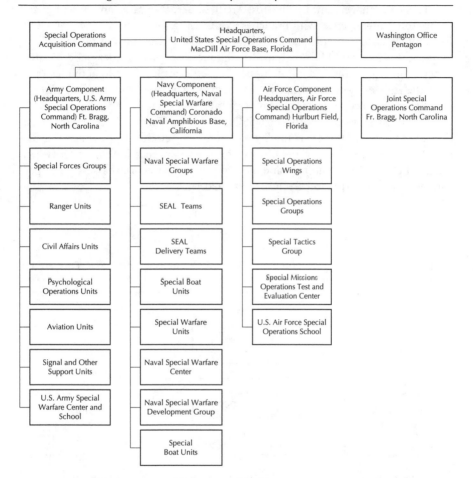

SOURCE: General Accounting Office, *Special Operations Forces: Opportunities to Preclude Overuse and Misuse,* (Washington, D.C.: GAO, 1997), p. 27.

internal defense, counterterrorism, civil affairs, psychological operations, humanitarian assistance, theater search and rescue, and other activities as specified by the President or the Secretary of Defense. In May 1995, at the direction of the President and the Secretary of Defense, counter proliferation was added to the list. Presently, the six key missions are counterproliferation, foreign internal defense, special reconnaissance, counterterrorism, unconventional warfare, and direct action.[46]

Intelligence responsibilities in the U.S. Special Operations Command are located in the Directorate of Intelligence and the USSOCOM Joint Intelligence

Center. Subordinate to the director and deputy director are three divisions— Intelligence Management, Intelligence Architecture, Programs and Systems; and Operational Intelligence, with branches as shown in Figure 5.10. The USOCOM Joint Intelligence Center began operations in 1994 and consists of four divisions, as shown in Figure 5.11—Analysis, Intelligence Systems, Imagery and Contingency Production, and Technical Support. In addition to the two activities in its title, the Imagery and Contingency Production Division also produces intelligence relevant to counterproliferation and information warfare.[47]

According to several reports, the USSOCOM has inherited the Army organization once known as the Army Intelligence Support Activity (ISA), which was disestablished qua ISA in June 1989. However, it appears that ISA's mission (which included clandestine collection and a variety of covert actions, assets), and personnel were transferred to USSOCOM in 1990.[48]

FIGURE 5.10   Organization of the U.S. Special Operations Command, Directorate of Intelligence

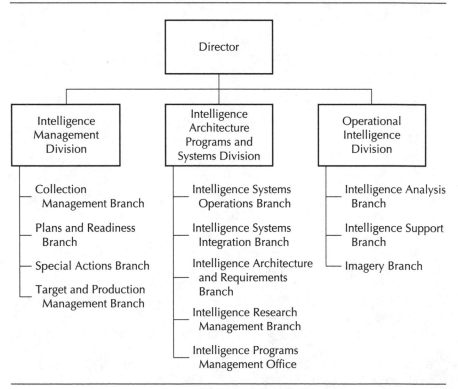

FIGURE 5.11   Organization of the USSOCOM Joint Intelligence Center

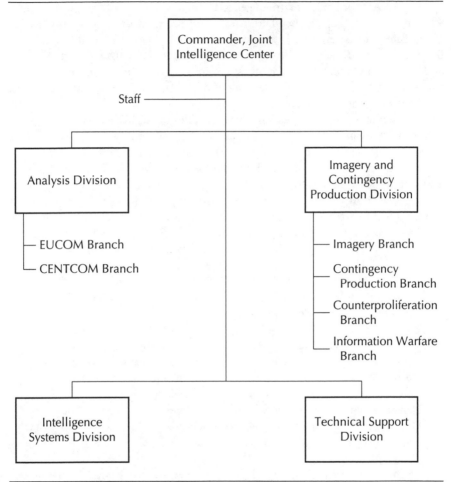

SOURCE: Department of Defense, *Joint Table of Distribution-Master, USSOCOM Joint Intelligence Center,* August 8, 1997.

U.S. STRATEGIC COMMAND

On September 27, 1991, President George Bush announced plans to disestablish the Strategic Air Command (SAC) and create two new commands to take over the SAC's functions. Operation of SAC aircraft would be assigned to the Air Combat Command, and nuclear strategic planning would be assigned to the new U.S. Strategic Command (STRATCOM).[49]

The STRATCOM's Senior Intelligence Officer is the Director of Intelligence, who manages the Intelligence Directorate and its seven divisions—Intelligence Plans, Intelligence Requirements, Special Security and Counterintelligence, Intelligence Systems, Intelligence Analysis and Reporting, Intelligence Applications, and Operations Intelligence. The divisions are grouped under two deputy directors, the Deputy Director for Intelligence and the Deputy Director for Intelligence Operations, as shown in Figure 5.12.

The Intelligence Plans Division is responsible for all USSTRATCOM intelligence policy, planning, programming and budgeting, and exercise and training activities. The Intelligence Requirements Division manages USSTRATCOM intelligence collection, processing, and exploitation programs. The Special Security and Counterintelligence Division is responsible for STRATCOM's Sensitive Compartmented Information (SCI) counterintelligence activities "and certain sensitive classified programs to ensure the security of the command." The Intelligence Systems Division manages and coordinates intelligence systems implementation and operates digital imagery dissemination and exploitation systems.[50]

The three divisions under the Deputy Director for Intelligence Operations constitute the Strategic Command Joint Intelligence Center (STRATJIC). The Intelligence Analysis and Reporting Division, through its Aviation, Defensive, Assessments, and Production Support branches:

- monitors, exploits, analyzes, reports and documents foreign aviation activity . . .
- monitors, analyzes, and reports on selected foreign countries' ground-based aerospace defense capabilities, including C^3, surface-to-air and anti-ballistic missiles, and air surveillance units and associated facilities
- analyzes and assesses military, political, and economic developments of the former Soviet Union, as well as countries involved in the acquisition, production and employment of weapons of mass destruction[51]

The Intelligence Applications Division (through its Mapping, Charting and Geodesy, Targeting Support, and Imagery Production branches) coordinates the command's MC&G requirements, produces classified imagery to develop the Single Integrated Operational Plan and for other purposes, and tasks and provides intelligence inputs to the Intelligence Directorate in support of operational planning. The Operational Intelligence Division operates the USSTRATCOM Indications and Warning Center, provides I&W support to internal and external customers, and provides operational intelligence for each Airborne Command Post Emergency Action Officer.[52]

U.S. TRANSPORTATION COMMAND

On October 1, 1987, the U.S. Transportation Command (TRANSCOM) was activated at Scott Air Force Base, Illinois. TRANSCOM is responsible for consolidating

FIGURE 5.12 Organization of the U.S. Strategic Command Intelligence Directorate and Joint Intelligence Center (STRATJIC)

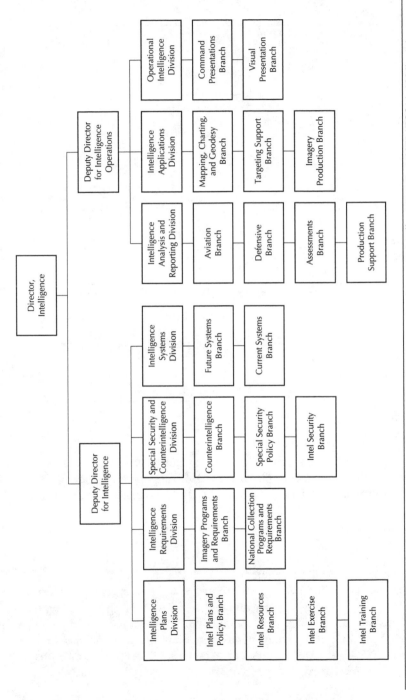

SOURCE: U.S. Strategic Command, *USSTRATCOM, Joint Manpower Program, Fiscal Year 1997* (Offut AFB, NE.: USSTRATCOM, 1996), p. 4.

FIGURE 5.13   Organization of the USTRANSCOM Joint Intelligence Center (JICTRANS)

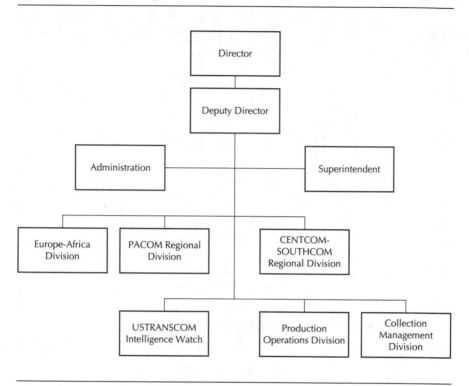

all U.S. strategic air, sea, and transportation during war or buildup to war and for exercising centralized control. TRANSCOM components include the Navy's Military Sealift Command, the Army's Military Traffic Management Command, and the Air Force Military Airlift Command.[53]

The Transportation Command's Intelligence Directorate develops and implements TRANSCOM intelligence policy, programs, doctrine, and organizational concepts.[54] TRANSCOM's Joint Intelligence Center (JICTRANS) is subordinate to the Intelligence Directorate and has five divisions—Europe-Africa, PACOM Regional, CENTCOM-SOUTHCOM Regional, Production Operations, and Collection Management. The structure of the JICTRANS is shown in Figure 5.13.

The first four divisions produce intelligence reports and briefings, a Daily Intelligence Summary, the Executive Intelligence Summary, Special Assessments, Contingency Planning Documents, Port Graphics, OPLAN Annexes, Transportation Planning Documents, and the Joint Theater Transportation Study.[55]

Notes

1. General Accounting Office, *Unified Command Plan: Atlantic and Southern Command Participation in 1995 Review* GAO/NSIAD–97-41-BR (Washington, D.C.: GAO, December 1996), p. 9.

2. Assistant Secretary of Defense (Command, Control, Communications, and Intelligence), *Plan for Restructuring Defense Intelligence*, March 15, 1991, p. 4.

3. Ibid.

4. On the disestablishment of the Fleet Intelligence Centers, see Arthur D. Baker III, "Farewell to the FICs," *Naval Intelligence Professionals Quarterly* (Winter 1992): 7–9.

5. William S. Cohen, *Defense Initiative Reform Report* (Washington, D.C.: U.S. Government Printing Office, November 1997), p. 76.

6. General Accounting Office, *Unified Command Plan*, pp. 9–10. U.S. Congress, House National Security Committee, *Hearings on National Defense Authorization Act for Fiscal Year 1997—H.R. 3230 and Oversight of Previously Authorized Programs, Authorization and Oversight* (Washington, D.C.: U.S. Government Printing Office, 1997), p. 862.

7. USACOM, "Atlantic Intelligence Command Organization," February 5, 1997.

8. Ibid.

9. Ibid.

10. U.S. Atlantic Command, USACOM Staff Instruction 5200.11, *United States Atlantic Command Organization, Missions and Functions* (Norfolk, Va.: USACOM, May 6, 1994), pp. S-1, S-13.

11. *United States Atlantic Command Organization, Missions and Functions*, p. T-11.

12. U.S. Congress, House Committee on Armed Services, *Hearings on HR 1816* (Washington, D.C.: U.S. Government Printing Office, 1983), p. 955.

13. "Intelligence Community Notes," *Defense Intelligence Journal* 1 (1992): 105–112.

14. U.S. Central Command, "The CENTCOM Perspective: CENTCOM/SOCOM Joint Intelligence Support Concept," 1992.

15. U.S. Central Command R 10–2, *U.S. Central Command Organization and Functions* (MacDill AFB, Fla.: USCENTCOM, March 1994), pp. 10–16, 10–19.

16. U.S. Central Command, "Joint Intelligence Center, Central," 1997.

17. U.S. Central Command, The CENTCOM Perspective.

18. U.S. Congress, House National Security Committee, *Hearings on National Defense Authorization Act for Fiscal Year 1997—H.R. 3230 and Oversight of Previously Authorized Programs, Authorization and Oversight*, p. 734; United States European Command, ED 40–1, "Intelligence Mission and Responsibilities," May 24, 1996.

19. European Command, ED 20–1, *Headquarters United States European Command Organization and Functions*, February 8, 1993, p. O-1.

20. Ibid., p. O-4.

21. Ibid., p. O-14.

22. European Command, *USEUCOM Plan for Theater Intelligence*, July 1, 1991, p. 2-3.

23. Ibid., p. 2-4.

24. European Command, ED 20–1, *Headquarters United States European Command Organization and Functions*, pp. U-4-9, U-4-13, U-4-27, U-43 to U-44.

25. European Command, *USEUCOM Plan for Theater Intelligence*, p. 2-1; European Command, "JAC Organization," 1997.

26. Commander in Chief, U.S. Pacific Command, *Organization and Functions Manual FY 86/87*, pp. 81–82.

27. Letter from K. Kibota, Chief, Administrative Support Division, Joint Secretariat, U.S. Pacific Command to author, October 8, 1991; "The New Boy on the Block," *Naval Intelligence Professionals Quarterly* (Spring 1992): 2; "West Coast Intelligence Consolidations," *Naval Intelligence Bulletin* (Fall/Winter 1990): 22–23.

28. Joint Intelligence Center, Pacific, *JICPAC Quick Reference Office and Function Guide* (Pearl Harbor, HI.: JICPAC, June 1996), pp. 11–12.

29. Ibid., pp. 12–13.

30. Ibid., pp. 14–15.

31. Ibid., pp. 15–16.

32. General Accounting Office, *Unified Command Plan*, pp. 9–10.

33. SOUTHCOM Regulation 10–1 (Draft), June 1998, p. D-1.

34. Ibid., pp. D-2, D-5.

35. U.S. Southern Command, SC Pamphlet 10-1, *Organization and Functions* (Miami, Fla.: SOUTHCOM, October 1997), p. J-1.

36. Ibid., pp. J-2 to J-3.

37. "Space Command," *Air Force Magazine*, May 1983, pp. 96–97.

38. Inspector General, Department of Defense, *U.S. Space Command: Inspection Report 94-INS–01* (Arlington, Va.: DOD IG, October 1993), p. 1.

39. United States Space Command, UMD 38–3, *HQ United States Space Command Organization and Functions* (Peterson AFB, Colo.: USSPACECOM, December 8, 1995), p. 15.

40. Ibid., p. 15.

41. Ibid., p. 16.

42. Ibid., p. 21; Headquarters, U.S. Space Command, *Initial Manning Document, FY 1986/87* (Peterson AFB, Colo.: USSPACECOM, 1985).

43. "Space Defense Operations Center Upgrades Assessment Capabilities," *Aviation Week & Space Technology*, December 9, 1985, pp. 67–73; United States Space Command, UMD 38–3, *HQ United States Space Command Organization and Functions*, p. 21; Headquarters, U.S. Space Command, *Initial Manning Document, FY 1986/87*.

44. Ronald Reagan, Memorandum for the Honorable Caspar W. Weinberger, Secretary of Defense, Subject: Establishment of Combatant Commands, April 13, 1987; Caspar Weinberger, Memorandum for the President, Subject: Establishment of the U.S. Special Operations Command, and the Specified Forces Command, April 16, 1987; General Accounting Office, *Special Operations Forces: Opportunities to Preclude Overuse and Misuse*, GAO/NSIAD–97–85, (Washington, D.C.: GAO, May 1997), p. 1.

45. General Accounting Office, *Special Operations Forces*, p. 2.

46. Ibid., pp. 6–7, 22.

47. Letter from Robert C. Mabry, USSOCOM Deputy Chief of Staff, to author, April 15, 1993; U.S. Special Operations Command, "Draft of JIC Structure," February 2, 1994; Department of Defense, Joint Table of Distribution-Master, USSOCOM Joint Intelligence Center, August 8, 1997.

48. See Jeffrey T. Richelson, "'Truth Conquers All Chains': The U.S. Army Intelligence Support Activity, 1981–1989," forthcoming.

49. "Intelligence Community Notes."

50. U.S. Strategic Command, *USSTRATCOM, Joint Manpower Program, Fiscal Year 1997* (Offut AFB, NE.: USSTRATCOM, October 15, 1996), pp. 16–18, 21–23.

51. Ibid., pp. 18–20.

52. Ibid., pp. 24–26.

53. James W. Canan, "Can TRANSCOM Deliver?" *Air Force Magazine*, October 1987, pp. 40–46.

54. U.S. Transportation Command, USTRANSCOM Pamphlet 20–2, "Organization and Functions," February 6, 1992, p. 12.

55. United States Transportation Command, USTRANSCOM Pamphlet 14–1, *JIC-TRANS*, (Scott AFB, Ill.: JICTRANS, December 1996), p. 2.

6

CIVILIAN INTELLIGENCE ORGANIZATIONS

The bulk of U.S. intelligence resources, whether in terms of personnel or dollars, lies in the hands of the national intelligence organizations and the military services. Some intelligence activities, however, are carried out by various branches of the civilian executive departments. Offices in the Departments of State, Energy, Treasury, Commerce, Justice, and Transportation collect and/or analyze intelligence on foreign political and military affairs, economic affairs, or narcotics trafficking. In some cases, the organizations, in addition to their primary responsibility to their department, also contribute to the national intelligence effort.

DEPARTMENT OF STATE INTELLIGENCE

With the dissolution of the Office of Strategic Services (OSS) after World War II, its research and analysis functions were transferred to the State Department. Those functions were carried out by the Interim Research and Intelligence Service. Two subsequent name changes and numerous reorganizations followed until the service was renamed the Bureau of Intelligence and Research (INR) in 1957.[1]

The INR employs approximately 360 individuals.[2] The bureau does not engage in clandestine collection, although it receives reports through normal diplomatic channels and conducts open source collection. However, it performs a variety of functions concerning operational matters, serving as liaison between the Department of State and the intelligence community, to ensure that the actions of the other intelligence agencies, such as the Central Intelligence Agency, are in accord with U.S. foreign policy.[3]

In terms of production, the INR faces in two directions. One direction is outward, where it is involved in interagency intelligence production efforts such as National Intelligence Estimates (NIEs) and Special Estimates (SEs). The second direction is inward—toward the State Department's internal organization. In this role the INR prepares a variety of intelligence products. The Secretary of State's *Morning Summary* is designed to inform the Secretary and his or her principal deputies of current events and current intelligence. The INR also prepares a variety of regional and functional summaries as well as single subject Intelligence Research Reports.[4]

The Director of INR is simultaneously the Assistant Secretary of State for Intelligence and Research. As shown in Figure 6.1, the Assistant Secretary is assisted by a Principal Deputy Assistant Secretary, a Deputy Assistant Secretary for Analysis, and a Deputy Assistant Secretary for Intelligence Policy, who supervise the INR's sixteen offices and two staffs. The Principal Deputy Assistant Secretary for Intelligence and Research is the second-ranking individual in the bureau and directly supervises the Office of Executive Director.[5]

The Deputy Assistant Secretary for Analysis supervises offices of analysis for six geographic regions: Africa; East Asia and the Pacific; Inter-American Affairs; the Near East and South Asia; Russia and Eurasia; and Europe and Canada. These offices primarily produce analyses of developments and issues that are, or will be, of concern to policymakers. The offices are also responsible for preparing regional and other special summaries and for contributing to intelligence community estimates and assessments. An analyst for the Office of Analysis for Europe and Canada might be asked to examine the situation in Germany, the future of democracy in Turkey, and/or the situation in Cyprus. An East Asia and Pacific analyst might be concerned with the role of the Chinese People's Liberation Army in domestic politics.[6]

The Deputy Assistant Secretary for Analysis is also responsible for the bureau's long-range analytical studies. He or she supervises the Office of Economic Analysis, the Office of the Geographer and Global Issues, the External Research Staff, and the Office of Analysis for Strategic, Proliferation, and Military Affairs, and the Office of Analysis for Terrorism, Narcotics, and Crime.[7]

The Office of Economic Analysis produces reports for policymakers on current and long-range issues involving international economic concerns such as foreign economic policies, business cycles, trade, financial affairs, food, population and energy, and economic relations between the industrialized countries and the developing nations. The Office of the Geographer and Global Issues prepares studies of policy issues associated with physical, cultural, economic, and political geography, U.S. maritime issues, and international boundaries and jurisdictional problems.[8]

The External Research Staff commissions those projects that cannot be done in INR. The Office of Strategic, Proliferation, and Military Affairs focuses on strategic forces of the acknowledged nuclear states (Russia, China, Britain, and France), the nuclear/ballistic missile activities of unacknowledged and aspiring nuclear nations, and regional military forces. The Office of Analysis for Terrorism, Narcotics, and Crime examines the structure, operations, and linkages of terrorist groups and drug cartels.[9]

The Deputy Assistant Secretary for Intelligence Policy supervises the Office of Intelligence Coordination, the Office of Intelligence Liaison, the Office of

FIGURE 6.1   Organization of the Bureau of Intelligence and Research

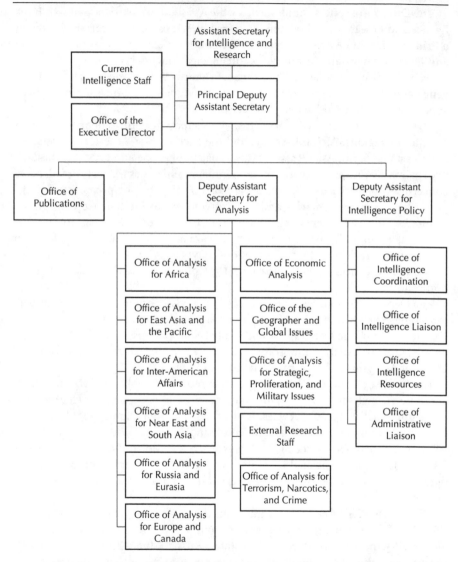

SOURCE: Bureau of Intelligence and Research, *INR: Intelligence and Research in the Department of State* (Washington, D.C.: Department of State, n.d.); *United States Department of State Telephone Directory* (Washington, D.C.: U.S. Government Printing Office, March 1998), pp. State 13–14.

Administrative Liaison, and the Office of Intelligence Resources. The Office of Intelligence Coordination works with the DIA and the FBI on matters of common interest and represents the State Department in community coordination of human and technical intelligence collection and production priorities. The Office of Intelligence Liaison coordinates proposals for covert action programs. Its basic responsibility in connection with such programs is to ensure "thorough consideration of their support of and implications for U.S. foreign policy."[10]

The Office of Intelligence Resources (OIR) provides staff support, representation, and coordination for the department's interests in the National Foreign Intelligence Program and budget. It works with other intelligence community agencies and other branches of the department and overseas missions in planning, tasking, and deploying, and evaluating technical collection activities. It also advises department offices on the use of intelligence produced by major technical collection systems. In 1992, the Director of the OIR advised the National Reconnaissance Office on how to handle the forthcoming declassification of its existence.[11]

DEPARTMENT OF ENERGY INTELLIGENCE

The Department of Energy's intelligence role can be traced to July 1946, when the National Intelligence Authority decided that the Atomic Energy Commission (AEC) had an appropriate foreign intelligence role and authorized AEC representation on the Intelligence Advisory Board. On December 12, 1947, the AEC's intelligence role was affirmed by National Security Council Intelligence Directive No. 1.[12]

The Energy Reorganization Act of 1974 transferred the AEC's intelligence responsibilities to the Energy Research and Development Administration, and the Department of Energy Organization Act of 1977 transferred them to the newly created Department of Energy. In April 1990, the Energy Department consolidated its intelligence functions by establishing an Office of Intelligence to bring under one roof the Offices of Foreign Intelligence, Threat Assessment, and Counterintelligence. A 1994 reorganization resulted in the redesignation of the office as the Office of Energy Intelligence within the Office of Nonproliferation and National Security, with the Office of Threat Assessment moved outside the new intelligence office.[13]

A 1998 reorganization split the OEI into two offices: an Office of Intelligence and a Office of Counterintelligence. The new offices report directly to the Secretary and Deputy Secretary of Energy. The counterintelligence office is responsible for counterintelligence programs throughout the Department of Energy, including the nuclear laboratories.[14]

As shown in Figure 6.2, the Office of Intelligence has five subordinate components: Intelligence Work for Others, the Special Technologies Program, the Nuclear Nonproliferation Division, the Energy Assessments Division, and the Intelligence Support Division.

FIGURE 6.2   Organization of the Office of Intelligence, Department of Energy

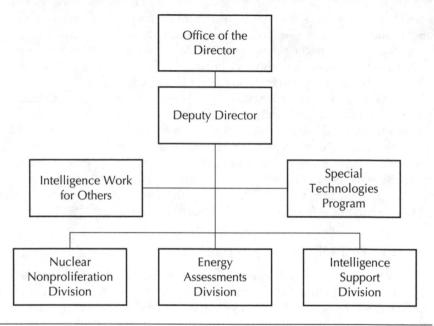

SOURCE: Department of Energy.

The Nuclear Nonproliferation Division studies and reports on foreign military and atomic and nuclear weapons programs for both intelligence and treaty monitoring purposes. During Operations Desert Shield and Desert Storm, the division provided the Joint Chiefs of Staff and the DIA with assessments of the Iraqi nuclear weapons program and its capabilities. It was also concerned with issues such as the command, control, and security of tactical and strategic nuclear weapons in Russia and other former Soviet states, the dismantlement of nuclear weapons in the former Soviet Union, the disposition of the nuclear materials removed from those weapons, and the proliferation potential (via a "brain drain") of the former Soviet republics.[15]

The Energy Assessment Division focuses on international developments that could affect the overall U.S. energy posture and the Strategic Petroleum Reserve. Special studies conducted by the office examined the prospects for disruption of energy supplies due to worldwide political, economic, and social instabilities. In addition, the division analyzed overall energy balances within Russia and other nations, focusing on total energy needs that might influence supply and demand. It also examined energy technologies that may have dual uses (civil and military) in support of foreign availability studies related to the DOE Military Critical Technologies List.[16]

The Office of Counterintelligence conducts counterintelligence risk assessments, including assessments of the Energy Department's susceptibility to economic espionage.[17] Recent Energy Department counterintelligence products have included *Statistical Analysis of Foreign Visits to DOE Facilities* (September 1993) and *Information Brokers* (August 1994). Counterintelligence newsletters and bulletins cover such topics as "Targeting of DOE Travelers."[18]

The Department of Energy is also responsible for the Lawrence Livermore Laboratory's intelligence program, which is conducted by the International Assessments Program, also known as the Special Projects or Z Division of Livermore's Nonproliferation, Arms Control, and International Security Directorate. Z Division was established in 1965 to analyze the Soviet nuclear weapons program and, shortly thereafter, the Chinese program. In the mid-1970s, Z Division began analyzing the proliferation of nuclear weapons to smaller nations. More recently, Z Division has also focused on the "control and accountability of nuclear weapons, materials, and technology in Russia." In addition, it has added chemical and biological weapons proliferation to the list of topics it examines.[19]

As indicated in Figure 6.3, Z Division consists of two major groups—Foreign Nuclear Programs and Global Issues. The Foreign Nuclear Programs Group consists of three subgroups—Former Soviet Union; China, Pakistan, India, and Israel; and the Rest of the World. The Global Issues Group also has three components—Suppliers; Counterproliferation, Regional Arms Control; and Information Operations, Science and Technology. These organizations provide:

- national capability assessments of potential proliferant countries
- analyses of state-of-the-art fuel cycle technologies, such as enrichment and reprocessing, that proliferants could use to acquire fissile material
- assessments of worldwide availability of related but nonnuclear weapons technology such as safety, arming, firing, and fusing systems
- assessments of the activities and behavior of nuclear supplier states and international organizations involved in nuclear commerce, safeguards, and physical security[20]

In addition to Z Division, the National Security Program Office (NSPO) at Oak Ridge National Laboratory also conducts intelligence assessments related to foreign nuclear activities. Within NSPO are four offices: Special Projects, Safeguards, Nonproliferation and Arms Control Assessments, and Program Operations and Support. The Nonproliferation and Arms Control Assessments Office produces intelligence assessments related to nonproliferation policy, nuclear export control, and arms control. It also conducts imagery exploitation.[21]

FIGURE 6.3   Organization of Z Division, Lawrence Livermore National Laboratory

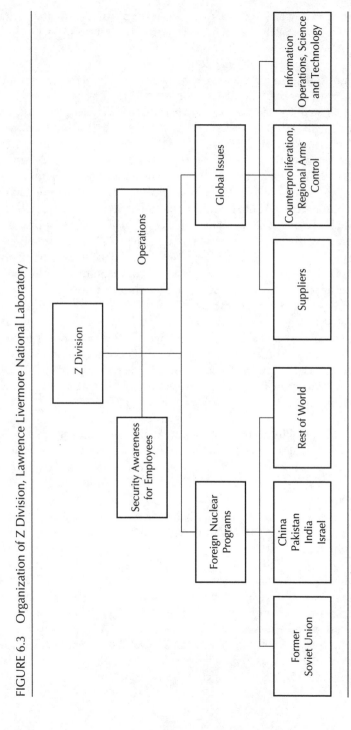

SOURCE: Department of Energy.

DEPARTMENT OF TREASURY INTELLIGENCE

The Office of Intelligence Support (OIS) is headed by the Special Assistant to the Secretary (National Security), who reports to the Secretary and Deputy Secretary. It was established in 1977, succeeding the Office of National Security, which had been created in 1961. The office began representing the Treasury with the intelligence community as a result of a 1971 presidential memorandum and became a member of the NFIB in 1972.[22]

The office overtly collects foreign economic, financial, and monetary data in cooperation with the Department of State. Its three primary functions are: providing intelligence related to U.S. economic policy to the Secretary of the Treasury and other Treasury officials; representing the Treasury on intelligence community committees and maintaining liaison with other elements of the intelligence community; and reviewing all proposed support relationships between the intelligence community and any Treasury office or bureau. As part of its participation on intelligence community committees and of its liaison role, the OIS develops intelligence requirements for the Treasury Department and disseminates them to the relevant intelligence agencies.[23]

Subordinate to the Special Assistant is the Senior National Intelligence Adviser, an Intelligence Support Coordinator, a Special Security Officer, seven National Intelligence Advisors, a Watch Office with six Watch Officers, and a Special Projects Manager. The National Intelligence Advisers are responsible for a variety of areas, countries, and regions; trade; energy; monetary affairs; National Foreign Intelligence Board support; and National Security Agency support.[24]

The Watch Office, provides around-the-clock coverage of national and international events and, outside of normal duty hours, is the Treasury focal point for alerting senior officials. The Watch Office also monitors cable traffic and delivers cables to Treasury executives and monitors press wire services and prepares a press summary for Treasury executives.[25]

DEPARTMENT OF COMMERCE INTELLIGENCE

Department of Commerce participation in intelligence activities has been heightened in the past twenty years by several factors—the concern over technology transfer to the Soviet Bloc and then the concern of the spread of advanced weapons technology. Intelligence is required concerning (1) those who wish to acquire such technology, (2) those who may attempt or are attempting to provide it, and (3) its accessibility from foreign sources.

At present, the Department of Commerce has two units with intelligence functions: the Office of Executive Support (OES) and the Office of Export Enforcement (OEE).

The Office of Executive Support, which is subordinate to the Office of the General Counsel, was established in October 1977 as the Office of Intelligence Liaison, "in order to improve the efficiency of intelligence support provided to the various administrations and bureaus in Commerce that have international responsibilities and foreign intelligence needs." A press release issued by the department at the time noted that the office's creation largely grew out of "three decades of intelligence community support of Commerce programs administering U.S. legislation on export controls, including both strategic commodities and advance technology." It further noted that intelligence reports had aided a number of other Department of Commerce activities, including trade negotiations with Communist countries, foreign shipping and fishing activities, and various aspects of international trade in industrial goods and commodities.[26]

Recently renamed the Office of Executive Support, the office provides day-to-day intelligence support to key Department of Commerce officials who have international policy or program responsibilities. This support includes preparation of a daily department foreign intelligence summary covering major international developments as well as briefings. Support also includes intelligence information and briefings for key departmental officials traveling abroad. Additionally, the office is responsible for reviewing and assessing Department of Commerce intelligence requirements. Based on the results of such assessments, it tasks the intelligence community to provide the necessary information.[27]

The OEE, formerly the Compliance Division of the Office of Export Administration, is subordinate to the Assistant Secretary for Export Enforcement. Its function is to ensure that the proper approvals have been obtained for the export of sensitive technology and to prevent unauthorized shipments of such technology.[28] The functions of the OEE's Intelligence Division include:

- receiving, interpreting, and analyzing intelligence and trade data to determine whether preventive, deterrent, or some other type of enforcement action [is] required or appropriate
- providing leads for ongoing investigations and assisting investigative personnel in the conduct of investigations
- disseminating intelligence information and analysis to agents of the OEE and other appropriate federal agencies
- applying qualitative and quantitative methodologies to establish patterns and profiles of diversion and acquisition
- collecting intelligence to assist in the conduct of prelicense checks and postshipment verifications[29]

DRUG ENFORCEMENT ADMINISTRATION INTELLIGENCE

The Drug Enforcement Administration (DEA)—which, like the Federal Bureau of Investigation (FBI), is part of the Department of Justice—operates in the United

States and abroad. DEA intelligence operations are the responsibility of the Administrator of the Intelligence Division. The division is responsible for:

- providing technical and operational intelligence products and services that identify the structure and members of international and domestic drug trafficking organizations and exploitable areas for enforcement operations
- preparing strategic intelligence assessments, estimates, and probes focusing on trafficking patterns, source country production, and domestic production and consumption trends
- developing intelligence that focuses on the financial aspects of drug investigations such as money-laundering techniques, drug-related asset discovery and forfeiture, and macroeconomic impact assessments of the illegal drug trade
- providing interagency intelligence support to other federal, state, and local law enforcement organizations and a variety of state and foreign drug intelligence clearinghouses and participating in the National Narcotics Interdiction System[30]

As Figure 6.4 illustrates, the DEA Intelligence Division, consists of three offices and one center. The Office of Investigative Intelligence is responsible for planning, organizing, coordinating, and implementing the DEA's investigative intelligence programs. The cocaine and heroin investigative units of the office's Investigative Intelligence Section, are responsible for identifying major traffickers and organizations engaged in cultivation, production, transportation, and distribution as well as in the laundering of drug proceeds.[31]

The Office of Intelligence Liaison and Policy designs the strategy and policy for DEA intelligence programs and coordinates their implementation. The Collection Requirements Unit of the office's Intelligence Policy and Program Section "identifies intelligence gaps and coordinates short and long-term intelligence probes to fulfill those needs," maintains a Collection Management Coordination program for interactive tasking of collection systems, and coordinates the DEA's imagery intelligence program. The office's Strategic Intelligence Section produces strategic intelligence assessments, studies, reports and estimates from both foreign and domestic sources. The section's Foreign Strategic Intelligence Units (Europe; Asia and Africa; Latin America) assess the drug situation in their areas of responsibility, including drug production capability and activity, transportation systems, makeup of trafficking groups, effectiveness of traffic interdiction, and local political attitudes regarding drug trafficking.[32]

In 1985 the DEA established the U.S. Southwest Border Intelligence Task Force, which supports DEA intelligence operations along the U.S.-Mexican border. The task force provides strategic assessments of all aspects of drug trafficking from

FIGURE 6.4 Organization of the DEA Intelligence Division

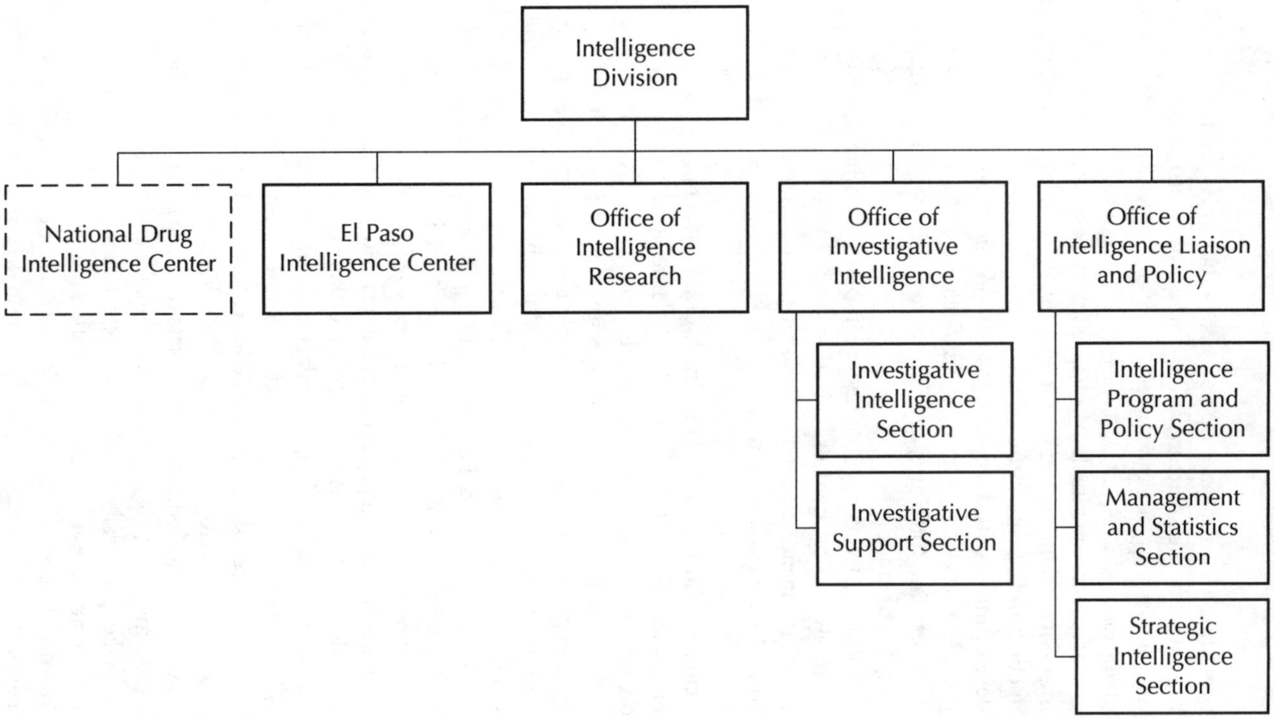

Mexico to the United States and—in conjunction with DEA field offices—collates, analyzes, and disseminates intelligence on major Mexican drug traffickers and their organizations.[33]

The Intelligence Division's Special Field Intelligence Program provides funding "to exploit highly specialized or unique collection opportunities against a wide variety of intelligence problems in foreign areas." The objective is to collect data on the entire narcotics raw material production process as well as on smuggling routes and methods, trafficking, and terrorist or financial matters relating to narcotics activities.[34]

According to the DEA's 1984 congressional budget submission, the agency had conducted intelligence probes in then West Germany that identified a sizable number of Turkish and Pakistani traffickers transporting Southwest Asian heroin to Western Europe. Likewise, DEA personnel conducting intelligence probes in Pakistan, Turkey, and Mexico were reported to have pinpointed illicit laboratory locations, identified the operators, and assessed the potential output of a number of sophisticated morphine, heroin, and opium production operations.[35]

FEDERAL BUREAU OF INVESTIGATION

The responsibilities of the Federal Bureau of Investigation (FBI) are predominantly in the criminal law enforcement, domestic counterterrorism, and domestic counterintelligence areas, with the last two responsibilities being performed by the bureau's National Security Division. The division also assumes some responsibility with regard to the collection of foreign intelligence in the United States.

Over the years the FBI has tried to expand its role in foreign intelligence collection. In 1939, President Franklin D. Roosevelt gave the FBI responsibility for the collection of intelligence in the Western Hemisphere and created a Special Intelligence Service (SIS) for this function. The SIS had approximately 360 agents, mostly in Mexico, Argentina, and Brazil. Although it was stripped of this function after the war, the bureau maintained representatives as Legal Attachés in ten embassies as of 1970. The attachés' official function was to be a liaison with national police forces on matters of common concern and to deal with Americans who found themselves in trouble with the law. In 1970 the bureau increased from ten to twenty the number of embassies with FBI representation and instructed agents to collect foreign intelligence, with particularly interesting intelligence being slugged HILEV (High Level) by overseas agents. Some material was distributed to high officials—for example, Henry Kissinger—outside normal channels. In the aftermath of J. Edgar Hoover's death and FBI revelations, the program was terminated and FBI representation abroad was reduced to fifteen embassies.[36]

At least two instances of FBI attempts to engage in foreign clandestine collection have come to light. During the investigation of the murder of former Chilean Defense Minister Orland Letelier, the FBI operated an undercover agent in Chile.

The agent told the FBI that the right-wing Partia y Libertad had contracted with Chilean narcotics traffickers to murder Letelier. The FBI agent, however, turned out to be a DEA informant who had been terminated and blacklisted years earlier for deception and moral turpitude. A more successful operation involved the FBI placement of a young woman informant in one of the first groups of U.S. leftists to visit China in the 1970s.[37]

The FBI does maintain a presence, in the form of legal attachés, overseas. The program has been expanding from the twenty-three offices and seventy agents overseas. In 1996, it was planned to add another twenty-three offices and fifty-nine additional agents over the following four years. By mid-1998, new offices had been opened in Tel Aviv, Cairo, Riyadh, Buenos Aires, Pretoria, Tallinn, Warsaw, and Kiev, with others in the planning stage or under consideration. The expansion was intended to permit closer liaison with foreign counterpart organizations, with respect to the investigation of international terrorism, narcotics trafficking, and organized crime.[38]

Although those offices are not authorized to conduct foreign intelligence activities, the FBI is involved in domestic activities to generate foreign intelligence. Executive Order 12333 allows the FBI to "conduct within the United States, when requested by the officials of the intelligence community designated by the President, activities undertaken to collect foreign intelligence or support foreign intelligence collection requirements of other agencies within the intelligence community."[39]

Thus, in September 1980 two FBI officials were briefed by the Joint Staff on intelligence requirements in support of a possible second attempt to rescue U.S. hostages in Iran. One of the officials was the Deputy Assistant Director for Intelligence, who was responsible for coordinating the use of non-U.S. persons in the United States for intelligence purposes. The Joint Staff asked the FBI officials for their assistance in developing information relevant to the rescue mission, instructing them to "seek any potential Iranian leads that they may spot for exploitation in the conduct of their programs."[40]

In the past, FBI foreign-intelligence related activities have also included wiretapping and break-ins. The FBI has operated wiretaps against numerous foreign embassies in Washington. FBI agents regularly monitored the phones in the offices of all Communist governments represented in Washington. Additionally, the phones in the offices of noncommunist governments were also tapped, especially when those nations were engaged in negotiations with the United States or when significant developments were taking place in those countries. At one point, the FBI tapped the phones of an ally's trade mission in San Francisco. In addition, the FBI has conducted break-ins at foreign embassies to obtain cryptanalytic material and other foreign intelligence.[41]

In August 1993, the FBI opened a National Drug Intelligence Center, headquartered in Jonestown, Pennsylvania. The 130-person staff reached 221 (of the authorized 257) by October 1, 1997. They included agents and analysts on leave from eleven agencies, including the CIA, the Defense Department, the DEA, and the Internal Revenue Service.[42]

NDIC's mission is to "coordinate and consolidate strategic organizational drug intelligence from national security and law enforcement agencies, in order to produce requested assessments and analyses regarding the structure, membership, finances, communications, transportation, logistics, and other activities of drug-trafficking organizations." The NDIC Intelligence Division is composed, in part, of three strategic organizational intelligence branches—the primary analytical units—that are organized by geographic and subject areas. The division also contains a Document Exploitation Branch, consisting of two teams that are deployed when requested by federal law enforcement agencies to review documents and computer data obtained from significant narcotics trafficking organizations.[43]

DEPARTMENT OF TRANSPORTATION INTELLIGENCE

The Transportation Department's Office of Intelligence and Security was established in 1990, based on a recommendation of the Presidential Commission on Aviation Security and Terrorism, which was set up after the Pan Am 103 bombing. The office, with Intelligence, Plans and Policy, and Security Divisions, is responsible for all strategic planning, coordination, and oversight of transportation intelligence and security.[44]

Notes

1. U.S. Congress, Senate Select Committee to Study Governmental Operations with Respect to Intelligence Activities, *Final Report, Book VI, Supplementary Reports on Intelligence Activities* (Washington, D.C.: U.S. Government Printing Office, 1976), pp. 271–276.

2. U.S. Congress, House Committee on Appropriations, *Departments of Commerce, Justice, and State, the Judiciary, and Related Agencies Appropriations for 1992, Part 3* (Washington, D.C.: U.S. Government Printing Office, 1991), p. 451.

3. U.S. Congress, House Committee on Foreign Affairs, *The Role of Intelligence in the Foreign Policy Process* (Washington, D.C.: U.S. Government Printing Office, 1980), p. 57.

4. *INR* (Washington, D.C.: Department of State, n.d.), pp. 2, 4.

5. Ibid., pp. 9, 10; *United States Department of State Telephone Directory* (Washington, D.C.: U.S. Government Printing Office, March 1998), pp. State 13–14.

6. *INR*, p. 10; *United States Department of State Telephone Directory*, pp. State 13–14; U.S. Congress, House Committee on Appropriations, *Departments of Commerce, Justice, and State, the Judiciary and Related Agencies Appropriations for FY 1987, Part 6* (Washington, D.C.: U.S. Government Printing Office, 1986), p. 351.

7. *INR*, p. 10; *United States Department of State Telephone Directory*, pp. State 13–14.

8. *INR* (Washington, D.C.: Department of State, 1983), pp. 12–13; U.S. Congress, House Committee on Appropriations, *Departments of Commerce, Justice, and State, the Judiciary and Related Agencies Appropriations for FY 1987, Part 6*, p. 351; *INR*, p. 4.

9. *INR* (1983), pp. 12–13; *INR*, p. 10.

10. *INR*, p. 8.

11. Ibid., p. 9; Jeffrey T. Richelson, "Out of the Black: The Disclosure and Declassification of the National Reconnaissance Office," *International Journal of Intelligence and Counterintelligence* 11, no. 1 (Spring 1998): 1–25.

12. Statement by Robert W. Daniel Jr., Director, Office of Intelligence, Department of Energy, in U.S. Congress, House Committee on Appropriations, *Energy and Water Development Appropriations for 1992, Part 6* (Washington, D.C.: U.S. Government Printing Office, 1991), pp. 819–836 at p. 820.

13. Ibid.; "Watkins Reorganizes DOE's Intelligence Work," *Washington Post*, April 18, 1990, p. A25; U.S. Congress, Senate Committee on Armed Services, *Department of Defense Authorization for Appropriations for Fiscal Years 1992 and 1993, Part 1* (Washington, D.C.: U.S. Government Printing Office, 1991), p. 657; Department of Energy, *National Telephone Directory* (Washington, D.C.: U.S. Government Printing Office, 1994), p. 46.

14. "Secretary Peña Strengthens DOE Intelligence Programs," *DOE News*, February 10, 1998.

15. U.S. Congress, Senate Committee on Armed Services, *Department of Defense Authorization for Fiscal Years 1992 and 1993, Part 1* (Washington, D.C.: U.S. Government Printing Office, 1991), p. 657; Daniel, in U.S. Congress, House Committee on Appropriations, *Energy and Water Development Appropriations for 1992, Part 6*, p. 823; Statement of Robert W. Daniel Jr., Director, Office of Intelligence, Department of Energy, in U.S. Congress, House Committee on Appropriations, *Energy and Water Appropriations for 1993, Part 6* (Washington, D.C.: U.S. Government Printing Office, 1992), p. 2081.

16. Daniel, in U.S. Congress, House Committee on Appropriations, *Energy and Water Development Appropriations for 1992, Part 6*, p. 823; Daniel, in U.S. Congress, House Committee on Appropriations, *Energy and Water Development Appropriations for 1993, Part 6*, p. 2195.

17. U.S. Congress, House Committee on Appropriations, *Energy and Water Development Hearings for 1997, Part 4* (Washington, D.C.: U.S. Government Printing Office, 1996), p. 441.

18. Department of Energy, Office of Intelligence, Office of Counterintelligence, *Statistical Analysis of Foreign Visits to DOE Facilities* (Washington, D.C.: DOE, September 1993); Department of Energy, Office of Intelligence, Office of Counterintelligence, *Information Brokers* (Washington, D.C.: DOE, August 1994); Department of Energy, Office of Counterintelligence, OCI Bulletin Number 93–007, "Targeting of DOE Travelers," 1993.

19. Lawrence Livermore National Laboratory, "Nonproliferation, Arms Control, and International Security," n.d.

20. U.S. Congress, House Committee on Armed Services, *Department of Energy: National Security and Military Applications of Nuclear Energy Authorization Act of 1984* (Washington, D.C.: U.S. Government Printing Office, 1983), p. 394.

21. Oak Ridge National Laboratory, National Security Program Office Organization Chart, February 1996; Oak Ridge National Laboratory, Organizational Charter for National Security Program Office, March 11, 1996.

22. "Treasury Department-Office of Intelligence Support," http://www.odci.gov/cia/other_links/wheel/tdois.html.

23. Ronald Reagan, "Executive Order 12333: United States Intelligence Activities," December 4, 1981, in *Federal Register* 46, no. 235 (December 8, 1981): 59941–54 at 59946; "Foreign Intelligence—It's More than the CIA," *U.S. News and World Report*, May 1, 1981, pp. 35–37; Department of the Treasury Order 100–3, "Functions of the Executive Secretariat," January 13, 1987, p. 2; Department of the Treasury, "Office of Intelligence Support," 1997.

24. Department of the Treasury, "OIS Organization Structure," n.d. (*circa* 1988); Department of the Treasury, "Office of Intelligence (OIS) Organization Structure," n.d. (*circa*

1992); Department of the Treasury Office of Intelligence Support Organization Chart, February 12, 1997.

25. Department of the Treasury, "Office of Intelligence Support."

26. United States Department of Commerce News G 77–194, "Commerce Establishes Office of Intelligence Liaison," October 12, 1977; Department of Commerce, Department Organization Order 10–6, Office of the General Counsel, March 7, 1996.

27. Department of Commerce, "Department Organization Order Series 10–6, Appendix A," June 10, 1981, p. 2.

28. Department of Commerce, Department Organization Order 50–1, Bureau of Export Administration, February 7, 1995, p. 5.

29. Department of Commerce, "Organization and Function Order 41–4, Assistant Secretary for Trade Administration," May 8, 1985, pp. 21–22.

30. Drug Enforcement Administration, *Annual Report, Fiscal Year 1986* (Washington, D.C.: DEA, 1986), pp. 9–10.

31. Memorandum from Thomas A. Constantine, Administrator to Paul V. Daly, Assistant Administrator, Intelligence Division, Subject: Reorganization of the Intelligence Division, June 7, 1996, pp. 3–7.

32. Ibid., pp. 18–19; 21–23.

33. Drug Enforcement Administration, *Annual Report Fiscal Year 1986*, p. 6.

34. U.S. Congress, House Committee on Appropriations, *Departments of Commerce, Justice, State, the Judiciary and Related Agencies Appropriations for 1984, Part 6* (Washington, D.C.: U.S. Government Printing Office, 1983), pp. 3, 21.

35. Ibid., pp. 22–23.

36. Sanford J. Ungar, *The FBI* (Boston: Little, Brown, 1976), pp. 225–226, 242.

37. Ibid., pp. 240–241; Taylor Branch and Eugene M. Proper, *Labyrinth* (New York: Viking, 1982), pp. 231, 350, 358.

38. R. Jeffrey Smith and Thomas W. Lippman, "FBI Plans to Expand Overseas," *Washington Post*, August 20, 1996, pp. A1, A14; Telephone conversation with Michael Kortan, FBI, March 27, 1998; Alan G. Ringgold, "The FBI's Legal Attaché Program," *The Investigator*, June 1997, p. 1.

39. Reagan, "Executive Order 12333: United States Intelligence Activities," Section 1.14, provision c, p. 59949.

40. JCS Joint Staff, Memorandum for the Record, Subject: Briefing of FBI Representatives, September 25, 1980.

41. Victor Marchetti and John Marks, *The CIA and the Cult of Intelligence* (New York: Knopf, 1974), p. 204; "Mole Tunnels Under a Soviet Consulate," *Newsweek*, August 15, 1983, p. 21; Douglas Watson, "Huston Says NSA Urged Break-Ins," *Washington Post*, March 3, 1975, pp. 1, 6.

42. Michael deCourcy Hinds, "Center for Drug Intelligence Opens, But Some Ask If It Is Really Needed," *New York Times*, November 17, 1993, p. A16; General Accounting Office, *An Overview of U.S. Counterdrug Intelligence Activities* (Washington, D.C.: GAO, 1998), p. 33.

43. General Accounting Office, *An Overview of U.S. Counterdrug Intelligence Activities*, pp. 31–32.

44. "Who's Who," *Intelligence Newsletter*, September 2, 1993, p. 8.

CIA headquarters, Langley, Virginia. Photo Credit: Central Intelligence Agency.

Natural Security Agency headquarters, Ft. George G. Meade, Maryland. Photo Credit: Department of Defense.

The headquarters of the National Reconnaissance Office in Chantilly, Virginia. Photo Credit: National Reconnaissance Office.

DIA's Defense Intelligence Analysis Center, Bolling AFB, Washington, D.C. Photo Credit: Department of Defense.

The National Maritime Intelligence Center (NMIC) in Suitland, Maryland. The NMIC houses the Office of Naval Intelligence (which absorbed the Naval Technical Intelligence Center, Task Force 168, and the Navy Operational Intelligence Center in 1993) along with Coast Guard and Marine Corps intelligence organizations. Photo Credit: U.S. Navy.

Headquarters, U.S. Army National Ground Intelligence Center (NGIC), Charlottesville, Virginia. NGIC was formed in 1995 with the merger of the Army Foreign Service and Technology Center and the Army Intelligence Threat Analysis Center. Photo Credit: FSTC.

7

IMAGERY COLLECTION, INTERPRETATION, AND DISSEMINATION

The use of overhead platforms to observe events on the earth can be traced to the French Revolution, when France organized a company of *aerostiers*, or balloonists, in April 1794. One balloon is said to have been kept in the air for nine hours while the group's commander made continuous observations during the Battle of Fleurus in Belgium.[1]

The United States made similar use of balloons during the Civil War, although little intelligence of value was obtained. By the latter part of the nineteenth century, Britain was conducting experiments using balloons as platforms from which to obtain "overhead photography." In January 1911, the San Diego waterfront became the first target of cameras carried aboard an airplane. That same year the U.S. Army Signal Corps put aerial photography into the curriculum at its flight training school. Between 1913 and 1915 visual and photographic reconnaissance missions were flown by the U.S. Army in the Philippines and along the Mexican border.[2]

During World War II the United States made extensive use of airplane photography using remodeled B-17 (Flying Fortress) and B-24 (Liberator) aircraft. The remodeled B-24, known as the F-7, carried six cameras internally—all triggered via remote control by an operator over the sealed rear bomb-bay doors. After the war, with the emergence of a hostile relationship with the Soviet Union, the United States began conducting photographic missions along the Soviet periphery. The aircraft cameras, however, could only capture images of territory within a few miles of the flight path.[3]

On some missions aircraft actually flew into Soviet airspace, but even those missions did not provide the necessary coverage of the vast Soviet interior. As a result, beginning in the early 1950s the United States began seriously exploring more advanced methods for obtaining images of targets throughout the Soviet Union. The result was the development, production, and employment of a variety of spacecraft and aircraft that permitted the U.S. intelligence community to closely monitor developments in the Soviet Union and other nations through overhead imagery.[4] In the years since the United States began operating such systems, their capabilities have improved in numerous ways. Satellites now have longer lifetimes, produce more detailed images, and transmit their imagery almost instantaneously.

In addition, the capabilities of spacecraft and aircraft have evolved from being limited to black-and-white visible light photography to being able to produce images using different parts of the electromagnetic spectrum, which is illustrated in Figure 7.1. As a result, imagery can often be obtained under circumstances (darkness, cloud cover) where standard visible-light photography is not feasible. In addition, employment of different portions of the electromagnetic spectrum, individually or simultaneously, expands the information that can be produced concerning a target.

Photographic equipment can be film-based or electro-optical. A conventional camera captures a scene on film by recording the varying light levels reflected from all of the separate objects in the scene. In contrast, an electro-optical camera converts the varying light levels into electrical signals. A numerical value is assigned to each of the signals, which are called picture elements, or pixels. The process transforms a picture (analog) image to a digital image that can be transmitted electronically to distant points. The signal can then be reconstructed from the digital to the analog format. The analog signal can be displayed on a video screen or made into a photograph.[5]

In addition to the visible-light portion of the electromagnetic spectrum, the near-infrared portion of the spectrum, which is invisible to the human eye, can be

FIGURE 7.1   The Electromagnetic Spectrum

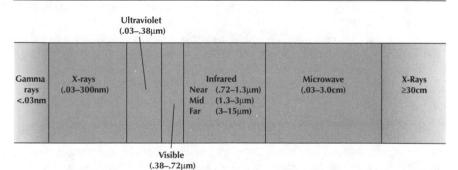

KEY: nm: nanometers (1nm = 10^{-9} meters)
   μm: micrometers (1μm = 10^{-6} meters)
   cm: centimeters (1cm = 10^{-2} meters)
SOURCE: James B. Campbell, *Introduction to Remote Sensing* (New York: Guilford), p. 24.

employed to produce images. At the same time, near-infrared, like visible-light imagery, depends on objects reflecting solar radiation rather than on their emission of radiation. As a result, such imagery can be produced only in daylight and in the absence of substantial cloud cover.[6]

Thermal infrared imagery, obtained from the mid- and far-infrared portions of the electromagnetic spectrum, provides imagery purely by detecting the heat emitted by objects. Thus, a thermal infrared system can detect buried structures, such as missile silos or underground construction, as a result of the heat they generate. Since thermal infrared imagery does not require visible light, it can be obtained under conditions of darkness—if the sky is free of cloud cover.[7]

Imagery can be obtained during day or night in the presence of cloud cover by employing an imaging radar (an acronym for *radio detection and ranging*). Radar imagery is produced by bouncing radio waves off an area or an object and using the reflected returns to produce an image of the target. Since radio waves are not attenuated by the water vapor in the atmosphere, they are able to penetrate cloud cover.[8]

Two types of imagery also important to intelligence analysts and military planners are multispectral imagery (MSI) and hyperspectral imagery (HSI). MSI is defined as "multiple discrete bands of digital electro-optical imagery collected simultaneously in different spectral regions that can be easily registered and exploited synergistically."[9]

Hyperspectral imagery employs at least sixty narrow (less than 10 nm), contiguous spectral bands, including the visible light, infrared, thermal infrared, ultraviolet, and radio wave portions of the electromagnetic spectrum. The data produced by examination of those bands will allow analysts to detect an object's shape, density, temperature, movement, and chemical composition.[10]

The six primary missions that hyperspectral imagery is expected to contribute to are: support to military operations; nonproliferation; counternarcotics; mapping, charting, and geodesy; technical intelligence; and civil applications. Specific applications are expected to include: determination of beach composition; location of amphibious obstacles; production of hydrography and bathymetry data; battle damage assessment; support of special operations; counter camouflage, concealment, and deception (CC&D); terrain analysis and mapping; trafficability analysis; vegetative cover and stress determination; and combat identification.[11]

COLLECTION

The most important means employed by the U.S. intelligence community for producing imagery are space systems. The United States has relied on a variety of spacecraft since the first successful reconnaissance satellite was launched in 1960. Some, such as the KH-8 (KEYHOLE-8), took highly detailed pictures of specific targets. In contrast, the KH-9 produced images of broader areas, allowing photo interpreters to examine a large area and select targets for closer inspection.

In December 1976, the KH-8 and KH-9 systems were joined by the KH-11, which became the sole type of intelligence imaging satellite operated by the United States between October 18, 1984 (when the last KH-9 mission concluded), and December 2, 1988.[12]*

The KH-11 represented a quantum leap in imagery capabilities because, in contrast to the KH-8 and KH-9, it could return its imagery in "near real-time." That is, rather than record images on film, with film canisters being deorbited once a reel of film was fully exposed, the KH-11 was an electro-optical system. Employing light-sensitive silicone diodes and charged couple devices (CCDs), the KH-11's optical system converted images into electronic signals that were transmitted to elliptically orbiting relay satellites and back to a ground station for near-instantaneous reconstruction.[13]

The origins of the KH-11, which was also known by the BYEMAN code names KENNAN and CRYSTAL, go back to the very origins of the U.S. satellite reconnaissance program. Intelligence and defense officials had always recognized that it would be desirable, particularly for indications and warning purposes, to have imagery data returned in near real-time. However, it was not until the late 1960s that technological developments made such a system a realistic possibility.[14]

In 1969, a study conducted by the DCI's Committee on Imagery Requirements and Exploitation (COMIREX)—*Implications of Near Real Time Imagery on Intelligence Production and Processes*—examined the potential utility of a near-real-time system. The study examined how such data could have been used during the Cuban Missile Crisis, the Six-Day War, and the Soviet invasion of Czechoslovakia. The ultimate result was a presidential decision to authorize development of the near-real-time system proposed by the Central Intelligence Agency.[15]

On December 19, 1976, the first KH-11 was launched from Vandenberg Air Force Base into an orbit of 164 by 329 miles. Another seven would be launched successfully, the last on November 6, 1988. The satellites were about 64 feet long and weighed about 30,000 pounds. Primarily as a result of employing an optical system that did not rely on a finite supply of film, KH-11 lifetimes far exceeded those of its film-return predecessors. Lifetimes of the KH-11 satellites grew from approximately two years for the early satellites to about seven years for its final versions.[16]

The satellites flew lengthwise, with the axis of the optical system parallel to the earth. The inclination of the satellites, approximately 97 degrees, meant they flew in a sun-synchronous orbit, so that the sun angle was the same each time the satellite was over a target. In the front was a downward-looking mirror that could

---

*The KH designation with respect to satellites actually referred to the *optical* system carried by the satellite, although it is often used to designated the satellite itself. NRO satellite programs have also been designated by a code name—GAMBIT in the cases of both the KH-7 and KH-8, and HEXAGON in the case of the KH-9. The use of the KH designations was terminated in 1987 because of repeated press disclosures of those designations. Hence, there is no "KH-12."

be flipped from side to side, allowing the area under observation to be changed from moment to moment. Two benefits resulted from that capability. One was that the menu of targets included not only areas under the spacecraft but areas to the sides and for hundreds of miles in front. In addition to expanding the intelligence community's ability to monitor a given target, it complicated foreign denial and deception activities. In addition, it permitted the production of stereoscopic images.

The final KH-11 was deorbited in 1996, after seven and a half years in orbit. By that time at least two satellites—advanced KH-11s—from the successor program had been placed in orbit—those launched on November 28, 1992, and December 5, 1995. A third advanced KH-11 was launched on December 20, 1996, into a 155 by 620 mile orbit, with an inclination of 97.9 degrees. These advanced KH-11s replaced their predecessors. All three advanced KH-11s were launched from Vandenberg Air Force Base, employing Titan IV boosters.[17]

The advanced KH-11 satellites have a higher orbit, particularly with respect to their apogee, than that exhibited by their predecessors—operating with perigees of about 150 miles and apogees of about 600 miles. In addition to a different orbit they have other capabilities. They contain an infrared imagery capability (originally code-named DRAGON), including a thermal infrared imagery capability, thus permitting imagery during darkness. The satellites also carry the Improved CRYSTAL Metric System (ICMS), which places the necessary markings on returned imagery to permit its full exploitation for mapping purposes.[18]

Additionally, the advanced KH-11 can carry more fuel than the original model, perhaps 10,000 to 15,000 pounds. This permits a longer lifetime for the new model—possibly up to eight years. A greater fuel supply also allows a greater ability to maneuver. Thus, an advanced KH-11 can operate at times in higher orbits to produce images covering a larger territory than is possible at lower altitudes—and then maneuver to lower orbits to produce higher-resolution imagery. The maneuvering capability could be employed in attempts to evade ASAT weapons or to defeat denial and deception activities.

The spacecraft fly in two orbital planes—a midday/midnight plane and a mid-morning/mid-evening plane. The designations are based on when each spacecraft crosses the equator in its sun-synchronous polar orbit. The second of the advanced KH-11s was placed in a midday/midnight plane, whereas the third was placed in a mid-morning/mid-evening plane, where it can provide repetitive imagery over mid-latitude targets during two periods of the day. Together, the two spacecraft are capable of imaging a target four times a day under different lighting conditions. The 1992 spacecraft supplements coverage from a slightly different orbit—having been moved out of the midday/midnight plane in the spring of 1996. The maneuver took it out of a sun-synchronous orbit, preventing standard lighting conditions over a target but expanding the number of targets that can be imaged in a single day.[19]

A second component of the U.S. space imaging fleet are satellites developed and deployed under a program first known as INDIGO, then as LACROSSE, and most recently as VEGA. Rather than employing an electro-optical system, they carry an imaging radar. The first two satellites that have been deployed are also known by the numerical designations 3101 and 3102, respectively.[20] The satellites closed a major gap in U.S. capabilities by allowing the U.S. intelligence community to obtain imagery even when targets are covered by clouds.

The first LACROSSE/VEGA was launched on December 2, 1988, from the space shuttle orbiter *Atlantis*. A second was orbited on March 8, 1991, from Vandenberg Air Force Base on a Titan IV. Satellite 3101 was deorbited in early 1997. The satellites have operated in orbits of approximately 400 miles and at inclinations of 57 and 68 degrees, respectively. A replacement for 3101 was scheduled to be launched in July 1997, but a faulty control valve that permitted a leak caused a postponement until October 24, 1997, when it was successfully placed in orbit.[21]

When conceived, the primary purpose envisioned for the satellite was monitoring Soviet and Warsaw Pact armor. Recent LACROSSE/VEGA missions included: providing imagery for bomb damage assessments of the consequences of Navy Tomahawk missile attacks on Iraqi air defense installations in September 1996; monitoring Iraqi weapons storage sites; and tracking Iraqi troop movements, such as the dispersal of the Republican Guard when the Guard was threatened with U.S. attack in early 1998. The satellites may also have been used to determine if submarines operating underwater could be located and tracked via radar imagery. LACROSSE/VEGA has a resolution of 3 to 5 feet, reportedly sufficient to allow discrimination between tanks and armored personnel carriers and identification of bomb craters of 6 to 10 feet in diameter.[22]

The LACROSSE/VEGA satellite that was launched in October 1997 may be the first of a new generation of radar imagery satellites. The new generation will apparently have greater resolution, and constellation size may be increased (presumably to three satellites).[23]

In the past several years, U.S. imagery satellites have been used to monitor a large number of activities and facilities around the world. As indicated in Table 7.1, they have imaged various targets in Russia; nuclear facilities in Iran, Algeria, and North Korea; two Libyan chemical warfare facilities during early stages of construction; Israeli-South African missile development activities; Israeli West Bank settlement construction; and drug production facilities.[24]

The targets and uses of satellite imagery can be further illustrated by some additional details:

- In 1996 a satellite image obtained while over central China showed one of five Chinese B-6D bombers that have been converted into air-refueling tankers. According to the Defense Intelligence Agency the tankers allow Chinese planes to fly well into the South China Sea.[25]

TABLE 7.1   Targets of U.S. Imagery Satellites, 1990–1998

	Target	*Year*
Algeria	Nuclear reactor	1991
Bosnia	Air-dropped aid bundles	1993
China	M-11 canisters	1995
	Fighter/refueling aircraft	1995/1996
	Nuclear test preparations	1996
	Aircraft/missile plants	1996
	IRBM Complexes	1996
Croatia	Aircraft/arms shipment	1994
Cuba	Russian Lourdes SIGINT facility	1990
	Russian freighter	1992
India	Pokharan nuclear test site	1995/1998
	Missile movement	1997
Iraq	Compliance evasion activities	1991
	Attacks on Shiite dissidents	1991
	Work on CBW facilities	1992
	Scud bunkers	1992
	Presidential palaces	1994
	Reconstruction operations	1995
Israel	West Bank settlements	1992
	Patriot missile batteries	1992
	Ramat David/Tel Nov air bases	1992
Laos	Military/narcotics convoy	1991
Lebanon	Hizballah Janta Camp	1992
Libya	Rabat chemical weapons facility	1990/1991
	Tarhuna chemical weapons facility	1996/1997
North Korea	Ballistic missiles	1990/1991
	Nuclear facility	1991
	Tunnel construction	1991
	Nuclear waste storage facility	1992
	Taepo-Dong IRBM mock-ups	1994
	Artillery deployments/DMZ	1995
	Nodong mobile launchers	1996/1997
Pakistan	M-11 canisters/Sargodha Air Base	1994
	M-11 production plant	1997
	Chagai Hills nuclear test site	1998
Russia	Military exercise	1992
	Train with SA-12 canisters	1996
	Urals underground military complex	1996
	Second Urals underground complex	1997
	Novaya Zemlya nuclear test site	1997
Rwanda	Refugee movements	1995
Ukraine	Aircraft carrier	1996
United States	Murrah Federal Building	1996

- Satellite photos of a military complex of China's Nachang Aircraft Company showed that equipment sold to China in 1994 for civilian purposes had been diverted to military use.[26]
- In late 1995, U.S. imagery satellites detected "a flurry of activity at (India's) Pokaran test site in the Rajasthan desert," causing concern that India was planning to test a nuclear device.[27]
- The Clinton administration showed satellite images to foreign leaders to demonstrate that Iraq has been rebuilding factories that could produce chemical weapons or missiles and armored vehicles.[28]
- In late May 1992, imagery satellites were used to monitor activity at Israel's Ramat David air base, in anticipation of a possible Israeli airstrike on Hizballah facilities. Satellites then monitored the aftermath of the Israeli strike of May 31 on the Hizballah Janta Camp in Lebanon.[29]
- In July 1996, satellite photographs showed that North Korea was adding more powerful, longer-range artillery along the demilitarized zone (DMZ) separating the two Koreas.[30]
- Satellite photographs showed that the layout of a plant in the suburbs of Rawalpindi, Pakistan, was similar to a M-11 rocket facility in Hubei province in central China.[31]
- U.S. imagery satellites monitored Russian construction of a huge underground military complex inside Yamanatau mountain in the Ural Mountains as well as a second underground facility at the same location.[32]
- In February 1998, it was reported that recent satellite photographs showed Iraqi forces—both Republican Guard and regular army units—throughout the country were increasing their war-fighting readiness within garrisons.[33]

Satellite imagery systems may eventually include a system nicknamed the 8X, designed to provide broad area coverage to tactical/battlefield commanders. The system is expected to produce images covering 800 to 1,000 square miles—eight times as much territory as other U.S. imagery satellites. After the Persian Gulf War of 1991, complaints were heard about the U. S. inability to simultaneously monitor significant parts of the battlefield. According to a DIA official, only the enemy's "large static defense strategy allowed us to track his numbers and disposition with acceptable accuracy." The lack of broad, synoptic, or near-simultaneous coverage made it difficult to fix the table of organization of some Iraqi units, led to an overestimate of Iraqi troop numbers, and contributed to the problems NATO countries confronted in trying to completely eliminate the mobile Scuds.[34]

The 8X program was reported to have been recommended by the National Reconnaissance Program Task Force for the Director of Central Intelligence, appointed by DCI Robert Gates in 1992 and chaired by his eventual successor, James Woolsey. The satellites have been variously reported to be an entirely new generation of satellites or a modification of the basic KH-11 design. It also has been reported that the satellites will have resolution sufficient to permit discrimination between specific types of tanks involved in a battle.[35]

Future imagery satellite constellations may also include, possibly even consist largely of, far smaller satellites than the 30,000 pound imagery spacecraft that became standard with the HEXAGON and KENNAN/CRYSTAL programs. The concept of employing significantly smaller satellites for imagery collection was strongly advocated by Rep. Larry Combest during his tenure (1995–1997) as chairman of the House Permanent Select Committee on Intelligence—a view not shared by all of the HPSCI committees, or by the Senate Select Committee on Intelligence. As a result the DCI was instructed to appoint a panel of experts to review the issue.[36]

Panel members included former NRO directors Robert Hermann (as chairman) and Martin Faga; former Air Force chief of staff, NRO official, and NSA director Lew Allen; scientist Sidney Drell; and four others. The panel's report supported a radical reduction in the size of most U.S. imagery satellites. The panel concluded that "now is an appropriate time to make a qualitative change in the systems architecture of the nation's reconnaissance assets," in part because "the technology and industrial capabilities of the country permit the creation of effective space systems that are substantially smaller and less costly than current systems." Thus, the panel saw "the opportunity to move towards an operational capability for . . . imagery systems, that consists of an array of smaller, cheaper spacecraft in larger number with a total capacity which is at least as useful as those currently planned and to transport them to space with substantially smaller and less costly launch vehicles."[37]

The panel concluded that satellites weighing 20 to 25 percent of current satellites, each with 40 to 50 percent of current planned capability, could well be feasible and desirable—and that the NRO should build a prototype to determine whether such an approach was actually feasible. Key advantages of such an approach, according to the panel, included robustness, flexibility, and the injection of new technologies and operational techniques. Thus, they argued that a constellation of smaller, cheaper, and individually less-capable satellites would reduce the risk to overall system capability if a single satellite was lost. In addition, with new satellites being produced on a more frequent basis, a new satellite would routinely be near completion whenever an operational system failed.[38]

Flexibility would be enhanced because "dividing the functions now on a single satellite on to smaller, separate satellites, the system can be re-balanced to achieve a different mix of capabilities without having to launch a system which includes all functions." As an example, the panel noted that "with a proliferated system, we could improve the revisit time for medium resolution coverage to respond to military operational needs without investing to better the revisit times for all of the other functions now on each satellite."[39]

A proliferated constellation would, according to the panel, also allow the quicker injection of new technologies as well as operational experimentation with different configurations "without the cataclysmic potential of perturbing all of the nation's capabilities. In addition, "by acquiring more, smaller, and cheaper systems, a smoother flow of delivered products is possible and a smaller work force is needed."[40]

One possible small imagery satellite for supporting military operations had been proposed by the Defense Advanced Research Projects Agency (DARPA). The satellite was originally designated STARLITE, an acronym for Surveillance, Targeting and Reconnaissance Satellite, and would be equipped with a synthetic aperture radar (SAR) and moving target indicator (MTI) capability. The proposed constellation consisted of at least twenty-four satellites (three each in eight different planes), with three spares, operating at 477 miles. The satellites would produce images of 40- by 50-square-mile swaths, with approximately 3-foot resolution. Within a single hour 17,980 miles could be imaged. It is also estimated that there would be a 90 percent probability of delivering an image of any point on earth between 65N and 65S latitudes within 15 minutes. The timeliness could be increased to 8 minutes with thirty-seven satellites, and 5 minutes with forty-eight satellites.[41]

In 1998, DARPA, NRO, and the Air Force agreed to jointly develop and, in 2003, launch an initial set of two SAR/MTI DISCOVER II satellites, as they were renamed, to test the technology involved. The constellation would be between twenty-four and forty-eight satellites, with the satellites providing 1-meter resolution and imaging 29,000 square kilometers per hour. These satellites are intended to provide the Air Force with an all-weather surveillance capability in support of precision weapons targeting, and such a constellation would sharply reduce revisit times over targets of interest. According to estimates, a twenty-four-satellite constellation would permit coverage of Iraq and North Korea more than 90 percent of the time, and nearly 100 percent of the time with forty-eight satellites.[42]

The U.S. intelligence community has also used imagery, including multispectral imagery, produced by two commercial systems—LANDSAT and SPOT. The LANDSAT program began in 1969 as an experimental National Aeronautics and Space Administration (NASA) program: the Earth Resources Technology Satellite (ERTS). The first ERTS launch took place in 1972. Currently there are two operating LANDSAT satellites—LANDSAT 4 and LANDSAT 5—launched in 1982 and 1984. LANDSAT 6 was launched in October 1993, but failed to achieve orbit. A Defense Department/NRO-NASA agreement to jointly procure and operate LANDSAT 7, equipped with multispectral sensors with 5-meter resolution, fell apart when NASA proved unable to fund its portion of the project. The Department of Defense proceeded to transfer its responsibility for the space segment back to NASA.[43]

LANDSATs 4 and 5 operate in 420-mile, sun-synchronous orbits, and each carries a Thematic Mapper (TM)—an upgraded version of the Multispectral Scanner (MSS) carried on earlier LANDSATs. In contrast to the MSS, which collected data in four broadly defined spectral regions, the TM records data from seven spectral bands. A typical LANDSAT image is 111 by 102 miles, providing significant broad-area coverage. However, the resolution of the images is approximately 98 feet—making them useful for only the coarsest intelligence tasks.[44]

SPOT, an acronym for Le Systeme Pour l'Observation de la Terre, is operated by the French national space agency. SPOT 1 was launched in 1986, followed by another three at approximately four-year intervals. SPOT satellites operate in about 500-mile orbits and carry two sensor systems. The satellites can return black-and-white (panchromatic) images with 33-foot resolution and multispectral images with 67-foot resolution. The images are of higher resolution than LANDSAT's but cover less territory—approximately 36 miles by 36 miles.[45]

Both LANDSAT and SPOT were employed for a variety of purposes during the Persian Gulf War. Ground forces found the multispectral data useful for identifying disturbances in the terrain (indicating possible passage of Iraqi forces), as well as for detecting wet areas that could slow down an advance. In addition, the "planning and execution of ground maneuvers, including the 'Left Hook,' were highly dependent on multispectral imagery." Naval forces employed it to identify shallow areas near coastlines for operational planning, to determine water depths, and to plan amphibious operations. Air Force planners used MSI data in conjunction with terrain elevation data to display attack routes and targets as they would appear. Subsequently, MSI data was used in support of operations in Haiti, Bosnia, and elsewhere.[46]

U.S. intelligence community use of commercial imagery will expand dramatically in the coming years, if the new generation of commercial imaging satellites lives up to expectations—which include images with 3-foot resolution. Such imagery and the reduced cost of attaining it when purchased commercially will permit the U.S. intelligence community to fill part of its needs via such commercial systems.

Among the commercial satellites that are expected to produce high-resolution imagery are the Ikonos satellites to be launched by Space Imaging Eosat (which also operates the LANDSAT satellites). The first of the satellites, scheduled to be launched in early 1999 from Vandenberg Air Force Base, is designed to generate 1-meter panchromatic and 4-meter multispectral images. A similar satellite is scheduled for launch in September 1999.[47]

Also promising to provide 1-meter panchromatic imagery and 4-meter multispectral imagery are the satellites to be developed by Earthwatch and Orbital Sciences. Earthwatch's Early Bird satellite, which was to return 3-meter resolution images, failed after only four days in orbit. A 1-meter resolution Quickbird satellite is scheduled for launch in late 1998 or 1999. Orbital Science's OrbView-4 satellite is to be launched in 2000. It is expected to have a three- to five-year lifetime and produce images covering 5-mile by 5-mile segments with 1-meter resolution. The satellite is also expected to produce hyperspectral images—as a result of an agreement with the Air Force that calls for Orbital Sciences to modify the satellite to serve as the first of a planned series of Space Technology Demonstration experiments, designated Warfighter-1, that will rely on commercial space activities to reduce costs. According to the agreement the Air Force will be provided with up to 800 hyperspectral images. However, in the last quarter of 1998 objections by the Defense Department and the intelligence community concerning the value of hyperspectral imagery to adversaries threatened to prevent Orbital Imaging from obtaining permission to include a hyperspectral capability on Orbview-4.[48]

Yet another partially commercial entrant is the Navy Earth Map Observer (NEMO) satellite, a joint venture of the Space Technology Development Corporation and the Naval Research Laboratory, to be launched in early 2000. It is expected to return 5-meter hyperspectral images, particularly of coastal areas. Its coastal focus reflects the Navy's shift in emphasis from deep-water to shallow-water operations in support of ground troops.[49]

The United States also employs a variety of aerial reconnaissance systems—manned and unmanned—to obtain overhead imagery. Aerial systems can supplement the coverage of satellites, provide a quick reaction capability, and produce imagery that can be more widely distributed than satellite imagery (under present security policy). In addition, while the satellite coverage of a particular area can be limited to the territory rotating under the satellite's orbit, aircraft can fly a route that focuses on a particular region.

The most important aerial system employed to collect imagery is the U-2.* The CIA and Lockheed began development of the U-2 in 1954, with the support of the Eisenhower administration's Technological Capabilities Panel. The aircraft became operational in 1956 and began overflying the Soviet Union in July of that year. The U-2 proceeded to return significant imagery of airfields, missile testing and training facilities, nuclear weapons storage sites, submarine production, and atomic facilities. The center of U-2 operations was Adana, Turkey, where U-2 operations were conducted by the 10-10 Detachment under the cover of the Second Weather Reconnaissance Squadron (Provisional). Overflights of the Soviet Union ended after the U-2 piloted by Francis Gary Powers was shot down on May 1, 1960, over the Soviet Union, and Powers survived to be put on trial.[50]

Even before that date the U-2 was employed against a variety of other targets. Thus, a U-2 mission was flown over Israel, Egypt, Jordan, Lebanon, and Syria in August 1956, and later in the decade a U-2 detected the site in the Negev desert where Israel's nuclear weapons production facility was under construction. In subsequent years, U-2s flew missions over, or along the borders of, Nicaragua, Cuba, the People's Republic of China, North Vietnam, North Korea, and Iraq. In the 1980s, U-2s regularly took pictures of military construction and arms depots in Nicaragua in order to document the buildup of forces there. During Operations Desert Shield and Desert Storm, U-2s flew more than 800 missions over

---

*The highly classified U-2 project was code-named AQUATONE, then CHALICE, and finally IDEALIST, when it was operated by the CIA. The Air Force designation for the U-2 is SENIOR YEAR.

the Persian Gulf region, enabling U.S. personnel to track Iraqi troop and armor buildups, assess bomb damage, survey Iraq for nuclear, chemical, and biological weapons sites, and monitor a massive Persian Gulf oil spill. On two occasions, U-2s provided warning of incoming Scud missiles.[51]

Today, there are thirty-five U-2s (including those that were originally produced under the TR-1 designation that was abandoned in October 1991), which come in two versions—the U-2R and U-2S. They have a wingspan of 103 feet, are 16 feet high, and 63 feet long. Standard speed is 410 knots, at altitudes of between 65,000 and 73,000 feet. They can remain in the air for nine to fourteen hours but are not refuelable. U-2s can perform a variety of imagery and SIGINT missions.[52]

The planes can carry a variety of imagery sensors, although not all at once. The nose can carry the SENIOR YEAR Electro-Optical Reconnaissance System (SYERS), which operates in both the visible-light and infrared bands, or the Advanced Synthetic Aperture Radar System II (ASARS-II). The SYERS can transmit its images in near real-time, if it is within 220 miles of its ground station. If it is outside that range, it can store the imagery and transmit it when it comes back within line of sight of the station. The station, designated SENIOR BLADE, controls the SYERS, as well as processing, exploiting, and reporting the imagery received. ASARS-II is an all-weather, day-night, standoff imaging system designed to detect, locate, classify, and, in some cases, identify enemy ground targets. The ASARS was developed to collect and process radar imagery in near real-time at 10-foot resolution. U-2S aircraft carry an upgraded ASARS-II with an improved moving target indicator (MTI) capability. U-2 aircraft equipped with the SENIOR SPUR system can transmit ASARS-II imagery via the Tracking and Data Relay Satellite (TDRS) system.[53]

The Q-Bay can carry either the H Camera System, the Optical Bar Camera (OBC), or the Intelligence Reconnaissance Imagery System III (IRIS III) camera. The H system is a framing camera with 66-inch focal length that can produce photographs with 6-inch resolution at its nadir, and with 12 to 18 inch resolution if the targets are 35 to 40 nautical miles from the aircraft flight path. The camera has also been fitted with an electro-optical capability. The Optical Bar Camera is a 30-inch focal length panoramic camera capable of providing full vertical or stereographic coverage with high resolution. IRIS III is an optical imagery system that uses a high-resolution panoramic camera with a 24-inch focal length and that can cover a 32-nautical-mile swath on both sides of the aircraft. Both the OBC and IRIS III are film-based systems, although they provide a broader view than the SYERS.[54]

All U-2 operations are directed by the 9th Reconnaissance Wing at Beale Air Force Base, which is subordinate to the Air Combat Command, as well as by theater commanders. Located at Beale are the 99th Reconnaissance Squadron for operational deployments and the 1st Reconnaissance Squadron for six-month qualification training. There are four overseas units: Operating Location-France (OL-FR) at Istres Le Tube air base, the 4402nd Reconnaissance Squadron (Provisional) at Prince Suttan air base in Saudi Arabia (relocated from Taif air base in October 1998); Detachment 1 at RAF Akrotiri on Cyprus; and the 5th Reconnaissance Squadron (RS) at Osan, Korea.[55]

Targets of the three U-2s flying from OL-FR (where they were relocated from RAF Fairfod in England in January 1996) include Bosnia, whereas those launching from Taif monitor Iraq for the UN and coalition forces. From May 1991 to early April 1996, U-2s flew 290 missions to monitor Iraqi compliance with postwar restrictions. Missions flown from RAF Akrotiri include those that monitored the 1973 Arab-Israeli peace accord. The 5th RS at Osan was the first U-2 unit to receive the MTI-equipped U-2S, to ease the task of monitoring the movement of missiles and heavy mortars that are moved in and out of North Korean mountain caves.[56]

Upgrades of the thirty-five remaining U-2s are planned to keep the aircraft in operation until 2020. A follow-on aircraft, presently designated the U-X, is expected to go into development around 2010, with the first aircraft to be delivered in 2018. It is conceived of as being operated in both manned and unmanned modes, providing multispectral, measurement and signature, imagery, and signals intelligence from anywhere in the world. It is likely to be a low-observable, high-speed aircraft, in order to make its arrival over a target unpredictable.[57]

With the collapse of the Soviet Union, the mission of the Navy's P-3C ORION aircraft, originally employed and equipped to detect and monitor Soviet submarines, has been employed on over-land imagery missions. The P-3C is the third generation P-3. The first model, the P-3A, was produced by shortening the airframe of an Electra airliner by 12 feet, equipping it with weapons, and giving it an increased fuel capacity.[58]

There are presently about 200 P-3Cs in the Navy's inventory. Squadron designations (VP-), locations, and inventories are listed in Table 7.2. The P-3C, according to one account, has "become a crucial photographic reconnaissance tool for operations to monitor peacekeeping in Bosnia and to track the new crisis in Albania." In a fourteen-month period in 1996 and 1997, P-3Cs were employed in 324 missions and examined 2,425 targets.[59]

Most P-3Cs carry standard cameras under the base of the plane as well as an infrared camera (the Infrared Detection System). But four P-3Cs are equipped with long-range, visible-light video cameras. Two of those cameras, designated CLUSTER RANGER and CAST GLANCE, are carried separately by a P-3C of Patrol Squadron 8 (VP-8), which flies out of NAS Sigonella in Italy. As of March 1997, the squadron was flying two daily missions over Albania and one over Bosnia. CLUSTER RANGER is capable of both black-and-white and color photography, while CAST GLANCE is restricted to black-and-white operations. In CLUSTER RANGER, a 40-inch focal length camera is used for wide-area surveillance. An 80-inch focal length lens has a narrow field of view and can be used to identify individuals with weapons, while remaining outside the range of antiaircraft artillery and shoulder-fired missiles. Both video and still pictures can be transmitted to

TABLE 7.2   Designations, Locations, and Inventories of P-3 Patrol Squadrons

Unit Designation	Location	Number of Aircraft
VP-1	NAF[a] Misawa, Japan	9
VP-4	NAS[b] Barbers Point, Hawaii	8
VP-5	NAS Jacksonville, Fla.	10
VP-8	NAS Brunswick, Maine	7
VP-8	NAS Jacksonville, Fla.	2
VP-9	NAS Barbers Point, Hawaii	6
VP-10	NAS Brunswick, Maine	5
VP-10	NAS Jacksonville, Fla.	2
VP-16	Keflavik, Iceland	4
VP-16	NS[c] Roosevelt Roads, P.R.	5
VP-26	NAS Sigonella, Italy	9
VP-30	NAS Jacksonville, Fla.	18
VP-40	NAS Whidbey Island, Wash.	6
VP-40	NAS Jacksonville, Fla.	1
VP-45	NAS Jacksonville, Fla.	7
VP-46	NAS Jacksonville, Fla.	1
VP-46	NAS Whidey Island, Wash.	7
VP-47	NAF Diego Garcia, BIOT	9
VP-47	NAF Kadena, Japan	1
VP-62	NAS Jacksonville, Fla.	8
VP-64	NAS Willow Grove, Pa.	8
VP-65	NAS Point Mugu, Calif.	9
VP-66	NAS Willow Grove, Pa.	9
VP-69	NAS Whidbey Island, Wash.	10
VP-91	NAR[d] Santa Clara, Calif.	7
VP-92	NAS Brunswick, Maine	9
VP-94	New Orleans, La.	9
		186

[a] Naval Air Facility
[b] Naval Air Station
[c] Naval Station
[d] Naval Air Reserve

SOURCE: Naval Aircraft Listing by Command, May 12, 1998.

ground commanders. On one flight, commanders at several locations in Bosnia and at the Combined Air Operations Center (CAOC) in Vicenza, Italy, received imagery.[60]

Upgrades to the P-3Cs are scheduled to begin in 1998. Improvements to the P-3C imaging capabilities will include a new generation of AVX-1 roll-on/roll-off, long-range, electro-optical video cameras, as well as an Inverse Synthetic Aperture Radar with a range of over 100 miles and capable of detecting an object as small as a submarine snorkel.[61]

In addition, to the U-2, SR-71, and P-3C, the United States operates a number of other manned aircraft that produce imagery. Modified C-130 aircraft, designated PACER COIN and operated by the Air Force and National Guard, provide "worldwide low-profile/clandestine imagery support for theater commanders, counternarcotics, and special operations." The four-engine turboprop aircraft can fly as low as 3,000 feet and as high as 26,000 feet at between 150 and 250 knots. They can fly for ten hours and provide high resolution day and night film imagery.[62]

Also producing imagery for counternarcotics missions are the Army's six EO-5 Airborne Reconnaissance Low aircraft. The four-engine turboprop flies at altitudes between 6,000 and 20,000 feet at 220 knots. It can fly for ten hours and is not refuelable during flight.[63]

Among the aircraft conducting reconnaissance missions for the Navy are specially modified F-14 fighters. F-14s are carrier-based jet aircraft that travel at between 400 and 500 knots, can fly at an altitude of between 500 and 50,000 feet, have a 500 nautical mile range, and can operate for two hours. The reconnaissance version of the F-14 is equipped with the Tactical Air Reconnaissance Pod System (TARPS), which provides film coverage in both standoff and penetration modes. At one time the TARPS consisted solely of film-based sensors—a serial frame camera, a panoramic camera, and a infrared imagery sensor—with no data link for real-time transmission.[64]

F-14s equipped with TARPS flew 279 missions during Operation Desert Storm. During a period of extremely low tides (January 28 through February 2, 1991) they were used to detect mines, and over land they photographed targets such as Iraqi Scud missile launch sites, storage bunkers, and the Al Qaim superphosphate fertilizer plant.[65] However, according to Admiral Thomas Brooks, Director of Naval Intelligence during Operation Desert Storm, the film-based TARPS "was totally inadequate" in providing satisfactory and timely bomb damage assessment.[66]

The Navy subsequently began deploying the TARPS-DI system, with one digital sensor, to permit transmission of the imagery to carriers. As of late April 1997, the Navy was in the process of buying twenty-four TARPS-DI sensor suites to upgrade the forty-seven existing TARPS pods. By August 1998, the Navy was planning the operational deployment of a more advanced imagery system, TARPS-CD (Completely Digital), which would digitize, on selected aircraft, all the cameras still employing film. Plans call for only a limited number of TARPS-CD sensors. By February 2000 the Navy expects to be operating four TARPS-CD systems, twenty-four TARPS-DI systems, and nineteen regular TARPS systems. At that time, the Navy was also considering proposing a further upgrade, TARPS-CD, which would digitize all the cameras still employing film.[67]

Three TARPS-equipped F-14s are assigned to one of two F-14 squadrons on each carrier air wing. Targets include land-based installations such as coastal defenses, lines of communications, and foreign ships.[68]

During the Persian Gulf War the United States relied on Unmanned Aerial Vehicles (UAVs)/Remote Piloted Vehicles (RPVs) in addition to manned reconnaissance aircraft. Six units employing Pioneer UAVs were deployed to the Middle

East—three with Marine Corps ground units, one attached to the Army's 7th Corps, and one each on board the battleships *Wisconsin* and *Missouri*. Each unit consisted of about five RPVs that could be controlled from fixed ground stations to a distance of 100 nautical miles and from portable stations to a distance of 40 nautical miles. Equipped with either television or forward-looking infrared sensors, the Pioneers operated day and night, making a total of 307 flights in Operation Desert Storm.[69]

The Navy employed the Pioneers for several purposes—hunting for mines; conducting reconnaissance in support of SEAL missions; and searching for Iraqi Silkworm missile sites, command and control bunkers, and antiaircraft artillery sites. Meanwhile, the Marines employed the RPVs in conjunction with attack aircraft for real-time targeting. A Pioneer spotted one of the first Iraqi probes into Saudi Arabia, west of Ras al-Kafki, on January 29, 1991.[70]

A second RPV system employed in the Gulf War was the Pointer. Five Pointer units, each with four air vehicles and two ground stations, operated in the Gulf area with Marine units and the Army's 82nd Airborne Division. Normally operating at an altitude of 500 feet, although it can reach 1,000 feet, the Pointer can fly for about an hour.[71]

Subsequently, UAVs came to represent a significant element in projected U.S. intelligence capabilities—extending beyond their use for purely tactical purposes. In February 1994, the CIA deployed a UAV unit to an Albanian base on the northern Adriatic coast to operate two specially modified General Atomics (GNAT) 750 UAVs. A primary mission of the unmanned reconnaissance craft was the monitoring of Serbian artillery emplacements in Bosnia.[72]

Today, there are three key UAV programs in operation or development. The GNAT 750-45, designated PREDATOR, is an advanced version of the UAVs flown over Bosnia by the CIA in 1994. Three of the vehicles were deployed to Gjader, Albania, from July to November 1995. Another three were deployed to Taszar, Hungary, in 1996, where they are operated by the Air Combat Command's 11th Reconnaissance Squadron.* An upgraded PREDATOR, of which seventeen will be built, has a 500 nautical mile range, a 450 pound payload, and carries electro-optical, infrared, or synthetic aperture imagery systems. It will be able to operate at 25,000 feet for over twenty hours.[73]

During the late summer and early fall of 1996, the PREDATORs based at Taszar monitored mass grave sites near Sarajevo. In September 1996 the UAVs also monitored election activities in Bosnia, and in October they monitored the deployment of peacekeeping forces. Imagery could be transmitted to ground commanders as well as to the United States, employing Joint Broadcast Satellites. In October 1998 PREDATORs were designated for surveillance duty over Kosovo.[74]

---

*The Air Force activated the 15th Reconnaissance Squadron in 1997. Both squadrons are headquartered at Indian Springs Auxiliary Field, near Nellis AFB, Nevada. By 2004, they will split ownership of forty-five Predators. ("USAF Activates Its Second UAV Squadron," *Jane's Defence Weekly*, August 13, 1997, p. 11).

Plans call for building ten GLOBAL HAWK (RQ-4A) UAVs. The vehicles will have a 3,000 nautical mile radius and carry a 1,860 pound payload and electro-optical, infrared, and SAR imaging systems. They will be able to stay on station for 20 hours (if flown to maximum radius) at an altitude of 65,000 feet. Data can be transmitted to ground stations below or to relay satellites for relay to the United States or other locations. First deliveries of operational vehicles could take place in 2001.[75]

Four copies of a stealthy UAV, DARK STAR (RQ-3A), will also be built, according to current plans, which may well change in 1999. The vehicles are intended to "provide critical imagery intelligence from highly defended areas." The DARK STARs will have an over 500 nautical mile radius, a payload of 1,287 pounds, and will carry either electro-optical or SAR sensors. They will be able to operate for over eight hours, at over 45,000 feet. Data can be transmitted to ground stations below or to relay satellites for relay to the United States or other locations.[76]

PROCESSING AND INTERPRETATION

As noted above, imagery can be obtained by relying on single portions of the electromagnetic spectrum (visible light, infrared, radio) or by combining a number of bands into a single image (multispectral, hyperspectral, or ultraspectral imagery). However the imagery is obtained, it requires processing and interpretation to convert it into intelligence data.

Computers can be employed to improve the quantity and quality of the information extracted. Obviously, digital electro-optical imagery arrives in a form that facilitates such operations. But even analog imagery obtained by a conventional camera can be converted into digital signals. In any case, a computer disassembles a picture into millions of electronic Morse code pulses and then uses mathematical formulas to manipulate the color contrast and intensity of each spot. Each image can be reassembled in various ways to highlight special features and objects that were hidden in the original image.[77] Such processing allows:

- building multicolored single images out of several pictures taken in different bands of the spectrum, making the patterns more obvious
- restoring the shapes of objects by adjusting for the angle of view and lens distortion
- changing the amount of contrast between objects and backgrounds
- sharpening out-of-focus images
- restoring ground details largely obscured by clouds
- conducting electronic optical subtraction, in which earlier pictures are subtracted from later ones, making unchanged buildings in a scene disappear while new objects, such as missile silos under construction, remain
- enhancing shadows
- suppressing glint[78]

Such processing plays a crucial role in easing the burden on photogrammetrists and imagery interpreters. Photogrammetrists are responsible for determining the size and dimensions of objects from overhead photographs, using, along with other data, the shadows cast by the objects. Photo interpreters are trained to provide information about the nature of the objects in the photographs—based on information as to what type of crates carry MiG-29s, for instance, or what an IRBM site or fiber optics factory looks like from 150 miles in space. Such information is provided in interpretation keys such as those listed in Table 7.3. Thus, an interpreter might see a picture with excavations, mine headframes, derricks, piles of waste, conveyor belts, bulldozers, and power shovels, but with just a few buildings. His key would suggest that this is a mine. Special kinds of equipment, the tone or color of the waste piles and the ore piles as well as knowledge of local geology might further indicate that this was a uranium mine.[79]

The ultimate utility of any imaging system is a function of several factors—the most prominent being spatial resolution. A simple measure of spatial resolution is the minimum size an object must be in order to be measurable and detectable by photo analysts. The "higher" the resolution, the greater the detail that can be extracted from an image. It should also be noted that resolution is a product of several factors—including the optical or imaging system, atmospheric conditions, and orbital parameters.[80]

The degree of resolution required depends on the specificity of the intelligence desired. Five different interpretation tasks have been differentiated. *Detection* involves locating a class of units or objects or an activity of interest. *General identification* involves determining a general target type, and *precise identification* involves discrimination within target type of known types. *Description* involves

TABLE 7.3   Joint Imagery Interpretation Keys

World Tanks and Self-Propelled Artillery	Major Surface Combatants
World Towed Artillery	Minor Surface Combatants
General Transportation Equipment	Mine Warfare Types
World Tactical Vehicles	Amphibious Warfare Types
Combat Engineer Equipment	Naval Auxiliaries
World Mobile Gap and River Crossing Equipment	Intelligence Research Vehicles
Coke, Iron, and Steel Industries	Shipborne Electronics
Chemical Industries	Shipborne Weapons
World Electronics	Airfield Installation
World Missiles and Rockets	Petroleum Industries
Military Aircraft of the World	Atomic Energy Facilities
Submarines	

SOURCE: Defense Intelligence Agency Regulation 0-2. "Index of DIA Administrative Publications," December 10, 1982, pp. 35–36.

specifying the size-dimension, configuration-layout, components-construction, and number of units. *Technical intelligence* involves determining the specific characteristics and performance capabilities of weapons and equipment.[81] Table 7.4 gives estimates of the resolution required for interpretation tasks.

Factors other than resolution that are considered significant in evaluating the utility of an imaging system include coverage speed, readout speed, analysis

TABLE 7.4   Resolution Required for Different Levels of Interpretation

Target	Detection	General Identification	Precise Identification	Description	Technical Intelligence
Bridge	20 ft.	15 ft.	5 ft.	3 ft.	1 ft.
Communications radar/radio	10 ft./10 ft.	3 ft./5 ft.	1 ft./1 ft.	6 in./6 in.	1.5 in./6 in.
Supply dump	5 ft.	2 ft.	1 ft.	1 in.	1 in.
Troop units (bivouac, road)	20 ft.	7 ft.	4 ft.	1 ft.	3 in.
Airfield facilities	20 ft.	15 ft.	10 ft.	1 ft.	6 in.
Rockets and artillery	3 ft.	2 ft.	6 in.	2 in.	.4 in.
Aircraft	15 ft.	5 ft.	3 ft.	6 in.	1 in.
Command and control hq.	10 ft.	5 ft.	3 ft.	6 in.	1 in.
Missile sites (SSM/SAM)	10 ft.	5 ft.	2 ft.	1 ft.	3 in.
Surface ships	25 ft.	15 ft.	2 ft.	1 ft.	3 in.
Nuclear weapons components	8 ft.	5 ft.	1 ft.	1 in.	.4 in.
Vehicles	5 ft.	2 ft.	1 ft.	2 in.	1 in.
Land minefields	30 ft.	20 ft.	3 ft.	1 in.	—
Ports and harbors	100 ft.	50 ft.	20 ft.	10 ft.	1 ft.
Coasts and landing beaches	100 ft.	15 ft.	10 ft.	5 ft.	3 in.
Railroad yards and shops	100 ft.	50 ft.	20 ft.	5 ft.	2 ft.
Roads	30 ft.	20 ft.	6 ft.	2 ft.	6 in.
Urban area	200 ft.	100 ft.	10 ft.	10 ft.	1 ft.
Terrain	—	300 ft.	15 ft.	5 ft.	6 in.
Surfaced submarines	100 ft.	20 ft.	5 ft.	3 ft.	1 in.

SOURCES: Adapted from U.S. Congress, Senate Committee on Commerce, Science, and Transportation, *NASA Authorization for Fiscal Year 1978, Part 3* (Washington, D.C.: U.S. Government Printing Office, 1977), pp. 1642–1643; and Bhupendra Jasani, ed., *Outer Space— A New Dimension in the Arms Race* (Cambridge, Mass.: Oelgeschlager, Gunn & Hain, 1982), p. 47.

speed, reliability, and enhancement capability. Coverage speed is the area that can be surveyed in a given amount of time; readout speed is the speed with which the information is processed into a form that is meaningful to imagery interpreters; and reliability is the fraction of time in which the system produces useful data. Enhancement capability refers to whether the initial images can be enhanced to draw out more useful data.

Digital satellite imagery can also be employed in some esoteric ways. Such data, when combined with elevation data, can be used to produce a three-dimensional image of the landscape of an area of interest—whether it be Serbia or south Beirut. The capability, first developed at the Jet Propulsion Laboratory, can be used to familiarize individuals—from national leaders to military personnel to clandestine intelligence personnel—with a particular geographical area.

In the spring of 1994, the CIA acquired an additional capability. Once a three-dimensional view of an area has been created, an individual can use a joystick to wander around the area as well as inside the three-dimensional buildings. Such an orientation experience is particularly useful to inspectors and intelligence officers—who benefit from the experience of moving around a building or area before entering it.

DISSEMINATION

At one time, when imagery was obtained solely by film-based cameras, there was a simple dissemination sequence. Imagery was returned in satellite capsules or on aircraft when they returned from a mission. The film was then transported to the relevant national (e.g., CIA NPIC), departmental (DIA), service (FTD), or command (PACOM) imagery interpreters. The imagery interpretation reports produced, as well as the reports incorporating the imagery-derived intelligence, were then disseminated to the appropriate groups and individuals. For much of the history of the satellite reconnaissance program, this was a very restrictive set of individuals—in part because film-return systems were not terribly useful in the heat of battle, with the long delays between the imaging of a target and the intelligence reaching military commanders.

However, the advent of real-time digital imagery dramatically increased the potential value of the imagery obtained from national systems for military commanders and combatants. Further, digital imagery could be transmitted with greater ease. As a result, the dissemination today involves a variety of possibilities.

The dissemination sequence for digital imagery begins, of course, with the downlinking of the imagery data from a spacecraft or aircraft to a ground station. In some cases, the downlink may be direct; in others, the process may require a relay because the ground station is not in line of sight of the satellite.

For the KH-11 and advanced KH-11 the primary ground station is the Mission Ground Site at Fort Belvoir, Virginia, about 20 miles south of Washington. It is a large, windowless, two-story concrete building officially known as the Defense Communications Electronics Evaluation and Testing Activity (DCEETA), and also known as Area 58. While initially the Fort Belvoir site was the only downlink for the KH-11, additional sites were added—apparently in Hawaii and Europe.[82]

The signals arriving at the Mission Ground Site have been relayed from one or more types of communications satellite. The elliptically orbiting Satellite Data System satellites were employed as relays at the beginning of the program, and their successors have continued that mission. In addition, the geosynchronous, Defense Satellite Communications System (DSCS) satellites may also be used to relay advanced KH-11 data.[83]

In contrast, the signals from the LACROSSE/VEGA system are relayed via NASA's Tracking and Data Relay Satellites (TDRSs), of which there are three in orbit. The signals are then transmitted to a ground station at White Sands, New Mexico.[84]

In the future, a joint military–civilian National Space Communications System may handle relay of intelligence, military, and civilian communications.[85]

U-2 flights over Bosnia usually downlink their information—electro-optical and radar imagery, as well as SIGINT—to the "Mobile Stretch" (MOBSTR) ground station in the theater, which can view the imagery (and analyze the electro-optical imagery, using a system designated SENIOR BLADE) and route it locally. It also relays it to the Deployable Ground Station-2 (DGS-2) at Beale Air Force Base, California. DGS-1 is headquartered at Langley Air Force Base, Virginia, and is partly deployed to Saudi Arabia. The data-link sensors, the U-2, and the DGS collectively constitute the Contingency Airborne Reconnaissance Systems (CARS). The Air Combat Command's 13th Intelligence Squadron manages CARS and its imagery products.[86]

Present plans call for the creation of a Common Imagery Ground/Surface System (CIGSS) that will serve as a ground station/downlink for all aerial imagery platforms.87

Primary Transmission Systems link Washington (or other locations in the United States) to military command headquarters or facilities in the United States and overseas. The first node in these systems has been either the Defense Satellite Communications System (DSCS) or the now-defunct Fleet Satellite Communications System (FLTSATCOM). One primary transmission system is the Digital Imagery Transmission System (DITS), which links Washington with the U.S. Central Command headquarters at MacDill Air Force Base, Florida.[88]

The successors to the FLTSATCOM system, the Navy's UHF Follow-On (UFO) spacecraft, are being employed as part of a Global Broadcast Service (GBS). GBS will provide a near global capability to forward NRO imagery to a wider spectrum of users than in the past. NRO helped set up a "GBS Phase 1" demonstration, which involved the transmission of imagery and other data to U.S. forces in Bosnia. The first GBS Phase 2 satellite (UFO F8) was launched in March 1998. The second and third are scheduled for launch in early 1999. Imagery will be uplinked to the satellites from ground stations in Hawaii, Virginia, and Europe.[89]

Secondary Transmission Systems allow military commands that have received imagery from primary distribution systems or other means to relay such data to subordinate units. One secondary imagery transmission system is the Central Command Imagery Transmission System (CITS). Among its components is the Portable Receive and Transmit System (PORTS). The U.S. Central Command's PORTS reached initial operational capability in 1987.[90]

A Secondary Transmission System also exists within the European Command. The EUCOM Secondary Imagery Transmission System (EUCOMSITS) network consists of five SITS nets composed of Air Force ICON (Image Communications and Operations Node), Fleet Imagery Support Terminals (FISTs), PORTS Imagery Processing Systems, ancillary devices, and interconnecting communications circuits.[91]

During Operation Desert Shield, at least twelve different secondary imagery dissemination systems were brought into the theater, including the DIA-purchased Digital Video Imagery Transmission System (DVITS) and the Air Force's Tactical Digital Facsimile (TDF). Of the twelve systems deployed, only four were interoperable.[92]

In addition to receiving data via primary and secondary dissemination systems, U.S. forces deployed overseas may also receive data directly from certain collection systems. Among the most prominent systems reported to be involved in the direct readout of data is the CONSTANT SOURCE UHF receipt and exploitation system. The terminals can be used to process the data in ways appropriate for specific missions—airlift, counter-air, interdiction, close-air support, and electronic countermeasures/suppression of enemy air defenses.[93]

The Fleet Imagery Support Terminals (FISTs) on U.S. aircraft carriers, which transmit imagery from shore locations to ships, from ship to shore, from ship to ship, or from shore to shore, may also receive data directly from space systems. Key Army units also have an imagery reception capability, including seven Tactical High-Mobility Terminals that permit the transmission of static photographs down to the location of the terminals.[94]

Eventually, it may be possible to send real-time satellite imagery as well as signals intelligence directly into the cockpits of tactical aircraft. Experiments intended to lead to such an option were under way in early 1993. In addition, real-time information from satellites may be used in the future to cue missiles fired from aircraft at enemy radar systems. Under a program designated TALON SWORD, tests conducted in April 1993 used intelligence data to directly cue missiles fired at simulated enemy radars by F-16 and EA-6B aircraft. Another phase of TALON SWORD involves transmitting satellite intelligence into F-15E cockpits for targeting enemy positions with smart bombs.[95]

Another program, TALON LANCE, would equip aircraft with a computer package that would allow high-speed processing of space intelligence data. TALON LANCE-equipped aircraft would be able to locate and identify an enemy on the ground or in the air. The aircraft crew could then decide whether to attack or avoid contact long before the aircraft's normal on-board sensors could detect the enemy.[96]

TALON SHOOTER encompasses a number of programs, including Project STRIKE, to provide threat, target, and weather information to the cockpit, "to make space a reality for operational aircraft." In July 1995, it was tested on B-1B and F-15E aircraft.[97]

Notes

1. William E. Burrows, *Deep Black: Space Espionage and National Security* (New York: Random House, 1986), p. 28.

2. Ibid., p. 32.

3. See Jeffrey T. Richelson, *American Espionage and the Soviet Target* (New York: William Morrow, 1987), p. 16.

4. Donald E. Welzenbach, "From the U-2 to Corona and Those Who Searched for Invisibility," in *CORONA: Between the Sun & the Earth—The First NRO Reconnaissance Eye in Space*, ed. Robert A. McDonald (Baltimore, Md.: The American Society for Photogrammetry and Remote Sensing, 1997), pp. 135–140.

5. Farouk el-Baz, "EO Imaging Will Replace Film in Reconnaissance," *Defense Systems Review* (October 1983): 48–52.

6. Richard D. Hudson Jr. and Jacqueline W. Hudson, "The Military Applications of Remote Sensing by Infrared," *Proceedings of the IEEE* 63, no. 1 (1975): 104–128; James B. Campbell, *Introduction to Remote Sensing* (New York: Guilford, 1987), p. 26.

7. Hudson and Hudson, "The Military Applications of Remote Sensing by Infrared"; Bruce G. Blair and Garry D. Brewer, "Verifying SALT," in *Verification and SALT: The Challenge of Strategic Deception*, ed. William Potter (Boulder, Colo.: Westview, 1980), pp. 7–48; Campbell, *Introduction to Remote Sensing*, p. 26.

8. Homer Jensen, L. C. Graham, Leonard J. Porcello, and Emmet N. Leith, "Side-Looking Airborne Radar," *Scientific American*, October 1977, pp. 84–95.

9. Defense Intelligence Agency, *Multispectral Applications—A Significant New Resource for Warfighting Planning and Execution, The Final Report on the Joint DIA–OSAF/DSPO Merit Program for Evaluating Landsat, SPOT and Aircraft Multispectral Imagery* (Washington, D.C.: DIA, 1988), p. 1-1.

10. Curtiss O. Davis, *Hyperspectral Imaging: Utility for Military, Science, and Commercial Applications* (Washington, D.C.: Naval Research Laboratory, October 15, 1996).

11. Ibid.

12. The KH-10, which was the camera system for the Manned Orbiting Laboratory (MOL), never became operational, since the MOL program was canceled before the first flight. For a history of the KEYHOLE program, see Jeffrey T. Richelson, *America's Secret Eyes in Space: The U.S. KEYHOLE Spy Satellite Program* (New York: Harper & Row, 1990).

13. Richelson, *America's Secret Eyes in Space*, pp. 128–131.

14. Ibid.

15. Ibid., p. 126; Private information.

16. Richelson, *America's Secret Eyes in Space*, p. 362.

17. "Secret Payload Launched on Titan IV," *Washington Times*, November 30, 1992, p. A2; "Sixth Titan 4 Launched," *Aviation Week & Space Technology*, December 7, 1992; Vincent Kiernan, "Titan 4 Launches Spy Satellite from Vandenberg AFB," *Space News*, December 7–13, 1992, p. 26. Richelson, *America's Secret Eyes in Space*, p. 231; "First 'Announced' NRO Payload," *Spaceflight* 39, no. 3 (March 1997): 77; William Harwood, "Titan Boosts

Military Payload," *Space News*, December 11–17, 1996, p. 26; "Titan Launch at Vanden-berg," *Aviation Week & Space Technology*, December 11, 1995, p. 20; Craig Covault, "Advanced KH-11 Broadens U.S. Recon Capability," *Aviation Week & Space Technology*, January 6, 1997, p. 24. At least two previous launches were initially believed to be advanced KH-11 spacecraft. The first, launched on August 1989, appears, reasonably conclusively, to be a follow-on to the Satellite Data System relay system. The second, launched on February 28/March 1, 1990, has behaved in ways that lead space observers to question its mission as an imaging satellite.

18. Richelson, *America's Secret Eyes in Space*, p. 231; Private information.

19. Covault, "Advanced KH-11 Broadens U.S. Recon Capability."

20. Bob Woodward, *Veil: The Secret Wars of the CIA, 1981–1987* (New York: Simon & Schuster, 1987), p. 221; Private information.

21. "Space Reconnaissance Dwindles," *Aviation Week & Space Technology*, October 6, 1980, pp. 18–20; "Navy Will Develop All-Weather Ocean Monitor Satellite," *Aviation Week & Space Technology*, August 28, 1978, p. 50; Craig Covault, "USAF, NASA Discuss Shuttle Use for Satellite Maintenance," *Aviation Week & Space Technology*, December 17, 1984, pp. 14–16, "Washington Roundup," *Aviation Week & Space Technology*, June 4, 1979, p. 11; Robert C. Toth, "Anaheim Firm May Have Sought Spy Satellite Data," *Los Angeles Times*, October 10, 1982, pp. 1, 32; Bill Gertz, "New Spy Satellite, Needed to Monitor Treaty, Sits on Ground," *Washington Times*, October 20, 1987, p. A5; Woodward, *Veil*, p. 221; Bill Gertz, "Senate Panel Asks for Radar Funds," *Washington Times*, April 5, 1988, p. A4; Craig Covault, "Atlantis' Radar Satellite Payload Opens New Reconnaissance Era," *Aviation Week & Space Technology*, December 12, 1988, pp. 26–28; "Valve Work Delays Another Titan Flight," *Space News*, August 18–31, 1997, p. 2; Vincent Kiernan, "Satellite Buffs Conclude That Titan Launch Carried Lacrosse," *Space News*, April 8–14, 1991, p. 22; Philip S. Clark, "Satellite Digest," *Spaceflight* 40, January 1998, pp. 35–36.

22. Gertz, "New Spy Satellite, Needed to Monitor Treaty, Sits on Ground"; Covault, "Atlantis' Radar Satellite Payload Opens New Reconnaissance Era"; "Radar Satellite Assesses Raids," *Aviation Week & Space Technology*, September 16, 1996, p. 26; David Fulghum and Craig Covault, "U.S. Set to Launch Upgraded Lacrosse," *Aviation Week & Space Technology*, September 20, 1996, p. 34; William Claiborne, "Taiwan-Born Scientist Passed Defense Data," *Washington Post*, December 12, 1997, p. A23; Craig Covault, "Secret Relay, Lacrosse NRO Spacecraft Revealed," *Aviation Week & Space Technology*, March 23, 1998, pp. 26–28.

23. Fulghum and Covault, "U.S. Set to Launch Upgraded Lacrosse."

24. Craig Covault, "Recon Satellites Lead Allied Intelligence Effort," *Aviation Week & Space Technology*, February 4, 1991, pp. 25–26; Bill Gertz, "S. Africa to Test Ballistic Missile," *Washington Times*, May 3, 1991, p. A3; Bill Gertz, "Laotian Military Smuggling Drugs," *Washington Times*, April 25, 1991, p. A11; Bill Gertz, "Soviets Testing Rail-Mobile Rocket," *Washington Times*, April 12, 1991, p. A5; Bill Gertz, "China Helps Algeria Develop Nuclear Weapons," *Washington Times*, April 11, 1991, p. A3; David E. Sanger, "Furor in Seoul over North Korea's Atomic Plant," *New York Times*, April 16, 1991, p. A3; Bill Gertz, "Satellites Spot Poison Bomb Plant in Libya," *Washington Post*, March 5, 1991, p. 3; "International," *Military Space*, January 27, 1992, p. 6.

25. Bill Gertz, "Beijing Creates Military Monster," *Washington Times*, April 10, 1997, pp. A1, A10.

26. Jeff Gerth, "Officials Say China Illegally Sent U.S. Equipment to Military Plant," *New York Times*, April 23, 1997, pp. A1, A9.

27. Tim Weiner, "U.S. Suspects India Prepares for Nuclear Test," *New York Times*, December 15, 1995, p. A6.

28. Elaine Sciolino, "U.S. Says It's Won Votes to Maintain Sanctions on Iraq," *New York Times*, March 5, 1995, pp. 1, 9.

29. Boerfink MHE to 26 IW et al., Subj: TFC Southern Region Disum (SORD) NR 146–92, May 26, 1992, pp. 3–4; Boerfink MHE to 26 IW et al., Subj: TFC Southern Region Disum (SORD) NR 211–92, July 30, 1992.

30. Bill Gertz, "N. Korea Masses Artillery at Border," *Washington Times*, July 25, 1996, pp. A1, A9.

31. Douglas Waller, "The Secret Missile Deal," *Time*, June 30, 1997, p. 58.

32. Michael R. Gordon, "Despite Cold War's End, Russia Keeps Building a Secret Complex," *New York Times*, April 16, 1996, pp. A1, A6; Bill Gertz, "Moscow Builds Bunkers Against Nuclear Attack," *Washington Times*, April 1, 1997, pp. A1, A16; Bill Gertz, "Russian Nuke Shelters Don't Concern Pentagon," *Washington Times*, April 2, 1997, p. A6.

33. Bill Gertz, "Hidden Iraqi Scuds Threaten Israel, Gulf Countries," *Washington Times*, February 11, 1998, pp. A1, A12.

34. R. Jeffrey Smith, "Senators, CIA Fight over $1 Billion," *Washington Post*, July 16, 1993, p. A4; David A. Fulghum, "Key Military Officials Criticize Intelligence Handling in Gulf War," *Aviation Week & Space Technology*, June 24, 1991, p. 83.

35. James Risen and Ralph Vartabedian, "U.S. Launches Costly Overhaul of Spy Satellites," *Los Angeles Times*, September 28, 1995, pp. A1, A11; "KH-11s Recons Modified," *Aviation Week & Space Technology*, October 9, 1995, p. 28.

36. Walter Pincus, "Congress Debates Adding Smaller Spy Satellites to NRO's Menu," *Washington Post*, October 5, 1995, p. A14; Joseph C. Anselmo, "House, Senate at Odds Over Intel Small Sats," *Aviation Week & Space Technology*, November 13, 1995, pp. 24–25; "When in Doubt Appoint a Panel," *Aviation Week & Space Technology*, January 1, 1996, p. 19.

37. Small Satellite Review Panel, Memorandum for: Director of Central Intelligence, Subject: Small Satellite Review Panel, July 1996, pp. 1–2.

38. Ibid., p. 3.

39. Ibid.

40. Ibid., p. 4; In 1998 the NRO decided to delay any introduction of small satellites, which had been envisioned to occur in 2003 or 2004, by at least one year because projected costs were higher than originally anticipated. See Joseph C. Anselmo, "Imagery Satellite Costs Prompt NRO Delay," *Aviation Week & Space Technology*, May 25, 1998, p. 24.

41. "NRO Opens Up to New Satellite System Ideas," *Jane's Defence Weekly*, July 30, 1997, p. 23; "DARPA Eyes Low-Cost Radar Satellite Constellation," *Aerospace Daily*, June 2, 1997, pp. 341–342; David A. Fulghum and Joseph C. Anselmo, "DARPA Pitches Small Sats for Tactical Reconnaissance," *Aviation Week & Space Technology*, June 9, 1997, pp. 29–31.

42. "DARPA/USAF/NRO Plan Space-Based SAR/MTI Development," *Aerospace Daily*, March 19, 1998, pp. 416–417; Warren Ferster, "Military to Get Satellite Control," *Space News*, March 16–22, 1998, pp. 1, 20; Ernest Blazar, "Inside the Ring," *Washington Times*, March 26, 1998, p. A10.

43. Bob Preston, *Plowshares and Power: The Military Use of Civil Space* (Washington, D.C.: NDU Press, 1994), pp. 55–56; Liz Tucci, "Landsat 7 to Carry Instrument with 5-Meter Resolution," *Space News*, November 2–8, 1992, p. 23; Ben Ianotta, "Who Will Finance the Sensor," *Space News*, January 3–9, 1994, p. 3; Ben Ianotta, "New Landsat Sensor Debated," *Space News*, July 19–25, 1993, p. 23; NASA/DOD, *National Aeronautics and Space*

Administration (NASA) and the Department of Defense (DOD) Landsat 7 Transition Plan, February 24, 1994.

44. Campbell, *Introduction to Remote Sensing,* pp. 137–138; HQ United States Space Command, *Command History, January 1990–December 1991, Narrative* (Peterson AFB, Colo.: USSPACECOM, n.d.), pp. 83–84.

45. Campbell, *Introduction to Remote Sensing,* pp. 149–153; HQ U.S. Space Command, *Command History, January 1, 1990–December 31, 1991,* p. 307; "Spot 4 Images Released," *Aviation Week & Space Technology,* April 13, 1998, p. 75.

46. HQ U.S. Space Command, *Command History, January 1, 1990–December 31, 1991,* pp. 309–310; James R. Asker, "U.S. Navy's Haiti Maps Merge Satellite Data," *Aviation Week & Space Technology,* October 17, 1994, p. 49; Ben Ianotta and Steve Weber, "Space-Based Data Found Useful in Haiti," *Space News,* September 26-October 2, 1994, p. 6.

47. Joseph C. Anselmo, "Space Imaging Readies 1-Meter Satellite," *Aviation Week & Space Technology,* May 19, 1997, p. 26; "Ikonos 1 Undergoes Tests as Launch Nears," *Space News,* May 11–17, 1998, p. 19; "Commercial Developments," *Aviation Week & Space Technology,* June 29, 1998, p. 17.

48. Warren Ferster, "USAF Imaging Deal to Bolster OrbView Program," *Space News,* August 18–31, 1997, p. 8; Joseph C. Anselmo, "Spot Sees Little Threat From 1-Meter Systems," *Aviation Week & Space Technology,* March 16, 1998, p. 43; Joseph C. Anselmo, "Commercial Satellites Zoom in on Military Imagery Monopoly," *Aviation Week & Space Technology,* September 22, 1997, pp. 75–77; "News Breaks," *Aviation Week & Space Technology,* April 13, 1998, p. 21; Earthwatch, "Earthwatch Forges Ahead Without Early Bird 1 Satellite," April 7, 1998; Warren Ferster, "Security Issues Stall Hyperspectral Effort," *Space News,* September 14–20, 1998, pp. 1, 28.

49. Warren Ferster, "Navy Near Imagery Deal," *Space News,* December 8–14, 1997, pp. 1, 42; "NEMO: Navy Earth Map Observor," http://www.pxi.com/NEMO/public/mission.html.

50. Chris Pocock, *Dragon Lady: The History of the U-2 Spyplane* (Shrewsbury, England: Airlife, 1989), pp. 18–32.

51. Seymour Hersh, *The Samson Option: Israel's Nuclear Arsenal and Foreign Policy* (New York: Random House, 1991), pp. 52–54; Dino Brugioni, *Eyeball to Eyeball: The Inside Story of the Cuban Missile Crisis* (New York: Random House, 1991), p. 33; Pocock, *Dragon Lady,* pp. 90–106, 143–163; Howard Silber, "SAC U-2s Provided Nicaraguan Pictures," *Omaha World Herald,* March 10, 1982, p. 2; Frank Oliveri, "The U-2 Comes in from the Cold," *Air Force Magazine,* September 1994, pp. 45–50.

52. Defense Airborne Reconnaissance Division, *Manned Airborne Reconnaissance Division* (Washington, D.C.: DARO, 1995), p. 24; Secretary of the Air Force, Office of Public Affairs, United States Air Force Fact Sheet 83–5, "U-2," 1983; Maj. Gen. Kenneth R. Israel, Director, DARO: *Supporting the Warfighter, NMIA Defense Intelligence Status '96* (Washington, D.C.: DARO, November 19, 1996), p. 20; Oliveri, "The U-2 Comes in from the Cold."

53. Michael A. Dornheim, "U-2 Runs at Frenzied Pace in New World Order," *Aviation Week & Space Technology,* April 29, 1996, pp. 55–56; Coy F. Cross, *The Dragon Lady Meets the Challenge: The U-2 in Desert Storm* (Beale AFB, Calif.: 9th Strategic Reconnaissance Wing, 1995), p. 15; Chris Pocock, "U-2: The Second Generation," *World Airpower Journal* 28 (Spring 1997): 50–99.

54. "More Eyes," *Aviation Week & Space Technology,* February 3, 1997, p. 21; Cross, *The Dragon Lady Meets the Challenge,* pp. 16–17; Lt. Col. Charles P. Wilson, *Strategic Reconnaissance in the Middle East: Is Manned High Altitude Aerial Reconnaissance Still Needed?*

(Washington, D.C.: Washington Institute for Near East Policy, 1997), p. 23.

55. Dornheim, "U-2 Runs at Frenzied Pace in New World Order"; "U-2s in France," *Washington Post*, January 6, 1996, p. A13; "Current U-2 News," http://www.the point.net/~jstone/u2news.html.

56. Tony Capaccio, "On Loan to U.N., U-2s Fly Nearly 300 Iraqi Missions," *Defense Week*, April 29, 1996, p. 16; "News Breaks," *Aviation Week & Space Technology*, November 21, 1994, p. 23; "More Eyes"; "U-2s in France"; "U-2s Deployed to French Base," *Aviation Week & Space Technology*, January 15, 1996, p. 61.

57. Robert Wall, "USAF Begins Search for U-2 Replacement," *Aviation Week & Space Technology*, February 23, 1998, p. 105.

58. David Miller, *An Illustrated Guide to Modern Sub Hunters* (New York: ARCO, 1984), p. 125; George A. Wilmoth, "Lockheed's Antisubmarine Warfare Aircraft: Watching the Threat," *Defense Systems Review* 3, no. 6 (1985): 18–25.

59. "Upgrades for P-3s to Begin in 1998," *Aviation Week & Space Technology*, March 31, 1997, p. 33.

60. *P-3C Orion Update Weapon System* (Burbank, Calif.: Lockheed, n.d.), p. 18; Lori A. McClelland, "Versatile P-3C Orion Meeting Growing ASW Challenge," *Defense Electronics*, April 1985, pp. 132–141; Nicholas M. Horrock, "The Submarine Hunters," *Newsweek*, January 23, 1984, p. 38; David A. Fulghum, "Airborne Video Stars As Intelligence Tool," *Aviation Week & Space Technology*, March 31, 1997, pp. 31–32.

61. "Upgrades for P-3s to Begin in 1998."

62. Defense Airborne Reconnaissance Office, *Manned Airborne Reconnaissance Division*, p. 4.

63. Ibid., p. 10; U.S. Congress, Senate Armed Services Committee, *Department of Defense Authorization for Appropriations for Fiscal Year 1997 and the Future Years Defense Programming, Part 1* (Washington, D.C.: U.S. Government Printing Office, 1997), p. 500.

64. Defense Intelligence Agency, *Capabilities Handbook, Annex A to the Department of Defense Plan for Intelligence Support of Operational Commanders*, (Washington, D.C.: DIA, March 1983), pp. 162–163.

65. Ibid. Barbara Starr, "TARPS Was Weak Link in BDA," *Jane's Defence Weekly*, August 3, 1991, p. 190.

66. Starr, "TARPS Was Weak Link in BDA."

67. William B. Scott, "F-14 Digital TARPS Captures Target Images," *Aviation Week & Space Technology*, July 1, 1996, p. 53; "U.S. Navy Eyes Future Growth for TARPS," *Aerospace Daily*, April 28, 1997, p. 158; "U.S. Navy to Field TARPS-CD, Eyes Future Upgrades," *Aerospace Daily*, June 5, 1998, pp. 374–375; "U.S. Navy to Build Three Additional TARPS-CD Pods," *Aerospace Daily*, August 24, 1998, p. 296.

68. Defense Intelligence Agency, *Capabilities Handbook, Annex A*, p. 162;

69. "Gulf War Experience Sparks Review of RPV Priorities," *Aviation Week & Space Technology*, April 22, 1991, pp. 86–87.

70. Ibid.

71. Ibid.

72. David A. Fulghum and John D. Morocco, "CIA to Deploy UAVs in Albania," *Aviation Week & Space Technology*, January 31, 1994, pp. 20–22; "Gnats Weathered Out," *Aviation Week & Space Technology*, February 14, 1994, p. 19.

73. Israel, *NMIA Defense Intelligence Status '96, Supporting the Warfighter*, p. 21; Defense Airborne Reconnaissance Office, *UAV Annual Report FY 1996*, (Washington, D.C.: DARO, November 6, 1996), pp. 7, 9, 18.

74. Defense Airborne Reconnaissance Office, *UAV Annual Report FY 1996*, pp. 9, 21; "World News Roundup," *Aviation Week & Space Technology*, June 15, 1998, p. 41.

75. Israel, *NMIA Defense Intelligence Status '96, Supporting the Warfighter*, p. 21; Defense Airborne Reconnaissance Office, *UAV Annual Report FY 1996*, pp. 13, 31; Michael A. Dornheim, "Global Hawk Begins Flight Test Program," *Aviation Week & Space Technology*, March 9, 1998, pp. 22–23; Defense Airborne Reconnaissance Office, *UAV Annual Report FY 1997*, 1997, p. 32.

76. Israel, *NMIA Defense Intelligence Status '96, Supporting the Warfighter*, p. 21; Defense Airborne Reconnaissance Office, *UAV Annual Report FY 1996*, pp. 13, 22, 31; Defense Airborne Reconnaissance Office, *UAV Annual Report FY 1997*, p. 34; "Falling Ax," *Aviation Week & Space Technology*, August 24, 1998, p. 21; "Dark Hawk," *Aviation Week & Space Technology*, June 22, 1998, p. 23; David A. Fulghum, "Dark Star Beats Problems, Scores Successful Flight," *Aviation Week & Space Technology*, July, 6, 1998, p. 25; Michael A. Dornheim, "Many Changes Made to Dark Star," *Aviation Week & Space Technology*, July, 6, 1998, pp. 26–27.

77. Paul Bennett, *Strategic Surveillance* (Cambridge, Mass.: Union of Concerned Scientists, 1979), p. 5.

78. Richard A. Scribner, Theodore J. Ralston, and William D. Mertz, *The Verification Challenge: Problems and Promise of Strategic Nuclear Arms Control Verification* (Boston: Birkhauser, 1985), p. 70; John F. Ebersole and James C. Wyant, "Real-Time Optical Subtraction on Photographic Imagery for Difference Detection," *Applied Optics* 15, no. 4 (1976): 871–876.

79. Scribner et al., *The Verification Challenge*, p. 69.

80. Campbell, *Introduction to Remote Sensing*, p. 226; James Fusca, "Space Surveillance," *Space/Aeronautics* (June 1964): 92–103.

81. U.S. Congress, Senate Committee on Commerce, Science and Transportation, *NASA Authorization for Fiscal Year 1978, Part 3* (Washington, D.C.: U.S. Government Printing Office, 1977), pp. 1642–1643.

82. Bamford, "America's Supersecret Eyes in Space"; Paul Stares, *Space and National Security* (Washington, D.C.: Brookings, 1987), p. 18. It is notable that the uplinks for the NRO Global Broadcast System are located in Hawaii, Europe, and Virginia.

83. Bamford, "America's Supersecret Eyes in Space"; Stares, *Space and National Security*, p. 18.

84. Robert C. Toth, "Anaheim Firm May Have Sought Spy Satellite Data," *Los Angeles Times*, October 10, 1982, pp. 1, 32.

85. Warren Ferster, "NRO Studies Relay Satellites," *Space News*, September 1–7, 1997, pp. 1, 19.

86. "CARS Gives Real-Time Recon," *Aviation Week & Space Technology*, April 29, 1996, p. 57.

87. Israel, *NMIA Defense Intelligence Status '96, Support to the Warfighter*, p. 46; DARO, *UAV Annual Report FY 1996*, p. 27.

88. Central Command, *United States Central Command 1987 Command History*, March 27, 1990, p. II-26.

89. Craig Covault, "'Info War' Advanced by Navy GBS Satcom," *Aviation Week & Space Technology*, March 23, 1998, p. 28.

90. Central Command, *U.S. Central Command 1987 Command History*, p. II-36.

91. Space Applications Corporation, *European Command Secondary Imagery Transmission System (EUCOMSITS)* (Vienna, Va.: Space Applications Corporation, June 1989).

92. U.S. Congress, House Committee on Armed Services, *Intelligence Successes and Failures in Operation Desert Shield/Storm* (Washington, D.C.: HASC, 1993), p. 20.

93. AFSPACECOM Public Affairs, "AFSPACECOM Assists in Mideast Response," n.d.

94. U.S. Congress, House Appropriations Committee, *Department of Defense Appropriations for 1992, Part 6* (Washington, D.C.: U.S. Government Printing Office, 1991), p. 470.

95. "AF Would Send Real-time Recce Satellite Images to Tactical Planes," *Aerospace Daily*, January 8, 1993, p 1; James R. Asker, "F-16, EA-6B to Fire Missiles Cued by Intelligence Satellites," *Aviation Week & Space Technology*, April 19, 1993, p. 25; Ben Iannotta, "Space to Play Bosnian Role," *Space News*, May 10–16, 1993, pp. 1, 2; Tony Capaccio, "Air Force Pushes 'In Your Face from Outer Space'" *Defense Week*, July 12, 1993, pp. 1, 8.

96. David A. Fulghum, "Talon Lance Gives Aircrews Timely Intelligence from Space," *Aviation Week & Space Technology*, August 23, 1993, p. 71; Capt. Michelle Dietrich, "Talon Lance Supports Warfighters," *Guardian*, August 1993, pp. 6–7.

97. Col. Jack Fry, Air Force Space Command Space Warfare Center, *AF TENCAP Programs* (AF TENCAP Briefing to AFSAB—New World Vistas Space Applications Panel), March 15, 1995; William B. Scott, "USAF to Broadcast Mission Data to Cockpit," *Aviation Week & Space Technology*, June 5, 1995, p. 23.

8

SIGNALS INTELLIGENCE

Signals intelligence (SIGINT) is traditionally considered one of the most important and sensitive forms of intelligence. The interception of foreign signals can provide data on diplomatic, military, scientific, and economic plans or events as well as on the characteristics of radars, spacecraft, and weapons systems.

SIGINT can be broken down into two basic components: communications intelligence (COMINT) and electronics intelligence (ELINT). As its name indicates, COMINT is intelligence obtained through the interception, processing, and analysis of the electronic communications of foreign governments or organizations, excluding radio and television broadcasts. The communications may take a variety of forms, such as voice, Morse code, radio-telephone, or facsimile, and may be either encrypted or transmitted in the clear.

The targets of COMINT operations are varied. The most traditional COMINT target is diplomatic communications—the communications from each nation's capital to its diplomatic establishments around the world. The United States has intercepted and deciphered the diplomatic communications of a variety of nations—for example, Britain's communications during the 1956 Suez Crisis, Iraq's communications to its embassy in Japan in the 1970s, and Libya's communications to its East Berlin People's Bureau prior to the bombing of a West Berlin nightclub in 1985.[1]

The United States also targets communications between different components of a large number of governments—on some occasions both components are located within the country being monitored, but on others at least one is located outside national boundaries. Communications frequently targeted include those between government and/or ministry officials; a ministry or agency and its subordinate units throughout the country and abroad; weapons production facilities and various military or government officials; military units, especially during exercises and operations, and higher authorities; and police and security forces and their headquarters. More specifically, the United States COMINT effort targets communications between the Chinese Ministry of Defense and subordinate military units; Russian military units; the Pakistani Atomic Energy Commission and

Pakistani nuclear facilities; the President of Egypt and his subordinates (including the time when Egypt was holding the hijackers of the *Achille Lauro*); and Israeli officials in Tel Aviv and Israeli representatives on the West Bank.

In 1968, intercepted voice communications in the Beijing Military Region indicated a field exercise involving the 4th Armored Division. In 1980, U.S. intercepts of Soviet communications led to a fear that the Soviets were about to invade Iran. COMINT played a significant role in preparing a 1982 study on Indian heavy water shortages. Intercepts allowed the United States to piece together the details concerning the sinking of a Soviet submarine in the North Pacific in 1983, and in 1988 intercepted Iraqi military communications led U.S. officials to conclude that Iraq had used chemical weapons in its war with Iran. After the Iraqi invasion of Kuwait in August 1990, COMINT and other intelligence reports indicated that some Saudi leaders were considering attempting to pay off Saddam Hussein. In September 1994, the United States intercepted communications from Haitian dictator Raoul Cedras, in which he said he would determine his response to President Clinton's demands based on the reaction of the American public to the president's forthcoming speech on U.S. Haitian policy. Intercepts of Chinese diplomatic communications in 1996 and thereafter raised the question of whether the PRC had attempted to funnel money to American politicians for use in their campaigns. A January 1997 intercept of Israeli diplomatic communications led to an FBI investigation of a possible Israeli penetration of the U.S. government. More recently, COMINT was a significant factor in monitoring the activities of Osama Bin Laden's associates.[2]

At times, entire sets of targets may be dropped or coverage of others dramatically increased. In the early 1970s, the United States dropped COMINT coverage of the Soviet civil defense network (although it was later resumed). In 1983 it began an all-source intelligence program (that included COMINT) to improve intelligence on the Soviet prison-camp system, with the specific intent of issuing a study that would embarrass the Soviets. The intelligence was intended to determine the location of the camps, the conditions, and the number of political prisoners. In recent years, COMINT coverage of targets related to nuclear and ballistic missile proliferation has increased dramatically. At the same time, the closure of a number of listening posts in Germany and elsewhere in Europe indicates significantly decreased eavesdropping activities directed at Eastern Europe.

As noted above, governmental communications do not exhaust the set of COMINT targets. The communications of political parties and of corporations involved in the sale of technology related to advanced weapons developments may also be targeted. In addition, the communications of terrorist groups are targeted—both to permit understanding of how the group functions and of the personalities of its leaders and to allow prediction of where and how it will attempt to strike next.

Another major set of COMINT targets are those associated with economic activity (of both the legal and illegal variety)—the communications of international banking firms and narcotics traffickers, for example. In 1970, the predecessor to

the Drug Enforcement Administration informed the NSA that it had "a requirement for any and all COMINT information which reflects illicit traffic in narcotics and dangerous drugs." Specific areas of interest included organizations and
individuals engaged in such activities, the distribution of narcotics, cultivation
and production centers, efforts to control the traffic in narcotics, and all violations of U.S. laws concerning narcotics and dangerous drugs.[3]

Electronic intercept operations are intended to produce electronics intelligence
(ELINT) by collecting the noncommunication signals of military and civilian
hardware, excluding those resulting from atomic detonations. Under the NSA's
Project KILTING, all ELINT signals are stored in computerized reference files
containing the most up-to-date technical information about the signals.

The earliest of the ELINT targets were World War II air defense radar systems.
The objective was to gather sufficient information to identify the location and operating characteristics of the radars—and then to circumvent or neutralize them
during bombing raids (through direct attack or electronic countermeasures). The
information desired included frequencies, signal strengths, pulse duration, pulse
repetition, and other specifications. Since that time, intelligence, space tracking,
and ballistic-missile-early-warning radars joined the list of ELINT targets.

In the early 1950s the primary targets were Soviet bloc (including PRC) radars.
Russian radars remain a target, although a less critical one. Monitoring Russian
radars also has an arms control verification aspect, since the 1972 Anti-Ballistic
Missile (ABM) Treaty restricts the use of radars in an "ABM mode." Today, Iraqi,
Iranian, North Korean, and PRC radars are among the prime targets.

A subcategory of ELINT is Foreign Instrumentation Signals Intelligence
(FISINT). Foreign instrumentation signals are electromagnetic emissions associated with the testing and operation of aerospace, surface, and subsurface systems
that have military or civilian applications. Such signals include, but are not limited to, those from telemetry, beaconing, electronic interrogators, tracking/fus-
ing/aiming/command systems, and video data links.[4]

A subcategory of FISINT is Telemetry Intelligence (TELINT). Telemetry is the
set of signals by which a missile or missile component sends back data about its
performance during a test flight. The data relate to structural stress, rocket motor
thrust, fuel consumption, guidance system performance, and the physical conditions of the ambient environment. Intercepted telemetry can provide data used
to estimate the number of warheads carried by a given missile, its payload and
throw-weight, the probable size of its warheads, and the accuracy with which the
warheads are guided at the point of release from the missile's post-boost vehicles.[5]

The ease with which communications or electronic signals can be intercepted
and understood depends on three factors: the method of transmission, the frequencies employed, and the encipherment (or lack thereof) used to conceal signals' meanings from unauthorized personnel.

The most secure method of transmission is by cable, either via landlines or
ocean cables. Communications or other signals transmitted in this manner can-

not be snatched out of the air. Interception of cable traffic has involved physically tapping into the cables or the use of "induction" devices placed in the proximity of the cables and the maintenance of the equipment at the point of access. This option might be impossible in the case of hardened and protected internal land-lines—the type that carry much high-priority secret command and control communications. Also it is not clear how feasible it is to productively tap fiber-optic cables.

A tremendous volume of communications is sent via satellite systems—for example, domestic and international telephone messages and military and business communications are regularly transmitted via satellite using ultra, very, super, and extremely high frequencies (UHF, VHF, SHF, and EHF). Thus, the United States and other nations have established major programs for the interception of communications transmitted via satellite. By placing satellite dishes at the proper locations, technicians can intercept an enormous volume of traffic. Whereas ground station antennas can direct the signals to a satellite with great accuracy, satellite antennas are smaller and the signals they send back to earth are less narrowly focused—perhaps covering several thousand square miles.[6]

Oftentimes, communications are transmitted partly by satellite and partly via microwave towers. In other cases—particularly in the case of telephone calls within a country, as in Canada—microwave towers serve as the entire means of transmission and reception. As one observer has written with regard to microwave relay towers: "With modern communications, 'target' messages travel not simply over individually tappable wires . . . but as part of entire message streams . . . and have voice, telegram, telex and high speed data bunched together."[7]

Microwave signals can be intercepted by two means: (1) ground stations near the invisible line connecting the two microwave towers and (2) space collection systems, if the area of transmission is within the footprint of the system.

Radio is the most traditional means for the transmission of signals—including communications, missile telemetry, and foreign instrumentation signals. The accessibility of radio signals to interception often depends on the frequencies upon which the signal is transmitted and the signal's geographic location. Messages transmitted at lower frequencies (ELF, VLF, LF, HF) travel for long distances since they bounce off the atmosphere and will come down in locations far from the transmitting and intended receiving locations. In contrast, data sent at higher frequencies will "leak" through the atmosphere and out into space. To intercept such signals, intercept stations must be within line of sight of the radio communications. The curvature of the earth can therefore make monitoring from ground-based sites impossible. Former CIA Deputy Director for Intelligence Sayre Stevens wrote of the Soviet ballistic missile defense test center at Sary Shagan: "It lies deeply enough within the USSR to make it difficult to monitor from peripheral intelligence gathering sites along the border. Because flight test operations at Sary Shagan can be conducted well below the radio-horizon from such external monitoring locations, the Soviet Union has been able to conceal the details of its activities at Sary Shagan for many years."[8] Under such conditions geosynchronous space collection systems may be necessary to gather the signals.

Two additional methods of communication that are targets of interception operations are walkie-talkie and radio-telephone communications. Walkie-talkie communications are employed during military exercises as well as during emergency situations such as Chernobyl. Radio-telephone communications are used by government officials as they travel in their limousines. Since walkie-talkie traffic, particularly in Russia and China, may occur over areas not accessible to ground stations, satellite interception may be required. Radio-telephone traffic in contrast, is particularly common in national capital areas, where embassy-based listening posts are often found.

Once intercepted, signals have to be processed. If communications are sent without encipherment or scrambling, then the only processing will be translation. Communications may be sent in the clear either because they are considered to be of too little importance to justify the time and expense involved in protecting them or because the method of transmission (e.g., cable) is believed to be immune to interception.

Electronic signals sent in the clear still need to be interpreted. Thus, telemetry signals on all channels may be transmitted as numbers. The variables being measured and the units of measurement must be inferred by correlating data on missile maneuvers with the intercepted telemetry. For example, measurement may be made concerning different types of events: one-time events (e.g., the firing of explosive bolt or separation of RVs from the post-boost bus), discontinuous events (e.g., adjustments to the guidance system during flight), and continuous events (e.g., fuel flow, motor burn, or acceleration of the missile during the boost phase). These events can be expressed in terms of absolute values, arbitrary values (on a one-to-ten scale), relative values (percentages), or inferential values. It will not necessarily be evident what particular characteristic an intercepted reading refers to or the particular values that are being used. A fuel tank reading may be given as "30," which could refer either to a tank that is 30 percent full or 30 percent empty. The temperature in the rocket combustion chamber can be measured from the temperature of another part known to have a specific temperature relative to that in the chamber.[9]

Communications or electronic signals may be either encrypted or scrambled, complicating the process of turning the intercepted signals into intelligence. Diplomatic communications are traditionally enciphered. The sophistication of the encipherment and the quality of the operators determine whether the encipherment can be broken. Conversations via radio and radio-telephone are frequently scrambled. Soviet leaders started to have their radio-telephone conversations scrambled after they became aware of a U.S. operation to intercept those conversations. Noncommunications signals may also be encrypted—as were a large portion of Soviet missile telemetry signals.

The U.S. SIGINT effort is a massive one and employs space and airborne collectors, ground stations, covert listening posts, surface ships, and submarines.

SPACE COLLECTION

The United States operates signals intelligence satellites in three different types of orbit—low-earth, geosynchronous, and highly elliptical ("Molniya").

Since 1962 the Air Force has been operating low-earth orbiting satellites designed to intercept signals emitted by Soviet, Chinese, and other nations' air defense, ABM, and early-warning radars.* The first of these heavy ferret satellites was launched by a Thor-Agena-B on February 21, 1962. Between the first launch and July 16, 1971, sixteen of these satellites were launched, about one to three satellites per year, with inclinations ranging from 75 to 82 degrees. The sixteen satellites involved three different generations—three successful launches in the first generation, nine in the second generation (with a first launch in January 1963 and the final launch in January 1968), and four in the third generation.[10]

A second class of ferrets was put into operation beginning in August 1963. Whereas each satellite in the first class had been launched as a primary payload, the satellites in the second class were piggybacked on launch vehicles carrying imaging satellites. The orbits of both classes evolved in a similar fashion—with initial orbits of approximately 180 by 250 miles giving way to near circular orbits of around 300 miles. The ferrets were usually arranged in constellations of four to maximize their utility for direction-finding.[11]

From 1972 until 1988 the only ferret launches were as secondary payloads. One set of ferret satellites, designated 989, were launched along with KH-9 imagery satellites (which were launched from 1971 to 1984) as well as with a class of SIGINT satellites designated JUMPSEAT (discussed below).

On September 5, 1988, the first satellite of what was intended to be a new four-satellite constellation of ferrets was launched. The new-generation ferret was the primary payload on a Titan II launched from Vandenberg Air Force Base. It was placed into an 85-degree inclined, 500-mile circular orbit. This launch was followed by similar Titan II launches on September 5, 1989, and April 25, 1992. However, in 1993 three Titan II boosters that had been designated for a "classified user" were reassigned to the Strategic Defense Initiative Organization (now the Ballistic Missile Defense Organization).[12]

---

*In the fall of 1997 the NRO and the Navy disclosed that the Navy began operating ferret satellites in 1960, with the launch of a system with the designation Galactic Radiation and Background (GRAB). A follow-on system was code-named POPPY. (See Naval Research Laboratory, *GRAB: Galactic Radiation and Background, First Reconnaissance Satellite* (Washington, D.C.: NRL, 1997); Dwayne A. Day, "Listening from Above: The First Signals Intelligence Satellite," *Spaceflight*, forthcoming.

That action apparently reflected a decision noted in a draft version of the Joint Chiefs of Staff "Roles and Missions" report that the missions being performed by two existing national satellites systems would be performed by a single new system. That system would be a follow-on to the advanced version of the PARCAE ELINT ocean surveillance satellite. PARCAE (as well as the advanced PARCAE satellite constellation), first launched in 1976, and its associated ground sites has the unclassified designation CLASSIC WIZARD.

The present CLASSIC WIZARD Global Surveillance System, as it is referred to in one Naval Security Group Command Instruction, had its origins in U.S. Navy studies started in 1968 to investigate the feasibility of a dedicated ocean surveillance satellite system. In 1970, the Chief of Naval Operations ordered a study of overall ocean surveillance requirements. This project resulted in a five-volume, Naval Research Laboratory *Ocean Surveillance Requirements Study*. In turn, the study produced Program 749, a study that focused on the development of high-resolution, phased-array radars that would allow all-weather ocean surveillance monitoring as well as detection of low-trajectory, sea-launched missiles.[13]

Despite the emphasis of these initial studies, the ocean surveillance satellite that resulted, PARCAE, lacked radar capability. Rather, it was a passive interceptor, equipped with a passive infrared scanner and millimeter wave radiometers, as well as radio-frequency antennas capable of monitoring radio communications and radar emissions from submarines and ships. It used passive interferometry techniques (the use of interference phenomena) to determine the location of ships—that is, the craft could compute a ship's position from data on radar or radio signals provided by several antennas.[14]

The PARCAE system consisted of a mother ship and three subsatellites tethered to the mother ship. The basic techniques involved in using multiple spacecraft to eavesdrop on and detection find Soviet surface vessels and submarines were first demonstrated using three NRL spacecraft launched on December 14, 1971. The subsatellites were relatively small, each measuring approximately 3 by 8 by 1 feet. The largest surface area on one side was covered by solar cells, and four spherical objects on the end of the metal booms were believed to be sensors.[15]

PARCAE satellites were launched from Vandenberg Air Force Base into a near-circular, 63-degree inclined orbit with an altitude of approximately 700 miles. At that altitude, the spacecraft could receive signals from surface vessels more than 2,000 miles away. Given that there was a displacement of approximately 1,866 miles between passes PARCAE could provide overlapping coverage on successive passes.[16]

There were eight operational clusters put in orbit between 1976 and May 15, 1987. An increased rate in the 1980s led the Navy to request and receive funds for antenna upgrades at all CLASSIC WIZARD ground stations. Those stations, colocated with Navy Regional Reporting Centers, were located at Diego Garcia, British Indian Ocean Territory; Guam; Adak, Alaska; Winter Harbor, Maine; and Edzell,

Scotland. Information received at the stations could be quickly transmitted to regional ocean surveillance centers and via satellite to a main downlink in the Washington area. In recent years the Adak and Edzell sites have closed down, and Army and Air Force SIGINT personnel now are colocated with Naval SIGINT personnel at the remaining sites—further indicating that the CLASSIC WIZARD system focuses on more than naval targets. Army participation began in the mid-1980s under a program known as TRUE BLUE (which also involved Army participation at other sites). In 1995, Detachment 1 of the Air Intelligence Agency's 692nd Intelligence Group was established on Guam to participate in the CLASSIC WIZARD program, described in an Air Intelligence Agency publication as a "joint global surveillance reporting system."[17]

Customers of CLASSIC WIZARD data, such as commanders of U.S. fleets, can specify, via an automated system, specific data that they require—with respect to area of interest, signals of interest, and units of interest.[18]

The first advanced PARCAE system was deployed during a June 1990 shuttle mission, launched from Cape Canaveral. The second advanced PARCAE was carried into orbit by a Titan IV, launched in November 1991 from Vandenberg Air Force Base. In both cases the satellites were deployed in orbits similar to those of PARCAE satellites. However, it appears that there is no mother ship attached to the triplets. An August 1993 launch from Vandenberg produced an explosion shortly after takeoff that destroyed the booster and the spacecraft. A successful advanced PARCAE launch followed—although not until May 12, 1996.[19]

Shortly after the explosion it was reported that the NRO and the Navy planned to develop a new generation of spacecraft with improved detection capabilities. The new generation will apparently be even more of dual system—employed against both land- and sea-based targets—than the advanced PARCAE.[20]

In the late 1960s and early 1970s the NRO began orbiting two geosynchronous systems—CANYON and RHYOLITE (subsequently renamed AQUACADE), developed by the Air Force Office of Special Projects and the CIA, respectively. The first CANYON was launched on August 1968 from Cape Canaveral into a orbit with a perigee of 19,641 miles, an apogee of 22,853 miles, and a 9.9 degree inclination. Controlled from a ground station at Bad Aibling, Germany, the satellite was America's first high-altitude SIGINT system and first COMINT satellite. Six additional launches would follow, concluding with a 1977 launch.[21]

In 1970, the first of four RHYOLITE spacecraft would be placed into geosynchronous orbit—although closer to achieving a pure geostationary orbit (0 degree inclination, 22,300 miles for both perigee and apogee) than CANYON. Rather than communications intelligence, RHYOLITE's primary function was intercepting the telemetry signals from Soviet and Chinese offensive and defensive missile tests, ASAT tests, and space launches. One satellite station was apparently located near the Horn of Africa, at 69 degrees east, to receive telemetry signals transmitted from liquid-fueled Intercontinental Ballistic Missiles (ICBMs) launched from Tyuratam in a northeasterly direction toward the Kamcahtka Peninsula impact zone. Another station was over Borneo, at 115 degrees east, to monitor Soviet solid-propellant missiles such as the SS-16 ICBM and SS-20 IRBM, launched from Plesetsk.[22]

In addition to intercepting the telemetry signals from Soviet and Chinese missile tests, the RHYOLITE satellites had a significant COMINT capability. Their use for COMINT purposes was dramatically increased on orders from President Nixon and Henry Kissinger, once they were made aware of the capability. The satellites apparently were used to intercept Soviet and Chinese telephone and radio communications across the UHF, VHF, and microwave frequency bands. Walkie-talkie communications generated by Soviet military exercises, which fell in the VHF/UHF range, also were regularly monitored by RHYOLITE satellites. Beyond the Soviet Union, RHYOLITE satellites, whose footprints collectively covered virtually the entire world outside of the Western Hemisphere, intercepted communications from China, Vietnam, Indonesia, Pakistan, and Lebanon.[23]

The CANYON and RHYOLITE/AQUACADE programs led, eventually, to follow-on programs originally code-named CHALET and MAGNUM. The final satellites deployed under those programs may still be active, given the extraordinarily long lifetime exhibited by some high-altitude SIGINT satellites.[24]

On June 10, 1978, the first CHALET satellite, was placed into an orbit similar to those inhabited by the CANYON satellites. Subsequently, after disclosure of the program in the press in 1979, it was renamed VORTEX. In 1987, its name was again changed to MERCURY after another disclosure. The final MERCURY was destroyed as a result of a 1998 launch failure.[25]

CHALET's original mission was strictly COMINT. However, after the loss of ground stations in Iran and the discovery that information on RHYOLITE had been sold to the KGB, CHALET was modified to allow it to intercept Soviet telemetry. The first modified CHALET was launched on October 1, 1979 (by which time it was known as VORTEX). Subsequent launches, not all successful, occurred on October 1, 1981; January 31, 1984; September 2, 1988; May 10, 1989; and September 4, 1989.[26]

The primary targets of VORTEX, for most of the program's existence, were in the Soviet Union. In particular, they included the communications of Soviet missile and nuclear RDT&E sites, defense-related ministries, and defense industries. At the height of the VORTEX operations, there were at least three operating VORTEX satellites—one covering Eastern Europe and the western USSR, another the central USSR, and the third the eastern portion of the USSR.[27]

Each also covered non-Soviet targets in its footprint—including Israel, Iran, and other Middle Eastern countries. Thus, the VORTEX ground station at Menwith Hill in the United Kingdom was heavily involved in supporting Operations Desert Shield and Desert Storm. In 1989 it received a Joint Meritorious Unit Award from Secretary of Defense Dick Cheney for "meritorious achievement from May 1987 to 1 September 1988"—a period that matches U.S. naval operations in the Persian Gulf.[28]

On January 25, 1985, the first satellite developed under the MAGNUM program was launched from the space shuttle Discovery, into a geosynchronous orbit. By the time of launch the program had been redesignated ORION. The second and final MAGNUM/ORION spacecraft was placed into orbit on November 22, 1989, also from a space shuttle orbiter. The satellites were reported to weigh about 6,000 pounds and have two huge parabolic antennas. One is intended to intercept communications and telemetry signals, the other to relay the intercepted material to earth. The first ORION may have been stationed over Borneo, the second over the Horn of Africa.[29]

Even if still operational, the final VORTEX and ORION spacecraft are certainly nearing the end of their lifetimes. Thus, in 1994 the NRO began launching two new generations of geosynchronous SIGINT satellites. Titan IV boosters placed the new SIGINT satellites in orbit on August 25, 1994; May 14, 1995; April 24, 1996; and May 8, 1998.[30]

It appears that the launches involve two distinct programs, with the first and third launches being from the same program. The ground processing equipment for that program is designated RAMROD. The system associated with RAMROD has been described as providing "near real-time reporting of highly sensitive, perishable data to national and tactical commanders," and consisting of two "strings," each with a "specific geographic reporting area." There is also under development a SIGINT satellite system, at one time designated INTRUDER, which is expected to perform the mission of all existing, high-altitude SIGINT satellites.[31]

Unlike VORTEX, ORION, and its successors, a third class of SIGINT satellites did not operate in geosynchronous orbit. Rather, the first generation of this class—designated JUMPSEAT—was launched into a 63-degree, highly inclined, elliptical orbit (200 by 24,000 miles) from Vandenberg Air Force Base. Approximately six JUMPSEATs were launched after the initial launch on March 20, 1971, with a final launch in 1987. In its highly elliptical orbit, JUMPSEAT "hovered" over the Soviet Union for eight to nine hours at a time, intercepting communications and electronic signals from the northern Soviet Union as well as from Molniya communications satellites that operated in the same orbit. When paired with 989 ferret satellites the combination was first designated YIELD and then (from 1982) WILLOW.[32]

A far more advanced version of JUMPSEAT, code-named TRUMPET, was launched on May 3, 1994. That launch culminated a ten-year effort to orbit the new satellite and a three-year effort from the time it first reached its launch pad at Cape Canaveral. A second launch followed on July 10, 1995. The satellites weigh about 10,000 pounds. Like JUMPSEAT, TRUMPET operates in a highly inclined, elliptical orbit, although with a more extensive mission. Although the intelligence community wished to leave the satellites in storage, feeling that the cost of operation and maintenance was not worth benefit in the post–Cold War world, congressional overseers directed otherwise. The program has been canceled—although, with the three launches in 1994, 1995, and 1997 (the final launch), data will be available from the satellites into the next century.[33]

SIGINT satellite operations are supported by several specialized ground stations—located at Buckley Air National Guard Base, Colorado; Menwith Hill, United Kingdom; Bad Aibling, Germany, and Pine Gap, Australia.

The Buckley site serves as a ground station for three satellite programs—ORION, TRUMPET, and the system whose ground processing equipment is designated RAMROD.* Although Buckley has been one of three stations associated with the ORION program, it is apparently the sole ground station for TRUMPET—whose orbit permits it to operate in view of the Buckley station when it is over the Northern Hemisphere. It is the most important of the two ground stations associated with RAMROD, "providing 75% of all information reported by the RAMROD system worldwide."[34]

From 1972 to 1974 NSA began augmenting its listening posts at Menwith Hill (which it took over from the Army in 1966) and Bad Aibling. One objective was to make Menwith Hill the primary ground station for the forthcoming CHALET system. Information received at Menwith Hill from the remaining operational VORTEX satellites can be transmitted directly to Fort Meade via DSCS satellite. In addition, Menwith Hill also serves as the ground station for the new generation of SIGINT satellites launched in May 1995, whose ground processing equipment is designated RUTLEY. Bad Aibling served as the ground station for the CANYON program and more recently as the European ground station for the MAGNUM/ ORION system, receiving intercepts of telemetry from Tyuratam and Plesetsk. Responsibility for the operation of Menwith Hill and Bad Aibling was transferred to the Army Intelligence and Security Command in 1994 and 1995, although representatives of the other services' SIGINT organizations are also involved in operation of the facility—such as the Air Intelligence Agency's 451st Intelligence Squadron at Menwith Hill and 402nd Intelligence Squadron at Bad Aibling.[35]

The Joint Defence Space Research Facility at Pine Gap, Australia, was established to serve as the ground control station and downlink for the RHYOLITE satellite located over Borneo and subsequently was assigned the same mission for the ORION satellite over Borneo. It may have assumed a similar mission for one of the satellites associated with the RAMROD system. The facility consists of at least seven large radomes, a huge computer room, and about twenty other support buildings. The radomes (the first of which were built in 1968 and which resemble gigantic golf balls with one of their ends sliced off) are made of Perspex and mounted on a concrete structure. They were intended to protect the enclosed antennas against dust, wind, and rain and to hide some of the operational elements of the antennas from Soviet reconnaissance satellites.[36]

---

*Ground processing equipment associated with SIGINT satellites is given an unclassified designation beginning with R. Thus the designations for ground processing equipment for various SIGINT satellites have included RAINFALL (RHYOLITE), RUNWAY (VORTEX), ROSTER (MAGNUM), and RUFFER (JUMPSEAT/TRUMPET).

The computer room is divided into three principal sections. The Station-Keeping Section is responsible for maintaining the satellites in geosynchronous orbit and for correctly aligning them toward targets of interest. The Signals Processing Office receives the signals transmitted from the satellite and transforms them into a form that can be used by the analysts in the Signals Analysis Section.[37] In 1996 plans to upgrade Pine Gap were announced by the U.S. and Australian governments.[38]

The future U.S. SIGINT constellation may look very different from the present one. In 1998 the NRO was developing an Integrated Overhead SIGINT Architecture (IOSA) that, according to its director, "will improve SIGINT performance and avoid costs by consolidating systems, utilizing medium lift launch vehicles whenever possible and using new satellite and data processing technologies." The IOSA is to be followed in about a decade by an IOSA 2.[39]

AIRBORNE COLLECTION

Each of the three major military services operates aircraft for the collection of strategic and tactical signals intelligence. The 55th Wing of the Air Combat Command (ACC), headquartered at Offutt Air Force Base, Nebraska, is responsible for the operations of the Air Force's RC-135 fleet. Personnel to operate the sensors, analyze the data, and disseminate it are provided by Air Intelligence Agency Intelligence Squadrons and Air Combat Command Reconnaissance Squadrons. Tasking is the responsibility of both AIA and the National Security Agency.

There have been twelve versions of the plane. The first RC-135, an RC-135B, joined the Strategic Air Command's reconnaissance fleet in December 1965. This step began the process of replacing thirty obsolescent RB-47Hs and ERB-47Hs that were then "performing the ELINT portion of the Global Peacetime Airborne Reconnaissance Program."[40]

The size of the RC-135 fleet has been growing in recent years, partly due to congressional action, and now stands at twenty-three. Sixteen of the operational RC-135s are RC-135V/W RIVET JOINT aircraft. These and other models of the RC-135 have an overall length of 129 feet, a wingspan of 131 feet, and an overall height of 42 feet. At its operational altitude, 34,990 feet, the plane cruises at 558 miles per hour. It can be refueled in the air, which it requires after ten hours, and stay aloft for thirty hours.[41]

The RIVET JOINT aircraft fly missions, designated BURNING WIND, that intercept both communications and electronic signals. One system carried by the plane is the Automatic Electronic Emitter Locating System (AEELS), which scans each side of the aircraft to identify and locate emitters of interest. It can reportedly locate, analyze, and identify a radar within seconds—although not with sufficient precision to permit targeting of smart weapons. The data can then be transmitted via secure voice link, the Tactical Information Broadcast Service (TIBS), or the Tactical Digital Information Link (TACDIL). The Multiple Communications Emitter Location System (MUCELS) employs four large saucer-shaped antennas below and forward of the wing. A second MUCELS array consists of ten blade-and-hook antennas clustered just to the rear of the wing.[42]

The RIVET JOINT aircraft operate from five primary locations: Offut Air Force Base, Nebraska (with intelligence personnel supplied by the AIA's 97th Intelligence Squadron, and electronic warfare personnel by the ACC's 343rd Reconnaissance Squadron); RAF Mildenhall, United Kingdom (488th Intelligence Squadron and 95th Reconnaissance Squadron); Souda Bay, Crete (an Operating Location of the 488th IS); Kadena Air Base, Okinawa (390th Intelligence Squadron and 82nd Reconnaissance Squadron); and Al Kharj, Saudi Arabia. The 488th Intelligence Squadron supplies Serbo-Croat linguists in support of Bosnia operations.[43]

With the end of the Cold War, the targets of RIVET JOINT missions have changed considerably. During 1995 and 1996, 79 percent of those missions were conducted in support of joint task force operations in the Middle East (Iraq) and Bosnia. Thus, on February 22, 1995, a RIVET JOINT aircraft flew the 1,000th mission in support of Operation Southern Watch, the enforcement of United Nations sanctions against Iraq. On July 17, 1995, a RIVET JOINT from Mildenhall flew the 700th Adriatic mission—three years after the beginning of those missions in support of Operation Provide Promise. (The 1,000th mission would be flown in October 1996). Another 19 percent were targeted on Cuba, the Mediterranean (particularly Libya) and the Pacific (including North Korea, China, and Vietnam). The remaining 2 percent of the flights involved training and exercises.[44]

Two RC-135s are RC-135U versions, which bear the designation COMBAT SENT and fly missions designated HAVE TERRA and HAVE UNION. The planes fly at the same speed and altitude as the RIVET JOINTs, although with a different mission—the provision of "signal parametrics used for the development of radar warning receivers, EW [electronic warfare] systems, threat system simulators, [and] mission planning." The signal parametrics include power, pulse, and polarization data. The primary sensor carried on the COMBAT SENT aircraft is the Precision Power Measurement System, which determines the absolute power, power pattern, and polarization of selected target emitters. In addition, a high-resolution camera and television and radar sensors are in the tail and are used when the occasion permits. One COMBAT SENT plane is equipped with a system known as COMPASS ERA, which contains infrared thermal imaging, interferometer-spectrometer, and spectral radiometer sensors. Among the targets of the COMBAT SENT planes that flew, during the Cold War, along the periphery of the Soviet Union and other Warsaw Pact countries, were the ODD PAIR, SIDE NET, and TOP STEER radar systems.[45]

The final component of the RC-135 fleet are the RC-135S models, designated COBRA BALL, which fly BURNING STAR missions. The aircraft COBRA BALL fleet will grow to three as the result of modifications of the former RC-135X aircraft that had been used by the Ballistic Missile Defense Organization. The COBRA BALLs had been based at Eielson Air Force Base, Alaska, until late 1991, and often operated from Shemya, when the COBRA BALL mission was transferred to Offutt Air Force Base.[46]

COBRA BALL missions, which number about 100 per year, are directed at obtaining intelligence on foreign missile tests—including Russian, Chinese, Indian, and Israeli. Thus, in January 1994 a COBRA BALL was deployed off the Bay of Bengal, within forty-eight hours from its base on Diego Garcia, to monitor an upcoming Indian test. Aircraft stationed at Souda Bay, Greece, can be employed to monitor Israeli and Iranian missile tests. In 1996, COBRA BALL aircraft monitored Chinese tests near Taiwan, Indian tests, and several Russian tests. In May 1997, a COBRA BALL monitored the test of a North Korean, anti-ship missile.[47]

Among the systems carried by the RC-135S aircraft is the Advanced Telemetry System (ATS), which automatically searches a portion of the frequency band and makes a digital record of all signals present. The operator of the ATS system allocates its collection resources to reentry vehicle links and records all telemetry detected.[48]*

Supplementing the operations of the RIVET JOINT aircraft are Air National Guard C-130 aircraft that carry the SENIOR SCOUT SIGINT system—a roll-on/roll-off package used to provide COMINT to theater commanders, counternarcotics operations, and special operations. The four-engine turboprop planes, operated by the 169th Intelligence Squadron, Utah Air National Guard, fly at between 20,000 and 26,000 feet, at a speed of 250 knots.[49]

In addition to their imagery capabilities, U-2 aircraft can also be equipped with SIGINT sensors. SENIOR RUBY is a near-real-time ELINT collection, processing, and reporting system that provides information (including type and location) on radar emitters within line of sight of the U-2R. It can handle a large number of emitters simultaneously and send its data to a Ground Control Processor colocated with the COMINT Transportable Ground Intercept Facility (TGIF).[50]

SENIOR SPEAR is a near-real-time COMINT collection, processing, and reporting system that provides line-of-sight collection capability—out to 300 nautical miles—from the aircraft. When flown together, the SENIOR RUBY and SENIOR SPEAR systems constitute SENIOR GLASS. Data collected by the U-2 SIGINT systems can be transmitted via satellite across the world via the SENIOR SPAN data link, carried in a dorsal fairing on the top of the aircraft.[51]

U-2 missions have been flown from several bases against a variety of targets. From Patrick Air Force Base, Florida, U-2Rs have flown collection missions against Cuba. The main targets are Cuban army, air force, and navy communications, with the intercepts being transmitted to Key West Naval Air Station, Florida. U-2Rs have flown from RAF Akrotiri (Operating Location OLIVE HARVEST) to intercept signals from Syria, Egypt, and Israel. The data are then uplinked to a DSCS satellite

---

*The MASINT sensors on COBRA BALL aircraft are discussed in Chapter 9.

for transmission to the Remote Operations Facility, Airborne (ROFA). From Osan Air Base, South Korea, SENIOR SPEAR U-2s fly OLYMPIC GAME missions to intercept Chinese and North Korean communications, with the intercepted communications being downlinked to an Air Intelligence Agency unit at Osan.[52]

The Navy operates two types of aircraft for SIGINT purposes—the land-based EP-3E ARIES (Airborne Reconnaissance Integrated Electronics System) II, a modification of the P-3, and the carrier-based ES-3A SHADOW. Each aircraft is operated by two Fleet Air Reconnaissance Squadrons. In recent years, such aircraft have been increasingly used in overland operations.

The twelve-aircraft EP-3E ARIES II fleet is evenly divided between Fleet Air Reconnaissance Squadrons One (VQ-1) and Two (VQ-2). In July 1994, VQ-1 headquarters was relocated from NAS Agana, Guam to NAS Whidbey Island, Washington. VQ-1's area of responsibility stretches from the West Coast of the United States to the East Coast of Africa and the Arabian Gulf. Its detachments are located at Bahrain, UAE; Misawa, Japan; Kadena, Japan; and Osan, Republic of Korea.[53]

The EP-3Es are four-engine turboprops that fly at altitudes up to 28,000 feet, can fly for up to twelve hours, and have a range of 3,400 nautical miles. The plane is distinguished from the Orion by a flat circular radome under the fuselage, and it lacks the long, thin MAD boom at the tail. The COMINT and ELINT collection and dissemination tasks on the EP-3E are performed by the personnel at thirteen positions. Position 8 looks for the beam width, pulse repetition, frequency, and other characteristics of radar systems. Position 9 is responsible for the search for signals associated with early warning, ground control intercept, fire control, and other radars. Position 10 conducts detailed analysis of the higher-band radar signals that are associated with fighters such as the Su-27 and MiG-29. The operator can often determine that a radar has locked on to a target. The Position 11 operator receives data from the longest range equipment and generally will be the first to detect radars, which are then assigned to other analysts. Position 12 is reserved for the ELINT supervisor, who coordinates the data collected. Position 13 integrates electronic and communications intelligence and is responsible for disseminating the data to other aircraft, operational headquarters, and intelligence organizations via the Tactical Information Broadcast Service and other data links. Position 14 supervises the communications intercept specialists in positions 15 through 19. Position 20 is used for special scientific and technical collection and analysis.[54]

VQ-1 targets include foreign surface and submarine activity (in support of Carrier Battle Groups) as well as land-based radars and UHF/VHF communications systems.[55] By 1993, VQ-1 operations targeted on the PRC became its highest priority in the Western Pacific. It flew "nationally and fleet tasked collection efforts against the PRC and also provided I&W [Indications and Warning] of PRC military activity to several transiting battle groups." During 1993, VQ-1 operations were also directed at collecting information on the changes in the Russian military in the wake of the collapse of the Soviet Union.[56]

In 1996, VQ-1 flew 1,319 sorties, involving "both nationally and fleet tasked SRO [Sensitive Reconnaissance Operations] and I&W missions, in support of DESERT STRIKE, SOUTHERN WATCH, VIGILANT WARRIOR, and VIGILANT SENTINEL." Its operating areas included the "North Arabian Sea, Gulf of Oman, Arabian Gulf, Overland Saudi Arabia, Sea of Japan, Sea of Okhotsk, Indian Ocean, South China Sea, East China Sea, Luzon Strait, Gulf of Thailand, Overland Korea, and the Western Pacific. As a result of operations in those areas VQ-1 "intercepted and processed 2,911 signals of tactical significance from target-country naval, airborne, and land-based emitters," as well as located seventy-two non-friendly submarines.[57]

VQ-2 headquarters are located at Rota, Spain. It reports to the Commander, Task Force Sixty-Seven; to the Commander, Sixth Fleet for operational requirements; and to the Commander, Fleet Air Mediterranean for administrative matters.[58]

VQ-2 is assigned six EP-3Es and operates detachments at Naval Air Station, Sigonella, Italy; Stuttgart, Germany; and Souda Bay, Crete. Planes are also periodically deployed to RAF Wyton and RAF Akrotiri, Cyprus. From those locations the planes fly missions over the Mediterranean, the Baltic, the Caribbean, the North Atlantic, and the Norwegian Sea. COMINT missions flown in the Western European area are code-named FLOOR DOOR, whereas ELINT missions are code-named FLOOR LEADER.[59]

In the summer of 1990, VQ-2 provided electronic reconnaissance support during the evacuation of 2,000 noncombatant personnel from Liberia in Operation SHARP EDGE. From August 1990 to April 1991, the squadron provided combat reconnaissance during Operations DESERT STORM, DESERT SHIELD, PROVEN FORCE, and PROVIDE COMFORT. A 1997 Mediterranean mission might involve eavesdropping on military, government, and police communications in North Africa, primarily Algeria and Libya. In 1997, EP-3Es from the Souda Bay detachment conducted missions to monitor the crisis in Albania.[60]

Fleet Air Reconnaissance Squadrons Five (VQ-5) and Six (VQ-6), located at NAS North Island, California, and NAS Cecil Field, Florida, respectively, are each responsible for half of the Navy's fleet of sixteen ES-3A SHADOW, carrier-based SIGINT aircraft. The two-engine turboprop flies at an altitude of between 25,000 and 35,000 feet (although it can reach 40,000 feet) and at a speed of 420 knots, can stay aloft for eight hours, and can be refueled in flight.[61]

The first ES-3A was delivered for testing in February 1992. The plane was conceived as part of the Navy's Battle Group Passive Horizon Extension System (BGPHES), which seeks to provide the battle group commander with over-the-horizon (OTH) tactical intelligence without electronic emissions, which would reveal the battle group's existence to an enemy. The ES-3A is able to relay intercepted data to terminals aboard selected vessels.[62]

VQ-5's home port changed from Agana, Guam, to North Island NAS, San Diego, in October 1994. It consists of four deployable detachments, three of which (BRAVO, CHARLIE, and DELTA) are located at North Island and support

CONUS-based west coast carrier air wings. Detachment FIVE (formerly ALPHA) supports the Carrier Air Wing Five at the Naval Air Facility, Misawa, Japan.[63]

For administrative purposes VQ-6 reports to the Commander, Sea Control Wing, U.S. Atlantic Fleet at NAS Cecil Field. However, guidance for its operations comes from elsewhere. Thus, according to its 1996 command history, VQ-6:

provide[s] real-time signals intelligence to tactical commanders for air, surface, and ground operations. [It] performs airborne reconnaissance in support of Battle Group Commanders against all potential enemies. Carrier based detachments deploy throughout the Caribbean and Mediterranean Sea as well as the Atlantic and Indian Oceans to satisfy Joint Chiefs of Staff (JCS), Theater CINC, National Security Agency (NSA) and Fleet intelligence requirements.[64]

VQ-6's ES-3As are employed by four detachments: Alpha, Bravo, Charlie, and Delta. In 1994, Detachment Alpha, operating from the USS *Saratoga,* flew over 100 overland reconnaissance missions over Bosnia-Herzegovina. Detachment Bravo, flying from the USS *George Washington,* flew seventy-eight missions over Bosnia as well as more than fifty missions in the Arabian Gulf area in support of operations SOUTHERN WATCH and VIGILANT WARRIOR. ES-3As from the USS *Eisenhower,* operated by Detachment Charlie, covered targets in the vicinity of the Arabian Gulf, the Mediterranean, and the Adriatic. Those planes—flying over Bosnia-Herzegovina, the Arabian Gulf, Saudi Arabia, and Kuwait—primarily provided tactical, overland, C2W reconnaissance and targeting for Battle Groups. Support to UN and NATO operations, including DENY FLIGHT, PROVIDE COMFORT, and SHARP GUARD, included providing positive identification and localization of threats to UN/NATO forces.[65]

In 1995, Detachment Delta, operating from the USS *Theodore Roosevelt,* conducted long-range strike support, accompanying Air Force aircraft and tankers from the Red Sea to the Iraqi border. In addition, the detachment's ES-3As conducted "real world SIGINT strike support . . . during Operation Deliberate Force in Bosnia-Herzegovina. The detachment also participated in operations SOUTHERN WATCH, DENY FLIGHT, COILED COBRA, and INFINITE MOONLIGHT. The entire ES-3 fleet is scheduled to be retired in 2000 for budgetary reasons.[66]

Two further airborne SIGINT systems are operated by the Army: the RC-12 GUARDRAIL and the RC-7B/Airborne Reconnaissance Low—Multifunction (ARL-M). The RC-12s are two-engine turboprops that can fly as low as 20,000 or as high as 32,000 feet at 130 knots and operate for up to five hours. The planes comes in a variety of models—the RC-12H, RC-12K, RC-12N, RC-12P, and RC-12Q. They carry remotely controlled, ground-based intercept and direction-finding systems to exploit HF, VHF, and UHF voice communications. They also carry Global Positioning System receivers, which permit location of data to within 60 feet. An adjunct to the RC-12 is the Remote Relay System (RRS). Intercepted SIGINT data will be downlinked to the RRS, where it can automatically be relayed by satellite to any location where the appropriate receiving equipment can be set up.[67]

RC-12s are deployed in groups of twelve. One group is located in Korea, assigned to the 3rd MI Battalion (AE) of the 501st MI Brigade in Korea, and another is assigned to the 1st MI Battalion (AE) of the 205th MI Brigade, subordinate to V Corps in Germany, and has been employed to support Operation JOINT ENDEAVOR. The third group is assigned to the 224th MI Battalion (AE) of the 525th MI Brigade under the 18th Airborne Corps at Fort Bragg, North Carolina. A fourth group is under construction.[68]

The RC-7B/ARL-M is a four-engine turboprop that flies at altitudes between 6,000 and 20,000 feet at 220 knots and has a ten-hour endurance. The ARL-M is a modification of the ARL aircraft that were dedicated to either imagery or SIGINT missions exclusively. It carries HF, VHF, and UHF receivers. Originally designed to satisfy SOUTHCOM intelligence requirements, its mission was to "provide low profile signals intelligence and imagery collection support for counter-narcotics." Of the Army's five ARL-Ms, three are assigned to Korea. In addition to SIGINT equipment, they carry a variety of imagery sensors—SAR, MTI, infrared, and electro-optical. The planes mission includes watching military and civilian movements near the demilitarized zone.[69]

As of early 1998 the Army envisioned replacing the RC-12 and RC-7B in 2008 and 2009 with a new intelligence gathering aircraft, carrying an Aerial Common Sensor (ACS). The ACS would detect the emanations from radars, intercept communications, and gather imagery with electro-optical and SAR sensors.[70]

GROUND STATIONS

Beginning in the late 1940s the United States began establishing ground stations from which to monitor the Soviet Union and Eastern Europe. This network changed composition over the years and grew to include stations targeted on China, Vietnam, North Korea, the Middle East, Central America, and other areas. As the Cold War and then the Soviet Union ended, dramatic cutbacks were made in the NSA/SCE overseas network—particularly in Europe, as the Warsaw Pact and fear of a U.S.-Soviet conflict disappeared. Thus, the 1990s has seen the close-down of major U.S. SIGINT facilities in Italy (San Vito), Germany (Field Station Berlin, Field Station Augsburg, as well as a number of lesser tactical stations), the United Kingdom (RAF Chicksands—returned to the U.K. government), and Turkey (Field Station Sinop—returned to the Turkish government).[71]

In addition, the NSA has established three Regional SIGINT Operations Centers to receive data from manned and unmanned SIGINT sites in particular regions. These sites are manned by personnel from each of the three major SCE's (Army Intelligence Security Command, Naval Security Group Command, and Air Intelligence Agency). NSA and Marine Support Battalion personnel may also be present.

The RSOCs include the Medina Regional SIGINT Operations Center (MRSOC) at Medina Annex, Lackland, Texas, which focuses on Central and South America as well as the Caribbean. The units present at the MRSOC are INSCOM's 748th MI Battalion; AIA's 93rd Intelligence Squadron; Naval Security Group Activity (NSGA), Medina; and Company H of the Marine Support Battalion. The Kunia Regional SIGINT Operations Center at Kunia, Hawaii, is focused on Asia. It is staffed by representatives of INSCOM's 703rd Military Intelligence Battalion, the Naval Security Group Command, and the AIA. The third RSOC is the Gordon Regional SIGINT Operations Center (GRSOC) at Fort Gordon, Georgia, which focuses on Europe and the Middle East. It hosts INSCOM's 513th MI Brigade (with three subordinate battalions: the 201st, 202nd, and 297th), 702nd MI Group (with a subordinate 721st MI Battalion); AIA's 31st Intelligence Squadron; NSGA, Fort Gordon; and Company D, Marine Support Battalion.[72]

Among the remaining stations in the SIGINT ground station network are those in Alaska, Japan, the United Kingdom, Germany, Thailand, and Korea.

Shemya Island, Alaska (also the home to the COBRA DANE radar)—which is approximately 400 miles across the Bering Sea from the Russian eastern seaboard—was the home for many years, and may still be, of the Anders Facility. Run by the Bendix Field Engineering Corporation for the NSA, the facility's Pusher antenna monitored Russian communications in the Far East.[73]

Elmendorf Air Force Base, located in Anchorage, is the home of a Naval Security Group Command unit, the 6981st Electronic Security Group of the Air Intelligence Agency, and an AN/FLR-9 "Elephant Cage" antenna. The AN/FLR-9 consists of three circular arrays, each made up of antenna elements around a circular reflecting screen. In the middle of the triple array is a central building containing the electronic equipment used for form directional beams for monitoring and direction-finding. The entire system is about 900 feet in diameter. The AIA contingent has monitored Russian Far Eastern military activity through voice, Morse, and printer intercepts and probably continues to do so.[74]

The equipment at Misawa Air Base in Japan is also targeted on the Russian Far East and probably on North Korea and China. Four miles northwest of Misawa is the "Hill," on which a 100-foot AN/FLR-9 antenna is situated. The base and its antenna lie at the northern tip of Honshu Island, about 500 miles west of Vladivostok and 400 miles south of Sakhalin Island. Misawa is a major base and employs representatives of all four services' cryptological elements. There is a 900-person detachment from the 6920th Electronic Security Group of the AIA, a 700-person detachment from the Naval Security Group Command (NSGC), 200 representatives from the Army's Intelligence and Security Command (INSCOM), and eighty representatives from Company E, Marine Support Battalion.[75]

Misawa is also the site of Project LADYLOVE, which involves the interception of communications transmitted via several Russian satellite systems, including Molniya, Raduga, and Gorizont. Also involved is the tri-service Menwith Hill station, located 8 miles west of Harrogate in Yorkshire. The station is located on 562 acres and consists of a large array of satellite-tracking aerials. Under Project MOONPENNY, a variety of Russian satellite communications are intercepted by Menwith Hill's satellite dishes. Finally, the Bad Aibling Station in Germany—with Army, Navy, and Air Force SIGINT personnel—also targets Russian satellite communications.[76]

In addition to its SATCOM intercept and satellite ground station missions, Bad Aibling has two additional functions. Employing Rhombic and Pusher antennas, the Bad Aibling station conducts high-frequency direction-finding (HFDF) and communications intercept operations covering Eastern Europe and what was the southwestern portion of the Soviet Union. It also serves as the initial reception site for data from two unmanned locations on Cyprus and Oman. The Cyprus station consists of a Pusher HF antenna set up by the NSA at Episkopi Sovereign Base Area to cover targets in the Middle East and the southern portion of the former Soviet Union. The Abut Sovereign Base Area, home to a British SIGINT operation, also serves as a base of operations for NSA equipment designed to monitor military activity in the Near East and the southern former Soviet Union.[77]

A second set of stations are those directed against the activities of Asian Communist nations. Two of those stations—Khon Kean, Thailand, and Taegu, South Korea—are unmanned, with the intercepted data being transmitted to the Kunia RSOC. The Khon Kean facility was apparently set up in the fall of 1979 to correct a shortfall of intelligence during the China-Vietnam war earlier that year. The Taegu facility, run for the NSA by the Bendix Field Engineering Group, is equipped with a Pusher HF antenna and targeted against communications in China, North Korea, and South Vietnam.[78]

Located at Pyong Taek, Korea, is the 751st Military Intelligence Battalion (formerly U.S. Army Field Station Korea), a 304-person contingent with three detachments at different operating locations: Detachment J (at Koryo-Son Mountain on the island of Kangwna), Detachment K (at Kanak-San Mountain, six miles from the Demilitarized Zone (DMZ), and Detachment L (on Yawol-San Mountain, within 1,500 meters of the DMZ). Collectively, the installations target a variety of North Korean COMINT and ELINT targets.[79]

Latin America, and particularly Central America, became a target of increased importance during the Reagan administration. Although Central America is no longer a priority, Cuba continues to be a major concern. At Lackland Air Force Base, Medina Annex, San Antonio, are contingents from INSCOM's 748th Military Intelligence Battalion) and AIA's 6948th Electronic Security Squadron. SIGINT sites in Florida used to include a NSGA at Homestead Air Force Base, which monitored Cuban HF military communications. Although Homestead has closed, the antennas operated by the 749th Military Intelligence Company and NSGA at Key West, and the NSGA at Pensacola, Florida, still target Cuba and the Caribbean.[80]

Two SIGINT stations on U.S. territory outside of the continental United States contribute to SIGINT operations targeted on Latin America. More than 100 members of the Guantanamo Naval Security Group Activity are stationed at

Guantanamo Bay, Cuba. Employing an AN/FRD-10, the unit intercepts Cuban and Russian military communications in and around Cuba and the Caribbean Basin. A 430-person Naval Security Group Activity at Sabana Seca, Puerto Rico, which also uses an AN/FRD-10, targets naval traffic, diplomatic communications for all of Central and South America, and international leased carrier (e.g., INTELSAT) traffic.[81]

Also involved in the targeting of satellite communications from Sabana Seca is Detachment 2 from the AIA 544th Intelligence Group (headquartered at Falcon Air Force Base, Colorado Springs), whose SATCOM intercept mission is designated CORALINE (the station also conducts HF-DF operations). Other detachments of the 544th involved in similar SATCOM intercept operations are Detachment 3 at Sugar Grove, West Virginia, and Detachment 4 at Yakima Research Station, Washington. The Yakima site targets the Pacific INTELSAT/COMSAT satellite and probably the INMARSAT-2 mobile communications satellite. The intelligence it produces is designated COWBOY. The NSA facility at Sugar Grove, with 30-, 60-, 105-, and 150-foot satellite antennas intercepts the signals being sent by the INTELSAT/COMSAT satellite over the Atlantic and intended for the INTELSAT/COMSAT ground station at Etam, West Virginia. Its mission, designated TIMBERLINE, is officially described as directing "satellite communications equipment supporting research and development for multi-service national missions."[82]

Various Naval Security Group activities operate land-based SIGINT stations that conduct HF/DF monitoring of naval activity. Those operations support national and naval intelligence collection objectives, general ocean surveillance, and search and rescue operations. The stations generally use the AN/FRD-10 antenna array, which has a nominal range of 3,200 nautical miles. The network, originally known as CLASSIC BULLSEYE, underwent a multi-year modernization program in the early 1990s, designated CLASSIC CENTERBOARD. The modifications resulted in the renaming of the network as CROSSHAIR, and in the reduction of net control stations from three (Atlantic, Pacific, Naval Forces Europe) to one, located at NSGA Northwest, Virginia. In recent years, a number of stations in the worldwide network have been closed—including those at Edzell, Scotland; Terceira, Portugal; Hanza, Okinawa; and Adak, Alaska.[83]

The present network includes the NSGA at Sugar Grove, West Virginia, and the NSGA at Northwest, Virginia. Both use AN/FRD-10s to monitor naval traffic in the Middle Atlantic. Farther north, the NSGA in Winter Harbor, Maine, employs an AN/FRD-10 to monitor naval activity in the North Atlantic.[84]

A NSG unit at Diego Garcia operates a Pusher antenna directed at monitoring naval traffic in the Indian Ocean area. Stations in Guam and along the west coast of the United States also play a substantial role in monitoring naval activity in the Pacific. The NSG Detachment at Guam employs an AN/FRD-10 and is responsible for high-frequency direction coverage of Russian, PRC, and Vietnamese naval activity in the western Pacific. At Wahiawa, Hawaii, an NSG unit also employs an AN/FRD-10 to monitor naval traffic around the Hawaiian Islands as well as to collect international leased carrier and other communications for the Pacific region. At Imperial Beach, California, sixty members of the NSGA from San Diego operate an AN/FRD-10.[85]

EMBASSY AND CONSULAR INTERCEPT SITES

In addition to the ground-based listening posts such as those described above, which use large tracts of land, there is a set of posts that are located in and on top of U.S. embassies and consulates. Such listening posts allow the United States to target the internal military, political, police, and economic communications of the nation in which the embassy or consulate is located. The listening posts, known as Special Collection Elements, are operated by a joint CIA-NSA organization—the Special Collection Service, which was established as such in the late 1970s. About forty-five U.S. embassies and consulates host such elements.[86]

The best known of the embassy listening posts is the one located in Moscow. In the late 1960s and early 1970s, this post intercepted the radio-telephone conversations of Soviet Politburo members—including General Secretary Leonid Brezhnev, President Nikolai Podgorny, and Premier Alexei Kosygin—as they drove around Moscow. Traffic from the interception operation was transmitted to a special CIA facility a few miles from the agency's Langley, Virginia, headquarters.[87]

Originally, the conversations simply needed to be translated, since no attempt had been made to scramble or encipher the conversations. After a 1971 disclosure in the press concerning the operation, which was code-named BROADSIDE, the Soviets began enciphering their limousine telephone calls to plug leaks. Despite that effort, the United States was able to intercept and decode a conversation between General Secretary Brezhnev and Minister of Defense A. A. Grechko that took place shortly before the signing of the SALT I treaty. Grechko assured Brezhnev that the heavy Soviet SS-19 missiles under construction would fit inside the launch tubes of lighter SS-11 missiles, making the missiles permissible under the SALT treaty.[88]

In general, however, the intelligence obtained, code-named GAMMA GUPY, was less than earthshaking. According to a former intelligence official involved in the operation, the CIA "didn't find out about say, the invasion of Czechoslovakia. It was very gossipy—Brezhnev's health and maybe Podgorny's sex life." At the same time the official said that the operation "gave us extremely valuable information on the personalities of top Soviet leaders."[89]

Undoubtedly, during the abortive coup of August 1991, the listening post was part of the effort to eavesdrop on the communications of those attempting to replace the Gorbachev government and those resisting the coup. Among the communications monitored by the United States were those from the Chairman of the KGB and the Minister of Defense, both coup plotters.[90]

Other covert listening posts are located in the U.S. embassies in Tel Aviv, Buenos Aires, Santiago, and Karachi. The Tel Aviv outpost is targeted on Israeli military and national police communications. Thus, the United States has closely followed police activities directed at the Palestinians. The presence of a U.S. eavesdropping site has not gone unnoticed by Israeli officials, as a large number of antennas are visible on the roof of the Tel Aviv embassy.[91]

The Buenos Aires post was used to target the communications of the Argentine General Staff during the Falklands crisis—information that would be quickly passed to the British. The eavesdropping operation in the Karachi consulate yielded intelligence on drug trafficking, terrorist networks, and the Pakistani nuclear program.[92]

SURFACE SHIPS

The United States has employed surface ships for the collection of signals intelligence against both land-based and sea-based targets. In the 1950s destroyers and destroyers' escorts were employed in intercept operations against land-based targets. In 1961 and 1965, respectively, two new types of ships were deployed—Auxiliary General Technical Research (AGTR) and Auxiliary General Environmental Research (AGER) ships. Transfer of the SIGINT mission to those ships was a response to the fears of some Navy officials that stationing a destroyer off a foreign shore, especially that of a hostile nation, would be a provocation. However, the bombing of the AGTR USS *Liberty* by the Israelis during the 1967 war and the seizure of the USS *Pueblo* by North Korea in 1969 led to the eventual termination of the AGTR and AGER programs.[93]

In the 1980s the United States began employing Spruance-class destroyers and frigates to collect intelligence concerning Nicaragua and El Salvador. The 7,800-ton destroyer *Deyo*, as well as its sister ship *Caron*, were stationed in the Gulf of Fonseca. The ships could monitor suspected shipping, intercept communications and encrypted messages, and probe the shore surveillance and defense capabilities of other nations. Both ships remain in operation.[94]

A Ticonderoga-class cruiser, the USS *Yorktown*, which has operated in the Black Sea, is outfitted with electronic equipment that can monitor voice communications and radar signals. Such systems were used during a 1986 mission into the Black Sea to determine if new radars had been deployed onshore and to check the readiness of Soviet forces. In a previous expedition, the *Yorktown*'s equipment was used in part to monitor aircraft movements within the Soviet Union.[95]

Two now-retired Navy frigates that were stationed in the Pacific were used against targets in Nicaragua, El Salvador, and Honduras in the 1980s. One ship—the 3,900-ton *Blakely*—is a Knox-class frigate commissioned in 1970; the other—the 3,400-ton *Julius A. Furei*—is a Brooke-class, guided-missile frigate. The missions involved homing in on and recording voice and signal communications, locating transmitting stations, logging ships' movements, and studying their waterlines to help determine if they were riding low in the water when entering port and high when exiting—indicating the unloading of cargo.[96]

Frigates were also used for monitoring telemetry from missile tests. It was reported in 1979 that "American ships equipped with sensitive listening gear . . . patrol the North Atlantic, where they collect telemetry broadcast by the new Soviet submarine-launched missiles tested in the White Sea, northeast of Finland." Likewise, on the night of August 31, 1983, when the United States was expecting the Soviet Union to test an SS-X-24 missile, the frigate *Badger* was stationed in the Sea of Okhotsk.[97]

Ship-based ocean surveillance operations employ equipment that allows the detection, classification, and location of hostile ships, aircraft, and submarines by exploiting their command and control communications. The data collected are analyzed on board and transmitted to Net Control Centers for correlation.[98]

During the 1980s and early 1990s the intercept equipment operated on Navy cruisers and destroyers was code-named CLASSIC OUTBOARD. In the 1990s the Navy began installing the COMBAT DF system on frigates and the newest cruisers and destroyers. COMBAT DF relies on a gigantic antenna built into the hull of a ship to intercept signals and determine the location of long-range, high-frequency radios.[99]

UNDERSEAS COLLECTION

The use of submarines for intelligence-gathering purposes had its genesis in the later years of the Eisenhower administration. Known by a variety of code names, the best known of which is HOLYSTONE, the program has been one of the most sensitive intelligence operations of the United States.[100]

HOLYSTONE, which has also been known as BINACLE and BOLLARD, and most recently as BARNACLE, began in 1959 and has involved the use of specially equipped electronic submarines to collect electronic communications and photographic intelligence. The primary target through 1991 was the former Soviet Union, but at times countries such as Vietnam and China have been targets of the operations, which occasionally have involved penetration of Soviet, Chinese, and Vietnamese 3-mile territorial limits.[101]

It was reported in 1975 that each mission lasted about ninety days. Crew members were given cover stories, such as being part of an undersea geodetic survey project that was using sonar to study ocean water temperatures to support data collected by satellites. The crews were forbidden to use any active electronic or sonar gear while on a HOLYSTONE mission, so as to avoid detection by Soviet antisubmarine warfare devices. In addition, hatches were tied down to prevent rattling.[102]

Missions conducted through 1975 apparently provided vital information on the Soviet submarine fleet—its configuration, capabilities, noise patterns, missiles, and missile-firing capabilities. One mission involved obtaining the "voice autographs" of Soviet submarines. Using detailed tape recordings of noise made by submarine engines and other equipment, analysts from the Naval Scientific and Technical Intelligence Center (now part of the Office of Naval Intelligence) were able to develop a methodology for the identification of individual Soviet submarines, even those tracked at long range under the ocean. The analysts could then follow the submarine from its initial operations to its decommissioning.[103]

HOLYSTONE operations also provided information about theater and strategic sea-based missiles. Some Soviet sea-based missiles were tested against inland targets to reduce U.S. observation. On occasion, HOLYSTONE submarines would penetrate close enough to Soviet territory to observe the missile launchings, providing information on the early stages of the flight. According to one government official, the most significant information provided by the missions was a readout of the computer calculations and signals put into effect by Soviet technicians before launching the missiles. Beyond that, the U.S. submarines also provided intelligence by tracking the flight and eventual landing of the missiles and relaying continuous information on guidance and electronic systems.[104]

The submarines were also able to bring back valuable photographs, many of which were taken through the submarine's periscope. In the mid-1960s, photographs were taken of the underside of an E-class submarine that appeared to be taken inside Vladivostok harbor.[105]

Most recent operations have employed, at various times, some of the thirty-eight nuclear powered Sturgeon-class submarines. The submarines have dimensions of 292 by 31.7 by 26 feet and carry SUBROC and antisubmarine torpedoes as well as Harpoon and Tomahawk missiles. With their 107-person complement (twelve officers and ninety-five enlisted personnel) the ships can travel at speeds of greater than twenty knots when surfaced and at more than thirty knots underwater and can reach a depth of 1,320 feet. Their standard electronic equipment includes a search radar and both active and passive sonar systems.[106]

Other operations have employed submarines from the more modern Los Angeles-class attack submarines. The subs are 362 by 33 by 32.3 feet, carry Tomahawk cruise missiles and between four and twenty-one torpedoes. They travel at thirty-two knots and carry a 133 personnel, including thirteen officers.[107]

The special equipment placed on submarines for HOLYSTONE/BARNACLE missions has included the WLR-6 Waterboy Signals Intelligence System. In the 1980s, the WLR-6 was replaced by a more advanced system known as SEA NYMPH, described in one document as "an advanced automatic, modular signals exploitation system designed for continuous acquisition, identification, recording, analysis and exploitation of electromagnetic signals." All the Sturgeon submarines carry a basic skeletal system that can be upgraded to full capacity when authorized.[108]

As late as early 1993 there was evidence that HOLYSTONE/BARNACLE operations continued. In February of that year, the USS *Baton Rouge*, a Los-Angeles class attack submarine, collided with a Russian submarine near the Kola Peninsula. It has been reported that the *Baton Rouge* was on an intelligence-gathering mission targeted on the Russian port of Murmansk.[109]

Another collision occurred on March 20, 1993, when the Sturgeon-class USS *Grayling* bumped into a Russian Delta III-class ballistic missile submarine in the

Barents Sea about 100 miles north of Murmansk. During a summit with Russian President Boris Yeltsin the following month, President Clinton apologized for the incident. He also ordered a review of the submarine reconnaissance operations.[110]

Although such operations may have been severely curtailed with respect to Russia, they may not have ceased altogether. In early December 1997, a Russian Typhoon submarine launched twenty SLBMs (Submarine Launched Ballistic Missiles) as part of a destruction routine under the START I treaty. Subsequently, the Russians charged that a submerged Los-Angeles class submarine monitored the event, although Navy officials indicated that it was not an American sub (leaving open the possibility that it was British).[111]

In any case, there are other targets. The Los Angeles-class subs USS *Topeka* and USS *Louisville* arrived in the Persian Gulf in November 1992 and January 1993, respectively. Their mission was to keep watch on Iran's new submarine fleet. When U.S. pilot Scott O'Grady was shot down over Bosnia in 1995, submarines intercepted communications among Bosnian Serbs hoping to capture the pilot. That same year, a submarine assigned to counternarcotics work in the eastern Pacific intercepted transmissions from a suspicious trawler—the transmissions helped the U.S. Coast Guard seize eleven tons of cocaine.[112]

Notes

1. Bill Gertz, "U.S. Intercepts from Libya Play Role in Berlin Bomb Trial," *Washington Times*, November 19, 1997, p. A13.

2. Defense Intelligence Agency, *Soviet and People's Republic of China Nuclear Weapons Employment Policy and Strategy*, March 1972, p. II-B-5; [author deleted], "Indian Heavy Water Shortages," [from an undetermined NSA publication], October 1982; George C. Wilson, "Soviet Nuclear Sub Reported Sunk," *Washington Post*, August 11, 1983, p. A9; David B. Ottaway, "Iraq Said to Have Expelled High-Level US Diplomat," *Washington Post*, November 17, 1988, p. A33; George J. Church, "Destination Haiti," *Time*, September 26, 1994, pp. 21–26; Christopher Andrew, *For the President's Eyes Only: Secret Intelligence and the American Presidency from Washington to Bush* (New York: HarperCollins, 1995), p. 520; David Johnston, "U.S. Agency Secretly Monitored Chinese in '96 on Political Gifts," *New York Times*, March 13, 1997, pp. A1, A25; Nora Boustany and Brian Duffy, "A Top U.S. Official May Have Given Sensitive Data to Israel," *Washington Post*, May 7, 1997, pp. A1, A28; Russell Watson and John Barry, "Our Target Was Terror," *Newsweek*, August 31, 1998, pp. 24–29.

3. John E. Ingersoll, "Request for COMINT of Interest to Bureau of Narcotics and Dangerous Drugs," in U.S. Congress, Senate Select Committee to Study Governmental Operations with Respect to Intelligence Activities, *The National Security Agency and Fourth Amendment Rights* (Washington, D.C.: U.S. Government Printing Office, 1976), pp. 152–155.

4. U.S. Congress, House Permanent Select Committee on Intelligence, *Annual Report* (Washington, D.C.: U.S. Government Printing Office, 1978), p. 38.

5. John Prados, *The Soviet Estimate: U.S. Intelligence Analysis and Russian Military Strength* (New York: Dial, 1982), p. 203; Farooq Hussain, *The Future of Arms Control, Part 4, The Impact of Weapons Test Restrictions* (London: International Institute for Strategic Studies, 1980), p. 44; Robert Kaiser, "Verification of SALT II: Art and Science," *Washington Post*, June 15, 1979, p. 1.

6. Deborah Shapley, "Who's Listening? How NSA Tunes in on America's Overseas Phone Calls and Messages," *Washington Post*, October 7, 1977, pp. C1, C4.

7. Ibid.

8. Sayre Stevens, "The Soviet BMD Program," in *Ballistic Missile Defense*, ed. Ashton B. Carter and David N. Schwartz (Washington, D.C.: Brookings Institution, 1984), pp. 182–221 at p. 192.

9. David S. Brandwein, "Telemetry Analysis," *Studies in Intelligence*, (Fall 1964): 21–29; Hussain, *The Future of Arms Control*, p. 46.

10. Private information; Anthony Kenden, "U.S. Reconnaissance Satellite Programs," *Spaceflight* 20, no. 7 (1978): 243ff; Philip Klass, *Secret Sentries in Space* (New York: Random House, 1971), p. 194.

11. Kenden, "U.S. Reconnaissance Satellite Programs"; Klass, *Secret Sentries in Space*, p. 194.

12. "Refurbished Titan Missile Orbits Secret Payload," *Washington Post*, September 6, 1988, p. A2; William J. Broad, "Military Launches First New Rocket for Orbital Loads," *New York Times*, September 6, 1988, pp. A1, B7; "New Military Satellites," *Aviation Week & Space Technology*, May 25, 1992, p. 13; "Mission Control," *Military Space*, June 15, 1992, p. 1; John Lancaster, "The Shroud of Secrecy—Torn," *Washington Post*, June 5, 1992, p. A29; "Navy Uses Space to Spot Stealth Fighter," *Military Space*, April 23, 1990, p. 1.

13. NAVSECGRU Instruction 5450.59A, *Mission, Functions and Tasks of Naval Security Group Command Detachment (NAVSECGRU Det.) Potomac, Washington, D.C.*, February 7, 1994; Kenden, "U.S. Reconnaissance Satellite Programs"; Janko Jackson, "A Methodology for Ocean Surveillance Analysis," *National War College Review* 27, no. 2 (September/October 1974): 71–89; "Navy Plans Ocean Surveillance Satellite," *Aviation Week & Space Technology*, August 30, 1971, p. 13; "Industry Observer," *Aviation Week & Space Technology*, February 28, 1972, p. 9.

14. "Navy Ocean Surveillance Satellite Depicted," *Aviation Week & Space Technology*, May 24, 1976, p. 22; "Expanded Ocean Surveillance Effort Set," *Aviation Week & Space Technology*, June 10, 1978, pp. 22–23; Mark Hewlish, "Satellites Show Their Warlike Face," *New Scientist*, October 1, 1981, pp. 36–40.

15. "Expanded Ocean Surveillance Effort Set"; Hewlish, "Satellites Show Their Warlike Face."

16. "Expanded Ocean Surveillance Effort Set"; Hewlish, "Satellites Show Their Warlike Face"; For further details on PARCAE, see Maj. A. Andronov, "Komischeskaya Sistema Radioteknicheskoy Razvedki VMS SShA 'Vayt Klaud,'" *Zarubezhnoye Voyennoye Obozreniyo* [*Foreign Military Review*] 7 (1993): 57–60.

17. Paul Stares, *Space and National Security* (Washington, D.C.: Brookings Institution, 1987), p. 188; United States Military Communications-Electronics Board, USMCEB Publication No. 6, *Message Address Directory* (Washington, D.C.: U.S. Government Printing Office, July 25, 1986), p. 48; U.S. Army Intelligence and Security Command, "Analysis of Project TRUE BLUE (U)—INFORMATION DF," May 28, 1985; Dan Marcella, "Det. 1 Builds Upon Operational Missions," *Spokesman*, October 1995, p. 20. The last reference also notes that Detachment 1 also would be involved in a second joint Army-Navy SIGINT effort known as Project MARLOCK.

18. CINCPACFLT Instruction S3251.1D, *Classic Wizard Reporting System*, September 23, 1991.

19. "U.S. Defense and Intelligence Space Programs," *Aviation Week & Space Technology*,

March 19, 1990, p. 37; Edward H. Kolcum, "Second Titan 4 Carries Secret Surveillance Satellite Into Orbit," *Aviation Week & Space Technology*, June 18, 1990, p. 27; "Sky Peepers Learn Titan Secrets," *Space News*, January 13–26, 1992, p. 2; "Air Force Launches Second Titan 4 from Vandenberg," *Aviation Week & Space Technology*, November 18, 1991, p. 20; Bruce Van Voorst, "Billion Dollar Blowup," *Time*, August 16, 1993, p. 41.

20. R. Jeffrey Smith and John Mintz, "Pentagon Plans Multibillion-Dollar Sea Spy Satellite System," *Washington Post*, August 7, 1993, p. A5; John R. Cushman Jr., "Pentagon Found to Have Ignored Congress in Buying Spy Satellite," *New York Times*, September 24, 1993, p. A14; Theresa Hitchens and Neil Munro, "Pentagon Review Might Terminate Nuclear Spy Plans," *Defense News*, October 18–24, 1993, p. 3; Ralph Vartabedian, "TRW Loses Key Military Jobs to Archrival," *Los Angeles Times*, July 26, 1994, pp. A1, A6; John Mintz, "Martin Gets Big Contract for Satellites," *Washington Post*, July 26, 1994, pp. D1, D5.

21. Christopher Anson Pike, "CANYON, RHYOLITE and AQUACADE: U.S. Signals Intelligence Satellites in the 1970s," *Spaceflight* 37, no. 11 (November 1995): 381–382; Private information.

22. Philip Klass, "U.S. Monitoring Capability Impaired," *Aviation Week & Space Technology*, May 14, 1979, p. 18; Victor Marchetti in *Allies* (a Grand Bay film directed by Marian Wilkinson and produced by Sylvia Le Clezio, Sydney, 1983).

23. Robert Lindsey, *The Falcon and the Snowman: A True Story of Friendship and Espionage* (New York: Simon & Schuster, 1979), p. 111; Desmond Ball, *Pine Gap: Australia and the US Geostationary Signals Intelligence Satellite Program* (Sydney: Allen & Unwin Australia, 1988), pp. 14–15.

24. The first planned follow-on program to RHYOLITE, ARGUS was canceled in the late 1970s.

25. Richard Burt, "U.S. Plans New Way to Check Soviet Missile Tests," *New York Times*, June 29, 1979, p. A3; William Burrows, *Deep Black: Space Espionage and National Security* (New York: Random House, 1986), p. 192; Craig Covault and Joseph C. Anselmo, "Titan Explosion Destroys Secret 'Mercury' Sigint," *Aviation Week & Space Technology*, August 17, 1998, pp. 28–30.

26. Hussain, *The Future of Arms Control, Part 4*, p. 42; Ball, *Pine Gap*, pp. 14–15; "U.S. Spy Satellite Falls Short on Orbit and Expectations," *New York Times*, September 4, 1988, p. 22; Edward H. Kolcum, "Titan 34D Upper Stage Failure Sets Back Pentagon Intelligence Strategy," *Aviation Week & Space Technology*, September 12, 1988, p. 26; "Correction," *Aviation Week & Space Technology*, June 5, 1989, p. 32; "Last Titan 3 Rocket Lofts a Secret Military Satellite," *Washington Post*, September 5, 1989, p. A2; Edward H. Kolcum, "Last Titan 34D, Transtage Launches Classified Military Spacecraft," *Aviation Week & Space Technology*, September 11, 1989, p. 41.

27. Private information.

28. Dick Cheney, Joint Meritorious Unit Award, June 23, 1989.

29. James Gerstenzang, "Shuttle Lifts Off with Spy Cargo," *Los Angeles Times*, January 25, 1985, pp. 1, 11; "Final Launch Preparations Under Way for Signals Intelligence Satellite Mission," *Aviation Week & Space Technology*, November 6, 1989, p. 24.

30. Steve Weber, "Third Straight Titan 4 Launch Success Buoys Martin," *Space News*, September 5–11, 1994, pp. 3, 21; James T. McKenna, "Martin, USAF Speed Titan 4 Processing," *Aviation Week & Space Technology*, September 12, 1994, pp. 54–55; James T. McKenna, "Titan 4 Lofts Classified Payload," *Aviation Week & Space Technology*, May 22, 1995; "DOD Titan 4 Launched," *Aviation Week & Space Technology*, April 29, 1996,

p. 28; "Titan on Defense Mission," *Aviation Week & Space Technology*, May 6, 1996, p. 16; Craig Covault, "Eavesdropping Satellite Parked Over Crisis Zone," *Aviation Week & Space Technology*, May 18, 1998, pp. 30–31.

31. Naval Security Group Activity Denver, *Annual Command History Report for 1996*, March 5, 1997, pp. 3–4; R. Jeffrey Smith, "As Woolsey Struggles, CIA Suffers," *Washington Post*, May 10, 1994, pp. A1, A7.

32. Seymour Hersh, *"The Target Is Destroyed": What Really Happened to Flight 007 and What America Knew About It* (New York: Random House, 1986), p. 4; Burrows, *Deep Black*, p. 223; Philip J. Klass, "NSA 'Jumpseat' Program Winds Down As Soviets Shift to Newer Satellites," *Aviation Week & Space Technology*, April 2, 1990, pp. 46–47; Private information.

33. James T. McKenna, "Titan 4/Centaur Orbits Classified Payload," *Aviation Week & Space Technology*, May 9, 1994, p. 24; "Titan/Centaur Lofts Classified Payload," *Aviation Week & Space Technology*, July 17, 1995, p. 29; Tom Bowman and Scott Shane, "Battling High-Tech Warriors," *Baltimore Sun*, December 15, 1995, pp. 1, 15; "News breaks," *Aviation Week & Space Technology*, November 17, 1997, p. 27; Private information.

34. Naval Security Group Activity Denver, *Annual Command History Report for 1996*, p. 4.

35. Ball, *Pine Gap*, pp. 27–28; Private information; "Bad Aibling—INSCOM's Newest Field Site," *INSCOM Journal*, October 1994, p. 3; Air Intelligence Agency, Mission Directive 1542: 402nd Intelligence Squadron, August 1, 1997; Air Intelligence Agency, Mission Directive 1517: 451st Intelligence Squadron, March 14, 1997.

36. Desmond Ball, *A Suitable Piece of Real Estate: American Installations in Australia* (Sydney: Hale & Iremonger, 1980), p. 59.

37. Ball, *Pine Gap*, pp. 67, 80.

38. Don Greenlees, "Pine Gap Upgrade Aims to Enhance US Alliance," *The Australian*, July 22, 1996, p. 5.

39. Statement of Keith R. Hall, "U.S. National Security Programs and Issues," National Reconnaissance Office Presentation to the Senate Armed Services Committee Strategic Force Subcommittee, March 11, 1998, http://www.nro.odci.gov; Joseph C. Anselmo, "NRO Embraces SIGINT Smallsats," *Aviation Week & Space Technology*, September 29, 1997, p. 35.

40. ACC Regulation 23–1, Volume 15, "Headquarters Air Combat Command Organization and Functions, Summary of Changes," October 23, 1992, p. 4; Untitled memo, *Declassified Documents Reference System (DDRS)*, 1982–001583.

41. U.S. Congress, General Accounting Office, *New RC-135 Aircraft Engines Can Reduce Cost and Improve Performance* (Washington, D.C.: GAO, August 1992), p. 384; Martin Streetly, "U.S. Airborne ELINT Systems, Part 3, The Boeing RC-135 Family," *Jane's Defence Weekly*, March 16, 1985, pp. 460–465; Defense Airborne Reconnaissance Office, *Manned Airborne Reconnaissance*, 1995, p. 20; David A. Fulghum, "Large, Diverse Crews Make RC-135 a Heavy Hitter," *Aviation Week & Space Technology*, June 24, 1996, pp. 61–62; U.S. Congress, Senate Select Committee on Intelligence, Report 105–24, *Authorizing Appropriations for Fiscal Year 1998 for the Intelligence Activities of the United States Government and the Central Intelligence Agency Retirement and Disability System and Other Purposes* (Washington, D.C.: U.S. Government Printing Office, 1997), p. 9.

42. "Specialized Equipment Key to Rivet Joint," *Aviation Week & Space Technology*, June 24, 1996, p. 59; David A. Fulghum, "Rivet Joint Carves Out New Combat Roles," *Aviation Week & Space Technology*, June 24, 1996, pp. 52–53.

43. Fulghum, "Large, Diverse Crews Make RC-135 a Heavy Hitter," pp. 61–62; Karina Jennings, "RJ Adriatic Operations," *Spokesman*, December 1996, pp. 11–12; Air Combat Command, ACCMD 23–108, "Reconnaissance Squadrons," June 25, 1993; Karian Jennings, "Vice Chief of Staff Visits Mildenhall; Flies Aboard RC-135 Rivet Joint," *Spokesman*, June 1996, pp. 24–25.

44. Fulghum, "Large, Diverse Crews Make RC-135 a Heavy Hitter"; Michael Harris, "Rivet Joint Flies 700th Adriatic Mission," *Spokesman*, November 1995, P. 27; "RC-135 Takes to the Sky," *Spokesman*, April 1995, p. 7; Jennings, "RJ Adriatic Operations."

45. Defense Airborne Reconnaissance Office, *Manned Airborne Reconnaissance Division*, p. 19; Capt. Paul Issler, "97th IS Participates in Recce Expo '96," *Spokesman*, September 1996, p. 15; Private information. References to the COMBAT SENT missions were found in the documents catalog of the Office of Air Force History, Bolling AFB, D.C.

46. Streetly, "U.S. Airborne ELINT Systems, Part 3"; "6985th Deactivates," *Spokesman*, July 1992, p. 10.

47. Jeffrey Richelson, "Cold War Recon Planes Find New Missions," *Defense Week*, September 5, 1995, pp. 6–7; "Recon Wing Famed for Skill, Endurance," *Aviation Week & Space Technology*, August 14, 1997, p. 53; Bill Gertz, "N. Korea Fires New Cruise Missile," *Washington Times*, June 30, 1997, pp. A1, A8.

48. Defense Intelligence Agency, *Capabilities Handbook, Annex A, to the Department of Defense Plan for Intelligence Support to Operational Commanders*, March 1983, p. 220.

49. Defense Airborne Reconnaissance Office, *Manned Airborne Reconnaissance Division*, p. 5; Frank Scheiber, "Senior Scout Era Ends for 94th IS," *Spokesman*, October 1994, pp. 8–9.

50. Chris Pocock, "U-2: The Second Generation," *World Airpower Journal* 28 (Spring 1997): 50–99; Defense Intelligence Agency, *Capabilities Handbook, Annex A, to the Department of Defense Plan for Intelligence Support to Operational Commanders*, pp. 254, 262.

51. Pocock, "U-2: The Second Generation"; Jim Coulter, "Senior Spear Maintenance Facility," *Spokesman*, January 1992, p. 10.

52. Private information.

53. Fleet Air Reconnaissance Squadron One, *1994 VQ-1 Command History*, March 23, 1995, pp. 2, 5; *Fleet Air Reconnaissance Squadron One, Naval Air Station Whidbey Island, Washington, Command Composition and Organization*, 1996, p. 1; Maj. Gen. Kenneth R. Israel, Director, DARO, *DARO: Supporting the Warfighter, NMIA Defense Intelligence Status '96*, November 19, 1996, p. 20.

54. "Flexibility, Endurance Are Valued EP-3 Assets," *Aviation Week & Space Technology*, May 5, 1997, pp. 50, 52; Defense Airborne Reconnaissance Office, *Manned Airborne Reconnaissance Division*, p. 11; Fleet Air Reconnaissance Squadron One, Naval Air Station, Whidbey Island, Washington, *Command Composition and Organization*, p. 1; Dick Van der Art, *Aerial Espionage: Secret Intelligence Flights by East and West* (New York: Arco/Prentice Hall, 1986), pp. 53–54; Private information.

55. Fleet Air Reconnaissance Squadron One, Naval Air Station, Whidbey Island, Washington, *Command Composition and Organization*, p. 1; Van der Art, *Aerial Espionage*, pp. 53–54; Private information.

56. Fleet Air Reconnaissance Squadron One, *1993 Command History*, April 8, 1994, p. 4.

57. Fleet Air Reconnaissance Squadron One, Naval Air Station, Whidbey Island, Washington, *Command Composition and Organization*, p. 4.

58. VQ-2 Instruction 5400.1N, *FAIRECONRON Two Standard Organization and Regulations Manual*, January 9, 1997, pp. 1–2.

59. Private information; Fleet Air Reconnaissance Squadron One, *1991 Command History*, n.d., p. 1; "Flexibility, Endurance Are Valued EP-3 Assets."

60. "Flexibility, Endurance Are Valued EP–3 Assets"; Fleet Air Reconnaissance Squadron Two, *Fleet Air Reconnaissance Squadron Two History*, n.d.

61. Defense Airborne Reconnaissance Office, *Manned Airborne Reconnaissance Division*, p. 12; Fleet Air Reconnaissance Squadron Six, *CY-95 Battle "B" Submission*, January 17, 1996, p. 10; Martin Streetly, "ES-3A, US Navy's New Listening Post," *Jane's Defence Weekly*, October 21, 1989, p. 872; "U.S. Navy to Begin Tests on New ES-3A Aircraft," *Defense News*, February 24, 1992, p. 43; "Navy Develops Electronic Intelligence Aircraft for Carrier Battle Groups," *Aviation Week & Space Technology*, September 11, 1989, pp. 62–63; "Fact and Justification Sheet: Fleet Air Reconnaissance Squadron Six (VQ-6), NAS Cecil Field, Florida," 1993; Office of Chief of Naval Operations, OPNAV Instruction C3501.280, Subject: Required Operational Capability (ROC) and Project Operational Environment (POE) for Fleet Air Reconnaissance Squadrons Five/Six (VQ-5/6), February 10, 1992, Enc. 1–3; Stephen H. Hardy, "Reaping the RF Harvest," *Journal of Electronic Defense* (December 1992): 34ff; Fleet Air Reconnaissance Squadron Five, "Lockheed ES-3A Shadow," n.d.

62. Streetly, "ES-3A, US Navy's New Listening Post,"; "U.S. Navy to Begin Tests on New ES-3A Aircraft"; "Navy Develops Electronic Intelligence Aircraft for Carrier Battle Groups"; "Fact and Justification Sheet: Fleet Air Reconnaissance Squadron Six (VQ-6), NAS Cecil Field, Florida"; Office of Chief of Naval Operations, OPNAV Instruction C3501.280, Subject: Required Operational Capability (ROC) and Project Operational Environment (POE) for Fleet Air Reconnaissance Squadrons Five/Six (VQ-5/6) Enc. 1–3; Hardy, "Reaping the RF Harvest."

63. Fleet Air Reconnaissance Squadron Five, *VQ-5 Command History for 1994*, April 20, 1995, Enclosure (1).

64. Fleet Air Reconnaissance Squadron Six, *Command History for CY 1996*, March 4, 1997, p. 1.

65. Fleet Air Reconnaissance Squadron Six, *Command History for CY 1994*, March 3, 1995, p. 2.

66. Fleet Air Reconnaissance Squadron Six, *CY-95 Battle "E" Submission*, January 17, 1996, p. 13; Fleet Air Reconnaissance Squadron Six, *Command History for CY-1995*, February 12, 1996, pp. 3–4; Robert Wall, "Facing Upgrade Costs, U.S. Navy Retires ES-3s," *Aviation Week & Space Technology*, June 8, 1998, pp. 40–41.

67. Defense Airborne Reconnaissance Office, *Manned Airborne Reconnaissance Division*, p. 18; Israel, *DARO:—Supporting the Warfighter*, p. 20; Private information; "News in Brief," *Jane's Defence Weekly*, July 22, 1989, p. 110; James W. Rawles, "Guardrail Common Sensor Comes on Line," *Defense Electronics*, October 1990, pp. 33–41.

68. Dennis Buley, *The US Army's Fleet of Special Electronic Mission Aircraft (SEMA)*, Version of March 14, 1997, http://www.jncpcs.com/dbuley/; Col. Ronald W. Wilson, "Eyes in the Sky: Aerial Systems," *Military Intelligence*, (July-September 1996): 16–18; William H. Arkin, Joshua M. Handler, Julia A. Morrissey, and Jacquelyn M. Walsh, *Encyclopedia of the U.S. Military* (New York: Harper & Row, 1990), p. 183.

69. Defense Airborne Reconnaissance Office, *Manned Airborne Reconnaissance Division*, p. 18; Israel, *DARO: Supporting the Warfighter—NMIA Defense Intelligence Status '96*, p. 20;

Wilson, "Eyes in the Sky"; Stacey Evers, "US Army Deploys Third Patrol Aircraft to Korea," *Jane's Defence Weekly*, August 20, 1987, p. 6; David A. Fulghum, "Army Spy Aircraft Watch North Korea," *Aviation Week & Space Technology*, November 24, 1997, pp. 58–59; David A. Fulghum, "Multisensor Observations Key to Army's RC-7," *Aviation Week & Space Technology*, November 24, 1997, pp. 60–61.

70. Robert Wall, "U.S. Army Considers Single Intelligence Aircraft," *Aviation Week & Space Technology*, February 23, 1998, pp. 102–103.

71. Susan Dowdee, "Farewell to the Last Outpost of Freedom," *INSCOM Journal*, April 1992, pp. 10–11; "6917th Bids San Vito Arrivederci," *Spokesman*, July 1993, pp. 14–15; T. K. Gilmore, "The 701st MI Brigade and Field Station Augsburg's Discontinuance and Farewell Ceremony," *INSCOM Journal*, March 1993, pp. 8–9.

72. Richard J. Fisher, "GRSOC," *INSCOM Journal*, July-August 1996, pp. 35–36; NAVSECGRU Inst. 5450.6A, Mission, Functions and Tasks of Naval Security Group Activity (NAVSECGRUACT) Medina, Texas, April 8, 1996; NAVSECGRU Inst. 5450.66, Mission, Functions and Tasks of Naval Security Group Activity (NAVSECGRUACT) Fort Gordon, Georgia, April 26, 1996; Verrell Jones, "Helping Those in Need," *Spokesman*, March 1997, p. 22; Staff Directory, HQ, US Army Signal Center and Fort Gordon, January 1, 1996; Jim Katzman, "Jaeger Returns to SIGINT Roots," *Spokesman*, July 1995, p. 18; Gabriel Marshall, "Medina Offers Multiservice Intelligence," *Spokesman*, July 1995, p. 15.

73. Private information.

74. Duncan Campbell, *The Unsinkable Aircraft Carrier: American Military Power in Britain* (London: Michael Joseph, 1984), p. 155; "British MP Accuses U.S. of Electronic Spying," *New Scientist*, August 5, 1976, p. 268; Department of the Army, Field Manual 34–40–12, *Morse Code Intercept Operations*, August 26, 1991, p. 4-4; "Northern Lights of Freedom," *Insight*, Spring 1991, pp. 16–18; Private information.

75. Hersh, *"The Target Is Destroyed,"* p. 47; "Company E Marine Support Batallion," http://www.misawa.af.mil/orgs/coe/history.htm.

76. Hersh, *"The Target Is Destroyed,"* p. 49; U.S. Congress, House Committee on Appropriations, *Military Construction Appropriations for 1981, Part 2* (Washington, D.C.: U.S. Government Printing Office, 1980), p. 875; David Morison, "Sites Unseen," *National Journal*, June 4, 1988, pp. 1468–1472; Duncan Campbell and Linda Melvern, "America's Big Ear on Europe," *New Statesman*, July 18, 1980, pp. 10–14; NAVSECGRU Instruction 5450.63, *Mission, Functions and Tasks of Naval Security Group Activity (NAVSECGRUACT) Bad Aibling, Germany*, October 25, 1995.

77. Private information.

78. Private information; Brian Toohey and Marian Wilkinson, *The Book of Leaks: Exposés in Defence of the Public's Right to Know* (North Ryde, Australia: Angus & Robertson, 1987), p. 135.

79. U.S. Army Field Station Korea, *Fiscal Year 1986, Annual Historical Report*, 1987, p. 2; Private information; History Office, U.S. Army Intelligence and Security Command, *Annual Historical Review: U.S. Army Intelligence and Security Command, Fiscal Year 1988* (Arlington, Va.: INSCOM, 1989), p. 105.

80. Private information; History Office, U.S. Army Intelligence and Security Command, *Annual Historical Review . . . Fiscal Year 1988*, p. 105; NAVSECGRU Inst. 5450.58B, Mission, Functions and Tasks of Naval Security Group Activity (NAVSECGRUACT) Pensacola, Florida, October 15, 1996.

81. Private information; U.S. Congress, House Committee on Appropriations, *Military Construction Appropriations for 1987, Part 2* (Washington, D.C.: U.S. Government Printing Office, 1986), p. 682.

82. "New Commander Takes Over Det. 4, 544th IG," *Spokesman*, March 1997, p. 27; 554th Intelligence Group, untitled, undated briefing; James Bamford, *The Puzzle Palace: A Report on NSA, America's Most Secret Agency* (Boston: Houghton-Mifflin, 1982), pp. 172–173; Nicky Hager, *Secret Power: New Zealand's Role in the International Spy Network* (Nelson, N.Z.: Craig Potton, 1996), p. 166; Air Intelligence Agency, *Air Intelligence Agency Almanac*, August 1997, pp. 30–32; U.S. Naval Security Group Activity Sabana Seca, *U.S. Naval Security Group Activity, Sabana Seca, Puerto Rico Command History for 1996*, February 28, 1997, p. 5; Naval Security Group Detachment Sugar Grove, *Naval Security Group Detachment, Sugar Grove History for 1991*, February 26, 1992; Private information.

83. NSG Inst. C3270.2, Bullseye Concept of Operations (U), June 30, 1989; NAVSEC-GRU Inst. C5450.27D, Mission, Functions, and Tasks of U.S. Naval Security Group Activity (NAVSECGRUACT) Hanza, Japan, September 5, 1995; Private information.

84. Private information.

85. Private information; U.S. Congress, House Committee on Appropriations, *Military Construction Appropriations for 1987, Part 2* (Washington, D.C.: U.S. Government Printing Office, 1986), p. 463.

86. Tom Bowman and Scott Shane, "Espionage from the Front Lines," *Baltimore Sun*, December 8, 1995, pp. 1A, 20A–21A.

87. Laurence Stern, "U.S. Tapped Top Russians' Car Phones," *Washington Post*, December 5, 1973, pp. A1, A16; Ernest Volkman, "U.S. Spies Lend an Ear to Soviets," *Newsday*, July 12, 1977, p. 7.

88. Stern, "U.S. Tapped Top Russians' Car Phones"; Volkman, "U.S. Spies Lend an Ear to Soviets"; Bill Gertz, "CIA Upset Because Perle Detailed Eavesdropping," *Washington Times*, April 15, 1987, p. 2A; Michael Frost and Michel Gratton, *Spyworld: Inside the Canadian and American Intelligence Establishments* (Toronto: Doubleday Canada, 1994), p. 60.

89. Jack Anderson, "CIA Eavesdrops on Kremlin Chiefs," *Washington Post*, September 16, 1971, p. F7.

90. Seymour Hersh, "The Wild East," *The Atlantic Monthly*, June 1994, pp. 61–86.

91. Howard Kurtz, "Pollard: Top Israelis Backed Spy Ring," *Washington Post*, February 28, 1987, p. A8.

92. Arthur Gavshon and Desmond Rice, *The Sinking of the Belgrano* (London: Secker & Warburg, 1984), p. 205 n. 5; Bownman and Shane, "Espionage from the Front Lines."

93. Trevor Armbrister, *A Matter of Accountability* (New York: Coward, McCann, 1970), p. 87; U.S. Congress, House Committee on Armed Services, *Inquiry into the U.S.S. Pueblo and EC-121 Incidents* (Washington, D.C.: U.S. Government Printing Office, 1969), pp. 1632, 1634; James Ennes, *Assault on the Liberty* (New York: Random House, 1980); Paul Backus, "ESM and SIGINT Problems at the Interface," *Journal of Electronic Defense* (July-August 1981): 23ff.

94. Richard Halloran, "2 U.S. Ships Enter Soviet Waters Off Crimea to Gather Intelligence," *New York Times*, March 19, 1986, pp. A1, A11; George C. Wilson, "Soviet Ships Shadowed U.S. Vessels' Transit," *Washington Post*, March 20, 1986, p. A33; Captain Richard Sharpe, ed., *Jane's Fighting Ships 1994–95* (Surrey, U.K.: Jane's Information Group Limited, 1994), p. 792.

95. Halloran, "2 U.S. Ships Enter Soviet Waters Off Crimea to Gather Intelligence"; Sharpe, *Jane's Fighting Ships 1994–95*, p. 768.

96. George C. Wilson, "U.S. Detects Slowdown in Shipments of Weapons to El Salvador," *Washington Post*, April 29, 1983, p. A13.

97. Richard Burt, "Technology Is Essential to Arms Verification," *New York Times*, August 14, 1979, pp. C1, C2; Murray Sayle, "KE 007: A Conspiracy of Circumstance," *New York Review of Books*, April 25, 1985, pp. 44–54.

98. Private information.

99. Robert Holzer and Neil Munro, "Navy Eyes Eavesdropping System," *Defense News*, November 25, 1991, p. 12.

100. Christopher Drew, Michael L. Millenson, and Robert Becker, "A Risky Game of Cloak-and-Dagger Under the Sea," *Chicago Tribune*, January 7, 1991, pp. 1, 8–9.

101. Seymour Hersh, "Submarines of U.S. Stage Spy Missions Inside Soviet Waters," *New York Times*, May 25, 1975, pp. 1, 42.

102. Seymour Hersh, "A False Navy Report Alleged in Sub Crash," *New York Times*, July 6, 1975, pp. 1, 26.

103. Hersh, "Submarines of U.S. Stage Spy Missions Inside Soviet Waters."

104. Ibid.

105. Ibid.

106. *Jane's Fighting Ships, 1983–1984*, p. 639.

107. Sharpe, *Jane's Fighting Ships 1994–95*, p. 774.

108. Private information.

109. "Pentagon Describes Damage to Sub After Arctic Collision," *New York Times*, February 28, 1992, p. A10; John H. Cushman Jr., "Two Subs Collide off Russian Port," *New York Times*, February 19, 1992, p. A6; Bill Gertz, "Russian Sub's Sail Damaged in Collision," *Washington Times*, February 27, 1992, p. A4; John Lancaster, "U.S., Russian Subs Collide in Arctic," *Washington Post*, February 19, 1992, pp. A1, A24.

110. Bill Gertz, "Clinton Apologizes for Sub Collision," *Washington Times*, April 5, 1993, p. A7; Sharpe, *Jane's Fighting Ships 1994–95*, p. 773.

111. "Moscow Files Complaint with U.S. Over Sub Incident," *Washington Post*, May 5, 1998, p. A16.

112. "Second U.S. Sub Monitors Iran's Fleet," *Washington Times*, February 12, 1993, p. A7; Sharpe, *Jane's Fighting Ships 1994–95*, p. 774; Richard J. Newman, "Breaking the Surface," *U.S. News & World Report*, April 6, 1998, pp. 28–42.

9

MEASUREMENT AND SIGNATURE INTELLIGENCE

Imagery and signals intelligence can trace their identities as collection disciplines back to at least the early twentieth century. The use of the term "measurement and signature intelligence" (MASINT) as a category encompassing a number of distinct collection activities is far more recent. The U.S. intelligence community first classified MASINT as a formal intelligence discipline in 1986.[1]

Measurement and signature intelligence is officially defined as:

> technically derived intelligence (excluding traditional imagery and signal intelligence) that, when collected, processed, and analyzed, results in intelligence that locates, tracks, identifies, or describes the signatures (distinctive characteristics) of fixed or dynamic target sources.[2]

Given the above definition, MASINT includes *all* remote technical collection, other than SIGINT and traditional imagery intelligence (which includes visible-light, radar, and infrared—but not multispectral, hyperspectral, or ultraspectral—imagery). MASINT's scope and diversity is indicated by the identification of its various components:

- radar (line of sight, bistatic, over-the-horizon)
- radio frequency (wideband electromagnetic pulse, unintentional radiation)
- geophysical (acoustic, seismic, magnetic)
- nuclear radiation (X-ray, gamma ray, neutron)
- materials (effluents, particulates, debris)
- electro-optical and infrared
- multi-, hyper-, and ultra-spectral imagery[3]

It should not be surprising that, given the diversity of the phenomena being monitored and the means employed to monitor them, MASINT can be employed in pursuit of a large number of missions—both strategic and tactical. Thus, MASINT mission areas include support to military operations, defense acquisition and force modernization, arms control and treaty monitoring, proliferation, counterterrorism, environmental intelligence, and counternarcotics. A more detailed breakdown is given in Table 9.1.

TABLE 9.1   MASINT Mission Areas

Support to Military Operations
   Precision Guided Munitions Targeting
   Intelligence Preparation of the Battlefield
   Naval and Ground Combat
   Space Control
   Search and Rescue
   Non-Cooperative Target Identification
   Mission Planning
   Indications and Warning
   Tactical Warning/Attack Assessment
   Theater Missile Defense
   Scud Hunting
   Air Defense
   Strike Warfare
   Peacekeeping
Defense Acquistion/Force Modernization
   Signatures
   Threat Defintion
   Countermeasures
Arms Control/Treaty Monitoring
   Missile
   Nuclear
   Chemical and Biological
Proliferation
   Missile
   Nuclear
   Chemical and Biological
   Advanced Conventional Weapons
Environment
   Natural Disasters
   Pollution
   Phenomena
Counterdrugs
   Production
   Transport
   Storage

SOURCE: John L. Morris, *MASINT: Progress and Impact, Brief to NMIA*, November 1996 (Slide 6).

Some MASINT missions are well known, even if not thought of in terms of MASINT collection—for example, the detection of acoustic signals from submarines that allows their tracking and identification, the collection and analysis of seismic signals from nuclear detonations, and the use of radars to detect and monitor Russian and Chinese missile tests.

Other, particularly tactical applications, are less appreciated. Thus, the collection of electro-optical spectral signatures from an aircraft's exhaust, the determination of the aircraft's radar cross section, and the gathering of its acoustic signatures can be used to collect varied data that would be useful in combat—range, speed, acceleration, climb rate, stability, turn radius, tactics, and proficiency. Such data can be loaded into an air defense system to aid in targeting such aircraft.[4]

It should be noted that MASINT's components lack the commonality of those of imagery or SIGINT. Visible-light, infrared, and radar imagery collection all result in an image from which intelligence is then extracted. Similarly, SIGINT, in whatever form, involves the interception of a transmitted electronic signal whose content is then mined for its intelligence value. There is no similar commonality between multispectral imagery and acoustic intelligence, or between the employment of radars for monitoring foreign missiles and the detection of X-rays from nuclear detonations. In many ways MASINT is more of a description of the product, stemming from a particular type of analysis of the data produced by a variety of collection activities than a coherent collection activity itself. In addition, measurement of objects and the identification of signatures is also a large portion of the work done by those interpreting and analyzing traditional imagery and signals intelligence data. Such observations, although important with respect to issues of the scope and organization of the MASINT effort, can, to a large extent, be put aside in surveying the collection systems that produce the data that is turned into measurement and signature intelligence.[5]

MASINT collections systems are operated in space, on aircraft, at ground stations, on surface ships, and below the oceans.

SPACE COLLECTION

At least four operational U.S. satellite systems carry MASINT sensors. Defense Support Program (DSP) satellites carry non-imaging infrared and nuclear detonation (NUDET) detection sensors, and Global Positioning System navigation satellites also carry NUDET detection sensors. The Defense Meteorological Satellite Program (DMSP) spacecraft have also been equipped with nuclear detection sensors. A non-imaging infrared sensor, code-named HERITAGE and with different characteristics than the one on DSP, has been carried on one, or more, type of elliptically orbiting satellite. In addition, research and development satellite programs designated COBRA BRASS and FORTE have also provided MASINT data.

The principal mission of the Defense Support Program satellites is to detect the launches of ICBMs and SLBMs using an infrared sensor to monitor the missile's plume. In the 1970s it was observed that DSP satellites could also detect the launches of intermediate-range ballistic missiles such as Scuds. Those missiles might be launched as part of a research and development program, a military exercise, or during an actual military conflict. DSP data thus provides information on the level of such activities and, in the case of war, the specific targets. In addition, analysis of DSP infrared data allows determination of what type of fuel is being burned and identification of the spectral signatures associated with different missile systems. DSP satellites have also provided intelligence on terrestrial events that generate sufficient infrared radiation—such as massive explosions of ammunition dumps, certain industrial processes, and aircraft explosions and crashes.[6]

The DSP satellites have also provided intelligence on foreign nuclear activity. The infrared sensor has detected the heat generated by surface nuclear tests. In addition, DSP satellites have also carried several nuclear detonation sensors. The satellites Advanced RADEC I sensor package consists of bhangmeters, atmospheric fluorescence detectors, and an X-ray locator system. The bhangmeters are optical sensors whose mission is to detect the bright flash that would result from the fireball of a nuclear explosion. The air fluorescence sensor would record the bright pulse of visible (fluorescence) radiation resulting from the interaction of thermal X-rays from a high-altitude or exoatmospheric nuclear explosion with the low-density air in the upper portions of the Earth's atmosphere. The X-ray locator employs several detectors to measure the direction and arrival time of X-rays from the near-Earth exoatmospheric nuclear detonations. The information provided by the most recent version of the locator (the Advanced Atmospheric Burst Locator—AABL) allows estimates of yield, location, height of burst, frequency of detonations, and timing. The estimates have a smaller range of uncertainty than the estimates produced by previous sensors, and the improved sensors are able to detect events below the threshold reached by earlier versions.[7]

There have been several generations of DSP satellites since the initial launch in November 1970. The present version, designated DSP-1, is a 33-foot-long, 10-foot-diameter spacecraft, weighing approximately 5,300 pounds. Detection is achieved by a 12-foot-long Schmidt telescope that is 39 inches in diameter. The telescope has a two-dimensional array of lead sulfide detectors at its focus to sense energy emitted by ballistic missile exhausts during the powered stages of their flights.[8]

DSP satellites are placed into geosyncrhonous orbit from Cape Canaveral, Florida. The three-satellite constellation, with two spares, that became standard in the late 1970s and through the 1980s has become a four-satellite constellation—with Atlantic, European, Indian Ocean, and Pacific slots. The ground segment includes three dedicated ground stations, a main operating base for six Mobile Ground Terminals at Fort Greeley, Colorado, and a DSP multipurpose facility at

Lowry Air Force Base, Colorado. The dedicated ground stations include the CONUS Ground Station at Buckley Air National Guard Base, Colorado; the Overseas Ground Station (also known as the Joint Defense Facility–Nurrungar) at Woomera Air Station, Australia; and the European Ground Station at Kapuan, Germany.[9]

The CONUS Ground Station is operated by the 2d Space Warning Squadron and receives data from Nurrungar as well as the other DSP satellites—either directly or via relay. Buckley also hosts Detachment 45 of the Air Force Technical Applications Center (AFTAC). AFTAC personnel stationed at Buckley are responsible for processing any nuclear detonation data provided by the nuclear detonation sensors aboard DSP spacecraft. The Nurrungar site is operated by the 5th Space Warning Squadron of the 821st Space Group of the U.S. Space Command. Data from Nurrungar to the United States are transmitted via both submarine cable and the Defense Satellite Communications System (DSCS) satellite stationed over the Western Pacific.[10]

The Nuclear Detonation (NUDET) Detection System (NDS) carried on board NAVSTAR Global Positioning System (GPS) satellites was developed to provide trans- and post-attack nuclear detonation monitoring. The primary function of the GPS satellites is to provide accurate locational data for targeting and navigational purposes; the NDS represents a major secondary function. The GPS satellites constellation consists of twenty-one operational satellites plus three active spares in near-circular 11,000-mile orbits with an inclination of 55 degrees. The satellites are deployed in six planes of four satellites each. This arrangement guarantees that at least four to six satellites are in view at all times from any point on or near the Earth.[11] Figure 9.1 shows the GPS constellation.

The NDS packages include X-ray and optical sensors, Bhangmeters, EMP sensors, and a data-processing capability that can detect a nuclear weapons detonation "anywhere in the world at any time and get its location down to less than [100 meters]." Data is reported on a real-time basis either directly to ground stations located at Diego Garcia; Kwajelein Atoll; Ascension Island; or Kaena Point, Hawaii.[12] Figure 9.2 shows a sample alert report for atmospheric tests detected by satellites.

Future GPS satellites—twenty-one Block IIR and thirty-three Block IIF—will continue to carry Bhangmeters, X-ray detectors, and dosimeters. Some or all of the IIF satellites will carry the NDS Augmentation Package (NAP) containing enhanced bhangmeters and signal processing techniques to achieve lower detection thresholds needed to support Comprehensive Test Ban Treaty monitoring requirements.[13]

DMSP satellites have hosted a variety of AFTAC sensors over the last several decades. These sensors have included the SSB Gamma Tracker (to track fallout and nuclear debris in the atmosphere), the SSB Gamma X-Ray Detector, the SSB/A X-Ray Spectrometer (for the detection of X-rays and gamma rays from bomb debris), as well as several that could monitor electromagnetic radiation.[14] The DMSP program will be merged with NOAA's civilian polar-orbiting weather satellite program. Whether the new satellites will possess any NUDET detection capability remains to be seen.

FIGURE 9.1   The NAVSTAR GPS Operational Constellation

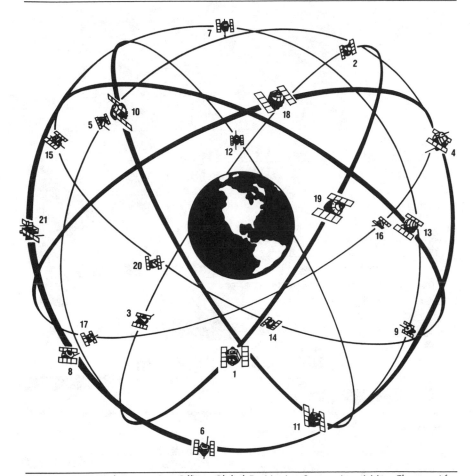

SOURCE: General Accounting Office, *Global Positioning System Acquisition Changes After Challenger's Accident* (Washington, D.C.: GAO, 1987), p. 12.

Since the mid-1970s one or both of the U.S. satellite systems in a "Molniya" orbit—the JUMPSEAT signals intelligence or Satellite Data System relay satellites—have carried infrared sensors as part of the HERITAGE program. The sensors were designed to detect infrared emissions in a narrower time frame than those of DSP—to allow detection of any short-burning anti-ballistic missiles that the Soviet Union might develop. They have thus provided additional non-imaging infrared intelligence to the intelligence community.[15]

Central MASINT Office multispectral and infrared experimental sensors, carried on NRO systems, have provided MASINT data, including data relevant

FIGURE 9.2   Sample Alert Report Text: Atmospheric

```
30                                      CENR 55-5    Attachment 12    28 May 1992


        Figure A12-1.  (U) Sample Alert Report Text:  Atmospheric
                       (This figure is classified SECRET)

SUBJECT:  ALERT _____  (U)

1.  (S) DATA RECORDED BY THE US ATOMIC ENERGY DETECTION SYSTEM (USAEDS) INDICATE AN ATMOSPHERIC NUCLEAR

EXPLOSION WITH A YIELD OF ABOUT _____ ( ____ ) KT

OCCURRED AT _____  _____

( ____ ) DEGREES _____ ( ____ ) MINUTES NORTH,

_____ ( ____ ) DEGREES

_____ ( ____ ) MINUTES EAST, AT _____ COLON

_____ ( _____ ) GMT ON _____ ( _____ ) _____ 19 ____ .

2.  (S) THE FOLLOWING SATELLITES/LOOK ANGLES (IN DEGREES) RECORDED THE EVENT:

_____/_____

_____/_____

_____/_____

3.  (S) THE LOCATION WAS OBTAINED FROM COMBINED INPUTS FRO███████████████████

4.  (S) SEISMIC DATA ARE/ARE NOT AVAILABLE FROM THIS EVENT.

5.  (S) THE PRELIMINARY ESTIMATE OF YIELD OF ABOUT _____ ( ____ ) KT, WITH AN UNCERTAINTY RANGE██

OF _____ ( ____ ) TO _____ ( ____ ) KT, IS BASED ON██████████A YIELD ESTIMATE OF

_____ ( ____ ) KT WAS OBTAINED FRO███████████████

6.  (S)  THE PRELIMINARY ESTIMATE OF HEIGHT OF BURST IS _____ ( _____ ) KILOMETERS.

7.  (S)  THE EARLIEST THAT████████████████████████████████████

_____ ( _____ ) _____ 19 ___.██████████

█████████████

8.  (U)  THE INFORMATION CONTAINED IN THIS DOCUMENT WILL BE SAFEGUARDED AS DIRECTED BY NATIONAL SECURITY DECISION

MEMORANDUM NO. 50.

DECL OADR.      OPR: AFTAC/DOB    INITIALS: _____ DATE: _____
=============================================================================
```

.b.(1)

SOURCE: AFTAC Regulation 55-5, "Alert Procedures," May 28, 1992.

to missile proliferation activities. The experiments are designated COBRA BRASS.[16]

AIRBORNE COLLECTION

Airborne MASINT systems are flown on Air Force and Navy aircraft that also serve as platforms for imagery and/or SIGINT sensors—including the RC-135S COBRA BALL, the P-3C ORION, and the P-3C REEF POINT. In addition, a number of aircraft serve as platforms for sensors that would detect evidence of nuclear, chemical, or biological warfare activities.

In addition to the Advanced Telemetry System discussed in Chapter 8, COBRA BALL aircraft carry two Medium-Wave Infrared Arrays (MIRA), a Real-Time Optical System (ROTS)—which records visible light images using a combination of eight acquisition and five tracking sensors—and a Large Aperture Tracking System (LATS), which has a 12-inch focal length telescope with finer resolution for small targets picked up by the LATS. Each MIRA system is made up of six infrared cameras, and each camera's field of view marginally overlaps those on either side to produce a panoramic picture of slightly less than 180 degrees. The arrays have been modified to permit detection of cooler targets. A COBRA BALL can locate a missile launch site within 100 yards, track missile flight at greater than 250 miles, and determine engine burnout and predict impact point within seconds.[17]

MASINT analysis of the data returned by COBRA BALL's infrared and optical sensors provides intelligence in a variety of areas. Analysis of the colors that appear around a reentry vehicle (RV) when heated by the friction of the Earth's atmosphere can reveal the materials that the RV is composed of and whether it has a hardened titanium warhead for penetrating deep targets. In addition, plotting the warheads flight path can indicate its speed and whether it can maneuver to avoid defensive missiles. Stability and accuracy of the RV can be estimated by calculating the speed-to-rotation ratio. Tracking the debris that surrounds a reentry vehicle allows analysts to extrapolate the quality of workmanship. Missiles manufactured during the Soviet era were "sloppy and dirty" and the warheads operated with "lots of debris."[18]

Prior to its extensive use for overland imagery purposes, the P-3C ORION, named after the Greek god of the hunt, was primarily an antisubmarine warfare aircraft. It is the third generation of the P-3 antisubmarine warfare aircraft that succeeded the Neptune P2V in the late 1950s. In its present configuration, the P-3C stands 33.7 feet high. It is 117 feet long and has a 99.7-foot wingspan. Its maximum speed is 473 miles an hour, and it has a service ceiling of 28,300 feet. Its endurance capability—sixteen hours—and maximum speed give it a range of 4,760 nautical miles. It can search up to 95,000 square nautical miles in an hour.[19]

The P-3C can carry up to eighty-four sonobuoys. Forty-eight of them are preset and loaded in external launch chutes prior to takeoff. The remaining thirty-six are carried internally and their operating channels can be chosen during the mission. For many of the sonobuoys, it is possible to select the operating depth and length of transmission time. The acoustic operators on the P-3C can monitor up to sixteen sonobuoys simultaneously. A sonar-type recorder stores all acoustic data for reference to reconstruct the missions in detail.[20]

In addition to the sonobuoys, there are several nonacoustic detection systems on the P-3C. Its Magnetic Anomaly Detector (MAD) is used in concert with the Submarine Anomaly Detector to determine whether known submarine magnetic profiles are present. To get a good MAD reading, the plane must fly 200 to 300 feet above the water. An airborne search radar, designated AN/APS-115, is used to detect radar returns from ships or submarines on the surface and pick out periscopes at the waterline.[21]

Five P-3C aircraft were specifically configured for the collection, analysis, and recording of high-quality acoustic data on Soviet submarines, sonars, and underwater communications equipment. These aircraft, known by the code name BEAR-TRAP, have a 4,000-nautical mile range, an operational altitude of 200 to 10,000 feet, and an endurance capability of twelve hours. Enhancements of BEARTRAP antisubmarine warfare capabilities during fiscal year 1994 focused on the littoral water/regional conflict environment.[22]

Another version of the P-3C, until recently designated REEF POINT, is a four-engine turboprop that can fly at 28,000 feet at 250 knots for up to twelve hours (but is not refuelable in flight). It is described as being engaged in "all-weather, worldwide multisensor scientific and technical collection of naval and littoral targets," in support of joint task force, fleet, and maritime operations. In addition to photographic, infrared, COMINT and ELINT sensors, it carries acoustic and nuclear intelligence sensors.[23]

The four REEF POINT aircraft are evenly split between Patrol Squadron Special Projects Unit One (VPU-1), whose home port is Brunswick, Maine, and Patrol Squadron Special Projects Unit Two (VPU-2), headquartered at Barbers Point, Hawaii. VPU-1 focuses on the Atlantic and Mediterranean, and VPU-2, which has about 200 personnel assigned to it, operates extensively throughout the Pacific and Indian Ocean theaters.[24]

At one time, aerial sampling was extensively employed to detect the atomic particles that would be emitted by an above-ground nuclear explosion or that might be "vented" by an underground test. Aircraft employed in aerial sampling operations included the U-2, the P-3, the WC-135, and the B-52. The WC-135s were equipped with the STARCAST camera system, designed to photograph high-speed objects in support of strategic research and development programs. Aerial sampling operations were conducted over the United States and the Southern Hemisphere. One version of the C-130, the HC-130, was outfitted with a sea water sampler for sorties flown against possible foreign underwater nuclear tests.[25]

Aircraft from the 55th Weather Reconnaissance Squadron (WRS) at McClellan Air Force Base, which operated six WC-135s, were used to monitor fallout from the 1986 Chernobyl accident, designated Special Event 86-05. The planes, which were deployed to RAF Mildenhall, flew missions over Germany, Switzerland, Italy, and the Mediterranean. A May 21, 1992, Chinese nuclear test at Lop Nor produced a large cloud of radioactive gas that, by early June, had passed over the Sea of Japan. A WC-135 flew the cloud to collect nuclear particles. A WC-135 was probably also used to monitor the effects of a plutonium leak from a nuclear plant in Siberia in July 1993.[26]

In recent years, the aerial sampling mission has virtually faded into oblivion. The C-130 sampling mission ended in 1990, and B-52 debris collection equipment was deactivated in 1993. Several WC-135s were transferred to Open Skies monitoring activities. In October 1993, the 55th WRS was deactivated. U-2 aircraft no longer carry aerial sampling equipment. At one point, all that remained was a single WC-135 stationed at Offutt Air Force Base, Nebraska. That plane was deployed to Diego Garcia to conduct aerial sampling missions (code-named CONSTANT PHOENIX) following the May 1998 Indian detonation of several nuclear devices. In the fall of 1998 whether that plane would remain operational was a subject of debate within the Clinton administration and of concern to several senators.[27]

Future airborne platforms may carry a variety of MASINT systems designed to detect chemical or biological warfare activities. One such system, developed by Los Alamos National Laboratory, is a laser-based device capable of detecting clouds of biological warfare agents at distances of nearly 20 miles. The system, which was tested in 1996, can scan up to 1 million acres per hour using laser pulses. Airborne contaminants reflect some of the laser light, which is picked up by a small telescope and focused on a sensitive light detector and computer analyzed.[28]

Lawrence Livermore National Laboratory has been involved in development of the Compact Airborne Multispectral Imager to provide spatial and spectral data on facilities suspected of being involved in chemical warfare activities. It has also worked on development of a more sensitive infrared spectrometer for airborne remote sensing of trace chemicals in the atmosphere, particularly those related to nuclear weapons production.[29]

In fall 1996, the Air Force's KC-135E Argus electro-optical test bed carried two lidar (light detection and ranging) systems—the Nonproliferation Airborne Lidar Experiment and the Lidar Airborne Remote Sensing (LARS)—designed to detect chemical warfare agents at ranges up to 62 miles.[30]

GROUND COLLECTION SYSTEMS

Intelligence collection systems operated from the ground that fall in the MASINT category focus on a variety of different targets and employ a significant variety of sensor systems. In addition, MASINT ground sensors include those employed for strategic purposes as well as for tactical purposes. Key MASINT ground collection systems include the radars operated by the Air Force Space Command for missile detection and tracking as well as the seismic stations operated by the Air Force Technical Applications Center to detect nuclear detonations. Whereas those systems produce strategic intelligence, the U.S. Army Intelligence and Security Command has, for a number of years, operated a number of tactical MASINT collection systems.

The radars operated by the Air Force Space Command and Air Intelligence Agency for missile detection and tracking include a mechanical radar at Diyarbakir, Turkey; the COBRA DANE phased array radar on Shemya, Alaska; the Norwegian-based CREEK CHART radar, and the COBRA SHOE radar, at a classified location.[31]

The primary purpose of the COBRA DANE radar, is "to acquire precise radar metric and signature data on developing [Russian] ballistic missile weapon systems for weapon system characteristics determination. The [Russian] developmental test to Kamchatka and the Pacific Ocean provide[s] the United States with the primary source for collection of these data early in the [Russian] developmental programs."[32]

Its corollary mission, missile warning, makes it part of the Integrated Tactical Warning and Attack Assessment (ITW/AA) network. COBRA DANE provides warning of all "Earth-impacting objects," including ballistic missiles targeted on the United States. Its secondary mission is space object tracking and identification.[33]

The COBRA DANE system consists of an AN/FPS-108 radar facility that measures 87 by 107 feet at its base; rises approximately six stories, or 100 feet, in height; and includes an attached, one-story, 87-square-foot Precision Measurement Equipment Laboratory (PMEL). This facility overlooks the Bering Sea from a 230-foot-high bluff in the northwestern section of Shemya.[34]

The most important characteristic of COBRA DANE is that it is a phased-array radar. To an observer depending only on his eyes or using binoculars, a phased-array radar is simply a dormant structure, sort of an electronic pyramid. This is in sharp contrast to the older, more traditional radar dish "sweeping its beam of microwave radiation along the horizon in search of distant objects." Rather COBRA DANE consists of 15,360 radiating elements that occupy 95 feet in diameter on the radar's face. Each element emits a signal that travels in all directions. When the signals are emitted at the same time, only targets in the immediate vicinity of the array's perpendicular axis are detectable. By successively delaying the signals by a fraction of a wavelength, however, one can "steer" the beam to detect objects away from the perpendicular axis.[35]

COBRA DANE, which replaced AN/FPS-17 and AN/FPS-80 mechanical radars, achieved initial operating capability on July 13, 1977. It can detect (with a 99 percent probability) and track a basketball-sized object at a range of 2,000 miles with a 120-degree field of view, extending from the northern half of Salkhalin Island to just short of the eastern-most tip of Russia near the Bering Strait. Its ability to provide information on the size and shape of the object, however, is available only over a 44-degree range centered on the upper portion of Kamchatka, as indicated in Figure 9.3. COBRA DANE can simultaneously track up to 100 warheads when operating in an intelligence collection mode. It can also be employed for early warning and space surveillance; in those modes it can track up to 300 incoming warheads and up to 200 satellites, respectively. The final near-Earth trajectory of Russian reentry vehicles is not visible to COBRA DANE, however, owing to line-of-sight constraints imposed by the curvature of the Earth.[36]

For many years, at Pirinclik Air Base, Turkey, a satellite operation of Diyarbakir Air Station, the United States operated two radars—an AN/FPS-17 detection radar and a AN/FPS-79 tracking radar. The AN/FPS-17 radar began operations in 1955, whereas the AN/FPS-79 began operations almost a decade later—in 1964.

FIGURE 9.3   Coverage of COBRA DANE Radar

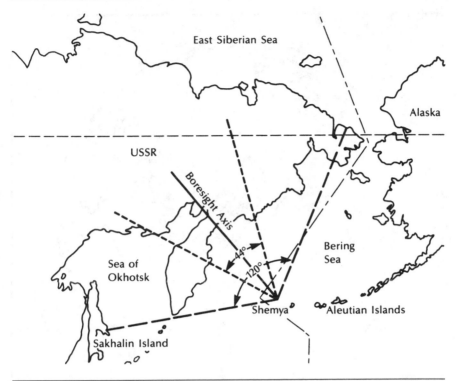

Located on a rocky plateau in southeastern Turkey, Pirinclik had its operations suspended from 1974 to 1978. During that time U.S. housekeeping personnel rotated one radar dish to prevent roller bearing damage while the Turks locked up a key piece of radar equipment to make sure the radar was inoperative.[37]

The base resumed operations on November 3, 1979, with its two radar antennas fixed permanently toward the northeast, where the Soviet border was 180 miles away. The electronic beams of the radar operated through a natural "duct" in the mountains around the plateau, picking up Russian missiles and space launches as they rose above the horizon. The AN/FPS-17 detection radar could detect an object 1 meter in diameter up to 5,000 miles away. After the AN/FPS-17 indicated that missile launch had taken place, the AN/FPS-79 tracking radar would "[swing] its white, round face in a noiseless arc in the same direction, ready to track missiles along their course." The radar's coverage is shown in Figure 9.4.

The radars were operated largely by civilian technicians hired by the contractor, General Electric. In addition to seventy contractor personnel, there were about

FIGURE 9.4   Range of Diyarbakir Radar

SOURCE: 21st Crew Training Squadron, *Space Operations Orientation Course* (Peterson AFB, Colo.: AFSPACECOM, 1991), p. 36.

145 Air Force personnel, mostly enlisted, and assigned to the Air Force Space Command's 19th Space Surveillance Squadron. In December 1995, the AN/FPS-17 was decommissioned, leaving the AN/FPS-79 tracking radar as the only radar still in operation at Pirinclik.[38]

Far less is known about two other land-based radars—COBRA SHOE and CREEK CHART. COBRA SHOE has been in operation since the late 1970s and may be an over-the-horizon (OTH) radar located at Ayios Nikolais, Cyprus. CREEK CHART is a United States Air Forces Europe project, of more recent origin, and located in Norway.[39]

A second set of ground stations are those operated for the Air Force Technical Applications Center (AFTAC) for the purposes of monitoring compliance with test ban treaties and the collection of nuclear intelligence. The Limited Test Ban

Treaty prohibits atmospheric testing; the Threshold Test Ban Treaty limits testing to underground tests of not more than 150 kilotons; and the pending Comprehensive Test Ban Treaty (CTBT) prohibits testing of any kind. According to an official history of AFTAC, the "only technique of the USAEDS [that is] truly effective in the detection of underground nuclear detonations" is the seismic technique.[40]

Seismic detection relies on the fact that nuclear detonations, like earthquakes, generate waves that travel long distances either by passing deep through the Earth (body waves) or by traveling along the Earth's surface (surface waves). Teleseismic body and surface waves can be recorded by seismometers or seismic arrays at significant distances (over 2,000 kilometers) from the point of detonation. When the waves arrive at a seismic station, the resulting motion of the ground is recorded by seismometers and converted into a seismogram.[41]

Analysis of the data involves distinguishing between earthquakes (which originate from two bodies of rock slipping past each other) and detonations (a point source), filtering out background and instrument noise, and converting the seismic signal into an estimate of explosive yield, when appropriate. The conversion requires not only application of a mathematical formula but also data concerning the geology of the test site—for a more stable geological structure will result in stronger body waves than a more molten structure.[42]

At distances of less than 625 miles from an event, explosions of greater than a few kilotons can easily be distinguished from earthquakes. At greater distances, such distinctions become far more difficult. Moreover, the actual recording of a seismic signal is disturbed by both instrumental and natural background noise, the latter setting a threshold of detectability. These limitations place a premium on situating monitoring stations or equipment in suitable locations and developing techniques to enhance the signal-to-noise ratio obtained at any location. The simplest form of Earth-based monitoring equipment is a seismometer, which basically consists of a magnet fixed to the ground and a spring-suspended mass with an electric coil. According to SIPRI, "When seismic waves move the ground and the magnet attached to it, they leave the mass with the coil relatively unaffected. The relative motion of the magnet and coil generates a current in the coil which is proportional to their relative velocity."[43]

One method of enhancing the signal-to-noise ratio is by placing several seismometers in an array. Arrays increase the data-set available for analysis in several ways, particularly because they can record the different arrival times of the seismic waves at the different seismometers.[44]

As a result of bilateral arrangements with the host governments to which AFTAC has turned over previously U.S.-run seismic stations, as well as of the provisions of the CTBT, AFTAC will have access to data from a larger number of sites than previously. The CTBT establishes an International Monitoring System (IMS), consisting of nationally run sites relying on seismic and other techniques. Data from those sites—such as ARCESS in Norway and KEV in Finland—as well as any additional data provided are transmitted to an International Data Center (IDC) in Vienna,

Austria. Under the provisions of the treaty each state party to the treaty will be able to receive all the data transmitted to the IDC.[45]

Even prior to the signing of the CTBT, AFTAC operations began to shift from a reliance on AFTAC-operated stations to a combination of AFTAC- and allied government-operated stations. The allied stations are often stations either previously operated by AFTAC or established by AFTAC for the host government. The seismic arrays and seismometers operated by or for AFTAC are distributed throughout the world. Each detachment possesses broadband seismic detection capabilities and is responsible for detecting, recording, and analyzing all seismic activity that occurs in its area of responsibility, twenty-four hours a day.[46]

AFTAC seismic detection is carried out by the AFTAC Distributed Subsurface Network (ADSN), which consists of six subsystems and support networks. The collection element of the ADSN is the Seismic Field Subsystem (SFS), which consists of equipment at Cambridge Bay, Canada (Equipment Location [EL] 079); Flin Flon, Canada (EL 244); Belbasi Seismic Research Station, Turkey (Detachment 301); Chiang Mai, Thailand (Detachment 415); Alice Springs, Australia (Detachment 421); Wonju Air Station, Korea (Detachment 452); Eielson Air Force Base, Alaska (Detachment 460), and the Southern U.S. Stations in Lajitas, Shafter, and Marathon, Texas (ELs 190, 191, 192). What used to be Detachment 313 at Sonseca, Spain, was turned over to the Spanish government in January 1996. Under the terms of a memorandum of understanding between AFTAC and the Spanish National Geographic Institute, AFTAC continues to receive data from the site, which includes two seismic arrays—a nineteen-instrument short-period array covering an area of about 125 square kilometers, and a six-instrument long-period array covering an area of about 1,250 square kilometers.[47]

Detachment 415 at Chiang Mai, Thailand, is actually operated by the Royal Thai Navy (RTN) Hydrographics Department, as a result of a memorandum of agreement between the U.S. Air Force and the RTN. The detachment has an eighteen-instrument short-period array for detecting vertical Earth motion. A five-instrument long-period array is used to detect vertical and horizontal Earth motion.[48]

Detachment 460 (Eielson Air Force Base) maintains forty-five seismic sites in seven arrays across Alaska, with the farthest site located 2,000 miles away Eielson. The geological data collected by the detachment is the largest joint data feed to the USAEDS. Detachment 452 (Wonju Air Station) is located 50 miles south of the Demilitarized Zone and operates the second largest seismic array. Two arrays are laid out over a 600-square-mile area in north central South Korea. A short-period array consisting of nineteen instruments detects vertical particle motion used for wave energy measurements. A long-period array consisting of six seismic instruments measures both vertical and horizontal earth particle motions and provides data used for event discrimination and wave energy measurements. Both arrays contribute to the refinement of seismic magnitude calculations.[49]

The installation at Alice Springs, Australia, code-named OAK TREE, is operated by Detachment 421. The installation is officially the Joint Geological and

Geophysical Research Station, although there is no Australian participation. An underground seismic array located about 1.5 miles northeast of the detachment consists of twenty-two detectors arranged in a circular pattern over about 7 miles. About thirteen of the seismometers are buried approximately 200 feet in the ground and designed to pick up the long-period waves that pass through the surface layer of the Earth. The remaining seismometers are buried 1.1 miles deep and tuned to detect the short-period waves that pass through the Earth's mantle and core. The seismometers are linked by cables to a central recording station where the signals are processed to provide an indication of the direction and speed at which they are traveling and the amplitude of the ground motion.[50]

AFTAC also obtains seismic data from stations it has set up in the Southern Hemisphere, but that are operated by foreign governments. This network—originally known as the Global Telemetered Seismic Network (GTSN), and subsequently as the Auxiliary Seismic Network (ASN)—is now known as the AFTAC Southern Network (ASN). The GTSN became operational in January 1995, and the ASN now consists of four stations in South America (Brazil, Paraguay, Argentina, Bolivia), four in Africa (South Africa, Botswana, Central African Republic, Ivory Coast), one in Antarctica, and an experimental station at the Albuquerque Seismological Laboratory (ASL) for testing and debugging.[51]

Figure 9.5 shows a sample alert report based on reporting from AFTAC seismic stations.

In addition to gathering seismic data, various AFTAC ground stations are part of a particulate sampling or Ground Filter Unit (GFU) network, established to back up and augment aerial sampling operations. The GFU is an electrically powered, ground-based, air filtering unit. The unit draws free air into a transition cone, which flows through a filter paper and is then emitted back into the atmosphere. The filter paper containing airborne particles from the atmosphere is then removed and forwarded for analysis and classification.[52]

One AFTAC site that is part of the GFU network is Detachment 460 at Eielson Air Force Base, Alaska. Detachment 460 also operates the B/20-5, an automated cryogenic distillation device that employs very low temperatures to isolate rare elements (gases) contained in the atmosphere. The unit is designed to operate continuously over any preset sample run of twenty-four hours (or a multiple thereof) for periods of up to seven days. Samples are collected in 800-cc metal containers that are forwarded to the McClellan Central Laboratory for analysis.[53]

The prospect of the requirement to monitor CTBT compliance has also led to plans to deploy additional systems for NUDET detection monitoring. The IMS to be established in support of CTBT monitoring envisions eighty ground-based radionuclide collection sites around the world, with the United States responsible for eleven. The key equipment at the sites will be Radionuclide Aerosol Sampler/Analyzers (RASAs), which push large volumes of air through six rolls of filter paper strips that, after a decay period, are mechanically passed through a gamma ray detector. The strips capture radioactive elements released into the atmosphere

FIGURE 9.5   Sample Alert Report Text: CIS/PRC Underground Test Site Events

CENR 55-5   Attachment 12   28 May 1992   31

      Figure A12-2. (U) Sample Alert Report Text: CIS/PRC Underground Test Site Events
                  (This figure is classified SECRET)

SUBJECT: ALERT _____ (U)

1. (S) DATA FROM _____ NORTH AMERICAN AND _____ OVERSEAS SEISMIC STATIONS OF THE US ATOMIC ENERGY DETECTION

SYSTEM (USAEDS) INDICATE AN UNDERGROUND EXPLOSION WITH A YIELD OF ABOUT _____ KT OCCURRED AT THE

_____ _____ _____ TEST SITE, _____ DEGREES _____ MINUTES NORTH

_____ DEGREES _____ MINUTES EAST, AT _____ GMT ON _____ 19___. THE ERROR ELLIPSE

ASSOCIATED WITH THE ABOVE LOCATION HAS A ███

███████████████████████████████████████

2. (S) DATA EVALUATED FROM _____ SATELLITES HAVING ██████████████████████████████████████

██████████ ITH THIS EVENT.

3. (S) THE PRELIMINARY ESTIMATE OF YIELD OF ABOUT _____ KT, WITH AN UNCERTAINTY RANGE ██████████ OF _____

TO _____ KT, IS BASED ON A SEISMIC MAGNITUDE (Mb) OF ABOUT _____ AND AN ASSUMPTION THE DETONATION OCCURRED

AT THE _____ TEST SITE, THE MAGNITUDE-YIELD FORMULA _____ WAS USED IN

DETERMINING THE YIELD.

4. (S) SURFACE WAVE DATA _____

_____.

5. (S) THE EARLIEST THAT ███

19___. AFTAC PLANS/DOES NOT PLAN TO CONDUCT ████████████████████████████████

6. (U) THE INFORMATION CONTAINED IN THIS DOCUMENT WILL BE SAFEGUARDED AS DIRECTED BY NATIONAL SECURITY DECISION

MEMORANDUM NO. 50.

_____

_____

           COORD: _____

           DATE: _____

           CLASSIFIED BY: AFTAC GSSCG 20 DEC 90
           DECLASSIFY ON: OADR

SOURCE: AFTAC Regulation 55-5, "Alert Procedures," May 28, 1992.

by a nuclear detonation, even days afterwards. By mid-1999, a similar system—the Automated Radioxenon Sample Analyzer (ARSA)—for gas sample collection and analysis should be in production.[54]

Another focus of research is infrasonic monitoring. The shock waves generated by nuclear detonations produce perturbations in certain levels of the ionosphere that can be detected by over-the-horizon radar. Infrasonic monitoring involves the use of a microphone array for long-range monitoring of very low-frequency sound waves generated by nuclear explosions that propagate in the upper levels of the atmosphere. It is expected that infrasonic arrays will be established in the Southern Hemisphere.[55]

Ground-based tactical MASINT systems have been developed and operated by the U.S. Army Intelligence and Security Command. Thus, during the 1989 fiscal year INSCOM MASINT systems, which appear largely to be infrared and electro-optical systems, included LANK BENCH/CEILING PRESS, LAND WATER/CEILING TABLE, GRAVEL WATER/LANDSMAN FAN, SUPER TIGER/CAIRN TRIUMPH, CAIRN EMPEROR, and TONE CASE/CEILING SEARCH.[56]

SEABORNE COLLECTION

The phased-array radar COBRA JUDY resides on the USNS *Observation Island*. The ship is operated by the Military Sealift Command, although AFTAC is responsible for radar operation. Emplaced on the 563-foot ship is a four-story turret on the aft deck that houses the major components of COBRA JUDY. The turret is essentially a 30-foot cube with one face tilted slightly inward. An antenna array 22.5 feet in diameter occupies an octagonal, raised area on the cube's slanting face. In addition, on top of the superstructure there are two, 32-foot diameter geodesic radomes containing a complex of passive receiving antennas funded by the NSA.[57]

The deployment of COBRA JUDY was designed to allow the monitoring of the final near-Earth trajectories of Soviet, now Russian, reentry vehicles during the portion of their flight not "visible" to COBRA DANE because of the Earth's line-of-sight constraints. In particular, the sensors provide information on the radar signatures of reentry vehicles and warheads. To enhance that capability, an X-band radar with parabolic dish antennas was added in 1985 to improve resolution and target separation—which may have resulted in the capability to distinguish between multiple warheads and penetration aids such as decoys and chaff.[58]

UNDERSEAS COLLECTION

As important as intelligence concerning Soviet surface naval activities was during the Cold War, intelligence concerning underseas activities was even more important. Although the Soviet Union placed the preponderance of its strategic nuclear weapons capability on land, it also maintained sixty-two submarines armed with SLBMs and in the late 1980s began to deploy the modern Typhoon SSBN armed with multiple warhead SS-N-20 missiles.

Additionally, Soviet attack submarines represented a threat to the U.S. SSBN fleet. In the midst of the transition from Poseidon to Trident submarines, the United States had only half of the number of SSBNs that the Soviet Union had—although the U.S. missiles were qualitatively superior to their Soviet counterparts.

Since the submarines played a more significant role in U.S. nuclear strategy than Soviet SSBNs played in Soviet strategy, it was imperative to detect and track any possible threats to U.S. SSBNs.

Much of the data gathered about foreign submarines comes under the heading of Acoustic Intelligence (ACOUSTINT)—intelligence derived from the analysis of acoustic waves radiated either intentionally or unintentionally by a submarine into the surrounding ocean. This category of intelligence includes the underwater acoustic waves from submarines, which can be used to determine the "signature" of those vehicles much in the same manner as voice autographs can be developed of individuals. The most important submarine detection and tracking system has been a global network of large, fixed, sea-bottom hydrophones that passively listen for the sounds generated by submarines. These arrays are collectively known as SOSUS (Sound Surveillance System), although only about two-thirds of the arrays were part of the SOSUS network proper. The other third are or were part of allied systems. The SOSUS system was described by one U.S. admiral in 1979 as the "backbone of our ASW [Antisubmarine Warfare] detection capability."[59]

The system was described by the Stockholm International Peace Research Institute (SIPRI) as follows:

> Each SOSUS installation consists of an array of hundreds of hydrophones laid out on the sea floor, or moored at depths most conducive to propagation, and connected by submarine cables for transmission of telemetry. In such an array a sound wave arriving from a distant submarine will be successively detected by different hydrophones according to their geometric relationship to the direction from which the wave arrives. This direction can be determined by noting the order in which the wave is detected at the different hydrophones. In practice, the sensitivity of the array is enhanced many times by adding the signals from several individual hydrophones after introducing appropriate time delays between them. The result is a listening "beam" that can be "steered" in various sectors of the ocean by varying the pattern of time delays. The distance from the array to the sound source can be calculated by measuring the divergence of the sound rays within the array or by triangulating from adjacent arrays.[60]

Two phenomena have made it possible to productively deploy a system such as SOSUS. One is that the decline in signal intensity is much less during propagation through the ocean than through the Earth, since the rate of absorption of sound energy in the ocean is very low. Second, the ocean has a layer of low-speed sound, called the SOFAR (Sound Fixing and Ranging) channel, that acts like a "waveguide." Sound energy moves horizontally in this channel, rather than downwards to the seafloor, where interaction with the bottom can cause significant attenuation. In addition, the waveguide effect limits the "geometrical spreading" attenuation of the sound wave. As a result, the effect of spreading increases only linearly with distance from the source, rather than as the square of the distance from the source (as occurs with seismic body waves).[61]

Development work on SOSUS began in the early 1950s, at which time the first hydrophone arrays were named CAESAR. Installation of the first SOSUS/CAESAR array was completed on the continental shelf off the east coast of the United States in the mid-1950s. Subsequent SOSUS arrays were installed elsewhere off the east coast, at Brawdy in Wales, and at other locations. The arrays have been progressively updated, and the technology is now in its fifth or sixth generation of development.[62]

The CAESAR arrays proved extremely effective during the Cuban Missile Crisis of October 1962, when every Soviet submarine in the area was detected and closely trailed. As a result, the United States decided to expand and upgrade the network. An array was established to cover the Greenland-Iceland-United Kingdom (GIUK) Gap, that is, the portion of the Atlantic through which Soviet submarines stationed at the Polyarnyy submarine base in the northwestern Soviet Union had to pass in order to head toward the United States. Even earlier warning has been provided by an array strung between Andoya, Norway, and Bear Island.[63]

By the late 1960s, several more arrays had been established. An upgraded variation of CAESAR—COLOSSUS—was deployed on the west coast of the United States, extending from the top of Alaska to the Baja Peninsula. COLOSSUS employed a more advanced form of sonar than CAESAR. Farther out in the Pacific, a 1,300-mile-long circular array code-named SEA SPIDER surrounds the Hawaiian Islands. Reportedly, it was this array that monitored and localized the breakup of the Soviet submarine that sank north of Hawaii in March 1968. Another Pacific array extended from Alaska and ran parallel to the Aleutian Islands. An array along the western side of the Kuril Islands allowed detection of Russian submarines exiting the naval base at Petropavlovsk or the Sea of Okhostk.[64]

Construction began on an array known as the Azores Fixed Acoustic Range (AFAR) in September 1968 off the island of Santa Maria, the southernmost of the Azores group. In May 1972 the system was commissioned by NATO with a dual mission—to track Soviet submarines approaching the Strait of Gibraltar or passing around the Cape of Good Hope. An array in the Bosporous strait between Yugoslavia and Turkey can detect submarines exiting the Black Sea port of Sevastapol. Yet another array was put in place next to the coast of Taiwan and the Philippines, and there is an Indian Ocean array in the vicinity of Diego Garcia. Other arrays were located off Turkey (in addition to the Bosporous array), Japan, Puerto Rico, Barbados, Canada (Argentia, Newfoundland), Italy, Denmark, Gibraltar, Galeta Island in Panama, and Guam.[65]

The hydrophones are sealed in tanks—approximately twenty-four to a tank— and cables transmit the data to shore facilities. The first step in converting the data collected by the hydrophones to finished intelligence occurs at Naval Facilities (NAVFACs) and Naval Regional Processing Centers (NRPCs), which are the initial recipients of the data. There has been a repeated reduction in the number of NAVFACs over the years. Among the NAVFACs still operating in 1993 were those at Adak, Alaska; Argentia, Newfoundland; Brawdy, Wales; Centerville Beach,

California; Whidbey Island, Washington; and Keflavik, Iceland. The Whidbey Island facility, with a staff of 200, receives remote data from unmanned relay centers at Coos Bay and Pacific Beach, provides analysis and processing of underwater signals, and transmits data to the Pacific Fleet around the clock. Plans call for a reduction in NAVFACs to five—with two in the Pacific and three in the Atlantic. Two of the Atlantic sites will be co-manned/owned with two allies—probably Canada (Argentia) and the United Kingdom (Brawdy).[66]

From the NAVFACs and NRPCs, the data has been sent by landline or communications satellite to Naval Ocean Processing Facilities at Damn Neck, Virginia, and Ford Island, Hawaii. Those facilities have been responsible for centralized reporting, correlation, localization, and tracking of submarine targets. It is intended that much of the data that used to be transmitted to NAVFACs from the arrays will now be transmitted via satellite to a central location—where it will remain unexamined.[67]

The data collected about each submarine detected—its sonar echo and the noises made by the engine, its cooling system, and the movement of its propellers—can be translated into a recognition signal. A distinctive pattern can be determined that indicates not only a particular type of submarine—an Alfa-class attack submarine instead of a Typhoon-class ballistic-missile-carrying submarine, for example—but also the individual submarine. Thus the data, when analyzed, operate much like fingerprints or voiceprints do to identify individuals.

Gradually, a fundamental change in Soviet submarine capabilities over the years reduced the value of SOSUS. The first three generations of Soviet sea-based ballistic missile submarines—the SS-N-4 Snark, the SS-N-5 Serb, and the SS-N-6 Sawfly—had ranges of between 350 and 1,600 nautical miles. Beginning in 1973—with the operation of the SS-N-8, which had a range of 4,200 nautical miles—Soviet subs did not have to exit Soviet home waters to hit targets in the United States. Soviet capability in this regard grew over the years, with the deployment of the SS-N-8 Mod 2, which has a range of 4,900 nautical miles, and of the SS-N-8 and SS-N-20, which have ranges of from 3,500 to 4,500 nautical miles. For several years subsequent to the Soviet collapse, Russian SSBNs have conducted fewer operations off the Atlantic and Pacific coasts, reducing the value of the SOSUS arrays covering those areas. However, more recently Russian subs have been identified off each U.S. coast.[68]

SOSUS has proved to be able to provide additional data about activities other than those taking place underwater. One additional capability is the detection and tracking of surface ships. An even more surprising capability demonstrated by SOSUS is the tracking and identification of aircraft flying over the ocean. This capability was first discovered in 1965 and 1966, when the Norwegian SOSUS station detected Soviet Bear-D bombers flying over the Norwegian Sea.[69]

The same properties that made SOSUS such a valuable tool in monitoring Soviet submarine activity also makes it possible to use it to detect nuclear detona-

TABLE 9.2 AFTAC Equipment Locations for Hydroacoustic Detection

EL Number	Location
69	NAVFAC Whidbey Island
70	NAVFAC Adak, Alaska
72	NAVFAC Bermuda
73	NAVFAC Argentia, Canada
74	NAVFAC Midway
92	NOPF Dam Neck, Virginia
135	NAVFAC Centerville Beach, California
145	NAVFAC St. Nicholas Island, Pt. Mugu, California
360	NAVFAC Keflavik, Iceland
423	NAVFAC Guam

tions, whether conducted underwater or near the oceans. Thus, at one time AFTAC used nine hydroacoustic stations around the world to provide coverage of the North Pacific Ocean, the Atlantic Ocean, and that part of the Antarctic Ocean adjacent to the South Atlantic Ocean. Eight of the stations were collocated with SOSUS. AFTAC equipment was connected as near to the hydrophone cable shore terminal as possible, bypassing all host electronics to the maximum extent. Digital data were then encrypted and transmitted over dedicated circuits via satellite links to the main Hydroacoustics Operations Center at AFTAC headquarters. Operated twenty-four hours a day, the hydroacoustic data center is tasked with identifying the source of each recorded wave. In a given year it receives data on over 650,000 events from both natural and man-made sources.[70]

AFTAC Hydroacoustic Equipment locations, as of 1992, are listed in Table 9.2.

Notes

1. U.S. Congress, House Permanent Select Committee on Intelligence, *IC 21: Intelligence Community in the 21st Century* (Washington, D.C.: U.S. Government Printing Office, 1996), p. 149.

2. Department of Defense Instruction Number 5105.58, *Management of Measurement and Signature Intelligence (MASINT)*, February 9, 1993, p. 1.

3. Ibid., p. 2; John L. Morris, *MASINT: Progress and Impact, Brief to NMIA*, November 19, 1996, Slide 1; Daniel B. Sibbet, "MASINT: Intelligence for the 1990s," *American Intelligence Journal*, (Summer/Fall 1990): 23–26.

4. Morris, *MASINT: Progress and Impact*, Slide 8; Capt. Chadwick T. Hawley, "MASINT: Supporting the Warfighter Today and Tomorrow!" *Communiqué*, May 1996, p. 14.

5. For a discussion of such issues, see U.S. Congress, House Permanent Select Committee on Intelligence, *IC 21: Intelligence Community in the 21st Century*, pp. 144–173; Office of the Inspector General, Department of Defense, *Evaluation Report on Measurement and Signature Intelligence*, PO 97–031 (Alexandria, Va.: DODIG, June 30, 1997).

6. Jeffrey T. Richelson, America's Space *Sentinels: DSP Satellites and National Security* (Lawrence: University Press of Kansas, forthcoming).

7. U.S. Congress, Senate Committee on Armed Services, *Department of Defense Authorization for Appropriations for FY 1981, Part 6* (Washington, D.C.: U.S. Government Printing Office, 1980), p. 3449; Science Applications International Corporation, *Fifty Year Commemorative History of Long Range Detection: The Creation, Development, and Operation of the United States Atomic Energy Detection System* (Patrick AFB, Fla.: Air Force Technical Applications Center, 1997), pp. 124–126.

8. Richelson, *America's Space Sentinels.*

9. Ibid.

10. Ibid.; Desmond Ball, *A Base for Debate: The U.S. Satellite Ground Station at Nurrungar* (Sydney: Allen & Unwin Australia, 1987), p. 50; "Space Group Activates, Serves As Space-Based Missile Warning Focal Point," *Guardian*, July 1996, p. 23.

11. U.S. Congress, General Accounting Office, *Satellite Acquisition: Global Positioning Acquisition Changes After Challenger's Accident* (Washington, D.C.: GAO, 1987), pp. 8, 29; David A. Turner and Marcia S. Smith, *GPS: Satellite Navigation and Positioning and the DOD's Navstar Global Positioning System* (Washington, D.C.: Library of Congress, 1994), p. 5; The Aerospace Corporation, *The Global Positioning System: A Record of Achievement*, n.d.

12. U.S. Congress, House Committee on Appropriations, *Department of Defense Appropriations for 1983, Part 5* (Washington, D.C.: U.S. Government Printing Office, 1982), p. 16; U.S. Congress, House Committee on Appropriations, *Department of Defense Appropriations for 1984, Part 8* (Washington, D.C.: U.S. Government Printing Office, 1983), p. 337; U.S. Congress, House Committee on Armed Services, *Department of Energy National Security and Military Applications of Nuclear Energy Authorization Act of 1984* (Washington, D.C.: U.S. Government Printing Office, 1983), pp. 383–384; Paul Stares, *Space and National Security* (Washington, D.C.: Brookings Institution, 1987), p. 29; Charles A. Zraket, "Strategic Command, Control, Communications and Intelligence," *Science*, June 22, 1984, p. 1309; "Navstar Bloc 2 Satellites to Have Crosslinks, Radiation Hardening," *Defense Electronics*, July 1983, p. 16; Department of the Air Force, *Supporting Data for Fiscal Year 1985* (Washington, D.C.: Department of the Air Force, 1984), pp. 394–395; AFSPACECOM Regulation 55–29, "Global Positioning System and Nuclear Detonation (NUDET) Detection System (GPS/NDS) Mission Requirements and Doctrine (MRD)," September 1, 1989, pp. 4, 6, 9; Turner and Smith, *GPS: Satellite Navigation and Positioning and the DOD's Navstar Global Positioning System*, p. 7.

13. Science Applications International Corporation, *Fifty Year Commemorative History of Long Range Detection*, p. 211; "GPS Sensor Added As Test Ban Monitor," *Space News*, May 13-19, 1996, p. 2.

14. Sylvia E. D. Ferry, *The Defense Meteorological Satellite System Sensors: An Historical Overview* (Los Angeles AFB, Calif.: DMSS Program Office, 1989), pp. 4–15.

15. Richelson, *America's Space Sentinels.*

16. FAS Space Policy Project, "COBRA BRASS," March 9, 1997, http://www.fas.org/spp/military/program/warning/cobrabrass.htm; U.S. Congress, House of Representatives, *National Defense Authorization Act for Fiscal Year 1996, Report 104–131* (Washington, D.C.: U.S. Government Printing Office, 1995), p. 122; Interview.

17. David A. Fulghum, "Endurance, Standoff Range Remain Crucial Attributes," *Aviation Week & Space Technology*, August 4, 1997, pp. 51–53.

18. David S. Fulghum, "Cobra Ball Revamped for Battlefield Missions," *Aviation Week & Space Technology*, August 4, 1997, pp. 48–50.

19. David Miller, *An Illustrated Guide to Modern Sub Hunters* (New York: Arco, 1984), p. 124; George A. Wilmoth, "Lockheed's Antisubmarine Warfare Aircraft; Watching the Threat," *Defense Systems Review* 3, no. 5 (1985): 18–25; U.S. Congress, Senate Committee on Armed Services, *Department of Defense Authorization for Appropriations for Fiscal Year 1986, Part 8* (Washington, D.C.: U.S. Government Printing Office, 1985), p. 4510; "P-3 ORION," http://www.history.navy.mil/planes/p3.htm.

20. Lori A. McClelland, "Versatile P-3C Orion Meeting Growing ASW Challenge," *Defense Electronics*, April 1985, pp. 132–141; Miller, *An Illustrated Guide to Sub Hunters*, p. 124; *P-3C Orion Update Weapon System* (Burbank, Calif.: Lockheed, n.d.), p. 17.

21. McClelland, "Versatile P-3C Orion Meeting Growing ASW Challenge"; *P-3C Orion Update Weapon System*, p. 18; Nicholas M. Horrock, "The Submarine Hunters," *Newsweek*, January 23, 1984, p. 38.

22. Private information; U.S. Congress, House Committee on Appropriations, *Department of Defense Appropriations for 1994, Part 1* (Washington, D.C.: U.S. Government Printing Office, 1993), p. 48.

23. Defense Airborne Reconnaissance Office, *Manned Airborne Reconnaissance Division*, 1995, p. 16.

24. Patrol Squadron Special Projects Unit Two, VPU-2 Inst. 5400.1H, "Squadron Organization and Regulations Manual (SORM)," February 7, 1995, p. 1-1; "Firms Specialize in Secret Aircraft," *Aviation Week & Space Technology*, August 4, 1997, p. 50.

25. Air Technical Applications Center, CENR 55–3, "Aerial Sampling Operations," October 22, 1982, pp. 2–7; Scott Weathers, Steve Greene, Greg Barge, Paul Schultz, and Chris Clements, *History of the 55th Weather Reconnaissance Squadron, July–December 1989* (McClellan AFB, Calif.: 55th WRS, December 31, 1989), p. 1.

26. Jerry King, Chris Lucey, Mike Lyons, Grant Phifer, and Leslie Yokoyama-Peralta, *History of the 55th Weather Reconnaissance Squadron, 1 Jan to 30 June 1986* (McClellan AFB, Calif.: 55th WRS, n.d.), p. 11; Bill Gertz, "Chinese Nuke Test Releases Gas Cloud," *Washington Times*, June 11, 1992, p. A5; James Rupert, "Plutonium Leak Reported at Russian Nuclear Plant," *Washington Post*, July 20, 1993, p. A14.

27. William B. Scott, "Sampling Missions Unveiled Nuclear Weapon Secrets," *Aviation Week & Space Technology*, November 3, 1997, pp. 54–57; Science Applications International Corporation, *Fifty Year Commemorative History of Long Range Detection*, pp. 66, 68; "USAF Aircraft Monitors Fallout of Nuclear Tests," *Jane's Defence Weekly*, May 20, 1998, p. 4; Bill Gertz, "Senators Back Keeping Atomic-Sniffing Jet," *Washington Times,* September 29, 1998, p. A6.

28. "Bug-Zapper Chopper," *Aviation Week & Space Technology*, May 6, 1996, p. 13.

29. Prepared statement of C. Bruce Tarter, U.S. Congress, Senate Armed Services Committee, *Department of Defense Authorization for Appropriations for Fiscal Year 1997 and the Future Years Defense Program, Part 7* (Washington, D.C.: U.S. Government Printing Office, 1997), p. 254.

30. William B. Scott, "Argus to Flight Test Chemical Detectors," *Aviation Week & Space Technology*, May 6, 1996, p. 26.

31. Brigadier General Frank B. Campbell, Director of Forces, USAF, "Air Force TIARA Programs: Intelligence Support to the Warfighter," 1995, p. 3; "COBRA DANE," http://www.fas.org/spp/military/programs/track/cobra_dane.htm.

32. Dr. Michael E. del Papa, *Meeting the Challenge ESD and the Cobra Dane Construction Effort on Shemya Island* (Bedford, Mass.: Electronic Systems Division, Air Force Systems Command, 1979), pp. 1–2.

33. AFSPACECOM Regulation 55–123, "Cobra Dane Tactical Requirements and Doctrine," December 15, 1992, p. 4.

34. del Papa, *Meeting the Challenge*, pp. 2–3.

35. Eli Brookner, "Phased-Array Radars," *Scientific American*, April 1985, pp. 94–102.

36. Philip J. Klass, "USAF Tracking Radar Details Disclosed," *Aviation Week & Space Technology*, October 25, 1976, pp. 41–46; del Papa, *Meeting the Challenge*, p. 38; Air Combat Command, *Searching the Skies: The Legacy of the United States Cold War Defense Radar Program* (Langley, Va.: ACC, 1997), p. 50.

37. Stanley G. Zabetakis and John F. Peterson, "The Diyarbakir Radar," *Studies in Intelligence* 8, no. 3 (Fall 1964): 41–47; Michael K. Burns, "U.S. Reactivating Bases in Turkey," *Baltimore Sun*, October 21, 1978, pp. 1, 23.

38. Air Force Space Command, *Command Organization and Chart Book*, April 1, 1997, n.p.; Michael Getler, "U.S. Intelligence Facilities in Turkey Get New Attention After Iran Turmoil," *Washington Post*, February 9, 1979, p. A15; Brian Orban, "Worldwide Support," *Guardian*, December 1995, pp. 3–6.

39. Air Force, "Cobra Shoe Program Element Description," 1978; Lt. Gen. Nikolai Brusnitsin, *Openness and Espionage* (Moscow, 1990), p. 23; Private information; Brig. Gen. Frank B. Campbell, Director of Forces, *Air Force TIARA Programs: Intelligence Support to the Warfighter*, 1995.

40. Science Applications International Corporation, *Fifty Year Commemorative History of Long Range Detection*, p. 71.

41. Ibid.

42. Ibid., p. 71.

43. Henry R. Myers, "Extending the Nuclear Test Ban," *Scientific American*, January 1972, pp. 13–23; Lynn R. Sykes and Jack F. Evernden, "The Verification of a Comprehensive Nuclear Test Ban," *Scientific American*, October 1982, pp. 47–55; "The Comprehensive Test Ban," in *SIPRI Yearbook, 1978: World Armaments and Disarmament* (New York: Crane, Russak, 1978), pp. 317–359 at p. 335.

44. "The Comprehensive Test Ban," p. 340.

45. Paul G. Richards and Won Young-Kim, "Testing the Nuclear Test Ban Treaty," *Nature*, October 23, 1997, pp. 781–782.

46. 3400 Technical Training Wing, *Introduction to Detection Systems* (Lowry Air Force Base: 3400 TTW, October 18, 1984), p. 17.

47. Science Applications International Corporation, *Fifty Year Commemorative History of Long Range Detection*, pp. 77–78; Air Intelligence Agency, *Air Intelligence Agency Almanac*, August 1997, pp. 36, 41; Amy Webb, "Changing Technologies, Times and Politics . . . ," *Spokesman*, April 1996, pp. 20–21; "Seismic Site Turned Over to Spanish Government," *Spokesman*, March 1996, p. 35; "Detachment 313-Sonseca, Spain," http://www.aftac.gov.

48. "Detachment 415-Chiang Mai," http://www.aftac.gov/.

49. Air Intelligence Agency, *Air Intelligence Agency Almanac*, pp. 37–38, 41; "Detachment 460-Eielson Air Force Base, Alaska," http//www.aftac.gov/; "Detachment 452-Wonju, Korea," http//www.aftac.gov/.

50. Desmond Ball, *A Suitable Piece of Real Estate: American Installations in Australia* (Sydney, Australia: Hale & Iremonger, 1980), pp. 84–85; Science Applications International Corporation, *Fifty Year Commemorative History of Long Range Detection*, p. 179; "Detachment 421—Alice Springs, Australia," http://www.aftac.gov/.

51. Science Applications International Corporation, *Fifty Year Commemorative History of Long Range Detection*, pp. 79–80; Amy Webb, "National Data Center Will Support Comprehensive Test Ban Treaty," *Spokesman*, October 1995, pp. 26–27.

52. Science Applications International Corporation, *Fifty Year Commemorative History of Long Range Detection*, pp. 84–85; 3400 Technical Training Wing, *Introduction to Detection Systems*, p. 17.

53. Science Applications International Corporation, *Fifty Year Commemorative History of Long Range Detection*, pp. 107–108; 3400 Technical Training Wing, *Introduction to Detection Systems*, p. 17.

54. "Test Ban Checking," *Aviation Week & Space Technology*, May 4, 1998, p. 13; William B. Scott, "Debris Collection Reverts to Ground Sites," *Aviation Week & Space Technology*, November 3, 1997, pp. 57–59.

55. U.S. Congress, Senate Committee on Appropriations, *Energy and Water Development Appropriations FY 1986, Part 2* (Washington, D.C.: U.S. Government Printing Office, 1985), pp. 1360–1361; Science Applications International Corporation, *Fifty Year Commemorative History of Long Range Detection*, p. 210.

56. History Office, U.S. Army Intelligence and Security Command, *Annual Historical Review, U.S. Army Intelligence and Security Command—Fiscal Year 1989* (Fort Belvoir, Va.: INSCOM, 1990), pp. 60–63.

57. Kenneth J. Stein, "Cobra Judy Phased Array Radar Tested," *Aviation Week & Space Technology*, August 10, 1981, pp. 70–73; "X-Band Expands Cobra Judy's Repertoire," *Defense Electronics* (January 1985): 43–44; Science Applications International Corporation, *Fifty Year Commemorative History of Long Range Detection*, p. 195.

58. Stein, "Cobra Judy Phased Array Radar Tested"; "X-Band Expands Cobra Judy's Repertoire."

59. Testimony of Admiral Metzel in U.S. Congress, Senate Committee on Armed Services, *Department of Defense Authorization for Appropriations for Fiscal Year 1980, Part 6* (Washington, D.C.: U.S. Government Printing Office, 1979), p. 2925.

60. Owen Wilkes, "Strategic Anti-Submarine Warfare and Its Implications for a Counterforce First Strike," in *World Armaments and Disarmament, SIPRI Yearbook 1979* (London: Taylor & Francis Ltd., 1979), p. 430.

61. Science Applications International Corporation, *Fifty Year Commemorative History of Long Range Detection*, p. 113.

62. U.S. Congress, House Committee on Appropriations, *Department of Defense Appropriations for Fiscal Year 1977, Part 5* (Washington, D.C.: U.S. Government Printing Office, 1976), p. 1255; Drew Middleton, "Expert Predicts a Big U.S. Gain in Sub Warfare," *New York Times*, July 18, 1979, p. A5; "Chapman Pincher, "U.S. to Set Up Sub Spy Station," *Daily Express*, January 6, 1973; Harvey B. Silverstein, "CAESAR, SOSUS and Submarines: Economic and Institutional Implications of ASW Technologies," *Ocean '78* (Proceedings of the Fourth Annual Combined Conference Sponsored by the Marine Technology Society and the Institute of Electrical and Electronics Engineers, Washington, D.C., September 6–8, 1978), p. 407.

63. U.S. Congress, House Committee on Appropriations, *Department of Defense Appropriations for Fiscal Year 1977, Part 5*, p. 1255; Middleton, "Expert Predicts a Big U.S. Gain in Sub Warfare."

64. Defense Market Survey, "Sonar-Sub-Surface-Caesar," *DMS Market Intelligence Report* (Greenwich, Conn.: DMS, 1980), p. 1; Clyde Burleson, *The Jennifer Project* (Englewood Cliffs, N.J.: Prentice-Hall, 1977), p. 17–18, 24–25; Joel S. Wit, "Advances in Antisubmarine Warfare," *Scientific American*, February 1981, pp. 36ff; Silverstein, "CAESAR, SOSUS, and Submarines."

65. Howard B. Dratch, "High Stakes in the Azores," *The Nation*, November 8, 1975, pp. 455–456; "NATO Fixed Sonar Range Commissioned," *Armed Forces Journal International*, August 1972, p. 29; "Atlantic Islands: NATO Seeks Wider Facilities," *International Herald Tribune*, June 1981, p. 75; Richard Timsar, "Portugal Bargains for U.S. Military Aid with Strategic Mid-Atlantic Base," *Christian Science Monitor*, March 24, 1981, p. 9; Wit, "Advances in Antisubmarine Warfare."

66. William Arkin and Richard Fieldhouse, *Nuclear Battlefields: Global Links in the Arms Race* (Cambridge, Mass: Ballinger, 1986), Appendix A; Ed Offley, "Turning the Tide: Soviets Score a Coup with Sub Progress," *Seattle Post-Intelligencer*, April 8, 1987, p. A5; USN-PLAD, p. 30 in United States Military Communications-Electronics Board, USMCEB Publication No. 6, Issue 25, *Message Address Directory* (Washington, D.C.: U.S. Government Printing Office, January 30, 1993); U.S. Congress, House Committee on Appropriations, *Department of Defense Appropriations for 1994, Part 1* (Washington, D.C.: U.S. Government Printing Office, 1993), p. 48; William J. Broad, "Scientists Oppose Navy Plan to Shut Undersea Monitor," *New York Times*, June 12, 1994, pp. 1, 18.

67. William E. Burrows, *Deep Black: Space Espionage and National Security* (New York: Random House, 1986), p. 180 n; USN-PLAD, pp. 28, 33 in U.S. Military Communications-Electronics Board, USMCEB Publication No. 6, *Message Address Directory* (Washington, D.C.: U.S. Government Printing Office, July 25, 1986); CINCPACFLT Instruction 5450.76, *Mission and Functions of Naval Ocean Processing Facility, Ford Island, Pearl Harbor, Hawaii*, February 22, 1985; Broad, "Scientists Oppose Navy Plan to Shut Down Ocean Monitor."

68. Robert P. Berman and John C. Baker, *Soviet Strategic Forces: Requirements and Responses* (Washington, D.C.: Brookings Institution, 1982), pp. 106–107; Bill Gertz, "Russian Sub Stalks Three U.S. Carriers," *Washington Times*, November 23, 1997, pp. A1, A5.

69. Office of the Chief of Naval Operations, OPNAVINST C3501.204A, Subj: Projected Operational Environment (POE) and Required Operational Capabilities (ROC) Statements for the Integrated Underseas Surveillance Systems (IUSS), March 14, 1995; Interview.

70. Science Applications International Corporation, *Fifty Year Commemorative History of Long Range Detection*, p. 114; 3400 Technical Training Wing, *Introduction to Detection Systems*, p. 18.

10

SPACE SURVEILLANCE

In addition to being concerned with events on land and sea, the U.S. intelligence community is concerned with events in outer space. An accurate understanding of the space activities of foreign nations is required for assessing foreign military space (including space intelligence) capabilities, selecting and implementing operations security measures, warning of actions (whether intended or unintended) that threaten U.S. space systems, warning of space systems or debris that could impact the Earth or other space systems (including space shuttles or the planned space station), developing plans for the interception of satellite communications, preparing and implementing plans to neutralize foreign space systems, and monitoring compliance with several treaties (including the Outer Space Treaty and ABM Treaty).[1]

The specific aspects of foreign space activities that are monitored include launch preparations and launch, deployment into orbit, mission, orbital parameters, maneuvering, deployment of subsatellites, breakup of satellites, and reentry of satellites or debris into the Earth's atmosphere. Space surveillance systems are also used to determine the size and other characteristics of space systems.[2]

During the Cold War, the driving force behind U.S. space surveillance activities was, of course, the Soviet Union. Of primary concern were the capabilities and employment of Soviet reconnaissance, navigation, communications, meteorological, and other military support satellites. The capabilities and orbits of Soviet reconnaissance satellites had to be factored into plans to provide operational security to U.S. military forces and research and development activities—including the plans of U.S. forces preparing for the April 1980 attempt to rescue U.S. hostages in Iran, as well as the highly classified aeronautical activities at Area 51 in Nevada. In addition, Soviet anti-satellite testing was a significant concern to U.S. military officials. Even non-military space activities, including space probes sent to Mars and Venus, were the targets of the U.S. intelligence community.[3]

In response to the intelligence threat from Soviet imagery satellites, the United States initiated the Satellite Reconnaissance Advanced Notice (SATRAN) program, also known by the nickname STRAY CAT, in 1966. The SATRAN program is presently part of the Satellite Reconnaissance Operations Security Program.[4]

The other main component of the program is the Navy's Fleet Support System/Satellite Vulnerability Program. By 1987 the Naval Space Surveillance System(NAVSPASUR) was providing satellite vulnerability information in four formats to Navy units:

- Large Area Vulnerability Reports (LAVR) provided satellite vulnerability information to units in established operating areas.
- Satellite Vulnerability Reports (SVR) provided tailored vulnerability information to units in a transit status or operating outside established operating areas.
- Safe Window Intelligence (SWINT) reports provided periods of time when the requesting units were not vulnerable to reconnaissance satellite coverage.
- One-line CHARLIE elements [which enable units to compute their own satellite vulnerability data] are provided to units having the Reconnaissance Satellite Vulnerability Computer (RSVC) program, allowing the units to compute their own satellite vulnerability data.[5]

In 1988 the Naval Space Command instituted the CHAMBERED ROUND program for support to deployed elements of the fleet and Fleet Marine Force. Under CHAMBERED ROUND, the Naval Space Command provides deployed naval forces with tactical assessments of hostile space capabilities and specific reactions to their operations. The support is tailored to a unit's specific equipment, geographic area of interest, and intentions during their predeployment workups or while they are in transit to the theater of operations.[6]

Although the collapse of the Soviet Union has resulted in a reduced Russian military space program, the remaining program is still of interest to the U.S. intelligence community. Operational security measures to prevent Russian imaging satellites from viewing particularly sensitive activities are still undertaken. Likewise, data concerning Russian communications satellites are still required to support U.S. satellite communications intercept activities.[7]

In addition, other nations have, for many years, made use of space systems, particularly for communications. By January 1992, seventeen nations other than the United States and Russia, as well as five international organizations, owned and operated seventy-seven commercial or civilian communications satellites. China has orbited spacecraft with photographic reconnaissance, electronic intelligence, meteorology, and communications missions. And in recent years the space activities of other nations have grown in size and scope. France has embarked on an ambitious intelligence satellite program that has already resulted in the launch of one reconnaissance satellite, with more planned. Israel has also launched a reconnaissance satellite. The growing number of foreign military space programs led Congress, in the 1993 fiscal year, to require the Office of the Secretary of Defense to produce a report on the proliferation of military satellites.[8]

In addition, the growth in the number of commercial imagery satellites, as well as the dramatic improvement in capabilities, although increasing the sources of imagery for the U.S. intelligence community, has further complicated the space monitoring and operational security missions. In 1990, aside from imagery sold by the Soviet Union before its collapse, the best commercial imagery available had a resolution of 33 feet. The new commercial imagery satellites promise to provide 1-meter imagery.[9]

Whereas the main means of observing activities on Earth is via overhead systems, both spacecraft and aircraft, the vast majority of space surveillance assets are located on the ground. The focal point of the U.S. space surveillance effort is the U.S. Space Command's Space Control Center (SCC), formerly the Space Surveillance Center (SSC), at Cheyenne Mountain Air Force Base. The SCC receives data from the three types of sensors—dedicated, collateral, and contributing—that make up the Space Surveillance Network (SSN). These systems track about 8,000 space objects.[10] In addition to the SSN, the U.S. employs additional systems for monitoring space activity.

DEDICATED SSN SENSORS

Dedicated SSN sensors are those reserved primarily for space surveillance.[11] They rely on a variety of techniques, including intermittent radar detection, optical collection, radio-frequency monitoring, and the establishment of an electronic radar fence.

Until the mid-1980s, the primary dedicated optical sensors consisted of series of Baker-Nunn cameras that operated in twilight or darkness, when the satellite was illuminated by the Sun but the Earth's surface was in darkness. Measurement of the satellite's position against a known star field produced precise locational data. Over the course of the program Baker-Nunn cameras were located at almost a dozen sites, although they were not all operational at the same time. The last two sites to close were those at San Vito, Italy (1991), and St. Margarets, New Brunswick (1992). Baker-Nunn cameras had also been located in Florida, Norway, Korea, California, and Chile.[12]

The central role of the Baker-Nunn camera in the U.S. space surveillance system has been assumed by the Ground-Based Electro-Optical Deep Space Surveillance (GEODSS), operated by four detachments of the 18th Space Surveillance Squadron (headquartered at Edwards Air Force Base, California)—Detachment 1 at Stallion Station, White Sands Missile Range, New Mexico; Detachment 2 at Diego Garcia Island, British Indian Ocean Territory; Detachment 3 at Maui, Hawaii; and Detachment 4 at Moron Air Base, Spain. The first three sites began operations in 1983, the Moron site, in 1997.[13] (Previously Detachment 2 was located at ChoeJong San, South Korea, and Diego Garcia was designated Detachment 4. The Korean site closed in 1993 as a result of poor tracking conditions.)[14]

The system provides the capability to optically track objects higher than 3,000 nautical miles, out to 22,000 nautical miles. It can detect objects 10,000 times dimmer than can be seen with the unassisted human eye. The ability of the GEODSS to reach geosynchronous altitude was demonstrated in 1985 when a GEODSS site photographed a Navy FLTSATCOM satellite. At geosynchronous altitude the GEODSS telescopes can detect a reflective object the size of a soccer ball. GEODSS is also able to search up to 17,400 square degrees per hour. Further, some GEODSS installations are close enough together to provide overlapping coverage as a means of overcoming poor weather at the nearby site.[15]

Like the Baker-Nunn system, GEODSS depends on the collection of light reflected by the objects under investigation and is operational only at night during clear weather. Additionally, sensitivity and resolution are downgraded by adverse atmospheric conditions. Unlike the earlier system, however, GEODSS is able to provide real-time data with a computer-managed instant video display of surveillance data. Further, the computer automatically filters stars from the night sky backdrop and then uses its memory of known space objects to determine the existence of new or unknown space objects, alerting the user when such objects are found.[16]

GEODSS consists of three telescopes at each site that work together under computer control. The Diego Garcia site has three 40-inch telescopes. The other sites have two 40-inch telescopes and a 15-inch telescope. The larger telescope is designed primarily for high-altitude searches of faint, slow-moving objects and is capable of examining up to 2,400 square degrees of the night sky each hour. The 15-inch telescope is employed mainly for low-altitude, wide-area searches of fast-moving objects and can search up to 15,000 square degrees per hour. Each telescope has a sensitive Ebiscon tube that registers the image of an object for real-time processing and a radiometer for optical signature characterization and identification.[17]

According to one account, "In a typical operational scenario that small telescope will be conducting a low-altitude, high-speed search, one of the large telescopes will be tracking an object at high altitude and the other large telescope will be tracking an object—at either high or low altitudes and collecting radiometric data." To locate an object, the system computes an object's position from information on its orbit and points the telescope to the required position. The operator may then pick out the spacecraft by locating a stationary object in a moving star field. The operator may also fix the telescope on the moving star background and collect camera frames that show a satellite streak building up.[18]

The television cameras feed their pictures into a computer that drives a display device. The computer automatically filters stars from the night sky backdrop, and the satellites appear on the display screen as streaks of light. GEODSS can transmit position and signature identification data to the SSC in Cheyenne Mountain in seconds.[19]

Prior to the closing of the Korea station, the stations' areas of coverage were: Stallion Station (165W–050W); Maui, Hawaii (010W–140E); Diego Garcia

(010E–130E); and ChoeJong San (070E–178E). GEODSS sensors were responsible for over 65 percent of all deep space object tracking and identification and provided almost worldwide coverage of the equator.[20]

A second set of dedicated sensors are those that constitute the Naval Space Surveillance System (NAVSPASUR), which has been in operation since 1961 and is presently operated by about 100 contractor personnel. The system, headquartered at Dahlgren, Virginia, detects and tracks satellites that pass through an electronic fence consisting of a fan-shaped radar beam with a 7,500-mile range, extending from San Diego, California, to Fort Stewart, Georgia. The beam cannot be steered; detection results when the satellite passes through the beam and deflects the beam's energy back to Earth, where it is detected by several arrays of dipole antennas—"a form of cheap, unsophisticated antenna not unlike a television receiving aerial."[21]

The central transmitter for the beam is located at Lake Kickapoo, Texas, and there are two smaller transmitting stations at Gilla River, Arizona, and Jordan Lake, Alabama. The six receiver stations—at San Diego, California; Elephant Butte, New Mexico; Red River, Arkansas; Silver Lake, Mississippi; Hawkinsville, Georgia; and Tattnall, Georgia—are all located, as are the transmitting stations, across the southern part of the United States, along a great circle inclined about 33 degrees to the equator. All satellites with an inclination greater than 33 degrees (about 80 percent of the current population) pass through this circle twice each day. The data obtained are then transmitted in real-time to NAVSPASUR headquarters and the Computation Center at Dahlgren.[22]

Objects in low-inclination orbit (which includes geosynchronous satellites) and very small objects are not routinely detectable with NAVSPASUR. It does have a longitudinal width that goes from Africa (less than 15 degrees west longitude) to beyond Hawaii (greater than 165 degrees west longitude) and is capable of "seeing" out beyond 22,000 miles. On a typical day the system will register more than 160,000 observations, most generated by satellites in near-Earth orbit. There are more than 100 satellites that no sensor other than the NAVSPASUR fence routinely detects.[23]

In June 1991 the Air Force Space Command closed down, for budgetary reasons, a mechanically steered AN/GPS-10 model radar, code-named COBRA TALON and located at San Miguel in the Philippines. The radar had a 60-foot dish and a range of 2,300 miles. In 1992 a similar radar, with a 30-foot dish, was to become operational at Saipan, Commonwealth of Northern Mariana Islands, but also became a victim of budgetary restrictions. The Saipan Space Surveillance Station was intended to be part of the three-site Pacific Radar Barrier (PACBAR), along with San Miguel and the ARPA Long-Range Tracking and Instrumentation Radar (ALTAIR) site discussed below.[24]

Two new sets of dedicated sensors were added to the Space Surveillance Network in the late 1980s and have undergone restructuring and downsizing in the 1990s. Space surveillance squadrons or detachments that have been closed in recent years include the 1st Space Surveillance Squadron at Verona Test Annex,

Griffiss Air Force Base, New York; and the 4th Space Surveillance Squadron at Lackland Air Force Base, Texas (with Detachments at San Vito dei Normanni, RAF Edzell, and Osan Air Base, Korea).[25]

The dedicated sensors previously operated by the 1st, 3rd, 4th, and 5th space surveillance squadrons are now operated only by the 3rd and 5th squadrons. The 3rd Space Surveillance Squadron, headquartered at Misawa Air Base, Japan, operates a Passive Deep Space Tracking System (DSTS). The DSTS is a system of passive antennas designed to receive active satellite transmissions, which can be used to locate, identify, and monitor operational spacecraft, including satellites in geosynchronous orbit.[26]

The squadron's sole detachment, Detachment 1 at Osan Air Base, Korea, operates a Passive Low Altitude Space Surveillance (LASS) system site—used primarily for gathering space intelligence and tracking space systems in near-Earth orbit. The 5th Space Surveillance Squadron at RAF Feltwell, United Kingdom, operates both DSTS and LASS systems.[27]

A new 4th Space Surveillance Squadron at Holloman Air Force Base, New Mexico, operates the Transportable Optical System (TOS), which was first tested at San Vito, Italy, in 1991. The TOS consists of a 21-inch telescope and electronic camera on a modified Nike-Ajax radar mount. The complete system can be crated and relocated in a C-141 transport.[28]

Also among the dedicated sensors is the 20th Space Surveillance Squadron's AN/FPS-85 phased array radar at Eglin Air Force Base, Florida, constructed in 1967. The radar, thirteen stories high and as long as a city block, has its principal axis aligned due south across the Gulf of Mexico and is capable of receiving and transmitting over an arc extending 60 degrees on either side. Most satellites pass through its beam, which has a range of 2,500 miles, twice a day. The radar provides tracking information on space objects in low-Earth orbit and has a limited deep-space capability.[29]

The AN/FPS-85 "consists of several thousand individual transmitters the power outputs of which are added together by controlling their phases to form a single beam which can be electronically swept across the sky in millionths of a second."[30]

The radar can search for unknown objects across 120 degrees of azimuth from horizon to zenith, while simultaneously tracking several already acquired targets. In a typical twenty-four-hour period, it can make 10,000 observations.[31]

COLLATERAL SSN SENSORS

Collateral sensors are used for space surveillance, but they are meant primarily for other missions—such as missile warning or intelligence collection.[32] Collateral sensors include those at Diyarbakir; Shemya, Alaska; Cavalier Air Station, North Dakota; at Antigua and Ascension Island; at the three Ballistic Missile Early Warning System (BMEWS) sites; and at the two remaining PAVE PAWS sites.

The BMEWS is designed primarily to track missiles and determine the number launched and their intended targets. The system is dispersed among three sites— Clear Air Force Station, Alaska; Thule Air Base, Greenland; and Fylingdales, Great Britain. The Air Force Space Command's 13th Space Warning Squadron at Clear Air Force Station operates an AN/FPS-50 Detection and AN/FPS-92 BMEWS Tracker radar. The 12th Space Warning Squadron at Thule operates an AN/FPS-123 phased array radar. The Fylingdales site, operated jointly with the RAF, is the home of an AN/FPS-126 phased array radar.[33]

Two of the original four PAVE PAWS (Perimeter Acquisition Vehicle Entry Phased Array Warning System) sites, those at and El Dorado Air Station in Texas and Robins Air Force Base in Georgia, have been placed in caretaker status, and the associated warning squadrons (8th and 9th) have been deactivated. The remaining squadrons and radars are located at Cape Cod Air Force Station (6th Space Warning Squadron) and Beale Air Force Base (7th Space Warning Squadron). Both the 6th and 7th squadrons operate AN/FPS-123 phased array radars, whose prime mission is warning of SLBM launches. But the radars also are employed for space surveillance and tracking and can provide limited metric observations of space objects and space object identification. They each have two arrays, providing a total coverage of 240 degrees out to 3,100 miles.[34]

The Perimeter Acquisition Radar Characterization System (PARCS), run by the 10th Space Warning Squadron at Cavalier Air Station, North Dakota, is a vestige of the U.S. ABM system that was dismantled in 1975. With a 3,100-mile range, the PARCS provides early warning and "also provides surveillance, tracking, reporting, and space object identification (SOI) support for space surveillance and intelligence operations."[35]

The phased array COBRA DANE (AN/FPS-108) and the mechanically steered AN/FPS-79 tracking radar, discussed in their MASINT role in Chapter 9, are also used as collateral sensors. The COBRA DANE has a 28,000-mile range, and the AN/FPS-79 has a range of 24,000 miles. With its coverage extending northward over an arc from Kamchatka to the Bering Strait, COBRA DANE can be used for tracking satellites in polar and near-polar orbits.[36]

Also among the collateral sensors are the mechanically steered radars at Antigua Island and Ascension Island. The primary mission of these radars is to provide launch support to the Eastern Test Range. The Antigua site provides data on satellites in low-Earth orbit, relying on a high-precision AN/FPQ-14 pulse tracker designed to track missiles and space objects. The AN/FPQ-14 is directly interconnected with other radars of the Eastern Space and Missile Center.[37]

On Ascension Island, located midway between the east coast of Brazil and the west coast of South Africa, are two radars. The primary radar is the AN/FPPQ-15 tracker, which provides space and missile launch support to the ESMC, near-Earth satellite observations to the Space Control Center, and narrow-band space object identification (SOI) data to the USSPACECOM intelligence components. The second radar is an AN/TPQ-18 tracker.[38]

CONTRIBUTING SSN SENSORS

Contributing sensors are those under contract or agreement to provide space surveillance data when requested by U.S. Space Command headquarters. Contributing sensors include two systems on Kwajelein Atoll, two radars in Massachusetts, and three sensors in Hawaii.[39]

The Advanced Research Projects Agency (ARPA) Lincoln C-Band Observable Radar (ALCOR) on Roi-Namur Island, Kwajalein Atoll, operated by the Army Space and Strategic Defense Command, consists of a 40-foot antenna and provides wideband radar imaging data for space object identification on low-Earth orbit satellites. Support to the SSN is on a noninterference basis with Kwajalein Missile Range support.[40]

A second radar located on Roi-Namur, the ARPA Long-Range Tracking and Instrumentation Radar (ALTAIR), is also operated by the Army Space and Strategic Defense Command. The ALTAIR is a 150-foot paraboloid antenna that provides metric data on spacecraft. The radar operates in a space surveillance mode for 128 hours per week.[41]

Also located on Roi-Namur are the TRADEX and MMW radars. Like ALTAIR, TRADEX is a low-frequency dish radar that can pick up incoming objects as soon as they come over Kwajelin's horizon at a distance of approximately 2,400 miles. Like ALCOR, MMW operates at a high frequencies, allowing it to image objects in space. MMW can detect details as small as 5 inches, which makes it of significant value to the intelligence community.[42]

The Millstone and Haystack radars, located about half a mile apart at Westford, Massachusetts, are operated by MIT's Lincoln Laboratory. The Millstone is a deep-space, large-dish tracking radar capable of tracking 1-square-meter targets at geosynchronous altitude. The Haystack radar is a high-quality imaging radar that can resolve objects as small as 1 foot in diameter in low-Earth orbit. It has been described in congressional hearings as providing "images of orbiting satellites that we can get from no other location." It is a "long-range, high altitude capable radar which provides extremely good intelligence data and now has a real-time operational reporting capability."[43]

The contributing sensors at Maui, Hawaii, together with the GEODSS system, constitute the Maui Space Surveillance Site. The Air Force Maui Optical System (AMOS) at Mt. Haleakala, Maui, is a photometric and laser facility assigned to the Air Force Materiel Command's Phillips Laboratory. Its basic mission is to conduct research and development of new and evolving electro-optical sensors as well as to provide support to the Air Force Space Command. It has also provided support to NASA and the Jet Propulsion Laboratory. AMOS experiments have included detection and tracking of orbital debris, observations of shuttle and satellite operations, and laser illumination of satellites.[44]

Mt. Haleakala's location, 10,000 feet above sea level, places AMOS's equipment above much of the atmosphere and the interference that results. The equipment includes a 5.2-foot Cassegrain telescope, a laser beam director, and an AMOS acquisition system. The space surveillance research and development work at AMOS includes metric, tracking, infrared space object identification, and compensated imaging.[45]

AMOS's laser was used to illuminate Soviet spacecraft at night for the purpose of telescope photography. It was also used to determine whether Soviet nuclear-powered radar ocean reconnaissance satellites were operating or properly shut down at the end of their missions. The visible wavelength images of the satellites produced by AMOS were good enough to show a Soviet reactor glowing red hot.[46]

AMOS's telescope has sufficiently high resolution to discern objects in the space shuttles' open payload bay. Such a capability could have been used to obtain intelligence on Soviet shuttle missions, had the Soviet program reached operational status. Its telescope has allowed identification of objects as small as 3.1 inches in diameter in geosynchronous orbit. Another optical sensor, AMOS Daylight Near-Infrared Imaging System (ADONIS), which underwent testing in 1993, extends AMOS capability to twenty-four hours a day.[47]

The mission of the AN/FPQ-14 at Kaena Point, Oahu, Hawaii, is to provide low-Earth satellite observation. The AN/FPQ-14 is tasked on a limited basis with supporting the space surveillance mission, primarily for high-priority objects requiring instantaneous observational data. The site is operated by civilians twenty-four hours per day, seven days per week. Kaena Point provides pointing data to the AMOS site.[48]

Collocated with the GEODSS and AMOS systems is the Maui Optical Tracking Identification Facility (MOTIF), code-named TEAL BLUE. MOTIF consists of two co-mounted, 48-inch, Cassegrain telescopes capable of both near-Earth and deep-space satellite tracking and object identification using visual light and long-wave infrared imaging. For satellites orbiting at 3,000 miles or less, MOTIF's sensors can measure reflectivity and heat emissions and provide images.[49]

As of 1990, images could be taken for only a few hours after sunset or before dawn, when the telescopes were in darkness and the satellites in the light. Planned improvements would allow one of the telescopes to operate for two hours before sunset or after sunrise by canceling out interference from the sun. As a result, the number of hours that MOTIF could be used daily would expand from six to ten.[50]

In 1997 the Air Force Material Command's Phillips Laboratory began testing another sensor at the Maui Complex—the Advanced Electro-Optical System (AEOS)—that is optimized for satellite tracking and space object identification. With a primary mirror 3.67 meters wide, it is expected to permit detection and tracking of 4-inch pieces of debris in low-Earth orbit at a range of 186 miles. Initial operating capability is expected in 1999.[51]

A second TEAL site at Malabar, Florida, is TEAL AMBER, consisting of similar telescopes to those at MOTIF, along with a laser radar (with eight laser transmitters). The two sites provide computer-enhanced, high-resolution, close-up photographs of Russian and Chinese spacecraft. It has also been reported that the system was used to photograph cosmonauts during of the extra-vehicular activities conducted from the SALYUT 6 space laboratory. Such photography implies a resolution of less than 40 inches.[52] The USSPACECOM has plugged the National Science Foundation UHF radar, developed by MIT's Lincoln Laboratory Electro-Optical Test Site at Socorro, New Mexico, into its network of deep-space sensors.[53]

The Space Surveillance Network makes an average of 45,000 sightings of orbiting objects each day. Twenty percent of the objects and debris cannot be reliably tracked. More than 16,000 objects have been catalogued. A commander in chief of the U.S. Space Command characterized the system as "predictive . . . rather than a constant surveillance system." Continuity on deep-space objects is sometimes difficult to maintain because the radars are part-time contributors and the optical and electro-optical sensors are restricted to nighttime, clear weather operation.[54]

ADDITIONAL SPACE SURVEILLANCE CAPABILITIES

The United States does not operate any space systems whose primary mission is the surveillance of other satellites. In 1983, development of a space-based space surveillance system was described by the Air Force Deputy Chief of Staff for Research, Development, and Acquisition as the "primary thrust of the Space Surveillance Technology Program." The system was to provide full-Earth orbit coverage, reduce overseas basing of sensors, and provide near real-time "operationally responsive coverage of objects and events in space." The envisaged Space-Based Surveillance System (SBSS) was to consist of four satellites in low-Earth orbit. The long-wave, infrared mosaic-staring sensor on each satellite would have viewed the volume of space from approximately 60 nautical miles to geosynchronous altitude. Subsequently, the SBSS program was absorbed into the Strategic Defense Initiative (SDI) program and renamed the Space Surveillance and Tracking System (SSTS). It then became one of many SDI systems that eventually succumbed to budget restrictions.[55]

The United States has for many years made use of two space systems to provide intelligence on foreign space activities. The possibility of employing U.S. imagery satellites to photograph Soviet satellites was raised no later than 1965, with respect to the KH-4. Over a decade later, KH-11 satellites were on occasion used in "space-to-space" imagery operations.[56] Presumably, its successor has also been employed for that purpose.

In addition, the Defense Support Program (DSP) satellites described in Chapter 9 have also proven useful in monitoring foreign satellites. The employment of DSP sensors to detect space objects, including satellites and their debris, has been designated FAST WALKER. Most FAST WALKERs have been routine observations of foreign spacecraft. The infrared readings obtained by DSP sensors, resulting from the reflection of sunlight off the spacecraft, provided analysts at the CIA, DIA, and Air Force Foreign Technology Division (now the National Air Intelligence Center) with data on spacecraft signatures and movements. Such data allowed analysts to estimate where the satellite was going and its mission.[57]

In addition, DSP sensors would provide data concerning the reentry of satellites or other man-made space platforms. In January 1978 DSP sensors detected the reentry of COSMOS 954, a Soviet ocean reconnaissance satellite, with a live nuclear reactor, that the Soviets could not control. Unable to boost it into an orbit that would keep it in space, the Soviets could only watch as the satellite's orbit decayed to the point that reentry took place. At the Aerospace Corporation, the DSP track of the reentry was subjected to mathematical analysis and the impact point determined. A field crew was dispatched to the approximate location in Canada where the analysts concluded the satellite would have crashed to Earth; the crew found a hunting party that had stumbled on the debris. In 1979 DSP sensors provided data on the reentry of Skylab, the 130,000-pound U.S. space station, whose reentry threatened various populated areas.[58]

Among the satellite movements and debris that the DSP detected from the early 1970s to early 1980s were those associated with the Soviet anti-satellite (ASAT) program. Between 1972 and 1982 the Soviets conducted sixteen anti-satellite tests. After an intercept satellite was placed in orbit by a SL-11 booster, ground controllers would maneuver the satellite so that after either one or two orbits it passed sufficiently near the target satellite to permit its own guidance system to take over. When in range an explosive charge aboard the intercept vehicle was detonated, sending a cloud of shrapnel at high speed to destroy the target. The DSP's monitoring of the launch, satellite movement, and aftermath contributed to U.S. intelligence analysis of the Soviet program.[59]

More recently a DSP satellite detected the descent of a malfunctioning Chinese FSW-1 reconnaissance satellite back to Earth and into the Atlantic.[60]

A new ground-based resource for space surveillance is presently designated HAVE STARE. Originally designed for intelligence gathering, it is expected to come on line in 1999 to track and catalog deep-space satellites and debris. It can also be used as an imaging radar to produce high-resolution images or pictures of whatever it is pointed at, or for spectral data collection, such as reading exhaust fumes of a jet engine to determine aircraft type. Presently at Vandenberg Air Force Base, it has been reported to be scheduled for deployment to Vardo, Norway, in mid-1999, where it would be operated by the Norwegian Military Intelligence Service.[61]

SIGINT SUPPORT TO SPACE SURVEILLANCE

In 1994, to provide improved SIGINT support to the space surveillance squadrons operating the DSTS and LASS systems, the Air Intelligence Agency established an 18th Intelligence Squadron (subordinate to the 544th Intelligence Group), with detachments located at the same sites as the space surveillance units. Since then

Detachment 1 of the 18th IS—at Verona Test Annex, Griffiss Air Force Base, New York—has been deactivated along with the Griffiss-based 1st Space Surveillance Squadron. Also deactivated was the 18th Intelligence Squadron's Detachment 5 at Edzell, along with the space surveillance activity at Edzell. Remaining are a new Detachment 1 at Holloman Air Force Base, New Mexico; Detachment 2 at Osan (where Detachment 1, 3rd Space Surveillance Squadron operates); Detachment 3 at Misawa (headquarters of the 3rd SPSS); and Detachment 4 at RAF Feltwell (home of the 5th SPSS).[62]

Notes

1. Air Force Space Command, *Space Surveillance Requirements* (Peterson AFB, Colo.: HQ AFSPC, July 10, 1995), pp. 7–8; General Accounting Office, *Space Surveillance: DOD and NASA Need Consolidated Requirements and a Coordinated Plan*, GAO/NSIAD 98–42 (Washington, D.C.: GAO, December 1997), p. 12.

2. Air Force Space Command, *Space Surveillance Requirements*, pp. 12–13.

3. See Lt. Col. Michael R. Mantz, *The New Sword: A Theory of Space Combat Power*, (Maxwell AFB, Ala.: Air University Press, 1995); Edna L. Jenkins and Dr. Paul W. Schumacher Jr., "Close Encounters: Parallel Processing Improves Space Debris Tracking," *Space Tracks*, Summer 1997, pp. 15–16; Dr. Paul W. Schumacher Jr., "Cataloging Space," *Space Tracks*, Fall 1997, pp. 10–13; Nicholas L. Johnson, *Soviet Military Strategy in Space* (London: Jane's Publishing, 1987); Nicholas L. Johnson and David M. Rodvold, *Europe and Asia in Space 1993–1994* (Colorado Springs, Colo.: Kaman Sciences Corporation, n.d.).

4. Aerospace Defense Command, *ADCOM Command & Control*, November 30, 1980, pp. 8–12; USSPACECOM Regulation 200–1, "Satellite Reconnaissance Operations Security Support Program," August 18, 1989.

5. USSPACECOM Regulation 200–1, "Satellite Reconnaissance Operations Security Support Program"; *Cryptologic Technician Training Series, Module 8 Fleet Operations— Electronic Warfare*, NAVEDTRA A 95–08–00–87 (Pensacola, Fla.: Naval Education and Training Command, 1987).

6. Lt. Frank Murphy, "Chambered Round," *Space Tracks*, March-April 1991, pp. 8–9.

7. "News Breaks," *Aviation Week & Space Technology*, March 15, 1993, p. 23.

8. Thomas G. Mahnken, "Why Third World Space Systems Matter," *Orbis*, Fall 1991, pp. 563–579; Johnson and Rodvold, *Europe and Asia in Space 1993–1994*, passim.

9. Joseph C. Anselmo, "Commercial Satellites Zoom in On Military Imagery Monopoly," *Aviation Week & Space Technology*, September 22, 1997, pp. 75–78;

10. AFSPACECOM Regulation 55–10, "2nd Space Wing (SWG) Satellite Operations," October 13, 1989, p. 6; Jess Hall, "Command Activates 21st SPW at Peterson," *Space Trace*, June 1992, p. 4; General Accounting Office, *Space Surveillance*, p. 10.

11. USSPACECOM Regulation 55–12, "Space Surveillance Network," June 1, 1992.

12. USSPACECOM Regulation 55–6, "Space Surveillance Network Data User Support," April 15, 1991, p. 10; AFSPACECOM 002–88, "Statement of Operational Need (SON): Space Surveillance (S2)," August 7, 1989, p. A1-1; Curtis Peebles, *High Frontier: The U.S. Air Force and the Military Space Program* (Washington, D.C.: U.S. Government Printing Office, 1997), pp. 39–41.

13. AFSPCMD 5–103, "Space Surveillance Squadrons (SPSS)," October 1, 1996; Peebles, *High Frontier*, pp. 39–40.

14. Vincent Kiernan, "Portuguese Balk at U.S. Radar, Leaving Air Force with Blind Spot," *Space News*, October 9, 1989, p. 12; Curtis Peebles, *High Frontier*, p. 40; General Accounting Office, *Space Surveillance*, p. 12.

15. David M. Russell, "NORAD Adds Radar, Optics to Increase Space Defense," *Defense Electronics*, July 1982, pp. 82–86; Lt. Col. William C. Jeas and Robert Anctil, "The Ground-Based Electro-Optical Deep Space Surveillance (GEODSS) System," *Military Electronics/Countermeasures*, November 1981, pp. 47–51; "GEODSS Photographs Orbiting Satellite," *Aviation Week & Space Technology*, December 5, 1985, pp. 146–147; Office of Technology Assessment, *Anti-Satellite Weapons, Countermeasures and Arms Control* (Washington, D.C.: U.S. Government Printing Office, 1985), p. 55; USSPACECOM Regulation 55–12, "Space Surveillance Network (SSN)," p. 15; Dr. T. S. Kelso, "Space Surveillance," *Satellite Times*, September/October 1997, pp. 68–69.

16. "U.S. Upgrading Ground-Based Sensors," *Aviation Week & Space Technology*, June 16, 1980, pp. 239–242; Russell, "NORAD Adds Radar, Optics to Increase Space Defense."

17. "U.S. Upgrading Ground-Based Sensors"; Science Applications International Corporation, *OUSD(A) Defense Space Systems Study, Final Report* (Falls Church, Va.: SAIC, March 1989), p. B-69; Lt. Col. Michael Muolo, *Space Handbook: A War Fighter's Guide to Space, Volume One* (Maxwell AFB, Ala.: Air University Press, 1993), pp. 98–99.

18. "U.S. Upgrading Ground-Based Sensors," p. 239; "GEODSS Photographs Orbiting Satellite."

19. Muolo, *Space Handbook: A War Fighter's Guide to Space, Volume One*, p. 99.

20. Ibid., pp. 98–99.

21. "Spacetrack," *Jane's Weapons Systems, 1982–1983* (London: Jane's Publishing, 1982), pp. 233–234; Russell, "NORAD Adds Radar, Optics to Increase Space Defense"; "The Arms Race in Space," *SIPRI Yearbook 1978: World Armaments and Disarmaments* (New York: Crane, Russak, 1978), pp. 104–130; Brendan Greeley Jr., "Navy Expanding Its Space Command to Bolster Readiness," *Aviation Week & Space Technology*, February 3, 1986, pp. 54–57; Office of the Chief of Naval Operations, OPNAV Instruction 5450.206, Subject: Naval Space Surveillance, Mission and Functions of, June 22, 1991; Schumacher, "Cataloging Space"; Gary R. Wagner, "High Desert Outpost," *Space Tracks*, Fall 1997, pp. 16–17; Roger Easton and Chester Kleczek, "Origins of Naval Space Surveillance," *Space Tracks*, May/June 1998, pp. 14–16.

22. "Spacetrack"; United States Space Command, "Space Surveillance Network (SSN)," p. 15; Schumacher, "Cataloging Space"; Kelso, "Space Surveillance."

23. Schumacher, "Cataloging Space"; "A Constant Vigil," *Space Tracks*, March/April 1998, p. 5.

24. USSPACECOM Regulation 55–6, "Space Surveillance Network Data User Support," p. 10; USSPACECOM Regulation 55–12, "Space Surveillance Network (SSN)," pp. 15–17; AFSPACECOM Regulation 23–58, "18th Surveillance Squadron (18 SURS)," September 10, 1990; Peebles, *High Frontier*, pp. 40–41.

25. "USAF Lists Force Structure, Realignment Changes," *Aerospace Daily*, July 6, 1995, pp. 14–15.

26. AFSPCMD 5–103, "Space Surveillance Squadrons (SPSS)."

27. Jesse Hall, "PASS Systems Enhance Surveillance Network," *Space Trace*, September 1992, p. 3; AFSPCMD 5–103, "Space Surveillance Squadrons (SPSS)."

28. Peebles, *High Frontier*, p. 40; AFSPCMD 5–103, "Space Surveillance Squadrons (SPSS)."

29. "AN/FPS-85," *Jane's Weapons Systems, 1982–1983*, pp. 505–506; "The Arms Race in Space," pp. 114–124 at p. 116; John Hambre et al., *Strategic Command, Control and Communications: Alternate Approaches for Modernization* (Washington, D.C.: Congressional Budget Office, 1981), p. 10; USSPACECOM Regulation 55–12, "Space Surveillance Network (SSN)," p. 15; Science Applications International Corporation, *OUSD(A) Defense Space Systems Study, Final Report*, p. B-68; AFSPCMD 5–103, "Space Surveillance Squadrons (SPSS)."

30. Owen Wilkes, *Spacetracking and Spacewarfare* (Oslo: International Peace Research Institute, 1978), p. 27.

31. Ibid.; Muolo, *Space Handbook: A War Fighter's Guide, Volume One*, p. 99.

32. USSPACECOM Regulation 55–12, "Space Surveillance Network."

33. "U.S. Upgrading Ground Sensors"; Paul Stares, *Space and National Security*, (Washington, D.C.: The Brookings Institution, 1987), p. 204; "The Arms Race in Space"; "Improved U.S. Warning Net Spurred," *Aviation Week & Space Technology*, June 23, 1980, pp. 38ff; USSPACECOM Regulation 55–12, "Space Surveillance Network (SSN)," p. 16; AFSPCMD 5–102, "Space Warning Squadron (SWS)," December 2, 1996.

34. "Pave Paws Radar," *Jane's Weapons Systems 1982–1983*, p. 501; "U.S. Upgrading Ground Sensors"; Stares, *Space and National Security*, p. 205; "Space Command Completes Acquisition of Pave Paws Warning Radar Installations," *Aviation Week & Space Technology*, May 18, 1987, pp. 128–129; Office of Legislative Liaison, Office of the Secretary of the Air Force, *Systems Information Briefs for Members of Congress* (Washington, D.C.: Department of the Air Force, 1987), p. 80; USSPACECOM Regulation 55–12, "Space Surveillance Network (SSN)"; Jesse Hall, "Command Activates 21 SPW at Peterson," *Space Trace*, June 1992, p. 4; Paul Tombarge, "On the Lookout," *Guardian*, October 1995, pp. 10–11; AFSPCM 5–102, "Space Warning Squadrons (SWS)"; Air Combat Command, *Searching the Skies: The Legacy of the United States Cold War Defense Radar Program* (Langley, Va.: ACC, 1997), p. 54; General Accounting Office, *Space Surveillance*, p. 11.

35. Stares, *Space and National Security*, p. 205; AFSPACECOM Regulation 23–46, "10th Missile Warning Squadron (MWS)," June 12, 1987; AFSPCMD 5–102, "Space Warning Squadrons (SWS)."

36. Stares, *Space and National Security*, p. 205; "The Arms Race in Space"; U.S. Air Force, "SAC Fact Sheet," August 1981.

37. USSPACECOM Regulation 55–12, "Space Surveillance Network (SSN)," p. 16; Science Applications International Corporation, *OUSD(A) Defense Space Systems Study, Final Report*, p. B-66.

38. USSPACECOM Regulation 55–12, "Space Surveillance Network (SSN)," p. 16; Science Applications International Corporation, *OUSD(A) Defense Space Systems Study, Final Report*, p. B-65.

39. USSPACECOM Regulation 55–12, "Space Surveillance Network (SSN)," p. 17.

40. Science Applications International Corporation, *OUSD(A) Defense Space Systems Study, Final Report*, p. B-62; USSPACECOM Regulation, "Space Surveillance Network (SSN)," p. 17.

41. Science Applications International Corporation, *OUSD(A) Defense Space Systems Study, Final Report*, p. B-63; USSPACECOM Regulation 55–12, "Space Surveillance Network (SSN)," p. 17.

42. Tony Reichhardt, "Catch a Falling Missile," *Air & Space*, December 1997/January 1998, pp. 26–37.

43. U.S. Air Force, "SAC Fact Sheet"; Defense Marketing Service, *Codename Handbook 1981* (Greenwich, Conn.: DMS, 1981), p. 168; Stares, *Space and National Security*, p. 205; U.S. Congress, House Committee on Appropriations, *Department of Defense Appropriations for 1981, Part 8* (Washington, D.C.: U.S. Government Printing Office, 1980), p. 241; Science Applications International Corporation, *OUSD(A) Defense Space Systems Study, Final Report*, p. B-71; USSPACECOM Regulation 55–12, "Space Surveillance Network (SSN)," p. 17.

44. Science Applications International Corporation, *OUSD(A) Defense Space Systems Study, Final Report*, p. B-64; Vincent Kiernan, "Air Force Begins Upgrades to Satellite Scanning Telescope," *Space News*, July 23–29, 1990, p. 8; "Air Force Maui Optical Station (AMOS)," http://www.fas.org/spp/military/program/ track/amos.htm.

45. Science Applications International Corporation, *OUSD(A) Defense Space Systems Study, Final Report*, p. B-64; Kiernan, "Air Force Begins Upgrades to Satellite Scanning Telescope."

46. Craig Covault, "Maui Optical Station Photographs External Tank Reentry Breakup," *Aviation Week & Space Technology*, June 11, 1990, pp. 52–53.

47. Ibid.; Bruce D. Nordwall, "Air Force Uses Optics to Track Space Objects," *Aviation Week & Space Technology*, August 16, 1993, pp. 66–68; Bruce D. Nordwall, "Optics/Laser Research Seeks to Improve Images," *Aviation Week & Space Technology*, August 16, 1993, p. 69.

48. Science Applications International Corporation, *OUSD(A) Defense Space Systems Study, Final Report*, pp. B-64, B-70.

49. Stares, *Space and National Security*, p. 204; John L. Piotrowski, "C3I for Space Control," *Signal*, June 1987, pp. 22–33; Science Applications International Corporation, *OUSD(A) Defense Space Systems Study, Final Report*, p. B-72; Kiernan, "Air Force Begins Upgrades to Satellite Scanning Telescope," p. 8.

50. Kiernan, "Air Force Begins Upgrades to Satellite Scanning Telescope."

51. William B. Scott, "Satellite-Tracking Telescope Readied for USAF Service," *Aviation Week & Space Technology*, July 21, 1997, p. 57; "Telescope That Tracks Satellites Is Unveiled," *Space News*, July 14–20, 1997, p. 22.

52. Joel W. Powell, "Photography of Orbiting Satellites," *Spaceflight* (February 1983): 82–83; Stares, *Space and National Security*, p. 204; "Request for Proposals–Air Force Space Technology Center," *SDI Monitor*, May 25, 1990, p. 125.

53. Stares, *Space and National Security*, p. 205; U.S. Air Force, "SAC Fact Sheet."

54. AFSPACECOM 002–08, "Statement of Operational Need (SON): Space Surveillance (S2)," p. 3; William J. Broad, "New Space Challenge: Monitoring Weapons," *New York Times*, December 8, 1987, pp. C1, C6.

55. U.S. Congress, House Committee on Appropriations, *Department of Defense Appropriations for 1984, Part 8* (Washington, D.C.: U.S. Government Printing Office, 1983), pp. 506–508; Craig Covault, "SDI Delta Space Experiment to Aid Kill-Vehicle Design," *Aviation Week & Space Technology*, September 15, 1986, pp. 18–19.

56. [Deleted], Chief Systems Analysis Staff, Memorandum for: Mr. William A. Tidwell, Subject; Use of KH-4 to Photograph Orbiting Satellites, October 1, 1965; Private information.

57. AFSPACECOM Regulation 55–55, "Space Based Sensor (SBS) Large Processing Station (LPS) and European Ground Station (EGS) Tactical Requirements Doctrine (TRD),"

September 30, 1992, p. 38; Interview. One exceptional sighting occurred on May 5, 1984, which has been suggested to represent a detection of a UFO by some in the UFO community. A detection did take place, but the object detected was of terrestrial origin. See Jeffrey T. Richelson, *America's Space Sentinels: DPS Satellites and National Security* (Lawrence: University Press of Kansas, forthcoming), chapter 7.

58. Gus W. Weiss, "The Life and Death of Cosmos 954," *Studies in Intelligence*, Spring 1978; Jack Manno, *Arming the Heavens: The Hidden Military Agenda for Space 1945–1995*, (New York, Dodd, Mead, 1984), p. 148; private information.

59. Stares, *Space and National Security*, pp. 85–87; Interviews.

60. Craig Covault, "Chinese Military Satellite Poses Falling-Debris Risk," *Aviation Week & Space Technology*, November 27, 1995, p. 56; "FSW-1 Sinks into Atlantic," *Aviation Week & Space Technology*, March 18, 1996, p. 62.

61. Brian Orban, "Worldwide Support," *Guardian*, December 1995, pp. 3–6; Gordon Van Vleet, "'STAREway' into Space," *Guardian*, October 1995, pp. 14–15; "HAVE STARE," http://www.fas.org/spp/ military/program/track/havestare.htm.

62. Jeff Qualls, "Vigilance on the High Frontier," *Spokesman*, March 1995, p. 13; Air Intelligence Agency, Bullet Background Paper on the 544th Intelligence Group, n.d.; Doug Karas, "AIA's 18th Intelligence Squadron," *Spokesman*, February 1997, p. 6; Air Intelligence Agency, Mission Directive 1520: 18th Intelligence Squadron, June 13, 1997.

11

HUMAN INTELLIGENCE

The increasing ability to collect intelligence via technical means has over the last several decades reduced the reliance on human sources; however, human sources are not inconsequential. Much valuable information, particularly that contained in documents, is accessible only through human sources. Such sources can be used to fill gaps—in some cases important gaps—left by technical collection systems.

Sometimes gaps will result because of the inherent limitations of technical systems—with proper security, many discussions will be immune to interception. Also, technical systems cannot photograph policy documents or weapons systems manuals locked in a vault. Nor can technical systems physically acquire weapons systems or weapons systems components.

A high priority for the U.S. intelligence community is to understand the decision processes involved in foreign, military, and economic policymaking in both hostile and friendly nations. An understanding of both the processes and people can lead to more accurate estimates of the course of action in given circumstances. Some data on such matters may be obtained by technical means, but there will be gaps that can be addressed only by human intelligence.

A further objective of human intelligence (HUMINT) activities is the acquisition of planning documents, technical manuals, contingency plans, and weapons systems blueprints. As Amrom Katz observed, "The analysts . . . want the designer's plan, notebooks, tests on components, tests of materials, conversation between designer and customer."[1] Although in most cases the analyst must settle for images and electronic data concerning test activities, it is often the designer's documentation that constitutes the "best evidence."

Obtaining a comprehensive overview of a particular program, whether it a be biological or nuclear weapons program, can be difficult to achieve relying solely on technical sources of information. It has been reported that in the experience of intelligence officials, a "program's workings become clear only when described by participants."[2]

Certain stages of military R&D are simply not available for technical monitoring. Once plans have reached the testing stage, a variety of U.S. technical collection systems can be employed. But when the weapon is being designed, and its characteristics debated, technical collection can be of very limited utility—particularly if communications security is stringent. It is desirable to know about the characteristics of weapons systems when they have reached the testing stage, but is also important to know whatever possible about activity in the design bureaus. Even nations that purchase weapons abroad may develop their own modified versions. Thus, Iraq developed modified versions of the Scuds that it purchased from the Soviet Union.

In the case of terrorist groups, drug cartels, underground political parties, and dictators, intelligence about intentions may be obtainable only through recruiting an inside source. Such a source may be able to cast light on a situation discovered by overhead photography—for example, the movement of troops toward a border.

HUMINT comes in two basic varieties: clandestine HUMINT and overt HUMINT. Clandestine HUMINT involves a secret relationship with a foreign source to provide classified data. Overt HUMINT involves open activities conducted by Defense attachés and State Department personnel as well as the debriefing of defectors, émigrés, and travelers.

Statistics derived from twelve 1994 intelligence reviews provide some measure, although not necessarily a perfect one, of the value of HUMINT. Of 376 specific intelligence issues, HUMINT was judged as making a "critical contribution" toward 205. In regard to terrorism, HUMINT items represented 75 percent of the critical items. The figures for other areas were: narcotics, over 50 percent; nonproliferation, over 40 percent; and international economics, over 33 percent.[3]

During the Persian Gulf War, overt HUMINT was employed, in real-time, "to nominate, target, and destroy key Iraqi command, control, communications, and other military targets." HUMINT was used, in conjunction with imagery, not only to aid in the destruction of facilities but to identify mosques and hospitals and permit U.S. war planners to avoid targeting such facilities. One source provided information that, according to an Army intelligence history, "significantly contributed to the impact of the air campaign, which undoubtedly saved many American and coalition lives."[4]

OFFICERS AND DIPLOMATS

Human sources include clandestine intelligence officers and their agents, attachés, diplomats, travelers, as well as defectors and émigrés. The core of U.S. human intelligence operations is composed of the intelligence officers of the CIA's Directorate of Operations. These officers are U.S. citizens who generally operate under the cover of U.S. embassies and consulates—an approach that provides them with secure communications (within the embassy and to other locations), protected files, and diplomatic immunity. Others operate under "non-official cover" (NOC). Such NOCs may operate as businessmen, sometimes under the cover of working at the overseas office of a U.S. firm. In 1995 it was reported that 110 CIA officers were serving as NOCs, and that RJR Nabisco, General Electric, IBM, Bank of America, Pan Am, Rockwell International, and other major corporations had allowed CIA officers to pose as overseas employees.[5]

The CIA officers seek to recruit foreign nationals as agents as well as to cultivate knowledgeable foreigners who may provide information, either as "unwitting" sources or outside of a formal officer-agent relationship.

CIA stations in foreign countries are headed by the Chief of Station (COS) and vary substantially in size, from just a few officers to more than 150, as was the case in the Philippines in the late 1980s. The COS and his or her officers operate under a variety of cover positions that vary from embassy to embassy, including political counselor, second secretary, and economic attaché. They also operate under the cover of a variety of offices in the embassy. Thus, in the late 1970s, the CIA station in London, the agency's largest liaison station, was staffed by some forty CIA officers who worked out of three cover offices—the Political Liaison Section; the Area Telecommunications Office, with a staff of between nine and thirteen at any one time; and the Joint Reports and Research Unit, with a staff of about thirty. Also operating from the embassy were representatives of the CIA's Foreign Broadcast Information Service, and the Office of the Special U.S. Liaison Officer (SUSLO). The latter served as the liaison between the National Security Agency and its British counterpart, the Government Communications Headquarters (GCHQ). Composed largely of NSA personnel, it did include some representatives of the CIA. The station is generally headed by a very senior CIA officer.[6]

In France, the Regional Reports Office, the Regional Administrative Support office, and the American Liaison Section served as cover offices in the late 1970s. In Italy, the Embassy Political Section and the United States Army Europe Southern Projects Unit served as covers, whereas in West Germany, the Office of the Coordinator and Adviser, the Research Office, the Records Office, and the Liaison Office performed that function. The CIA also made great use in Germany of the United States Army Europe (USAREUR) for cover. Among the units it used for cover were the U.S. Army Field Systems Office, the U.S. Army General Research Detachment, the U.S. Army Scientific and Technical Programming Detachment (Provisional), the U.S. Army Scientific Projects Group, the U.S. Army Security Evaluation Group, and the U.S. Army Technical Analysis Unit.[7]

The DHS officers, including the attachés who operate as part of the Defense Attaché System, constitute a second group of intelligence officers. The functions of the Defense attachés include:

- identifying and gaining cooperation of human sources believed to possess the ability to furnish intelligence information
- identifying and capturing collection opportunities represented by trade fairs, military demonstrations, parades, symposia, convocations, conferences, meetings, and the like

- traveling to identified geographic target areas to observe, photograph, and report information specifically needed by consumers/users
- identifying, establishing contact, and maintaining liaison with foreign military officers who, by virtue of rank, position, or assignment, can furnish potential intelligence information or are considered to be future leaders
- gaining and maintaining area reality to observe and report political, sociological, psychological, and economic developments of potential value in gauging military plans, capabilities, and intentions of foreign governments and their military forces and their stability
- identifying and gaining access to assist in the acquisition and exploitation of foreign military equipment and materiel[8]

In addition to cultivating sources and collecting open source material, Defense attachés may also engage in direct collection activities—which may constitute more than open observation, at least in the view of foreign security services.

In May 1986, the Nicaraguan government charged that two military officers, including the U.S. Embassy's military attaché, were discovered traveling without permits in a restricted war zone and suggested they were involved in espionage activity. The two were found traveling near the town of Siuna, a remote area in north central Nicaragua that had been a focus of combat between the Sandinista Army and guerrilla forces.[9]

In early 1987, Colonel Marc B. Powe, the attaché at the U.S. Embassy in Baghdad, was declared persona non grata and given two weeks to leave Iraq after he was accused of spying on and photographing truckloads of tanks and other military equipment in Kuwait in early December. Powe, who also served as attaché to Baghdad, had discovered a convoy of Soviet military equipment in Kuwait en route to Baghdad, and Kuwaiti authorities spotted him photographing the convoy and taking notes.[10]

In early 1989, two U.S. attachés, Col. Clifford Robert Ward and Maj. Robert Siegel, were apprehended on the perimeter of a Palestinian commando base, 25 miles from Damascus. Taken into custody by armed guerrillas of the Popular Front for the Liberation of Palestine—General Command (PFLP-GC), Ward and Siegel were reported to have been carrying cameras, maps, binoculars, and telephoto lenses.[11]

At the beginning of August 1995, two U.S. Air Force officers, Col. Joseph Wei Chan and Capt. Dwayne Howard Florenzie, were expelled from China after being apprehended on July 28 and accused of spying on restricted military zones along the southeastern coast of China. The two attachés, assigned to the U.S. Consulate General's office in Hong Kong, were charged with sneaking into restricted areas and "illegally acquiring military intelligence by photographing and videotaping" the areas before being detained "on the spot" by Chinese soldiers.[12]

The attachés had entered China on July 23 on visas issued for the purpose of consulting with officials at the U.S. Embassy in Beijing and the Consulate General in Guanghzhou. But their actual objective was reported to be the monitoring of ongoing Chinese military exercises north of Taiwan. The officers were said to be looking for Chinese SU-27 warplanes that had been moved to an airfield up the coast from Canton and close to Taiwan.[13]

The American officers were riding bicycles, wearing civilians clothes, had photographic equipment stored away in their backpacks, and were "observing" and "carrying along with the normal business" of military attachés when they were picked up by the Chinese, according to a Defense Department spokesman.[14]

Five months later, in early January 1996, a similar incident took place near a military base at Siaxi, in Guangdong province in southern China. The Chinese detained Air Force Col. Bradley Gerdes, the assistant military attaché, whose spying, Beijing said, had "seriously encroached upon China's sovereignty and compromised the national security of China."[15]

On January 8, Gerdes and a Japanese military attaché were stopped near a military area on Hainan Island, off the southern tip of China, after allegedly sneaking into a military airport near the city of Zhangjiang, the headquarters of the South China Fleet. Chinese authorities confiscated film and videotapes, according to a Foreign Ministry spokesman. The attachés may have been checking unconfirmed rumors of a temporary deployment of SU-27 fighter-bombers around Hainan Island, which China first used in an exercise off Taiwan in November 1995.[16]

In July 1998, Maj. Thomas Gillen, the deputy U.S. Army attaché in Mexico, and his assistant, conducted an information-gathering mission in Mexico's explosive Chiapis region. The trip resulted in their being detained for four and a half hours by suspicious residents of the remote village of Los Platanos, which had been the scene of fighting in June between local pro-government forces and the leftist Zapatista National Liberation Army.[17]

A third source of HUMINT reporting comes from Foreign Service officers stationed in U.S. embassies and consulates. These officers include those with political, economic, or cultural assignments. According to the 1995 congressional testimony of Undersecretary of State Peter Tarnoff, "The Foreign Service is a primary collector and producer of diplomatic and overseas reporting." That reporting, according to Tarnoff, accounts for a significant contribution, particularly in the political and economic areas, of the data that goes into national intelligence production.[18]

In certain situations, such individuals can provide valuable additional on-the-ground reporting. Thus, during late May and through June 1989, one important source of knowledge about the events unfolding in China was the reporting from U.S. diplomats stationed in Beijing.

For example, on June 3, 1989, a cable from the U.S. Embassy in Beijing to the State Department reported that "ten to fifteen thousand helmeted, armed troops moved into Beijing during the late afternoon/early evening hours of June 3." The same cable also reported, inter alia, on the location of troop trucks, the troops weapons, and that elite airborne troops were moving from the south. The cable also noted that the embassy had received reports of trucks surrounded and stopped by city residents. It also reported that Defense Attaché Office personnel were checking the western suburbs.[19]

AGENTS

Agents are foreign nationals recruited by U.S. intelligence officers to collect information either in their home country or in a third nation. Obviously, the identities of present U.S. agents are not known publicly. However, revelations of recent years indicate the types of recruits, many of whom were operating until quite recently, and the types of information acquired in this manner.

During the Cold War, the primary target was, of course, the Soviet Union. Despite the closed nature of Soviet society and the size and intensity of the KGB's counterintelligence operation, the CIA had a number of notable successes. The most significant was Colonel Oleg Penkovskiy, a Soviet military intelligence (GRU) officer with significant connections. In 1961 and 1962, Penkovskiy passed great quantities of material to the CIA and the British Secret Intelligence Service, including information on Soviet strategic capabilities and nuclear targeting policy. Additionally, he provided a copy of the official Soviet MRBM (Medium-Range Ballistic Missile) manual—which was of crucial importance at the time of the Cuban Missile Crisis.[20]

In subsequent years the CIA was able to penetrate the Soviet Foreign Ministry, Defense Ministry/General Staff, GRU, KGB, at least one military research facility, and probably several other Soviet organizations. Individuals providing data to the CIA included some stationed in the Soviet Union as well as some in Soviet consulates and embassies and some assigned to the United Nations or other international organizations. One unfortunate measure of success in terms of recruiting Soviet citizens was the number of Russian nationals that Aldrich Ames was able to compromise in his first few years as an agent for the KGB.[21]

Included in the group was one agent who had already been compromised by former CIA officer Edward Lee Howard—Adolf G. Tolkachev, an electronics expert at the Moscow Aviation Institute. Tolkachev was, according to a U.S. official, "one of our most lucrative agents"; he "saved us billions of dollars in development costs" by telling the United States about the nature of Soviet military aviation efforts. Over the years, Tolkachev passed on information concerning Soviet research efforts in electronic guidance and countermeasures, advanced radar, and stealth technologies. The information made it significantly easier for the United States to develop systems to counter Soviet advances. Tolkachev was arrested in 1985 and subsequently executed.[22]

Such operations have not ceased with the end of the Cold War and the collapse of the Soviet Union. In September 1995, a worker at a Defense Ministry research institute in St. Petersburg was arrested on suspicion of having provided the United

States with secret information on Russia's new attack submarine. In 1997 a former Russian diplomat was convicted of having spied for the United States since his recruitment in 1976.[23]

Evidence of U.S. operations in Europe, the Middle East, and Africa has emerged with respect to France, Germany, Israel, Egypt, the PLO, Iraq, Ethiopia, Ghana, and Iran.

In early 1997 the German government ordered a CIA officer expelled. According to one account the officer had been accused of trying to recruit senior German officials to provide information on high technology projects. According to another account, the officer was gathering information about a third country, probably Iran, and was ordered to leave because the operation had not been cleared with the German government.[24]

In 1993, in France, the CIA targeted Henri Plagnol, an adviser to Premier Edouard Balladur, although how successful they were is a matter of dispute. At approximately the same time, the agency also approached Thierry Mileo, who handled cable and satellite issues for Minister of Communications Alain Carignon, and offered him cash in exchange for information on the French negotiating strategy on telecommunications. In another instance, an employee of French Telecom, the national telephone company, was asked to "sell documents and information on France international structure and networks," according to the report of the French security service, the DST. Both targets reported the overtures to the DST, who encouraged them to continue contacts with the CIA officers. Among those involved in the operation was one NOC, who represented herself as an employee of a Texas foundation interested in world economics.[25]

An Israeli army officer, Maj. Yosef Amit, apparently began providing the CIA with information in 1982. In 1987 he was secretly sentenced to twelve years imprisonment for espionage. The Egyptian government has apparently been extensively penetrated by the CIA. The CIA has also had a variety of sources in the Palestine Liberation Organization.[26]

In 1985, it was reported that the CIA had a senior Ethiopian official on its payroll. In Ghana, several individuals were convicted of spying for the CIA in 1985: Felix Peasah—a security officer at the U.S. Embassy in Accra—and Theodore Atiedu—a police inspector with Ghana's Bureau of National Investigation— pleaded guilty. Also convicted were Stephen Balfour Ofusu—a former Chief Superintendent of Police, who gave government secrets to the CIA and arranged taps on the telephones of diplomatic missions and high-level government officials—and Robert Yaw Appiah—a technician with the Post and Telecommunications Corporation who gave a CIA officer copies of keys to utility hole covers.[27]

In April 1989, a number of Iranian military officers were arrested and charged with spying for the United States. Before the network, which was coordinated from Frankfurt, was detected, it apparently produced valuable military intelligence about Iranian operations in the Persian Gulf at a time when U.S. naval forces were confronting Iranian forces.[28]

The CIA's targets in Asia have included India, China, and the Philippines. In India six individuals were arrested for spying for the United States in 1977. The head of the operation was P. E. Mehta, who apparently confessed to selling information to U.S. Embassy officials between 1962 and 1977. Also arrested were K. K. Sareen, a former director at the Planning Commission who had also worked for the Soviet Union; E. L. Choudhuri of the State Trading Corporation; R. P. Varshney of the Planning Commission; Mahabir Prasid, personal secretary to Y. B. Chaven, when he was External Affairs Minister; and C. S. Balakrishanan, a clerk in the office of the Minister for Defense Production. Mehta received secret reports of the external affairs, chemicals, and petroleum ministries as well as information about India's main aircraft design and production center, plus drawings of Soviet-made guns, missiles, and radar.[29]

At least one CIA penetration of the Chinese establishment has involved someone with access to information concerning Chinese nuclear relations with a variety of foreign nations. That source reported on:

- China's nuclear exports to Argentina and South Africa
- Chinese technicians helping at a suspected Pakistani bomb development site
- Chinese scientific delegations who were spending a substantial amount of time at a centrifuge plant in Kahuta where Pakistani scientists were attempting to produce enriched uranium
- Pakistani scientists from a secret facility at Wah showing a nuclear weapon design to some Chinese physicists in late 1982 or early 1983, seeking Chinese evaluation of whether the design would yield a nuclear blast
- the triggering mechanism for the Pakistani bomb, which appeared to be very similar to one used by China in its fourth nuclear test[30]

Information about the Taiwanese program was also provided by a long-time agent, Col. Chang Hsien-Yi, the Deputy Director of the Institute for Nuclear Energy Research. Chang had been recruited by the CIA when he was a military cadet and had defected in 1987. The information he provided indicated that the Taiwanese were in the process of building a secret installation that could be used to produce plutonium. Construction of the installation would have violated Taiwanese commitments to the United States not to undertake nuclear weapons research. U.S. pressure forced the Taiwanese to stop work on the secret installation as well as to shut down its largest civilian reactor, which the United States felt had military potential.[31]

CIA assets in the Philippines have provided important information at crucial times. On September 17, 1972, a CIA asset in the Philippines informed the CIA station that Ferdinand Marcos was planning to proclaim martial law. Another asset provided a list of the individuals whom Marcos planned to arrest and imprison. In 1982, a CIA officer was able to locate a Philippine immigration official who was willing to provide the names of two doctors who visited the Philippines to treat Marcos, giving the agency a clue to the nature of Marcos's health problems.[32]

HUMINT operations in Latin American have targeted Cuba, El Salvador, Nicaragua, Colombia, and Argentina. The operations in Cuba highlighted the potential dangers of HUMINT operations. During 1987, Cuban television showed films of apparent CIA officers operating in Cuba picking up and leaving material at dead drops. The programs claimed that from September 1977 thirty-eight of the sixty-nine diplomats permanently accredited to the U.S. diplomatic mission in Havana had been CIA officers. Apparently, a significant number of Cubans had been operating as double agents, feeding information to the CIA under the supervision of Cuban security officials. The Cubans decided to reveal the operation as a result of the defection of a senior intelligence officer.[33]

In Central America, the head of El Salvador's Treasury Police, Nicolas Carranza, was an informant of the CIA in the late 1970s, having received more than $90,000 a year from the CIA for at least six years. In Nicaragua, General Reynaldo Perez Vega, the second-ranking officer in the National Guard under Anastasio Somoza, was a CIA asset.[34]

Allegations of CIA clandestine collection activities in Nicaragua came with the arrest, in March 1986, of three Nicaraguans accused of working to infiltrate the Interior Ministry. One of the three was a sublieutenant in the Interior Ministry who was allegedly recruited by the CIA while he was outside of Nicaragua in November 1983. He had been tasked to provide information on connections between the Sandinistas and leftist guerrillas in Colombia and El Salvador.[35]

Among those Haitians serving as paid agents of the CIA in the 1990s was Emmanuel (Toto) Constant, head of the Front for the Advancement and Progress of Haiti, better known as FRAPH—the acronym derived from the initials of its French name. Despite, its title FRAPH was described as a paramilitary "gang of thugs unusually vicious even by Haitian standards."[36]

The issue of recruiting, as CIA assets, individuals involved in serious criminal activity or human rights abuses became an issue internally in 1994, with respect to an asset in El Salvador. In 1995, it became a public issue when it was revealed that the CIA had employed a Guatemalan military officer, Julio Roberto Alpirez, who had been alleged to have been involved in the murder of an American innkeeper and a guerrilla fighter married to an American. That same year, the CIA severed contact with Colombian General Ivan Ramirez Quintero after receiving reports that he was involved in drug trafficking, right-wing paramilitary activities, and human rights violations. For several years before that Ramirez had been a key intelligence source for the CIA. He had received intelligence training in the United States in 1983 and had gone on to serve in several key intelligence posts. A two-year review of CIA assets resulted in the dropping of over 1,000 informants—90 percent of whom were judged to be unproductive, whereas the other 10 percent were judged to have been involved in serious criminal activity and/or human rights abuses.[37]

Overt and controlled (i.e., clandestine) sources for military intelligence organizations have also provided a variety of information. During the 1993 fiscal year, Army intelligence sources reported on: mass murders and other atrocities committed by Bosnian Serbs against Bosnian Muslims, the rise in membership of neo-Nazi organizations in Germany, the activities of the Algerian Front Islamique de Salvation (FIS), a planned campaign of violence against U.S. interests and personnel by a member of the Panama National Police, Russian directed energy programs, the status of Cuba's biological warfare program, the purchase of advanced tunnel boring equipment by North Korea, and a planned coup d'état in Afghanistan supported by Russia.[38]

DEFECTORS AND ÉMIGRÉS

Defectors and émigrés also sometimes serve as intelligence sources. The United States attaches major importance to the intelligence information that can be obtained via defectors. Thus, it has a coordinated Defector Program managed by the CIA-led Interagency Defector Committee (IDC).[39]

In the past, the prime defectors were Soviet bloc officials, such as scientists, diplomats, or intelligence officers. In the aftermath of the declaration of martial law in Poland, several Polish ambassadors defected to the West, bringing with them their knowledge of personalities, procedures, policies, and relations with the Soviet Union.

A defector may be able to settle disputes concerning matters of data acquired via technical collection systems. Thus, one defector was asked to:

> look at an elaborate analysis of something our cameras detected by chance when there was an abnormal opening in the clouds that normally covered a particular region. Learned men had spend vast amounts of time trying to figure out what it was and concluded that it was something quite sinister, an Air Force officer said. "Viktor took one look at it and convincingly explained why what we thought was so ominous was in fact comically innocuous."[40]

During the 1980s, CIA informants included defectors from Cuba and Nicaragua, such as Rafael Del Pino Diaz and Roger Miranda Bengoechea. Diaz apparently had held important aviation posts in the 1960s, including head of Cubana Airlines and the Cuban Aviation Agency. He also claimed to be the Cuban Air Force's Deputy Chief of Staff, although the Cuban government claimed he had been relegated to organizing a museum about the history of the Cuban Air Force.[41]

Roger Miranda Bengoechea, a senior military officer, was chief contact for all military advisers in Nicaragua—which probably gave him knowledge concerning the Cuban presence in that country. He had toured all Sandinista military bases the week prior to his defection. Miranda, who made frequent trips to Mexico for medical reasons, may have been passing information to the CIA before his defection. According to the Nicaraguan Defense Minister, Miranda had made copies of Air Force plans as well as documents concerning artillery brigades and other Managua installations.[42]

A senior Iraqi scientist, Khidhir Abdul Abas Hamza, who fled his country in 1994, provided the CIA with important details concerning the Iraqi nuclear program. Hamza, the highest-ranking scientist ever to defect from Baghdad, was able to provide information on the origins of the nuclear program, the role of foreign suppliers, the treatment of nuclear scientists in Iraq, and Iraqi success in perfecting methods for uranium enrichment.[43]

Today, the most desirable defectors would be those from Iraq, Iran, and North Korea. In the immediate aftermath of the 1991 Persian Gulf War, Iraqi defectors provided valuable information about the Iraqi nuclear weapons program. Then, in the summer of 1995, two of Saddam Hussein's sons-in-law defected to Jordan, where they were interrogated by U.S., presumably CIA, officials. One defector was Lt. Gen. Hussein Kamel Hassan, who headed the industry ministry and military industrialization program, which included the nuclear weapons and biological weapons program. The other, Lt. Col. Saddam Kamel Hassan, headed the presidential security detail. (Not surprisingly, after they decided to return to Iraq they were killed.)[44]

In 1997 two high-level North Korean officials defected. One was the country's chief ideologist, Hwang Jan Yop, who defected to South Korea. He reportedly told his South Korean, and then U.S., interrogators about North Korea's strategy for nuclear war, their nuclear and chemical weapons program, and about the identities of North Korean agents in South Korea. However, one Clinton administration official remarked that Hwang didn't have "as much knowledge as we hoped," and had "no direct knowledge of military matters." Some of his information was also characterized as "old, dated, not true."[45]

A more useful defector was Chang Sung Kil, the North Korean ambassador to Egypt prior to his defection to the United States in 1997. It was believed that Chang could provide the CIA with a "wealth of information about his country's sensitive dealings with Middle East nations." Of particular interest would be North Korean sales of Scud-B missiles to Egypt and of other arms to Iran and Syria. Some of that information may have been provided prior to his defection; it was reported that Chang had been recruited by the CIA well before his defection.[46] However, his defection would have allowed the CIA to debrief him at length about a variety of topics.

Other North Korean defectors include Ju-Hwal Choi, a former official of the Ministry of the People's Army, and Young-Hwan Ko, a former official of the Ministry of Foreign Affairs. They were able to tell a Senate committee (and presumably the CIA) about subjects such as the activities of the production and deployment of rockets by the 4th General Bureau, the production of chemical weapons by the 5th General Bureau, and North Korean missile exports.[47]

TRAVELERS

Travelers who are not necessarily intelligence officers may often be able to provide useful intelligence information. At one time, before the United States developed satellites to penetrate the Soviet interior, travelers played a more significant role in intelligence activities than they do today.[48]

Among present traveler collection programs is CREEK GRAB, a USAF program. USAFE Regulation 200-6 states that:

> During peacetime, USAF military and DAF [Department of the Air Force] civilian personnel, other US employees, and contractors may occasionally have opportunities to acquire information of intelligence value either while performing their normal duties or by pure chance . . . USAFE intelligence personnel must be able to respond effectively to unexpected opportunities for foreign intelligence collection in peacetime as well as wartime.[49]

Among those considered potential intelligence contributors are not just travelers but also amateur radio operators, persons in contact with foreign friends and relatives, and persons living adjacent to sites where foreign military aircraft have landed or crashed. Regulation 200-6 also specifies procedures for photographing aircraft, specifying that photographs could be obtained of the following items:

- cockpit interior
- weapons systems controls, panel instruments
- seat(s)
- weaponry
- electronics gear (avionics, radar, black boxes, etc.)
- propulsion system (air intake, variable geometry, fuel parts, and fuel tankage)
- documents, maintenance records[50]

CIA-trained military travelers have been used in Africa to provide political intelligence as well as information relevant in insuring the security of U.S. forces employed in humanitarian and peacekeeping operations. Specific information provided by the travelers has included threats to U.S. military personnel, the general security threat, as well as the status of airfields and ports. During political upheaval in one country, "the collectors provided extensive data on five neighboring countries, two of which were either considered or used as forward staging areas for US troops. The US military regularly relied on their detailed reporting on airports and air fields."[51]

The CIA's National Resources Division seeks to interview business people, tourists, and professionals, either because of specific contacts they may have had during their foreign travels or because of the sites of their travel—for example, Iran or China. The information sought may include the health and attitudes of a national leader, the military activities in a particular region, or the developments in foreign science and technology.[52]

Notes

1. Amrom Katz, "Technical Collection Requirements for the 1980s," in *Intelligence Requirements for the 1980s: Clandestine Collection,* ed. Roy Godson (New Brunswick, N.J.: Transaction, 1982), pp. 101–117 at pp. 106–107.

2. Judith Miller, "Baghdad Arrests a Germ Specialist," *New York Times,* March 24, 1998, pp. A1, A11.

3. John I. Millis, "Our Spying Success Is No Secret," *Wall Street Journal,* October 12, 1994, p. A15.

4. Office of the Deputy Chief of Staff for Intelligence, *Annual Historical Review, 1 October 1990 to 30 September 1991* (Washington, D.C.: ODCSI, 1993), pp. 4–10 to 4–12.

5. Robert Dreyfuss, "The CIA Crosses Over," *Mother Jones,* January-February 1995, pp. 40ff. The utility of NOCs is discussed in Walter Pincus, "Agencies Debate Value of Being Out in the Cold," *Washington Post,* January 12, 1996, p. A18.

6. Philip Agee and Louis Wolf, eds., *Dirty Work: The CIA in Western Europe* (Seacaucus, N.J.: Lyle Stuart, 1978), pp. 131–132.

7. Ibid., pp. 721–722; Private information.

8. Defense Intelligence Agency, *Capabilities Handbook, Annex A, to the Department of Defense Plan for Intelligence Support to Operational Commanders (U)* (Washington, D.C.: DIA, 1983), p. 352.

9. Nancy Nusser, "U.S. Officials Cited as Spies by Managua," *Washington Post,* May 10, 1986, p. A14.

10. Richard Mackenzie, "A Gulf War Intrigue: The Tale of the Colonel's Camera," *Washington Times,* April 20, 1987, p. 9A.

11. Nora Boustany and Patrick E. Tyler, "Syria Suspects U.S. Attachés Meant to Aid Israel," *Washington Post,* March 13, 1989, p. A28.

12. Steven Mufson, "China Expels Two U.S. Attachés Accused of Spying," *Washington Post,* August 3, 1995, pp. A1, A27.

13. Martin Sieff, "Two American Officers Ordered Out of China," *Washington Times,* August 4, 1995, p. A15.

14. Linda Chong, "Expelled Americans Arrive in Hong Kong," *Washington Times,* August 4, 1995, p. A15.

15. Tim Weiner, "China Detains U.S. Attaché and Seeks Recall," *New York Times,* January 17, 1996, p. A26; Steven Mufson, "U.S. and Japanese Attachés Detained Twice, China Says," *Washington Post,* January 18, 1996, p. A19.

16. Mufson, "U.S. and Japanese Attachés Detained Twice, China Says"; Martin Sieff, "Detained U.S. Military Aide to Be Sent Home from China," *Washington Times,* January 18, 1996, p. A13.

17. Molly Moore, "U.S. Attaché, Aide Stray Into Chiapis Face-Off," *Washington Post,* July 29, 1998, p. A17.

18. Undersecretary of State Peter Tarnoff, "Intelligence in Support of Foreign and National Security Policy in a Post–Cold War World," September 20, 1995, presentation to the U.S. Congress, Senate Select Committee on Intelligence.

19. Amembassy Beijing to Sec State Wash DC, Subject: SITREP No. 28: Ten to Fifteen Thousand Armed Troops Stopped at City Perimeter by Human and Bus Barricades, June 3, 1989.

20. See Jerrold L. Schecter and Peter S. Deriabin, *The Spy Who Saved the World: How a Soviet Colonel Changed the Course of the Cold War* (New York: Scribner's, 1992).

21. John Barron, *The KGB Today: The Hidden Hand* (New York: Reader's Digest Press, 1983), p. 428; Ernest Volkman, *Warriors of the Night: Spies, Soldiers and American Intelligence* (New York: Morrow, 1985), p. 224; David Martin, "A CIA Spy in the Kremlin," *Newsweek*, July 21, 1980, pp. 69–70; Ronald Kessler, "Moscow's Mole in the CIA," *Washington Post*, April 17, 1988, pp. C1, C4; Peter Samuel, "1977 Spy Data on SS-20's Cast Shadow Over INF Talks," *New York City Tribune*, November 17, 1987 p. 1; Walter Pincus, "U.S. May Have Discounted Some Soviet Missiles," *Washington Post*, April 17, 1988, p. A6; Peter Earley, *Confessions of a Spy: The Real Story of Aldrich Ames* (New York: Putnam, 1997), pp. 143–144; David Wise, *Nightmover: How Aldrich Ames Sold the CIA to the KGB for $4.6 Million* (New York: HarperCollins, 1995).

22. William Kucewicz, "KGB Defector Confirms Intelligence Fiasco," *Wall Street Journal*, October 17, 1985, p. 28.

23. "Russian Arrested as U.S. Spy," *Washington Post*, September 26, 1996, p. A22; "Russians Assail U.S. Spy 'Trick'," *Washington Post*, November 5, 1996, p. A15; Gareth Jones, "Russian Sentenced in Spying," *Washington Times*, July 4, 1997, p. A9.

24. William Drozdiak, "Bonn Expels U.S. Officials for Spying," *Washington Post*, March 9, 1997, pp. A1, A25; Walter Pincus, "Expelled CIA Agent Was Not Gathering Data on Germany, Sources Say," *Washington Post*, March 11, 1997, p. A11.

25. William Drozdiak, "France Accuses Americans of Spying, Seeks Recall," *Washington Post*, February 23, 1995, pp. A1, A20; Craig R. Whitney, "France Accuses 5 Americans of Spying: Asks They Leave," *New York Times*, February 23, 1995, pp. A1, A12; Walter Pincus, "Agencies Debate Value of Being Out in the Cold," *Washington Post*, January 12, 1996, p. A18.

26. Wolf Blitzer, "U.S. Changed Rules of the Spy Game," *Jerusalem Post International Edition*, March 28, 1987, pp. 1, 2; Bob Woodward, *Veil: The Secret Wars of the CIA, 1981–1987* (New York: Simon & Schuster, 1987), pp. 87, 161; David Hoffman, "Israel Army Major Was a Spy," *Washington Post*, June 3, 1993, p. A18.

27. Philip Smith, "Events Spark Speculation That Spy Swap Is Imminent," *Washington Post*, November 21, 1985, p. A16; "2 More Convicted in Ghana of Spying for CIA," *Washington Post*, November 23, 1985, p. A8; Woodward, *Veil*, p. 167.

28. Youssef M. Ibrahim, "Teheran Is Said to Arrest Officers on Charges of Spying for U.S.," *New York Times*, April 22, 1989, p. 5; Stephen Engelberg and Bernard E. Trainor, "Iran Broke C.I.A. Spy Ring, U.S. Says," *New York Times*, August 8, 1989, p. A6.

29. Sanjoy Hazarika, "In Secret Trial, India Sentences 6 for Spying for U.S.," *New York Times*, October 30, 1986, p. A5.

30. Jack Anderson and Dale Van Atta, "Nuclear Exports to China?" *Washington Post*, November 3, 1985, p. C7; Patrick E. Tyler and Joanne Omang, "China-Iran Nuclear Link Is Reported," *Washington Post*, October 23, 1985, pp. A1, A19; Joanne Omang, "Nuclear Pact with China Wins Senate Approval," *Washington Post*, November 22, 1985, p. A3; Patrick E. Tyler, "A Few Spoken Words Sealed China Atom Pact," *Washington Post*, January 15, 1986, pp. A1, A20–A21.

31. Stephen Engelberg and Michael R. Gordon, "Taipei Halts Work on Secret Plant to Make Nuclear Bomb Ingredient," *New York Times*, March 23, 1988, pp. A1, A15; Tim Weiner, "How a Spy Left Taiwan in the Cold," *New York Times*, December 28, 1997, p. A7.

32. Raymond Bonner, *Waltzing with a Dictator* (New York: Times Books, 1987), pp. 3, 5, 340.

33. "Cuban TV Purports to Show U.S. Spies," *Washington Times*, July 8, 1987, p. A8; Lewis H. Duiguid, "Spy Charges Strain U.S.-Cuban Ties," *Washington Post*, July 25, 1987, p. A17; Michael Wines and Roland J. Ostrow, "U.S. Duped by Cuban Agents, Defector Says," *Los Angeles Times*, August 12, 1987, pp. 1, 14.

34. Philip Taubman, "Top Salvador Police Official Said to Be CIA Informant," *New York Times*, March 22, 1984, pp. A1, A4; Stephen Kinzer, "Sandinistas Tap Heroine as Envoy, But Some in U.S. Oppose Her," *New York Times*, March 22, 1984, pp. A1, A4.

35. Stephen Kinzer, "Nicaragua Says It Has Cracked CIA Spy Ring," *New York Times*, March 15, 1986, p. 3.

36. George J. Church, "Lying Down with Dogs," *Time*, October 17, 1994, pp. 26–29.

37. R. Jeffrey Smith, "CIA Drops Over 1,000 Informants," *Washington Post*, March 2, 1997, pp. A1, A19; Douglas Farah and Laura Brooks, "Colombian Army's Third in Command Allegedly Led Two Lives," *Washington Post*, August 11, 1998, p. A14.

38. Department of the Army, Office of the Deputy Chief of Staff for Intelligence, *Annual Historical Review, 1 October 1992 to 30 September 1993* (Washington, D.C.: ODCSI, n.d.), pp. 4-32 to 4-42.

39. E. Howard Hunt, *Undercover: Memoirs of an American Secret Agent* (New York: Berkley, 1974), p. 80.

40. John Barron, *MIG Pilot* (New York: Avon, 1981), p. 186.

41. John M. Goshko and Julia Preston, "Defector Arrives for Debriefing: Cuba Plays Down Military Role," *Washington Post*, May 30, 1987, p. A3.

42. Glenn Garvin and John McCaslin, "Key Nicaraguan Aide Dubs Military Defector U.S. Spy," *Washington Times*, November 4, 1987, p. A10.

43. Judith Miller and James Risen, "Defector Describes Iraq's Atom Bomb Push," *New York Times*, August 15, 1998, pp. A1, A4; Judith Miller and James Risen, "C.I.A. Almost Bungles Intelligence Coup with Iraqi Refugee," *New York Times*, August 15, 1998, p. A4.

44. Daniel Williams, "U.S. Questions Top-Level Iraqis," *Washington Post*, August 12, 1995, p. A15; "Saddam's Sons-in-Law Talk to U.S. After Pair's Defection," *Washington Times*, August 12, 1995, p. A6; Kevin Fedavko, "Dead on Arrival," *Time*, March 4, 1996, p. 44; William J. Broad and Judith Miller, "Iraq's Deadliest Arms: Puzzles Breed Fears," *New York Times*, February 26, 1998, pp. A1, A10–A11.

45. Kevin Sullivan, "Key Defector Warns Again of North Korean War Plans," *Washington Post*, July 10, 1997, p. A23; Nicholas D. Kristof, "North Korean Defector's 'Spy List' Proves a Hot Topic in Seoul," *New York Times*, September 5, 1997, p. A9; Kevin Sullivan, "N. Korea Defector Takes Questions, Raises Them," *Washington Post*, July 11, 1997, p. A27; Bill Gertz, "Hwang Says N. Korea Has Atomic Weapons," *Washington Times*, June 5, 1997, p. A12.

46. R. Jeffrey Smith, "North Korean May Bring Arms Data," *Washington Post*, August 27, 1997, pp. A1, A24; Stephen Lee Myers, "Defecting Envoy from North Korea to Get U.S. Asylum," *New York Times*, August 21, 1997, pp. A1, A9; Bill Gertz, "CIA Seeks Missile Data from Defector," *Washington Times*, August 27, 1997, pp. A1, A10; "North Korean Defector Reportedly a CIA Agent," *Washington Times*, August 31, 1997, p. A2; Tony Emerson, "The CIA Lands a Big Fish," *Newsweek*, September 8, 1997, p. 54.

47. U.S. Congress, Senate Committee on Governmental Affairs, *Compilation of Hearings of National Security Issues*, Report 105–50, (Washington, D.C.: U.S. Government Printing Office, 1998), pp. 467–495.

48. See Jeffrey T. Richelson, *American Espionage and the Soviet Target* (New York: William Morrow, 1987), pp. 52–55.

49. USAFE Regulation 200–6, "CREEK GRAB," May 31, 1986, p. 2.

50. Ibid., p. 15.

51. The Central Intelligence Agency Lieutenant General Vernon A. Walters Award presented to The Operational Architect for a New Collection Capability, NMIA XXIV Anniversary & Awards Banquet, June 5, 1998, http://www.nmia.org/1998Awards/CIAAward98.htm.

52. Victor Marchetti and John Marks, *The CIA and the Cult of Intelligence* (New York: Dell, 1980), pp. 236–237.

12

OPEN SOURCES, TECHNICAL SURVEILLANCE AND EMPLACED SENSORS, AND MATERIEL EXPLOITATION

Significant intelligence concerning the political, military, and economic affairs of other nations can be obtained through means other than remote technical and human source collection. Included in this category are open sources, technical surveillance and emplaced sensors, and materiel exploitation.

Open source collection includes the acquisition of any verbal, written, or electronically transmitted material that can be legally acquired—which includes newspapers, magazines, and unclassified journals as well as the broadcasts of public radio and television stations and the varied material appearing on the Internet.

A significant portion of the intelligence gathered by the CIA and other intelligence units is acquired by means of electronic surveillance or emplaced sensors. The electronic surveillance usually takes the form of bugging or phone tapping. Although technical in nature, it is not a remote sensing activity and requires HUMINT personnel to install the surveillance devices.

Another significant aspect of intelligence collection revolves around "materiel exploitation"—the acquisition and analysis of foreign weapons, communications, and other systems. Such acquisition and analysis yield information that cannot be acquired by overhead photography, such as information on firearms and more detailed information on systems such as tanks, which can then be used to design countermeasures. Although the weapons designed for the Soviet armed forces are now far less threatening in the hands of the Russian armed forces, the Soviet (and Russian) export of a variety of weapons systems and technology to nations such as Iraq, Libya, Iran, and other nations makes intelligence on them of continuing relevance.

OPEN SOURCES

Open source collection has traditionally involved three separate activities: collection of legally available documents; open observation of foreign political, military, and economic activity; and the monitoring and recording of public radio and television broadcasts. In recent years additional sources of data have emerged in the form of electronic databases and the Internet. The statement of Roscoe Hillenkoeter, the Director of Central Intelligence in 1948, that "80 percent of intelligence is derived from such prosaic sources as foreign books, magazines and radio broadcasts, and general information from people with a knowledge of affairs abroad" remains approximately true today.[1]

In open societies, a variety of data concerning political, military, and economic affairs is available through newspapers, magazines, trade journals, academic journals, and government publications. These published sources may yield intelligence concerning the internal disputes plaguing a European political party, French arms developments, Japanese defense and trade policy, or advances in computer and laser technologies.

Of course, in a closed society much less information will be available. Most particularly, direct reporting on internal political and military affairs will be absent. Further, all reporting will be conducted under the direction of government propaganda guidelines. Even in a closed society, however, there is a significant amount of intelligence that can be gleaned from legally obtainable documents—including newspapers, magazines, collected speeches, academic journals, and even official documents on military affairs.

For several decades the prime focus of U.S. open source collection was the Soviet Union. From August 1947 through April 1951, all articles in Soviet scientific and technical journals were abstracted, and some were translated in full. As of 1952, there were eighty-seven Soviet journals available. In 1954, there were 165 available. A joint CIA-Air Force program selected fifty-eight journals of prime intelligence interest for cover-to-cover abstracting.[2]

By April of 1956 the number of available Soviet scientific and technical journals had virtually doubled again, to 328. Those journals contained information on Soviet research and development in, or related to, atomic energy, missiles, electronics, and atomic, biological, and chemical warfare. Upon close examination, it was determined that there were far more than fifty-eight journals of prime interest.[3]

The large volume of these publications led to two approaches. The Air Force conducted a cover-to-cover abstracting program for more than 100 journals. For other consumers, the CIA began issuing the twice-monthly *Scientific Information Report*, which sought to cover the entire range of Soviet bloc scientific literature. In addition to journals there were about 3,000 books and monographs per year that were surveyed for scientific and technical intelligence, along with two Soviet newspapers that regularly covered the subject.[4]

Translations of scientific reports or articles can be used in assessing foreign activities and capabilities as well as in providing support to U.S. research and development activities. Thus, in 1971 the Foreign Technology Division produced a translation of a paper by Pytor Ufimtsev of the Moscow Institute of Radio Engineering titled the "Method of Edge Waves in the Physical Theory of Diffraction." The paper became, according to Ben Rich, former head of the Lockheed Skunk Works, "the Rosetta Stone breakthrough for stealth technology."[5]

The U.S. intelligence community examined other components of Soviet open source literature for information of political and military intelligence value. In addition to general circulation organs such as *Pravda* and *Izvestia*, the CIA and other agencies would examine the eleven major Soviet military journals and approximately 500 books on military affairs published in the Soviet Union each year.[6]

The introduction of *glasnost* in the Soviet Union, and then the transformation of the Soviet Union into Russia, has dramatically increased the value of open source intelligence concerning that area of the world. Whereas before Mikhail Gorbachev's rise to power, political maneuvering was concentrated within a small and secretive elite, domestic politics in Russia are now conducted in public view, including the view of television cameras. Thus, even before the collapse of the Soviet Union, a senior governmental official observed, "It used to be that you'd go through reams of stuff, and just come up with dross. Now there's so much gold that [analysts] could work around the clock."[7]

The type of military intelligence that can now be obtained from Russian open sources is qualitatively different from that which could be acquired under the Soviet regime—both because of greater press freedom and the Russian desire to sell weaponry to remedy dire economic conditions. Thus, an August 1993 broadcast from Moscow reported on the threat that a lack of funding posed to the MiG-29M program. That same month *Rossiyskaya Gazeta* reported on an air defense missile demonstration at Kapustin Yar. In December 1993, in an unprecedented public announcement, the Russia government revealed that the first unit of their new fourth-generation SSN, to be named the SEVERODVINSK, was laid down. The November 4, 1994, issue of *Nezavisimaya Gazeta* included an interview concerning the future of the Russian strategic forces with a scientist employed by the Defense Ministry's 4th Central Scientific Research Institute. In early 1995, *Izvestia* contained "an unusually detailed description" of the silo-based Topol-M ICBM, including information on its accuracy as well as the time between launch command and the missile leaving its silo.[8]

In early 1997, a retired Russian colonel, in an article in the mass-circulation newspaper *Komsomolskaya Pravda*, wrote about the deterioration of the Russian command-and-control system. His article echoed the comments that Defense Minister Igor Rodionov made in a letter to President Yeltsin. The article was subsequently discussed in a CIA report outlining Rodionov's concerns about command and control.[9]

Russian open source material is also considered valuable with respect to understanding Russian organized crime. In 1997, the FBIS Gray Literature Coordinator wrote:

> The combination of Russian culture and Soviet past makes open source material particularly valuable for studying Russian organized crime and illuminates much about this criminal world. First, during the emergence of a relatively free press following the years of constricting CPSU control, the exposé became a popular style of reporting. Criminal groups are regularly portrayed and detailed by daring crime reporters, some of whom have paid with their lives. Second, because of the nexus of Russian crime, politics, and the media, Russian criminal leaders appear to be image conscious and often use the press to defend themselves as honest businessmen. At the same time, however, they rarely miss an opportunity to attack their opponents—viciously exposing other groups for their criminal ties and activity. Third, Russian criminals have in the past been motivated to attract Western business partners or allies. For this reason, they provide business data to various research firms that are publicly available—allowing interested parties to understand their business methods, sophistication, and business sense.[10]

Chinese open sources can also be exploited to produce intelligence. In a mid-1980s assessment the journal *Knowledge of Ships* was judged to generally provide low-quality and unreliable naval information but on occasion to contain useful data. One article, "The Role of the Guided Missile Speedboat in Engagement," stated that the "planners" were considering assigning an antiaircraft mission to one or two of the six boats in a typical OSA or KOMAR squadron.[11]

The Journal of Shipbuilding in China focused on research topics in marine engineering in considerable detail and demonstrated that the Chinese were actively exploiting U.S., British, Soviet, Japanese, and German work in the field. Examination of the journal also revealed that the instruments being employed by China for test purposes were of German, Japanese, and Chinese manufacture and that the Chinese experiments generally picked up where the exploited source stopped—either advancing the testing process a step further or seeking empirical verification of a theory propounded by the source.[12]

According to one analyst: "From the technical intelligence perspective the publication can be valuable in providing new information about the marine engineering topics of interest to China, an appreciation of the foreign sources being exploited by the Chinese and the results of their experiments in the field." This information, when combined with other intelligence, "offers a reasonably accurate assessment of where China stands in this area of technology."[13] Also of interest to intelligence analysis was a publication entitled *Contemporary Military Affairs*, in which the Pacific and Indian Ocean theaters of operation receive good coverage.[14]

Press reports may also provide useful information to those tracking the organization and operations of the People's Liberation Army. Thus, a February 4, 1987, report in the Xinhua press disclosed the existence of a training center for reserve paratroop personnel, apparently the first such center in China. The article stated that the center included a small airport, parachute training and drop zones, an area to stage tactical exercises, and lecture rooms.[15]

Chinese views on information warfare and the new military revolution can also be judged, at least in part, via reference to a variety of published sources. Those sources include *On Meeting the Challenge of the New Military Revolution* (by Lt. Gen. Huai Guomo), *Latest Trends in China's Military Revolution, Logical Concept of Information Warfare, Information Warfare and Training of Skilled Commanders*, and *Exploring Ways to Defeat the Enemy Through Information*.[16]

Today, the volume of open source material around the world dwarfs what was available only twenty years ago, in part due to the explosion in printed matter. The number of periodicals worldwide grew from 70,000 in 1972 to 116,000 in 1991. A 1997 CIA study on the Chinese media reported that there were over 2,200 newspapers, in contrast to forty-two—almost all party papers, limited to propaganda and official speeches—thirty years earlier. The same study estimated that 7,000 magazines and journals were being published in the PRC. As of December 1992, there were 1,700 newspapers that did not exist in 1989 published in Russia and the other former Soviet states. At that time, the CIA's Foreign Broadcast Information Service (FBIS) monitored more than 3,500 publications in fifty-five foreign languages.[17]

FBIS monitoring produces a wide variety of reports, including five-times-a-week compilations for Eurasia, Africa, Latin America, Western Europe, Eastern Europe, the Middle East, the Near East, and Asia. Once published in hard-copy versions, these reports are now available only on line (at wnc.fedworld.gov). Similarly, the CIA's Joint Publications Research Service (JPRS) produces weekday compilations concerning subjects such as "Science and Technology-Europe," and "Nuclear Proliferation." In addition, both the FBIS and the JPRS prepare special products for use by intelligence community analysts.[18]

CIA analysts can also tap directly into the full texts of more than 2,000 on-line journals, from the *African Economic Digest* to the *Yale Law Review*, via ROSE—the Rich Open Source Environment.[19]

The DIA and military service intelligence organizations acquire foreign S&T publications and materials, publications concerning foreign weapons systems, training and doctrine manuals, military organization and planning documents, and map and town plans. A database of foreign scientific and technical information references and abstracts contains about 10 million records, of which approximately 6 million are unclassified. Included in one of those databases, for example, are the transactions of the Third International Conference on Nuclear Technology Transfer. Papers presented at the conference included "Issues and Experiences in the Transfer of Nuclear Technology," "Advanced Reactor Concepts," and "The Nuclear Fuel Cycle."[20]

The massive volume of open source material that is available also has been affected by the information technology revolution, which has led to the creation of databases. As of late 1992, the CIA had identified 8,000 commercial databases worldwide. [21]

In addition to accessing databases both within and outside the Internet, an analyst can access a variety of material through the Internet. A report by an analyst with the Office of the Assistant Secretary of Defense for Special Operations and Low-Intensity Conflict concluded that the Internet could provide useful intelligence information by providing reports on current events, "analytical assessments by politically astute observers on or near the scene of those events, many of whom offer unique insights," and information about the plans and operations of politically active groups.[22]

The report also noted that "a great deal of message traffic on the Internet is idle chit-chat with no intelligence value" and that much of the accuracy of much of the information on the Internet would be suspect, requiring validation. As a result, an alternative use of the Internet would be to "cue higher confidence means of U.S. intelligence collection, by alerting us to potentially important factors and allowing us to orient and focus our collection more precisely."[23]

The monitoring of radio and television broadcasts can also be valuable. Through the FBIS and its partner, the BBC Monitoring Service, the United States obtains a vast amount of information concerning political, military, and economic events throughout the world. In 1988 the Air Force Intelligence Service observed that:

> broadcasts can provide information on development of new weapons systems, deployment and modifications of existing systems, military operations, daily life in the armed forces of foreign countries. High level personalities can be identified— the West can better understand a country's foreign and internal policies by viewing the broadcasts and analyzing statements by leadership.[24]

In a 1992 speech, then Deputy DCI Admiral William O. Studeman noted, "Each week FBIS monitors 790 hours of television from over 50 countries in 29 languages. Foreign TV programs, such as news programs and documentaries—give analysts a multi-dimensional feel for a country or material that other open source media cannot provide. TV allows us to broaden our knowledge of more restrictive societies."[25]

Just as the number of publications in China has increased dramatically so has the number of radio and television outlets. In late 1997, it was estimated that there were 700 broadcast TV stations, 3,000 cable stations, and 1,000 radio stations. During May 1989, U.S. monitoring of Chinese radio broadcasts provided important information on the support for the student protesters in Beijing. The reports indicated that 40,000 students, teachers, and writers in Chengdu marched in support of democracy in mid-May. Guangdong provincial radio reported a march of 30,000 students. Altogether, radio reports indicated that there had been demonstrations of more than 10,000 people in at least nine other provinces.[26]

During Operation Desert Shield, the CIA and other intelligence agencies found that the television appearances of Saddam Hussein and other Iraqi officials provided useful information. CIA doctors and psychologists examined interviews with Iraqi leaders to look for signs of stress and worry. DIA analysts studied TV reports, particularly those from Baghdad, that might show scenes with military vehicles in the background. They would freeze the frames and try to compare a vehicle's unit designation with the lists of Iraqi equipment in DIA computers in order to determine whether anything new had been added to the force.[27]

U.S. intelligence analysts have also studied transcripts of radio broadcasts "by both sides [in the Yugoslav crisis] to gain insights into the intensity of the conflict." At the theater/tactical level, in support of U.S. forces in the region, the intelligence component of the Army's 1st Infantry Division, headquartered in Tuzla, monitors Serbian, Bosnian, and Croatian media. It produces the daily *Tuzla Night Owl*, whose approximately ten pages contain excerpts of media reports on political, economic, and military developments in the region, such as "Investigation of Black Marketing Denied," "Bosnians Have Chemical Weapons?" and "Milosevic Pressures RS Socialist Party."[28]

In the early 1990s, FBIS monitoring stations were located at: Abidjan, Ivory Coast; Amman, Jordan; Asuncion, Paraguay; Bangkok, Thailand; Chiva Chiva, Panama; Hong Kong; Islamabad, Pakistan; Key West, Florida; London; Mbabane, Swaziland; Nicosia, Cyprus; Okinawa, Japan; Seoul, Republic of Korea; Tel Aviv, Israel; and Vienna, Austria.[29] The station in Key West targeted Cuban radio and television, with a particular interest in any information on Cuban military exercises.

To facilitate the collection and availability of open source information the intelligence community has established both management structures for the supervision of open source efforts as well as the Open Source Information System (OSIS)/ Intelink-U database. Information available through OSIS/Intelink-U includes *Armies of the World*, *CIA World Factbook*, *Patterns of Global Terrorism*, country handbooks, FBIS reports, trade show imagery and brochures, as well as data on foreign medical capabilities, worldwide health issues, land mines and demining, infectious diseases, and a number of other topics.[30]

TECHNICAL SURVEILLANCE AND EMPLACED SENSORS

The technical surveillance and emplaced sensor operations conducted by the CIA and other intelligence units constitute another important aspect of intelligence gathering. These methods supplement human intelligence activities and can provide detailed information not available by other means. Technical penetration of a residence offers twenty-four-hour coverage and captures the exact conversations that occur. Such operations in foreign embassies can provide information on the plans, policies, and activities of diplomats and intelligence agents.

Two prominent forms of technical surveillance are "bugs" and telephone taps. A bug, or audio device, which will transmit all conversations in a room to a monitoring site, is planted by experts from Directorate of Operations. Planting such a device is a complex operation involving surveillance of the site, acquisition of building and floor plans, and determination of the color of the interior furnishings and the color and texture of the walls. Activity in the room as well as the movements of security patrols are noted. When the information is acquired and processed, it will be employed to determine the time of surreptitious entry and the materials needed to install the device in such a way as to minimize the probability of a discovery.[31]

During the early 1970s one target of CIA audio devices was Nguyen Van Thieu, the President of South Vietnam. Presents given to Thieu by the CIA—television sets and furniture—came equipped with audio devices, allowing the agency to monitor his personal conversations. The CIA also attempted to install devices in the office and living quarters of the South Vietnamese observer to the Paris Peace Talks.[32]

Another Asian ally that has been subject to CIA and NSA technical penetration is South Korea. A substantial part of the evidence against Tongsun Park concerning his alleged attempts to bribe U.S. congressmen came from tape recordings of incriminating conversations inside the South Korean presidential mansion.[33]

Audio devices and telephone taps have, at least in the past, produced much of the CIA's intelligence on Latin America. A report on clandestine collection activities in Latin America during the 1960s revealed that the CIA had managed to place audio devices in the homes of many key personnel, including cabinet ministers.[34]

During E. Howard Hunt's tenure in Mexico City, the CIA bugged or tapped several Iron Curtain embassies. During his tenure in Uruguay, the CIA station conducted technical penetrations of embassies and the living quarters of key personnel. During Philip Agee's time in Uruguay, seven telephone lines were being monitored. Included were phones of the Soviet and Cuban embassies, consulates, and commercial offices.[35]

More recently, the CIA may have bugged the rooms of Iraqi and Iranian delegates to a November 1996 OPEC meeting in Vienna. Decorators found bugging devices in the walls at the hotel during a subsequent renovation. It was reported that the German Federal Intelligence Service (Bundesnachrichtendienst—BND) told its Austrian counterpart that the CIA eavesdropped on the delegates. In 1997 a member of the U.S. Embassy in Austria, presumably a CIA officer, left Austria after being arrested for wiretapping the phone of a North Korean diplomat in Vienna.[36]

In 1982 or 1983, a unit of INSCOM—then known as the Quick Reaction Team (QRT), and subsequently as the Technical Analysis Unit—placed an electronic listening device in a Panamanian apartment belonging to General Manuel Antonio Noriega. Paying bribes to the maids who cleaned the apartment, and to the guards who protected it, a QRT member was able to place a listening device in Noriega's conference room. The six 90-minute tapes that resulted did not produce any substantial intelligence information.[37]

QRT agents also bugged the apartment of a Cuban diplomat in Panama. When the diplomat was away, agents slipped into his apartment and wired it with microtransmitters; again the take was of little value.[38]

In 1983, the QRT targeted Soviet representatives on several occasions during their visit to the United States. Soviet officials who traveled to Livermore, California, home of the Lawrence Livermore National Laboratory, had their rooms bugged by QRT agents. The bugging was repeated when the Soviets moved on to Denver. This time the results were more useful—sensitive discussions were recorded and leads obtained on possible Soviet agents in the United States.[39]

A more daring operation, conducted by the CIA, was designated TAW, and involved the taping of KGB and GRU communication lines at Troitsk, about 25 miles southeast of Moscow. TAW ceased working around 1985, and could have been betrayed by Edward Lee Howard, Aldrich Ames, or both. Another technical surveillance operation that was betrayed to the Soviets around 1985 was designated ABSORB. The operation involved secretly placing Radiation Detection Devices with cargoes traveling on the Trans-Siberian railroad in order to pick up the radiation emitted from missiles in the vicinity of the train tracks, radiation that could be used to determine the number of warheads on each missile.[40]

Technical surveillance operations may also employ lasers. A laser beam can be directed at a closed window from outside and used to detect the vibrations of the sound waves resulting from a conversation inside the room. The vibrations can be transformed back into the words that were spoken. Such a device was successfully tested in West Africa in the 1960s, but at the time did not seem to function properly anywhere else except in the United States.[41] Subsequent technological advances have made it a viable intelligence collection technique.

Whereas technical surveillance devices are used to monitor communications, emplaced sensors are often designed to monitor noncommunications signals or emissions. Emplaced sensors may have the same purpose as sensors placed on spacecraft, aircraft, ships, or other mobile platforms. However, placing them covertly in a single location rather than on mobile platforms can offer two advantages. First, their proximity to the target may increase the value of the intelligence they produce. In many cases, no mobile platform operating from a distance could produce the necessary intelligence. Second, an emplaced sensor can monitor a facility or activity continuously.

Such operations are as sensitive as certain HUMINT operations, since if the target is aware of the operation it can be easily neutralized. There can also be significant risks for those involved in installing the sensors. Former DCI Stansfield Turner recalled the "very risky planting of a sensing device to monitor a secret activity in a hostile country. The case officer had to do the placement himself, escaping surveillance and proceeding undetected to a location so unusual that had he been found he would have undoubtedly paid with his life."[42]

In 1965 the CIA planted a nuclear monitoring device on the summit of Nanda Devi in Garhwal, India. The device was intended to monitor Chinese nuclear tests being conducted at China's Lop Nur nuclear test site, approximately 900 miles away. After it was swept away in an avalanche a second device was placed, in 1967, on the summit of the neighboring 22,400-foot Nanda Kot. That device remained in place for a year before being removed.[43]

In 1974 and 1975, and possibly subsequently, the U.S. Navy and Israel Defense Forces conducted a joint operation designated CLUSTER LOBSTER. The operation involved planting an acoustic and magnetic sensor/recorder package in the Strait of Gubal. The tapes yielded valuable information on Soviet mine-sweeping operations.[44]

East Germany was also the target of emplaced sensor operations. In one operation, nuclear detection equipment was installed in a series of road posts on an East German road. The equipment transmitted its data back to an antenna on a pile of rubble in West Berlin.* In another instance, seismic monitoring devices were placed underground near a road. The data they transmitted (to a satellite) allowed intelligence analysts to differentiate between seven different weight classes (e.g., jeep, passenger car, truck, tank).[45]

Some of the most exotic emplaced sensors were those used in an attempt to monitor various Soviet weapons programs. One was a round device camouflaged as a tree stump and discovered near a military facility that could transmit the data collected to a satellite. Another looked like a tree branch and was discovered in the late 1980s near a military airfield. According to a 1990 Soviet publication, it was an "automatic device for gathering intelligence on the parameters of the optronic control systems and laser sights used in the Air Force." The publication went on to state that the "optronic sensor enables it to receive scattered radiation from laser sights or missile control systems. The received laser beams are transformed into a numerical code and recorded by the electronic memory." The data could then be transmitted to a satellite.[46]

The Defense Intelligence Agency is developing Unattended Ground Sensors (UGS) and Unattended MASINT Sensors (UMS) (the latter code-named STEEL RATTLER), employing imagery and acoustic sensors to covertly monitor activity around critical targets such as North Korean nuclear facilities. UGS/UMS may eventually be used to monitor nuclear power plants, deeply buried bunkers, mobile missile launch sites, and weapons manufacturing facilities. A high-speed digital signal processor board inside the UGS would handle both the processing for the acoustic sensor and the image compression for the imager.[47]

MATERIEL EXPLOITATION

An important source of information comes from the acquisition of new or used foreign weapons systems, communications equipment, and other devices of mili-

---

*On one occasion the equipment stopped transmitting. KH-11 photography indicated the East Germans had pulled out all the posts for road repairs. After they were done, the East Germans obligingly replaced the posts, which resumed transmitting.

tary significance. In many cases information on small systems cannot be obtained by overhead reconnaissance or signals intelligence. In any case, possession of the actual system adds significant new information to whatever is already known. The acquisition and analysis—materiel exploitation—of such systems, a function of all military scientific and technical intelligence units, allows scientists to determine not only the capabilities of the system but how such capabilities are achieved. Such knowledge can then be exploited to improve U.S. systems as well as to develop countermeasures.

According to Army Regulation 381–26, materiel exploitation allows:

- production of scientific and technical intelligence in support of force, combat, and materiel development
- assessment of foreign technology, design features, and scientific developments for infusion into U.S. developmental efforts
- support of U.S. systems and developmental testing/operational testing by providing adversary systems for use in evaluating U.S. systems capabilities
- development of simulator systems in support of simulation of foreign systems[48]

During the course of the Cold War, U.S. materiel acquisition activities focused primarily on Soviet and Chinese systems. In Indonesia, in the 1960s, the CIA conducted an operation known as HABRINK. In one phase of the operation, CIA operatives entered a warehouse holding SAM-2 missiles, removed the guidance system from one of them, and took it with them. The acquisition allowed U.S. Air Force scientists to equip B-52s with appropriate countermeasures. HABRINK also obtained the designs and workings of numerous Soviet weapons—the surface-to-surface Styx naval missile, the W-class submarine, the Komar guided-missile patrol boat, a RIGA-class destroyer, a SVERDLOV cruiser, a TU-16 (BADGER) bomber, and a KENNEL air-to-surface missile.[49]

In a more recent version of HABRINK, the CIA purchased, from retired officers of the Indian Army and Air Force, details on weapons furnished to India by the Soviet Union. The Indian officers involved included an Army Major General, an Army Lieutenant Colonel, and an Air Vice Marshal.[50]

In 1979 the CIA and DIA planned Operation GRAY PAN, which was to involve the theft of a Soviet-made antiaircraft gun and armored personnel carrier that the Soviets had sold to the Iranian Army in 1978.[51]

The most significant ground forces equipment the CIA obtained during the Cold War was the T-72 tank; only the T-80 is newer. In 1981, the Army Intelligence Support Activity, in an operation code-named GRAND FALCON, attempted to obtain a T-72 and other equipment (including a MiG-25) from Iraq in exchange for U.S. 175-mm cannons. Ultimately, Iraqi officials vetoed the deal. A CIA attempt to acquire a T-72 from Romania also failed in 1981. Another unsuccessful ISA attempt to acquire a T-72, at the behest of Lt. Col. Oliver North, involved the attempted delivery of U.S.-made machine guns to Iran in October 1986 in exchange for a T-72 captured from Iraq. By March 1987 the CIA had acquired several T-72s.[52]

The United States acquired advanced Soviet aircraft from pilots who defected, or purchased the aircraft from third parties. Once obtained, the planes were examined thoroughly by Foreign Technology Division (FTD) officers and scientists. Thus, when a MiG-25 pilot defected from the Soviet Union with his plane, landing in Japan, examination of the airplane was a high priority. Before being returned to the Soviet Union, the entire MiG-25 was disassembled at Hyakuri Air Base in Japan. The engines, radar, computer, electronic countermeasures, automatic pilot, and communications equipment were placed on blocks and stands for mechanical, metallurgical, and photographic analysis.[53]

This examination, as well as the pilot's debriefing, sharply altered Western understanding of the plane and its missions. Among the discoveries was a radar more powerful that that ever installed in any other interceptor or fighter. In addition, the Soviet designers had used vacuum tubes rather than transistors.[54] (Although vacuum tubes represent a more primitive technology that transistors, they are resistant to the electromagnetic pulse [EMP] created by nuclear detonations.)

The MiG-25 was far from the first MiG obtained for purposes of exploitation. In early 1951 the Allied Air Force Commander in Korea was asked to make every effort to obtain a complete MiG-15 for analysis. As a result, a MiG that was shot down off Korea was retrieved within a short time. Portions of another MiG were recovered by helicopter. Air Technical Intelligence Center personnel landed, ran up to the crashed plane, threw grenades into it to separate assemblies small enough to carry, and left under hostile fire. In 1953, a defecting North Korean pilot flew an intact MiG-15 to South Korea.[55]

In some instances, Soviet equipment was sold to the United States by nominal Soviet allies—particularly Romania. During the final ten years of the Ceausescu regime, the CIA was able to buy advanced Soviet military technology through Ceausecsu's two brothers, one of whom was the Deputy Defense Minister. The equipment acquired from Romania included:

- the latest version of the Shilka, one of the more effective Soviet antiaircraft systems
- mobile rocket launchers that had been modified and improved by the Romanian military
- radar systems used in identifying targets and directing the firing of various Soviet AA weapons[56]

In other cases materiel exploitation follows from the completion of a recovery operation in which parts of a satellite that have returned to earth, or a crashed airplane, or a sunken ship are retrieved. During the 1960s, Project MOON DUST focused on the "national-level coordination of information concerning the decay and deorbit of space debris [including rocket boosters], regardless of country of origin." When sightings and/or recovery was considered possible, attachés were notified to maintain watch and consider action for recovery.[57]

In 1970 the United States recovered a nuclear weapon from a Soviet aircraft that crashed into the Sea of Japan; in 1971 the Navy recovered electronic eaves-dropping equipment from a sunken trawler; and in 1972 a joint U.S.-British oper-ation recovered electronic gear from a Soviet plane that had crashed earlier that year into the North Sea. In 1975, in Project JENNIFER, the CIA recovered half of a Golf-II submarine that had sunk northwest of Hawaii.[58]

The repeated recovery of Soviet test warheads that landed in ocean waters was known as Operation SAND DOLLAR. By international agreement, the Soviet Union was required to specify the impact areas for such tests. U.S. radars tracked the warheads to determine the precise points of impact. What appeared to be civilian drilling ships were sent to the Pacific test range after the tests had been completed to recover nose cones that had not self-destructed. Ships were guided to the proper locations by computers coordinated with U.S. satellites, and the ob-jects were located by sonar and magnetometer devices. Scientists at FTD then an-alyzed the design and construction of captured nose cones.[59]

In the aftermath of the 1973 Yom Kippur War, the United States received from Israel a variety of Soviet materiel. In addition to a Soviet AMD-500 mine, the Is-raelis provided SA-2, SA-3, SA-6, and SA-7 missiles.[60]

In 1983, during Operation BRIGHT STAR, personnel from INSCOM's 513th Military Intelligence Group were able to examine and evaluate Soviet and other foreign communications equipment that had been left behind in Somalia. The INSCOM personnel examined and repaired eighty-one pieces of Soviet and other foreign communications equipment.[61]

In the 1980s, the CIA acquired several advanced Soviet military helicopter gunships, specifically the Mi-24 HINDs, from both Pakistan and Chad. The heli-copters were obtained by Pakistan and Chad as a result of the defection of a Soviet pilot from Afghanistan and Chad's victory over Libya in their border war. It has been reported that as a result of acquiring the helicopters, the United States dis-covered how to penetrate the Mi-24s defense systems with Stinger surface-to-air missiles. In 1983, the Deputy Under Secretary of Defense had refused to sanction an operation to acquire a Mi-24 from Iraq in exchange for permission for Iraq to buy up to 100 Hughes helicopters because he believed that the background of the Iraqi intermediary meant that "the potential for causing embarrassment to the U.S. Government is too great."[62]

The end of the Cold War and the collapse of the Soviet Union did not in any way decrease the emphasis on acquiring Soviet and Russian-produced weapons systems. In addition to providing intelligence about innovative aspects of current Russian weapons systems, acquisition operations also provide a hedge against any future conflict. But of much greater importance is the extent to which Soviet weapons systems are the foundations for other nations' military arsenals, and

Russia continues to sell advanced weaponry. Thus, in 1990 the Soviet Union exported a variety of high-tech aircraft—the Su-7, Su-24, MiG-21, MiG-3, MiG-29, Mi-17, and Mi-24. In 1998 significant portions of the Iraqi, Libyan, North Korean, and Syrian air forces were made up by Soviet aircraft.[63]

In addition to aircraft, a large number of Third World nations also possess Soviet-made tanks and surface-to-air missiles. In particular, Soviet-produced SAMs form a significant part of the Iraqi, Syrian, Libyan, Iranian, Cuban, and North Korean arsenals.[64]

Thus, the vast analyses of Soviet weapons conducted by Army, Navy, and Air Force scientific and technical intelligence organizations during the Cold War served as the basis for understanding Iraqi capabilities during Operations Desert Shield and Desert Storm.

Hence, in April 1991 the Army received, from Germany, T-55 and T-72 tanks, assorted signals and communications equipment, and small battlefield weapons, automatic rifles, and mortars. The equipment had been inherited from the East German Army. In late 1992 the CIA was reported to be involved in a program of buying up high-technology weapons from former Soviet republics.[65]

Russia has also sought to export its most modern surface-to-air missile systems, the S-300 PMU (designated the S-10 GRUMBLE by the United States) and the S-300V (SA-12A/B GLADIATOR/GIANT). Not surprisingly, the United States has acquired both systems. It has also acquired, from Eastern European governments, 31 Scud-B missiles and four MAZ 543 transporter-erector-launchers, in a program designated WILLOW SAND. The missiles have been employed both in theater missile defense exercises and as subjects of intelligence exploitation by the DIA's Missile and Space Intelligence Center.[66]

In November 1997, it was announced that the United States had purchased from Moldova twenty-one MiG-29 aircraft, including fourteen MiG-29Cs—the most advanced model, and capable of carrying and launching nuclear missiles. The primary goal was allegedly to prevent their being sold to Iran, but the acquisition also "represented something of an intelligence coup," since the planes were the first MiG-29s to be acquired by the United States. The planes were quickly transported after the deal was arranged to the National Air Intelligence Center. It was suggested that of particular interest to analysts at the NAIC would be the nuclear wiring system and nuclear safeguards on the aircraft, since other versions obtained by the United States were not set up for the delivery of nuclear weapons.[67]

Notes

1. Roscoe H. Hillenkoeter, "Using the World's Information Sources," *Army Information Digest*, November 1948, pp. 3–6.

2. J. J. Bagnall, "The Exploitation of Russian Scientific Literature for Intelligence Purposes," *Studies in Intelligence* 2, no. 3 (Summer 1958): 45–49.

3. Ibid.

4. Ibid.

5. Bruce Ashcroft, "Air Force Foreign Materiel Exploitation," *American Intelligence Journal*, Autumn/Winter 1994, pp. 79–82; Ben Rich with Leo Janos, *Skunk Works* (Boston: Little, Brown, 1994), p. 19.

6. Andrew Cockburn, *The Threat: Inside the Soviet Military Machine* (New York: Random House, 1983), p. 22; Jonathan Samuel Lockwood, *The Soviet View of U.S. Strategic Doctrine* (New Brunswick, N.J.: Transaction, 1983), p. 5.

7. Michael Wines, "Kremlin Watchers Cope with Data Glut," *New York Times*, January 14, 1990, p. 14.

8. "Lack of Funding Threatens 'MiG–29M'," *FBIS-SOV–93–164*, August 26, 1993, pp. 32–33; "Air Missile Defense Demonstration Observed," *FBIS-SOV–93–164*, August 26, 1993, pp. 33–34; Office of Naval Intelligence, *Office of Naval Intelligence Command History 1994*, 1995, p. 55; "Top-Secret Scientist on Future of Strategic Rocket Forces," *FBIS-SOV–94–215*, November 7, 1994, pp. 34–35; "Topol-M Silo-Based SS–25 Upgrade Said More Accurate Than MX," *Aerospace Daily*, January 24, 1995, p. 113.

9. David Hoffman, "Cold-War Doctrines Refuses to Die," *Washington Post*, March 15, 1998, pp. A1, A24-A25.

10. Michael S. Moore, "Use of Open Source Material for Studying Russian Organized Crime," in *1997 Open Source Conference for the Intelligence and Law Enforcement Communities*, September 16–18, 1997, McLean, Virginia.

11. Carl B. Crawley, "On the Exploitation of Open Source Chinese Documents," *Naval Intelligence Quarterly* 2, no. 4 (1981): 7–9.

12. Ibid.

13. Ibid.

14. Ibid.

15. Intelligence Center, Pacific, *IPAC Daily Intelligence Summary 24–87*, February 6, 1987, p. 2.

16. M. Ehsan Ahrari, "Chinese Prove to Be Attentive Students of Information Warfare," *Jane's Intelligence Review*, October 1997, pp. 469–473.

17. Remarks by Admiral William O. Studeman, Deputy Director of Central Intelligence, to the First International Symposium on National Security and National Competitiveness: Open Source Solutions, December 1, 1992, McLean, Virginia, pp. 12, 20; Todd Hazelbarth, *The Chinese Media: More Autonomous and Diverse—Within Limits* (Washington, D.C.: CIA Center for the Study of Intelligence, September 1997), p. 1.

18. Herman L. Croom, "The Exploitation of Foreign Open Sources," Studies in Intelligence (Summer 1969): 129–136; Stephen Barr, "Monitoring Service Spared in Latest Cuts," *Washington Post*, February 6, 1997, p. A21.

19. Loch K. Johnson, *Secret Agencies: U.S. Intelligence in a Hostile World* (New Haven, Conn.: Yale University Press, 1996), p. 19.

20. Remarks by A. Denis Clift, Chief of Staff, Defense Intelligence Agency, to the First International Symposium on National Security and National Competitiveness: Open Source Solutions, December 1, 1992, McLean, Virginia, pp. 12, 20; *Transactions*, Third International Conference on Nuclear Technology Transfer, Madrid, Spain, October 14–18, 1985, p. III.

21. Remarks by William O. Studeman, p. 12.

22. Charles Swett, *Strategic Assessment: The Internet* (Washington, D.C.: Office of the Assistant Secretary of Defense for Special Operations and Low-Intensity Conflict, July 17, 1995), p. 25.

23. Ibid., p. 26.

24. Air Force Intelligence Service, "Video Intelligence (VIDINT)," 1988.

25. Remarks by William O. Studeman, p. 15.

26. Hazelbarth, *The Chinese Media*, p. 1; Robert Pear, "Radio Broadcasts Report Protests Erupting All Over China," *New York Times*, May 23, 1989, p. A14.

27. "Live, from Baghdad," *Newsweek*, September 24, 1990, p. 4.

28. Remarks by William O. Studeman, p. 5; 1st Infantry Division, *Tuzla Night Owl*, November 30, 1997, p. 1.

29. Joint Chiefs of Staff, United States Military Communications-Electronics Board, *Joint Department of Defense Plain Language Address Directory*, January 30, 1993, p. 32 in USMCEB Publication No. 6, Update 9-25 *Message Address Directory* (Washington, D.C.: Department of Defense, January 30, 1993).

30. Office of the Director, COSPO, *OSIS/INTELINK-U* Brochure, n.d.

31. Victor Marchetti and John Marks, *The CIA and the Cult of Intelligence* (New York: Knopf, 1974), p. 189.

32. John Stockwell, *In Search of Enemies: A CIA Story* (New York: Norton, 1978), p. 107; Thomas Powers, *The Man Who Kept the Secrets: Richard Helms and the CIA* (New York: Knopf, 1974), p. 189.

33. Steven Weissman and Herbert Krosney, *The Islamic Bomb* (New York: Times Books, 1981), p. 151.

34. Marchetti and Marks, *The CIA and the Cult of Intelligence*, p. 189.

35. E. Howard Hunt, *Undercover: Memoirs of an American Secret Agent* (New York: Berkley, 1974), pp. 80, 126; Philip Agee, *Inside the Company: A CIA Diary* (New York: Stonehill, 1975), pp. 346–347.

36. "Weekly notes . . . ," *Washington Times*, April 16, 1997, p. A10; "Intelligence monitor," *Jane's Intelligence Review*, July 1997, p. 336; Tim Weiner, "U.S. Diplomat Leaves Austria After Being Caught Wiretapping," *New York Times*, November 6, 1997, p. A10.

37. Steve Emerson, *Secret Warriors: Inside the Covert Military Operations of the Reagan Era* (New York: Putnam's, 1988), p. 111.

38. Ibid., p. 112.

39. Ibid., p. 116.

40. Pete Earley, *Confessions of a Spy: The Real Story of Aldrich Ames* (New York: Putnam, 1997), pp. 19, 117, 197.

41. Marchetti and Marks, *The CIA and the Cult of Intelligence*, pp. 190–191.

42. Stansfield Turner, *Secrecy and Democracy: The CIA in Transition* (Boston: Houghton Mifflin, 1985), pp. 59–60.

43. "The Indian Connection," *India Today*, December 31, 1983, p. 10; "$ Diplomacy," *India Today*, May 1–15, 1979, p. 107.

44. Naval Intelligence Command, *Naval Intelligence Command (NAVINTCOM) History for CY-1975, Basic Narrative*, 1976, p. 18.

45. Interview; "Seismic Sensors," *Intelligence Newsletter*, January 17, 1990, p. 2.

46. Lt. Gen. Nikolai Brusnitsin, *Openness and Espionage* (Moscow, 1990), p. 15; NBC, *Inside the KGB: Narration and Shooting Script*, May 1993, p. 39.

47. Barbara Starr, "Super Sensors Will Eye the New Proliferation Frontier," *Jane's Defence Weekly*, June 4, 1994, p. 19.

48. AR 381–26, "Army Foreign Materiel Exploitation Program," March 6, 1987, p. 3.

49. John Barron, *The KGB Today: The Hidden Hand* (New York: Reader's Digest, 1983), pp. 233–234; *Statement of Facts, United States of America v. David Henry Barnett*, K 80–0390, United States District Court, Maryland, 1980.

50. William J. Eaton, "CIA Reportedly Caught Buying Indian Military Secrets," *Los Angeles Times*, December 15, 1983, p. 4.

51. "What the U.S. Lost in Iran," *Newsweek*, December 28, 1981, pp. 33–34.

52. Emerson, *Secret Warriors*, p. 185; Michael Wines and Richard E. Meyer, "North Apparently Tried a Swap for Soviet Tank," *Washington Post*, January 22, 1987, p. A37; Richard Halloran, "U.S. Has Acquired Soviet T-72 Tank," *New York Times*, March 13, 1987, p. A12; Benjamin Weiser, "One That Got Away: Romanians Were Ready to Sell Soviet Tank," *Washington Post*, May 6, 1990, p. A30.

53. John Barron, *MIG Pilot* (New York: Avon, 1981), pp. 172–173.

54. Ibid.

55. Foreign Technology Division, *FTD 1917–1967* (Dayton, Ohio: FTD, 1967), p. 24.

56. Benjamin Weiser, "Ceaucescu Family Sold Military Secrets to U.S.," *Washington Post*, May 6, 1990, pp. A1, A30.

57. Air Force Office of the Assistant Chief of Staff, Intelligence, *History, Directorate of Collection, AFNIC, 1 July–31 December 1968*, pp. 250–251.

58. Clyde W. Burleson, *The Jennifer Project* (Englewood Cliffs, N.J.: Prentice-Hall, 1977), p. 47; "The Great Submarine Snatch," *Time*, March 31, 1975, pp. 20–27; William J. Broad, "Russia Says U.S. Got Sub's Atom Arms," *New York Times*, June 30, 1993, p. 4; "CIA Raising USSR Sub Raises Questions," *FBIS-SOV–92–145*, July 28, 1992, pp. 15–16.

59. Roy Varner and Wayne Collier, *A Matter of Risk* (New York: Random House, 1977), p. 26; Willard Bascom, *The Crest of the Wave: Adventures in Oceanography* (New York: Harper & Row, 1988), pp. 241–242; William J. Broad, *The Universe Below: Discovering the Secrets of the Deep Sea* (New York: Simon & Schuster, 1996), pp. 69–70.

60. Naval Intelligence Command, *Naval Intelligence Command History for CY-1973*, April 29, 1974, p. 20.

61. U.S. Army Intelligence and Security Command, *Annual Historical Review FY 1983*, September 1984, p. 72.

62. James Bruce, "CIA Acquires Soviet MI-24 and T-72," *Jane's Defence Weekly*, March 28, 1987, p. 535; James Brooke, "Chad, with Victories Is Awash in War Booty," *New York Times*, August 17, 1987, p. A4; Brig. Gen. Harry E. Soyster, Acting ACS for Intelligence, Memorandum Thru Director, Defense Intelligence Agency, For Deputy Under Secretary of Defense (Policy), Subject: Possible Acquisition Opportunity (U)—Action Memorandum, April 11, 1983; Gen. Richard O. Stilwell (Ret.), Deputy Undersecretary of Defense (Policy), Memorandum for the Assistant Chief of Staff for Intelligence, Department of the Army, (day and month illegible), 1983.

63. Statement of Rear Admiral Thomas A. Brooks, USN, Director of Naval Intelligence, before the Seapower, Strategic, and Critical Materials Subcommittee of the House Armed Services Committee on Intelligence Issues, March 7, 1991, p. 36; Paul Quinn-Judge, "CIA Buys Ex-Soviet Arms, US Aide Says," *Boston Globe*, November 15, 1992, pp. 1, 14; Bill Gertz, "Soviets Flee with Secrets," *Washington Times*, January 1, 1991, pp. A1, A6; "World

Military Aircraft Inventory," *Aviation Week & Space Technology*, January 12, 1998, pp. 222–238.

64. Quinn-Judge, "CIA Buys Ex-Soviet Arms, US Aide Says."

65. Richard H. P. Sia, "U.S. Army Gets Soviet Weapons from Germany," *Philadelphia Inquirer*, May 5, 1991, p. 14-E.

66. Nikolay Novichkov and Michael A. Dornheim, "Russian SA-12, SA-10 on World ATBM Market," *Aviation Week & Space Technology*, March 3, 1997, p. 59; David Hughes, "U.S. Army to Assess Russian SA-10 SAM System," *Aviation Week & Space Technology*, January 2, 1995, p. 60; Jeff Gerth, "In a Furtive, Frantic Market, America Buys Russian Arms," *New York Times*, December 24, 1994, pp. 1, 7; Barbara Starr, "USA Fields 'Scuds' to Test Theatre Missile Defense," *Jane's Defence Weekly*, May 7, 1997, p. 3.

67. Steven Lee Myers, "U.S. Is Buying MiG's So Rogue Nations Will Not Get Them," *New York Times*, November 5, 1997, pp. A1, A6; David A. Fulghum, "Moldovan MiG-29s To Fly for USAF," *Aviation Week & Space Technology*, November 10, 1997, pp. 37–38; Brian Barr and Rob Young, "Russian Aircraft Cross Borders: Moldovan MiGs Call NAIC Home," *Spokesman*, January 1998, pp. 4–5.

13

INTELLIGENCE SHARING

Despite its huge investment in technical and human intelligence activities, the United States relies on exchange and liaison arrangements with a variety of foreign nations for a significant portion of its intelligence. As then Defense Secretary Caspar Weinberger explained in 1985: "The United States has neither the opportunity nor the resources to unilaterally collect all the intelligence information we require. We compensate with a variety of intelligence sharing arrangements with other nations in the world."[1]

The United States can benefit in several ways with respect to such arrangements and liaison relationships. The ability to monitor events in a foreign country can be enhanced because an ally is particularly well situated to conduct a variety of technical collection operations against the target. The United States has often helped establish collection sites, in exchange for access to the information collected. In the case of nations where the United States has no diplomatic representation, allied intelligence services can run agents on behalf of the United States. Allies can also provide additional manpower to collect or process intelligence, particularly the vast quantities of intelligence produced by technical collection systems. In addition, the commentary and analysis presented by allied analysts via intelligence exchanges and conferences may help U.S. analysts improve their understanding of foreign developments. At the same time, there is at least one major risk involved in such arrangements. The cooperating service may be penetrated by an adversary, and the information provided by the United States might wind up in an adversary's hands.[2]

Some arrangements are long-standing, highly formalized, and involve the most sensitive forms of intelligence collection. Others are less wide-ranging and reflect limited common interests between the United States and particular nations. Thus, the United States has shared satellite intelligence concerning drug production with Mexico.[3] In addition, exchange arrangements may involve different components of the intelligence communities in the United States and other nations. Whereas some arrangements may involve links between the CIA and a nation's counterpart agency, others may involve cooperation between the NSA, the DIA, or the ONI and their foreign counterparts.

The most important arrangements are the bilateral and multilateral agreements between the United States and the United Kingdom, Australia, Canada, and New Zealand concerning the collection and distribution of signals intelligence and ocean surveillance data. The United States is also involved in intelligence sharing and cooperation, to varying degrees, with several East European nations, Israel, Japan, Norway, the People's Republic of China, and Russia. The United States also provides intelligence support to the United Nations and the International Atomic Energy Agency.

UKUSA

The U.S.-British military alliance in World War II necessitated a high degree of cooperation with respect to intelligence activities. It was imperative that the United States and Britain, as the main allied combatants in the European and Pacific theaters, established a coordinated effort in the acquisition of worldwide intelligence and its evaluation and distribution.

The most important aspect of that cooperation was in the area of signals intelligence. An apparently limited agreement on SIGINT cooperation was reached in December 1940. That was followed by the visit of four U.S. officers, including two members of the Army Signal Intelligence Service, to the British Government Code and Cipher School in January 1941. In June of that year the United States and Britain agreed to exchange signals intelligence concerning Japan. But it was not until October 2, 1942, that the United States and Britain signed an agreement for extensive cooperation in the area of naval SIGINT. That was followed by a May 17, 1943, agreement, generally known as the British-U.S. Communications Intelligence Agreement (BRUSA), that provided for extensive cooperation between the U.S. Army's SIGINT agency and the British Code and Cipher School. SIGINT cooperation also included Canada, Australia, and New Zealand.[4]

The intelligence relationships among Australia, Britain, Canada, New Zealand, and the United States that were forged during World War II did not end with the war. Rather, they became formalized and grew stronger. In 1946, William Friedman, America's premier cryptographer, visited British cryptographers to work out the mechanics of postwar consultation and cooperation. A U.S. Liaison Office was set up in London, and schemes were derived for avoiding the duplication of effort. It was agreed that solved material was to be exchanged between the two agencies. In addition, an exchange program was started under which personnel from each agency would work for two or three years at the other site.[5]

An event that occurred in 1948 set the stage for post–World War II signals intelligence cooperation: the formulation and acceptance of the UKUSA Agreement, also known as the UK-USA Security Agreement or "Secret Treaty." The primary emphasis of the agreement was to provide a division of SIGINT collection responsibilities between the First Party (the United States) and the Second Parties

(Australia, Britain, Canada, New Zealand).* The specific agencies now involved are the U.S. National Security Agency (NSA), the Australian Defence Signals Directorate (DSD), the British Government Communications Headquarters (GCHQ), the Canadian Communications Security Establishment (CSE), and the New Zealand Government Communications Security Bureau (GCSB).[6]

Under the present division of responsibilities the United States is responsible for SIGINT in Latin America, most of Asia, Russia, and northern China. Australia's area of responsibility includes its neighbors (such as Indonesia), southern China, and the nations of Indochina. Britain is responsible for the former Soviet Union west of the Urals, and Africa. The polar regions of Russia are the responsibility of Canada, and New Zealand's area of responsibility is the western Pacific. Specific tasking assignments are specified in the SIGINT Combined Operating List (SCOL).[7]

Britain's geographical position gives it a significant capability for long-range SIGINT collection against certain targets in Russia and former Soviet states such as the Ukraine. Britain's historical role in Africa led to its assumption of SIGINT responsibility for that area. Canada's responsibility for northern Russia stems from its geographical location, which gives it "unique access to communications in . . . northern [Russia]." The areas of responsibility for Australia and New Zealand clearly result from their geographical location.[8]

The UKUSA relationship (and its SIGINT aspect) is more than an agreement to coordinate separately conducted intelligence activities and share the intelligence collected. Rather, it is cemented by the presence of U.S. facilities on British, Canadian, and Australian territory; by joint operations (U.S.-U.K., Australian-U.S., U.K.-Australian) within and outside UKUSA territory; and, in the case of Australia, by the presence of U.K. and U.S. staff at all DSD facilities.[9]

The relationship also involves a computer-based tasking and exchange system, code-named ECHELON, that allows the various parties to request, via key words, data collected by the other's collection assets and to have it transmitted to the requesting party.[10]

In addition to specifying SIGINT collection responsibilities, the agreement addresses access to the collected intelligence and security arrangements for the handling of data. Standardized code words (e.g., UMBRA for the highest-level signals intelligence), security agreements that all employees of the respective SIGINT agencies must sign, and procedures for storing and disseminating code word material all are implemented under terms of the agreement.[11]

Thus, in 1967, the "COMINT Indoctrination" declaration, which all British-cleared personnel had to sign, included in the first paragraph the statement, "I declare that I fully understand the information relating to the manner and extent of the interception of communications of foreign powers by H. M. Government and

---

*There are also ten Third Parties to the treaty: Austria, Thailand, Japan, South Korea, Norway, Denmark, Germany, Italy, Greece, and Turkey.

other cooperating Governments, and intelligence produced by such interception known as Communications Intelligence (COMINT) is information covered by Section 2 of the Official Secrets Act 1911 (as amended)" [emphasis added].[12] These requirements for standardized code words (see Chapter 19), security arrangements, and procedures for the handling and dissemination of SIGINT material are detailed in a series of *International Regulations on SIGINT (IRSIG)* that was in its third edition as of 1967.

Despite numerous references to the agreements in print, officials of some of the participating governments have refused to confirm not only the details of the agreement but even its existence. Thus, on March 9, 1977, the Australian Opposition Defence Spokesman asked the prime minister:

- Is Australia a signatory to the UKUSA Agreement?
- Is it a fact that under this agreement, NSA operates electronic intercept stations in Australia?
- Does any other form of station operate in Australia under the agreement? If so, is it operated by an Australian or overseas authority or is it operated under some sort of joint authority?
- Will the [prime minister] identify the participating country or countries in any such agreement?

The prime minister refused to answer and referred to a previous response wherein he said the government would not confirm or deny speculation in that area. And the Australian D Notice, "Ciphering and Monitoring Activities," requests the media to refrain from publishing material on Australian collaboration with other countries in monitoring activities.[13]

Similarly, in the United States a 1982 Freedom of Information Act request to the NSA asking for "all documents from 1947 outlining United States–United Kingdom–Australia–Canadian–New Zealand cooperation in Signals Intelligence" brought the response, "We have determined that the fact of the existence or non-existence of the materials you request is in itself a currently and properly classified matter."[14]

In one case, U.S.–Canadian–British cooperation in the SIGINT area was the result of a U.S. inability to process the data produced by a U.S. COMINT satellite program. The program CANYON commenced operations with a launch in April 1968; that would be followed by five additional successful launches through 1977. The satellite produced such a heavy volume of intercepted communications that the U.S. recruited the British and Canadian SIGINT agencies to help in the processing, thus granting those two nations access to the intercepted communications. However, one of the individuals assigned by the British to work on the processing of the intercepts was Geoffrey Prime, who also reported to Soviet intelligence.[15]

In the case of Britain, the decision to cancel an indigenous SIGINT satellite program, code-named ZIRCON, was followed by a February 1987 decision to purchase a share in the ORION system at the cost of about $750 million. ZIRCON had originally been conceived by GCHQ director Brian Tovey "to keep the special relationship sweet and to take his organization into space."[16]

With regard to ocean surveillance, cooperation exists on a similar level to that in the SIGINT area, with British and Australian stations feeding into the U.S. Ocean Surveillance Information System (OSIS). Several Australian stations contribute significantly to OSIS. Those stations are located at Pearce, Western Australia; Cabarlah, Queensland; and Shoal Bay, New Territories. The Pearce station has as its primary purpose the monitoring of naval and air traffic over the Indian Ocean. In the early 1980s a Pusher antenna was installed for the purpose of intercepting, monitoring, direction finding, and analyzing radio signals in a portion of the HF band.[17]

The Cabarlah station on the east coast of Australia is operated by the DSD. Its main purpose is monitoring radio transmissions throughout the southwest Pacific. Thus, the station monitored Soviet intelligence-gathering trawlers that were watching the Kangaroo II naval exercise of October 1976.[18]

The most important station for monitoring the Southeast Asian area is the DSD station at Darwin (Shoal Bay), which originally had a very limited direction-finding capability. However, contracts signed in 1981 provided for the procurement of modern DF equipment to enable the station to "participate fully in the OSIS." Canadian stations at Halifax and a joint U.S.-British station on Ascension Island (which monitors naval traffic in the South Atlantic) contribute to the monitoring of naval movements in the Atlantic Ocean.[19]

Overhead maritime surveillance is the subject of the 1977 agreement between Australia, New Zealand, and the United States, the Agreement for the Coordination of Maritime Surveillance and Reconnaissance in the South-Southwest Pacific and Eastern Indian Oceans.[20]

In addition to cooperating on collection activities, the UKUSA nations are also involved in cooperative arrangements concerning defense intelligence analysis, holding periodic conferences dealing with a wide range of scientific and defense intelligence matters. Thus, U.S. analysts have participated in the Annual Land Warfare Technical Intelligence Conference, the International Scientific Intelligence Exchange, the Quadripartite Intelligence Working Party on Chinese Guided Missiles, and the Tripartite Defense Intelligence Estimates Conference.[21]

U.S., Canadian, and U.K. representatives regularly attend the Annual CAN-UKUS Maritime Intelligence Conference. Air Force intelligence representatives from each nation have also met to examine topics such as Soviet surface-to-air missiles. U.S. and U.K. military intelligence representatives have also participated in the U.S./U.K. Chemical Warfare Intelligence Conference and the U.S./U.K. Armor Conference (held at the CIA).[22]

The U.S. Armed Forces Medical Intelligence Center (AFMIC) has also been involved in medical intelligence exchanges with Australia, Canada, and the United Kingdom. AFMIC is a member of the Quadripartite Medical Intelligence Committee. Other members include the Canadian and U.S. medical liaison offices and the Australian scientific attaché.[23]

In 1974, a senior U.S. intelligence official wrote, with respect to U.S. participation:

> I believe that an objective study would show that the U.S. is ahead of the game, keeping [deleted] analysts informed of activities here allows them to channel their work into more productive areas. And, in spite of the small size of the [deleted] intelligence groups, they keep coming up with nuggets in the form of unique analysis which have been very helpful to us.[24]

In addition to positive intelligence links, the UKUSA nations also cooperate in matters of counterintelligence. Beginning in the 1950s, representatives of Canada, Australia, New Zealand, Canada, and the United Kingdom met every eighteen months for a week-long conference on counterintelligence matters of common interest. Subjects have included joint operations, research of old cases, investigation of penetrations, assessment of defectors, and technical and communications advances.[25]

CANADA

Canada and the United States have signed a variety of bilateral intelligence agreements and have worked together on a number of projects. U.S.-Canadian joint estimates produced in the late 1950s focused on Soviet capabilities and likely actions in the event of a major Soviet attack on North America. Thus, the document *Soviet Capabilities and Probable Courses of Action Against North America in a Major War During the Period 1 January 1958 to 31 December 1958*, as well as a similarly titled document prepared by the Canadian-U.S. Joint Intelligence Committee, assessed the Soviet threat to North America. These documents considered factors such as Communist bloc political stability and economic support; the internal threat to North America; Soviet nuclear, radiological, biological, and chemical weapons; aircraft, including bombers, transport aircraft, and tanker aircraft; guided missiles; naval weapons; electronics; ground, naval, and surface strength and combat effectiveness; Soviet worldwide strategy; and Soviet capabilities to conduct air and airborne missile, naval, amphibious, and internal operations against North America. Preparation of such estimates continues on a yearly basis under the title *Canadian–United States Intelligence Estimate of the Military Threat to North America*.[26]

Canada's SIGINT relationship with the United States is defined by the CANUS Agreement (as well as the UKUSA Agreement). On September 15, 1950, Canada and the United States exchanged letters giving formal recognition to the Security

Agreement Between Canada and the United States of America (which was followed exactly two months later by the Arrangement for the Exchange of Information between the U.S., U.K., and Canada).[27]

Negotiations for the CANUS Agreement had been taking place since at least 1948. There was some concern on the part of U.S. intelligence officials that original drafts of the agreement provided for too much exchange. Thus, a 1948 memorandum by the Acting Director of Intelligence of the U.S. Air Force noted that paragraph 6a of the proposed agreement "was not sufficiently restrictive. In effect, it provides for the complete exchange of information. Not only is it considered that the Canadians will reap all the benefits of complete exchange but wider dissemination of the information. It is believed that the exchange should be related to mutually agreed COMINT activities on a 'need to know' basis."[28]

In the 1970s, U.S.-Canadian SIGINT cooperation led the Canadian SIGINT organization to conduct a feasibility study of embassy-based eavesdropping operations. The overall program, code-named PILGRIM, involved eavesdropping operations in India, China, Venezuela, Mexico, the Soviet Union, Romania, Morocco, Jamaica, and the Ivory Coast.[29]

Canada has also been a partner in the Sound Surveillance System (SOSUS). Canada first became involved in SOSUS when one of its first Naval Facilities, located in Shelburne, Nova Scotia, was opened. In 1972, Canada expanded its role in SOSUS and sent a small detachment to work with U.S. personnel at the U.S. Naval Facility at Argentia, Newfoundland. By the early 1980s it had expanded to ninety personnel. As SOSUS expanded its capabilities in the 1970s, Canadian participation grew, with additional Canadian Forces personnel being assigned to the Naval Ocean Processing Facility at Dam Neck, Virginia, the Naval Facility at Bermuda, and at Headquarters, Commander, Undersea Surveillance Pacific, Ford Island, Hawaii. A Canadian detachment was also formed at the Whidbey Island Naval Facility. In 1994 the Canadian Offshore Surveillance Center at Halifax, Nova Scotia, opened to process all acoustical information gathered in Argentia.[30]

Another aspect of intelligence cooperation is the Canadian–United States Communications Instructions for Reporting Vital Intelligence Sightings (CIRVIS/MERINT), signed in March 1966. This agreement specifies the type of information to be reported by airborne or land-based observers—that is, information concerning:

- hostile or unidentified single aircraft or formations of aircraft that appear to be directed against the United States or Canada or their forces
- missiles
- unidentified flying objects
- hostile or unidentified submarines
- hostile or unidentified groups of military vessels
- individual surface vessels, submarines, or aircraft of unconventional design, or engaged in suspicious activity or observed in a location or on a course

that may be interpreted as constituting a threat to the United States, Canada, or their forces
- any unexplained or unusual activity that may indicate a possible attack against or through Canada or the United States, including the presence of any unidentified or other suspicious ground parties in the Polar Region or other remote or sparsely populated areas[31]

The agreement also specifies eleven types of information that should be provided in any MERINT report, including a description of the object sighted (covering each of nine different aspects of the object), a description of the course of the object and the manner of observation, and information on weather and wind conditions.[32]

The agreement specifies that seaborne vessels submit MERINT reports concerning such topics as:

- the movement of . . . unidentified aircraft (single or in formation)
- missile firings
- the movement of . . . unidentified submarines
- the movement of . . . unidentified groups of surface combatants
- any airborne, seaborne, ballistic, or orbiting object that the observer feels may constitute a military threat against the United States or Canada or may be of interest to military and civilian government officials
- individual surface ships, submarines, or aircraft of unconventional design or engaged in suspicious activities or observed in unusual locations
- any unexplained or unusual activity that may indicate possible attack against or through the United States or Canada, including the presence of any unidentified or suspicious ground parties in the Polar Region or other remote or sparsely populated areas[33]

EASTERN EUROPE

Since 1990, officials from the intelligence services of three East European countries—Czechoslovakia, Hungary, and Poland—have visited CIA headquarters. CIA officials have also visited those nations to provide advice on restructuring the agencies that were hostile services during the Cold War.[34]

The most significant links were established with the Polish civilian intelligence and security service, now known as the Office of State Security. Links were established immediately after the collapse of East European communism in 1989, and have grown gradually. Of particular value to the United States has been the presence of Polish intelligence officers and assets in countries where the United States has no diplomatic representation—including Iraq and Libya. The relationship was further enhanced by the Polish rescue of CIA agents stranded in Iraq prior to the Persian Gulf War.[35]

One concern in pursuing cooperation with the East European services is the extent to which former Communists remain in place. Their continued presence creates the fear that they might disclose sensitive information to nations such as Iraq or Libya or that any who served as KGB assets will continue to provide information to the Russian Foreign Intelligence Service (SVRR). Thus, the Polish Military Information Service has remained untouched since the collapse of communism. In Hungary, five different intelligence services are headed by former Communist officials.[36]

ISRAEL

One of the strongest Western intelligence links is that between the United States and Israel. These arrangements involve the Mossad (the Central Institute for Intelligence and Special Tasks), AMAN (the Israeli Defense Forces Intelligence Branch), and a variety of U.S. intelligence agencies—the CIA, the FBI, the DIA, the NSA, the National Air Intelligence Center, and the National Ground Intelligence Center.

The intelligence liaison between the United States and Israel dates back to 1951, when Prime Minister David Ben-Gurion arrived in the United States for a fundraising drive. Ben-Gurion also paid an unpublicized visit to DCI Walter Bedell Smith and his deputy, Allen Dulles. At that meeting, Ben-Gurion offered, and the CIA accepted, the concept of a liaison relationship between the U.S. and Israeli intelligence communities. In October 1951, James Jesus Angleton, then Director of the CIA's Staff A (Foreign Intelligence), arrived in Israel to establish a cooperative arrangement. Angleton would direct the liaison relationship with Israel until his forced retirement in 1975.[37]

Angleton had developed extensive contacts with future Israeli intelligence officials during his World War II activities in Europe with the Office of Strategic Services. In 1957, he set up a liaison unit to deal with the Mossad. This unit was made responsible for producing Middle East intelligence for both services. In addition, the CIA received intelligence from Mossad networks in the Soviet Union.[38]

By the early 1970s the United States and Israel established a joint debriefing operation to interview émigrés from the Soviet Union. The joint operation was located in Tel Aviv under Mossad auspices, with CIA officers participating.[39]

After Angleton's dismissal as counterintelligence chief in 1975, the liaison unit was abolished and the Israeli account was moved to the appropriate Directorate of Operations regional division of the CIA. The CIA also began to operate more independently of the Mossad. In the late 1970s the agency began operating on the West Bank.[40]

Through this liaison relationship, the U.S. intelligence community gained access to Soviet weapons systems and data on their wartime performance. Such exchanges took place after the 1967 and 1973 Arab-Israeli wars. Israel furnished the United States with captured Soviet air-to-ground and ground-to-air missiles and antitank weapons. Also furnished were Soviet 122- and 130-mm artillery pieces, along with ammunition for evaluation and testing. Additionally, extensive joint analyses conducted after the 1973 war produced eight 200- to 300-page volumes of intelligence. These analyses influenced subsequent developments in U.S. weapons tactics and military budgets.[41]

In early 1983 the Israeli government offered to share military intelligence gained during the war in Lebanon. The offer included details of an "Israeli invention" that was alleged by Prime Minister Menachem Begin to be the key to Israel's ability to destroy Syria's Soviet-made surface-to-air missiles during the war. However, Secretary of Defense Caspar Weinberger rejected a proposed agreement for sharing that information, feeling that it would have trapped the United States into undesirable long-range commitments to Israel. Administration officials argued that the information had already been learned through normal military contacts.[42]

As a condition for sharing the information, Israel insisted on sending Israeli experts to the United States with captured weapons for U.S. analysis, stipulating that the United States share the results of the analysis. Israel also insisted on the right to veto the transfer of information and analysis to third-party countries, including members of NATO, and on measures to ensure that the data remained secret. According to diplomats, the Israelis expressed fears that Soviet intelligence agents who had penetrated Western European governments would find out what Israel had learned and would then pass that information along to the Soviet Union's Arab allies. Subsequently, an agreement was reached that continued the flow of information.[43]

In late 1983, as the situation in Lebanon deteriorated and Syrian intransigence continued, the United States conducted a reassessment of U.S. policy in the Middle East. This effort resulted in the Top Secret, National Security Decision Directive 111, "Next Steps Toward Progress in Lebanon and the Middle East." The directive reportedly specified a "tilt" toward Israel and expanded U.S.-Israeli strategic cooperation.[44]

The expanded cooperation reportedly involved greater sharing of reconnaissance satellite data, including data on Saudi Arabia and Jordan. William J. Casey, in his first three years as CIA director (1981–1984), provided the Israelis with access to sensitive photographs and other reconnaissance information that they had been denied under the Carter administration. The head of AMAN from 1979 to 1983, Major General Yehoshua Saguy, said in early 1984 that the CIA was providing Israel with access to data from reconnaissance satellites, and "not only the information but the photos themselves." Under the Carter administration, DCI Stansfield Turner had refused to provide the satellite imagery that had been shared during George Bush's tenure as DCI in 1976–1977.[45]

After 1981, inside the Israeli intelligence community the satellite photos were often referred to as "Casey's gifts," and they were considered invaluable. After Israel used some of the photos to aid in targeting the Osirak reactor, Deputy DCI Bobby Ray Inman restricted Israeli access to photographs of targets within 250 miles of the Israeli border.[46]

Another aspect of the expanded cooperation was reported to be greater Israeli access to the "take" of Cyprus-based SR-71 flights. The United States had been sharing such data with Israel, Egypt, and Syria on a "highly selective basis" as a result of an agreement signed in 1974 after the October War of 1973. The information previously transmitted to Israel primarily concerned Egyptian or Syrian military developments but was now to be expanded to cover a "broader range."[47]

Israel did not, however, receive everything it wanted—including a dedicated satellite and a system of ground stations that would "directly access" the KH-11 as it passed over the Middle East.[48]

In return for intelligence from the United States, Israel supplied the U.S. with intelligence on the Middle East—including both reports from agents and finished intelligence analyses. Some U.S. officials were not impressed by the political intelligence, however. One CIA official said that he was "appalled at the lack of quality, of the political intelligence on the Arab world . . . Their tactical military intelligence was first rate. But they didn't know their enemy. I saw this political intelligence and it was lousy, laughably bad . . . It was gossip stuff mostly."[49]

The United States and Israel have also exchanged intelligence during crises situations. During the 1973 war, Israel received data obtained by the RHYOLITE satellite. In 1976 the United States supplied Israel with both aerial and satellite reconnaissance photographs of Entebbe airport to supplement the information obtained by Israeli agents in preparation for the Israeli hostage rescue mission. During the 1985 hijacking of the *Achille Lauro*, Israel provided the United States with the location of the ship on several occasions, the location of the ship's hijackers when they were in Egypt, and the identification number and call sign of the plane carrying the hijackers seconds after it took off from Egypt.[50]

The United States and Israel also exchanged intelligence during Operations Desert Shield and Desert Storm. Israel provided the United States with data on Iraqi air defenses, and the United States granted Israel increased access to U.S. satellite imagery. Once again, Israel pressed for establishment of a receiving station to allow real-time access.[51]

In October 1997, it was reported that the AMAN had provided the CIA and the DIA with a report stating that China's Great Wall Industries was providing Iran with "telemetry infrastructure" to support a program to develop two medium-range ballistic missiles.[52]

Israel has also assisted the United States in its efforts to discover further details of Iraqi nuclear, chemical, and biological warfare activities. Israeli imagery interpreters have analyzed overhead photography obtained by U.S. U-2 aircraft operating in support of the UN Special Commission (UNSCOM). The Israelis analyzed the imagery in light of data contained in Israeli databases about the U-2 targets. Israeli intelligence personnel have also processed other forms of data obtained by UNSCOM and provided the commission with raw reports from defectors and other human sources. In September 1994, Israel provided UNSCOM with details concerning the deception and concealment activities of the Special Security Organization, headed by Saddam's son, Qusay.[53]

JAPAN

Japan has an extensive intelligence exchange relationship with the United States. One aspect of that relationship is the sharing of signals intelligence, as indicated by the Japanese sharing of Soviet communications intercepted by a unit on Wakkania on the night the Soviets shot down Korean Airlines Flight 007. The United States maintains SIGINT facilities on Japanese territory and in return shares SIGINT information of mutual interest.[54] The Japan-U.S. SIGINT relationship is a formal one, with Japan being one of ten Third Parties to the UKUSA Agreement.

Japan has received satellite photographs from U.S. authorities. In 1982, Secretary of Defense Caspar Weinberger presented the chief of the Japanese Defense Agency with satellite photographs "showing a Japanese-made floating dock being used in the repair of the Soviet aircraft carrier *Minsk*."[55] The revelation was made to convince the Japanese that technology made available to the Soviets for non-military purposes was being misused.

In addition, it is likely that the Japanese Defense Agency receives, on a regular basis, satellite photographs or at least satellite photograph-derived information. Such information would concern naval movements in the vicinity of Japan as well as North Korean military and nuclear research activity.

A substantial amount of U.S.-Japanese intelligence cooperation has focused on SIGINT concerning naval activities. In 1972, the U.S. Naval Intelligence Command began discussions with the CIA, the NSA, and the DIA that led to the expansion of SIGINT exchange with the Japanese Maritime Self-Defense Force (JMSDF) regarding Soviet and Chinese naval activities. In addition, under the terms of Project COMET, Japan provided the United States with foreign material recovered from the Sea of Japan.[56]

One vehicle for such cooperation is the CINCPACFLT-JMSDF Intelligence Exchange Conference. Likewise, the Intelligence Liaison and Production Section of the Intelligence Division, U.S. Naval Forces, Japan, is responsible for coordinating the Commander in Chief, U.S. Pacific Fleet, and the Commander, U.S. Naval Forces, Japan intelligence exchange, with the Chief of the Intelligence Division, Maritime Staff Office, and the Intelligence Officer, CINCSDFLT (Commander in Chief, Self-Defense Fleet).[57]

Information derived from U.S. worldwide ocean surveillance assets—especially from ocean surveillance satellites and the SOSUS network—can substantially increase the effectiveness of Japan's surface ship and submarine detection efforts. Information likely to be passed on to Japan includes much of that coming into the fleet ocean surveillance information center at Kamiseya, Japan. At the same time, the Japanese share information obtained by their sonar array and their P-3Cs.

NORWAY

Intelligence cooperation between the United States and Norway dates back to the 1950s, when Norway served as the launching site for GENETRIX reconnaissance balloons and as a base for U-2 operations. By early 1963, Norway was the site of Project SOUTH SEA—"an integrated technical collection system intended for operation in northern Norway to monitor Soviet submarine-launched missiles." The system consisted of electronic intelligence, infrared, and photographic equipment connected to a missile tracking system.[58]

The project was first approved in November 1961, and development continued throughout 1962. By February 1963 SOUTH SEA was undergoing testing and checkout. It subsequently became a significant element in the U.S.-Norwegian intelligence relationship.[59]

Norway not only provided a desirable location from which to monitor Soviet naval activities in the Barents Sea but was also well located to monitor the Soviet missile and space launch center at Plesetsk, as well as Soviet nuclear testing activities at Novaya Zemlaya and Semipalatinsk. The SIGINT stations are still in operation, monitoring Russia and other former member states of the Soviet Union, and particularly Russian ICBM and SLBM tests. They are operated by the Norwegian SIGINT agency, but they were erected by and are operated for the NSA. According to Victor Marchetti, a former U.S. intelligence official, CIA and NSA personnel were regularly on assignment at those stations in the 1960s. Although U.S. personnel are no longer assigned there, and the NSA no longer provides funding for the stations (as it did until the collapse of the Soviet Union), Norway does pass the information it acquires on to the United States.[60]

One of the stations is at Vadso, a small fjord town in Norway's arctic region close to the former Soviet border. Somewhere between several hundred and 1,500 of the towns 5,000 residents are said to work at the intercept station. There are four intercept locations at Vadso. The station conducts high-frequency (HF) listening primarily by means of monopole antennas, within which is a further array of monopoles. The large array is 492 feet in diameter. About 2 miles to the southeast is a smaller circular antenna array with an outer ring that is 82 feet in diameter and consists of twelve dipoles. An inner ring consists of six dipoles, and there is a hut in the center of the array. The array's location apart from the main HF site suggests that it is used for transmission rather than reception. The location of the antenna arrays on the northern shore of Varangerfjord gives them uninterrupted overseas propagation paths all the way to the Soviet Union.[61]

In addition to the circular arrays, there are two VHF-UHF interception sites in the Vadso area. The main site is at the summit of a 397-foot hill. The site is the home of a variety of VHF-UHF antennas known as Yagis, log-periodic arrays (LPAs), vertical wire dipoles, and broadband dipoles. Four of the antennas are pointed in the direction of Murmansk and the associated complex of naval and air facilities—one toward Wickel; two to the coast; and one northeast, toward the Barents Sea. The antennas at the smaller site also point toward Russia. It has been reported that Vadso has the capability of intercepting voice communications from Russian pilots down to their ground controllers.[62]

Also in the very north of Norway are Viksjofell and Vardo. At Viksjofell, on a 1,476-foot-high hill only 3 miles from the former Soviet border, is a concrete tower with a geodesic radome. On the side of the tower facing toward the border is a semi-cylindrical extension apparently made of the same material as the radome and mounted by a VHF Adcock direction-finding antenna. The Viksjofell facility appears to be a very sophisticated VHF installation, and it might be presumed that the dome contains a moveable dish antenna that can be constantly rotated in either a scanning mode or a tracking mode. Installations of this type are capable of monitoring all VHF-SHF frequencies, including ground-based and air-based radars, communications, and missile command and control links.[63]

At Vardo there is a tower identical to the one at Viksjofell, except that the external direction-finding and log-periodic antennas are absent. Vardo can intercept signals from Plesetsk. Another likely target in the past was telemetry from Soviet SLBM tests in the Barents Sea. The Soviet navy tested the SS-N-18 missile as well as the Typhoon-based SS-N-20 missile from the White Sea and Barents Sea. The Viksjofell station apparently was established in 1972 and the one at Vardo in 1971, at the same time that an earlier submarine-launched missile, the SS-N-8, became operational. In December 1988, according to a 1990 Soviet publication, a phased array radar was installed at Vardo. The radar is designated CREEK CHART by the United States.[64]

Also scheduled for deployment at Vardo is a space surveillance radar, possibly with a secondary missile detection and warning role, designated HAVE STARE by the U.S. Air Force. Originally intended as an intelligence radar, it was transferred from the intelligence budget during the 1993 fiscal year, at the direction of Congress. The system is to be financed by the United States and Norway and operated by the Norwegian Military Intelligence Service. Its Norwegian designation is GLOBUS II. A 132-foot-tall radome to enclose the mechanical antenna is scheduled to be completed in 2000.[65]

At Skage (in Namdalen) and Randaberg (near Stavanger, on Norway's western coast) there are arrays similar to the smaller of the Vardo arrays. These arrays probably are used mainly to intercept HF communications from Russian ships, submarines, and long-range marine reconnaissance aircraft in the Norwegian Sea. The two stations are probably operated as pairwise units to allow triangulation of emitter locations.[66]

PEOPLE'S REPUBLIC OF CHINA

The PRC's intelligence relationship with the United States had its origins in the April 1970 visit to Beijing of National Security Adviser Henry Kissinger. Kissinger presented his hosts with communications intelligence and high-resolution satellite imagery concerning Soviet forces on China's border.[67]

In May 1978, Morton Abramowitz, Deputy Assistant Secretary of Defense for International Security Affairs, accompanied National Security Adviser Zbigniew Brzezinski to Beijing. In a meeting with a senior Chinese defense official, Abramowitz gave a highly classified briefing on the deployment of Soviet forces along the Chinese border and pulled out of his briefcase satellite photographs of Soviet military installations and armor facing China. China continued to receive such photography.[68]

The Abramowitz meeting led to the most important element of the U.S.-PRC intelligence cooperation—two SIGINT stations in western China, located at Qitai and Korla in the Xinjiang Uighur Autonomous Region, that could monitor the telemetry from Soviet ballistic missile tests and space launches. The United States initially suggested setting up such posts in 1978, prior to the establishment of diplomatic relations. At first, the Chinese, apparently concerned about cooperating too closely with the United States, were reluctant to agree. The issue was raised again after the overthrow of the Shah of Iran in January 1979 and the resulting deactivation of key U.S. intelligence sites in that country. In an April 1979 meeting with a visiting U.S. Senate delegation, PRC Vice Premier Deng Xiaoping indicated that China was willing to use U.S. equipment "to monitor Soviet compliance with a proposed new arms limitation treaty." Deng also indicated that the monitoring stations would have to be run by the Chinese and that the data would have to be shared with the PRC.[69]

The United States and the PRC reached a basic agreement during a secret visit to Beijing by DCI Stansfield Turner during January 1980. Collection operations began that fall. The stations were constructed by an office of the CIA's Directorate of Science and Technology, which sent personnel to train the Chinese technicians, and which periodically sent advisers and service technicians as required. The initial equipment allowed for the interception of telemetry from Soviet missile test and space shots conducted from two major Soviet launch sites—at Tyuratam near the Aral Sea and at Sary Shagan near Lake Balkash. Although they are somewhat farther from Tyuratam than the Iranian sites were, the Chinese sites are closer to the Sary Shagan ABM test site. The sites continued to operate throughout the Tienanmen Square crisis of 1989 and beyond. They are apparently still in operation.[70]

Recent visible signs of U.S.-PRC intelligence ties have been the visits of the Director of the DIA, in 1994, and of then DCI John Deutch on October 15–17, 1996. According to a CIA spokesman, the purpose of Deutch's visit was "to exchange views on global trends and concerns, and to discuss transnational threats."[71]

RUSSIA

Even before the change in relations between the United States and the Soviet Union that followed Mikhail Gorbachev's assumption of power, there was limited intelligence exchange between the two Cold War adversaries.

In the early 1980s the "Gavrilov Channel," named after an 18th century Russian poet, was established. In 1984, the CIA requested the KGB's help in determining the fate of the CIA Station Chief in Beirut, William Buckley, who had been kidnapped by the Iranian-supported Islamic Jihad. In 1988, KGB officials approached the CIA station chief in Moscow about reopening the channel.[72]

By late 1988, both nations agreed they would exchange intelligence on narcotics shipments headed for each other's territory as well as information on the methods used by traffickers to conceal illicit drugs.[73]

The next year, DCI William Webster announced that the U.S. and Soviet governments had discussed exchanging information concerning international terrorism. In 1990, following the Iraqi invasion of Kuwait, the CIA sought KGB cooperation in attempting to build an international coalition in opposition to the Iraqi action. The Soviet Union began to provide the United States with data about Iraqi weapons capabilities, Iraqi air defenses, and Iraqi communications networks. The Soviets may also have provided information on Iraqi military officials. Later that year, in October, the acting DCI, Richard Kerr, noted that the CIA was "quite willing to talk and discuss with the KGB those areas were we have a common interest, whether they are terrorism or narcotics or issues of proliferation."[74]

In 1991 the KGB approached the CIA for information on the death of Leonid Nikitenko, the KGB's counterintelligence chief in Brazil. In October 1992, DCI Robert Gates journeyed to Moscow to discuss intelligence sharing. In addition to meeting with President Yeltsin, Gates met with Yevgeniy Primakov and General Fyodor Ladygin—the heads of the Russian Foreign Intelligence Service (SVRR) and Chief Intelligence Directorate of the General Staff (GRU), respectively. Intelligence sharing was probably discussed with respect to terrorism, narcotics, Islamic fundamentalism, and the proliferation of ballistic missiles and weapons of mass destruction. Gates may have also met with officials of the Ministry of Security. Even before his trip, agreements had been reached with that organization to share certain intelligence information.[75]

The U.S. Embassy noted of the visit that "the possibility of contact and joint activity between the Russian and American intelligence services was discussed." During the visit, SVRR chief Primakov observed, "The exchange of intelligence is crucial. If an intelligence service has information about terrorist acts planned against the citizens of other countries, it must give its partners this information. We will do this."[76]

The discussions may have produced specific agreements for intelligence sharing, possibly formalizing already existing exchanges on subjects such as the advanced weaponry of former Soviet client states. Further discussions concerning sharing information on terrorism, proliferation, and drug trafficking took place during DCI James Woolsey's August 1993 visit to Moscow.[77]

On at least one occasion the United States provided intelligence to Russia to influence policy rather than as part of an exchange. In 1995 the United States provided Russia with intelligence on Iran, in hopes of persuading President Yeltsin to drop Russia's plans to build nuclear reactors in Iran. The intelligence related to Iranian imports and smuggling of material related to building an atomic bomb.[78]

U.S.-Russian cooperation has also extended to the field of nuclear detonation detection and treaty monitoring. In July 1994, technicians from the Russian Special Monitoring Service (SMS), with assistance from AFTAC technical specialists, deployed portable seismic data acquisition systems on the banks of the Dubna River. The devices were used by the SMS to conduct field surveys of candidate seismic stations that would be used in monitoring the CTBT.[79]

In the fall of 1995, Col. General Yevgeniy P. Maslin, the Commander of the Central Directorate of the Russian Ministry of Defense (responsible for nuclear weapons programs), as well as the chief and deputy chief of the SMS, visited AFTAC and some of its facilities for a tour, discussions, and briefings. At that time, Maslin expressed his interest in the "creation of a bilateral agreement covering exchange of information from a variety of different collection systems such as space-based and radionuclide operations."[80]

UNITED KINGDOM

Bilateral intelligence relations between the United States and the United Kingdom include human intelligence, signals intelligence, and radio and television broadcast monitoring. The British-United States Communications Intelligence Agreement (BRUSA) is still in force and regulates the bilateral part of the British-U.S. SIGINT relationship.

A second highly formalized arrangement consists of an agreement to divide up, on a geographic basis, the responsibility for monitoring public radio and television broadcasts—mainly news and public affairs broadcasts. The specific organizations involved are the British Broadcasting Corporation (BBC) Monitoring Service and the CIA's Foreign Broadcast Information Service (FBIS). Together, these two organizations monitor most of the world's significant news reports and other broadcasts. Both the BBC Monitoring Service and the FBIS have a network of overseas stations that operate with varying degrees of secrecy to gather raw material.[81]

Post–World War II cooperation between the BBC Monitoring Service and the United States was formalized in 1947, as the result of an exchange of letters between the head of the Foreign Broadcast Information Branch of the CIA's Office of Operations and head of the BBC Monitoring Service. The basic provisions were noted in a 1950 document, the two-page "FBIS-BBC Reciprocal Agreement, Basic Provisions." The agreement divided the monitoring tasks among the small number of stations then operating, provided for FBIS personnel to be stationed at BBC headquarters to select material, and required FBIS to provide material to satisfy BBC requirements. It also provided for a joint planning FBIS-BBC Monitoring Service Coordination Committee.[82]

The 1950 document also noted that "the organization of mutually complimentary operations requires continuous consultation and cooperation between the Services in respect to the location of monitoring stations, the allocation of monitoring coverage, the standardization of operational principles and procedures, their communications networks, and all other matters of mutual concern."[83]

The cooperation began as an openly acknowledged arrangement. Thus, the BBC Annual Report for 1948–1949 noted: "There [is] close cooperation between the BBC's Monitoring Service and its American counterpart, the Foreign Broadcast Information Branch of the United States Central Intelligence Agency, and each of the two services maintained liaison units at each other's stations for the purpose of a full exchange of information."[84]

The area of responsibility for the Monitoring Service is roughly equivalent to the GCHQ's area of responsibility for SIGINT collection—Europe, Africa, and western Russia. Thus, the Monitoring Service maintains a remotely controlled listening post on the top of the British Embassy in Vienna to monitor VHF radio and television broadcasts originating in Hungary and Czechoslovakia. It also maintains listening posts in Accra, Ghana, and Abidjan, Ivory Coast. In 1976–1977 the Monitoring Service turned over responsibility for monitoring Far East broadcasts to the FBIS. To compensate, it stepped up its reporting of events in Portugal and Spain to meet CIA requirements.[85]

The United Kingdom has also had significant access to U.S. satellite imagery, beginning with the CORONA program. In 1996 it was reported that Britain was going to provide part of the funding for a new generation of U.S. imagery satellite, which would allow it greater access to the resulting imagery.[86]

THE UNITED NATIONS AND THE INTERNATIONAL ATOMIC ENERGY AGENCY

The United States has shown satellite imagery to the U.N. Security Council as evidence of Iraqi violations of the cease-fire agreement. At a private briefing on June 26, 1991, U.S. intelligence officials showed the council's members satellite images of uranium-enrichment machinery being moved around on trucks or being buried to avoid detection by U.N. inspectors.[87]

The photographs showed uncrated calutrons, which are used in electromagnetic isotope separation, being moved onto trucks just before U.N. inspectors arrived at the sites. The satellite images also showed that sometimes the Iraqis buried equipment at the sites. When they were dug up, the holes would be filled with fresh earth so there would be no radioactive traces left in the soil.[88]

More important, U.S. intelligence, including imagery and SIGINT, has been used to guide the movements of U.N. inspectors. Thus, the inspectors' trip that ended in a standoff in September 1991, as well as other trips, was guided largely by tips from U.S. intelligence. David A. Kay, who headed the U.N. inspection effort, told the Senate Foreign Relations Committee that "without that data, we would not have been able to operate" against Iraqi deception efforts. He also observed that "the lesson of Iraq, where you combine that information with an international inspectorate, is one that I find encouraging."[89]

The specific value of U.S. U-2 imagery to the work UNSCOM was described by U.S. Ambassador Rolf Ekeus:

> The data [the U-2] provides is fundamental to UNSCOM planning. The images also reveal the hiding of production equipment and the movement of such equipment. It can systematically cover large areas of Iraq, revealing new facilities and production sites. The dynamic use of the U-2 is an insurance policy against the expansion of production facilities.[90]

The U.S. intelligence community also may receive intelligence windfalls as a result of international inspections. In 1995 the Jordanian government turned over to the CIA several dozen Russian gyroscopes and accelerometers for analysis. The Jordanians had seized the equipment, which Iraq was trying to secretly import from Russia, at the request of the United Nations. The parts were diverted from some of Russia's most advanced ICBMs.[91]

In November 1993 a team of inspectors from the International Atomic Energy Agency (IAEA) conducted an examination of previously unchecked buildings at Iranian nuclear sites, looking for evidence of a clandestine nuclear weapons program. The targets of the unannounced inspection included sites that the U.S. intelligence community suspected might be involved in nuclear-related work—isolated and camouflaged buildings, surrounded by tall-wire fencing and tight security. The U.S. intelligence community also benefits from IAEA reporting. Information on the contents of an Iraqi reactor led U.S. analysts involved in evaluating the Iraqi nuclear program to the conclusion that Iraq was trying to develop a pulonium 210-initiator.[92]

Notes

1. Declaration of the Secretary of Defense, *United States of America v. Jonathan Jay Pollard*, defendant, United States District Court for the District of Columbia, Criminal No. 86-, p. 22.

2. See Jeffrey T. Richelson, "The Calculus of Intelligence Cooperation," *International Journal of Intelligence and Counterintelligence* 4, no. 3 (Fall 1990): 307–324; H. Bradford Westerfield, "America and the World of Intelligence Liaison," *Intelligence and National Security* 11, no. 3 (July 1996): 523–560; Commission on the Roles and Capabilities of the United States Intelligence Community, *Preparing for the 21st Century: An Appraisal of U.S. Intelligence* (Washington, D.C.: U.S. Government Printing Office, 1996), p. 128.

3. American Embassy, Mexico, to State Department, Subject: Weekly Narcotics Roundup: August 13–17, August 22, 1990, p. 1.

4. On the British-U.S. World War II SIGINT alliance, see Bradley F. Smith, *The Ultra-Magic Deals* (Novato, Calif.: Presidio, 1993). On Canadian participation, see John Bryden, *Best Kept Secret: Canadian Secret Intelligence in the Second World War* (Toronto: Lester, 1993). On Australian-New Zealand involvement, see Jeffrey T. Richelson and Desmond

Ball, *The Ties that Bind: Intelligence Cooperation Among the UKUSA Countries* (Boston: Allen & Unwin, 1985), pp. 3–4; and Desmond Ball, "Allied Intelligence Cooperation Involving Australia During World War II," *Australian Outlook* 32, no. 4 (1978): 299–309.

5. Ronald Clark, *The Man Who Broke Purple* (Boston: Little, Brown, 1977), p. 208.

6. Ball, "Allied Intelligence Cooperation Involving Australia During World War II"; Duncan Campbell, "Threat of the Electronic Spies," *New Statesman*, February 2, 1979, pp. 140–144; John Sawatsky, *Men in the Shadows: The RCMP Security Service* (New York: Doubleday, 1980), p. 9n; Transcript of "The Fifth Estate—The Espionage Establishment," broadcast by the Canadian Broadcasting Company, 1974.

7. Private information; Seymour Hersh, *"The Target Is Destroyed": What Really Happened to Flight 007 and What America Knew About It* (New York: Random House, 1986), p. 48n.

8. Chapman Pincher, *Inside Story: A Documentary of the Pursuit of Power* (New York: Stein & Day, 1979), p. 157; Sawatsky, *Men in the Shadows*, p. 9n.

9. Desmond Ball, *A Suitable Piece of Real Estate: American Installations in Australia* (Sydney: Hale & Iremonger, 1980), p. 40.

10. See Nicky Hager, *Secret Power: New Zealand's Role in the International Spy Network* (Nelson, N.Z.: Craig Potton, 1996),.pp. 42–56.

11. Campbell, "Threat of the Electronic Spies."

12. See Richelson and Ball, *The Ties that Bind*, pp. 148–149.

13. Paul Kelly, "NSA, the Biggest Secret Spy Network in Australia," *The National Times*, May 23–28, 1977.

14. Letter, Eugene Y. Yeates, Director of Policy, National Security Agency, to the author, December 7, 1982.

15. Christopher Anson Pike, "CANYON, RHYOLITE and AQUACADE: US Signals Intelligence Satellites in the 1970s," *Spaceflight* 37, no. 11 (November 1995): 381–383; Mark Urban, *UK Eyes Alpha: The Inside Story of British Intelligence* (London: Faber and Faber, 1996), p. 58; Private information.

16. Urban, *UK Eyes Alpha*, pp. 60–63; Duncan Campbell, "The Parliamentary Bypass Operation," *New Statesman*, January 23, 1987, pp. 8–12.

17. Desmond Ball, "The U.S. Naval Ocean Surveillance Information System (NOSIS)—Australia's Role," *Pacific Defence Reporter*, June 1982, pp. 40–49.

18. Ibid.

19. "Britania Scorns to Yield," *Newsweek*, April 19, 1982, pp. 41–46.

20. Centre for Peace Studies, The University of Auckland, "New Zealand's International Military Connections: Agreements and Arrangements," 1986.

21. Joint Intelligence Organization, *Fourth Annual Report, 1974* (Canberra: JIO, 1974), pp. F1–F2; Department of the Army, Office of the Deputy Chief of Staff for Intelligence, *Annual Historical Review, 1 October 1993 to 30 September 1994*, n.d., pp. 6–11.

22. Navy Field Operational Office, *Command History for CY 1981*, April 15, 1982, p. 5; Assistant Chief of Staff for Intelligence, Air Force, *History of the Assistant Chief of Staff, Intelligence Hq., United States Air Force, 1 July 1974–31 December 1974*, n.d., p. 9; Department of the Army, Office of the Assistant Chief of Staff, Intelligence, *Annual Historical Review, 1 October 1985–30 September 1986*, n.d., pp. 4–5.

23. Armed Forces Medical Intelligence Center, *Organization and Functions of the Armed Forces Medical Intelligence Center* (Ft. Detrick, Md.: AFMIC, April 1986), p. vii.

24. David S. Brandwein, "Confessions of a Former USIB Committee Chairman," *Studies in Intelligence* 18, no. 2 (Summer 1974): 43–50.

25. Tom Mangold, *Cold Warrior, James Jesus Angleton: The CIA's Master Spy Hunter* (New York: Simon & Schuster, 1991), p. 292.

26. Canadian-U.S. Joint Intelligence Committee, *Soviet Capabilities and Probable Course of Action Against North America in a Major War Commencing During the Period 1 January 1958 to 31 December 1958* (Washington, D.C.: CIA, March 1, 1957), *Declassified Documents Reference System (DDRS)* 1981–169A; U.S. Congress, Senate Committee on Armed Services, *Department of Defense Authorization for Appropriations for Fiscal Year 1984, Part 5* (Washington, D.C.: U.S. Government Printing Office, 1983), p. 2708.

27. *Canada–U.S. Arrangements in Regard to Defence, Defence Production, Defence Sharing* (Washington, D.C.: Institute Policy Studies, 1985), p. 31.

28. Walter Agee, Deputy Director of Intelligence, "Memorandum for the Coordination of Joint Operations: Proposed U.S.-Canadian Agreement," Military Reference Branch, National Archives, RG 341, Entry 214, File Nos. 2-1900 through 2-1999.

29. Mike Frost as told to Michel Gratton, *Spyworld: Inside the Canadian and American Intelligence Establishments* (Toronto: Doubleday Canada, 1994), pp. 15, 274–275.

30. Lt. Rodney R. Bickford, "Canadian Undersea Surveillance," *Proceedings*, March 1995, pp. 70–71.

31. Joint Chiefs of Staff, *Canadian–United States Communications Instructions for Reporting Vital Intelligence Sightings (CERVIS/MERINT)* (Washington, D.C.: JCS, March 1966), p. 2-1.

32. Ibid., pp. 2-4 to 2-6.

33. Ibid., p. 3-1.

34. Jane Perlez, "Touchy Issue of Bigger NATO: Spy Agencies," *New York Times*, January 5, 1998, p. A3.

35. Ibid.

36. Ibid.

37. Andrew Cockburn and Leslie Cockburn, *Dangerous Liaisons: The Inside Story of the U.S.-Israeli Covert Relationship* (New York: HarperCollins, 1991), p. 41.

38. Judith Perera, "Cracks in the Special Relationship," *The Middle East* (March 1983): 12–18.

39. Cockburn and Cockburn, *Dangerous Liaisons*, p. 187.

40. Ibid.

41. Richard Halloran, "U.S. Offers Israel Plan on War Data," *New York Times*, March 13, 1983, pp. 1, 13.

42. Edmund Walsh, "Begin Offers to Give War Intelligence to U.S.," *Washington Post*, October 15, 1982, p. A18; Richard Halloran, "U.S. Said to Bar Deal with Israel," *New York Times*, February 10, 1983, pp. A1, A7.

43. Halloran, "U.S. Said to Bar Deal with Israel"; Bernard Gwertzman, "Israelis to Share Lessons of War with Pentagon," *New York Times*, March 22, 1983, pp. 1, 12.

44. National Security Decision Directive 111, "Next Steps Toward Progress in Lebanon and the Middle East," October 28, 1983. The directive has been released in heavily sanitized form. The tilt toward Israel is reported in Bernard Gwertzman, "Reagan Turns to Israel," *New York Times Magazine*, November 27, 1983, pp. 62ff.

45. Bob Woodward, "CIA Sought 3rd Country Contra Aid," *Washington Post*, May 19, 1984, pp. A1, A13.

46. "Statement of Bobby Ray Inman on Withdrawing His Nomination," *New York Times*, January 19, 1994, p. A14.

47. "U.S. to Share More Recon Data, Tighten Air Links with Israel," *Aerospace Daily*, December 8, 1983, pp. 193–194.

48. Ibid.

49. Charles Babcock, "Israel Uses Special Relationship to Get Secrets," *Washington Post*, June 15, 1986, p. A1.

50. "How the Israelis Pulled It Off," *Newsweek*, July 19, 1976, pp. 42–47; David Halevy and Neil C. Livingstone, "The Ollie We Knew," *The Washingtonian*, July 1987, pp. 77ff.

51. Theodore Sanger, "The Israelis: A Not Very Hidden Agenda," *Newsweek*, September 10, 1990, p. 20; Gerald F. Sieb and Bob Davis, "Fighting Flares Again at Saudi Town; Allied Planes Attack Big Iraqi Column," *Wall Street Journal*, February 1, 1991, p. A12; Martin Sieff, "Israelis Press U.S. for Direct Access to Intelligence Data," *Washington Times*, November 28, 1992, p. A7.

52. Bill Gertz, "U.S. Offers Deal to Stop China's Nuke Sales," *Washington Times*, October 14, 1997, pp. A1, A11.

53. Barton Gellman, "Israel Gave Key Help to U.N. Team in Iraq," *Washington Post*, September 29, 1998, pp. A1, A12.

54. Hersh, "*The Target is Destroyed*," pp. 63–72.

55. "U.S. Warns Japan Not to Increase Soviet Military Power," *Xinhua General Overseas News Service*, March 30, 1982.

56. Naval Intelligence Command, *Naval Intelligence Command (NAVINTCOM) History for CY-1972*, August 1, 1973, p. 35; Naval Intelligence Command, *Naval Intelligence Command (NAVINTCOM) History for CY-1973*, p. 48.

57. U.S. Naval Forces, Japan, COMNAVFORJAPAN Staff Instruction 5450.1G, *Staff Organization Manual*, May 13, 1983, p. V-5.

58. Curtis Peebles, *The Moby Dick Project: Reconnaissance Balloons over Russia* (Washington, D.C.: Smithsonian, 1991), p. 169; Rudolf Tamnes, *The United States and the Cold War in the High North* (Oslo: Ad Notam, 1991), pp. 126–127; Assistant Chief of Staff for Intelligence, *History: Directorate of Collection Office, ACS, Intelligence, 1 January–30 June 1963*, n.d., p. 2; further details on SOUTH SEA are contained in Olav Riste and Arnfinn Moland, *Top Secret: The Norwegian Intelligence Service, 1945–1970* (London: Frank Cass, forthcoming).

59. Assistant Chief of Staff for Intelligence, *History: Directorate of Collection Office, ACS, Intelligence, 1 January–30 June 1963*, p. 2.

60. F. G. Samia, "The Norwegian Connection: Norway (Un)willing Spy for the U.S.," *Covert Action Information Bulletin*, June 1980, pp. 4–9.

61. Ibid.; R. W. Apple Jr., "Norwegians, Ardent Neutralists, Also Want Their Defense Strong," *New York Times*, August 5, 1978, p. 2; Owen Wilkes and Nils Petter Gleditsch, *Intelligence Installations in Norway: Their Number, Location, Function and Legality* (Oslo, Norway: Peace Research Institute Oslo, 1979), pp. 17–20.

62. Wilkes and Gleditsch, *Intelligence Installations in Norway*, pp. 24–26; Hersh, "*The Target is Destroyed*," p. 4.

63. Wilkes and Gleditsch, *Intelligence Installations in Norway*, p. 20.

64. Ibid., p. 35; Hersh, "*The Target Is Destroyed*," p. 42; Nikolai Brusnitsin, *Openness and Espionage* (Moscow, 1990), p. 23; Private information.

65. "HAVE STARE," http://www.fas.org/spp/military/program/track/havestare.htm; Daniel Dupont, "Air Force 'HAVE STARE' Radar May Be Deployed Along Russian Border,"

Inside Missile Defense, April 15, 1998; Lt. Col. William R. Price, Air Force Space Command, "HAVE STARE Beddown (U) (Your SSS, 8 Nov 93)," November 9, 1993.

66. Wilkes and Gleditsch, *Intelligence Installations in Norway,* p. 20.

67. John Newhouse, *War and Peace in the Nuclear Age* (New York: Knopf, 1989), p. 224.

68. Nayan Chandra, *Brother Enemy: The War After War* (New York: Harcourt, Brace, Jovanovich, 1983), p. 280; "Washington Round-Up," *Aviation Week & Space Technology,* March 19, 1984, p. 15; Daniel Southerland, "U.S. Navy Call at Chinese Port Symbolizes Growing Military Relationship," *Washington Post,* November 5, 1986, pp. A23, A29.

69. Philip Taubman, "U.S. and Peking Jointly Monitor Russian Missiles," *New York Times,* June 18, 1981, pp. 1, 14; Murrey Marder, "Monitoring Not So-Secret-Secret," *Washington Post,* June 19, 1981, p. 10.

70. Robert C. Toth, "U.S., China Jointly Track Firings of Soviet Missiles," *Los Angeles Times,* June 18, 1981, pp. 1, 9; David Bonavia, "Radar Post Leak May Be Warning to Soviet Union," *London Times,* June 19, 1981, p. 5; George J. Lardner Jr. and R. Jeffrey Smith, "Intelligence Ties Endure Despite U.S.-China Strain," *Washington Post,* June 25, 1989, pp. A1, A24; Robert M. Gates, *From the Shadows: The Ultimate Insider's Story of Five Presidents and How They Won the Cold War* (New York: Simon & Schuster, 1996), p. 123.

71. Barry Schweid, "CIA Chief Visits China to Discuss Arms, Terror," *Washington Post,* October 22, 1996, p. A11.

72. James Risen, "Ghosts of the KGB: Tales of the Last of the Soviet Spies," *Los Angeles Times,* December 31, 1997, pp. A1, A8.

73. "Glasnost for Drugs," *U.S. News and World Report,* November 28, 1988, p. 18.

74. Risen, "Ghosts of the KGB"; Bill Gertz, "Joint CIA-KGB Targeting of Terrorism Talked About," *Washington Times,* April 7, 1989, p. A4; Tim Weiner and Mark Thompson, "Soviets Give U.S. Significant Intelligence Help," *Philadelphia Inquirer,* January 26, 1991, pp. 1A, 6A; Gerald F. Sieb, "CIA's Acting Chief Says U.S. Is Ready to Cooperate with Soviet Spy Agency," *Wall Street Journal,* October 4, 1991, p. A4.

75. Risen, "Ghosts of the KGB"; Margaret Shapiro, "Ex-KGB, CIA Talk of Sharing," *Washington Post,* October 19, 1992, pp. A14, A22; Bill Gertz, "Gates Plans Moscow Talks on CIA-KGB Cooperation," *Washington Times,* September 10, 1992, p. A9; Private information.

76. Shapiro, "Ex-KGB, CIA Talk of Sharing"; Janet Guttsman, "CIA Director Seeks Russia's Assistance on Terrorism, Drugs," *Washington Times,* October 19, 1992, p. A8.

77. "CIA Takes on a Client," *Los Angeles Times,* August 12, 1993, p. A10.

78. Steven Greenhouse, "U.S. Gives Russia Secret Data on Iran to Fight Atom Deal," *New York Times,* March 3, 1995, pp. A1, A9.

79. Science Applications International Corporation, *Fifty Year Commemorative History of Long Range Detection: The Creation, Development, and Operation of the United States Atomic Energy Detection System* (Patrick AFB, Fla.: AFTAC, 1997), p. 204.

80. Fred Hagans, "Russian Officers Visit AFTAC, TOD," *AFTAC Monitor,* Sept./Oct./Nov. 1995, p. 18.

81. Duncan Campbell and Clive Thomas, "BBC's Trade Secrets," *New Statesman,* July 4, 1980, pp. 13–14.

82. Lousie D. Davison, "Historical Note on the 'Agreement' Between the Foreign Broadcast Information Service (CIG/CIA) and the British Broadcasting Corporation Monitoring Service, 1947," August 23, 1971; "FBIS-BBC Reciprocal Arrangement, Basic Provisions," 1950.

83. "FBIS-BBC Reciprocal Agreements, Basic Provisions."

84. Campbell and Thomas, "BBC's Trade Secrets."

85. Ibid.

86. Acting Assistant Director, Special Activities, DR/CIA, Memorandum for: Special Requirements Staff, DD/R, Subject: Accessibility of LANYARD Take to the British, 31 January 1963; James Adams, "Britain in Spy Satellite Talks," *Sunday Times*, January 14, 1996.

87. Paul Lewis, "U.S. Shows Photos to Argue Iraqi Hides Nuclear Material," *New York Times*, June 27, 1991, p. A12.

88. Ibid.

89. Melissa Healy, "U.N. Sleuth Credits Allied Data on Iraq," *Los Angeles Times*, October 18, 1991, p. A12.

90. Quoted in Lt. Col. Charles B. Wilson, *Strategic Reconnaissance in the Middle East: Is Manned High Altitude Reconnaissance Still Needed?* (Washington, D.C.: Washington Institute for Near East Policy, 1997), p. 49.

91. R. Jeffrey Smith, "U.N. Inspectors or Spies?" Iraq Data Can Take Many Paths," *Washington Post*, February 16, 1998, pp. A1, A20.

92. Steve Coll, "Nuclear Inspectors Check Sites in Iran," *Washington Post*, November 20, 1993, pp. A13, A16; Private information.

14

ANALYSIS AND PRODUCTION

Just as the U.S. intelligence collection effort is vast and distributed across a number of different organizations, the effort to produce finished intelligence is extensive and involves a number of different organizations and results in a large array of intelligence products.

As noted in earlier chapters, intelligence production organizations include the Central Intelligence Agency, the Defense Intelligence Agency, the Bureau of Intelligence and Research, the National Imagery and Mapping Agency, the National Ground Intelligence Center, the National Air Intelligence Center, the Office of Naval Intelligence, the Energy Department's Office of Intelligence, Lawrence Livermore's Z Division, and the unified command joint intelligence centers.

The products produced by these organizations can be characterized in a number of ways. One way is by reference to the designated consumers. Thus, there are national products (for the President and the National Security Council), departmental products(for the Departments of State, Defense, Energy), and military service/ military commands products(for the Army or the European Command). An alternative approach is to distinguish the outputs by the nature of the product—current intelligence, warning intelligence, estimative and analytical intelligence, periodicals, and databases and maps. The second approach is more reflective of the reality that the consumers for many products include individuals spread across the government—thus, Anthony Lake, President Clinton's first national security adviser, read not only the *President's Daily Brief* each morning but also the Secretary of State's *Morning Summary*. Likewise, an analyst who is responsible for producing finished intelligence on nuclear proliferation or a policymaker who helps formulate decisions in the area may receive intelligence reports from the intelligence components of the National Intelligence Council, the Joint Atomic Energy Intelligence Committee, the CIA, the DIA, and the Department of Energy—as well as other organizations. And the analyst's report, wherever he or she is located, may find its way not only to departmental readers but to those in other departments and at the national level.

CURRENT INTELLIGENCE

Current intelligence is intelligence pertinent to a topic of immediate interest—such as military movements in Beijing during early June 1989 or a terrorist attack in Israel. Such intelligence is generally transmitted without the opportunity for prolonged evaluation that is possible in other types of reports; it is also more likely to be a product based on one or two sources rather than to be an all-source product.

A variety of products, whose sensitivity and consumers vary, fall into the current intelligence category. The most restricted and sensitive current intelligence publication is the *President's Daily Brief*—"a compilation of current intelligence items of high significance to national policy concerns prepared six days a week by CIA." The *PDB* is tailored to meet the daily intelligence requirements as defined by the President. Because it contains information from the most sensitive U.S. sources it has been the most restricted of current intelligence products—at times being distributed only to the President, the Vice President, the Secretaries of State and Defense, the national security adviser, the chairman of the Joint Chiefs of Staff, and possibly a few other key officials.[1]

According to Cord Meyer, a former CIA official, in the hands of the DCI the *PDB* "is a powerful tool for focusing the attention of the President on potential crisis areas and for alerting him to situations that may require rapid policy adjustment. Occasionally, when fresh intelligence sheds new light on a complex problem an annex is attached to the *PDB* to give the President more extensive background for the decisions he has to make."[2]

The size and structure of the *PDB* may change from president to president. Under Gerald Ford the brief was rather lengthy, but it was reduced to a maximum of about fifteen pages under Jimmy Carter, although DCI Stansfield Turner occasionally appended longer "trend pieces" at the end. Carter would often write in the margins of the *PDB* to request more information. Most recently, it has been reported to run between five and seven pages, to contain one article that takes a more in-depth look at a future issue, and sometimes to have a document—possibly containing a transcript of a communications intercept, or overhead imagery—attached.[3]

The second daily current intelligence publication is the *National Intelligence Daily* (NID). The NID was the idea of former DCI William Colby, who had repeatedly recommended during the mid-1960s that the CIA's daily intelligence report, then known as the *National Intelligence Digest*, be issued in newspaper format to emphasize the more important items and to offer its readers a choice between a headline summary and in-depth reports. Colby's interest was sufficient to lead him to join, on every evening possible, the editorial conference that determined subjects to be carried in the next day's edition. Subsequently, the newspaper format was judged to be too inflexible, and the publication reverted to a magazine format.[4]

The NID is currently produced six days a week by the CIA's Directorate of Intelligence, in consultation with the DIA, the INR, and the NSA, and distributed to several hundred officials. Dissenting views are noted either in the text of the article or in a separate paragraph. There is no classification limit, although the *NID* is produced in various versions with different classifications and is tailored to different consumers, with some versions being cabled to major U.S. military commands and selected U.S. posts overseas.[5]

The November 12, 1975, issue of the NID was classified TOP SECRET RUFF UMBRA, indicating the presence of both sensitive communications intelligence and data based on satellite imagery. It contained the following front-page headlines: "Motion to Impeach President Gaining Support in Argentina," "Disorders Seen in Aftermath of Whitlam Firing," "Military Leader Warns Turkey on Violence," "Morocco, Spain Discuss Sahara," and "Israel is Exaggerating Gravity of Deteriorating Trade Situation." A more recent NID, that of May 9, 1985, contained a review of Libya on the first anniversary of the May 8, 1984, attempted coup, in which Qaddafi's barracks had been attacked. According to the NID, Libyan dissident and exile groups led by the National Front for the Salvation of Libya were planning to blow up a military installation in Libya to demonstrate their ability to attack Qaddafi on Libyan soil.[6]

A relatively recent current intelligence product is the *Daily Economic Intelligence Brief* (DIEB), a CIA prepared, five-days-a-week compilation of articles on economic issues of current significance. The brief is tailored to meet the requirements of senior economic policymakers at the cabinet or deputy secretary level.[7]

The State Department's Bureau of Intelligence and Research produces the *Secretary's Morning Summary* seven days a week. It includes approximately a dozen brief reports with comment and three or four longer articles—all related to policy issues. A supplementary *Weekend Edition* covers selected issues in detail. Topics of the *Weekend Edition* have included "China's Forecast: Cloudy with Summer Storm Possible" (February 9–10, 1991) and "China's Defense Conversion: Lessons for the USSR?" (June 29–30, 1991). In addition to limited dissemination within the State Department, the *Summary* is also provided to the White House, the National Security Council, and key ambassadors.[8]

The Defense Department's premier current intelligence product is the *Military Intelligence Digest* (MID), which began publication in 1993. It is produced in a magazine format and published Monday through Friday. The MID is a joint DIA-military service intelligence-unified command publication that contains items likely to be of interest to national-level policymakers on military or military-related topics. General areas covered include regional security, nuclear security and proliferation, and strategy and resources. The January 24, 1997, issue carried a report on a Russian program code-named FOLIANT, which concerned the production of a highly lethal nerve gas agent, A-232. The February 2, 1998, issue carried a report on Iraqi concealment of Scud missiles.[9]

Two additional Defense Department current intelligence products are the *NMJIC Executive Highlights* (EH) and the *Defense Intelligence Terrorism Summary* (DITSUM). The EH is published Monday through Friday based on data from the DIA and the NSA and contains articles on crisis or near crisis situations. It is intended to keep the Secretary of Defense, the chairman of the Joint Chiefs of Staff, and other key decisionmakers informed of developments that might require immediate action by the United States.[10]

The DITSUM is a compilation of information and analyses concerning terrorism threats and developments that could affect DOD personnel, facilities, and interests. DITSUM articles include brief terrorism notes, regional terrorism developments, and in-depth special analyses. It also contains a monthly terrorism review by combatant commands. The DITSUM is distributed Monday through Friday in the Washington area in hard copy form and in an electronic message version to military commands outside the area.[11]

Two specialist current intelligence products are *The SIGINT Digest* and the *World Imagery Report*. The former is distributed in hard copy form on weekdays in the Washington area, and electronically to customers in the field, and contains the most significant daily intelligence derived from SIGINT. *The World Imagery Report* is a video-format compilation of current intelligence items derived from imagery collection.[12]

The military services and unified commands also produce their own current intelligence products. Two current intelligence publications are the *Air Force Intelligence Daily* and the *Air Force Intelligence Morning Highlights*. The U.S. Space Command produces two daily publications—the USSPACECOM *Space Intelligence Notes* (SPIN) and the USSPACECOM *Strategic Posture Aerospace Threat Summary* (SPATS). The SPIN provides a summary of foreign space activity, whereas the SPATS provides information on the status of strategic posture indicators. An event-generated report is the *USSPACECOM Intelligence Report*, which contains data on the deorbiting of foreign satellites, launch notification messages, and preliminary launch assessments.[13]

Current intelligence may also be conveyed by video rather than paper or electronic formats. The DIA distributes finished intelligence via television through the Defense Intelligence Network (DIN), known formally as the Joint Worldwide Intelligence Communications System. For approximately twelve hours a day, five days a week, the DIN broadcasts Top Secret reports to defense intelligence and operations officers at the Pentagon and nineteen other military commands in the United States.[14]

In addition to having anchors who report finished intelligence, the DIN also shows satellite reconnaissance photos, reports communication intercepts, and carries reports from defense attachés overseas. Reporting begins at 6:15 A.M., with a 30-minute "Global Update." At 6:45 the head of the DIA Directorate for Intelligence (J-2) conducts a 45-minute interview show that features visiting briefers who give classified reports on developing events. "Global Update" resumes at 8:00 A.M. and continues at the top of each hour, updated as required and interspersed with special features. In addition, there are regular features such as "Regional Intelligence Review," and "Military Trends and Capabilities."[15]

WARNING INTELLIGENCE

Warning intelligence products "identify and focus on developments that could have sudden and deleterious effects on U.S. security or policy." Among the national-level products that are dedicated specifically to warning intelligence is *The Warning Watchlist*, a weekly report that tracks and assigns probabilities to potential threats to U.S. security or policy interests within the following six months.[16]

A product that can be initiated by the National Intelligence Officer for Warning or, through that office, by an element of the intelligence community is the *Warning Memorandum*. The memorandum is a special warning notice that focuses on "a potential development of particularly high significance to U.S. interests." It is forwarded to the DCI and simultaneously to the principal members of the National Foreign Intelligence Board for a telephone conference, a process that is completed within several hours. The DCI must then decide whether to disseminate the memorandum to policymakers, to commission a National Intelligence Estimate on the subject, or both.[17]

A third national-level product is the *Monthly Warning Report for the CINCs*, which is a summary of key warning issues that have arisen in intelligence community meetings over the previous month.[18]

The Defense Intelligence Agency also issues a number of regular and special warning reports designed to guide U.S. commands around the world. *The Weekly Intelligence Forecast* and the *Weekly Warning Forecast Report* include assessments from the various commands. In addition, *The Quarterly Warning Forecast* reviews a wide range of potential events that could affect U.S. security interests. The DIA and the commands also publish two ad hoc products as issues arise: the *Warning Report*, an assessment of a specific warning issue that is considered to require the immediate, specific attention of senior U.S. officials within the Washington area; and the *Watch Condition Change*, a notification of a change in the threat level presented by a specific warning problem.[19]

Defense Warning System Forecasts are a set of DIA periodicals that "provide evaluation of critical threat issues that could reach crisis proportions in the period covered." *The Weekly Warning Forecast* covers the following two-week period, whereas *The Quarterly Warning Forecast* focuses on the two- to six-month period. The *Annual Warning Forecast* focuses on the coming year. The forecasts are distributed in hard copy to members of the Defense Warning System and other decisionmakers in the Washington area and in message form to other recipients.[20]

ESTIMATIVE AND ANALYTICAL INTELLIGENCE

The best-known estimative intelligence products are the National Intelligence Estimates (NIEs), which attempt to project existing military, political, and economic trends into the future and to estimate for policymakers the likely implications of these trends. In 1980, the House Committee on Foreign Affairs described an NIE as "a thorough assessment of a situation in the foreign environment which is relevant to the formulation of foreign, economic, and national security policy, and which projects probable future courses of action and developments."[21]

Based on inputs from the intelligence community, the NIEs are produced by the National Intelligence Council and formally approved by the National Foreign Intelligence Board (NFIB). NIEs are intended for a variety of customers, from the president and the National Security Council to other senior policymakers to analysts.[22]

By the late 1950s an NIE numbering system was in place in which a two- or three-digit term indicated the country or region of the estimate (e.g., 11 for the Soviet Union, 13 for China), a one- or two-digit term indicated the subject (e.g., 1 for space, 2 for atomic energy), and the final set of numbers indicated the year that the estimate was produced. The numbering system was abandoned in the aftermath of the collapse of the Soviet Union, and the numerical designations of current NIEs are determined only by the year produced and the number of estimates produced previously in that year.

NIEs produced during the final years of Soviet rule include NIE 11-3/8-89 (*Soviet Forces and Capabilities for Strategic Nuclear Conflict Through the 1990s*), 11-7-89 (*Soviet Aerodynamic Counterstealth and Stealth Capabilities*), 11-18-89 (*The Soviet System in Crisis: Prospects for the Next Two Years*), and 11-34-89 (*Trends and Developments in Warsaw Pact Theater Forces and Doctrine Through the 1990s*).[23]

In late December 1991, in the aftermath of the failed coup in the Soviet Union, the intelligence community was commissioned to produce at least ten new NIEs concerning subjects in the Soviet Union such as food, fuel, the consumer distribution system, economic stagnation, and the potential for civil disorder, ethnic strife, military conditions, control over nuclear weapons and technology, and nuclear forces.[24]

NIE's focusing on other subjects and areas of the world that were produced in the 1980s included *Nicaragua: Prospects for Sandinista Consolidation* (February 1985), *Nicaragua: Prospects of Insurgency* (March 1986), *State-Sponsored Terrorism, Terrorist Use of Chemical and Biological Warfare*, and *The International Narcotics Trade: Implications for U.S. Security* (November 1985).[25]

More recent NIEs include *The Global Energy Environment into the Next Century* (1990); *North Korea: Outlook for War and Warning* (1993); NIE 95-19, *Emerging Missile Threats to North America During the Next Fifteen Years* (1995); *The Foreign Terrorist Threat in the United States* (1995); NIE 97-8, *Monitoring the Comprehensive Test Ban Treaty over the Next Ten Years* (1997), as well as 1993 NIEs on the North Korean nuclear weapons program and the intelligence community's ability to monitor the Chemical Weapons Convention. During the 1994 fiscal year NIEs were completed or started on South Africa, Zaire, Iraq, Sub-Saharan Africa, European peacekeeping trends, Russia and former Soviet states, France, the former Yugoslavia, and Greece-Turkey. The intelligence community also produces an annual NIE on global humanitarian emergencies.[26]

In recent years the number of NIEs has dropped significantly. By late 1997, the number produced annually was 60 percent less than the number produced in the mid-1990s.

NIEs are distilled into a separate *President's Summary*, which is distributed to the highest levels of the foreign policymaking community. Other national estimative products include *Special Estimates* (formerly Special National Intelligence Estimates [SNIEs]), "short, tightly focused papers . . . designed to provide consumers with policy-relevant analysis needed under a short deadline," and *Update Memorandums*, which update a previous NIE "when new evidence, analysis, or perspective is available." In addition, *NIC Memorandums* (NICMs) are mini-NIEs, longer than Special Estimates but shorter than NIEs. A 1994 Special Estimate focused on Russian government failures to halt the spread of Russian arms and weapons technology.[27]

For many years, the DIA produced a DOD version of the NIEs and SNIEs—the Defense Intelligence Estimates (DIEs) and Special Defense Intelligence Estimates (SDIEs). Those estimates were originated in late 1969 or early 1970 as a means of expressing independent DIA judgments on estimative issues prior to U.S. Intelligence Board meetings. The estimates often covered topics similar to those covered by NIEs and SNIEs; however, they also tended to deal in depth with military issues that were treated only briefly in NIEs and SNIEs. Being departmental estimates, they were produced without interdepartmental coordination.[28]

The DIEs and SDIEs were replaced by Defense Intelligence Assessments in the late 1980s. The assessments are intended to respond to "broad consumer interest by presenting comprehensive analysis on a policy-relevant event, situation, issue, or development in 5 to 25 pages." The assessments are targeted at planning and policy staffs at various levels.[29]

Assessments have included *USSR: Advanced Conventional Munitions on the Future Battlefield* (1990), *Implications of Directed Energy Weapons in a Ground Combat Environment over the Next Twenty Years* (1990), *South Africa: Defense Forces Transition to Majority Rule* (1991), *East Africa in the 1990s: The Evolving Challenge to United States Security* (1990), and *Balkan Instability—Europe's Vulnerable Underbelly* (1991).[30]

A second DIA estimative product is the *Defense Intelligence Report*, "a concise report that addresses a topic of interest to senior policymakers and commanders."[31]

Estimative intelligence produced by the State Department's Bureau of Intelligence and Research is sometimes contained in the Bureau's Intelligence Research Report series but is mainly found in memorandums circulated within the department. The Drug Enforcement Administration also produces an estimative product—the annual *Narcotics Intelligence Estimate* and a compendium of worldwide production, smuggling, and trafficking trends and projections.[32]

The CIA's Directorate of Intelligence, the DIA, the INR, and other agencies also produce a variety of reports and studies whose main focus is the analysis of political, economic, military, or social matters. CIA analytical products, such as Intelligence Assessments, have included *Political Stability: The Narcotics Connection* (March 1987), *South Africa: The Dynamics of Black Politics* (March 1987), *The Abu Nidal Terror Network: Organization, State Sponsors, and Commercial Enterprises* (July 1987), *Chemical and Biological Weapons: The Poor Man's Atomic Bomb* (December 1988), *Rising Political Instability Under Gorbachev: Understanding the Problem and Prospects for Resolution* (April 1989), *Gorbachev's Future* (May 23, 1991), and *Arms Transfers to State Sponsors of Terrorism.*[33]

By 1995, the CIA produced three basic types of analytical reports. The *Special Intelligence Report* (SIR) is a very brief, highly focused analysis of an event or topic of major significance, prepared for high-level policymakers. The *Intelligence Memorandum* (IM) is also oriented toward policymakers but provides a somewhat more detailed analysis of key issues. A third category, the *Intelligence Report* (IR) actually includes a variety of items, including Research Reports, Tactical Action Reports, Leadership Assessments, Sanctions Monitoring Reports, Situation Reports, and Handbooks.[34]

Recent CIA reports include *Rodionov's Concerns about Nuclear Command and Control, Prospects for Unsanctioned Use of Russian Nuclear Weapons,* a report on the links between the Russian Mafia and the banking industry, and a report on the Russian biological warfare program.[35]

Analytical studies by the State Department's INR were, for many years, published under three titles: *Current Analyses, Assessments and Research,* and *Policy Assessments.* Those studies analyzed recent or ongoing events, assessed prospects and implications for the following six months, assessed past trends or projected events beyond six months, or analyzed the context or results of past policies or assessed policy options. The distinct series were subsequently merged into a single *Intelligence Research Report* series.[36]

INR reports over the past decade have included: *French Nuclear Strategy and Nuclear Forces: An Update* (June 30, 1987), *Soviet-Cuban Relations Smolder Over Perestroyka and Rectification* (1988), and *China: Aftermath of the Crisis* (July 27, 1989).

The military service intelligence organizations also produce their own analytical reports, sometimes as designated (by the DIA) producers within the Defense Intelligence Production Program. The Office of Naval Intelligence has produced reports such as *Chinese-Space Based Remote Sensing Programs and Ground-Processing Capabilities* (September 1994), *Worldwide Threat to U.S. Navy and Marine Forces (deleted) Volume II: Country Study—China* (December 1993), and *Chinese Exercise Strait 961: 8–25 March 1996* (May 1996). In 1995 it produced Special Intelligence Studies on *Algeria: Air Defenses; Fixed-Wing and Helicopter Threat to Expeditionary Forces; Iraqi Threat to Naval Forces–95;* and *Cuban Helicopter Operations, Training, and Tactics;* as well the *Maritime Surveillance Capabilities Study—Iran.* The Air Force's Foreign Technology Division (now NAIC) produced, under DIA auspices, *Technological Base Resources—China: The Chinese Aviation Industry Design and Development Process and Resources* (1989) and *Threat to Air Operations: North*

Korea. The Army organizations that were merged to establish the NGIC produced *Chinese High Precision Artillery Munitions* (March 1994), and *Technology Alert: Chinese Military Operations Research* (March 1994).[37]

PERIODICALS

A substantial part of the outcome of the intelligence analysis effort is conveyed in a variety of weekly or monthly publications. Thus, the CIA publishes the *Economic Intelligence Weekly* (EIW), which analyzes major foreign economic developments and trends and is distributed to top and mid-level policymakers. The offices within the CIA's Directorate of Intelligence also publish periodic collections of articles, ranging from weekly to monthly, which may have either a regional or topical focus, depending on the publishing office. Included among those publications are the *European Monthly Review,* the bimonthly *Arms Trade Report,* and the *International Energy Statistical Quarterly.*[38]

Three additional periodicals are published by DCI centers. *The Terrorism Review* is a monthly publication of the CIA's Counterterrorist Center that addresses current trends in international terrorism activity and methods. It also tracks international terrorist incidents. Articles that appeared in the *Review* when it was published on a weekly basis included "Italian Leftist Terrorism: Defeated But Not Destroyed" (November 23, 1983), "The Shia Urged Toward Martyrdom" (January 24, 1985), "Iran: Spreading Islam and Terrorism," (March 1, 1984), "Islamic Jihad: Increasing Threat to U.S. Interests in Western Europe" (February 2, 1984), and "The Surprising Absence of the Red Brigades" (March 25, 1985).[39]

The *International Narcotics Review* is published monthly by the CIA's Crime and Narcotics Center and evaluates worldwide developments related to narcotics. In addition, the *Proliferation Digest* is published monthly by the Directorate of Intelligence, and *NPT [Non-Proliferation Treaty] Vote Preferences at a Glance as of . . .* is published monthly by the CIA's Nonproliferation Center, with contributions from all offices in the intelligence directorate.[40]

A number of other periodicals are also produced by the State Department's Bureau of Intelligence and Research. Among those most recently established is *Peacekeeping Perspectives,* a biweekly journal on multilateral conflict management and humanitarian operations. It provides the government's only comprehensive review of current or projected peacekeeping operations or humanitarian issues.[41]

Shortly before the attempted coup in the Soviet Union, INR journals included *African Trends; East-Asia Pacific Dynamics, Economic Commentary; Inter-American Highlights; Soviet-East European Review; Strategic Forces Analysis Biweekly; War Watch Weekly;* and *Western Europe and Canada—Issues and Trends.* Each journal consisted of short essays, brief analyses of intelligence reporting, and selected chronologies.[42]

Regular DEA intelligence publications include the *Monthly Digest of Drug Intelligence* and *Quarterly Intelligence Trends.* The Air Force produces the *Air Force Intelligence Weekly,* which contains a synopsis of current events and developments from a political-military perspective. On a weekly basis, the U.S. Space Command produces the *USSPACECOM Defense Intelligence Space Order of Battle*, which summarizes the status of Russian, PRC, and Indian satellites.[43]

BIOGRAPHIES, REFERENCE DOCUMENTS, AND DATABASES

Both the CIA and DIA devote extensive effort to prepare biographical sketches of key civilian and military officials, respectively. The sketches serve as both reference and analytical documents, providing basic information on the individual, as well as exploring his or her motivations and attempting to provide explanations for past and likely future actions.

Before the demise of the Soviet Union, the CIA produced *Biographic Handbooks* that provided biographies of key Soviet officials who made and implemented policy, as well as biographies of many lesser individuals. Thus, the April 1977 *Biographic Handbook, USSR, Supplement IV* included profiles on twenty-one officials, including the chief editor of *Pravda*, the chairman of the State Committee for Prices, the Minister of Construction, and the chairman of the Board for the State Bank.[44] The biography of Eduard Shevardnadze, then a Georgian party official and later foreign minister, is shown as Figure 14.1.

A few years earlier, in 1974, the CIA prepared a nine-page *Biographic Report* on Yitzhak Rabin, who served as Israeli prime minister on a number of occasions, including in the 1990s. The report contained seven subheadings: "Prime Minister," "The Sons of Founding Generation," "Military Hawk/Political Dove," "The General as Ambassador," "Exodus' Hero," "Strong Belief and Extreme Caution," and "A Fighting Family."[45]

The DIA prepares biographic sketches of foreign military officers, even junior officers. The agency prepared its first sketch of Andres Rodriguez, for example, no later than April 1966, at which time he was commander of the 1st Cavalry Division of the Paraguayan Army. In February 1989, he led the coup that deposed Paraguay's long-time dictator, Alfredo Stroessner.[46]

Each sketch usually runs several single-spaced pages and provides information on the subject's position, significance, politics, personality, personal life, and professional career. An August 1994 sketch of Gen.-Lt. Aleksander Lebed—then commander of the 14th Army, Moldova, and subsequently Boris Yeltsin's national security adviser—noted that he continued to retain his post despite "a public stance that regularly tests his superiors' tolerance for insubordination." It also noted that his "penchant for controversy almost cost him his job in August 1994 after the publication of an interview in which he characterized Yeltsin as a 'minus' and endorsed the Pinochet model of military rule." The personal data section characterized him as a "persuasive speaker" who gives the impression of being experienced in dealing with the press. The final section traced his career in the airborne forces until his appointment as 14th Army commander. The sketch is reproduced as Figure 14.2.

FIGURE 14.1   Biography of Eduard Shevardnadze

USSR   **Eduard Amvrosiyevich SHEVARDNADZE**
First Secretary, Central Committee, Communist Party of Georgia

One of the youngest regional Party leaders in the Soviet Union, Eduard Shevardnadze (pro-
nounced shevardNAHDzeh) became first secretary of the Georgian Communist Party in
September 1972, at the age of 43. He was a newcomer to the Georgian Party hierarchy,
having served in the government for the previous 7 years as republic minister of internal
affairs, charged with the preservation of law and order. The chief factor in Shevardnadze's
promotion was his experience as a police administrator.

In the Soviet Union, Georgia has long been known as an enclave of high living and
fast runners. Its most important economic activity, wine production, is one of the oldest
and the best loved branches of Georgian agriculture. Georgians are freedom loving and
individualistic; they have always lived by looser rules than other Soviet nationalities, first
because former Premier Josif Stalin (himself a Georgian by birth) indulged them, and later,
apparently, because the pattern had been established.

Disciplinarian in a Loose Republic

Former police official Shevardnadze, who has nurtured an image as a firm, austere discipli-
narian (the Georgians refer to him as the "boss"), has tried since 1972 to overturn the habits
of generations regarding easy virtue, political corruption, underground capitalism and heavy
drinking. The Georgians are not giving in easily. Shevardnadze's cleanup campaign met
with early and continued foot dragging, and during his first years as Georgian Party leader
he encountered considerable bureaucratic opposition. Speakers at an August 1973 Party
Plenum hinted at disorders among the public at large, and rumors of anonymous threats
against Shevardnadze and his family were prevalent throughout 1973.

Several recent developments indicate that Shevardnadze's cleanup campaign in Georgia
has been intense, broad and continuous. An underground Soviet publication that appeared
in 1975 claimed that nearly 25,000 persons had been arrested in Georgia in the past 2 years.
(A Soviet who visited Georgia in late 1974 reported that 13,000 Party and Komsomol members
had been arrested.) In addition, the republic's second secretary, Al'bert Churkin, was dis-
missed in April 1975 for gross errors and shortcomings.

During 1976 there was a series of bomb and arson attacks in the republic as Shevardnadze
continued his all-out campaign against corruption, nationalism and ideological deviation
in Georgia. The attacks may have been intended to blacken Shevardnadze's reputation by
showing his inability to control the Georgian situation; there were rumors that the first
secretary was on the way out because of the disorders. A long hard-hitting report delivered
by Shevardnadze in July 1976 seemed to indicate that despite the disturbances he was still
in control. His repeated allusions to approval of his campaign by the central authorities
in Moscow, however, betrayed a certain unease about his authority in the republic.

Views on Agriculture

In 1975, when Georgia was suffering from the Soviet Union's general harvest failure,
Shevardnadze set forth several new ideas on agriculture. In a report delivered to a local
Party meeting, he attacked the existing program for construction of large mechanized livestock
facilities—a pet project of top Soviet agricultural officials—and proposed instead to divert
a part of the material and money to help expand the feed base. Shevardnadze also made
several proposals designed to strengthen the position of individual farmers. For example,

(continues)

FIGURE 14.1   *(continued)*

he asked that the feed allotment be ensured for livestock owned by individuals; that unwanted land (swamp lands or rocky areas) be turned over to the population, with technical assistance and fertilizer provided by the state; and that individual farmers form cooperative associations. Little has been heard of these proposals since 1975, but they are indicative of Shevardnadze's surprisingly pragmatic leadership style, which may serve him well in the face of continuing political problems in his republic.

Early Life and Career

A native Georgian, Eduard Amvrosiyevich Shevardnadze was born on 25 January 1928. He was the son of a teacher and was educated as a historian at a pedagogical intitute, but he began his career as a Komsomol functionary in 1946. He rose through the ranks to become first secretary of the Georgian Komsomol Central Committee in December 1957. Shevardnadze was elected a nonvoting member of the Bureau of the Georgian Party Central Committee, his first Party post, in 1958; and 3 years later he advanced from nonvoting to voting membership on the Bureau of the All-Union Komsomol Central Committee.

Political Eclipse and Recovery

In 1961 Shevardnadze was released without explanation as Komsomol chief and removed from his position on the Party Bureau. His career in eclipse, he served for 3 years in minor Party posts in Tbilisi, the Georgian capital. He began his political comeback in 1965, when he was appointed Georgian minister for the protection of public order, a title later changed to minister of internal affairs. His career may have benefited at this stage from an association with Aleksandr Shelepin, at that time a member of the Communist Party of the Soviet Union (CPSU) Politburo: When Shevardnadze became Georgian Komsomol chief, Shelepin was first secretary of the All-Union Komsomol, and when he was named minister, Shelepin's influence in Moscow was at its peak.

In July 1972 Shevardnadze was elected a voting member of the republic's Party Bureau and first secretary of the Tbilisi City Party Committee. Shevardnadze did not serve as first secretary for long—2 months later he became Georgian Party chief. He has been a Deputy to the USSR Supreme Soviet since 1974.

Travel

While he was Komsomol first secretary, Shevardnadze made several trips abroad to attend youth conferences, visiting Belgium, Tunisia and France. Since becoming republic first secretary, he has increased his contacts with foreign officials through travel and attendance at official functions. During 1974 he headed a CPSU delegation to the Austrian Communist Party Congress, attended a dinner in Moscow given by CPSU General Secretary Leonid Brezhnev for the President of France, met with Senator Edward Kennedy in Georgia, and traveled with Politburo member Nikolay Podgorny to Sofia. He accompanied Brezhnev to the Hungarian Party Congress in March 1975.

Shevardnadze has a brother, Ippokrat, who has been active in the Georgian Party apparatus. No further personal information on Shevardnadze is currently available.

CIA/DDI/OCR
JZebatto   1 April 1977

SOURCE: Central Intelligence Agency, *Biographic Handbook USSR, Supplement 4* (Washington, D.C.: CIA, April 1977).

FIGURE 14.2   Biography of General-Lieutenant Aleksander Ivanovich Lebed

Biographic Sketch

RUSSIA
General-Lieutenant Aleksander Ivanovich *LEBED*
August 1994

(U) *NAME:* General-Lieutenant (U.S. major general equivalent) Aleksander Ivanovich *Lebed* (LEH-bed).

(U) *POSITION:* Commander, 14th Army, Moldova (since June 1992).

(U)   1992

(CNF) *SIGNIFICANCE:* Aleksandr Lebed, the fiery and controversial commander of Russian forces in the Transdnestr region of Moldova, continues to retain his post despite a public stance that regularly tests his superiors' tolerance for insubordination. Although senior Russian officials largely credit him with bringing an end to the hostilities between Moldova and the breakaway self-declared Transdnestr Republic in 1992, he has repeatedly angered President Boris Yeltsin and Defense Minister Pavel Grachev by making public statements that undercut Moscow's initiatives in Moldova and by voicing disapproval of the Russian government's leadership in the national security and military reform arena. Lebed's penchant for controversy almost cost him his job in August 1994 after the publication of an interview in which he characterized Yeltsin as a "minus" and endorsed the Pinochet model of military rule. After an abortive attempt to oust the rebellious general, Grachev was forced to backtrack and allow Lebed to remain in place, albeit with a commitment to rename the 14th Army an Operational Group of the General Staff and reduce its central staff somewhat. It is believed that Lebed has been able to retain his post because of his support in the officer corps, local backing, and strong command abilities:

■ Lebed's decisive style of leadership and support for Transdnestr autonomy has earned him considerable popularity among local Russian military personnel and residents of the Transdnestr region, who overwhelmingly elected him to the Transdnestr legislature in September 1993. The attempt by the Russian high command to remove Lebed as 14th Army Commander unleashed a storm of protest from Lebed's officers, who threatened to ignore Moscow's orders to abolish the 14th Army.

■ Lebed is highly regarded among many members of the Russian officer corps for his command experience, success in preserving peace in Moldova, and willingness to voice his frustrations with the political leadership in Russia publicly. Many officers probably agree with Lebed's assertions that without his leadership, the situation in Moldova might rapidly disintegrate into chaos. Yeltsin and Grachev may believe that firing Lebed would cost them support among a military already angered by the military's loss of societal status, privileges, and cutbacks in personnel and funding.

(CNF) Lebed's defiant stance puts under considerable strain his longstanding career ties with Grachev, his onetime patron. The two served together in the 1970s as training officers at the Ryazan Higher Airborne Command School, in the same paratroop regiment in Afghanistan in the early 1980s, and as leading officers of the Airborne Forces during the early 1990s. During the August 1991 coup attempt, Lebed and Grachev were in close contact, deciding how and where to deploy paratroop units in Moscow and remaining on the sidelines until it became clear which side would win.

FIGURE 14.2 *(continued)*

CONFIDENTIAL
NOFORN

General-Lieutenant Aleksander Ivanovich *LEBED*

(C/NF) Although Lebed has been a prominent advocate of sovereignty for the Transdnestr Republic, he has regularly clashed publicly with the Transdnestr leadership since 1993; he says the leadership is corrupt and incompetent and has called for its resignation. In October 1993, he resigned his seat in the local legislature in protest over allegations that the Transdnestr government supported the hardline opponents of Yeltsin in the showdown between the executive and legislative branches in Moscow during autumn 1993. Lebed has, while stepping up the war of words with the Transdnestr leadership, moderated his rhetoric against the Moldovan government.

(C) *PERSONAL DATA:* Lebed was born 20 April 1950. A native of Novocherkassk, he once told a Western journalist that he witnessed the violent suppression of food riots in that city in 1962. According to a U.S. official, Lebed is a persuasive speaker who gives the impression that he is fully in control and who is experienced in dealing with the press. The same official states that Lebed has a sense of humor and likes to tell jokes. Lebed and his wife, Inna, have two sons and a daughter. Lebed – whose father served in World War II as a sergeant – has two younger brothers also in the military, including Aleksey, who, as of 1993, was a paratroop regiment commander serving in the 14th Army. The general's English language ability is unknown.

(U) *CAREER:* Lebed has spent most of his career in the Airborne Forces. After failing to gain admittance to the Armavir Flight School in the 1960s, he joined the Airborne Forces and graduated from the Ryazan Higher Airborne Command School in 1973. Lebed subsequently remained at the school for an additional 8 years to train officer cadets; for part of this time, his superior was Grachev, who was also an instructor at the Ryazan School. From 1981 until 1982, Lebed served as a paratroop battalion commander in Afghanistan, then returned to the Soviet Union to attend the Frunze Academy, which he completed in 1985. He then commanded a paratroop regiment (1985-86) and was deputy commander of an airborne formation (1986-88). From 1989 until 1990, Lebed commanded the 106th Guards Airborne Division; he led this unit into a variety of ethnic hotspots during this period, including Georgia and Azerbaijan. The general was deputy commander of Airborne Forces during 1991-92.

PREPARED BY: ████████████████████████████████

CONFIDENTIAL

Sketches of Iraqi military officials completed prior to the Persian Gulf War include those for Lt. Gen. Husayn Rahsid Mohammad Hasan (December 18, 1990), chief of the General Staff at the time; and Lt. Gen. Ayyad Futayih Khalifa Al Rawi (October 18, 1990), commander of the Iraqi Republic Guard forces.[47]

The DIA also produces or delegates production of the *Defense Intelligence Reference Document* (DIRD) series. A DIRD can be a one-time or recurring (often encyclopedic) study on military forces and force capabilities, infrastructure, facilities, systems and equipment, or associated topics for military planning and operations. A DIRD may consist of foldout wall charts intended as reference aids or be a more typical book-length publication.[48]

A May 1995 DIRD, produced by the National Ground Intelligence Center, concerned *Nonlethal Technologies—Worldwide*. The eighty-one-page document covered such topics as nonlethal chemical effectors, nonlethal biotechnical effectors, nonlethal acoustic effectors, nonlethal electromagnetic effectors, kinetic nonlethal effectors, and nonlethal information effectors. Under the nonlethal electromagnetic effectors, it examined laser weapons in the former Soviet Union, United Kingdom, Armenia, France and Germany, China, Iraq, Israel, and Jordan. A 1996 DIRD, focused on *Foreign Oceanographic Research and Development with Naval Implications—China*.[49]

Notes

1. Central Intelligence Agency, *A Consumer's Guide to Intelligence* (Washington, D.C.: CIA, July 1995), p. 30; Walter Pincus, "PDB, the Only News Not Fit for Anyone Else to Read," *Washington Post*, August 27, 1994, p. A7; Cord Meyer, *Facing Reality: From World Federalism to the CIA* (New York: Harper & Row, 1980), p. 352; Zbigniew Brezezinski, *Power and Principle: Memoirs of the National Security Adviser, 1977–1981* (New York: Farrar, Straus & Giroux, 1983), p. 224.

2. Meyer, *Facing Reality*, p. 352.

3. Loch K. Johnson, "Making the Intelligence 'Cycle' Work," *International Journal of Intelligence and Counterintelligence* 1, no. 4 (Winter 1986–1987): 1–23; Pincus, "PDB, the Only News Not Fit for Anyone Else to Read."

4. William Colby with Peter Forbath, *Honorable Men: My Life in the CIA* (New York: Simon & Schuster, 1978), p. 354; Letter, Arthur S. Hulnick, CIA Office of Public Affairs, to author, April 7, 1988; Nathan Nielsen, "The National Intelligence Daily," *Studies in Intelligence* 20 (Spring 1976): 39–51.

5. Central Intelligence Agency, *A Consumer's Guide to Intelligence*, p. 30; Meyer, *Facing Reality*, pp. 352–354; Private information.

6. Brian Toohey and Dale Van Atta, "How the CIA Saw the 1975 Crisis," *National Times*, March 28–April 3, 1982, pp. 16ff; Bob Woodward, *Veil: The Secret Wars of the CIA, 1981–1987* (New York: Simon & Schuster, 1987), pp. 410–411.

7. Central Intelligence Agency, *A Consumer's Guide to Intelligence*, p. 30.

8. Ibid.

9. Ibid.; Susan McFarland and Mike Zwicke, "MID: Providing Insights for Policymakers and Warfighters," *Communiqué*, September 1996, pp. 12–13; Bill Gertz, "Russia Dodges

Chemical Arms Ban," *Washington Times*, February 4, 1997, pp. A1, A20; Bill Gertz, "Hidden Iraqi Scuds Threaten Israel, Gulf Countries," *Washington Times*, February 11, 1998, pp. A1, A12.

10. Central Intelligence Agency, *A Consumer's Guide to Intelligence*, p. 31.

11. Ibid.

12. Ibid.

13. AFSPACECOM Regulation 200–1, "Air Force Space Command Unit Intelligence Program," February 17, 1989, p. 7; Air Force Intelligence Agency, AFIAR 23–1, "Organizations and Functions, Air Force Intelligence Agency (AFIA)," June 7, 1990, p. F-6.

14. George Lardner Jr. and Walter Pincus, "On This Network, All the News Is Top Secret," *Washington Post*, March 3, 1992, pp. A1, A9.

15. Ibid.

16. Central Intelligence Agency, *A Consumer's Guide to Intelligence*, p. 36.

17. Ibid.

18. Ibid.

19. Ibid., pp. 36–37.

20. Ibid., p. 37.

21. U.S. Congress, House Committee on Foreign Affairs, *The Role of Intelligence in the Foreign Policy Process* (Washington, D.C.: U.S. Government Printing Office, 1980), p. 235.

22. Central Intelligence Agency, *A Consumer's Guide to Intelligence*, p. 35.

23. Office of Naval Intelligence, *Office of Naval Intelligence 1989 Command History*, n.d., Intelligence Analysis Division section, pp. 1–2; U.S. Congress, Senate Select Committee on Intelligence, *Nomination of Robert M. Gates to Be Director of Central Intelligence* (Washington, D.C.: U.S. Government Printing Office, 1991), p. 131.

24. John M. Broder, "CIA Scrambles to Evaluate Breakaway Soviet Republics," *Los Angeles Times*, December 12, 1991, p. A14; Sam Vincent Meddis, "Soviet Disunion Keeps U.S. Spymasters Busy," *USA Today*, December 11, 1991, p. 6A.

25. U.S. Congress, Senate Select Committee on Intelligence, *Nomination of Robert M. Gates to Be Director of Central Intelligence*, pp. 121, 123; Private information; Peter Kornbluh, *Nicaragua: The Price of Intervention* (Washington, D.C.: Institute for Policy Studies, 1987), p. 243, n. 22; Woodward, *Veil: The Secret Wars of the CIA*, p. 400; Brian Barger and Robert Parry, "Nicaraguan Rebels Linked to Drug Trafficking," *Washington Post*, December 27, 1985, p. A22; Office of Naval Intelligence, *Office of Naval Intelligence (ONI) Annual History 1985, Annex C*, September 1986, p. 4; U.S. Congress, *Department of Energy and Water Development Appropriations for 1992, Part 6* (Washington, D.C.: U.S. Government Printing Office, 1991), p. 828.

26. Department of the Army, *Office of the Deputy Chief of Staff for Intelligence Historical Review, 1 October 1992 to 30 September 1993*, n.d., p. 6-4; Department of the Army, *Office of the Deputy Chief of Staff for Intelligence Historical Review, 1 October 1994 to 30 September 1995*, n.d., p. 3-23; Department of the Army, *Office of the Deputy Chief of Staff for Intelligence Historical Review, 1 October 1993 to 30 September 1994*, n.d., pp. 6-6, 6-8; U.S. Congress, Senate Select Committee on Intelligence, *Intelligence Analysis of the Long-Range Missile Threat to the United States* (Washington, D.C.: U.S. Government Printing Office, 1997), p. 14; Martin Sieff, "N. Korea Has Nuke or Is Close to It, CIA Believes," *Washington Times*, December 22, 1993, p. 12; Stephen Engelberg with Michael R. Gordon, "Intelligence Study Says North Korea Has Nuclear Bomb," *New York Times*, December 26, 1993, pp. 1, 8; U.S. Congress, Senate Select Committee on Intelligence, *Current and Projected National Security*

Threats to the United States (Washington, D.C.: U.S. Government Printing Office, 1997), pp. 38, 87–88.

27. Central Intelligence Agency, *A Consumer's Guide to Intelligence*, p. 35; Bill Gertz, "Yeltsin Can't Curtail Arms Spread," *Washington Times*, September 27, 1994, p. A3.

28. Harold P. Ford, *Estimative Intelligence: The Purposes and Problems of National Intelligence Estimating* (Washington, D.C.: Defense Intelligence College, 1989), p. 136.

29. Central Intelligence Agency, *A Consumer's Guide to Intelligence*, p. 31.

30. Title pages obtained under Freedom of Information Act.

31. Central Intelligence Agency, *A Consumer's Guide to Intelligence*, p. 35.

32. Ibid.; U.S. Congress, House Committee on Appropriations, *Departments of Commerce, Justice and State, the Judiciary and Related Agencies Appropriations for FY 1986, Part 7* (Washington, D.C.: U.S. Government Printing Office, 1985), p. 492.

33. Bill Gertz, "NATO Candidates Armed Rogue States," *Washington Times*, February 19, 1997, pp. A1, A16. Other titles are obtained from documents released by CIA.

34. Central Intelligence Agency, *A Consumer's Guide to Intelligence*, p. 34.

35. Bill Gertz, "Mishaps Put Russian Missiles in 'Combat' Mode," *New York Times*, May 12, 1997, pp. A1, A10; Bill Gertz, "Most of Russia's Biggest Banks Linked to Mob, CIA Says," *Washington Times*, December 5, 1994, pp. A1, A12; Bill Gertz, "16 Biological Weapons Sites Identified in Ex-Soviet Union," *Washington Times*, March 3, 1992, p. A3; Bill Gertz, "Renegades Pose Nuke Danger," *Washington Times*, October 22, 1996, pp. A1, A18.

36. Central Intelligence Agency, *A Consumer's Guide to Intelligence*, p. v.

37. Documents obtained under the Freedom of Information Act; Office of Naval Intelligence, *Office of Naval Intelligence Command History 1995*, 1996, pp. 54–55; Department of Defense Inspector General, *Final Report on the Inspection of Scientific and Technical Intelligence Production*, IR 96–005, April 11, 1996, p. 21.

38. Central Intelligence Agency, *A Consumer's Guide to Intelligence*, pp. 32–33.

39. Ibid., p. 33; issues of *Terrorism Review* partially released under the Freedom of Information Act; Vernon Loeb, "Where the CIA Wages Its New War," *Washington Post*, September, 1998, p. A17.

40. Central Intelligence Agency, *A Consumer's Guide to Intelligence*, p. 33.

41. Ibid., p. 34.

42. Central Intelligence Agency, *A Consumer's Guide to Intelligence* (Washington, D.C.: CIA, 1993), p. 22.

43. AFSPACECOM Regulation 200–1, "Air Force Space Command Unit Intelligence Program," p. 7; Air Force Intelligence Agency, AFIAR 23–1, "Organizations and Functions, Air Force Intelligence Agency (AFIA)," p. F-6.

44. Central Intelligence Agency, *Biographic Handbook USSR, Supplement IV*, April 1977.

45. Central Intelligence Agency, *Biographic Report: Yitzhak RABIN, Prime Minister of Israel*, June 1974.

46. Defense Intelligence Agency, "Biographic Sketch: Andres Rodriguez," April 1966.

47. Sketches obtained under the Freedom of Information Act.

48. Central Intelligence Agency, *A Consumer's Guide to Intelligence* (1995), p. 32.

49. National Ground Intelligence Center, *Nonlethal Technologies—Worldwide (U)*, NGIC–1147–101–95, May 1995, pp. vii–ix; Office of Naval Intelligence, *Foreign Oceanographic Research and Development with Naval Implications*, 1996.

15

COUNTERINTELLIGENCE

Counterintelligence is often associated with the catching of spies. However, it is necessary to distinguish between *counterintelligence* and *counterespionage*. Counterespionage is a narrower activity than counterintelligence and is concerned simply with preventing a foreign government's illicit acquisition of secrets. Counterintelligence is concerned with understanding, and possibly neutralizing, all aspects of the intelligence operations of foreign nations.

Counterintelligence was defined by President Reagan's Executive Order 12333, which is still in force, as both "information gathered" and "activities conducted" in order "to protect against espionage, other intelligence activities, sabotage or assassination conducted on behalf of foreign powers, organizations or persons, or international terrorist activities but not including personnel, physical documents or communications security."[1]

Thus, as defined in Executive Order 12333, counterintelligence incorporates a wide range of activities not strictly in the counterintelligence tradition. The definition stresses the *counter* aspect and lets the term *intelligence* represent activities below the conventional military level, including terrorist attacks and sabotage, irrespective of whether they are performed by an intelligence organization. Some would also consider counterdeception and counter-illicit technology transfer to be part of the list of counterintelligence subcategories.[2] Such a view essentially combines traditional counterintelligence, positive intelligence designed to counter any form of hostile activity, and a framework (counterdeception) for the analysis of positive intelligence.

The traditional notion of counterintelligence, the one that will be used here, focuses on information gathered and activities conducted with the purpose of understanding and possibly neutralizing the activities of foreign intelligence services (which may include denial and deception and illicit technology transfer). In this view there are four basic functions of counterintelligence activity:

- collection of information on foreign intelligence and security services and their activities through open and clandestine sources

- the evaluation of defectors
- research and analysis concerning the structure, personnel, and operations of foreign intelligence and security services
- operations for the purpose of disrupting and neutralizing intelligence and security services engaging in activities hostile to the United States

TARGETS

Even foreign intelligence communities with which the U.S. intelligence community has the closest relations—such as the British and Canadian communities—will be the subject of collection and analysis by the CIA and other counterintelligence agencies. It is necessary to establish a base of knowledge about such communities to guide relations with them. There will, however, be limitations on what are considered acceptable methods of collection.

In addition, some nations that are allies of the United States also employ their intelligence services to engage in activities—such as industrial espionage—inimical to U.S. interests. Most prominently, the French Directorate General of External Security (DGSE) has penetrated several U.S. companies, including IBM, Texas Instruments, and Bell Textron. A French government document apparently obtained by the CIA indicated a broad effort to obtain information about the work of U.S. aerospace companies. Other allies, including Germany, Israel, Japan, and South Korea, also are involved in economic espionage.[3] Thus, the United States may seek both to collect intelligence on those operations as well as to neutralize them.

Of course, the intelligence communities of other nations often are involved in operations inimical to U.S. national security, as well as economic, interests. The Russian, Israeli, South Korean, and Chinese intelligence services have penetrated the CIA, the FBI, the Office of Naval Intelligence, and other national security institutions—as indicated by the cases of Aldrich Ames (CIA), Harold Nicholson (CIA), Earl Edwin Pitts (FBI), Larry Wu-Tai Chin (CIA), Robert S. Kim (ONI), Jonathan Pollard (Naval Investigative Service), and Peter Lee (Los Alamos National Laboratory). Collectively, Ames, Nicholson, and Pitts were able to provide information about the identities of Soviets/Russians providing intelligence to the CIA, about technical surveillance operations (ABSORB and TAW, discussed in Chapter 12), and about the identities of CIA personnel. Pollard provided an enormous number of documents, including over 800 Top Secret documents. Among his CIA duties, Chin "reviewed, translated and analyzed classified documents from covert and overt human and technical collection sources," and Peter Lee examined the feasibility of detecting submerged submarines via radar imagery.[4]

In addition, it has been reported that the Russian Foreign Intelligence Service (SVRR) has spied on personnel of the UN Special Commission responsible for investigating Iraq's compliance with its pledge to eliminate its capacity for producing weapons of mass destruction, and that the SVRR may have passed some of the information collected to Iraq. Meanwhile, the Russian Federal Security Service (FSB) has recruited Russian scientists from technological institutes and weapons factories to train Iranian scientists in missile development.[5]

The continued presence of a Soviet communications intelligence facility at Lourdes, Cuba, also represents a significant target for U.S. counterintelligence. The facility, whether or not it provided Moscow with advanced knowledge of U.S. war plans during Operation Desert Storm, is one of the world's largest intercept facilities and capable of intercepting a wide variety of commercial and government communications within the United States and between the United States and Europe.[6] The SIGINT activities of a number of other countries will similarly be targets for U.S. collection.

The intelligence services of nations such as Iran, Iraq, and North Korea, in addition to any espionage operations in the United States, also operate against U.S. interests outside of the United States. Thus, Iraqi intelligence successfully spied on UN weapons inspectors in 1996 and 1997, and after learning of the inspector's targets moved quickly to hide suspected weapons caches. Iraqi intelligence also recruited a member of the German Foreign Ministry to provide data during the Gulf War, including Western assessments of Iraq's missile capabilities.[7]

According to testimony by then DCI John Deutch, Iranian agents contacted officials at nuclear facilities in Kazakhstan on several occasions, attempting to acquire nuclear-related materials. In 1992, Iran unsuccessfully approached the Ulba Metallurgical Plant to obtain enriched uranium. The following year, three Iranians believed to have connections to Iran's intelligence service were arrested in Turkey while seeking to acquire nuclear material from smugglers from the former Soviet Union.[8]

In 1997 it was reported that Iranian agents in Bosnia were engaged in extensive operations and had infiltrated the U.S. program to train the Bosnian Army. In addition, for several years the VAVAK component of the Iranian Ministry of Intelligence and Security has been leaving a trail of dead bodies across Europe and the Middle East—the result of a campaign to assassinate Iranian dissidents. The campaign is orchestrated by a Committee for Special Operations, which includes the country's spiritual leader, president, foreign minister, and high security officials.[9]

COLLECTION

Information concerning the activities of foreign intelligence and security services comes from a variety of sources. Open sources concerning friendly and hostile services may include official government documents (e.g., telephone directories, brochures, yearly reports, parliamentary hearings, and reports of commissions of inquiry), books, articles in magazines, and newspapers. Examples of such sources include Russian newspaper articles on that nation's reconnaissance satellites, investigative books on the German Federal Intelligence Service (BND), and official publications such as the Canadian Security Intelligence Review Committee's annual report on the Canadian Security Intelligence Service.[10]

In the case of closed societies, open source material is limited; nevertheless, even in these countries analysts may get some useful insights into high-ranking personnel or some aspects of internal operations from occasional government-approved accounts of intelligence and security service actions.

Information about friendly services may also come from liaison and training arrangements. Thus, Dominic Perrone of the U.S. Military Liaison Office, U.S. Embassy, Rome, was able, in 1978, to gather inside information on the effectiveness, or lack thereof, of the newly established intelligence and security services (the SISMI, or Military Security and Information Service, and the SISDE, or Democratic Security and Information Service) from several sources inside the Italian government. As a result, Perrone was able to prepare a 4,000-word report for the DIA that indicated that the resources devoted to SISDE's antiterrorist activities were making effective counterespionage impossible, that the commander of SISDE was not qualified for the job, and that both SISDE and SISMI were performing poorly.[11]

Liaison with allied services also provides information about the activities of hostile services—such as when the French Directorate for Territorial Surveillance (DST) provided the CIA with information about its agent—Vladimir Vetrov, code-named FAREWELL—in Directorate T of the KGB. Beginning in 1981, FAREWELL provided the DST with more than 4,000 documents on Soviet scientific and technical espionage, including information on the Soviet Union's plans to steal Western technological secrets and on internal assessments of its covert technology acquisition activities. Specifically, FAREWELL provided: (1) a complete, detailed list of all Soviet organizations involved in scientific and technical intelligence; (2) reports on Soviet plans, accomplishments, and annual savings in all branches of the military industry due to illegal acquisition of foreign technology; (3) a list of all KGB officers throughout the world involved in scientific and technical espionage; and (4) the identities of the principal agents recruited by the officers of "Line X" in ten Western nations, including the United States, West Germany, and France. French President François Mitterrand informed President Reagan about FAREWELL in 1981 and gave him a sample of the intelligence material the agent had transmitted. Several weeks later, the head of the DST, Marcel Chalet, visited Vice President Bush in Washington to discuss FAREWELL.[12]

Two types of human sources may provide useful information. The first is the agent who holds an official position within a hostile service. This type is either a mole (someone recruited prior to their entry into the service—such as Kim Philby) or a "defector-in-place" (someone who agrees to provide information after having attained an intelligence or security position—such as FAREWELL). An individual may agree to provide information for ideological or financial reasons or as the result of coercion or blackmail, which might be based on evidence of sexual or financial misbehavior.

The United States had some significant successes during the Cold War in penetrating the Soviet military intelligence organization, the Chief Intelligence Directorate of the Soviet General Staff (GRU). In the late 1950s and early 1960s, Peter

Popov and Oleg Penkovsky, both colonels in the GRU, volunteered their services to the CIA. In addition to providing detailed information on the physical layout of the GRU's headquarters, they identified GRU agents and described their personalities. The CIA also began receiving information in the early 1960s from GRU officer Dmitri Polyakov, code-named GTBEEP by the CIA and TOP HAT by the FBI. Polyakov, who reached the rank of Major General, was eventually betrayed by Aldrich Ames and was executed in 1988. Indeed Polyakov was only one of a number of CIA sources, recruited in the 1970s and early 1980s, in the Soviet intelligence apparatus (primarily the KGB) who was betrayed by Ames.[13]

The CIA also apparently penetrated the Indian Research and Analysis Wing (RAW), India's principal foreign intelligence agency. In 1987 a senior RAW official, K. V. Unnikrishnan, was reported to have been stationed in Madras, where he was responsible for coordinating Tamil insurgency activities. Unnikrishnan was reportedly blackmailed with compromising photographs of himself and a "stewardess."[14]

The second type of human source is the defector. Defectors provide information concerning various aspects of an intelligence or security service's structure, operations, and leadership. The CIA certainly reaped an intelligence bonanza when Maj. Hunter Bolanos of the Nicaraguan Directorate General of State Security (Direccion General de Serguidad del Estado, DGSE) defected in 1983. For almost all of the period between January 1980 and May 7, 1983, Bolanos had special responsibility for surveillance of the U.S. Embassy and CIA activities in Nicaragua. He provided information on the structure of the DGSE, the number of Nicaraguans in the DGSE (2,800–3,000), the presence of foreign advisers to the DGSE (seventy Soviets, 400 Cubans, forty to fifty East Germans, twenty to twenty-five Bulgarians), and on the Soviet provision of sophisticated bugging devices.[15]

Similarly, senior intelligence officers who have defected from Cuba and China have provided the United States with new information on intelligence and counterintelligence operations in those nations. In June 1987, Maj. Florentino Apillaga Lombard defected to the United States from the Cuban DGI (General Directorate of Intelligence) and proceeded to inform CIA officials that the great majority of CIA "assets" in Cuba were actually double agents working for the Cuban government. In 1986, Yu Zhensan, the former head of the Foreign Affairs Bureau of the PRC's Ministry of State Security, defected and provided the United States with extensive information about Chinese intelligence operations abroad, including the names of Chinese agents, as well as the names of suspected agents from other nations working in China. Before defecting, he apparently provided the United States with information leading to the arrest of Larry Wu-Tai Chin, an employee of the CIA's Foreign Broadcast Information Service who was a long-term Chinese mole.[16]

During the course of the Cold War, the United States benefited from information provided by a substantial number of KGB and GRU defectors. As a result, the CIA was able to develop a detailed, albeit not complete, picture of the structures and activities of those organizations.

Before his redefection, KGB official Vitaly Yurchenko provided the CIA with information concerning several Soviet penetrations of the U.S. intelligence community—information that led to the discovery that former CIA officer Edward Lee Howard and former NSA employee Ronald Pelton had been providing information to the Soviet Union. He also stated that Pelton and naval spy John Walker were the KGB's most prized assets in the United States.[17]

In June 1986, it was reported that the head of KGB operations in North Africa and KGB liaison to the Palestine Liberation Organization, Oleg Agraniants, had defected to the United States. Agraniants, who may have been working for the CIA for the three years prior to his defection, apparently supplied the names of KGB agents in Tunisia, Algeria, Morocco, and Libya.[18]

The changing domestic situation in the Soviet Union during the Gorbachev era and the subsequent collapse of the Soviet Union led to the defection of numerous KGB officers. Thus in 1990, Igor Cherpinski, reportedly the KGB station chief in Belgium, defected. In 1991, Sergei Illarionov, a KGB colonel based in Genoa, defected and helped Western security services identify KGB espionage networks in Europe. Recent non-Soviet defectors have included Majid Giaka, a Libyan intelligence officer who provided information on the 1988 bombing of Pan Am Flight 103.[19]

Beyond human sources, technical collection also provides data of value for counterintelligence. Intercepted communications from within a country or to embassies overseas can reveal either the activities of the internal security service or the intelligence activities of the foreign intelligence service. Thus, the United States interception and decoding of Soviet communications traffic in the 1940s paid off significantly in the late 1940s, 1950s, and beyond when the traffic was decrypted as part of the VENONA project. From the 1960s until the collapse of East Germany, the targets of the U.S. Army's Field Station Berlin included the communications of the East German Ministry of State Security. In addition, intercepts of signals from foreign reconnaissance satellites can provide information on what targets are being imaged by those satellites.[20]

Satellite imagery is decidedly less useful than either human sources, open sources, or COMINT in providing information about most activities of foreign intelligence services. It can, however, provide information on the precise location and layout of intelligence and security service complexes—information that may prove particularly useful if a direct attack on such facilities is authorized. Thus, reconnaissance flights in support of U.N. inspectors have provided information on the regional centers of the Iraqi Special Security Organization. In addition, satellite imagery can provide information on the presence of SIGINT facilities and ground stations such as the GRU LOW EAR intercept dishes.[21]

EVALUATION OF DEFECTORS

The evaluation and debriefing of defectors is another important aspect of counterintelligence operations. The United States has provided political asylum to officials from the Soviet Union and Russia, China, Nicaragua, Cuba, and a number of Eastern European nations. When the defector is not an intelligence officer, the debriefers seek information on the policies and leaders of whatever government component employed the defector. In addition to eliciting information, the debriefers seek to determine the reliability of the information offered.

When the defector has been employed by a foreign intelligence service, the debriefers attempt to extract the maximum information possible on the structure, functions, agents, operations, procedures, and leaders of the defector's intelligence community, as well as to determine the defector's reliability. They try to obtain the information as soon as possible so that if a response is necessary, action can be taken before the hostile intelligence service realizes its officer or agent has defected. When dealing with defectors from hostile intelligence services, the debriefers must determine where the officer's knowledge ends and where exaggeration or fabrication in the face of depleted information begins. Complicating the debriefers' task is the fact that many defectors hold back information as insurance for continued protection.[22]

The inability to determine conclusively the bona fides of defectors can lead to paralysis of intelligence collection operations in one or more nations, the creation of unwarranted suspicion about and damage to the careers of valuable intelligence officers, and the failure to fully exploit potentially valuable information provided by a clandestine source or a defector.

Thus, the 1962 defection of KGB officer Anatoli Golitsin to the CIA in Helsinki, Finland, combined with the suspicions of CIA counterintelligence chief James Angleton, produced a mole hunt that ruined the career of several CIA officers, led other KGB defectors to be treated with unjustified suspicion, and helped immobilize CIA clandestine collection operations in the Soviet Union throughout much of the 1960s.[23]

In the case of Vitaly Yurchenko, the CIA Counterintelligence Staff was faced with assessing whether he was a legitimate defector who changed his mind or a plant who intended to redefect from the beginning. Yurchenko, a KGB staff officer with twenty-five years of service, requested political asylum in the United States at the U.S. Embassy in Rome on August 1, 1985.[24]

From August 1975 until August 1980, Yurchenko was the security officer at the Soviet Embassy in Washington. There, he was responsible for ensuring the security of Soviet establishments and citizens in Washington, for protecting classified information, and for handling foreign visitors. In September 1980, he was transferred to the First Chief Directorate. From that date until March 1985 he was chief of Fifth Department of Directorate K, where, among other security functions, he was responsible for investigating suspected espionage incidents involving KGB staff personnel and information leaks concerning the First Chief Directorate. From April to July 1985, he was deputy chief of the First Department, which carried out operations against the United States and Canada.[25]

Three months after his defection, Yurchenko appeared at a press conference at the Soviet Embassy in Washington, claiming to have been kidnapped, drugged, and kept in isolation at a CIA safe house in Fredricksburg, Virginia. His "escape" was due, according to Yurchenko, to a "momentary lapse" by his captors. (In fact, he walked out of a Georgetown restaurant without opposition from his CIA escort.) Two days later, Yurchenko, after a visit by U.S. officials to determine he was acting of his own free will, flew back to Moscow. In Moscow, he held a two-hour press conference at which he and other Soviet officials accused the United States of "state terrorism." Subsequent reports that he had been executed were proved incorrect when he was discovered walking on a Moscow street.[26]

Following Yurchenko's defection, U.S. officials speculated on the reasons for his actions. If Yurchenko was a plant who had planned to redefect from the beginning, KGB motives could have been to gather information on CIA treatment and debriefing of defectors, or to embarrass the CIA and discourage CIA acceptance of defectors. Among those suggesting that Yurchenko was a plant were President Reagan, Senator Patrick Leahy (then vice chairman of the Senate Select Committee on Intelligence), and other officials who considered Yurchenko's information to be largely "historical."[27]

Others suggested that Yurchenko had been a legitimate defector who had changed his mind. Reasons given for an actual change included his rejection by the wife of a Soviet official stationed in Canada, with whom Yurchenko had had a relationship (and whom he visited almost immediately after his arrival in the United States); the great publicity generated by his defection; a general homesickness for "Mother Russia" often experienced by Soviet defectors; and a specific longing to be reunited with his family—especially his sixteen-year-old son. Among those doubting a staged defection was then FBI chief William H. Webster, who said that Yurchenko had provided the United States with valuable information on the roles of Edward Lee Howard and Ronald Pelton.[28]

In early 1993, DCI Robert Gates stated that the CIA had concluded that Yurchenko was a bona fide defector. According to Gates: "My view, and I think the view of virtually everybody in this building, is that Yurchenko was genuine. He provided too much specific information, including in the counterintelligence arena, that has been useful, for him, in my judgement to have been a plant."[29]

RESEARCH AND ANALYSIS

It is fundamental to both intelligence and counterintelligence missions that there exists a store of knowledge concerning the personalities, past operations, structure, and activities of other nations' intelligence and security services. Only with such knowledge can positive intelligence collection operations be planned and conducted effectively. Likewise, only with such knowledge can effective penetration and disruption and neutralization activities be conducted.

The most significant research on foreign intelligence services conducted within the U.S. intelligence community are those reports prepared by the CIA's Counterintelligence Center (CIC), which is the successor to the Counterintelligence Staff. The CIC prepares reports ranging from fifty to one hundred pages on all intelligence communities of interest, both hostile and friendly. The reports detail the origins of the intelligence services, their structure, function, and mode of operation, and the arrangements for control by higher authority.

Thus, the forty-seven-page study, *Israel: Foreign Intelligence and Security Services*, published in March 1977, focused in its first section on the background and development of the Israeli services, objectives, and structure; the relationship between the government and the services; and professional standards. The second, third, and fourth sections focused on the three major Israeli intelligence and security units— the Mossad, the Shin Bet, and AMAN, respectively. In each case, the report examined the service's function, organization, administrative practice (including training), and methods of operation. Additionally, liaison with other Israeli and foreign services was considered. The three penultimate sections examined the Foreign Ministry's Research and Political Planning Center, the National Police, and key officials, and the final section commented on principal sources. The study's table of contents is shown as Figure 15.1.[30]

A 1984 study entitled *Soviet Intelligence: KGB and GRU* discussed the background and development of the Soviet services, national intelligence objectives and structure, the relationship between the Communist Party/government and the services, the internal security and counterintelligence operations of the KGB, and the foreign operations of the KGB and GRU.[31]

The intelligence structure of Russia is significantly different from that of the Soviet Union. Today there are four key services: the Russian Foreign Intelligence Service (SVRR), the Federal Security Service (FSB), the Federal Agency for Government Communications and Information (FAPSI) and the Chief Intelligence Directorate of the General Staff (GRU).[32] Any present studies of the Russian services will examine their Soviet heritage, the transition from Soviet structure to the present Russian structure—during which services have been established, abolished, and renamed—their present organization, size, targets, and the key personalities in those services.

Such a study will be a far more detailed examination of the questions that appeared in the unclassified September 1992 CIA study, *The Russian Security Services: Sorting Out the Pieces*. The seven-page study contains a diagram of the evolution of the Russian services (except the GRU) between August 1991 and September 1992, a brief description of the organizations at the time of publication, and short biographies of the service heads.[33]

Other intelligence communities will be of even more concern, and those of greatest concern often include a fairly large number of distinct agencies. Thus any study of the Iraqi community will focus on the history, structure, operations, and leadership of the numerous Iraqi intelligence agencies, which include the Special Security Service, the General Intelligence Directorate, the Military Intelligence Service, the General Security Service, Project 858, and the Military Security Service.[34]

Counterintelligence studies are also prepared by the Defense Intelligence Agency and military service intelligence and security components. The DIA prepared a

November 15, 1978, Intelligence Appraisal titled *Italy: Reorganization of Intelligence and Security Services*, which discussed the background and structure of Italy's intelligence and security services, key personalities, intelligence reforms, and outlook for the future. Studies prepared by the Army Intelligence and Threat Analysis Center, absorbed into the National Ground Intelligence Center in 1995, included: *Italy: A Counterintelligence Assessment* (April 1984), which reviewed the various intelligence and security services of the Italian government as well as various threats—including terrorism, wartime sabotage, and espionage; *The DST: An Organization*

FIGURE 15.1   Table of Contents for *Israel: Foreign Intelligence and Security Services*

TABLE OF CONTENTS

SECRET

(continues)

FIGURE 15.1   (continued)

FIGURES

SOURCE: Central Intelligence Agency, *Israeli Foreign Intelligence and Security Services* (Washington, D.C.: CIA, March 1977).

in Flux (September 1986); *France: A Counterintelligence Assessment* (June 1981); *GRU Activity in Washington, D.C. Area* (April 1983); and *The Cuban Intelligence Threat in Panama* (May 1978).[35]

NEUTRALIZATION

The neutralization of the activities of hostile intelligence services can be accomplished by various means. Penetrations of a hostile service can be used not only to gather information but to damage the service's operations. In 1980 the Polish civilian intelligence and security service, the SB, began receiving classified information from James D. Harper, a Silicon Valley engineer. Harper, via his wife, who worked for a southern California defense contractor, obtained copies of well over 100 pounds of classified reports—which he sold to the SB for more than $250,000. Most of the documents pertained to the U.S. Minuteman missile and ballistic missile defense programs and were classified Confidential or Secret. Documents sold to the SB included the 1978 *Minuteman Defense Study (Final Report)*, the 1981 *Report on the Task Force on U.S. Ballistic Missile Defense*, and a 1978 Martin Marietta Corporation study entitled *Endoatmospheric Nonnuclear Kill Technology Requirements and Definition Study*. Harper was detected by a CIA penetration of the SB. When arrested he was preparing to deliver an additional 150 to 200 pounds of documents.[36]

A second way to neutralize a hostile intelligence service is by passing information to a third country that will lead that country to take action against the officers and agents of the hostile service. In many cases the CIA passes such information on as a natural result of its liaison with a friendly security service—such as when it provided the British Security Service with information on East German intelligence operations in the United Kingdom. When GRU officer Sergei Bokhane, who had been stationed in Greece, defected, he provided information on at least three Greeks involved in spying for the Soviet Union. Included was Michael Megalokonomos, who, when apprehended, was in possession of a codebook, a microfilm reading device, a radio for picking up special frequencies, and instructions on how to work a radio transmitter. Also named by Bokhane was Nikos Pipitsoulis, who sold an electrical device to Soviet officials for $43,000. In addition, a lieutenant commander working in the data processing unit at Greek defense headquarters was involved in passing information to the Soviet Union. The information provided to the CIA by Bokhane was passed on to Greek security authorities, leading to the arrest of the three agents.[37]

On other occasions the recipient of the information may itself be a hostile nation. In the spring of 1983, when the Iranian Communist (Tudeh) Party had been closed down, the CIA provided a list of Soviet agents and collaborators operating in Iran to the Khomeini regime and its security service (SAVAMA). As a result, eighteen Soviet diplomats were expelled, 200 suspects executed, and Tudeh Party leaders imprisoned.[38]

Another method of neutralization entails running double agents. One CIA double agent operation that came to light is one that backfired. In 1959, Captain Nikolai Federovich Artamanov, the youngest commanding officer of a destroyer in Soviet naval history, defected to Sweden. Information about Artamanov was transferred to the United States by the CIA station chief in Sweden.[39]

Artamanov was subsequently recruited by the Office of Naval Intelligence (ONI) to come to the United States. In his debriefing, he provided the ONI with information on the Soviet use of travelers for intelligence collection, Soviet nuclear strategy, and Soviet destroyer tactics against submarines. Subsequently, he was given a new name, Nicholas Shadrin, and a position as a translator in the Naval Scientific and Technical Intelligence Center. In 1966 two events of importance occurred. Shadrin went to work for the Defense Intelligence Agency and was also approached by a Soviet intelligence officer who tried to recruit him. Shadrin did not close the door on the officer but reported the offer to the FBI. After initial hesitation, Shadrin was persuaded to become a double agent, to "accept" the Soviet offer and feed the KGB CIA-doctored disinformation.[40]

Among the reasons for U.S. pressure on Shadrin to accept the double agent role was that his recruiter, "Igor," was believed to be a Soviet defector-in-place who had been assigned the task of recruiting Shadrin. Successful completion of his mission, said Igor, would help propel him to a new position—chief of the KGB's American Department.[41]

After several years of pretending to work for the KGB, Shadrin began to make trips abroad to meet his controller. He never returned from a December 20, 1975, meeting in Vienna. According to temporary defector Vitaly Yurchenko, Shadrin was, by accident, fatally chloroformed while struggling in the backseat of a sedan with Soviet agents trying to spirit him out of Austria.[42]

The military, particularly the Army, also runs double agent operations. As noted in Chapter Three, the clandestine counterintelligence activities of the services was not transferred to the Defense HUMINT Service, along with HUMINT activities. According to U.S. Army Regulation 381-47, offensive counterintelligence operations, such as double agent operations, "may require engagement in unorthodox operations and activities. These unorthodox activities may be at variance with recognized standards or methods normally associated with the military Service. They will be undertaken only when authorized by the commander of a counterintelligence unit or higher authority."[43]

Double agent operations often are initiated after a member of the U.S. armed forces reports an approach made by a foreign intelligence officer. In 1984, there were 481 incidents of soldiers being approached by people suspected of being Soviet bloc intelligence officers or sympathizers.[44]

Under the direction of counterintelligence authorities, the service personnel maintain contact with the foreign intelligence officers, providing a combination of factual low-grade and false, but apparently valuable, information supplied by the military services. Such operations yield information on the intelligence targets of hostile services; allow identification of the intelligence officers and agents of hostile services; tie up hostile service resources; and permit the transmission of disinformation concerning the plans and capabilities of U.S. military forces. The INSCOM agents involved in such operations bear code names such as ROYAL MITER, LANCER FLAG, HOLE PUNCH, LARIAT TOSS, CANARY DANE, and LANDSCAPE BREEZE.[45]

One operation involved Chief Warrant Officer Janos Szmolka, who had left Hungary to become a U.S. citizen. Szmolka eventually joined the U.S. Army and was stationed in West Germany. From there, he went on authorized leaves to Budapest to visit his mother in 1978 and 1979. On his third trip he was approached by a man described as a Hungarian intelligence officer who offered to insure better living conditions for Szmolka's family in exchange for information.[46]

Szmolka returned to West Germany and reported the offer to his superiors. For the next four years, under the direction of Army counterintelligence officers, he was in contact with Hungarian agents in Europe and the United States. In 1980, under normal rotation procedures, he was transferred to the States; and in 1982, when the Army desired to uncover the Hungarian intelligence network in the United States, Szmolka was instructed to inform the Hungarians, through coded letters, that he had valuable information to turn over. On April 17, 1982, he went to the Confederate monument in Augusta, Georgia, near his post at Fort Gordon, to meet a Hungarian agent. Federal agents arrested Otto A. Gilbert, an expatriate Hungarian and naturalized U.S. citizen, and charged him with espionage. Gilbert received a reduced sentence in exchange for information about Hungarian intelligence.[47]

Notes

1. Ronald Reagan, "Executive Order 12333: United States Intelligence Activities," December 4, 1981, in *Federal Register* 46, no. 235 (December 8, 1981): 59941–55 at 59943.

2. For example, William Harris, "Counterintelligence Jurisdiction and the Double Cross System by National Technical Means," in *Intelligence Requirements for the 1980s: Counterintelligence*, ed. Roy Godson (New Brunswick, N.J.: Transaction, 1980), pp. 53–82.

3. Jay Peterzell, "When 'Friends' Become Moles," *Time*, May 28, 1990, p. 50; "Parlez-Vous Espionage?" *Newsweek*, September 23, 1991, p. 40; Douglas Jehl, "U.S. Expanding Its Effort to Halt Spying by Allies," *New York Times*, April 30, 1993, pp. A1, A10; R. Jeffrey Smith, "U.S. to Protest Industrial Spying by Allies," *Washington Post*, April 30, 1993, p. A39; ABC, "World News Tonight," April 29, 1993; John J. Fialka, *War by Other Means: Economic Espionage in America* (New York: Norton, 1997); Peter Schweizer, *Friendly Spies: How America's Allies Are Using Economic Espionage to Steal Our Secrets* (New York: Atlantic Monthly Press, 1993); General Accounting Office, *Weaknesses in U.S. Security Arrangements with Foreign-Owned Defense Contractors* GAO/NSIAD-96-64 (Washington, D.C.: GAO, February 1996), pp. 22–26.

4. David Wise, *Nightmover: How Aldrich Ames Sold the CIA to the KGB for $4.6 Million* (New York: HarperCollins, 1995); Nicholas Eftimiades, *Chinese Intelligence Operations* (Annapolis, Md.: Naval Institute Press, 1994), pp. 21–37; "Physicist Admits Spying for

China," *Washington Times*, December 10, 1997, p. A9; *United States of America v. Larry Wu-Tai Chin aka Chin Wu-Tai* in the United States District Court for the Eastern District of Virginia, Alexandria Division, Criminal No. 85–00263-A, January 2, 1986, pp. 2–3, 14.

5. R. Jeffrey Smith, "Did Russia Sell Iraq Germ Warfare Equipment?" *Washington Post*, February 12, 1998, pp. A1, A35; Daniel Williams, "Russian Spy Agency Linked to Iran," *Washington Post*, March 23, 1998, p. A14; Bill Gertz, "U.S. Official Claims Russia Cutting Aid to Iran on Missiles," *Washington Times*, March 11, 1998, p. A5.

6. Juan O. Tamayo, "Soviets Spied on Gulf War Plans from Cuba, Defector Says," *Miami Herald*, April 3, 1998, p. 21A; William Rosenau, "A Deafening Silence: US Government Policy and the Sigint Facility at Lourdes," *Intelligence and National Security* 9, no. 4 (October 1994): 723–734.

7. Tim Weiner, "U.S. Says Iraq Spied on Inspectors to Know When to Hide Weapons," *New York Times*, November 25, 1997, pp. A1, A6; Alan Cowell, "German Ministry Official Spied for Iraq in Gulf War," *New York Times*, November 18, 1997, p. A14.

8. John Deutch, "The Threat of Nuclear Diversion," Statement for the Record to the Permanent Subcommittee on Investigations of the Senate Committee on Governmental Affairs, March 20, 1996, p. 4.

9. Mike O'Connor, "Spies for Iranians Are Said to Gain a Hold in Bosnia," *New York Times*, November 28, 1997, pp. A1, A8; Alan Cowell, "Berlin Court Says Top Iran Leaders Ordered Killings," *New York Times*, April 11, 1997, pp. A1, A10; Carl Anthony Wege, "Iranian Intelligence Organizations," *International Journal of Intelligence and Counterintelligence* 10, no. 3 (Fall 1997): 287–298; U.S. Department of State, *Patterns of Global Terrorism, 1997* (Washington, D.C.: U.S. Government Printing Office, 1998), p. 31.

10. "Russian Newspaper Says Spy Satellite Was Expensive Test Dummy," *Aerospace Daily*, June 11, 1997, p. 399; Security Intelligence Review Committee, *Annual Report 1995–1996* (Ottawa: SIRC, 1996); Erich Schmidt-Eenboom, *Schnüffler ohne Nase: Der BND—Die Unheimliche Macht im Staate* (Dusseldorf: ECON Verlag, 1993).

11. Dominic Perrone, "I&SS, Status of SISDE/SISMI Anti-Terrorist Orientation," *Covert Action Information Bulletin* (April-May 1979), pp. 6–9.

12. Theirry Wolton, *Le KGB en France* (Paris: Bernard Grasset, 1986), pp. 248–249.

13. Tom Mangold, *Cold Warrior, James Jesus Angleton: The CIA's Master Spy Hunter* (New York: Simon & Schuster, 1991), pp. 227–236; David Wise, *Molehunt: The Secret Search for Traitors That Shattered the CIA* (New York: Random House, 1991), pp. 153–154; David Wise, *Nightmover*, pp. 105, passim.

14. Iderjit Badhwar, "Spy-Catching," *India Today*, September 20, 1987, p. 33.

15. Don Oberdorfer and Joanne Omang, "Nicaraguan Bares Plan to Discredit Foes," *Washington Post*, June 19, 1983, pp. 1, 4.

16. Jack Anderson and Dale Van Atta, "Cuban Defector Impeaches CIA Spies," *Washington Post*, March 21, 1988, p. B15; Jack Anderson and Dale Van Atta, "CIA Recruits Were Castro's Agents," *Washington Post*, March 23, 1988, p. D11; Jack Anderson and Dale Van Atta, "CIA, Cubans in Looking-Glass War," *Washington Post*, March 25, 1988, p. E5; "Chinese Official Said Exposer of CIA Turncoat," *Washington Post*, September 5, 1986, p. A18; Michael Wines, "Spy Reportedly Unmasked by China Defector," *Los Angeles Times*, September 5, 1986, pp. 1, 12; Daniel Southerland, "China Silent on Reported Defection of Intelligence Official," *Washington Post*, September 4, 1986, p. A30.

17. "Did Yurchenko Fool the CIA?" *Newsweek*, November 18, 1985, pp. 34–39.

18. "High-Ranking KGB Agent Defects," *Washington Post*, June 20, 1986, p. A5.

19. "Defection of KGB Agent Causes Stir," *Washington Times*, June 6, 1990, p. A11; Bill Gertz, "CIA Learning from KGB Defector," *Washington Times*, March 5, 1992, p. A3; George J. Lardner Jr., "Libyan Named as Informer in Bombing," *Washington Post*, September 18, 1992, p. A30.

20. Robert Louis Benson and Michael Warner, eds., *VENONA: Soviet Espionage and the American Response 1939–1957* (Washington, D.C.: National Security Agency/Central Intelligence Agency, 1996); Markus Wolf with Ann McElvoy, *Man Without a Face: The Autobiography of Communism's Greatest Spymaster* (New York: Times Books, 1997), p. 294; Private information.

21. Barton Gellman, "Raids May Strike at Power Structure," *Washington Post*, February 17, 1998, pp. A1, A9; Jeffrey T. Richelson, *America's Secret Eyes in Space: The US KEYHOLE Spy Satellite Program* (New York: Harper & Row, 1990), p. 245.

22. Ralph Blumenthal, "Moscow Moves Rapidly in Defections to the U.S.," *New York Times*, November 7, 1985, p. A12.

23. See Wise, *Molehunt: The Secret Search for Traitors That Shattered the CIA*; Mangold, *Cold Warrior—James Jesus Angleton: The CIA's Master Spy Hunter*.

24. Central Intelligence Agency, "Vitaly Sergeyevich Yurchenko," November 8, 1985, p. 1.

25. Ibid., pp. 2–3.

26. "Did Yurchenko Fool the CIA?"; Celestine Bohlen, "Yurchenko Regales Moscow Audience," *Washington Post*, November 15, 1985, p. A33; "How Yurchenko Bade C.I.A. Adieu," *New York Times*, November 7, 1985, p. A12; Stephen Engelberg, "U.S. Is Convinced That K.G.B. Agent Wants to Go Home," *New York Times*, November 6, 1985, pp. A1, A12.

27. "Did Yurchenko Fool the CIA?"; Stephen Engelberg, "President Sees a Soviet 'Ploy' in 3 Defections," *New York Times*, November 7, 1985, pp. A1, A12; Stephen Engelberg, "Washington Ponders Yurchenko: A Troubled Spy or Actor?" *New York Times*, November 10, 1985, p. 20; Bob Woodward, "CIA Takes Serious Look at Theory That Yurchenko Was Double Agent," *Washington Post*, November 20, 1985, p. A35; Stephen Engelberg, "U.S. Aides Split on Yurchenko's Authenticity," *New York Times*, November 8, 1985, p. A10.

28. John Mintz, "FBI Chief Doubts Defection of Yurchenko Was Staged," *Washington Post*, December 2, 1985, pp. A1, A14; Joel Brinkley, "Publicity Said to Have Upset Defector," *New York Times*, November 14, 1985, p. A12; Christopher Wren, "K.G.B. Man Reportedly Met with Envoy's Wife," *New York Times*, November 9, 1985, p. 4; Arkady N. Shevchenko, "A Lesson of the Yurchenko Affair," *New York Times*, November 12, 1985, p. 35; Dale Russakof, "In Yurchenko Case, Truth Remains a Covert Factor," *Washington Post*, November 10, 1985, pp. A1, A40–41.

29. "Gates Call '85 Defector Bona Fide," *Washington Post*, January 16, 1993, p. A7.

30. Central Intelligence Agency, *Israel: Foreign Intelligence and Security Services* (Washington, D.C.: CIA, March 1977).

31. Central Intelligence Agency, *Soviet Intelligence: KGB and GRU* (Washington, D.C.: CIA, 1984).

32. See Amy Knight, *Spies Without Cloaks: The KGB's Successors* (Princeton, N.J.: Princeton University Press, 1996); J. Michael Waller, *Secret Empire: The KGB in Russia Today* (Boulder, Colo.: Westview Press, 1994).

33. Central Intelligence Agency, *The Russian Security Services: Sorting Out the Pieces* (Washington, D.C.: CIA, September 1992).

34. Sean Boyne, "Inside Iraq's Security Network, Part One" *Jane's Intelligence Review*, July 1997, pp. 312–314.

35. Documents obtained under the Freedom of Information Act.

36. "Partners in Espionage," *Security Awareness Bulletin*, August 1984, pp. 1–8; Linda Melvern, David Hebditch, and Nick Anning, *Techno-Bandits: How the Soviets Are Stealing America's High-Tech Future* (Boston: Houghton Mifflin, 1984), p. 242; Affidavit of Allen M. Power, Federal Bureau of Investigation, submitted to State and Northern District of California, City and County of San Francisco, October 16, 1983, pp. 1–2; "For Love of Money and Adventure," *Time*, October 31, 1983, pp. 39–40; Howard Kurtz, "California Man Charged with Spying," *Washington Post*, October 18, 1983, pp. A1, A4; David Wise, "How Our Spy Spied Their Spy," *Los Angeles Times*, October 23, 1983, pp. 1, 6.

37. "Greece Charges Three as Spies After U.S. Tip," *Washington Post*, September 17, 1985, p. A29.

38. Bob Woodward and Dan Morgan, "Soviet Threat Toward Iran Overstated, Casey Concluded," *Washington Post*, January 13, 1987, pp. A1, A8.

39. Henry Hurt, *Shadrin: The Spy Who Never Came Back* (New York: McGraw-Hill, 1981), p. 52.

40. Ibid., pp. 52–82; 140–151.

41. Ibid., pp. 120–151.

42. Ibid., p. 206; Patrick E. Tyler, "Missing U.S. Agent Dead," *Washington Post*, October 30, 1985, p. A9.

43. AR 381–47, "U.S. Army Offensive Counterintelligence Operations," May 15, 1982, p. 7.

44. Richard Halloran, "Overtures to Soldiers to Spy for Soviet Bloc Said to Rise," *New York Times*, June 29, 1985, pp. A1, B5.

45. "Former Counterspy for Army Is Indicted on Subversion Charges," *New York Times*, April 10, 1984, p. A20.

46. Ibid.

47. Ibid.

16

COVERT ACTION

Traditionally, covert action involves activities designed to influence foreign governments, events, organizations, or persons in support of U.S. foreign policy in such a way that the involvement of the U.S. government is not apparent. During the Reagan and Bush administrations, the practice of the "overt-covert operation" emerged—the clearest examples being the attempt to overthrow the Sandinista government and the support provided to the Afghan resistance.

During the course of the Cold War U.S. covert operations included: (1) political advice and counsel; (2) subsidies to individuals; (3) financial support and technical assistance to political parties or groups; (4) support to private organizations, including labor unions and business firms; (5) covert propaganda; (6) training of individuals; (7) economic operations; and (8) paramilitary or political action operations designed to overthrow or support a regime; and, up until the mid-1960s, (9) attempted assassination.[1]

Many of those activities, such as paramilitary or political action operations, have had high visibility and have been designed to achieve a specific objective— for example, the overthrow of a regime or the defeat of an insurgent force. Many behind-the-scenes political support and propaganda activities have also been designed to achieve a specific objective, such as the electoral defeat or victory of a political candidate or party. Other low-visibility operations involving propaganda or aid to individuals or organizations have been less directed toward achieving a specific objective in the near term than toward the enhancement of long-term U.S. objectives and the countering of similar Soviet activities. A high-visibility operation might also be conducted without expectation of "success." When the United States began aiding the Afghan rebels, for example, there was no expectation of actually inducing Soviet withdrawal, only of draining Soviet resources and keeping international attention on the Soviet role in Afghanistan.

Thus, beginning in 1946, and extending for various periods of time, the United States, principally through the Central Intelligence Agency, engaged in a wide variety of covert action operations. These included support to political parties and labor unions in France and Italy; support to resistance groups in the Soviet Union;

masterminding the overthrow of the Guatemalan and Iranian governments; a full-scale covert action campaign (including attempted assassination) directed against the Cuban regime of Fidel Castro; political action in an attempt to prevent Salvador Allende from becoming president of Chile and then to remove him once he attained that position; propaganda operations directed against the Soviet SS-20 deployments in Europe and against the Sandinista regime; paramilitary operations in Afghanistan and Nicaragua; and political support operations in El Salvador and Panama.[2]

COVERT ACTION IN THE POST–COLD WAR ERA

The collapse of the Soviet Union and its Eastern European satellites is only one of several factors that have reshaped the nature of post–Cold War covert action operations. One consequence of the Soviet collapse was the end of a worldwide ideological conflict—a conflict that led to covert support of publications in Western Europe and elsewhere that advanced Western democratic values and sought to undermine the propaganda of the Soviet Union and other Marxist entities. In contrast, no similar worldwide *ideological* conflict is being waged between the United States and its allies on one side and Iran, Iraq, North Korea, and Libya on the other, although a clash of civilizations has been posited.[3]

In addition, activities such as the support of political parties or broadcasting that would have been conducted as covert operations are now, often, done overtly. Thus, the National Endowment for Democracy provided support to Nicaraguan political parties who ran against the Sandinistas in the 1990 election. A September 22, 1989, National Security Directive declared that "the Department of State shall undertake a vigorous *overt* program to support a free and fair election process. Every effort will be made, consistent with U.S. law, to assist the democratic opposition to compete effectively with the Sandinista regime." Further, the directive specified that "there shall be *no covert* assistance to political or other groups in Nicaragua in the upcoming election campaign."[4]

In 1995, the Agency for International Development began providing funds, which totaled $26 million by May 1998, to Indonesian human rights and free speech groups, including the Indonesia Legal Aid Society, headed by a leading figure in the Indonesian democracy movement. Altogether AID provided funds to thirty nongovernmental organizations in Indonesia.[5]

Likewise, some of the broadcast operations, such as Radio Free Asia and Radio Free Iran (approved by Congress in 1997), are openly acknowledged and funded rather than being conducted as covert operations.[6]

The emergence of a number of rogue states that previously might have been restrained by the Soviet Union has also had an impact. Whereas undermining them politically at home is one objective of U.S. covert action policy, an equally or more critical concern may be impeding the acquisition of technologies that facilitate the production of weapons of mass destruction (WMD) or even destroying facilities that are employed to produce such weapons.

Third, there are three major transnational targets—proliferation of weapons of mass destruction, terrorism, and international narcotics trafficking—that can be distributed across the world and were of lesser concern during most of the Cold War. Thus, proliferation can involve the acquisition of technologies and information from Europe, their transportation (by physical or electronic means) to the acquiring nation, and, finally, the exploitation of the technologies to produce weapons of mass destruction. Likewise, terrorism may be planned and practiced in Lebanon or Syria, funded through Switzerland, and carried out in London, Paris, or New York. Finally, narcotics trafficking involves leadership, production facilities, transportation, transit points, and delivery to a variety of nations. In each case there are a number of points that operations can be directed at, and a number of techniques that can be employed, in an attempt to disrupt or neutralize such operations.

There are several other additional aspects to post–Cold War covert action operations. The greater prevalence of underground targets—established to avoid overhead surveillance as well as protect the facility from attack—adds a new dimension to any paramilitary operation that seeks to destroy such targets. In addition, new means may be available for covert operators to employ. Among the most prominent new techniques is information warfare, which can be employed to deprive hostile parties of the financial resources needed to perform terrorist acts or acquire WMD technologies.[7]

The changes in both targets and techniques available means that organizations equipped to perform covert action operations extend beyond the CIA. Information warfare operations are carried out by the NSA and by the three service information warfare organizations. In addition, the United States Special Operations Command and its subsidiary organizations (discussed in Chapter 5) can also play a significant, indeed primary, role in operations designed to neutralize WMD or narcotics production facilities.

IRAN

The NSC-directed covert operation that ended in the Iran-Contra affair was highly publicized, but other covert operations—directed by the CIA—were not. CIA operations during the Reagan and Bush years were designed to aid Iranian paramilitary and political exile groups, counter Soviet influence in Iran, and give the United States a role of its own in the event that the Khomeini regime fell. The initial goal was to knit together a coalition of exile groups and their supporters still in Iran so that if the opportunity arose they could be a significant factor in shaping the future of Iran.[8]

The covert action included providing several million dollars to units composed largely of Iranian exiles in eastern Turkey. The larger of the paramilitary groups had 6,000 to 8,000 men under the command of former Rear Admiral Ahmad Madani, the commander of the Iranian navy under the Shah, who was court-martialed for "being against the government." Madani was the first defense minister in the Khomeini regime. The second unit, which consisted of less than 2,000 men, was commanded by General Bahram Aryana, chief of staff of the Iranian army under the Shah. The paramilitary groups were intended to perform two functions. In the event of a Soviet invasion of Iran they could harass the flanks of the Soviet armed forces, and in the event of a civil war or domestic upheaval they would be able to enter Iran to protect and bolster any centrist forces.[9]

The CIA was also reported to be financing Iranian exile groups said to be situated principally in France and Egypt. Support was made available to groups both on the Left (up to but not including Bani-Sadr) and the Right (up to but not including the monarchist factions).[10]

The CIA established and financed a radio station in Egypt to broadcast anti-Khomeini information. In 1987, regular features included reports on long food lines, pockets of opposition and small uprisings against the clergy and revolutionary guards, torture and killings by the government, and gains made by Iranian Communists and agents of the Soviet Union. In September 1986, the CIA provided a miniaturized suitcase television transmitter for a clandestine broadcast to Iran by the Shah's son. The broadcast disrupted two channels of Iranian television for 11 minutes at 9 P.M. on September 5.[11]

In addition, the CIA supplied information to Iraq to aid the country in its war with Iran. The CIA secretly supplied Iraq with detailed intelligence to assist with Iraqi bombing raids on Iran's oil terminals and power plants. In 1984, when some feared that Iran might overrun Iraq, the United States began supplying Iraq with intelligence that reportedly enabled Iraq to calibrate mustard gas attacks on Iranian ground troops.[12]

In early 1985, Iraq began receiving regular satellite information from Washington, particularly after Iraqi bombing raids. It is not clear whether the Iraqis were receiving actual photos or information derived from the photos at that point.[13]

In any case, in August 1986 the CIA established a direct, top secret, Washington-Baghdad link to provide the Iraqis with better and more timely satellite intelligence. The Iraqis would thus receive information from satellite photos "several hours" after a bombing raid in order to assess damage and plan the next attack. By December 1986 the Iraqis were receiving selected portions of the actual photos taken by KH-11 and SR-71 overhead platforms. According to one account, some of the information or images provided were incomplete or doctored—inflating the size of the Soviet troop strength on the Iranian border—in order to further the Reagan administration's goals.[14]

IRAQ

The August 2, 1990, the Iraqi invasion of Kuwait brought to an unsuccessful conclusion attempts by the Reagan and Bush administrations to transform the nature of Saddam Hussein's regime. Before, during, and after Operation Desert Storm, the United States sought to partially fulfill its goals in Iraq through covert action.

Shortly after the Iraqi invasion, the CIA began training Kuwaitis in Saudi Arabia with the objective of increasing the scope and effectiveness of resistance attacks on Iraqi forces, including attacks on military convoys and the killing of sentries at key installations.[15]

Also receiving CIA support was the Iraqi National Accord (INA/Wifaq), based in Jordan. Its 80–100 members included several prominent Iraqi army officers and former officials of Saddam's government. The key figures in establishing the INA were Salah Omar Ali Tikriti—a former member of Iraq's ruling Baathist Party, who had once been Iraq's information minister but split with Saddam when Iraq invaded Kuwait—and former military intelligence chief Ayad Alawi, who had left Iraq in 1971.[16]

It was reported that George Bush signed three Presidential Findings in January 1991 with respect to Iraq. One authorized CIA-sponsored propaganda and deception operations. A second allowed the CIA to work with Army Special Forces to resupply and support resistance forces in Kuwait. The third gave the CIA authority to aid rebel factions inside Iraq in an attempt to destabilize Hussein's government.[17]

With U.S. encouragement, the INA established the *Voice of Free Iraq*, which began broadcasting in January 1991. The station, located on the outskirts of Jedda, was managed by forty Iraqi expatriates and protected by armed Saudi guards. Broadcasting on four frequencies, it called for the withdrawal of Iraqi forces from Kuwait, the overthrow of Hussein, and the creation of a democratic Iraqi state.[18]

The station continued to operate after the conclusion of Desert Storm. During March 1991 it called on Iraqi army officers to "champion your people's uprising" and counseled rebels to form a unified military command "to swoop in on the regime of the Saddam Hussein gang and destroy it."[19]

In May 1991, President Bush signed a new Presidential Finding on Iraq. The finding did not include support for an attempt to initiate an Afghan-style covert action to inflict major losses on the Republican Guard and help split the rest of the military from Saddam, for fear of rupturing the international coalition. The finding did authorize support for three options—encouraging Kurdish groups to trigger a "rolling coup" that moved southward from territory under their control; employing economic sanctions to create the atmosphere in Iraq that could lead to a "silver bullet" assassination by a lone security official or family member; or promoting a palace coup against Saddam and aides by disgruntled Republican Guards or Iraqi security units.[20]

In late 1991 a Presidential Finding authorized CIA contacts with Iraqi military leaders and opposition groups in an attempt to organize a successful coup that would unseat Hussein. The finding also provided for increased funding for propaganda broadcasts into Iraq and authorized $30 million for this purpose from a special contingency fund.[21]

By March 1992 the CIA had launched an operation to undermine the Iraqi economy by flooding Iraq with counterfeit money. The CIA systematically dumped large amounts of forged dinars—of two relatively low denominations that circulated extensively. The forged currency was apparently smuggled into Iraq from Jordan, Iran, and Turkey by agents and unwitting merchants. The fake currency further contributed to Iraq's severe inflation problem.[22]

In late May or early June 1992, the House Permanent Select Committee approved $40 million in funding to help overthrow Hussein. The money was intended to expand and strengthen a number of opposition groups and individuals inside Iraq. The money was also intended to finance opposition groups outside Iraq, increase an anti-Hussein propaganda program carried out through clandestine radio stations, allow publication of leaflets and other printed propaganda, and finance the spreading of disinformation inside Iraq.[23]

The key group to be funded was the Iraqi National Congress (INC) whose formation was announced in Vienna in June 1992, by which time the INA had become less potent, due to the split between its two founders. The INC was formed as an umbrella group in attempt to bring together several elements of the Iraqi opposition, including two rival Kurdish groups based in northern Iraq—Massoud Barzani's Kurdish Democratic Party (KDP) and Jalal Talabani's Patriotic Union of Kurdistan (PUK). Also joining the umbrella group was the Amman-based Iraqi National Accord. Initial holdouts, Shiite groups joined after President Bush expanded the no-fly zone in southern Iraq.[24]

The INC proceeded to set up television and radio stations to broadcast anti-Saddam propaganda into Baghdad, published miniaturized versions of anti-Saddam books, and occasionally sent CIA-provided unmanned aerial vehicles over Iraqi cities to drop propaganda leaflets. Each of the Kurdish groups also used the CIA funds to establish separate militia. In 1994 the INC published a fake issue of *Babil*, the daily newspaper owned by Saddam's son, Uday. Distributed in Baghdad, it revealed a number of Saddam's atrocities. However, the operation backfired. Rather, than fueling opposition to Saddam, the information on the atrocities only increased the population's fear of the Iraqi dictator.[25]

In the fall of 1994 the CIA established a base near the Turkish border, manned by agency officers and members of the Army Special Forces, to monitor INC operations. Teams of four to ten agents each lived there for an average of six weeks, with the formal mission of monitoring the INC and gathering intelligence. However, they also began providing military training and light weaponry to the INC at their own initiative, and they were not instructed to stop doing so by CIA headquarters.[26]

According to one of the CIA officers stationed in northern Iraq, the initial intent of the operation was to reduce Saddam's control over Iraq to the point where he was "nothing more than the mayor of Baghdad." That objective was to be achieved by "hollowing out" the Iraqi army and establishing a political and administrative structure in the north.[27]

That strategy was apparently succeeded by one, emanating from higher authorities, that called for an attempt to quickly end Saddam's reign. A target date of March 4, 1995, was established for a coordinated strike on the Iraqi garrisons at Mosul and Kirkuk. The attacking forces were to include 20,000 Kurdish guerrillas, 1,000 soldiers from the INC, and 1,000 armed followers of the Iraqi Communist Party, according to a former chief of Iraqi military intelligence who defected. The expectation was that Saddam, after going on full alert, would discover that his troops would not fight for him.[28]

However, on March 3, a CIA officer informed the prospective attackers that the group had been penetrated by Saddam's security forces, that the operation risked failure, and that there would be no U.S. involvement or support—in particular, there would be no air cover as promised by the plan's originator. The information split the Kurdish forces and led to the withdrawal of Barzani's KDP forces. The forces of Talabani's PUK attacked two Iraqi divisions and captured 700 men, but the offensive fizzled.[29]

In August 1995, the defection of two of Saddam's sons-in-law, including Hussein Kamel, chief of weapons procurement, convinced the CIA that Saddam was growing weaker. As a result the CIA shifted a portion of its Iraq covert action resources to the Iraqi National Accord, which had been advertising itself as a potential architect of a quick and clean decapitation of the top Iraqi leadership.[30]

In January 1996, President Clinton signed a finding expanding the covert action campaign. The finding authorized the CIA to provide weapons, to organize some military training, and to install intelligence gathering equipment in support of groups trying to unseat Hussein. It also authorized acts of sabotage within Iraq.[31]

The coup plotting directed by the INA failed to produce the desired results. In June 1996, Saddam's security forces arrested more than 100 officers and security men who had been plotting to overthrow his regime. His security forces had apparently penetrated the group by watching or capturing some of the key couriers between INA headquarters in Amman and its recruits in Baghdad.[32]

Disaster struck again in late August. This time the target was the INC operation based in northern Iraq. The defection of Barzani's KDP from the anti-Saddam forces to an alignment with Saddam, which may have taken place substantially earlier, allowed the Iraqi army to roll into Erbil, where the INC and CIA base was located. The CIA officers were forced to flee, leaving behind a TV-radio station that had broadcast anti-Saddam propaganda into Iraq for eleven hours each day. Also left behind were 1,500 members of the Iraqi National Congress and 100 employees of the radio station.[33]

Iraqi security forces proceeded to loot the INC headquarters, seizing high-tech communications equipment and computers. They also executed more than 100 members of the INC. Also, only twelve of the radio station's employees survived.[34]

Subsequently plans for both covert and overt political action to undermine Saddam were proposed. A CIA plan, which had not been approved at the time it was reported, called for recruiting Kurdish and Shiite agents to destroy or damage key components of Iraqi economic and political power, such as utility plants or government broadcast facilities. It also called for increasing political pressure on Iraq via propaganda programs such as Radio Free Iraq. The ultimate objective of the plan is to undermine Saddam by demonstrating that he is not invincible, strengthening the internal opposition and igniting a rebellion inside the Iraqi dictator's inner circle.[35]

In addition a group of Republican Senators voted to add a $38 million package of programs that was also intended to undermine Saddam. In addition to $5 million to fund Radio Free Iraq, the funds would be used for humanitarian aid for areas in northern and southern Iraq where the regime does not exercise control ($20 million), for political support to the democratic opposition ($10 million for leadership training and for the revival of cooperation between the different groups), and for an attempt to get the U.N. to approve an international criminal tribunal for "indicting, prosecuting and punishing Saddam Hussein and other Iraqi officials responsible for crimes against humanity."[36]

Subsequently, the House of Representatives authorized an even greater expenditure—$97 million—for direct aid to Iraqi dissident groups, including military equipment and training. The House also approved $2 million for radio and television broadcasts designed to undermine the Iraqi regime. The goal is to create an opposition army that would capture lightly defended areas in southern and western Iraq, encourage large-scale defections from the Iraqi army, and finally topple Saddam's government. Although the legislation—*Iraqi Liberation Act of 1998*—was also approved by the Senate it may never be implemented as a result of Clinton administration opposition—due to concerns over the chances of success as well as the drain it would create on U.S. weapons stocks.[37]

LIBYA

In addition to authorizing an NSC disinformation operation, Ronald Reagan authorized a CIA covert operation to undermine the Libyan regime. The plan involved CIA assistance to other countries in North Africa and the Middle East that opposed Mu'ammar Qaddafi. Authorized in a fall 1985 Presidential Finding, the program's first objective was to disrupt, preempt, and frustrate Qaddafi's subversive and terrorist plans. Beyond that, the CIA hoped to lure him into some foreign adventure or terrorist exploit that would give a growing number of Qaddafi opponents in the Libyan military a chance to seize power or justify a military response by Algeria or Egypt.[38]

Another CIA operation, code-named TULIP, involved support for anti-Qaddafi exile movements, including the National Front for the Salvation of Libya, and for the efforts of other countries such as Egypt.[39]

In 1988 the CIA began an operation to destabilize Qaddafi's regime via U.S.-trained Libyan commandos. The program, which began in the final months of the Reagan administration, provided military aid and training to 600 former Libyan soldiers at a base outside the Chadian capital of Ndjamena. The Libyan force consisted of soldiers who had been captured in 1988 border fighting between Libya and Chad. The commandos never actually launched a serious military operation. After the Chad government fell in December 1990, the force was moved to Zaire and then to Kenya. The commandos were disarmed before leaving Chad and subsequently permanently disbanded.[40]

MEXICO AND PERU

The CIA is involved in training both the Mexican and Peruvian military as part of the U.S. counternarcotics strategy. The U.S. Army has been providing training to over 1,000 Mexican military officers in an effort to establish an elite counternarcotics unit. The CIA has been giving extensive intelligence support to a group of about ninety Mexican officers, who will be part of the Center for Anti-Narcotics Investigation. The support includes intelligence, training, and equipment.[41]

The intelligence provided is, however, carefully scrubbed, because of the mistrust that exists as a result of the linkages between senior Mexican officials and international narcotics traffickers. One U.S. official told the *Washington Post* that "While intelligence sharing is significant there is no free flow . . . We send information that has been scrubbed, that safeguards our interests."[42]

In Peru, thirty American military instructors are reportedly involved in one of the most ambitious anti-drug programs the Defense Department has undertaken in Latin America. The trainers are drawn from the SEALs, Army Special Forces, Marines, and Coast Guard. They are training and equipping a Peruvian counter-drug unit that would operate on water and land, with the objective of cutting off the flow of cocaine from Peru to Colombia via the Amazon. The CIA will provide the Peruvian trainees—selected from the country's navy, marines, and anti-drug police—with specialized intelligence training.[43]

TRANSNATIONAL TARGETS/MULTINATIONAL TARGETS

As noted above transnational activities, such as proliferation, terrorism, and narcotics trafficking represent a far more important target of covert action than during the Cold War. As one account noted, "Major covert actions are now being aimed at disrupting terrorist plans, stopping narcotics shipments or fouling up financial transaction of missile makers."[44] In addition, certain operations may be directed simultaneously at a number of nations.

At least three types of operations have been identified against transnational/multinational targets:

- computer warfare has been employed to disrupt terrorist plans, stop narcotics shipments, or interfere with the financial transactions of missile producers
- the military R&D operations of governments such as North Korea, Iraq, and Iran have been sabotaged by having European, Asian, and other suppliers sell them faulty parts that will eventually fail
- exports and imports to and from Libya and Iraq have been spiked with extraneous matter—such as putting water in oil—to create dissatisfaction with consumers[45]

Notes

1. "The Bissell Philosophy," appendix to Victor Marchetti and John Marks, *The CIA and the Cult of Intelligence* (New York: Knopf, 1974), p. 387; U.S. Congress, Senate Select Committee to Study Governmental Operations with Respect to Intelligence Activities, *Alleged Assassination Plots Involving Foreign Leaders* (Washington, D.C.: U.S. Government Printing Office, 1976).

2. For histories of U.S. covert action, see Roy Godson, *Dirty Tricks or Trump Cards: U.S. Covert Action and Counterintelligence* (Washington, D.C.: Brassey's, 1995); John Prados, *Presidents' Secret Wars: CIA and Pentagon Covert Operations from World War II Through the Persian Gulf War* (Chicago: Elephant Paperbacks, 1996); Gregory F. Treverton, *Covert Action: The Limits of Intervention in the Postwar World* (New York: Basic Books, 1987).

3. Samuel P. Huntington, *The Clash of Civilizations and the Remaking of World Order* (New York: Simon & Schuster/Touchstone, 1997).

4. George Bush, National Security Directive 25, "U.S. Policy Toward the February 1990 Nicaragua Election," September 22, 1989; It should be noted that a Secret Annex to NSD 25, "[deleted] NSD–25 on U.S. Policy Towards the February 1990 Nicaraguan Election," was issued on the same day as NSD 25.

5. Tim Weiner, "U.S. Has Spent $26 Million Since '95 on Suharto Opponents," *New York Times*, May 20, 1998, p. A11.

6. U.S. Congress, Senate Committee on Foreign Relations, *Broadcasting to China: Applying the Lessons from European Freedom Radios* (Washington, D.C.: U.S. Government Printing Office, 1992); U.S. Congress, Senate Committee on Foreign Relations, *The Radio Free China Act, S. 2985* (Washington, D.C.: U.S. Government Printing Office, 1992); Kennon H. Nakamura and Susan B. Epstein, *Radio Free Asia* (Washington, D.C.: Congressional Research Service, June 3, 1994); Elaine Sciolino, "Pleased Yet Wary, U.S. Offers Gestures of Support for Iran," *New York Times*, March 26, 1998, pp. A1, A10; Elaine Sciolino, "White House Agrees to Radio Broadcasts to Iran," *New York Times*, April 15, 1998, p. A3.

7. Walter Pincus, "CIA Turns to Boutique Operations, Covert Action Against Terrorism, Drugs, Arms," *Washington Post*, September 14, 1997, p. A6; Craig Covault, "Cyber Threat Challenges Intelligence Capability," *Aviation Week & Space Technology*, February 10, 1997, pp. 20–21.

8. Leslie H. Gelb, "U.S. Said to Aid Iranian Exiles in Combat and Political Units," *New York Times*, March 7, 1982, pp. 1, 12.

9. Ibid.

10. Ibid.

11. Ibid.; Bob Woodward, "CIA Curried Favor with Khomeini Exiles," *Washington Post*, November 19, 1986, pp. A1, A28.

12. Bob Woodward, "CIA Aiding Iraq in Gulf War," *Washington Post*, December 15, 1986, pp. A1, A18–A19.

13. Ibid.

14. Ibid.; Stephen Engelberg, "Iran and Iraq Got 'Doctored' Data, U.S. Officials Say," *New York Times*, January 12, 1987, pp. A1, A16.

15. Nick B. Williams Jr. and Robin Wright, "CIA Training Kuwait to Harass Iraqis," *Los Angeles Times*, August 31, 1990, pp. A1, A8.

16. Kevin Fedarko, "Saddam's CIA Coup," *Time*, September 23, 1996, pp. 42–44; R. Jef-

frey Smith and David B. Ottaway, "Anti-Saddam Operation Cost CIA $100 Million," *Washington Post*, September 15, 1996, pp. A29–A30.

17. Paul Bedard and Warren Strobel, "Bush Again Urges Ouster of Saddam," *Washington Times*, April 4, 1991, pp. A1, A10; Michael Wines, "C.I.A. Joins Military Move to Sap Iraqi Confidence," *New York Times*, January 19, 1991, p. 7.

18. Wines, "C.I.A. Joins Military Move to Sap Iraqi Confidence"; Barton Gellman, "Kurds Contend U.S. Encouraged Rebellion Via 'Voice of Free Iraq,'" *Washington Post*, April 9, 1991, p. A17; Michael Wines, "Kurd Gives Account of Broadcasts to Iraq Linked to the C.I.A.," *New York Times*, April 6, 1991, pp. 1, 5; Elaine Sciolino, "Radio Linked to C.I.A. Urges Iraqis to Overthrow Hussein," *New York Times*, April 16, 1991, p. A9.

19. Gellman, "Kurds Contend U.S. Encouraged Rebellion Via 'Voice of Free Iraq.'"

20. Smith and Ottaway, "Anti-Saddam Operation Cost CIA $100 Million."

21. Patrick E. Tyler, "Saudis Press U.S. for Help in Ouster for Iraq's Leader," *New York Times*, January 19, 1992, pp. 1, 10; Patrick E. Tyler, "Plan on Iraq Coup Told to Congress," *New York Times*, February 9, 1992, pp. 1, 16; John M. Broder and Robin Wright, "CIA Authorized to Target Hussein," *Los Angeles Times*, February 8, 1992, pp. A1, A11.

22. Christy Campbell and Adrian Porter, "U.S. Carrier Moves Toward Iraq Targets," *Washington Times*, March 16, 1992, pp. A1, A6; Youssef M. Ibrahim, "Fake-Money Flood Is Aimed at Crippling Iraq's Economy," *New York Times*, May 27, 1992, pp. A1, A6.

23. Elaine Sciolino, "Greater U.S. Effort Backed to Oust Iraq," *New York Times*, June 2, 1992 p. A3.

24. Smith and Ottaway, "Anti-Saddam Operation Cost CIA $100 Million"; Christopher Dickey and Gregory L. Vistica, "Mission Impossible," *Newsweek*, September 23, 1996, pp. 38–39.

25. Smith and Ottaway, "Anti-Saddam Operation Cost CIA $100 Million"; Fedarko, "Saddam's CIA Coup."

26. Dickey and Vistica, "Mission Impossible"; Jim Hoagland, "How CIA's Secret War on Saddam Collapsed," *Washington Post*, June 26, 1997, pp. A1, A21.

27. Hoagland, "How CIA's Secret War on Saddam Collapsed."

28. Ibid.

29. Ibid.; Dickey and Vistica, "Mission Impossible."

30. Smith and Ottaway, "Anti-Saddam Operation Cost CIA $100 Million.

31. Tim Weiner, "Iraqi Offensive into Kurdish Zone Disrupts U.S. Plot to Oust Hussein," *New York Times*, September 7, 1996, pp. 1, 6; Smith and Ottaway, "Anti-Saddam Operation Cost CIA $100 Million."

32. Smith and Ottaway, "Anti-Saddam Operation Cost CIA $100 Million"; Dickey and Vistica, "Mission Impossible."

33. Fedarko, "Saddam's CIA Coup."

34. Ibid.; R. Jeffrey Smith, "CIA Operation Fell with Iraqi City," *Washington Post*, September 8, 1996, pp. A1, A28.

35. Tim Weiner, "C.I.A. Drafts Covert Plan to Topple Hussein," *New York Times*, February 26, 1998, p. A11.

36. Walter Pincus, "Senators Urge Undermining of Saddam," *Washington Post*, March 11, 1998, p. A6.

37. Sean Scully, "House Strongly Backs Anti-Saddam Activities," *Washington Times*, October 6, 1998, p. A4; Vernon Loeb, "Congress Stokes Visions of War to Oust Saddam," *Washington Post*, October 29, 1998, pp. A1, A6.

38. Bob Woodward, "CIA Anti-Qaddafi Plan Backed," *Washington Post*, November 3, 1985, pp. A1, A19.

39. Bob Woodward, *Veil: The Secret Wars of the CIA, 1981–1987* (New York: Simon & Schuster, 1987), p. 411.

40. Clifford Krauss, "Failed Anti-Qaddafi Effort Leaves U.S. Picking up the Pieces," *New York Times*, March 12, 1991, p. A15; "Have Rebels, Will Travel," *Newsweek*, March 26, 1991, p. 43.

41. Tim Golden, "U.S. Helps Mexico's Army Take a Big Anti-Drug Role," *New York Times*, December 29, 1997, pp. A1, A10; Douglas Farah and Dana Priest, "Mexican Drug Lord is U.S.-Bred," *Washington Post*, February 26, 1998, pp. A1, A20.

42. Farah and Priest, "Mexican Drug Lord is U.S.-Bred"; Bill Gertz, "CIA Links Mexico's Interior Minister to Drug Lords," *Washington Times*, February 5, 1998, pp. A1, A16; Douglas Farah and Molly Moore, "2,000 Miles of Disarray in Drug War," *Washington Post*, March 9, 1998, pp. A1, A15.

43. Douglas Farah, "Pentagon Helps Peru Fight Drugs," *Washington Post*, April 22, 1998, pp. A1, A18.

44. Pincus, "CIA Turns to Boutique Operations, Covert Action Against Terrorism, Drugs, Arms."

45. Ibid.

U.S. Satellite photgraph of Shifa Pharmceutical Plant, Sudan. This degraced photo was released after the U.S. attack in August 1998 on the plant in retaliation for attacks on two U.S. embassies in Africa. Photo Credit: U.S. Department of Defense.

Defense Communications Electronics Evaluation and Testing Activity at Fort Belvoir, Virginia, the U.S. receiving station for KH-11 and advanced KH-11 imagery. Photo Credit: Robert Windrem.

The U-2 reconnaissance aircraft. U-2s first began operating in 1956 and are still in service, performing both imagery and SIGINT missions. Photo Credit: Lockheed.

The GLOBAL HAWK UAV is expected to carry electro-optical, infrared, and synthetic aperture sensors. It will be capable of operating up to 3,000 nautical miles from its launch point and staying on station for twenty-four hours. Photo Credit: Teledyne Ryan Aeronautical.

With the end of the Cold War, P-3 aircraft have been used not only for ocean surveillance missions but for overland imagery collection. Photo Credit: Lockheed.

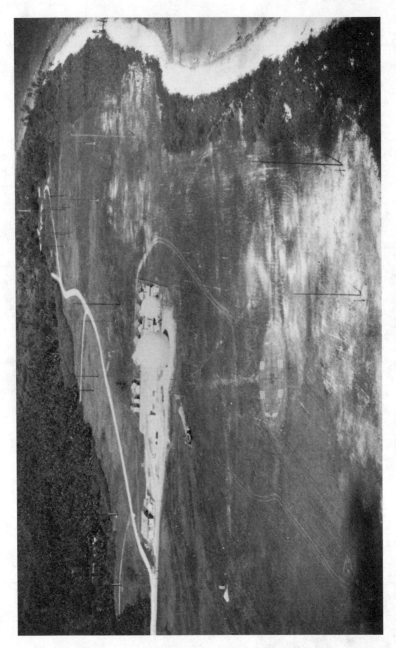

Diego Garcia, British Indian Ocean Territory, hosts a contingent from the Naval Security Group Command. They operate a ground station in the CLASSIC WIZARD satellite system as well as land-based intercept equipment. Photo Credit: Bob Windrem.

Menwith Hill has served as the ground station for the VORTEX SIGINT satellite and is now the ground station for a new SIGINT satellite program. Photo Credit: Duncan Campbell.

Joint Defense Space Research Facility at Alice Springs, Australia (Pine Gap), the ground control station for RHYOLITE and ORION satellites. Photo Credit: Desmond Ball.

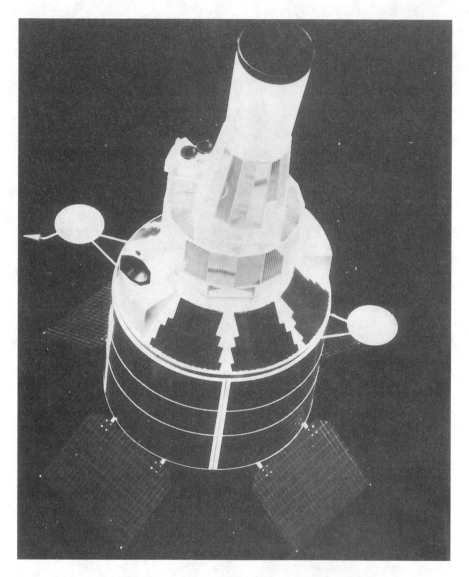

An artist's drawing of the Defense Support Program satellite. Although the primary function of DSP satellites is the detection of foreign missile launches, they also provide data used in the production of measurement and signature intelligence (MASINT). Photo Credit: U.S. Air Force.

COBRA DANE phased array radar, Shemya Island. COBRA DANE is used to track Russian missile warheads as they descend to earth during tests. Photo Credit: Raytheon.

The Teal Blue space surveillance site in Hawaii. Photo Credit: Bob Windrem.

The COBRA JUDY phased array radar on the USNS *Observation Island* has been used to monitor the end phase of Soviet and Russian ballistic missile tests. Photo Credit: Raytheon.

FIGURE 16.1   Some of the analytical products of the U.S. intelligence community.

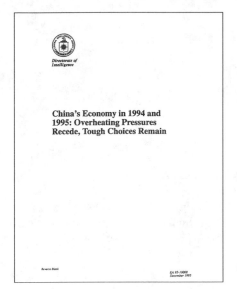

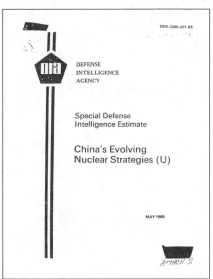

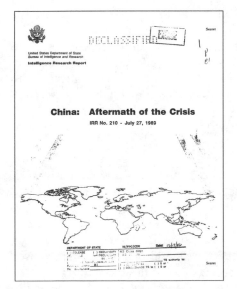

17

MANAGEMENT AND DIRECTION

Given the number of intelligence agencies, services, and offices, the conflicting and diverse supervisory executive departments, and the wide range of intelligence activities, it is clear that the U.S. intelligence community requires coordination and control to guide its work. Furthermore, the highly sensitive nature of some of its activities requires approval by high-level officials. Thus, it is not surprising that over the past fifty years an elaborate system of directives, committees, offices, plans, and programs have been established.

The system can be divided into three basic categories. Executive orders, presidential directives, NSC directives, departmental and agency regulations establish the basic mission and structure of the intelligence community and its components. Individuals, committees, and offices implement and formulate directives, seek to resolve conflicts, provide advice and counsel, and establish collection and analysis priorities. Finally, there are the plans, programs, and requirements documents that establish objectives or specify resource allocation for the attainment of specific collection or analysis tasks.

ORDERS, DIRECTIVES, AND REGULATIONS

The orders, directives, and regulations that guide the activities of the intelligence community all stem from documents issued by the president and the National Security Council (NSC). These documents represent the apex of the system and come in two varieties—unclassified executive orders and (often classified) presidential/NSC directives. The title of the second type of document changes with presidential administrations. Thus, Bill Clinton's Presidential Decision Directives (PDDs) were National Security Directives (NSDs) in the Bush administration, National Security Decision Directives (NSDDs) in the Reagan administration, Presidential Directives (PDs) in the Carter administration, National Security Decision Memoranda (NSDMs) in the Nixon and Ford administrations, and National Security Action Memoranda (NSAM) in the Kennedy and Johnson administrations.[1] Although new administrations often issue directives superseding the directives of

an earlier administration, it is also the case that the directives issued in one administration may remain in force in one or more succeeding administrations.

Executive orders governing the intelligence community were issued in the Ford,
Carter, and Reagan administrations. Although the orders reflected some different
concerns, they often overlapped with previous orders. Since no executive order on
intelligence was issued during the Bush administration or has been issued during
the Clinton administration, President Reagan's Executive Order 12333, "United
States Intelligence Activities" of December 4, 1981, is still operative. It is divided
into three parts: Goals, Direction, Duties, and Responsibilities with Respect to the
National Intelligence Effort; the Conduct of Intelligence Activities; and General
Provisions.[2] Part 1 authorizes the establishment of National Foreign Intelligence
Advisory Groups, specifies the agencies and offices that constitute the intelligence
community, defines their general functions, and lists the duties and responsibilities
of the senior officials of the community.

Part 2, on the conduct of intelligence activities, establishes procedures and
restrictions concerning the collection of information abroad and in the United
States concerning U.S. persons. It also establishes (or continues) procedures concerning the assistance to law enforcement authorities and human experimentation, and it prohibits U.S. involvement in assassinations. Part 3 deals with congressional oversight, implementation, and definitions.

Changes in the content of the executive orders have been the product of three
factors: different modes of NSC organization, revelations concerning abuses by
the intelligence community, and differing attitudes concerning domestic intelligence activities. Thus, Gerald Ford's executive order, "United States Foreign Intelligence Activities," of February 18, 1976, imposed restrictions on physical and
electronic surveillance activities, experimentation, and assistance to law enforcement authorities in response to the 1974–1975 revelations concerning various
CIA, FBI, and NSA activities. It also specified for the first time that "no employee
of the United States Government shall engage in, or conspire to engage in, political assassination."[3]

The Carter executive order was primarily concerned with restrictions and oversight. The Reagan executive order loosened some of those restrictions, allowing
the collection of "significant foreign intelligence" within the United States by the
CIA so long as the collection effort was not undertaken for the purpose of acquiring information concerning the domestic activities of U.S. persons.[4]

In addition to an executive order governing the intelligence community, each
president has generally also issued an order concerning national security information. The orders have dealt with classification levels and authority, downgrading
and declassification, safeguards for classified information, and implementation of
their provisions. The most recent of these orders is President Clinton's Executive
Order 12958, "Classified National Security Information," of April 17, 1995. Included
among the order's provisions is the requirement that within five years of the order's
issuance all classified information in records more than twenty-five years of age and

determined to be of historical value be released, irrespective of whether the records have been reviewed—unless they are exempted by an agency head under one of nine specific exemptions. It also requires each agency that has originated classified information to establish a program for systematic declassification.[5]

The usually classified presidential directives on intelligence matters tend to deal with specific areas of intelligence operations—intelligence community organization and procedures, covert operations, and space reconnaissance, for example.

At least seven Reagan NSDDs concerned intelligence matters. NSDD-17 of January 4, 1982, "National Security Directive on Cuba and Central America," dealt with covert operations in that region. NSDD-19 of January 12, 1982, is entitled "Protection of Classified National Security Council and Intelligence Information," and NSDD-22 of January 29, 1982, concerned the "Designation of Intelligence Officials Authorized to Request FBI Collection of Foreign Intelligence." NSDD-42 of July 4, 1982, "National Space Policy," dealt, in part, with space reconnaissance. NSDD-84 of March 11, 1983, "Safeguarding National Security Information," specified new security review requirements for individuals permitted access to code word information. NSDD-159 of January 18, 1985, specified "Covert Action Policy Approval and Coordination Procedures"; NSDD-196 of November 1, 1985, concerned "Counterintelligence/Countermeasure Implementation Task Force"; NSDD-202, "Soviet Noncompliance with Arms Control Agreements," of December 20, 1985, dealt, in part, with the impact of a new methodology for assessing the yield of Soviet nuclear weapons tests; NSDD-204 of December 24, 1985, concerned "Transfer of National Intelligence Collection Tasking Authority"; and NSDD-286 dealt with covert action procedures.[6]

Bush administration National Security Directives concerning intelligence matters included a February 1989 NSD on support to the Afghan resistance; NSD-30 of November 2, 1989, on "National Space Policy"; an August 1990 NSD on covert action directed against Iraq; the October 5, 1990, NSD-47 on "Counterintelligence and Security Countermeasures"; NSD-63 of October 21, 1991, on "Single Scope Background Investigations"; and NSD-67 on intelligence priorities.[7]

The only two known Clinton Presidential Decision Directives to deal directly with intelligence matters are PDD-24 on "U.S. Counterintelligence Effectiveness," which was the product of an interagency review mandate by Presidential Review Directive-44, and PDD-35 on intelligence priorities.[8]

Both executive orders and presidential directives deal with subjects in fairly general terms and do not necessarily cover the full scope of intelligence activities. Guidance across much of the spectrum of intelligence activities comes in the form of National Security Council Intelligence Directives (NSCIDs).

NSCIDs offer guidance to the entire intelligence community, and the Director of Central Intelligence (DCI) in particular, concerning specific aspects of U.S. intelligence operations. The NSCID numbering system is unlike that for Presidential Decision Directives or their predecessors, which are numbered according to the sequence in which they are issued. In general, an NSCID number is assigned to a particular topic, and subsequent revisions of the NSCID bear the same number—although the topic assigned to a particular number may change over time, or one topic may be subsumed under another. NSCIDs were first issued in 1947 and have been updated numerous times since then. Sometimes revisions have been of selected documents; other times an entire group has been revised. As of 1987 the last major revision appears to have been completed on February 17, 1972, when updated versions of all eight NSCIDs were issued. The numbers and names of those NSCIDs are listed in Table 17.1. A 1970s project to establish a single omnibus NSCID was never completed.

NSCID No. 1, "Basic Duties and Responsibilities," was first issued in 1947 and subsequently updated in 1952, 1958, 1961, 1964, and 1972. The NSCID No. 1 of February 17, 1972, assigned four major responsibilities to the DCI:

1. planning, reviewing, and evaluating all intelligence activities and the allocation of all intelligence resources
2. producing national intelligence required by the President and national consumers
3. chairing and staffing all intelligence advisory boards
4. establishing and reconciling intelligence requirements and priorities with budgetary constraints[9]

NSCID No. 1 also (1) instructs the DCI to prepare and submit to the Office of Management and Budget (OMB) a consolidated budget, (2) authorizes the issuance of Director of Central Intelligence Directives as a means of implementing the NSCIDs, and (3) instructs the DCI to protect sources and methods.[10]

NSCID No. 2 of February 1972, makes the DCI responsible for planning how the overt collection and reporting capabilities of the various government departments will be utilized and makes the CIA responsible for conducting, as a service of common concern, radio broadcast monitoring. The Department of State is charged with overt collection of political, sociological, economic, scientific, and

TABLE 17.1   NSCIDs Issued on February 17, 1972

Number	Title
1	Basic Duties and Responsibilities
2	Coordination of Overt Activities
3	Coordination of Intelligence Production
4	The Defector Program
5	U.S. Espionage and Counterintelligence Activities Abroad
6	Signals Intelligence
7	Critical Intelligence Communications
8	Photographic Interpretation

technical information; military-pertinent scientific and technical intelligence; and economic intelligence.[11]

The 1972 version of NSCID No. 3 makes the Department of State responsible for the production of political and sociological intelligence on all countries and economic intelligence on the countries of the "Free World." It makes the Department of Defense (DOD) responsible for the production of military intelligence and scientific and technical intelligence pertinent to the missions of DOD components. The CIA is assigned responsibility for economic and scientific and technical intelligence plus "any other intelligence required by the CIA."[12] In practice, this clause has meant that the CIA is heavily involved in the production of political and military intelligence, especially strategic intelligence. In addition, atomic energy intelligence is decreed, by NSCID No. 3, to be the responsibility of all National Foreign Intelligence Board (NFIB) agencies.[13]

Originally, NSCID No. 4 concerned Priority National Intelligence Objectives (PNIOs)—a system for prioritizing collection efforts. The PNIO system has been eliminated; hence, NSCID No. 4 now bears the title "The Defector Program" and presumably concerns the inducement of defections and the responsibilities of the CIA and other agencies in the program.[14]

NSCID No. 5, "U.S. Espionage and Counterintelligence Activities Abroad" is the successor to versions issued in 1947, 1951, 1958, and 1961. The directive authorizes the DCI to "establish the procedures necessary to achieve such direction and coordination, including the assessment of risk incident upon such operations as compared to the value of the activity, and to ensure that sensitive operations are reviewed pursuant to applicable direction."[15]

NSCID No. 6, "Signals Intelligence," serves at the charter for the NSA. The February 1972 version was still in force as of 1987. It defines the nature of SIGINT activities and directs the Director of NSA (DIRNSA) to produce intelligence "in accordance with objectives, requirements and priorities established by the Director of Central Intelligence and the United States Intelligence Board." It further authorizes the DIRNSA "to issue direct to any operating elements engaged in SIGINT operations such instructions and assignments as are required. All instructions issued by the Director under the authority provided in this paragraph shall be mandatory, subject only to appeal to the Secretary of Defense."[16]

NSCID No. 7 establishes the Critical Intelligence Communications (CRITIC) system. This system governs procedures and criteria for the transmission of particularly important intelligence to top officials, including the president, within the shortest possible period of time. The information may concern an imminent coup, the assassination of a world leader, or, as in September 1983, the shooting down of a civilian airliner. The information acquired may be via HUMINT, SIGINT, or IMINT. It has been NSA's goal to have a CRITIC message on the president's desk within 10 minutes of the event.[17]

The original NSCID No. 8 was issued on May 25, 1948, and was entitled "Biographic Data on Foreign Scientific and Technological Personalities." Before the end of 1961, the NSCID dealt, instead, with "Photographic Interpretation." NSCID No. 8 of February 1972 continued the National Photographic Interpretation Center (NPIC) as a service of common concern to be provided by the DCI. Additionally, it specified that the Director of the NPIC is to be selected by the DCI with the concurrence of the Secretary of Defense.[18] Creation of the National Imagery and Mapping Agency presumably required the production of a new NSCID No. 8, although no information on the new version is available.

The NSCIDs state, in general terms, the responsibilities of the DCI and other components of the intelligence community. One provision of NSCID No. 1 authorizes the DCI to issue more detailed directives—Director of Central Intelligence Directives (DCIDs)—in pursuit of the implementation of the various NSCIDs. DCIDs are keyed to the NSCIDs from which they follow, according to the NSCID numbering system. Thus, DCID 1/3 is the third DCID issued pursuant to NSCID No. 1.*

DCIDs in the 1/ series about which information is available include DCIDs 1/2, 1/3, 1/5, 1/7, 1/8, 1/10, 1/11, 1/13, 1/14, 1/15, 1/16, 1/17, 1/18, 1/19, 1/21, and 1/22. DCID 1/2 of January 21, 1972, "U.S. Intelligence Requirements Categories and Priorities," provided guidance for planning and programming for the subsequent five years. It identified intelligence targets in terms of the information needed "to enable the U.S. intelligence community to provide effective support for decision-making, planning and operational activities of the U.S. government."[19] DCID 1/3 of May 18, 1976, entitled "Committees of the Director of Central Intelligence," outlined the basic composition and organization of the committees and authorized the DCI to designate their chairmen. DCID 1/5 of May 1976 dealt with "Data Standardization for the Intelligence Community." DCID 1/7 of June 15, 1996, "Security Control on the Dissemination of Intelligence Information," imposed restrictions on the dissemination of intelligence to immigrant aliens and foreign governments. DCID 1/8 of May 6, 1976, "The National Foreign Intelligence Board," established the board as the successor to the United States Intelligence Board. A more recent version of DCID 1/8 was issued on January 28, 1982.[20]

DCID 1/10 of January 18, 1982, is entitled "Security Policy Guidance on Liaison Relationships with Foreign Intelligence Organizations and Foreign Security Services." DCID 1/11 of July 15, 1982, spelled out the mission, functions, and composition of the now defunct Security Committee, and DCID 1/17 of May 18, 1976, did the same for the Human Resources Committee. Another now defunct NFIB committee, the Committee on Imagery Requirements and Exploitation (COMIREX) was the main subject of DCID 1/13, "Coordination of the Collection and Exploitation of Imagery Intelligence." DCID 1/15 of May 15, 1976, concerned "Data Standardization for the Intelligence Community."[21]

---

*More precisely, DCID 1/3 fills the third slot in the set of DCIDs issued pursuant to NSCID NO. 1. DCIDs are not numbered according to when they are issued. Thus, a DCID 1/3 may be issued after DCID 1/8 and replace an earlier DCID 1/3. The title or subject matter may vary.

Security standards are the subject of six DCIDs. DCIDs 1/14 and 1/19 are concerned with the protection of Sensitive Compartmented Information (SCI). DCID 1/14 of April 14, 1986, is entitled "Minimum Personnel Security Standards and Procedures Governing Eligibility for Access to Sensitive Compartmented Information." The directive focuses on personnel security standards, investigative requirements, the implications of various outside activities on security, the determination of access eligibility, continuing security programs, and security violations. DCID 1/16 deals with "Guidance on SCI Automated Systems." DCID 1/19, "SCI Administrative Guidance," focuses on the handling and accountability of SCI, and DCID 1/20 concerns "Security Policy Concerning Travel and Assignment of Personnel with Access to Sensitive Compartmented Information." DCID 1/21 is titled "SCI Physical Security Guidance," and DCID 1/22 is concerned with "Technical Surveillance Countermeasures."[22]

DCID 1/18 of May 18, 1976, "Recognition of Exceptional Service to the U.S. Intelligence Community," established criteria for the National Intelligence Distinguished Service Medal, the National Intelligence Medal of Achievement, and the Intelligence Community Certificate of Distinction.

DCID 2/1 of March 8, 1960, concerned the "Coordination of Overt Collection Abroad." By late 1982, DCID 2/1 bore the title, "Relationship with Nongovernmental Organizations and Individuals within the U.S. for Foreign Intelligence Purposes." It undoubtedly provided guidance for the CIA's domestic contact operations. DCID 2/8 of January 31, 1984, concerned "Coordination of Overt Collection Abroad." DCID 2/9 of June 1, 1992, bore the title, "Management of National Imagery Intelligence," and defined the function and responsibilities of the Central Imagery Office. DCID 2/11 of April 6, 1993, "Management of National Measurement and Signature Intelligence," gives the Central MASINT Office the authority to provide, for "the common concern," MASINT on behalf of the intelligence community. DCID 2/13-1 states that the Justice Department will be informed before there is notification to Congress on intelligence matters that involve law enforcement information.[23]

DCIDs in the 3/ series have involved implementation of NSCID No. 3, "Coordination of Intelligence Production." These directives have dealt with the production of National Intelligence Estimates as well as the establishment of numerous NFIB committees to facilitate production of intelligence in specific areas. Early versions of DCID 3/1 (July 8, 1948), 3/2 (September 13, 1948), and 3/5 (September 1, 1953) were entitled, respectively, "Standard Operating Procedures for Departmental Participation in the Production and Coordination of National Intelligence"; "Policy Governing Departmental Concurrences in National Intelligence Reports and Estimates"; and "Production of National Intelligence Estimates."[24]

Later DCIDs in the 3/ series defined the mission and functions of the Economic Intelligence Committee (3/1), the Joint Atomic Energy Intelligence Committee (3/3), the National Intelligence Producers Council (3/3 of March 30, 1983), the Guided Missile and Astronautics Intelligence Committee (3/4), the Scientific and Technical Intelligence Committee (3/5), the Human Resources Committee (3/7 of October 12, 1982), the Critical Intelligence Problems Committee (3/8 of April 6, 1983), the Technology Transfer Intelligence Committee (3/13 of December 3, 1981), the Information Handling Committee (3/14 of May 4, 1982), the Foreign Language Committee (3/15 of March 5, 1982), and Community Personnel Coordination Committee (1989). The most recent known versions of DCIDs 3/1 (January 28, 1982), 3/2 (January 18, 1982), and 3/3 (June 1, 1992) chartered the National Foreign Intelligence Board, National Foreign Intelligence Council, and the Community Management Staff, respectively.[25]

DCID 3/29 of June 2, 1995, provides procedures for the establishment and review of Special Access Programs pertaining to intelligence activities and restricted collateral information. It states that the DCI or DDCI shall determine whether to create, modify, or terminate special access programs.[26]

DCIDs 4/1 and 4/2 of May 1976 concerned the "Interagency Defector Committee" and the "The Defector Program Abroad." DCIDs in the 5/ series include 5/1 of December 19, 1984, "Espionage and Counterintelligence," 5/2 of May 1976, "U.S. Clandestine Foreign Intelligence and Counterintelligence Liaison," and DCID 5/6 on "Intelligence Disclosure Policy." DCID 6/1 of May 12, 1982, focuses on the functions, composition, and mission of the SIGINT Committee. DCID 7/1 of August 1976 dealt with "Handling of Critical Information."[27]

Both the DCI and Director of NSA are authorized to issue directives concerning aspects of the signals intelligence effort. The DCI issues Communications Intelligence Supplementary Regulations, whereas the Director of NSA issues U.S. Signals Intelligence Directives.[28]

The most important departmental regulations and directives on intelligence matters are DOD Directives, which concern both intelligence policies and the operations of specific units. Hence, DOD Directive 3310.1, "International Intelligence Agreements," includes the following specifications:

1. The Deputy Under Secretary of Defense (Policy) . . . is the principal within the Department of Defense responsible for oversight, coordination, and policy review of intelligence matters relating to agreements with foreign parties.
2. The Director, Defense Intelligence Agency (DIA) shall exercise, for the Department of Defense, approval authority (which may not be further delegated) to negotiate and conclude non-SIGINT intelligence agreements.[29]

A related DOD Directive C-5230.23 of November 18, 1983, on "Intelligence Disclosure Policy," specifies the functions of various DOD officials in the disclosure process. Thus, the Director of DIA is to "coordinate within and for the Department of Defense, proposed disclosures of classified U.S. intelligence to senior foreign officials" and the Deputy Undersecretary of Policy is to "resolve conflicts among DOD components relating to disclosure of classified U.S. intelligence to senior foreign officials."[30]

Other DOD directives and instructions concerning intelligence policy include "Signals Intelligence" (S-3115.7, January 25, 1983); "Management of Measurement and Signature Intelligence," (Instruction 5105.58, February 9, 1993) "Implementation of National Security Council Intelligence Directive No. 7" (S-5100.19, July 9, 1987); "The Security, Use and Dissemination of Communications Intelligence (COMINT)" (S-5200.17, January 26, 1965); "Coordination and Reporting of Foreign Intelligence Related Contacts and Arrangements" (S-3315.1, March 23, 1984); "Foreign Materiel Program" (S-3325.1, September 18, 1986); "Transfer of National Intelligence Collection Authority" (S-3325.2, June 18, 1987); "Protection of Classified National Security Council and Intelligence Information" (5230.21, March 21, 1982); "Support to Department of Defense Offensive Counterintelligence Operations" (S-5240.9, November 18, 1989).[31]

These directives may represent initial DOD implementation of NSCID, DCID, or presidential directives. Thus, S-5100.19 represents initial implementation of NSCID No. 7 (on critical intelligence); Directive 3310.1 represents the implementation of DCID 1/10 (on liaison relationships); and Directive 3325.2 represents implementation of NSDD-204 (on transfer of tasking authority).

Other DOD Directives specify the mission and functions of the National Reconnaissance Office (TS-5105.23, March 27, 1964); the National Security Agency and Central Security Service (S-5100.20, December 23, 1971); the Defense Intelligence Agency (5105.21, February 18, 1997); the National Imagery and Mapping Agency (5105.60, October 11, 1996); the Defense Special Missile and Astronautics Center (S-5100.43, April 27, 1964); and the Armed Forces Medical Intelligence Center (6240.1-R, April 1986).[32]

Military service and command regulations also state intelligence policies as well as define the mission and functions of service intelligence units. Among Air Force instructions, mission directives, and policy directives governing intelligence activities are those listed in Table 17.2. Those governing specific agencies include Air Force Mission Directive (AFMD) 15, "Air Intelligence Agency" (December 1995); and AFMD 49, "Air Force Technical Applications Center" (March 1996). Army Regulations (ARs) governing intelligence units and activities are listed in Table 17.3.

The most detailed regulations and directives are those issued by the intelligence units themselves. These directives seek to implement the broader DOD and military service directives by adopting the guidelines, restrictions, and procedures mandated by those broader directives and by specifying the internal structure and organization of the unit and the functions of its components.

Among the over sixty INSCOM regulations is INSCOM Regulation 10-2, "Organization and Functions, United States Army Intelligence and Security Command," of May 5, 1995, which is 125 pages long and enumerates the functions of

TABLE 17.2   Selected Air Force Instructions and Directives Concerning Intelligence Activities

Document	Title	Date
AFI10-1103	Sensitive Reconnaissance Programs	April 1994
AFPD14-1	Air Force Intelligence Planning and Operations	October 1995
AFI14-102	International Intelligence Agreements	October 1993
AFI14-208	Intelligence Support to the Air Force Acquisition Process	March 1994
AFPD14-3	Control, Protection, and Dissemination of Intelligence Information	January 1993
AFMD 15	Air Intelligence Agency	December 1995
AFMD 49	Air Force Technical Applications Center	March 1996

SOURCE: Air Force Index 2, "Numerical Index of Standard and Recurring Air Force Publications," August 1, 1996.

TABLE 17.3   Selected Army Regulations (ARs) Concerning Intelligence Activities

AR	Title	Date
10-53	U.S. Army Intelligence and Security Command	June 15, 1978
381-1	Control of Dissemination of Intelligence Information	Feb. 12, 1990
381-3	Signals Intelligence	Jan. 15, 1982
381-10	Army Intelligence Activites	July 1, 1984
381-26	Army Foreign Materiel Exploitation Program	May 27, 1991
381-171	International Intelligence Agreements	Oct. 21, 1986
381-172	Counterintelligence Force Protection to Source Operations and Low Level Source Operations	Feb. 1995

SOURCE: Department of the Army, Information Management Pamphlet 25-30, *Consolidated Index of Army Publications and Blank Forms,* October 1992, pp. K1, L3, M3; Department of the Army, Office of the Deputy Chief of Staff for Intelligence, *Annual Historical Review, 1 October 1994 to 30 September 1995,* n.d., pp. 3-17 to 3-18.

each of the deputy chiefs of staff and the divisions, branches, and offices that make up the organization. Likewise, the Air Force Technical Application Center (AFTAC) publications index lists over fifty directives and instructions covering administrative practices, organization and mission, personnel operations, collection activity, R&D, security, and supply.[33]

INDIVIDUALS, COMMITTEES, AND OFFICES

No matter how thorough the documents and directives described above or the plans described below are in stating the responsibilities and subjects for collection and analysis, they will, for several reasons, be insufficient as complete guides. First, every document leaves some room for interpretation. Second, attainment of the objectives specified will require coordination and cooperation on a regular basis. Hence, it is necessary to maintain a structure that facilitates such coordination and cooperation. Third, it is necessary to see that the components of the intelligence community are performing their activities within the restrictions imposed on them—that is, that the activities planned to attain specified objectives are acceptable to higher authorities. Fourth, some management structure is needed to generate the directives, plans, and programs under which the intelligence community operates. Finally, changing circumstances will require an alteration in preconceived plans and priorities.

At the top of the management system, which includes individuals, committees, and offices, are the President and the National Security Council committees. The first of these committees was established in 1948 by NSC 10/2 and was known as the 10/2 Panel. In subsequent years, as the panel was recreated and its membership and functions altered or maintained, it was renamed the 10/5 Panel (NSC 10/5, October 23, 1951), the Operations Coordinating Board (NSC 5412, NSC 5412/1 of March 12–15, 1954), the 5412 Group or Special Group (NSC 5412/2, December 28, 1955), and the 303 Committee (NSAM 303, June 2, 1964). In 1959 the Special Group became responsible for approval of sensitive air and naval reconnaissance missions. Subsequently, it also became an approval authority for satellite reconnaissance activities.[34]

With the signing of National Security Decision Memorandum 40, "Responsibility for the Conduct, Supervision and Coordination of Covert Action Operations," on February 17, 1970, the Director of Central Intelligence was required to "obtain policy approval for all major and/or politically sensitive covert action operations through the 40 Committee." The memorandum also called for an annual review of all covert action programs previously approved.[35]

In addition to the 40 Committee, the Nixon administration created the National Security Council Intelligence Committee (NSCIC), which was responsible for supervising the intelligence activities not under the purview of the 40 Committee. By creating the NSCIC, Nixon acknowledged that there were intelligence issues of importance in addition to covert action and reconnaissance operations. These issues included the need to make the intelligence community more responsive to policymakers, the establishment of intelligence priorities, and the allocation of resources.[36]

The basic two-committee system was continued by the Ford and Carter administrations. With Executive Order 11905, President Ford established the Committee on Foreign Intelligence (CFI) and the Operations Advisory Group (OAG).

The CFI was given control over budget preparation and resource allocation for the National Foreign Intelligence Program (NFIP), whereas supervision of covert operations was the responsibility of the OAG. In the Carter administration, the Special Coordination Committee (SCC) and Policy Review Committee (PRC) each had intelligence responsibilities. The SCC had jurisdiction over covert operations and counterintelligence matters. The PRC-Intelligence (PRC-I) was concerned with the preparation of a consolidated national intelligence budget and with resource allocation for the entire intelligence community. Among the concerns of PRC-Space was the subject of space reconnaissance.[37]

Ronald Reagan established Senior Interagency Groups (SIGs), including the Senior Interagency Group-Intelligence (SIG-I). SIG-I was given the responsibility of advising and assisting the NSC with respect to intelligence policy and intelligence matters. It was chaired by the DCI, and its members included the Assistant to President for National Security Affairs, the Deputy Secretary of State, the Deputy Secretary of Defense, and the chairman of the JCS. In addition to the statutory members, provision was made for attendance by heads of organizations with direct interest in the activities under consideration. When meeting to consider counterintelligence activities, the membership of the group was augmented by the Director of the FBI and the Director of the National Security Agency. When meeting to consider sensitive intelligence collection activities, the SIG-I's membership was augmented as required by the head of each organization within the intelligence community directly involved in the activity in question.[38]

Under the Bush administration a series of Policy Coordinating Committees was established within the NSC to handle substantive areas, including intelligence. The PCC-Intelligence was chaired by the DCI. In addition, a PCC-Special Activities, chaired by the NSC Senior Director for Intelligence Programs, was also established to "coordinate the development and conduct of special activities."[39]

President Clinton established, via Presidential Decision Directive 2 (PDD-2), a NSC Principals Committee "as the senior interagency forum for consideration of policy issues affecting national security," and a NSC Deputies Committee (NSC/DC) to serve "as the senior sub-Cabinet interagency forum for consideration of policy issues affecting national security." The DCI serves on the former and the Deputy DCI on the latter. PDD-2 does specify that when the NSC/DC meets "on sensitive intelligence activities, including covert actions, the attendees shall include the appropriate senior representative of the Attorney General."[40]

The directive also authorized the NSC/DC to create a system of Interagency Working Groups (IWGs) and specified that any IWG-Intelligence should be chaired by a NSC representative.[41]

Subsequently, the Brown commission recommended, and Congress legislated, the creation of a NSC committee—the Committee on Foreign Intelligence (CFI)—to oversee, monitor, and supervise intelligence activities. Plans to establish such a committee were, according to a NSC spokesperson, already under way. The committee is chaired by the Assistant to the President for National Security Affairs and has as members the DCI, the Secretaries of State and Defense, and "other members as the President may designate."[42]

The CFI's responsibilities include:

- identifying the intelligence required to address the national security interests of the United States as specified by the President
- establishing priorities (including funding priorities) among the programs, projects, and activities that address such interests and requirements
- establishing policies relating to the conduct of intelligence activities of the United States, including appropriate roles and missions for the elements of the intelligence community and appropriate targets of intelligence collection activities[43]

Responsibility for the management of the intelligence community emanates, in two different but not totally distinct directions, from the President and the NSC. One direction is toward the DCI, the other toward the Secretary of Defense. Both, of course, are guided by the provisions of the NSCIDs.

The DCI is the statutory head of the intelligence community. Executive Order 12333 instructs him to:

1. act as the primary adviser to the President and the NSC on national foreign intelligence
2. develop such objectives and guidance for the intelligence community as will enhance capabilities for responding to expected future needs for national foreign intelligence
3. promote the development and maintenance of service of common concern by designated intelligence organizations on behalf of the intelligence community
4. ensure implementation of special activities
5. coordinate foreign intelligence and counterintelligence relationships between agencies of the intelligence community and the intelligence or internal security services of foreign governments
6. ensure the establishment by the intelligence community of common security and access standards for managing and handling foreign intelligence systems, information, and products
7. ensure that programs are developed which protect intelligence sources, methods and analytical procedures
8. establish uniform criteria for the determination of relative priorities for the transmission of critical national foreign intelligence and advise the Secretary of Defense concerning the communications requirements of the intelligence community for the transmission of such intelligence
9. establish appropriate staffs, committees, or other advisory groups to assist in the execution of the director's responsibilities

10. have full responsibility for production and dissemination of national foreign intelligence, and authority to levy analytical tasks on departmental intelligence production organizations, in consultation with those organizations' policymakers

11. ensure the timely exploitation and dissemination of data gathered by national foreign intelligence collection means

12. establish mechanisms that translate national foreign intelligence objectives and priorities approved by the NSC into specific guidance for the intelligence community, resolve conflicts in tasking priority, and provide for the development of plans and arrangements for transfer of required collection tasking authority to the Secretary of Defense when directed by the President

13. develop, with the advice of the program managers and departments and agencies concerned, the consolidated National Foreign Intelligence Program budget

14. monitor National Foreign Intelligence Program implementation, and, as necessary, conduct program and performance audits and evaluation

15. together with the Secretary of Defense, ensure that there is no unnecessary overlap between national foreign intelligence programs and Department of Defense intelligence programs consistent with the requirement to develop competitive analysis, and provide to and obtain from the Secretary of Defense all information necessary for this purpose[44]

The responsibilities of the DCI, as stated in Executive Order 12333, and the National Security Act of 1947, have not been matched by the power to fulfill these responsibilities. As DCI Richard Helms noted in 1969, although the DCI was theoretically responsible for 100 percent of U.S. intelligence activities, he controlled less than 15 percent of the intelligence community's assets, whereas almost 85 percent were controlled by the Secretary of Defense and the JCS. And, until the signing of PD-17 during the Carter administration, the DCI had neither budgetary or day-to-day management control. Despite DCI Stansfield Turner's wishes, management control of the National Reconnaissance Office and the National Security Agency remained with the Secretary of Defense. The DCI did receive full and exclusive authority to approve the National Foreign Intelligence Program budget, which includes the Department of Defense portion—made up of the General Defense Intelligence Program, the National Reconnaissance Program, Navy Special Reconnaissance Activities, the Consolidated Cryptologic Program, and the Defense Foreign Counterintelligence Program. An attempt in 1996 to give the DCI more control over budget execution failed.[45]

A number of individuals and organizations help the DCI fulfill his responsibilities. In addition to the Deputy DCI, whose traditional task is to manage the CIA for the DCI, several additional positions were created by Congress in 1996. One of these positions—the Deputy Director for Community Management (DDCI/CM), which replaced the Executive Director for Intelligence Community Affairs—was first filled in 1998. The three other positions—the Assistant Director for Collection, the Assistant Director for Analysis and Production, and the Assistant Director for Administration, whose creation was opposed by the Clinton administration—had not been filled at the time Congress held hearings on the nominee for the DDCI/CM position. However, the nominee announced that she was "fully committed to using the Assistant DCI positions for Analysis and Production and Collection to exercise strong leadership over the collection and production communities."[46]

Also serving in a community-wide role is the Associate Director for Military Support, a position created to facilitate intelligence community support for military operations. Subordinate to the associate director is the Office of Military Affairs (OMA). The OMA, which is jointly staffed by the CIA and the military, posts representatives to the unified commands, selected military components, and senior service colleges; it deploys CIA representatives to National Intelligence Support Teams (NISTs) in support of U.S. forces overseas and provides responses to requests for information and analytical products.[47]

Seven organizations help the DCI fulfill his responsibilities: the Community Management Staff (CMS), the National Intelligence Council (NIC), the National Intelligence Collection Board (NICB), the National Intelligence Production Board (NIPB), the National Counterintelligence Policy Board (NCIPB), the National Foreign Intelligence Board (NFIB), and the Intelligence Community Executive Committee (IC/EXCOM).

The CMS was created in June 1992 by DCID 3/3 to replace the Intelligence Community Staff, which was a descendant of the National Intelligence Programs Evaluation Staff (created in 1963), as well as of the more recent Resource Management Staff. According to the directive, the CMS is responsible for "developing, coordinating, and implementing DCI policy and exercising DCI responsibilities" with respect to:

A. intelligence policy and planning
B. National Foreign Intelligence Program and budget development, evaluation, justification, and monitoring
C. intelligence requirements management and evaluation
D. performance of such other functions and duties as determined by the DCI[48]

The CMS operates under the direction of the Deputy Director for Community Management. As of September 1997, it was authorized to maintain up to 303 people on its staff. The CMS is divided into three offices—Resource Management; Systems and Architecture; and Requirements and Evaluation.[49]

The Resource Management Office is responsible for National Foreign Intelligence Program budget development, evaluation, justification, and monitoring. The Requirements and Evaluation Office is responsible for translating the requirements of intelligence community customers into national intelligence needs, for integrating the efforts of the collection disciplines to address these needs, and for evaluating the intelligence community's performance in satisfying them. The Systems and Architecture Office is responsible for strategic planning to define long-range objectives and priorities for the intelligence community as well as the means for assessing the community's progress toward the goals.[50]

The Requirements and Evaluation Office is supported by the National Intelligence Collection Board (NICB). The board, which is composed of senior officials "representing the intelligence collection disciplines and the principal Intelligence Community production offices," was established to "act as a forum for integrating the efforts of the separate collection disciplines and issuing guidance to collectors."[51]

The CMS is also responsible for coordinating the activities of four other entities. It oversees the Advanced Technology Office, which is responsible for coordinating science and technology matters pertaining to the NFIP Advanced Research and Development Program. It provides executive secretariat and other support to the Advanced Research and Development Committee, which advises the DCI on the overall National Intelligence Advanced R&D Program and on technologies that will best contribute to national intelligence objectives. It also supervises the Foreign Language Coordinator, who is responsible for coordinating intelligence community foreign language issues, including the recruitment and training of linguists, technology exchange, and an annual strategic plan.[52]

The third of the organizations supervised by the CMS, the Quality Council Secretariat, supports the Intelligence Community Quality Council "in its efforts to broaden and deepen the application of quality management in the Intelligence Community." Finally, the CMS oversees the activities of the Intelligence Systems Secretariat (ISS), a DCI-Deputy Secretary of Defense initiative aimed at improving the interoperability of automated intelligence systems operated by the intelligence community and the Department of Defense.[53]

The National Intelligence Council (NIC) is the DCI's principal means of producing National Intelligence Estimates, Special Estimates, and Interagency Intelligence Memoranda. The council consists of a chairman, twelve National Intelligence Officers responsible for specific geographic and substantive areas, and an Analytic Group consisting of approximately fifteen analysts.[54]

The National Intelligence Production Board (NIPB), formerly known as the Intelligence Producers Council (IPC), operates under the NIC, is chaired by the chairman of the NIC, and is composed of senior intelligence community production managers, including the chairmen of the DCI production committees. In addition to advising the DCI on all production matters, it "oversees several Community programs that focus on minimizing unnecessary duplication of effort and maximizing efforts to meet consumer needs."[55]

The National Counterintelligence Policy Board was established in May 1994 by PDD-24 and consists of senior executive representatives from the DCI/CIA, the FBI, the Defense Department, the State Department, and the Justice Department, plus a military service counterintelligence component and the NSC staff. The board will consider, develop, and recommend counterintelligence policy and planning directives to the president's national security adviser.[56]

Subordinate to the policy board is the National Counterintelligence Operations Board. The operations board consists of representatives from the CIA; the FBI; the Defense, State, and Justice Departments; the military service counterintelligence components; and the Chief of the National Counterintelligence Center.[57]

While the CMS and the NIC are subordinate to the DCI, the National Foreign Intelligence Board (NFIB) and the Intelligence Community Executive Committee (IC/EXCOM) provide advice and counsel to the DCI and serve as his principal means of coordinating intelligence community activities and attaining consensus on major issues.

The NFIB is the successor to the U.S. Intelligence Board (USIB), which was formed in 1958 by the merger of the Intelligence Advisory Committee and the Communications Intelligence Board. The functions of the NFIB, as defined in DCID 1/8 of May 6, 1976, consist of:

A. [the] review and coordination of national intelligence products
B. [the] maintenance of effective interface between intelligence producers and consumers and the development of procedures for continuing identification of consumer needs for intelligence
C. the establishment of appropriate objectives, requirements and priorities for substantive intelligence
D. the review of requirements coordination and operational guidance for intelligence collection systems
E. the protection of sensitive intelligence sources and methods and sensitive intelligence information
F. the development as appropriate, of policies regarding arrangements with foreign governments on intelligence matters
G. such other matters as the Director of Central Intelligence may refer to the Board for advice[58]

The DCI serves as chairmen of the NFIB. The board's other members include the Directors of the NSA, the DIA, the NIMA, and the Bureau of Intelligence and Research, and the Deputy Director of the CIA, as well as representatives of FBI, Department of Energy, and Department of Treasury intelligence components. The Director of the NRO attends as necessary. The Deputy Chief of Staff for Intelligence, Army; the Director of Naval Intelligence; the Air Force Director of Intelligence, Surveillance, and Reconnaissance; and the Director of Intelligence for the Marine Corps sit on the board as observers.[59]

The NFIB's predecessor, the USIB, operated through an elaborate committee structure. It was observed in 1974, before the NFIB replaced the USIB, that through the committee structure the USIB

> lists the targets for American intelligence and the priority attached to each one, coordinates within the intelligence community the estimates of future events and enemy

strengths, controls the classification and security systems for most of the U.S. government, directs research in the various fields of technical intelligence, and decides what classified information will be passed on to foreign friends and allies.[60]

The committee structure also served as a means of informing the members of the intelligence community on particular matters (e.g., weapons and space systems) and providing support to agencies outside the intelligence community.

In 1976, in the interval between the abolition of the USIB and the creation of the NFIB, the USIB committees were redesignated as DCI committees. Present DCI committees include the National SIGINT Committee, the Technology Transfer Intelligence Committee (TTIC), the Economic Intelligence Committee (EIC), the Foreign Intelligence Priorities Committee (FIPC), the Critical Intelligence Problems Committee (CIPC), the Scientific and Technical Intelligence Committee (STIC), the Information Handling Committee (IHC), the Joint Atomic Energy Intelligence Committee (JAEIC), the Weapons and Space Systems Intelligence Committee (WSSIC), the Foreign Language Committee, the Narcotics Intelligence Issues Committee (NIIC), the Interagency Intelligence Committee on Terrorism (IICT), the Interagency Defector Committee (IDC), the Measurement and Signature Intelligence (MASINT) Committee, the Warning Committee, the Community Nonproliferation Committee (CNC), the Open Source Committee (OSC), the Community Counterintelligence and Security Countermeasures Committee (CCSCC), and the Advanced Research and Development Program Committee.[61]

In 1992, three of the committees—the JAEIC, the WSSIC, and STIC—were made directly responsible to the National Intelligence Council. In addition, several other committees now operate within the agencies they supervise. Thus, the National SIGINT Committee is now "within NSA," while the MASINT Committee operates under the DIA's Central MASINT Office.[62]

The SIGINT Committee was formed in 1962 by the merger of the COMINT and ELINT Committees. It reviews and validates all proposed requirements before they are levied on the NSA. The Technology Transfer Intelligence Committee (TTIC) was created in 1981 to deal with what was perceived to be a growing hemorrhage of critical technology to the Soviet Union. The TTIC, which operates through two subcommittees (the Subcommittee on Exchanges and the Subcommittee on Export Control) draws on scientific and technical analysts throughout the military intelligence services and elsewhere in the intelligence community.[63]

The TTIC's functions are to:

A. advise the DCI on the effectiveness of the Intelligence Community's role in support of U.S. Government policy on technology transfer issues
B. as directed, prepare coordinated intelligence assessments on the significance of technology transfer and, as appropriate, their implications to national security
C. advise appropriate U.S. government departments and agencies of the technology transfer implications of foreign intelligence equities involved in exchange pro-

grams and commercial contacts with nationals from designated foreign countries and recommend changes as appropriate

D. provide foreign intelligence support on export control issues to appropriate U.S. Government agencies

E. monitor all technology transfer intelligence concerning foreign efforts to acquire U.S. and Western technology and provide appropriate analyses to U.S. Government organizations concerned with protection and countermeasures, including counterintelligence organizations

F. provide priority guidance to collection systems on technology transfer issues

G. establish an exchange of information with all departments and agencies concerned with the technology transfer program to ensure that utility of the Intelligence Community's activities is maintained[64]

The TTIC's products have included "Soviet Requirements for Western Technology: A Forecasting Methodology" (May 1987), "National Security and Export Controls: A Decision Aid (September 1988), and "Israel: Marketing U.S. Strategic Technology" (September 1990).[65]

The Economic Intelligence Committee (EIC) was first established in 1948 as a subsidiary of the Intelligence Advisory Committee. It is responsible for assisting the DCI in the production of foreign economic intelligence and provides support to agencies charged with formulating U.S. international economic policy. The Subcommittee on Requirements and Coordination of the EIC produces the Economic Alert List (EAL), which highlights the current economic information needs of all agencies participating in the Combined Economic Reporting Program (CERP).[66]

The Critical Intelligence Problems Committee (CIPC) was created in 1958—as the Critical Collection Problems Committee (CCPC)—to examine, as its name suggests, particularly difficult collection problems regardless of the technique involved. In 1971, one subject considered by the CCPC was narcotics intelligence, and it has a permanent Narcotics Working Group.[67]

According to DCID 3/8 of April 6, 1983, the committee is to identify:

A. the specific intelligence requirements and shortfalls associated with the critical intelligence problem under review

B. current and programmed collection, processing, and production resources directed against the critical intelligence problem

C. options for adjustments in collection, processing, and production efforts which could be accomplished within existing resources, and the associated impact such adjustments would have on the Intelligence Community's ability to respond to other priority intelligence needs

D. recommendations for new initiatives which could increase collection, processing, and production efforts against the critical intelligence problem, noting which options would require programming of supplemental funding actions[68]

In 1975 the CIPC prepared the "Study on Intelligence Activities Against International Terrorism." In 1985 it sponsored a conference on combat intelligence analysis and produced at least three studies—on combat intelligence analysis, cruise missile collection, and Strategic Defense Initiative intelligence. Two years later it prepared a study on "Soviet Enigma Satellites."[69]

The Foreign Intelligence Priorities Committee (FIPC) is the executive agent for managing the DCI's statement of "Foreign Intelligence Requirements Categories and Priorities" in DCID 1/2. An October 20, 1986 order by the FIPC raised the collection of intelligence related to American MIAs to "Priority One." Although that priority level is formally reserved for information considered "vital to U.S. survival," the order waived the definition for the POW-MIA issue.[70]

The Foreign Language Committee has three basic responsibilities, to:

A. appraise the effectiveness of programs to recruit, train, and retain personnel with adequate foreign language competence for elements of the Intelligence Community

B. recommend to the DCI new initiatives to be undertaken to ensure the continuing availability within the Intelligence Community of requisite foreign language competence

C. coordinate replies to all queries from Congressional committees concerning the Community's overall foreign language competence[71]

The Warning Committee is chaired by the National Intelligence Officer for Warning. Its members include the Directors of the DIA and the NSA, the CIA Deputy Director for Intelligence, and the Assistant Secretary of State for Intelligence and Research. The committee meets weekly to discuss a variety of warning issues and to coordinate warning products.[72]

The DCI Advanced Research and Development Committee has worked with research and development authorities in the imagery, energy, and defense sectors to produce a Critical Technologies List that would guide investment decisions in key areas such as sensors, communications, data storage and management, advanced processing, and enabling technology.[73]

The Information Handling Committee (IHC) is responsible for all aspects of information handling—supervising research and development of information handling systems, developing rules and procedures for the exchange of information between agencies, and establishing education and training programs in information science. Its subcommittees include the Geographic Information Systems Subcommittee and the Access Control Subcommittee.[74]

The DCI's Interagency Intelligence Committee on Terrorism (IICT), which operates under the oversight of the Community Counterterrorism Board of the CIA's Counterterrorist Center, advises and assists the DCI in "coordinating national intelligence on terrorism issues and [promoting] effective use of intelligence resources for [counterterrorism]." The committee has representatives from forty-two agencies, distributed across the intelligence, law enforcement, military, and regulatory communities.[75]

The IICT has six subcommittees—Research and Development; Technical Countermeasures; Chemical, Biological, Radiological Threat; Warning; Analytic Training; Requirements—and one group, the Information Advisory Handling Group. In May 1996, the IICT published a report entitled "Aum Shinrikyo: Insights to the Chemical and Biological Terrorist Threat."[76]

The Intelligence Community Executive Committee (IC/EXCOM), was created as the National Foreign Intelligence Council under the Reagan administration. The council evolved out of the NFIB and deals with priorities and budgets. As with the NFIB, the DCI is designated a chairman and the Deputy DCI as vice chairman representing the CIA. Other members include the vice chairman, JCS; Director, NSA; Director, DIA; Assistant Secretary of State, INR; Director, NRO; Director, NIMA; chairman, NIC; Assistant Secretary of Defense for C^3I; and Deputy Director of Central Intelligence for Community Management.[77]

The IC/EXCOM "advises the DCI on priorities and objectives for the National Foreign Intelligence Program budget; intelligence policy and planning; and IC management and evaluation."[78]

The Secretary of Defense's role in the management of intelligence activities is exercised through an Assistant Secretary of Defense, the Joint Space Management Board, and an executive committee and a review board.

For a number of years, responsibility for oversight of Defense Department intelligence activities was assigned to the Assistant Secretary of Defense for Command, Control, Communications, and Intelligence [ASD (C^3I)]. DOD Directive 5137.1 specifies that the ASD (C^3I) is responsible for assessing the responsiveness of intelligence products in satisfying DOD requirements. The Assistant Secretary is also charged with establishing policy and providing direction to DOD components with respect to surveillance, warning, and reconnaissance architectures; intelligence programs, systems, and equipment; and counterintelligence operations.[79]

In November 1997 Secretary of Defense William S. Cohen announced his intention, in response to the recommendations of the Defense Reform Initiative Report, to disestablish the ASD(C^3I) position. Oversight of intelligence responsibilities would be assigned to a new Assistant Secretary of Defense (Intelligence), who would oversee the intelligence, counterintelligence, security countermeasures, information operations, warning, reconnaissance, and intelligence-related activities of the department. The new Assistant Secretary would also supervise the operations of the NIMA, the NSA, the DIA, the NRO, and the Defense Security Service—which would (and did) replace the Defense Investigative Service.[80]

However, in the face of adverse reaction to the elimination of the C^3I office, Cohen reversed course. The ASD (C^3I) position was actually strengthened and the office's mandate expanded—as was recommended in a report by former ASD(C^3I) Duane Andrews. The new office assumed some of the responsibilities of the Defense Airborne Reconnaissance Office as well as those of the office of the Deputy Undersecretary of Defense (Space); both offices were disestablished at approximately the same time.[81]

As a result of the decision there are four Deputy ASDs (C³I), responsible for C⁴ISR (Command, Control, Communications, Computers, Intelligence, Surveillance, and Reconnaissance); Policy and Implementation; Security and Information Operations; and Intelligence. The office of the DASD (C⁴ISR) will include a Directorate for Intelligence, Surveillance, and Reconnaissance Systems, responsible for aerial and space systems. The DASD (C³I/Intelligence) will, among other responsibilities, supervise the operations of the DIA.[82]

Supervision of military space procurement decisions, including intelligence satellite procurement, is now the responsibility of the Joint Space Management Board (JSMB). Located within the Department of Defense, the JSMB was established by the joint agreement of the Secretary of Defense and the DCI in December 1995. The JSMB provides "overall policy and program guidance for defense and intelligence space programs, to include review and approval of trade-offs among requirements, programs, and resources." It also reviews and approves defense and intelligence space policies, architectures, and program plans for consistency with JSMB policy and program guidance. In addition, the JSMB is "charged with establishing the integration of defense and intelligence space architectures."[83]

The JSMB is co-chaired by the Under Secretary of Defense for Acquisition and Technology and the Deputy Director of Central Intelligence. The full membership of the JSMB includes twenty-five individuals, including representatives of the military services, acquisition offices, the CIA, the NRO, the NIMA, the INR, the DIA, and the U.S. Space Command. The JSMB Executive Committee is vested with full authority to act for the Secretary of Defense and the DCI within the terms of the charter. It consists of the JSMB co-chairs, the vice chairman of the JCS, and the Deputy Director of Central Intelligence for Community Management.[84]

An executive committee, probably called the National Special Navy Program Executive Committee, supervises sensitive underseas intelligence programs. It is chaired by the DCI and reports to the Secretary of Defense. Foreign materiel acquisition activities are carried out under the guidance of the Foreign Materiel Program Review Board (FMPRB). The board is co-chaired by the DASD (Intelligence) and the Under Secretary of Defense for Policy; its other members include the Under Secretary of Defense (Acquisition); the Director, Program Analysis and Evaluation; the Director, Operational Test and Evaluation; the OSD Comptroller; and the Director of the DIA.[85]

Another mechanism for the coordination of military intelligence is the Military Intelligence Board (MIB), chaired by the Director of the DIA. The board was established on August 15, 1961, to assist in the development of the DIA activation plan and in the selection of personnel. However, it remained in existence as a mechanism for coordinating Defense positions on DOD intelligence issues among the Director of the DIA, the Joint Staff J2, and the service intelligence chiefs.[86]

The MIB coordinates intelligence support to military operations as well as provides a forum for discussion and development of coordinated military intelligence positions on issues going before the NFIB and IC/EXCOM. It also provides oversight and direction to the defense intelligence functional managers for collection, production, and infrastructure.[87]

The MIB meets approximately once a week and has considered topics such as intelligence support to Operation Desert Storm, intelligence support to the European Command, Operation Joint Endeavor, Iraq, Korea, the NIMA Implementation Plan, the Quadrennial Defense Review, and National Intelligence Estimates.[88]

MIB members, in addition to the Director of the DIA, include the Deputy Director, DIA; the Directors of the NSA and the NIMA, and the service intelligence chiefs. In addition, the Deputy Assistant Secretary of Defense (Intelligence), the CIA's Associate Deputy Director for Operations (Military Affairs), and the intelligence director for the JCS participate in the MIB. There are three groups associated with the MIB (although they are not subordinate to it). They are the Council of Defense Intelligence Producers, the Military Target Intelligence Committee, and the Council on Functional Management.[89]

PROGRAMS

In any given year, there must be a specific allocation of resources in order to produce the intelligence required by decisionmakers and other government officials. Three programs govern the allocation of resources: the National Foreign Intelligence Program (NFIP), the Joint Military Intelligence Program (JMIP), and the Tactical Intelligence and Related Activities Program (TIARA).

The NFIP encompasses all national foreign intelligence activity. The nonmilitary components of the NFIP are the Central Intelligence Agency Program, the State Department Intelligence Program, the Community Management Staff, and the Intelligence Elements of the FBI, the Department of Energy, and the Department of the Treasury. There are five DOD components: the Consolidated Cryptologic Program (CCP), the General Defense Intelligence Program (GDIP), the Navy Special Reconnaissance Activities, the National Reconnaissance Program, and the Defense Foreign Counterintelligence Program.[90]

The CCP is managed by the NSA and includes all SIGINT resources in the NFIP. The GDIP includes all non-SIGINT, non-reconnaissance programs. Specifically, the GDIP includes eight activities:

1. general military intelligence production
2. imagery collection and processing
3. HUMINT
4. nuclear monitoring
5. R&D procurement

6. field support
7. general support
8. scientific and technical intelligence production

The CCP and GDIP, when combined, form the Consolidated Defense Intelligence Program.

The Navy Special Reconnaissance Activities Program allocates attack submarines (SSNs) and other craft for sensitive reconnaissance missions. The National Reconnaissance Program specifies the spending, procurement, and operational activities of the NRO on satellites and aircraft.[91]

The Joint Military Intelligence Program (JMIP) was established in 1995 to "improve the effectiveness of DOD intelligence activities when those activities involve resources from more than one DOD Component; when users of the intelligence data are from more than one DOD Component; and/or when centralized planning, management, coordination, or oversight will contribute to the effectiveness of the effort."[92]

There are three major program aggregations within the JMIP: the Defense Cryptologic Program (DCP), the Defense Imagery and Mapping Program (DIMAP), and the Defense General Intelligence and Applications Program (DGIAP). Each program is made up of resources that had previously been funded within the TIARA program. The DGIAP consists of five subordinate programs—the Defense Airborne Reconnaissance Program (DARP), the Defense Intelligence Counterdrug Program (DICP), the Defense Intelligence Agency's Tactical Program (DIATP), the Defense Space Reconnaissance Program (DSRP), and the Defense Intelligence Special Technologies Program (DISTP).[93]

The Deputy Secretary of Defense serves as the Program Executive for the JMIP and chairs the Defense Intelligence Executive Board (DIEB), which serves as the senior management body providing planning, programming, and budget oversight of the JMIP.[94]

Creation of the JMIP stripped the TIARA program of two of its three elements—the Defense Space Reconnaissance Program (formerly the Defense Reconnaissance Support Program) and the Tactical Cryptologic Program—leaving the Reconnaissance, Surveillance, and Target Acquisition component.

In 1995 the Air Force TIARA program was divided into five components: Battle Management (JOINT STARS); Processing and Dissemination (including CONSTANT SOURCE, the Combat Air Intelligence System, and the Combat Intelligence System); Surveillance and Reconnaissance (including SPACETRACK, PACER COIN, and SENIOR SCOUT); Tactical Warning/Attack Assessment (including the SLBM Radar Warning System, Defense Support Program, and the Ballistic Missile Early Warning System); Manpower and Training (including the U.S. Space Command's Space Warfare Center); and Scientific and Technical Collection (the COBRA JUDY sea-based phased array radar).[95]

Notes

1. A compilation of declassified National Security directives on microfiche is National Security Archive, *Presidential Directives on National Security from Truman to Clinton* (Alexandria, Va.: Chadwyck-Healey, 1994).

2. Ronald Reagan, "Executive Order 12333: United States Intelligence Activities," December 4, 1981, in *Federal Register* 46, no. 235 (December 8, 1981): 59941–59954.

3. Gerald Ford, "Executive Order 11905: United States Intelligence Activities," February 18, 1976, in *Weekly Compilation of Presidential Documents* 12, no. 8 (1976): 234–243.

4. Jimmy Carter, "Executive Order 12036: United States Intelligence Activities," *Federal Register* 43, no. 18 (January 24, 1978): 3675–3698.

5. President William J. Clinton, Executive Order 12958, "Classified National Security Information," April 17, 1995, in *Federal Register* 60, no. 76 (April 20, 1995): 19832–19834. The automatic declassification provision ran into at least a temporary roadblock in the fall of 1998. See George Lardner Jr., "Automatic Declassification Halted," *Washington Post,* October 16, 1998, p. A25.

6. On NSDD–17, see Raymond Bonner, "President Approved Policy of Preventing 'Cuba Model' States," *New York Times,* April 7, 1983, pp. 1, 16; On NSDD–42, see U.S. Congress, House Committee on Science and Technology, *National Space Policy* (Washington, D.C.: U.S. Government Printing Office, 1982), p. 13; NSDDs 17, 19, 22, 42, 84, 196, 202, and 204 were obtained, in whole or in part, under the Freedom of Information Act by the National Security Archive. NSDD–159 was released during the Iran-Contra hearings.

7. Elaine Sciolino, "Pakistan Keeping Afghan Aid Role," *New York Times,* February 26, 1989, p. 15; "Saudi Help for the CIA," *Newsweek,* September 10, 1990, p. 6; Bill Gertz, "Despite Thaw in Cold War, Bush Heats Up Counterspy Operations," *Washington Times,* October 24, 1990, pp. A1, A6; Edward D. Shaefer Jr., *Strategic Planning for the Office of Naval Intelligence: Vision and Direction for the Future* (Washington, D.C.: Office of Naval Intelligence, 1992), p. 10.

8. National Security Council, Fact Sheet, "U.S. Counterintelligence Effectiveness," May 1994; William J. Clinton, "Remarks at the Central Intelligence Agency in Langley, Virginia, July 14, 1995," White House, July 14, 1995. PDD–35 established six priority ranks as tiers— 0: crisis coverage; 1: countries that are enemies/potential enemies; 1A: topics of highest priority; Tier 2: other countries of high priority; Tier 3: low priority countries (some coverage); Tier 4: low priority countries (not covered). See Defense Science Board, *Defense Mapping for Future Operations* (Washington, D.C.: Office of the Under Secretary of Defense for Acquisition and Technology, 1995), p. E-9.

9. NSCID No. 1, "Basic Duties and Responsibilities," February 17, 1972, *Declassified Documents Reference Service (DDRS),* 1976–167G.

10. Ibid.

11. NSCID No. 2, "Coordination of Overt Collection Activities," February 17, 1972, *DDRS* 1976–253D.

12. NSCID No. 3, "Coordination of Intelligence Production," February 17, 1972, *DDRS* 1976–253E.

13. Ibid.

14. U.S. Congress, House Permanent Select Committee on Intelligence, *Annual Report* (Washington, D.C.: U.S. Government Printing Office, 1978), p. 70.

15. NSCID No. 5, "U.S. Espionage and Counterintelligence Activities Abroad," February 17, 1972, *DDRS* 1976–253F.

16. Department of Justice, *Report on Inquiry into CIA-Related Electronic Surveillance Activities* (Washington, D.C.: Department of Justice, 1976), pp. 77–78.

17. National Security Agency/Central Security Service, *NSA/CSS Manual 22–1* (Ft. Meade, Md.: NSA, 1986), p. 1; Department of Defense Directive S-5100.9, "Implementation of National Security Council Directive No. 7," March 19, 1960; James Bamford, *The Puzzle Palace: A Report on NSA, America's Most Secret Agency* (Boston: Houghton Mifflin, 1982), p. 104; Seymour M. Hersh, *"The Target Is Destroyed": What Really Happened to Flight 007 and What America Really Knew About It* (New York: Random House, 1986), p. 53.

18. NSCID No. 8, "Photographic Interpretation," February 17, 1972, *DDRS* 1976–253G.

19. Department of Justice, *Report on Inquiry into CIA-Related Electronic Surveillance Activities*, p. 100.

20. DCID 1/3, "Committees of the Director of Central Intelligence," May 18, 1976; DCID 1/4, "Intelligence Information Handling Committee," May 18, 1976; U.S. Congress, House Permanent Select Committee on Intelligence, *Annual Report*, p. 70; Enclosure 1 of DOD Instruction 5230.22, *Control of Dissemination of Intelligence Information*, April 1, 1982; DCID 1/18, "The National Foreign Intelligence Board," May 6, 1976; HQ USAF, ACS, I, INOI–11–3, "Intelligence Community Boards, Councils and Committees," December 30, 1983; DCID 1/7, "Security Controls on the Dissemination of Intelligence Information," June 15, 1996.

21. Reference (d) to Department of Defense Directive 3310.1, "International Intelligence Agreements," October 22, 1982; DCID 11/1, "Security Committee," July 15, 1982; DCID 1/17, "Human Resources Committee," May 18, 1976; DCID 1/13, "Coordination of the Collection and Exploitation of Imagery Intelligence," February 2, 1973, *DDRS* 1980–132D; DCID 1/15, "Data Standardization for the Intelligence Community," May 18, 1976.

22. U.S. Congress, House Permanent Select Committee on Intelligence, *Security Clearance Procedures in the Intelligence Agencies* (Washington, D.C.: U.S. Government Printing Office, 1979), pp. 25–29; U.S. Congress, House Permanent Select Committee on Intelligence, *Espionage Laws and Leaks* (Washington, D.C.: U.S. Government Printing Office, 1979), p. 276; Working Group on Computer Security, *Computer and Telecommunications Policy* (Washington, D.C.: National Communications Security Committee, July 1981), p. 158; DCID 1/14, "Minimum Personnel Security Standards and Procedures Governing Eligibility for Access to Sensitive Compartmented Information," April 14, 1986; Department of Energy Order 5636.2, "Security Requirements for Classified Automatic Data Processing Systems," January 10, 1980; USSPACECOM Regulation 200–1, "The Security, Use and Dissemination of Sensitive Compartmented Information (SCI)," August 31, 1990; Naval Intelligence Activity, *Calendar Year 1991 History, Naval Intelligence Activity (NIA), 1 January–30 September 1991*, 1992, p. 4; "Changes Ahead for Security," *INSCOM Journal*, September 1993, pp. 38–39.

23. DCID 2/1, "Coordination of Overt Collection Abroad," March 8, 1960, *DDRS* 1980–131B; USCINCPAC Instruction S3821.55F, *Foreign Materiel Collection and Exploitation Program in the United States Pacific Command (USPACOM)*, April 27, 1992; DCID 2/9, "Management of National Imagery Intelligence," June 1, 1992; U.S. Congress, House

Permanent Select Committee on Intelligence, *IC 21: Intelligence Community in the 21st Century* (Washington, D.C.: U.S. Government Printing Office, 1996), pp. 149, 165, 287; Office of the Inspector General, Department of Defense, PO 97–031, *Evaluation Report on Measurement and Signature Intelligence* (Alexandria, Va.: DODIG, June 30, 1997), p. 2.

24. John Prados, *The Soviet Estimate: U.S. Intelligence Analysis and Russian Military Strength* (New York: Dial, 1982), pp. 306–307.

25. DCID 3/1, "Production and Coordination of Foreign Economic Intelligence," May 18, 1976; U.S. Congress, House Permanent Select Committee on Intelligence, *Annual Report*, pp. 35, 49; DCID 3/2, "Production of Atomic Energy Intelligence," April 23, 1965, *DDRS* 1980–131G; DCID 3/4, "Production of Guided Missile and Astronautics Intelligence," April 23, 1965, *DDRS* 1980–132A; DCID 3/3, "Community Management Staff," June 1, 1992; USAF, Air Force Assistant Chief of Staff, Intelligence, "Intelligence Community Boards, Councils, and Groups," January 9, 1989; Department of Army, Office of the Deputy Chief of Staff for Intelligence, *Annual Historical Review, 1 October 1989–30 September 1990*, n.d., p. 11-11.

26. DCID 1/7, "Security Controls on the Dissemination of Intelligence Information," April 12, 1995, p. 2; Information Security Oversight Office, *Final Report on the Verification Inspection of the National Security Agency*, IR 96–03, February 13, 1996, p. 13.

27. U.S. Congress, House Permanent Select Committee on Intelligence, *Annual Report*, pp. 42, 70–71; DCID 6/1, "SIGINT Committee," May 12, 1982; USCINCPAC Instruction S3821.55F, *Foreign Materiel Collection and Exploitation Program in United States Pacific Command (USPACOM)*; John Deutch, Memorandum for Intelligence Community Principals, Subject: Revision of Director of Central Intelligence Directive 1/7, "Security Controls on the Dissemination of Intelligence Information," April 16, 1996.

28. U.S. Congress, House Permanent Select Committee on Intelligence, *Security Clearance Procedures*, p. 29.

29. Department of Defense 3310.1, "International Intelligence Agreements," October 22, 1982.

30. Department of Defense Directive C–5230.23, "Intelligence Disclosure Policy," November 18, 1983.

31. Department of Defense 5025.1-I, *DOD Directives System Annual Index* (Washington, D.C.: DOD/NTIS, January 1993), pp. 2-34, 2-56, 2-71 to 2-72.

32. Ibid., pp. 2-52 to 2-59; Department of Defense Directive TS–5105.23, "National Reconnaissance Office," March 27, 1964; DOD Directive 5105.60, "National Imagery and Mapping Agency," October 11, 1996; DOD Directive 5105.21, "Defense Intelligence Agency," February 18, 1997.

33. United States Army Intelligence and Security Command, Index of Administrative Publications and Command Forms, May 3, 1994; INSCOM Regulation 10–2, "Organization and Functions, United States Army Intelligence and Security Command," May 5, 1995; HQ Air Force Technical Applications Center, Center Index 2, Numerical Index of Standard and Recurring Center Publications, April 1, 1997.

34. Emmanuel Adler, "Executive Command and Control in Foreign Policy: The CIA's Covert Activities," *Orbis* 23 (1979): 671–696; U.S. Congress, Senate Select Committee to Study Governmental Operations with Respect to Intelligence Activities, *Final Report: Book 1, Foreign and Military Intelligence* (Washington, D.C.: U.S. Government Printing Office, 1976), p. 53.

35. National Security Decision Memorandum 40, "Responsibility for the Conduct, Supervision and Coordination of Covert Action Operations," *DDRS* 1976–297A.

36. U.S. Congress, Senate Select Committee to Study Governmental Operations with Respect to Intelligence Activities, *Final Report, Book 1: Foreign and Military Intelligence*, p. 61.

37. Lawrence J. Korb, "National Security Organization and Process in the Carter Administration," in *Defense Policy and the Presidency: Carter's First Years*, ed. Sam C. Sarkesian (Boulder, Colo.: Westview, 1979); Ford, "Executive Order 11905: United States Intelligence Activities."

38. NSDD–2, "National Security Council Structure," January 12, 1982; National Defense University, *Publication 5—Intelligence for Joint Forces* (Norfolk, Va.: Armed Forces Staff College, August 1985), pp. 2-1 to 2-2.

39. George Bush, National Security Directive-1, Organization of the National Security Council System, January 30, 1989; George Bush, National Security Council Directive-10, Creation of New Policy Coordinating Committees, May 7, 1989.

40. William J. Clinton, Presidential Decision Directive-2, Organization of the National Security Council, January 20, 1993.

41. Ibid.

42. U.S. Congress, Public Law 104–293, *Intelligence Authorization Act for Fiscal Year 1997*, October 11, 1996, 110 Stat. 3424–75; P. J. Crowley, National Security Council, Telephone conversation, March 17, 1998.

43. U.S. Congress, Public Law 104–293, *Intelligence Authorization Act for Fiscal Year 1997*, 110 Stat. 3424–75.

44. Reagan, "Executive Order 12333: United States Intelligence Activities," pp. 59943–59944.

45. Victor Marchetti and John Marks, *The CIA and the Cult of Intelligence* (New York: Knopf, 1974), pp. 98–99; Caspar Weinberger, *FY 1983 Report of Secretary of Defense Caspar Weinberger* (Washington, D.C.: U.S. Government Printing Office, 1982), p. III-8; Walter Pincus, "Spy Chief's Grasp Reaches Other Pockets," *Washington Post*, April 25, 1996, p. A29; R. Jeffrey Smith, "Clinton to Sign Bill Giving CIA Three New Managers," *Washington Post*, October 5, 1996, p. A4.

46. "Empty Posts at C.I.A.," " *New York Times*, August 25, 1997, p. A15; White House, Office of the Press Secretary, Statement by the President, October 11, 1996; Smith, "Clinton to Sign Bill Giving CIA Three New Managers"; Joan A. Dempsey, "Testimony to the Senate Select Committee on Intelligence for the Confirmation of the Deputy Director of Central Intelligence for Community Management, Joan A. Dempsey," May 20, 1998, p. 5.

47. Director of Central Intelligence, *Persian Gulf War Illnesses Task Force, Lessons Learned: Intelligence Support on Chemical and Biological Warfare During the Gulf War and On Veterans' Illness Issues*, December 1997, p. 2.

48. DCID 3/3, "Community Management Staff," June 1, 1992.

49. Ibid.; Central Intelligence Agency, "What's News at CIA," July 16, 1992; U.S. Congress, PL–102–496, *Intelligence Authorization Act for Fiscal Year 1993* (Washington, D.C.: U.S. Government Printing Office, 1992), p. 106 Stat. 3182; Central Intelligence Agency, *A Consumer's Guide to Intelligence* (Washington, D.C.: Central Intelligence Agency, 1995), p. 41; U.S. Congress, *Public Law 104–293* (Washington, D.C.: U.S. Government Printing Office, 1996), p. 110 Stat. 3463.

50. Central Intelligence Agency, *A Consumer's Guide to Intelligence*, p. 41.

51. DCID 3/3, "Community Management Staff."

52. Central Intelligence Agency, *A Consumer's Guide to Intelligence*, pp. 41–42.

53. Ibid.

54. Ibid.

55. Ibid., p. 43; National Intelligence Council, *A Guide to the National Intelligence Council*, 1994, p. 41; U.S. Congress, Senate Select Committee on Intelligence and House Permanent Select Committee on Intelligence, *S.2198 and S.421 to Reorganize the United States Intelligence Community* (Washington, D.C.: U.S. Government Printing Office, 1993), p. 15.

56. National Security Council Fact Sheet, "U.S. Counterintelligence Effectiveness," p. 2.

57. Ibid.

58. DCID 1/8, "National Foreign Intelligence Board," May 6, 1976.

59. DIA Regulation 50–17, "Release of Classified DOD Intelligence to Non-NFIB U.S. Government Agencies," July 26, 1978; Central Intelligence Agency, *A Consumer's Guide to Intelligence*, pp. 39, 41.

60. Marchetti and Marks, *The CIA and the Cult of Intelligence*, pp. 81, 84.

61. Letter, Lee S. Strickland, CIA Information and Privacy Coordinator, to the author, June 5, 1987; Naval Intelligence Command, *Naval Intelligence Command Historical Review, 1976*, 1977, p. 3; Office of Naval Intelligence, *Office of Naval Intelligence (OP–92) Command History 1990*, n.d., Assistant for Counternarcotics Section, p. 2; Department of the Army, Office of the Deputy Chief of Staff for Intelligence, *Annual Historical Review, 1 October 1987–30 September 1988*, n.d., p. 2–37; Eagle Research Group, *ERG Support to OTA* (Arlington, Va. ERG, December 14, 1990), p. 11; Central Intelligence Agency, *A Consumer's Guide to Intelligence*, pp. 53–57.

62. Telephone conversation between a representative of the CIA Office of Public and Agency Information and the author, December 10, 1993.

63. National Academy of Sciences, *Scientific Communication and National Security* (Washington, D.C.: National Academy Press, 1983), pp. 72, 141–142.

64. DCID 3/13, "Technology Transfer Intelligence Committee," December 3, 1981.

65. Edward T. Pound, "U.S. Sees New Signs Israel Resells Its Arms to China, South Africa," *Wall Street Journal*, March 13, 1992, pp. A1, A6.

66. Central Intelligence Agency, *A Consumer's Guide to Intelligence*, p. 53; Konrad Ege, "CIA Targets African Economies," *Counter Spy* (July-August 1982): 30–38.

67. Department of Justice, *Report on Inquiry into CIA-Related Electronic Surveillance Activities*, pp. 72–73; Office of Naval Intelligence, *Office of Naval Intelligence (ONI) Annual History 1985*, 1986, pp. 5, 9.

68. DCID 3/8, "Critical Intelligence Problems Committee," April 6, 1983.

69. Office of Naval Intelligence, *Office of Naval Intelligence (ONI) Annual History 1985*, p. 9; Edward C. Mishler, *History of the Air Force Office of Special Investigations 1 July 1975–31 December 1976, Volume I, Narrative* (Washington, D.C.: AFOSI, 1978), p. 23.

70. Central Intelligence Agency, *A Consumer's Guide to Intelligence*, p. 54; Bob Woodward and John Mintz, "Despite Vast U.S. Hunt, Perot Says POWs Held," *Washington Post*, June 21, 1992, p. A18.

71. DCID 3/15, "Foreign Language Committee," March 5, 1982.

72. Central Intelligence Agency, *A Consumer's Guide to Intelligence*, p. 36.

73. Director of Central Intelligence, *Annual Report FY 1994, Director of Central Intelligence*, September 1995, p. 7.

74. DCID 3/14, "Information Handling Committee," May 4, 1982; Naval Intelligence Activity, *Calendar Year 1991 History, Naval Intelligence Activity (NIA) 1 January–30 September 1991*, 1992, p. 6; Putney *History of the Air Force Intelligence Service, 1 January–31 December 1983, Volume 1, Narrative and Appendices*, p. 95.

75. General Accounting Office, *Combating Terrorism: Federal Agencies' Efforts to Implement National Policy and Strategy*, GAO/NSIAD–97–254, September 1997, pp. 22, 32.

76. Ibid., p. 23; U.S. Congress, Senate Select Committee on Intelligence, *Current and Projected National Security Threats to the United States* (Washington, D.C.: U.S. Government Printing Office, 1997), p. 51.

77. Central Intelligence Agency, *A Consumer's Guide to Intelligence*, p. 41.

78. Ibid.

79. DOD Directive 5137.1, Assistant Secretary of Defense for Command, Control, Communications, and Intelligence, February 12, 1992.

80. Department of Defense, *Defense Reform Initiative Report* (Washington, D.C.: DOD, 1997), pp. 58–60.

81. George I. Seffers, "Pentagon Responds To Outcry Over C³I," *Space News*, February 16–22, 1998, pp. 3, 42; "DOD Space, Airborne Reconnaissance Oversight Combined," *Aerospace Daily*, March 20, 1998, p. 2420; "Wedding Bells," *Aviation Week & Space Technology*, March 23, 1998, p. 25; Duane P. Andrews, *A Recommended Blueprint for the ASD (C³I) and CIO in Response to DRI Directive #17*, March 11, 1998.

82. Warren Ferster, "Pentagon Overhauls Space Policy Structure," *Space News*, May 18–24, 1998, p. 4; Bryan Bender, "USA Gets New Focal Point for All Military C4ISR," *Jane's Defence Weekly*, May 20, 1998, p. 9.

83. William J. Perry and John Deutch, "Charter for Joint Space Management Board," December 14, 1995.

84. Ibid. The Andrews study (note 81) recommended elimination of this board, noting (p. 21): "This board is made up of 24 senior officials, three ex officio members, and two executive secretaries: such a body cannot efficiently provide integrated program planning, efficient resource allocation, or accountable management for the nation's national security space program."

85. U.S. Congress, Senate Select Committee to Study Governmental Activities with Respect to Intelligence Activities, *Final Report, Book I: Foreign and Military Intelligence*, p. 335; U.S. Congress, House Committee on Appropriations, *Department of Defense Appropriations for 1994, Part 1* (Washington, D.C.: U.S. Government Printing Office, 1993), p. 45; Private information.

86. Lt. Col. Steve Palm, "DOD's Military Intelligence Board," *Communiqué*, April/May 1997, p. 13.

87. Ibid.

88. Ibid.

89. Ibid.

90. Weinberger, *FY 1983 Report of Secretary of Defense Caspar Weinberger*, p. III-88; Department of Defense Inspector General, *Defense Intelligence Agency Inspection Report 91-INS–06*, 1991, p. 14.

91. Department of Defense, Memorandum for Correspondents No. 264-M, September 18, 1992.

92. DOD Directive 5205.9, "Joint Military Intelligence Program," April 7, 1995.

93. Ibid.; U.S. Congress, House of Representatives, Report 105–508, *Intelligence Authorization Act for Fiscal Year 1999* (Washington, D.C.: U.S. Government Printing Office, 1998), p. 7.

94. DOD Directive 5205.9, "Joint Military Intelligence Program."

95. Brig. Gen. Frank B. Campbell, Director of Forces, USAF, "Air Force TIARA Programs: Intelligence Support to the Warfighter," 1995.

18

MANAGING INTELLIGENCE COLLECTION AND COVERT ACTION

Management of three different types of collection—imagery, SIGINT, and HUMINT—reflects both the commonality and diversity of the operations and collection systems the intelligence community employs. Both imagery and SIG-INT are collected by satellites as well as aircraft—which can be involved in international incidents. At the same time, SIGINT is also collected by ground stations, ships, and submarines—which are not employed, to a significant extent, for the acquisition of imagery. And, of course, human collection is a quite different method of collection.

Managing covert action is yet another aspect of the management task. Inadequate management can result not only in an inefficient use of resources but in political disaster.

MANAGING SATELLITE IMAGING

For many years, the actual job of translating general imagery collection priorities into the targeting of systems against installations or activities had been the responsibility of the Committee on Imagery Requirements and Exploitation (COMIREX). COMIREX was established on July 1, 1967, by Director of Central Intelligence Directive 1/13 as the successor to the Committee on Overhead Reconnaissance (COMOR). COMOR's responsibilities included coordination of collection requirements for the development and operation of all imaging satellites. As these programs grew, the number of photographs increased substantially, resulting in serious duplication of imagery exploitation activities. One solution to this problem involved replacing COMOR with COMIREX. COMIREX's membership consisted of representatives from all USIB/NFIB agencies, plus the intelligence chiefs of the Army, Navy, and Air Force. The committee was staffed by personnel from the CIA and the DIA.[1]

The functions of COMIREX were summarized by former COMIREX chairman Roland S. Inlow:

COMIREX performs the interagency coordination and management functions needed to direct photographic satellite reconnaissance, including the process of deciding what targets should be photographed and what agencies should get which photos to analyze. It also evaluates the needs for, and the results from, photographic reconnaissance, and oversees security controls that are designed to protect photography and information derived from photography from unauthorized disclosure.[2]

COMIREX dealt with three basic questions with regard to the establishment of targets and priorities:

1. What installations/areas were to be imaged?
2. What systems were to be targeted on specific installations/areas?
3. What was to be the frequency of coverage?

When the United States operated a single type of imaging satellite system (the KH-11), COMIREX's decision problem with regard to the second question was simple, but as advanced KH-11 and LACROSSE/VEGA satellites joined the constellation, the decision became more complicated. In any case, there are always significant areas of contention among consumers over priorities and targeting. In addition, there are a multitude of technical questions with regard to the imagery of targets that must be factored into decisions concerning items 1 and 2—including the angle and altitude at which the image is to be obtained.

Conflicts over satellite imagery targeting priorities can occur for a variety of reasons. Current intelligence requirements can conflict with more long-term requirements—as when coverage of the Iran-Iraq battlefield meant bypassing some opportunities for monitoring the Iraqi nuclear program. Strategic and tactical intelligence requirements may also conflict. Day-to-day coverage, revealing movements of troops or weapons and small changes in capabilities, may be of interest to military commanders; at the national level, in the absence of a crisis, such information is of little interest. COMIREX served to prioritize the claims of the CIA, the DIA, the military services, and other consumers with the objective of distributing a strictly limited resource in such a way as to at least minimally satisfy the legitimate requests of several competitive bureaucracies.

In the area of imagery exploitation, COMIREX allocated interpretation tasks among the National Photographic Interpretation Center, the CIA's Office of Imagery Analysis, the imagery exploitation components of the DIA, and the military service intelligence organizations. The basic division of labor was spelled out in COMIREX's National Tasking Plan for Imagery Processing and Exploitation.[3] With NIMA's absorption of NPIC, the CIA's Office of Imagery Analysis, and the DIA's imagery exploitation component, NIMA now must decide between which interpretation tasks it will perform itself, and which it will assign to military service intelligence organizations.

Following its creation, the Central Imagery Office assumed responsibility for tasking satellites and exploitation components. According to DCID 2/9 of June 1,

1992, "Management of National Imagery Intelligence," the CIO was to "perform those Intelligence Community responsibilities previously vested in COMIREX." Tasking was to be done by a central imagery tasking authority "in accordance with intelligence requirements established by the DCI in peacetime and the Secretary of Defense in wartime." The CIO was also to produce the *National Tasking Policy for Imagery Exploitation* to allocate interpretation tasks among the different agencies.[4] NIMA's Central Imagery Tasking Office is the successor to the CIO tasking function.

Among the innovations in imagery tasking that took place during the 1970s was COMIREX's establishment of the COMIREX Automated Management System (CAMS). CAMS used operations research procedures to take the requirements from different customers and create a tasking plan to optimize satellite operations in pursuit of those requirements and established priorities. In 1996 NIMA established the Requirements Management System to supersede CAMS. The system can be accessed from eighty locations throughout the world.[5]

MANAGING SIGINT

Management of the United States SIGINT System (USSS) is vested in the Director of the NSA by National Security Council Directive No. 6. The most recently available version of that directive, the version of February 17, 1972, was still operative as of 1987.[6] In addition to defining the components of SIGINT—COMINT and ELINT—the directive states:

> The Secretary of Defense is designated as Executive Agent of the Government for the conduct of SIGINT activities in accordance with the provisions of this directive and for the direction, supervision, funding, maintenance and operation of the National Security Agency. The Director of the National Security Agency shall report to the Secretary of Defense, the Director of Central Intelligence, and the Joint Chiefs of Staff. The Secretary of Defense may delegate, in whole or part, authority over the Director of the National Security Agency within the Office of the Secretary of Defense.
>
> It shall be the duty of the Director of the National Security Agency to provide for the SIGINT mission of the United States, to establish an effective unified organization and control of all SIGINT collection and processing activities of the United States, and to produce SIGINT in accordance with the objectives, requirements and priorities established by the Director of Central Intelligence Board. No other organization shall engage in SIGINT activities except as provided for in this directive.
>
> Except as provided in paragraphs 5 and 6 of this directive (re unique responsibilities of CIA and FBI) the Director of the National Security Agency shall exercise full control over all SIGINT collection and processing activities . . . The Director of the National Security Agency is authorized to issue direct to any operating elements engaged in SIGINT operations such instructions and assignments as are required. All instructions issued by the Director under the authority provided in this paragraph shall be mandatory, subject only to appeal to the Secretary of Defense . . .

The Armed Forces and other departments and agencies often require timely and effective SIGINT. The Director of the National Security Agency shall provide such SIGINT . . .

The intelligence components of the individual departments and agencies may continue to conduct direct liaison with the National Security Agency in the interpretation and amplification of requirements and priorities established by the Director of Central Intelligence (emphasis in original).[7]

One means of managing the SIGINT systems is via the U.S. Signals Intelligence Directives (USSIDs) issued by the Director of the NSA. The numbering scheme for the directives is keyed to the different types of subject matter covered by the directives. Thus, the USSID numbering system can be described as follows:

USSID	1–99	Policy
USSID	100–199	Collection
USSID	200–299	Processing
USSID	300–399	Analysis and Reporting
USSID	400–499	Standards
USSID	500–599	Administration
USSID	600–699	Training
USSID	700–799	ADP
USSID	1000–	Tasking[8]

A listing of known USSIDs is given in Table 18.1.

As indicated in the extract from NSCID No. 6 above, although the Secretary of Defense is the executive agent, and the Director of the NSA is the program manager of the USSS, requirements and priorities are to be established by the NFIB and the National SIGINT Committee. The committee is the successor to a series of predecessors. As of 1950, prior to the creation of the NSA, the work was divided between the Armed Forces Security Agency Council's Intelligence Requirements Committee (AFSAC/IRC) and the U.S. Communications Intelligence Board's Intelligence Committee (USCIB/IC). The AFSAC/IRC was primarily responsible for targeting and setting priorities for intercepts of military traffic. The USCIB/IC was primarily concerned with non-military traffic.[9]

Following the creation of the NSA, NSCID No. 9 of December 9, 1952, reconstituted the USCIB to operate under the Special Committee of the NSC for COMINT, which consisted of the Secretary of State, the Secretary of Defense, and the Attorney General, and was assisted by the DCI. In 1958, when the USCIB and the Intelligence Advisory Committee were merged into the USIB, two committees were created: the COMINT Committee and the ELINT Committee (by

TABLE 18.1 U.S. Signals Intelligence Directives

Number	Title/Subject	Date
3	SIGINT Security	August 1972
4	SIGINT Support to Military Commanders	July 1, 1974
18	Limitations and Procedures in Signals Intelligence Operations of the USSS	May 18, 1976
40	ELINT Operating Policy	October 1970
52	SIGINT Support to Electronic Warfare Operations	n.a.
56	Exercise SIGINT	n.a.
58	SIGINT Support to MIJI	n.a.
101	COMINT Collection Instructions	Dec. 1, 1989
110	Collection Management Procedures	Dec. 18, 1987
150	SIGINT Numerical Tasking Register	Feb. 1, 1985
240	ELINT Processing, Analysis, and Reporting	n.a.
300	SIGINT Reporting	n.a.
301	Handling of Critical (CRITIC) Information	Nov. 25, 1987
302	SIGINT Alert Systems	n.a.
316	Non-Codeword Reporting System	June 19, 1987
319	Tactical Reporting	n.a.
325	AIRBOAT Procedures	n.a.
326	Electronic Warfare Mutual Support Procedures	n.a.
341	Technical ELINT Product Reporting	n.a.
369	Time-Sensitive SIGINT Reporting	n.a.
402	Equipment and Manning Standards for SIGINT Positions	Sept. 8, 1986
404TM	Technical Extracts from Traffic Analysis (TEXTA)	Dec. 14, 1988
505	Directory of SIGINT Organizations	n.a.
550	Technical SIGINT Support Policies, Procedures, and Responsibilities	n.a.
601	Technical Support for Cryptologic Training	n.a.
602	Specialized Operational Training	n.a.
701	Sanitizing and Declassifying ADP Storage Devices	Sept. 30, 1976
702	Automatic Data Processing Systems Security	Sept. 1980
1045	SIGINT Tasking for USM-45, Misawa	Jan. 16, 1980
1600	SIGINT Tasking for US Army Tactical SIGINT Units	June 7, 1989

SOURCES: U.S. Congress, House Permanent Select Committee on Intelligence, *Annual Report* (Washington, D.C.: U.S. Government Printing Office, 1978), pp. 70, 72; Working Group on Computer Security, *Computer and Telecommunications Security* (Washington, D.C.: National Communications Security Committee, July 1981), pp. 110, 157; Defense Intelligence College, *Instructional Management Plan: Advanced Methods of Intelligence Collection,* March 1984; Department of the Army AR 350-3, "Tactical Intelligence Readiness Training (RED-TRAIN)," November 20, 1984, p. 7; Department of the Army, *FM 34-1, Intelligence and Electronic Warfare Operations,* July 1987, Ref. 2; Department of the Army, *FM 34-40-12, Morse Code Intercept Operations (U),* August 26, 1991, Ref. 3; U.S. European Command, ED 40-6, Operations and Administration of JIC, April 25, 1989; Private information.

means of DCID 6/1 and DCID 6/2, respectively, both issued on October 21, 1958). The ELINT and COMINT Committees were merged to form the SIGINT Committee by DCID 6/1 of May 31, 1962.[10]

The responsibilities of the SIGINT Committee are extensive, as indicated by DCID 6/1 of May 12, 1982, reprinted as Figure 18.1. They include developing specifications for SIGINT collection requirements, monitoring the responsiveness of U.S. and cooperating foreign SIGINT agencies, and developing policies for the conduct of SIGINT liaison and the security of SIGINT-obtained information. In the 1993 fiscal year key SIGINT Committee activities included the development of a new architecture for SIGINT satellites, the review and approval of selected allied relationships, the review of foreign military sales requests, and several special evaluations.[11]

Prior to the Middle East war in 1973, the USIB SIGINT Committee recommended that the Middle East be a priority target for intelligence collection if hostilities erupted. The NSA was asked to evaluate the intelligence collected and to determine appropriate targets. Upon the outbreak of war, the NSA implemented these policies under the SIGINT Committee's guidance. The committee discussed and approved the DIA's recommendation to change the primary target of one collector.[12]

In addition to validating requirements and tasking collection assets, the SIGINT Committee examines the relationships between U.S. SIGINT agencies and foreign agencies. Thus, in 1972 the committee developed a new set of objectives regarding SIGINT relations with Japan.[13]

The SIGINT Committee operated for many years with two permanent subcommittees, which remain in existence—the SIGINT Requirements Validation and Evaluation Subcommittee (SIRVES) and the SIGINT Overhead Reconnaissance Subcommittee (SORS). SIRVES was established in the 1970s, as a successor to the Evaluation Subcommittee, to, among other things, oversee the National SIGINT Requirements System (which is discussed in more detail below). SIRVES has restructured the key SIGINT requirements covering the former USSR and Eastern Europe.[14]

SORS was established in the 1960s, with the arrival of satellite collection. It is "responsible for receipt, approval, and subsequent generation of intelligence guidance in response to tasks to be levied on national resources [i.e., space systems]" and "continually monitors requirements and provides collection and processing guidance for both long- and short-term needs."[15]

In the mid-1990s two new groups were established—the Weapons and Space Systems Advisory Group (WSSAG) and the National Emitter Intelligence Subcommittee (NEIS). The WSSAG was created to "coordinate SIGINT on foreign weapons and space systems," whereas the NEIS is concerned with SIGINT production on foreign radars and other non-communications signals. The committee may also employ working groups and task forces on a short-term basis—such as the Third Party Ad Hoc Working Group of 1972.[16]

A second DCI committee that might on occasion have input on the subject of SIGINT requirements is the Critical Intelligence Problems Committee (CIPC).

FIGURE 18.1 DCID 6/1, The SIGINT Committee

SECRET
NOFORN

DIRECTOR OF CENTRAL INTELLIGENCE DIRECTIVE[1]
SIGINT Committee
(Effective 12 May 1982)

Pursuant to the provisions of Section 102, the National Security Act of 1947, and Executive Order 12333, there is established a Signals Intelligence (SIGINT) Committee.

1. Mission

The mission of the SIGINT Committee is to advise and assist the Director of Central Intelligence (DCI) and the Director, National Security Agency (DIRNSA) in the discharge of their duties and responsibilities with respect to Signals Intelligence as specified in Executive Order 12333, to monitor and assist in coordinating within the Intelligence Community the accomplishment of objectives established by the DCI, and to promote the effective use of Intelligence Community SIGINT resources.

2. Functions:

Under the general guidance of the Deputy Director of Central Intelligence, the SIGINT Committee shall:

a. advise the DCI on the establishment of SIGINT requirements, priorities, and objectives;

b. develop statements, based on the DCI's objectives and priorities, of collection and exploitation requirements for COMINT, ELINT, foreign instrumentation signals, nonimagery infrared, coherent light, and nonnuclear electromagnetic pulse (EMP) sources. (These statements will provide guidance for resource programming, mission planning, and reporting. Each statement should take into account practical limitations, costs, and risk factors.)

c. monitor and evaluate the responsiveness of present and programmed United States and cooperating foreign SIGINT resources to United States needs for intelligence information;

d. monitor the impact on SIGINT programs of information needs levied by intelligence comsumers;

e. advise and make recommendations on the dissemination and sanitization of SIGINT or information derived therefrom and the release of disclosure of SIGINT or derived information to foreign governments or international organizations in which the United States Government participates;

f. develop and recommend to the DCI policies, directives, and guidance for the conduct of SIGINT arrangements with foreign governments;

g. assess and report to the DCI on the potential impact on current and future United States SIGINT capabilities of providing cryptographic assistance to foreign governments; and

---

[1]This directive supersedes DCID No. 6/1, 18 May 1976.

SECRET

Classified by: DCI
Declassify on: OADR

FIGURE 18.1   (continued)

SECRET
NOFORN

h. review, develop, and recommend to the DCI policies for the protection, through classification and compartmentation, of COMINT, ELINT, and other SIGINT or of information about them or derived from them and procedures enabling United States Government entities outside of the Intelligence Community to receive and use SIGINT.

3. Intelligence Community Responsibilities

Upon request of the Committee Chairman, Intelligence Community elements shall provide information pertinent to the Committee's mission and functions within DCI-approved security safeguards.

4. Composition and Organization

The Committee Chairman will be appointed by the Director of Central Intelligence.

The members of the committee will be representatives designated by Intelligence Community principals.

The Chairman will establish subcommittees or task forces as required.

With the approval of the DCI, the Committee Chairman may invite representatives of relevant United States Government entities to participate as appropriate.

The Committee will be supported by an Executive Secretariat.

William J. Casey
Director of Central Intelligence

SECRET

On January 31, 1972, the DCI requested the Critical Collection Problems Committee (CCPC), as the CIPC was then known, to conduct a review of intelligence efforts against narcotics. In a section entitled "SIGINT Information on Narcotics and Dangerous Drugs," the CCPC report of October 1972 noted in part:

1. No SIGINT resources are dedicated solely to the intercept of narcotics information. The SIGINT which is now being produced on the international narcotics problem is a by-product of SIGINT reporting on other national requirements. . . .
5. The effective use of SIGINT information in support of ongoing operations while at the same time protecting the source has been a problem.
6. Successful usage of the SIGINT product is largely contingent upon close collaboration between the SIGINT producers and the appropriate customer agencies.

The CCPC therefore recommended that the "NSA, in conjunction with the interested customers, particularly BNDD and Customs, make appropriate determination of what COMINT support is required on the narcotics problem and that the requisite priorities be established through the SIGINT Committee."[17]

As noted above, under congressional pressure a National SIGINT Requirements System was established in 1975, after USIB approval. Under this system, the NFIB must conduct a formal community review and approval procedure for each requirement before it can be validated and placed on a National SIGINT Requirements List (NSRL). The NSRL is today the basic guidance document for the NSA and specifies SIGINT targets according to well-defined priorities, including cross-references to DCI and other national requirements documents. The system does not, however, prevent the Director of the NSA from determining which specific signals to intercept in fulfillment of requirements. Nor does it prevent the Secretaries of State and Defense or military commanders from directly tasking the NSA in a crisis and then informing the DCI and SIGINT Committee afterward.[18]

The yearly statement of objectives, requirements, and priorities are given in the yearly Consolidated Cryptologic Program (CCP) and Defense Cryptologic Program, formerly the Tactical Cryptologic Program (TCP). The TCP "was established in 1979 to correct the problem of disparate requirements competing for limited available funding within the NFIP which resulted in inadequate treatment of Service tactical support needs."[19]

MANAGING SENSITIVE RECONNAISSANCE MISSIONS

Reconnaissance conducted by satellite is relatively nonintrusive because it does not require actual violation of a target nation's airspace. Further, with the exception of Russia, no nation possesses means of destroying U.S. satellites. And even during the Cold War, the likely costs to the Soviet Union of interfering in an obvious ways with such satellites was likely to be far greater than the potential benefits.

When airborne overflights or air, sea, or submarine missions close to a nation's borders are involved, the potential for an international incident is much greater. Early Cold War aircraft reconnaissance missions directed at the Soviet Union involved this risk because they approached or penetrated the margins of Soviet and East European territory to collect a variety of intelligence, including the signatures and operating frequencies of air defense systems.[20]

Over the years incidents occurred involving air and sea missions. In 1962, during the Cuban Missile Crisis, one U-2 strayed into Soviet territory and another was shot down during a flight over Cuba. In 1967 the Israeli Air Force bombed the USS *Liberty* while it was collecting signals intelligence in the midst of the Six Day War. In 1968 the USS *Pueblo* was seized by North Korea during a SIGINT mission off the North Korean coast, and in 1969 an EC-121 SIGINT aircraft was shot down by North Korean forces while it patrolled off the same coast. The North Koreans also made hundreds of attempts to shoot down overflying SR-71s. In addition, there have been several incidents involving U.S. submarines conducting HOLYSTONE-type missions, including collisions with Soviet submarines.[21]

The U.S. system for the management of these missions reflects many considerations. Many of the missions are conducted in support of and proposed by the unified and specified commands. Others are clearly designed to provide national intelligence. In either case, such missions could cause an international incident, and thus they require national-level approval and close monitoring.

As noted in Chapter 17, special Navy reconnaissance programs are the initial responsibility of the "National Special Navy Program Executive Committee," chaired by the DCI and reporting to the Secretary of Defense. Missions originating from the commanders in chief of the unified commands go through a chain of supervisory offices and divisions, beginning with the command's Joint Reconnaissance Center (JRC).

Until recently, a national Joint Reconnaissance Center operated as part of the J-3 (Operations) Directorate of the Joint Chiefs of Staff and collocated with the National Joint Military Intelligence Center.[22]

The JRC was established in 1960 after the loss of an RB-47 over the Barents Sea. In the aftermath, President Eisenhower assigned General Nathan Twining the task of avoiding a repetition. The Air Force proposed that it become the executive agent, a proposal strongly resisted by the Navy. Finally, the JRC was established as part of the J-3 on October 24, 1960.[23]

The JRC acted as an initial approval authority for reconnaissance plans developed by unified, specified, and theater commands. It also developed a Joint Reconnaissance Schedule (JRS)—which was "several inches thick and filled with hundreds of pages of highly technical data and maps"—monitored the progress of the missions, and provided the National Military Command Center with real-time information regarding the status and disposition of forces, mission activity, and other reconnaissance related information. Figure 18.2 shows a 1980 request related to planning for a possible second mission to rescue U.S. hostages in Iran.

FIGURE 18.2 SR-71 Mission Request

THE JOINT CHIEFS OF STAFF ~~SECRET~~
WASHINGTON, D.C. 20301

3 November 1980

THE JOINT STAFF

MEMORANDUM FOR DIRECTOR, JOINT RECONNAISSANCE CENTER

Subject: SR 71 Mission Request

1. (U) (TS) Request consideration be given to conducting several SR 71 surveillance missions of the Persian Gulf during the next 3-6 weeks.

2. (U) (TS) Purpose of mission is to determine locations of major oil rig concentrations and typical flow pattern of Gulf shipping to assist in selection of low level air penetration routes.

3. (U) (TS) Recognize that missions could raise Soviet/Iran/ME speculation; however, given irregular scheduling, direct association with any US military planning will probably be low. On the other hand, periodic SR 71 missions would provide "reason" for increased tanker support in the area prior to the execution of any US military contingency action.

JAMES B. VAUGHT
Major General, USA

~~TOP SECRET~~

CLASSIFIED BY JCS, J-3▮
DECLASSIFY ON 3 NOV 2000

The JRC, operating through three branches, performed several functions:

- receiving, reviewing, evaluating, and submitting for approval to the JCS the reconnaissance plans, programs, and schedules originated by the commanders of the unified and specified commands, the military services, and other governmental agencies
- preparing the planning guidance for the execution of reconnaissance operations of special significance or sensitivity

- reviewing intelligence support plans, and preparing policy guidance, planning, analysis, and review of reconnaissance related activities that support trans- and post-SIOP nuclear operations
- monitoring the missions approved by the JRC and insuring that all incidents were brought to the attention of appropriate authorities
- displaying on a current basis all peacetime military reconnaissance and some other sensitive operations[24]

Those functions are now performed by the Reconnaissance Operations Division (ROD) of the J-3 Directorate, as the JRC has been retitled.[25] As indicated in Figure 18.3, the ROD consists of three branches (Administrative, Airborne, and Maritime) and several liaison offices.

FIGURE 18.3 Organization of the Reconnaissance Operations Division

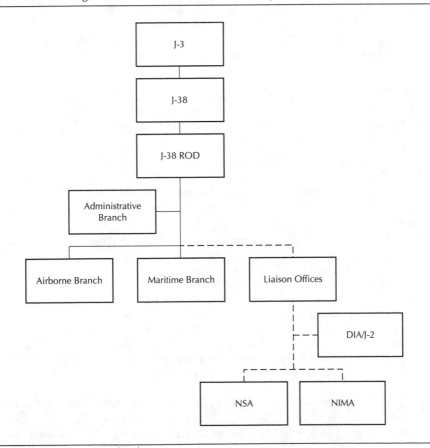

SOURCE: Department of Defense.

MANAGING HUMINT

Human source collection requires a diverse set of management arrangements to deal with a variety of sources, including foreign service officers, clandestine agents, and defectors, as well as nongovernmental sources.

The titles of NSCID No. 4 of February 4, 1972, "The Defector Program," and two DCIDs—4/1, "The Interagency Defector Committee," and 4/2, "Defector Program Abroad"—suggest the importance with which defectors were viewed during the Cold War. In addition to defining a variety of terms (defectors, inducement, potential defector, disaffected person, walk-in, refugee, and escapee), the directives also stated that "defection, particularly from the USSR, should be encouraged and induced, employing both conventional and unconventional means, whenever there is a net advantage to U.S. interests" and that the United States should:

1. encourage and induce the defection of the maximum number of persons from the USSR and of Soviet nationals outside the USSR
2. continue, and if possible expand, effort to encourage and induce the defection of key members of elite groups of countries other than the USSR who may qualify as defectors

In addition, DCID 4/2 suggested that recruitment in place be carefully considered before any U.S. department or agency took action to induce defection. When an individual did defect, the first priority was to determine whether the defector possessed any information indicating the imminence of hostilities.[26]

NSCID No. 4 and the associated DCIDs were written long before the collapse of the Soviet Union. However, defectors from other hostile nations, Communist and noncommunist, are still considered of importance. Thus, as noted in Chapter 11, in the aftermath of Operation Desert Storm, Iraqi defectors provided valuable information on the Iraqi nuclear program.

NSCID No. 5, "U.S. Espionage and Counterintelligence Abroad," of February 17, 1972, gave the DCI primary responsibility for coordination of clandestine collection activities. Paragraphs 2a and 2b authorized the DCI to

establish the procedures necessary to achieve such direction and coordination, including the assessment of risk incident upon such operations as compared to the value of the activity, and to ensure that sensitive operations are reviewed pursuant to applicable directives [and to] coordinate all clandestine activities authorized herein and conducted outside the United States and its possessions, including liaison that concerns clandestine activities or that involves foreign clandestine services.[27]

At the DCI committee level, these responsibilities belonged to the Human Resources Committee (HRC). This committee was first proposed in 1970 by Gen. Donald Bennett, Director of the DIA, as a means of providing a national-level forum to coordinate both overt and clandestine human source collection. It was not established immediately, however, because of objections from the CIA's Directorate of Plans. In addition to falling victim to the bureaucratic "territorial imperative," the directorate sought to minimize the number of individuals with access to information concerning clandestine sources. As a result, DCI Richard Helms established an ad hoc task force to study the problem of human source collection. After a year of study, the task force recommended the establishment of a USIB committee on a one-year trial basis—a suggestion endorsed by the President's Foreign Intelligence Advisory Board (PFIAB) in a separate study. In June 1974, the committee attained permanent status as the Human Sources Committee, and in 1975 its name was changed to the Human Resources Committee.[28]

The committee's functions were specified by DCID 3/7 of October 12, 1982. They were:

A. to examine problems and consider possible improvements in collection and procedures for dissemination of intelligence obtained by human resources and to provide recommendations to the DCI related thereto

B. to encourage and promote collection activities and coordination among human resources collection agencies concerning the allocation of effort and responsibility for the satisfaction of foreign intelligence needs[29]

Through its Assessments Subcommittee, the HRC conducted community-wide assessments of human source reporting in individual countries. In 1976 and 1977 the subcommittees of the HRC included those for Collection Program Evaluation; Research and Development; Organization, Training, and Advisory; Planning and Programming; and Guidance and Requirements.[30]

The guidelines establishing the committee specifically avoided giving it responsibility for reviewing the operational details or internal management of the individual departments or agencies. Departments and agencies were authorized to withhold "sensitive" information from the committee and to report directly to the DCI.[31]

As of 1975, the HRC had "only just begun to expand community influence over human collection," issuing a general guidance document called the Current Intelligence Reporting List (CIRL). The military made some use of the document, but the CIA's Directorate of Operations instructed CIA stations that the list was provided only for reference and did not constitute collection requirements for CIA operations.

During 1977 the committee provided the U.S. Ambassador in Iran, William Sullivan, with a short prioritized list of items of national intelligence interest. The list was developed by the HRC with the advice of the National Intelligence Officer for the Near East and South Asia. The chairman of the HRC, in his cover letter, expressed his hope that the list would "be of some use . . . as a coordinated interagency expression of the most important information Washington needs."[33]

In addition to the HRC, the now defunct Intelligence Community Staff played a role in HUMINT tasking. During the 1970s it began to issue the National

Human Intelligence Collection Plan. The plan included an advisory for HUMINT collectors, such as Foreign Service officers, who are outside the NFIP. Apparently, it included a variety of subplans for specific subject areas. Thus, in 1988 there were National HUMINT Collection Plans for Space, Soviet Naval Forces, Soviet Strategic Forces, and Soviet S&T. The plan's effect was limited by being only one of several guidance documents levied on human source collectors.[34]

More recently, several initiatives have been launched to improve coordination of clandestine collection. In 1992 a National HUMINT Requirements Tasking Center (NHRTC), replacing the HRC, was established within the CIA's Directorate of Operations to allocate collection tasks between all HUMINT agencies. Then DCI Robert Gates described the center as "an integrated interagency mechanism for tasking human intelligence requirements to that part of the community that has the best chance of acquiring the information at least cost and risk."[35]

The center—which consists of senior representatives from the DIA, the State Department, and the CIA, and a staff of about twelve drawn from the military and three CIA directorates (Intelligence, Operations, and Science and Technology)—has three key areas of responsibility:

- identifying information needs from policymakers, the military, science and technology centers, law enforcement, and analysts
- establishing collection priorities for collection and reporting
- tasking requirements to the most suitable collector and assessing their capability to respond to these requirements[36]

The principal products of the center are National HUMINT Collection Directives (NHCDs), which define the requirements for HUMINT collection and tasking. They attempt to focus on the succeeding two-year period, although many are periodically updated. As of late 1997, there were over 100 current NHCDs on countries and transnational issues. Issues covered in the directives included support to military operations, weapons of mass destruction, advanced conventional weapons, and counterterrorism.[37]

If the subject of a NHCD requires more detailed treatment, which may occur with technical subjects such as proliferation, intelligence community analysts write a Collection Support Brief (CSB), which is appended to the directive.[38]

NHRTC guidance is binding on the clandestine and overt HUMINT collections components of the CIA Directorate of Operations and the Defense HUMINT Service. It is advisory with respect to collection elements outside the intelligence community, such as the Foreign Commercial Service of the Department of Commerce and Department of State embassy reporting.[39]

Also of note is DCID 2/3 of July 25, 1963, entitled "Domestic Exploitation of Nongovernmental Organizations and Individuals," which vests in the CIA responsibility for managing the domestic exploitation program. The CIA is instructed to determine the foreign intelligence potential of nongovernmental organizations and individuals, to serve as coordinator for other government agencies, and to disseminate to intelligence departments and agencies all foreign intelligence information obtained through the program.[40]

MANAGING COVERT ACTION

Management of U.S. covert action programs involves procedures and review groups within the CIA and the NSC. To initiate a covert action, a Presidential Finding is required by the Hughes-Ryan Amendment to the Foreign Assistance Act of 1961. Under that and subsequent regulations, the finding must state that the President has determined that the "operation in a foreign country . . . is important to the national security of the United States" and then go on to describe the scope (the country or countries that are the target) of the operation and what the operation involves. Findings must also specify each U.S. government entity that will participate in any significant way in the program's implementation and whether any third party will participate in the program in any significant way; findings may not authorize violation of the Constitution or any U.S. statute.[41] Figure 18.4 shows one of the findings signed in pursuit of the attempt to establish contact with Iranian "moderates."

Findings are initially prepared within the CIA's Directorate of Operations, either as a result of a directorate initiative or in response to requests from the DCI, who in turn may be responding to a presidential request. Before a proposed finding leaves the Directorate of Operations it is reviewed by the Covert Action Planning Group (CAPG), composed of the Associate Deputy Director for Operations, senior staff chiefs, and those individuals who have a substantive responsibility for the finding and its eventual implementation. If approved by the CAPG, the finding is sent on to the top echelon of CIA management for review and recommendations and then to the DCI.[42]

Under the Reagan administration, if the proposed finding was approved by the DCI it would go to the Planning and Coordination Group (PCG) of the NSC, which consisted of senior representatives of the State Department, Defense Department, and the NSC. If the PCG supported the finding, it sent a favorable recommendation to the National Security Planning Group (NSPG). Approval of the NSPG then resulted in a Presidential Finding. NSDD 159, of January 18, 1985, "Covert Action Policy Approval and Coordination Procedures," specified that all intelligence findings be written and circulated among the eight senior members of the NSPG before being put into effect.[43]

Since 1991, under Title V of the National Security Act, Presidential Findings must be in writing and may not confer retroactive authorization for covert activities— except in emergencies when oral findings may be used for up to twenty-four hours.[44]

FIGURE 18.4 Presidential Finding on Iran

Finding Pursuant to Section 662 of
The Foreign Assistance Act of 1961
As Amended, Concerning Operations
Undertaken by the Central Intelligence
Agency in Foreign Countries, Other Than
Those Intended Solely for the Purpose
of Intelligence Collection

I hereby find that the following operation in a foreign country (including all support necessary to such operation) is important to the national security of the United States, and due to its extreme sensitivity and security risks, I determine it is essential to limit prior notice, and direct the Director of Central Intelligence to refrain from reporting this Finding to the Congress as provided in Section 501 of the National Security Act of 1947, as amended, until I otherwise direct.

SCOPE	DESCRIPTION
Iran	Assist selected friendly foreign liaison services, third countries and third parties which have established relationships with Iranian elements, groups, and individuals sympathetic to U.S. Government interests and which do not conduct or support terrorist actions directed against U.S. persons, property or interests, for the purpose of: (1) establishing a more moderate government in Iran, (2) obtaining from them significant intelligence not otherwise obtainable, to determine the current Iranian Government's intentions with respect to its neighbors and with respect to terrorist acts, and (3) furthering the release of the American hostages held in Beirut and preventing additional terrorist acts by these groups. Provide funds, intelligence, counter-intelligence, training, guidance and communications and other necessary assistance to these elements, groups, individuals, liaison services and third countries in support of these activities.
	The USG will act to facilitate efforts by third parties and third countries to establish contact with moderate elements within and outside the Government of Iran by providing these elements with arms, equipment and related materiel in order to enhance the credibility of these elements in their effort to achieve a more pro-U.S. government in Iran by demonstrating their ability to obtain requisite resources to defend their country against Iraq and intervention by the Soviet Union. This support will be discontinued if the U.S. Government learns that these elements have abandoned their goals of moderating their government and appropriated the material for purposes other than that provided by this finding.

The White House
Washington, D.C.
Date January 17, 1986

Notes

1. DCID 1/13, "Coordination of Collection and Exploitation of Imagery Intelligence," February 2, 1973, *Declassified Documents Reference System (DDRS)*, 1980–132D; DCID 1/13, "Committee on Imagery Requirements and Exploitation," July 1, 1967, *DDRS* 1980–132B; U.S. Congress Senate Select Committee to Study Governmental Operations with Respect to Intelligence Activities, *Final Report, Book I: Foreign and Military Intelligence* (Washington, D.C.: U.S. Government Printing Office, 1976), p. 85.

2. Roland S. Inlow, "An Appraisal of the Morison Espionage Trial," *First Principles* 11, no. 4 (May 1986): 1–5.

3. CINCPACFLT Instruction S3822.1E, *PACOM Imagery Reconnaissance Procedures and Responsibilities*, July 5, 1983, p. 1; HQ EUCOM Directive No. 40–4, "Exploitation and Dissemination of Time-Sensitive Imagery," November 4, 1983, p. 1.

4. DCID 2/9, "Management of National Imagery Intelligence," June 1, 1992.

5. Walter Pincus, "Space Imagery Overhaul Aims at Better Data and Easier Access," *Washington Post*, January 20, 1998, p. A7.

6. National Security Agency, *NSA Transition Briefing Book* (Ft. Meade, Md.: NSA, 1980), not paginated; National Security Agency/Central Security Service, *NSA/CSS Manual 22–1* (Ft. Meade, Md.: NSA, 1986), p. 1.

7. Department of Justice, *Report on CIA-Related Electronic Surveillance Activities* (Washington, D.C.: Department of Justice, 1976), pp. 77–79.

8. Private information.

9. George A. Brownell, *The Origins and Development of the National Security Agency* (Laguna Hills, Calif.: Aegean Park Press, 1981), p. 3.

10. James Bamford, *The Puzzle Palace: A Report on NSA, America's Most Secret Agency* (Boston: Houghton Mifflin, 1982), p. 50; Department of Justice, *Report on CIA-Related Electronic Surveillance Activities*, p. 91; DCID 6/1, "Communications Intelligence Committee," October 21, 1958, *DDRS* 1980–130C; DCID 6/2, "Electronics Intelligence Committee," October 21, 1958, *DDRS* 1980–130D; DCID 6/1, "SIGINT Committee," May 1, 1962, *DDRS* 1980–131D.

11. Office of the Deputy Chief of Staff for Intelligence, *Office of the Deputy Chief of Staff for Intelligence, Annual Historical Review, 1 October 1992 to 30 September 1993*, n.d., p. 4-4.

12. U.S. Congress, Senate Select Committee to Study Governmental Operations with Respect to Intelligence Activities, *Final Report, Book I, Foreign and Military Intelligence*, p. 85.

13. Naval Intelligence Command, *Naval Intelligence Command (NAVINTCOM) History for CY-1972*, August 1, 1973, p. 20.

14. Department of the Army, Office of the Assistant Chief of Staff for Intelligence, *Annual Historical Review, 1 October 1984–30 September 1985*, p. 2-30; Office of the Deputy Chief of Staff for Intelligence, *Annual Historical Review, 1 October 1990–30 September 1991*, 1993, p. 4-34; Lois G. Brown, "National SIGINT Committee," *NSA Newsletter*, February 1997, p. 2.

15. Department of the Army, Office of the Assistant Chief of Staff for Intelligence, *Annual Historical Review, 1 October 1984–30 September 1985*, p. 2-30; Office of the Deputy Chief of Staff for Intelligence, *Annual Historical Review, 1 October 1990–30 September 1991*, 1993, p. 4-34; Brown, "National SIGINT Committee."

16. Brown, "National SIGINT Committee"; Naval Intelligence Command, *Naval Intelligence Command (NAVINTCOM) History for CY-1972*, p. 19.

17. Department of Justice, *Report on CIA-Related Electronic Surveillance Activities*, pp. 101–103.

18. U.S. Congress, Senate Select Committee to Study Governmental Activities with Respect to Intelligence Activities, *Final Report, Book I, Foreign and Military Intelligence*, pp. 85–86; U.S. Congress, House Permanent Select Committee on Intelligence, *Annual Report*, (Washington, D.C.: U.S. Government Printing Office, 1978), p. 55; Stephen J. Flanagan, "The Coordination of National Intelligence," in *Public Policy and Political Institutions: United States Defense and Foreign Policy—Policy Coordination and Integration*, ed. Duncan Clarke (Greenwich, Conn.: JAI, 1985), p. 177.

19. National Security Agency, *NSA Transition Briefing Book*, not paginated.

20. See Jeffrey T. Richelson, *American Espionage and the Soviet Target* (New York: Morrow, 1987), pp. 120–126.

21. Bamford, *The Puzzle Palace*, pp. 184–185, 216–231; U.S. Congress, House Committee on Armed Services, *Inquiry into the U.S.S. Pueblo and EC-121 Plane Incidents* (Washington, D.C.: U.S. Government Printing Office, 1969); "Radar Detector Aboard SR-71 Alerted Plane Missile Attack," *New York Times*, August 29, 1983, p. 3.

22. U.S. Congress, House Appropriations Committee, *Department of Defense Appropriations for 1994, Part 1* (Washington, D.C.: U.S. Government Printing Office, 1993), p. 37.

23. Col. Thomas G. Shepherd, Chief, Reconnaissance Programs Division J-3, Memorandum for the Record: "Conversation between Colonel Earnest R. Harden (USAF Ret.) and Colonel Thomas G. Shepherd, OJCS/JRC, 11 August 1977," August 12, 1977.

24. Joint Chiefs of Staff, JCS Publication 4, *Organization and Functions of the Joint Chiefs of Staff* (Washington, D.C.: U.S. Government Printing Office, 1985), pp. III-3-28 to III-3-29.

25. Charles P. Wilson, *Strategic Reconnaissance in the Middle East: Is Manned High-Altitude Aerial Reconnaissance Still Needed?* (Washington, D.C.: The Washington Institute for Near East Policy, 1997), pp. 13–14.

26. DCID 4/2, "The Defector Program Abroad," June 26, 1959, in *Documents from the Espionage Den (53): U.S.S.R., The Aggressive East*, section 4 (Tehran: Muslim Students Following the Line of the Imam, n.d.), pp. 4–11; U.S. Congress, House Permanent Select Committee on Intelligence, *Annual Report*, p. 70.

27. NSCID No. 5, "U.S. Espionage and Counterintelligence Activities Abroad," February 17, 1972, *DDRS 1976–253F*.

28. U.S. Congress, Senate Select Committee to Study Governmental Operations with Respect to Intelligence Activities, *Final Report, Book I, Foreign and Military Intelligence*, p. 85 n. 42.

29. DCID 3/7, "Human Resources Committee," October 12, 1982.

30. U.S. Congress, Senate Select Committee to Study Governmental Operations with Respect to Intelligence Activities, *Final Report, Book I, Foreign and Military Intelligence*, pp. 86–87; Department of the Army, Office of the Assistant Chief of Staff for Intelligence, *Annual Historical Review, 1 October 1976–30 September 1977*, n.d., pp. 28–34.

31. U.S. Congress, Senate Select Committee to Study Governmental Operations with Respect to Intelligence Activities, *Final Report, Book I, Foreign and Military Intelligence*, p. 86.

32. Ibid.

33. Scott Armstrong, "Intelligence Experts Had Early Doubts About Shah's Stability," *Washington Post*, February 2, 1982, pp. 1, 9.

34. Flanagan, "The Coordination of National Intelligence," p. 177; Navy Operational Intelligence Center, *Command History for CY 1987*, May 20, 1988, p. 7.

35. Remarks by Robert M. Gates, Director of Central Intelligence, to Association of Former Intelligence Officers, Boston, November 14, 1992, p. 5.

36. Teresa M. Jones, "The National HUMINT Requirements Tasking Center," *Communiqué*, October/November 1997, pp. 11–12.

37. Ibid.

38. Ibid.

39. U.S. Congress, House Permanent Select Committee on Intelligence, *IC 21: Intelligence Community in the 21st Century* (Washington, D.C.: U.S. Government Printing Office, 1996), p. 194 n.

40. DCID 2/3, "Domestic Exploitation of Nongovernmental Organizations and Individuals," July 25, 1963, *DDRS* 1980–131E.

41. U.S. Congress, House Select Committee to Investigate Covert Arms Transactions with Iran and Senate Select Committee on Secret Military Assistance to Iran and the Nicaraguan Opposition, *Report of the Congressional Committees Investigating the Iran-Contra Affair with Supplemental, Minority, and Additional Views* (Washington, D.C.: U.S. Government Printing Office, 1987), pp. 376–377; Caspar Weinberger, Memorandum to the Secretary of the Army, Subject: DOD Support [to CIA Special] Activities, June 13, 1983, p. 1; U.S. Congress, Senate Select Committee on Intelligence, *U.S. Actions Regarding Iranian and Other Arms Transfers to the Bosnian Army, 1994–1995* (Washington, D.C.: SSCI, 1996), p. 3.

42. Wilhelm G. Hinsleigh, "Covert Action: An Update," *Studies in Intelligence* (Spring 1986).

43. Ibid.; NSDD 159, "Covert Action Approval and Coordination Procedures," January 18, 1985; NSDD 266, "Implementation of the Recommendations of the President's Special Review Board," March 31, 1987, p. 7.

44. U.S. Congress, Senate Select Committee on Intelligence, *U.S. Actions Regarding Iranian and Other Arms Transfers to the Bosnian Army, 1994–1995*, p. 3.

19

MANAGING INFORMATION ACCESS AND ANALYSIS

The U.S. intelligence collection effort produces an enormous volume of information, particularly from its numerous technical collection systems. Collection, however, is only an intermediary step in the intelligence process—between the formulation of requirements and the production of finished intelligence. Thus, the information collected must be channeled to those who process and analyze the data at the CIA's Directorate of Intelligence, the National Imagery and Mapping Agency, the Defense Intelligence Agency, the State Department's Bureau of Intelligence and Research, and the intelligence analysis components of the military services.

The same information, either in its raw or processed and analyzed form, must also be made available to a wide variety of individuals—policymakers, policy implementers, strategists, contractors, and consultants—who need it in order to perform their jobs. Information is also made available to U.S. allies under treaty or other arrangements for intelligence sharing. At the same time, much of the information needs to be protected, since its disclosure might reveal nonobvious targets of collection and/or collection capabilities—disclosures that could lead to effective countermeasures and precautions and the denial of such information in the future. Hence, it is necessary to establish guidelines for the classification and distribution of intelligence information, as well as for access to that information by both U.S. and foreign governments.

Although the numerous analytical intelligence units have distinct functions, it is still necessary to manage the analytical process on a community-wide basis. Aside from the avoidance of undesired duplication where the potential for such duplication exists, officials must ensure that intelligence production is responsive to the requirements of national and departmental leaders. The intelligence community must have mechanisms to deal with analytical problems, and agencies working on similar problems must maintain an adequate degree of cooperation on a day-to-day basis. Further, coordinating the production of national estimates is a delicate process involving several agencies with differing perspectives.

MANAGING INFORMATION ACCESS

The basic means of managing or controlling access to intelligence information are delineated in the classification system, which defines different levels of sensitivity and restricts access to those who have been cleared at that level and have a "need to know." The best known classifications are those used to restrict access to a wide range of national security information: Confidential, Secret, and Top Secret.

Confidential information is defined as information "the unauthorized disclosure of which could be expected to cause damage to the national security that the original classification authority is able to identify or describe." Secret information differs from Confidential information in that the expected damage would be "serious." In the case of Top Secret information, the damage would be "exceptionally grave."[1]

In theory, at least, access for an individual with clearance at a certain level is further restricted to the information the individual needs to know in order to perform his or her job. In some cases the need-to-know principle is implemented by compartmenting certain sets of data—such as that concerning specific operations or individuals. Thus, the Army Intelligence and Security Command's offensive counterintelligence operations are designated by a special code word used to restrict access to information about those operations. Similar operations conducted by the Air Force Office of Special Investigations have had the designation SEVEN DOORS. Information about sensitive or clandestine attaché collection activities involving non-U.S. sources or foreign materiel acquisition projects is sent via the DOD RODCA channel.[2]

The CIA's Directorate of Operations maintains several dozen compartments for the transmission of human source reports. The compartments are informally designated "blue border" or "blue stripe" material (for the blue stripes on the border of the cover sheet to any document containing such material). The CIA's Soviet Bloc Division used compartments such as REDWOOD, REDCOAT, and RYBAT. Among the documents classified SECRET RYBAT was a January 9, 1973, message from the Chief of the Soviet Bloc Division to Chiefs of Station and Base on "Turning Around REDTOP [Soviet Bloc] Walk-ins."[3]

In addition to the traditional Confidential, Secret, and Top Secret classifications, the intelligence community employs classifications for information that falls into the Sensitive Compartmented Information (SCI) category. According to a 1984 report by the NFIB Security Committee:

> Sensitive Compartmented Information is data about sophisticated technical systems for collecting intelligence and information collected by those systems. The characteristics of the systems that necessitated the development of SCI programs are (a) that compared to conventional intelligence activities employing human sources, many more people normally must know sensitive information in order to develop, build and operate the systems and to analyze the material they collect; (b) that they generally produce large quantities of accurate, detailed intelligence, which is needed and relied

upon by senior planners and policymakers, and which, by its nature is extremely frag-
ile, in that it reveals the characteristics of the systems that collect it; and (c) that they
are extremely vulnerable to adversary countermeasures, i.e. denial or deception.[4]

The systems that generate such SCI are imaging and signals intelligence satellites; aircraft such as the U-2 and RC-135; submarines involved in special Navy reconnaissance activities; and ground stations involved in the interception of foreign signals. Information about imaging and signals intelligence satellites also
falls into the SCI category.

Traditionally, a more stringent background investigation was required to gain
access to SCI than was required to gain access to Top Secret information. The
logic was that whereas denial of a Top Secret clearance required the presence of a
well-defined character or personality defect that posed a threat to national security, "no risk is tolerable where SCI is involved and individuals who have been
granted Top Secret clearances may be denied approval for access to SCI." National
Security Directive 63, of October 21, 1991, established the practice of single-scope
background investigations, which allow the same minimum standards for Top Secret and SCI background investigations. The directive does not prohibit more
stringent requirements for access to SCI, however. Thus, an SCI screening interview might delve into an individual's family, financial, sexual, drug, criminal, political, travel, mental health, and physical histories. Moreover, it is still the case
that the physical security measures used to protect SCI—particularly the holding
of SCI in vault areas from which it is not permitted to be removed—are more extensive than those used to protect Top Secret information.[5]

The first public hint of the existence of such a category occurred during the
Senate hearing on the Gulf of Tonkin Resolution in 1964, when Senate Foreign
Relations Committee Chairman William Fulbright inquired into the source of a
report that North Vietnamese patrol boats were about to attack the *Turner Joy* on
the night of August 4, 1964. Defense Secretary Robert McNamara, Fulbright, and
Senators Frank Lausche and Albert Gore engaged in the following colloquy:

McNamara   We have some problems because the [committee] staff has not
been cleared for certain intelligence.

Lausche   I do not understand that. The members of our staff are not
cleared?

Fulbright   All of those who have worked on this matter, but he is talking of
a special classification of intelligence communications . . .

Gore   Mr. Chairman, could we know what particular classification that is? I
had not heard of this super classification.

McNamara   Clearance is *above* Top Secret for the particular information
on the situation [emphasis added].[6]

The "above Top Secret" category dealt with communications or signals intelligence (rather than intelligence communications), and McNamara revealed that it was called Special Intelligence (SI).[7] SI is one of several categories of SCI.

The institutionalization of such categories and clearances, particularly SI, can be traced to the successful interception and decryption of Japanese, German, and Italian signals during World War II by the United States and Great Britain. The machine by which the United States was able to decode Japanese diplomatic messages was known as PURPLE, and the intelligence produced as a result was designated MAGIC. Distribution of MAGIC material was sharply restricted by George Marshall, who drew up a "Top List" of those authorized to have access. The list was restricted to President Roosevelt; the Secretaries of State, War, and the Navy; and the Directors of Military and Naval Intelligence. Among those not on the list was the commander of U.S. Naval Forces at Pearl Harbor, Admiral Husband Kimmel.[8]

The British also instituted a code word system to guard the fact that they were able to decrypt German and Italian military intelligence communications. The most sensitive military material was originally designated PEARL, ZYMOTIC, SWELL, and SIDAR. Later, the British settled on three code words—ULTRA, PEARL, and THUMB—to indicate material of special sensitivity. Eventually, PEARL and THUMB were combined into a single code word—PINUP.[9]

In addition to intercepting Japanese diplomatic communications, the United States also spent considerable effort in intercepting and trying to decipher Japanese military communications. The United States employed several code names to represent the product of such activity. DEXTER was the code word used for intercepts of the highest-level traffic—for example, Admiral Yamomoto's travel plans. CORRAL indicated less sensitive intercepts. RABID was used to indicate Traffic Analysis intelligence. With the signing of the BRUSA Communications Intelligence Agreement in May 1943, which standardized signals intelligence procedures between the United States and Britain, ULTRA was made a prefix to each classification, so that the code words became ULTRA DEXTER, ULTRA CORRAL, and ULTRA RABID.[10]

Although the outbreak of World War II required a significant expansion of those with a need to know ULTRA information, extraordinary security procedures were maintained and distribution was restricted as much as possible. Thus, the British maintained a system of Special Liaison Units to facilitate the transmission of ULTRA from the Government Code and Cypher School in Bletchley to military commanders. It was required that those with knowledge of ULTRA remain outside the battle areas to avoid any chance of capture. On occasions where exceptions were made and ULTRA-cleared personnel did risk capture, they carried cyanide pills to allow them to commit suicide to avoid interrogation.[11]

Within the SCI category are several sets of clearances—the most common being Special Intelligence (SI), GAMMA (G), TALENT-KEYHOLE (TK), and BYEMAN (B).

As McNamara indicated, the SI category concerns signals intelligence. Just as there were different ULTRA levels (for the United States), there are different compartments of the SI category corresponding to different levels of sensitivity. UMBRA is the successor to a long line of code words, including DINAR and TRINE, that designated the most sensitive SI material. Less sensitive is the SPOKE compartment, which might contain information from intercepts of PLO communications. Least sensitive is the information in the MORAY compartment.[12]

To express these differing levels of sensitivity, a page containing only UMBAR SCI will be stamped TOP SECRET UMBRA; a page containing only SPOKE SCI will be stamped SECRET SPOKE; and a page containing only MORAY SCI will be stamped SECRET MORAY. While the use of the Top Secret and Secret prefixes may appear to imply that UMBRA, SPOKE, and MORAY are simply "need-to-know" compartments of those conventional classifications, such a conclusion is inconsistent, with, among other things, the fact that greater physical security measures are taken to protect a SECRET MORAY or SECRET SPOKE document than are taken for a plain Top Secret document.[13]

Further designators are employed by the NSA for especially sensitive UMBRA information. GAMMA is a designator that was reserved exclusively for intercepts of Soviet communications until 1969, when the NSA received orders to use the same methods and procedures to monitor the communications of U.S. antiwar leaders. At one point, there were at least twenty GAMMA designations, including GILT, GOAT, GULT, GANT, GUPY, GABE, GYRO, and GOUT, each of which referred to a specific operation or method. As noted in Chapter 8, GAMMA GUPY referred to the interception of radio-telephone conversations being conducted by Soviet leaders as they were driven around Moscow in their limousines. GAMMA GOUT referred to the material obtained by interception of South Vietnamese government communications.[14] Thus, a document might bear the classification of TOP SECRET UMBRA GAMMA GYRO.

At one time, there was a DELTA compartment of UMBRA for intercepts relating to Soviet military operations, such as the location of Soviet submarines or aircraft operations. DELTA categories included DACE, DICE, and DENT.[15]

SI documents might also bear a code word indicating that the SIGINT was obtained from a Third Party to the UKUSA Agreement. DRUID designates a Third Party intercept. Other designations indicate the specific nations involved: JAEGER (Austria), ISHTAR (Japan), SETEE (Korea), DYNAMO (Denmark), RICHTER (Germany), and DIKTER (Norway).[16]

The TK or TALENT-KEYHOLE clearance restricts access to information concerning the product of certain overhead collection systems—specifically, imaging and signals intelligence satellites and the U-2. Compartments within the TK system include RUFF, ZARF, and CHESS. RUFF pertains to information produced by imaging satellites; ZARF indicates ELINT obtained by satellite; and CHESS designates certain U-2 photography. Thus, the December 1986 final report of the DCI Mobile Missile Task Force Intelligence Requirements and Analysis Working Group is classified TOP SECRET RUFF ZARF UMBRA.[17]

In practice, SI and TK clearances, which both permit access to the product of technical collection systems, are almost awarded jointly. Hence, the term "SI-TK clearance" is more common than the terms "SI clearance" or "TK clearance." Although, an SI-TK clearance gives individuals access to the product of sensitive intelligence systems, it does not grant access to information concerning the systems themselves. Information about the type of system, its location, name, orbit, or capabilities is not accessible to an individual simply on the basis of an SI-TK clearance. Clearances for such information were traditionally granted on a system-by-system basis, with each system having a specific code word. Each code word represented a compartment of the BYEMAN system. POPPY, CANYON, RHYOLITE, AQUACADE, CHALET, VORTEX, MERCURY JUMPSEAT, MAGNUM, ORION, and TRUMPET are BYEMAN compartments used for past and present SIGINT satellites, often with several different words being used over time for a single system. CORONA, ARGON, LANYARD, GAMBIT, KENNAN, CRYSTAL, INDIGO, LACROSSE, and VEGA are code names associated with past and present imaging satellites. PARCAE was the BYEMAN code name for the first major set of ocean surveillance satellites.[18]

Individual systems still have their own code names. However, as a result of the 1993 BYEMAN Compartmentation Restructure study, a single major compartment was established, with access to specific programs on a need-to-know basis.[19]

In recent years, two new clearances that appear to be widely held in the SCI world were established. One of these is SPECTRE,* which is concerned with intelligence relating to terrorist activities. The other, the subject matter of which is not known, is LOMA.[20]

According to one document, additional CIA, NSA, and Navy SCI compartments are CS, PM, VER, SNCP, and M. PM and VER may correspond to two Navy (and possibly NSA) SCI compartments—PANGRAM and VERDANT. SNCP referred to the Special Navy Control Program, which employed submarines to collect intelligence in or near the territorial waters of the Soviet Union, as discussed in Chapter 8. M also represented a Navy SCI system—MEDITATE—that concerned information about IVY BELLS-type operations. In recent years, the terms Naval Activities Support Program (NASP) and DNI's Special Access Program (DSAP) appear to have replaced SNCP and MEDITATE, respectively.[21]

A code word classification specific to the NSA is Very Restricted Knowledge (VRK). The classification was established in November 1974 by the Director of the NSA "to limit access to uniquely sensitive SIGINT activities and programs."[22]

---

*Those familiar with the James Bond novels will recognize SPECTRE as the acronym for the Special Executive for Counterintelligence, Terrorism, Revenge, and Extortion. It is reasonable to assume that the code word was not chosen by U.S. intelligence officials by coincidence.

The classification system described above, as well as personnel and security standards for access to and handling of intelligence information, is defined in a series of executive orders, national security decision directives, National Security Council Intelligence Directives (NSCIDs), Director of Central Intelligence Directives (DCIDs), and DOD Directives. Additionally, several DCI committees are concerned with the security of the information acquired as well as that of sources and methods.

As noted in Chapter 17, since the Eisenhower administration most administrations have issued an executive order on national security information. Since President Bush did not, the order that was still in force as of January 1993 was Ronald Reagan's 1982 executive order. In April 1993, President Clinton signed Presidential Review Directive 29 on "National Security Information," which set forth a review process to be completed prior to the issuance of a new executive order.[23]

President Clinton signed Executive Order 12958, "Classified National Security Information," on April 17, 1995. Part 1 of the order defines classification levels (Top Secret, Secret, Confidential) and specifies the officials (by position) who can classify information or delegate the authority to do so. This section also specifies the identification and markings that are to be shown on the face of all classified documents and the basic rules concerning the duration of classification.[24]

In addition, part 1 defines the types of information that shall be considered for classification and establishes limitations on classification. Information may be considered for classification if it concerns:

A. military plans, weapons systems, or operations
B. foreign government information
C. intelligence activities (including special activities), intelligence sources or methods, or cryptology
D. foreign relations or foreign activities of the United States, including confidential sources
E. scientific, technological, or economic matters relating to the national security
F. United States government programs for safeguarding nuclear materials or facilities
G. vulnerabilities or capabilities of systems, installations, projects or plans relating to national security[25]

Section 1.8, which deals with limitations on classification, forbids classification to "conceal violations of law, inefficiency, or administrative error; prevent embarrassment to a person, organization, or agency; restrain competition; or prevent or delay the release of information that does not require protection in the interest of national security."[26]

The remaining parts of the order deal with derivative classification (part 2), declassification and downgrading (part 3), safeguarding (part 4), and implementation and review (part 5). Section 4.4 of part 4 specifies that a Special Access Program can, unless otherwise authorized by the president, be established only by the Secretaries of State, Defense, and Energy, and the Director of Central Intelligence, or their principal deputies. It also requires that the number of such programs be kept to a minimum and that they be established only upon a specific finding that:

1. the vulnerability of, or threat to, specific information is exceptional; and
2. the normal criteria for determining eligibility for access applicable to information classified at the same level are not deemed sufficient to protect the information from unauthorized disclosure; or
3. the program is required by statute[27]

The Reagan administration issued two NSDDs concerning the control of intelligence information: NSDD-19 of January 12, 1982, "Protection of Classified National Security Council and Intelligence Information," and NSDD-84 of March 11, 1983, "Safeguarding National Security Information."[28]

NSDD-19 required advanced senior-level approval for all contacts with the news media that would involve discussions about classified National Security Council (NSC) or classified intelligence information. It also specified that the number of officials with access to documents relating to NSC matters be kept to a minimum and that, in the event of unauthorized disclosure of such information, government employees with access to the information would be subject to investigation. The investigations could employ all legal methods.[29]

Because of NSDD-19, those granted access to classified NSC information were required to sign a cover sheet acknowledging access and agreeing to "cooperate fully with any lawful investigation by the United States Government into any unauthorized disclosure of classified information contained therein."[30]

A February 12, 1982, memo from the Assistant to the President for National Security Affairs, William Clark, superseded NSDD-19. It continued the language on the cover sheet as well as the requirement to minimize the number of officials with access to NSC information but made no mention of obtaining approval of press contacts.[31]

NSDD-84 specified that all government officials and employees with access to SCI sign a nondisclosure agreement providing for prepublication review of any of their writings or speeches dealing with subjects relating to SCI—for example, START verification. Beginning in 1981, individuals with access to SCI had been required to sign Form 4193, which provided for lifetime prepublication review of all SCI-related writings, "including works of fiction, which contain or purport SCI or that I have reason to believe are derived from SCI." After promulgation of NSDD-84, Form 4193 was revised to expand the requirement so that individuals would also have to submit writings that contained or purported to contain, "any classified information from intelligence reports or estimates; or . . . any information concerning intelligence activities, sources, or methods."[32]

As a result of congressional opposition, President Reagan suspended the pre-publication review portion of the revised 4193. However, employees were still required to sign the prior version of Form 4193 before being granted access to SCI.[33] The present SCI form is shown as Figure 19.1.

NSCID No. 1 of February 17, 1972, "Basic Duties and Responsibilities," authorized the Director of Central Intelligence to

> disseminate national intelligence and interdepartmental intelligence on a strictly controlled basis to foreign governments and international bodies upon his determination after consultation with the United States [now National Foreign] Intelligence Board, that such action would substantially promote the security of the United States, provided such dissemination is consistent with existing statutes and Presidential policy, including that reflected in international agreements.[34]

NSCID No. 1 also makes the DCI responsible for developing policies and procedures for the protection of intelligence, intelligence sources, and methods from unauthorized disclosure. In carrying out these responsibilities, DCIs have issued several DCIDs concerning personnel matters, physical security, and the dissemination of intelligence information to foreign governments.

The version of DCID 1/7 issued in 1987, "Control of Dissemination of Intelligence Information," was, according to a 1995 DCI memo, "written to constrain dissemination to the most strict need-to-know basis."[35] Newer versions of DCID 1/7, issued in 1995 and 1996, were intended to reflect a risk management approach to imposing restrictions on dissemination, to allow for a wider dissemination of intelligence within the government and to contractors, and to eliminate restrictions that were believed to have outlived their usefulness.

Thus, DCID 1/7 of April 12, 1995, "Security Controls on the Dissemination of Intelligence Information," offered some relief to the long-standing "third agency rule" that prohibited the dissemination of intelligence beyond a recipient agency without the consent of the originating agency. Under the new DCID, intelligence community components consent to the use of their intelligence in intelligence products of other components and to the dissemination of the products within the executive branch, except as specifically restricted by controls defined in the directive. The DCID also allowed dissemination to intelligence community contractors, within specific guidelines in the directive.[36]

The directive did not eliminate the originator control of all information. The ORCON (shorthand for Dissemination and Extraction of Information Controlled By Originator) marking could be used but "only on classified intelligence that clearly identifies or would reasonably permit ready identification of intelligence sources or methods that are particularly susceptible to countermeasures that would nullify or measurably reduce their effectiveness."[37]

The directive also permitted continued use of the PROPIN (CAUTION-PROPRIETARY INFORMATION INVOLVED) and NOFORN (NOT RELEASABLE TO FOREIGN NATIONALS) markings. PROPIN has been used to identify information

FIGURE 19.1 Sensitive Compartmented Information Nondisclosure Statement

---

SENSITIVE COMPARTMENTED INFORMATION NONDISCLOSURE STATEMENT

PRIVACY ACT STATEMENT

AUTHORITY: EO 9397, November 1943 (SSN).

PRINCIPAL PURPOSE(S): The information contained herein will be used to precisely identify individuals when it is necessary to certify their access to sensitive compartmented information.

ROUTINE USE(S): Blanket routine uses, as published by Defense Intelligence Agency in the Federal Register.

DISCLOSURE: Voluntary; however, failure to provide requested information may result in delaying the processing of your certification.

SECTION A

An Agreement Between _____ and the United

(Printed or Typed Name)

1. Intending to be legally bound, I hereby accept the obligations contained in this Agreement in consideration of my being granted access to information or material protected within Special Access Programs, hereinafter referred to in this Agreement as Sensitive Compartmented Information (SCI). I have been advised that SCI involves or derives from intelligence sources or methods and is classified or in the process of a classification determination under the standards of Executive Order 12356 or other Executive order or statute. I understand and accept that by being granted access to SCI, special confidence and trust shall be placed in me by the United States Government.

2. I hereby acknowledge that I have received a security indoctrination concerning the nature and protection of SCI, including the procedures to be followed in ascertaining whether other persons to whom I contemplate disclosing this information have been approved for access to it, and I understand these procedures. I understand that I may be required to sign subsequent agreements upon being granted access to different categories of SCI. I further understand that all my obligations under this Agreement continue to exist whether or not I am required to sign such subsequent agreements.

3. I have been advised that unauthorized disclosure, unauthorized retention, or negligent handling of SCI by me could cause irreparable injury to the United States or be used to advantage by a foreign nation. I hereby agree that I will never divulge anything marked as SCI or that I know to be SCI to anyone who is not authorized to receive it without prior written authorization from the United States Government department or agency (hereinafter Department or Agency) that last authorized my access to SCI. I understand that it is my responsibility to consult with appropriate management authorities in the Department or Agency that last authorized my access to SCI, whether or not I am still employed by or associated with that Department or Agency or a contractor thereof, in order to ensure that I know whether information or material within my knowledge or control that I have reason to believe might be SCI, or related to or derived from SCI, is considered by such Department or Agency to be SCI. I further understand that I am also obligated by law and regulation not to disclose any classified information or material in an unauthorized fashion.

4. In consideration of being granted access to SCI and of being assigned or retained in a position of special confidence and trust requiring access to SCI, I hereby agree to submit for security review by the Department or Agency that last authorized my access to such information or material, any writing or other preparation in any form, including a work of fiction, that contains or purports to contain any SCI or description of activities that produce or relate to

4. *(Continued)* have reason to believe are derived from SCI, that I contemplate disclosing to any person not authorized to have access to SCI or that I have prepared for public disclosure. I understand and agree that my obligation to submit such preparations for review applies during the course of my access to SCI and thereafter, and I agree to make any required submissions prior to discussing the preparation with, or showing it to, anyone who is not authorized to have access to SCI. I further agree that I will not disclose the contents of such preparation to any person not authorized to have access to SCI until I have received written authorization from the Department or Agency that last authorized my access to SCI that such disclosure is permitted.

5. I understand that the purpose of the review described in paragraph 4 is to give the United States a reasonable opportunity to determine whether the preparation submitted pursuant to paragraph 4 set forth any SCI. I further understand that the Department or Agency to which I have made a submission will act upon them, coordinating within the Intelligence Community when appropriate, and make a response to me within a reasonable time, not to exceed 30 working days from date of receipt.

6. I have been advised that any breach of this Agreement may result in the termination of my access to SCI and removal from a position of special confidence and trust requiring such access, as well as the termination of my employment or other relationships with any Department or Agency that provides me with access to SCI. In addition, I have been advised that any unauthorized disclosure of SCI by me may constitute violations of United States criminal laws, including the provisions of Sections 793, 794, 798, and 952, Title 18, United States Code, and of Section 783(b), Title 50, United States Code.. Nothing in this Agreement constitutes a waiver by the United States of the right to prosecute me for any statutory violation.

7. I understand that the United States Government may seek any remedy available to it to enforce this Agreement, including, but not limited to, application for a court order prohibiting disclosure of information in breach of this Agreement. I have been advised that the action can be brought against me in any of the several appropriate United States District Courts where the United States Government may elect to file the action. Court costs and reasonable attorneys' fees incurred by the United States Government may be assessed against me if I lose such action.

8. I understand that all information to which I may obtain access by signing this Agreement is now and will remain the property of the United States Government unless and until otherwise determined by an appropriate official or final ruling of a

DD FORM 1847-1, DEC 91 (EG) PREVIOUS EDITIONS ARE OBSOLETE. Designed using Perform Pro, WHS/DIOR, Jun 94

(continues)

434

FIGURE 19.1 (continued)

8. *(Continued)* court of law. Subject to such determination, I do not now, nor will I ever, possess any right, interest, title or claim whatsoever to such information. I agree that I shall return all materials that may have come into my possession or for which I am responsible because of such access, upon demand by an authorized representative of the United States Government or upon the conclusion of my employment or other relationship with the United States Government entity providing me access to such materials. If I do not return such materials upon request, I understand this may be a violation of Section 793, Title 18, United States Code.

9. Unless and until I am released in writing by an authorized representative of the Department or Agency that last provided me with access to SCI, I understand that all the conditions and obligations imposed upon me by this Agreement apply during the time I am granted access to SCI, and at all times thereafter.

10. Each provision of this Agreement is severable. If a court should find any provision of this Agreement to be unenforceable, all other provisions of this Agreement shall remain in full force and effect. This Agreement concerns SCI and does not set forth such other conditions and obligations not related to SCI as may now or hereafter pertain to my employment by or assignment or relationship with the Department or Agency.

11. These restrictions are consistent with and do not supersede conflict with or otherwise alter the employee obligations, rights, or liabilities created by Executive Order 12356; Section 7211 of Title 5, United States Code (governing disclosures to Congress); Section 1034 of Title 10, United States Code, as amended by the Military Whistleblower Protection Act (governing disclosure to Congress by members of the military);

11. *(Continued)* (governing disclosures of illegality, waste, fraud, abuse or public health or safety threats); the Intelligence Identities Protection Act of 1982 (50 USC 421 et seq.) (governing disclosures that could expose confidential Government agents), and the statutes which protect against disclosure that may compromise the national security, including Section 641, 793, 794, 798, and 952 of Title 18, United States Code, and Section 4(b) of the Subversive Activities Act of 1950 (50 USC Section 783(b)). The definitions, requirements, obligations, rights, sanctions and liabilities created by said Executive Order and listed statutes are incorporated into this agreement and are controlling.

12. I have read this Agreement carefully and my questions, if any, have been answered to my satisfaction. I acknowledge that the briefing officer has made available Sections 793, 794, 798, and 952 of Title 18, United States Code, and Executive Order 12356, as amended, so that I may read them at this time, if I so choose.

13. I hereby assign to the United States Government all rights, title and interest, and all royalties, remunerations, and emoluments that have resulted, will result, or may result from any disclosure, publication, or revelation not consistent with the terms of this Agreement.

14. This Agreement shall be interpreted under and in conformance with the laws of the United States.

15. I make this Agreement without any mental reservation or purpose of evasion.

16. TYPED OR PRINTED NAME *(Last, First, Middle Initial)*	17. GRADE/RANK/SVC	18. SOCIAL SECURITY NO.	19. BILLET NO. *(Optional)*
20. ORGANIZATION	21. SIGNATURE		22. DATE SIGNED *(YYMMDD)*

FOR USE BY MILITARY AND GOVERNMENT CIVILIAN PERSONNEL

SECTION B

The execution of this Agreement was witnessed by the undersigned, who accepted it on behalf of the United States Government as a prior condition of access to Sensitive Compartmented Information.

23. TYPED OR PRINTED NAME *(Last, First, Middle Initial)*	24. ORGANIZATION
25. SIGNATURE	26. DATE SIGNED *(YYMMDD)*

FOR USE BY CONTRACTORS/CONSULTANTS/NON-GOVERNMENT PERSONNEL

SECTION C

The execution of this Agreement was witnessed by the undersigned.

27. TYPED OR PRINTED NAME *(Last, First, Middle Initial)*	28. ORGANIZATION
29. SIGNATURE	30. DATE SIGNED *(YYMMDD)*

SECTION D

This Agreement was accepted by the undersigned on behalf of the United States Government as a prior condition of access to Sensitive Compartmented Information.

31. TYPED OR PRINTED NAME *(Last, First, Middle Initial)*	32. ORGANIZATION
33. SIGNATURE	34. DATE SIGNED *(YYMMDD)*

DD FORM 1847-1, DEC 91 (BACK)

provided by a commercial firm or private individual under an explicit or implicit understanding that the information would be protected as a proprietary trade secret or proprietary data. The 1995 directive noted that the NOFORN marking might be used on intelligence that "if released to foreign governments or nationals, could jeopardize intelligence sources or methods, or when it would not be in the best interest of the United States." One document that was classified SECRET NO-FORN ORCON PROPIN is the 1977 CIA study entitled *Israel: Foreign Intelligence and Security Services*. Its NOFORN control marking was assigned for a variety of reasons, including the documents likely impact on U.S.-Israeli relations if its content became available to the Israeli government. When the study was made public in 1979, after its seizure by Iranian militants from the U.S. Embassy in Tehran, it caused acute embarrassment to both the Israeli and U.S. governments because it alleged that Israeli intelligence agencies had blackmailed, bugged, wiretapped, and offered bribes to U.S. government employees in an effort to gain sensitive information. An Israeli spokesman denounced the allegations as "ridiculous." [38]

The 1995 directive did eliminate two long-time designations—NOCONTRACT (NOT RELEASABLE TO CONTACTORS/CONSULTANTS) and WNINTEL (Warning Notice-Intelligence Sources or Methods Involved). The first was eliminated due to the new policy that permitted release of intelligence to contractors under specified conditions. The latter was abolished because it "was always used in conjunction with one or more other control markings and added no value to understanding the content of the material."[39]

A little over a year after the 1995 DCID 1/7 was issued a new version replaced it. The policy section of the new directive explained that it was DCI policy that "intelligence be 'written for the consumer,' allowing for the widest dissemination of timely, tailored intelligence possible." It also noted that the "intelligence control markings established herein may only be used to identify and restrict dissemination of specific intelligence derived from sensitive sources and methods and signify that originator approval is required for additional dissemination or foreign release."[40]

This 1996 directive continued the 1995 directive's emphasis on taking a risk management approach to the restriction of intelligence, offering relief from the "third agency rule" and making intelligence accessible to contractors. It also continued to permit the use of the ORCON and PROPIN designations under the same conditions as the 1995 directive.[41]

The 1996 DCID also added two new designations to the set of obsolete markings. The REL (RELEASE AUTHORIZED TO . . .) category, used to indicate specific countries that intelligence data might be released to, was eliminated, as was the NOFORN category. In the place of NOFORN, a more restrictive US ONLY category was established "to identify that limited amount of intelligence which an originator has determined falls" in the category of intelligence that may not be disclosed as identified in DCID 5/6 on "Intelligence Disclosure Policy." In a covering memo to the 1996 DCID 1/7, DCI John Deutch noted that it was his hope that "US ONLY, would not become another NOFORN, a marking which was overused, redundant, and eventually, completely ineffective."[42]

A new provision of the 1996 DCID concerns dissemination and disclosure under emergency conditions. It specifies certain emergency situations (for example, a Joint Chiefs of Staff declaration of an alert condition of defense emergency, or an immediate threat by hostile forces to U.S. persons or facilities) that "warrant dissemination of intelligence to organizations and individuals not routinely included in such dissemination." It also specifies the specific conditions under which dissemination would be authorized—conditions that include a lack of time to obtain approval through normal intelligence disclosure channels.[43]

The 1996 DCID 1/7 notes that

> it is the policy of the DCI that intelligence may be shared with foreign governments, and international organizations or coalition partners consisting of sovereign states to the extent such sharing promotes the interests of the United States, does not pose unreasonable risk to U.S. foreign policy or national defense, and is limited to a specific purpose and normally of limited duration.[44]

However, the details of the policy governing intelligence sharing are the subject of DCID 5/6, "Intelligence Disclosure Policy." As of April 1996, the most recent revision of DCID 5/6 was that of May 26, 1983, although a new version was scheduled to be completed by the end of May 1996. The 1983 version contained a section entitled "Intelligence Which May Not Be Disclosed."[45]

As its title indicates, DCID 1/10 of January 18, 1982, "Security Policy Guidelines on Liaison Relationships with Foreign Intelligence Organizations and Foreign Security Services," establishes procedures concerning liaison relationships with foreign organizations, including the exchange of information.

Personnel and physical security have been the subject of several DCIDs, including: DCID 1/14 of April 14, 1986, "Minimum Personnel Security Standards and Procedures Governing Eligibility for Access to Sensitive Compartmented Information"; DCID 1/19 "Uniform Procedures for Administrative Handling and Accountability of Sensitive Compartmented Information"; DCID 1/20, "Security Policy Concerning Travel and Assignment of Personnel with Access to Sensitive Compartmented Information"; and DCID 1/21, "Physical Security Standards for Sensitive Compartmented Information Facilities."

DCID 1/14 specifies that the "granting of access to SCI shall be controlled under the strictest application of the 'need-to-know' principle and all individuals who are given access are required, as a condition of gaining access, to sign an agreement that they will not disclose that information to persons not authorized to receive it."[46]

The directive also stipulates that, except under special circumstances (which include liaison arrangements), individuals to be given SCI access, as well as their families, must be U.S. citizens. It requires that intended recipients undergo a Special Background Investigation (SBI) before being awarded SCI access—an investigation that, until NSD-63 was signed, was certain to be more extensive, in theory, than the background investigation for a Top Secret clearance. After the initial investigation, a periodic reinvestigation is conducted at least every five years. Additionally, the directive requires all departments employing personnel with SCI access to institute security programs that involve security education, security supervision, and security review.[47]

According to DCID 1/14, items to be considered in determining eligibility for access to SCI include: loyalty, close relatives and associates, sexual considerations, cohabitation, undesirable character traits, financial irresponsibility, alcohol abuse, use of illegal drugs and drug abuse, emotional and mental disorders, law violations, security violations, and involvement in outside activities.[48]

DCID 1/19 concerns physical security issues such as the establishment of vault facilities for holding SCI; intrusion detection; communications, computer, and data-processing security systems relating to the transmission of SCI; and other physical security systems. It also regulates the location of vault facilities in exposed or combat areas. Thus, the directive requires that "all electronic equipment which is used to process or transmit Sensitive Compartmented Information (SCI) shall meet national standards for TEMPEST."[49]

DCID 1/20 specifies that "no person with access to SCI will be assigned or directed to participate in a hazardous activity, as defined herein, until he or she has been afforded a defensive security briefing and/or risk of capture briefing."[50] The directive also requires that all individuals with access to SCI who plan unofficial travel through hazardous countries must give prior notification of all planned travel, receive a defensive security briefing, immediately contact certain U.S. authorities if detained or subjected to harassment, and report any unusual incidents to the appropriate security official upon return.[51]

On the basis of the executive orders, presidential directives, NSCIDs, and DCIDs, the Departments of Defense, State, Treasury and others produce implementation directives and manuals. Included are DOD Instruction 5230.22, "Control of Dissemination of Foreign Intelligence"; DIA Regulation 50-10, "Control of Dissemination of Foreign Intelligence"; DIA Manual 50-3, *Physical Security Standards for Construction of Sensitive Compartmented Information Facilities*.[52]

MANAGING THE ANALYTIC PROCESS

Management of the analytic process takes two basic forms. Management of the production of national intelligence reports—including the National Intelligence Estimates (NIEs) and the Special Estimates (SEs)—is the most visible of these. But in addition to the national estimates and reports, the U.S. intelligence community, as is clear from Chapter 14, produces a vast amount of finished intelligence on military, economic, political, and scientific and technical topics.

Although much of this intelligence is not "national" in the sense of being produced for national policymakers, it is important to the attainment of national security objectives.

Extensive intelligence production on atomic energy problems, space and weapons systems, and economic, social, and political matters provides input to national estimates as well as supplies detailed information needed by officials in various departments. Thus, it is necessary to ensure that departmental intelligence production is consistent with national priorities.

As with other types of intelligence activities, management of the analytical process is handled through NSCIDs, DCIDs, requirements documents, and various committees.

NSCIDs No. 1 and No. 3 are the general guidance documents for all aspects of intelligence production. Section 6 of NSCID No. 1 defines national intelligence as intelligence required for the formulation of national security policy, concerning more than one department or agency, and transcending the exclusive competence of a single department or agency. It authorizes the DCI to produce national intelligence and disseminate it to the president, the NSC, and other appropriate U.S. government components. In addition, this section stipulates that national intelligence must carry a statement of abstention or dissent of any NFIB member or intelligence chief of a military department who disagrees with the intelligence findings.[53]

NSCID No. 3 of February 17, 1972, "Coordination of Intelligence Production," distinguishes between different types of intelligence—basic intelligence, current intelligence, departmental intelligence, interdepartmental intelligence, and national intelligence—and assigns responsibilities for the production of basic and current intelligence to the CIA and a variety of other agencies.

The directive also specifies that:

A. The Department of State shall produce political and sociological intelligence on all countries and economic intelligence on countries of the Free World.

B. The Department of Defense shall produce military intelligence. This production shall include scientific, technical, and economic intelligence directly pertinent to the mission of the various components of the Department of Defense.

C. The Central Intelligence Agency shall produce economic, scientific and technical intelligence. Further, the Central Intelligence Agency may produce such other intelligence as may be necessary to discharge the statutory responsibilities of the Director of Central Intelligence.[54]

The directive assigns to all NFIB members charged with the production of finished intelligence the responsibility of producing atomic energy intelligence. In addition, when an intelligence requirement is established for which there is no existing production capability, the DCI, in consultation with the NFIB, is responsible for determining which departments or agencies of the intelligence community can "best undertake the primary responsibility as a service of common concern."[55]

On the basis of NSCIDs No. 1 and No. 3, the DCI issues DCIDs in the 1/ and 3/ series to further implement the NSCIDs. The original DCIDs governing the national intelligence production process were issued in July and September 1948. DCID 3/1 of July 8, 1948, "Standard Operating Procedures for Departmental Participation in the Production and Coordination of National Intelligence," required, except under exceptional circumstances, that, upon initiation of a report or estimate, the CIA inform departmental intelligence organizations of:

1. the problem under consideration
2. the nature and scope of the report or estimate involved
3. the scheduled date of issuance of the first draft
4. the requirements for departmental contributions . . .
5. the date upon which such departmental action should be completed[56]

Under normal procedures the CIA was to prepare an initial draft and then furnish copies to departmental intelligence organizations with a request for review and preparation. If the comments received indicated differences of opinion, the CIA was instructed to arrange for an informal discussion with departmental personnel. The CIA was then to prepare a final draft and distribute it to departmental intelligence organizations for concurrence or statements of substantial dissent, which would be incorporated in the final paper.

DCID 3/2 of September 13, 1948, complemented 3/1. Entitled "Policy Governing Departmental Concurrences in National Intelligence Reports and Estimates," the directive specified three options for departmental intelligence organizations: concur, concur with comment, or dissent. It further stated the considerations that should be involved in choosing among the options.[57]

Subsequently, DCIDs 3/1 and 3/2 were superseded by DCID 3/5 of September 1, 1953, entitled "Production of National Intelligence Estimates." The directive reflected the changes that had occurred in the intervening years—particularly the establishment of the Board of National Estimates (BNE) and the Intelligence Advisory Committee (IAC)—and required the BNE to present a production program for NIEs and SNIEs to the IAC every year by January 1.[58]

In 1950 an Office of National Estimates (ONE) was established within the CIA's Directorate of Intelligence. This office, tasked with drafting national and special national estimates, consisted of the Board of National Estimates and its staff. The board consisted of between seven and twelve senior officials with expertise in particular areas who were initially drawn from academia and subsequently from the CIA.[59]

The board was serviced initially by fifty professional analysts, subsequently by thirty. In theory, the board reacted to specific requests from the NSC, and in emergencies this was often the case. Thus, several SNIEs were commissioned during the Cuban Missile Crisis. However, the subject of the NIEs became routine on the basis of the board's judgment as to the requirements of policymakers.[60]

The process for drafting NIEs was established by DCI 3/1. It included initial drafting by BNE/ONE, interagency review, revision, and submission to the USIB with dissenting footnotes, if any. During the process, the BNE operated in collegial fashion, taking collective responsibility for the estimates produced and exercising collective judgment in approving them.[61]

The ONE suffered a decline in prestige and influence during the Nixon administration for a variety of reasons, including Henry Kissinger's unhappiness with its product. In June 1973, John Huizenga, the BNE chairman, was forced to retire. DCI William Colby decided not to replace him and abolished the ONE.[62] Colby gave two reasons for his decision:

> One, I had some concern with the tendency to compromise differences and put out a document which was less sharp than perhaps was needed in certain situations. Second, I believed that I needed the advantage of some individuals who could specialize in some of the major problems not just as estimative problems but as broad intelligence problems. They could sit in my chair, so to speak, and look at the full range of an intelligence problem: Are we collecting enough? Are we processing the raw data properly? Are we spending too much money on it? Are we organized right to do the job?[63]

Colby created the National Intelligence Officer (NIO) system, whereby specific individuals were held solely responsible for producing a particular estimate. In a 1987 memo on "The Integrity and Objectivity of National Foreign Estimates," the then Deputy Director for Intelligence, Richard J. Kerr, observed:

> The role of the *National Intelligence Officer*, in our judgment, is critical. An impartial estimative process requires the full expression of views by participating agencies and the clear identification for our consumers of areas of agreement and, often most importantly, disagreement. In order to fight what is often an unhealthy desire to reach consensus, the NIO must, above all, see himself as a manager of the process, the one who ensures that the tough questions are addressed, that consensus views represent real agreement, and not papered-over differences, and that minority views are fully expressed. It has been our experience that when the NIO subordinates this responsibility to the advocacy of a particular analytic line that the integrity of the estimative process suffers.[64]

NIOs are recruited mainly, but not exclusively, from the CIA and from specialists in a specific functional or geographic area. The number of NIOs, originally thirteen, went to eight, then seventeen, and then to the present twelve.

In the mid-1980s, in addition to three at-large NIOs, there were NIOs for Africa, East Asia, Europe, the Near East and South Asia, Latin America, the USSR, Counterterrorism, Science and Technology, Economics, General Purpose Forces, Strategic Programs, Warning, Foreign Denial and Intelligence Activities, and Narcotics.

The responsibilities of the NIO for Foreign Denial were summarized by one former holder of that position:

The responsibilities for the National Intelligence Officer for Foreign Denial and Intelligence Activities focuses on the question and issue of what are foreign governments doing to deny us the capabilities of collecting certain intelligence, to analyze the degree to which that has been done, to make recommendations as to how that might be alleviated. The intelligence activities aspect of it is related to that, but also includes such items as foreign disinformation programs, what are people doing to make it difficult for us to get at the truth.[65]

Today, there are NIOs for Europe; Russia and Eurasia; the Near East and South Asia; Africa; East Asia; Latin America; Strategic and Nuclear Programs; General Purpose Forces; Warning; Economics and Global Issues; Science and Technology; and Special Activities.[66]

The NIOs with regional responsibilities focus on issues such as: emerging relationships among the states of the former Soviet Union; the Arab-Israeli peace process; Cuba and Haiti; Central European reform; emerging economics in Southeast Asia; and the transition to democracy in South Africa.[67]

The NIO for Strategic and Nuclear Programs is responsible for producing studies on the current and future strategic forces of the former Soviet states and China; C^3 and the safety of nuclear weapons; chemical, biological, and strategic missile programs throughout the world; treaty monitoring; and space programs. The portfolio of the NIO for General Purpose Forces includes worldwide conventional ground, air, and naval forces; regional military relationships; current and future advanced conventional weapons balances; and the monitoring of assessments of conventional and chemical weapons arms control.[68]

The NIO for Science and Technology focuses on future technologies for weapons and military systems; nuclear materials disposition and disposal; information infrastructure issues; and technology sales and exports. The NIO for Economics and Global Issues reports on bilateral and regional economic developments; world economic trends; economic reform and transition to market economies; population and other demographic issues, as well as environmental issues.[69]

The responsibilities of the NIO for Warning include producing analytical reports on regional conflicts triggered by ethnic, religious, or national differences; proliferation threats involving weapons of mass destruction; and transnational threats such as terrorism, narcotics, and technology transfer. The NIO for Special Activities assists the DCI and DDCI on special projects, often involving technical issues, including encryption, aviation safety, information operations, and declassification. He or she also serves as the principal adviser to the DCI on a number of presidentially appointed commissions, such as the Moynihan commission on secrecy.[70]

Initially, NIOs were purposely not given a staff but were expected to draw on the resources of the CIA, the DIA, the INR, and other analytical units to produce the required estimates. On January 1, 1980, with the establishment of the National Intelligence Council (NIC), the NIOs were given not only a collective existence but also a staff.[71] The NIOs are specifically tasked with:

1. becoming knowledgeable of what substantive intelligence questions policy-makers want addressed
2. drawing up the concept papers and terms of references for the NIE
3. participating in the drafting and draft review of the NIE
4. chairing coordinating sessions and making judgments on substantive questions in debate
5. ensuring that the final text accurately reflects the substantive judgment of the DCI[72]

In addition to the NIEs, the NIOs are responsible for the Special Estimates, Interagency Intelligence Memoranda (IIMs), and Special IIMs.

When created, the BNE/ONE was firmly a part of the CIA. Under DCI John McCone the BNE was attached to the DCI's office and made responsible to him alone. During the Carter administration, the NIOs became part of the National Foreign Assessment Center (NFAC) and hence were placed under the direct control of the CIA's Deputy Director for National Foreign Assessment.[73]

One of the Reagan administration's earliest actions concerning intelligence was the downgrading of the NFAC to its previous identity—that is, the Directorate of Intelligence. With that change, the NIOs were once again placed under the control of the DCI. According to the Director of the NFAC at the time, John McMahon, that was a decision that

> the Director and I debated long and hard because at the time I was in charge of national foreign assessments, and I did not want it to happen out of the symmetry of management. The Director wanted to have it because he felt that intelligence was so vital, so important that it should not be left to one person to manage and control. And so by having the NIOs separate and under himself, he could insure that he could get a balanced view coming out of the agency on one hand and the rest of [the] intelligence community and [the] NIOs on the other. And it was just his way of assuring that all alternative views bubbled to the top.[74]

Subsequently, the NIC was moved back within the Directorate of Intelligence. In 1992, however, DCI Robert Gates announced plans to move the NIC out of the CIA and into an independent facility. In addition, a post of Vice Chairman for Evaluation and a subordinate Evaluation Group (subsequently Staff) were established to conduct postmortems on previous estimates to assess the quality and accuracy of the work and to work with NIOs to determine critical intelligence gaps. The estimates production program is managed by the Vice Chairman for Estimates, who is responsible for ensuring that all draft estimates encompass dissents and that alternative scenarios take into account potential dramatic unanticipated developments.[75]

Subordinate to the Vice Chairman for Estimates is the Analytic Group. The group is responsible for supervising the production of NIEs, the President's NIE Summary, NIE Update Memoranda, Intelligence Community Assessments, and

NIC Memoranda. Its staff redrafts, edits, and monitors production of estimates from the initial outline through community coordination.[76]

Gates also transferred three DCI production committees—the Joint Atomic Energy Intelligence Committee (JAEIC), the Weapons and Space Systems Intelligence Committee (WSSIC), and the Scientific and Technical Intelligence Committee (STIC)—to the NIC.[77]

The Joint Atomic Energy Intelligence Committee was created to "foster, develop and maintain a coordinated community approach to the problems in the field of atomic energy intelligence, to promote interagency liaison, and to give added impetus and community support to the efforts of individual agencies."[78]

In 1965, DCID 3/3, "Production of Atomic Energy Intelligence," noted that atomic energy intelligence is the responsibility of all NFIB committees and further declared that "the mission of the Joint Atomic Energy Intelligence Committee (JAEIC) shall be to foster, develop and maintain a coordinated community approach to the problems in the field of atomic energy intelligence, to promote interagency liaison and to give impetus and community support to the efforts of individual agencies."[79]

The JAEIC meets twice a month to discuss items related to nuclear intelligence. It specific responsibilities are classified but certainly include: assessing the adequacy of the U.S. nuclear monitoring program and its ability to effectively monitor compliance with various nuclear testing treaties; evaluating the methodology used in estimating the yield of foreign nuclear detonations; assessing major developments in the nuclear weapons programs of the nuclear powers; considering the possible impact of nuclear energy programs on proliferation in nations not yet possessing nuclear weapons; providing national decisionmakers with advice on the possible authorization of U.S. foreign sales in the nuclear energy area; and providing warning of a country "going nuclear."[80]

Its products have included a 1976 assessment of "The Soviet Atomic Energy Program," a 1989 assessment of Iraq's ability to build an atomic weapon, and the 1992 study on the "Geology of the Qingir Underground Nuclear Test Site." It may also commission work, such as the tasking of Z Division to produce a study on the state of nuclear materials security in Russia. JAEIC components include a Nuclear Test Intelligence Subcommittee and a Nuclear Weapons Logistics Working Group.[81]

The Weapons and Space Systems Intelligence Committee was created in 1956 as the Guided Missile Intelligence Committee and subsequently became the Guided Missile and Astronautics Intelligence Committee (GMAIC). According to DCID 3/4, "Production of Guided Missiles and Astronautics Intelligence," the committee's membership consists of representatives of all NFIB agencies, plus Army, Navy, and Air Force representatives. Its chairman is named by the DCI with the approval of the NFIB, and the CIA provides secretarial support. In addition to coordinating the guided missile and astronautics intelligence activities of the intelligence community, during the Cold War, the WSSIC performed technical studies on Soviet missiles as *inputs* to the NIEs. These papers were coordinated in the same manner as NIEs but were directed at informing the intelligence community. The WSSIC also assigns designators and code names for such systems.[82]

Table 19.1 lists subcommittees and panels of the WSSIC. The Biological and Chemical Warfare Working Group, the predecessor to the Chemical and Biological Warfare Intelligence Subcommittee, reviewed all available intelligence concerning the suspected biological warfare incident at Sverdlovsk in 1979. It concluded that there was a high probability that the Soviets still had some anthrax for biological warfare purposes and that they maintained an active biological warfare program at the Sverdlovsk facility. Previous committee products included "Soviet Medium Tank Developments" (1976), "Low Altitude Air Defense Capabilities of Soviet Nuclear Equipped SAMs" (August 1976), and "Soviet ICBM Silo Hardness Estimates" (November 1976). A more recent product was a report concluding that Chinese supplied M-11s in Pakistan should be considered operational.[83]

The Scientific and Technical Intelligence Committee (STIC) is responsible for "advising and assisting the DCI with respect to the production, coordination, and evaluation of intelligence on foreign scientific and technical developments that could affect U.S. national security."[84]

TABLE 19.1   Subcommittees and Panels of the Weapons and Space Systems Intelligence Committee

Subcommittee	Last Reference
Ballistic Missile Systems	1990
Naval Weapons Systems	1990
Ground Weapons	1990
Electronic Warfare	1995
Aviation	1990
Air Defense	1990
Space Systems	1991
GLONASS Panel	1991
Space Proliferation Panel	1995
Chemical and Biological Warfare Intelligence	1990
CBWIS Chemical Agent Panel	1991
Command, Control, and Communications	1991
Rest of World C3I Panel	1991
Sub-HF Panel	1991
CROSSBOW C3SS Data Base	1991

SOURCES: U.S. Army Deputy Chief of Staff for Intelligence, *Annual Historical Review, 1 October 1989–30 September 1990*, n.d., pp. 6–25; Naval Maritime Intelligence Center, *Naval Maritime Intelligence Center Command History 1991*, 1992, pp. 11, 14, 34; Air Force Intelligence Agency, *History of the Air Force Intelligence Agency, 18 April 1987–31 December 1989, Volume 1, Narrative and Appendices*, 1990, p. 79; Office of Naval Intelligence, *Office of Naval Intelligence Command History 1994*, 1995, p. 41.

STIC subcommittees, working groups, and panels have included the Collection Subcommittee (STIC-C), the Open Sources Subcommittee, the Information Technologies Working Group, the Technology Forecasting Working Group, the Computer Working Group, the Electro-Optics Working Group, the Directed Energy Weapons Working Group, the Signal Processing Working Group, the Technology Processing Working Group, the Electronics Working Group, the Electro-Optics and Technology Working Group, the Life Sciences Working Group, the Radar and Optical Steering Group, the Radar Subcommittee, the Multispectral High Energy Laser Panel, the Scientific and Technical Information Support Program Committee, the Scientific and Technical Thermal Applications Group, and the Multispectral/Laser Applications Group.[85]

In the 1991 fiscal year the Collection Subcommittee examined "existing and planned approaches to S&T intelligence collection, identified gaps, and provided a forum for discussion of S&T collection issues."[86]

STIC products have included "Soviet R&D Related to Particle Beam Weapons" (October 1976), "Collection Guide: Chinese Students and Visitors from Important Institutes Seeking Critical Technologies" (1986), and "A Preliminary Assessment of Soviet Kinetic Energy Weapons Technology" (1986).

Notes

1. President William J. Clinton, Executive Order 12958, "Classified National Security Information," April 17, 1995, in *Federal Register* 60, no. 76 (April 20, 1995): 19825–19843 at 19826.

2. *Documents from the U.S. Espionage Den (52): U.S.S.R., The Aggressive East,* section 3-2 (Tehran: Muslim Students Following the Line of the Imam, n.d.), pp. 46–94; Army Regulation 381–47, "U.S. Army Offensive Counterintelligence Operations," May 15, 1982, p. B-1.

3. Philip Agee, *Inside the Company: CIA Diary* (New York: Stonehill, 1975), p. 68; *Documents from the U.S. Espionage Den (52): U.S.S.R., The Aggressive East,* section 4, p. 28.

4. NFIB Security Committee, "Sensitive Compartmented Information: Characteristics and Security Requirements," June 1984, p. 1.

5. Ibid., p. 3; National Security Directive 63, "Single Scope Background Investigations," October 21, 1991; U.S. Strategic Command, USSTRATCOM Administrative Instruction 321–28, *Sensitive Compartmented Information (SCI) Personnel Security Operating Policy and Procedures,* June 30, 1992, pp. 25–27; Defense Intelligence Agency, *Physical Security Standards for Construction of Sensitive Compartmented Information Facilities (DIAM 50–3)* (Washington, D.C.: DIA, February 1990).

6. Quoted in David Wise, *The Politics of Lying: Governmental Deception, Secrecy, and Power* (New York: Viking, 1973), p. 86.

7. Ibid.

8. Ronald Lewin, *The American Magic: Codes, Ciphers and the Defeat of Japan* (New York: Farrar, Straus & Giroux, 1928), p. 17; Anthony Cave Brown, *The Last Hero* (New York: Times Books, 1982), p. 193.

9. James Bamford, *The Puzzle Palace: A Report on NSA, America's Most Secret Agency* (Boston: Houghton Mifflin, 1982), p. 314; Nigel West, *MI 6: British Secret Intelligence Service*

Operations, 1909–1945 (London: Weidenfeld and Nicolson, 1983), p. 163; Cave Brown, *The Last Hero*, p. 182; David Martin, *Wilderness of Mirrors* (New York: Harper & Row, 1980), p. 15.

10. Bamford, *The Puzzle Palace*, p. 314.

11. F. W. Winterbotham, *The Ultra Secret* (New York: Harper & Row, 1974), pp. 88–89.

12. Wise, *The Politics of Lying*, p. 83; Jack Anderson, "Syrians Strive to Oust Arafat as PLO Chief," *Washington Post*, November 10, 1982, p. D22; Bob Woodward, "ACDA Aide Faulted on Security," *Washington Post*, November 4, 1986, pp. A1, A16; National Intelligence Council, *National Intelligence Daily (Cable)*, December 13, 1983.

13. Bamford, *The Puzzle Palace*, p. 120.

14. Bob Woodward, "Messages of Activists Intercepted," *Washington Post*, October 13, 1975, pp. 1, 14; Seymour Hersh, *The Price of Power: Kissinger in the Nixon White House* (New York: Summit, 1983), p. 183.

15. Woodward, "Messages of Activists Intercepted."

16. Seymour Hersh, *"The Target is Destroyed": What Really Happened to Flight 007 and What America Knew About It* (New York: Random House, 1986), p. 4; Private information.

17. James Ott, "Espionage Trial Highlights CIA Problems," *Aviation Week & Space Technology*, November 27, 1978, pp. 21–22; Gregory A. Fossedal, "U.S. Said to Be Unable to Verify Missile Ban," *Washington Times*, November 18, 1987, p. A6; Dale Van Atta, "The Death of the State Secret," *New Republic*, February 18, 1985, pp. 20–23.

18. William Burrows, *Deep Black: Space Espionage and National Security* (New York: Random House, 1986), p. 23; Bob Woodward, *Veil: The Secret Wars of the CIA, 1981–1987* (New York: Simon & Schuster, 1987), pp. 221–224, 402–403; Private information.

19. Admiral David Jeremiah et al., *Report to the Director National Reconnaissance Office: Defining the Future of the NRO for the 21st Century, Final Report*, August 26, 1996, p. 171.

20. U.S. Strategic Command, *Organization and Functions Manual*, August 17, 1992, p. 61; Private information.

21. HQ USAF, ACS, I, INOI 205–4, "Designation of Special Security Officer (SSO), TK Control Officer (TCO), Gamma Control Officer (GCO), and Bravo Control Officer (BCO)," March 15, 1985, p. 2.

22. Inspector General, Department of Defense, *Final Report on the Verification Inspection of the National Security Agency*, IR–96–03 (Arlington, Va.: DOD IG, February 13, 1996), p. 13.

23. William J. Clinton, Presidential Review Directive 29, "National Security Information," April 26, 1993.

24. Clinton, Executive Order 12985, "Classified National Security Information," April 17, 1995, pp. 19826–19828.

25. Ibid., p. 19827.

26. Ibid., p. 19829.

27. Ibid., p. 19837.

28. Ronald Reagan, National Security Decision Directive 19, "Protection of Classified National Security Council and Intelligence Information," January 12, 1982; Ronald Reagan, National Security Decision Directive 84, "Safeguarding National Security Information," March 11, 1983.

29. Ronald Reagan, National Security Decision Directive 19, "Protection of Classified National Security Council and Intelligence Information."

30. Ibid.; William P. Clark, Assistant to the President for National Security Affairs, Memorandum for the Secretary of State et al., "Implementation of NSDD–19 on Protection of Classified National Security Council and Intelligence Information," February 2, 1982.

31. Clark, Assistant to the President for National Security Affairs, Memorandum for the Secretary of State et al., "Implementation of NSDD–19 on Protection of Classified National Security Council and Intelligence Information."

32. U.S. Comptroller General, General Accounting Office, *Information and Personnel Security: Data on Employees Affected by Federal Security Programs* (Washington, D.C.: GAO, 1986), p. 2; "Revised Form 4193," August 24, 1983.

33. U.S. Comptroller General, *Information and Personnel Security*, p. 2; On the NSDD–84 saga, see Angus Mackenzie, *Secrets: The CIA's War at Home* (Berkeley: University of California Press, 1997), pp. 103–133; U.S. Congress, House Committee on Government Operations, *Review of the President's National Security Decision Directive 84 and the Proposed Department of Defense Directive on Polygraph Use* (Washington, D.C.: U.S. Government Printing Office, 1984).

34. NSCID No. 1, "Basic Duties and Responsibilities," February 17, 1972, *Declassified Documents Reference Systems (DDRS)*, 1976–167G.

35. Admiral William O. Studeman, Acting DCI, Memorandum for: Intelligence Community Executive Committee Principals, Subject: Revised DCID 1/7, *Security Controls on the Dissemination of Intelligence Information*, April 12, 1995.

36. Director of Central Intelligence Directive 1/7, "Security Controls on the Dissemination of Intelligence Information," April 12, 1995, p. 3.

37. Ibid.

38. Ibid.; Scott Armstrong, "Israelis Have Spied on U.S., Secret Papers Show," *Washington Post*, February 1, 1982, pp. A1, A18; "Israel Calls Report on CIA Findings Ridiculous," *Washington Post*, February 3, 1982, p. 10.

39. Director of Central Intelligence Directive 1/7, "Security Controls on the Dissemination of Intelligence Information," p. 10; William O. Studeman, Acting DCI, Memorandum for: Intelligence Community Executive Committee, Subject: Revised DCID 1/7, *Security Controls on the Dissemination of Intelligence Information*.

40. Director of Central Intelligence Directive 1/7, "Security Controls on the Dissemination of Intelligence Information," June 15, 1996.

41. Ibid., pp. 4, 9–10.

42. Ibid., pp. 11, 14; John Deutch, Director of Central Intelligence, Memorandum for: Intelligence Community Executive Committee Principals, Subject: Revision of Director of Central Intelligence Directive 1/7, "Security Controls on the Dissemination of Intelligence Information," April 16, 1996.

43. Director of Central Intelligence Directive 1/7, "Security Controls on the Dissemination of Intelligence Information," p. 12.

44. Ibid., p. 7.

45. Ibid., pp. 7, 11.

46. DCID 1/14, "Minimum Personnel Security Standards and Procedures Governing Eligibility for Access to Sensitive Compartmented Information," April 4, 1986, Annex A.

47. Ibid.

48. Ibid., p. 7.

49. Defense Intelligence Agency, *Physical Security Standards for Sensitive Compartmented Information Facilities* (DIAM 50–3) (Washington, D.C.: DIA, 1980), p. i; Defense Intelligence Agency, *Physical Security Standards for Construction of Sensitive Compartmented Information Facilities* (DIAM 50–3), (Washington, D.C.: DIA, 1990); USAF AFR 20–7, "Sensitive Compartmented Information (SCI) Security System," October 16, 1992.

50. DCID 1/20, "Security Policy Concerning Travel and Assignment of Personnel with Access to Sensitive Compartmented Information (SCI)," July 20, 1987, p. 2.

51. Ibid.

52. Ibid., entire text; Department of Defense Instruction 5230.22, *Control of Dissemination of Intelligence Information*; Defense Intelligence Agency Regulation 50–10, "Control of Dissemination of Foreign Intelligence," May 11, 1977.

53. NSCID No. 1, "Basic Duties and Responsibilities."

54. NSCID No. 3, "Coordination of Intelligence Production," February 17, 1972. *DDRS* 1976–253E.

55. Ibid.

56. DCID 3/1, "Standard Operating Procedures for Departmental Participation in the Production and Coordination of National Intelligence," July 8, 1948.

57. DCID 3/2, "Policy Governing Departmental Concurrences in National Intelligence Reports and Estimates," September 13, 1948.

58. DCID 3/5, "Production of National Intelligence Estimates," September 1, 1953.

59. Lawrence Freedman, *U.S. Intelligence and the Soviet Strategic Threat* (Princeton, N.J.: Princeton University Press, 1986), p. 31.

60. Ibid.

61. DCID 3/1, "Standard Operating Procedures for Departmental Participation in the Production and Coordination of National Intelligence."

62. Freedman, *U.S. Intelligence and the Soviet Strategic Threat*, p. 54.

63. Ibid.

64. Richard J. Kerr, Deputy Director for Intelligence, Memorandum for Chairman, National Intelligence Council, Subject: The Integrity and Objectivity of National Foreign Intelligence Estimates, May 12, 1987, p. 1. The memo is reprinted in U.S. Congress, Senate Select Committee on Intelligence, *Nomination of Robert M. Gates,* vol. 2 (Washington, D.C.: U.S. Government Printing Office, 1992), pp. 106–108.

65. *United States of America v. Samuel L. Morison*, U.S. District Court, Baltimore, Case Y–84–00455, October 8–16, 1985, p. 1025.

66. National Intelligence Council, *A Guide to the National Intelligence Council*, 1994, p. 4; Information provided by CIA Public Affair Staff.

67. National Intelligence Council, *A Guide to the National Intelligence Council*, pp. 16–27.

68. Ibid., pp. 28–31.

69. Ibid., pp. 35–39.

70. Ibid., pp. 32–35; Information provided by the CIA Public Affairs office, April 15, 1998.

71. U.S. Congress, House Select Committee on Intelligence, *U.S. Intelligence Agencies and Activities: Fiscal Costs and Procedures, Part I* (Washington, D.C.: U.S. Government Printing Office, 1975), p. 389; U.S. Congress, House Committee on Foreign Affairs, *The Role of Intelligence in the Foreign Policy Process* (Washington, D.C.: U.S. Government Printing Office, 1980), p. 135.

72. U.S. Congress, House Committee on Foreign Affairs, *The Role of Intelligence in the Foreign Policy Process*, p. 230.

73. Freedman, *U.S. Intelligence and the Soviet Strategic Threat*, p. 31.

74. U.S. Congress, Senate Select Committee on Intelligence, *Nomination of John N. McMahon* (Washington, D.C.: U.S. Government Printing Office, 1982), pp. 48–49.

75. Robert M. Gates, Director of Central Intelligence, "Statement of Change in CIA and Intelligence Community," April 1, 1989, pp. 21, 22.

76. National Intelligence Council, *A Guide to the National Intelligence Council*, pp. 39, 44.

77. U.S. Congress, Senate Select Committee on Intelligence and House Permanent Select Committee on Intelligence, *S. 2198 and S.421 to Reorganize the United States Intelligence Community* (Washington, D.C.: U.S. Government Printing Office, 1993), p. 15.

78. DCID 3/3, "Production of Atomic Energy Intelligence," April 23, 1965, *DDRS* 1980–131G.

79. DCID 3/3, "Production of Atomic Energy Intelligence."

80. The JAEIC's role in evaluating the U.S. capability to monitor compliance with the Threshold Test Ban Treaty is mentioned in Attachment to Memorandum, Holsey G. Handyside, Deputy Assistant Secretary, International Nuclear and Technical Programs, Department of Energy for Leslie H. Brown, Senior Deputy Assistant Secretary for Oceans and International, Environmental and Scientific Affairs, Department of State, "Responses to Congressional Questions on Nuclear Explosives," March 7, 1980.

81. U.S. Congress, House Committee on Energy and Commerce, *Nuclear Nonproliferation: Failed Efforts to Curtail Iraq's Nuclear Weapons Program* (Washington, D.C.: U.S. Government Printing Office, 1992), p. 20; William J. Broad, "Warning on Iraq and Bomb Bid Silenced in '89," *New York Times*, April 20, 1992, pp. A1, A5; NIE 11–3/8–76, *Soviet Forces for International Conflict Through the Mid-1980s, Volume 1, Key Judgements and Summary*, 1976, p. iii; Air Force Intelligence Agency, *History of the Air Force Intelligence Agency, 18 April 1987–31 December 1989, Volume 1, Narrative and Appendices*, 1990; Air University, Special Bibliography Series, Special Bibliography No. 207, Supplement No. 5, *China: Military Capabilities* (Maxwell AFB, Ala.: Air University, February 1993), p. 14; Andrew and Leslie Cockburn, *One Point Safe* (New York: Anchor Books, 1997), p. 188; R. Jeffrey Smith, "U.S. Officials Acted Hastily in Nuclear Test Accusation," *Washington Post*, October 20, 1997, pp. A1, A6–A7.

82. DCID 3/4, "Production of Guided Missile and Astronautics Intelligence," April 23, 1965, *DDRS* 1980–132A; John Prados, *The Soviet Estimate: U.S. Intelligence Analysis and Russian Military Strength* (New York: Dial, 1982), pp. 59–61, 202; U.S. Congress, House Committee on Appropriations, *Department of Defense Appropriations for 1978, Part 1* (Washington, D.C.: U.S. Government Printing Office, 1977), p. 224.

83. Department of the Army, Office of the Assistant Chief of Staff for Intelligence, *Annual Historical Review, 1 July 1975–30 September 1976*, n.d., pp. 39–40; NIE 11–3/8–76, *Soviet Strategic Forces for International Conflict Through the Mid-1980s, Volume 1, Key Judgments and Summary*, p. iii; Andrew Koch, "Pakistan Persists with Nuclear Procurement," *Jane's Intelligence Review*, March 1997, pp. 131–133.

84. Central Intelligence Agency, *A Consumer's Guide to Intelligence*, p. 57.

85. Diane T. Putney, *History of the Air Force Intelligence Service, 1 January–31 December 1984* (Ft. Belvoir, Va.: AFIS, n.d.), pp. 335–336; Department of the Air Force, *Headquarters Publication 21–1: Department of the Air Force Organization and Functions (Chartbook)*,

March 1986, p. 6–23; Diane T. Putney, *History of the Air Force Intelligence Service, 1 January–31 December 1983* (Ft. Belvoir, Va.: AFIS, n.d.), p. 340; Naval Intelligence Support Center, *Naval Intelligence Support Center Command History, 1982*, p. VII-II; Department of the Army, Office of the Deputy Chief of Staff for Intelligence, *Annual Historical Review, 1 October 1989–30 September 1990*, Glossary 11; Naval Intelligence Support Center, *Naval Intelligence Support Center Command History, 1981*, n.d., p. VIII-6; Office of Naval Intelligence, *Office of Naval Intelligence Command History*, 1997, p. 25.

86. Department of the Army, Office of the Deputy Chief of Staff for Intelligence, *Annual Historical Review, 1 October 1990 to 30 September 1991*, n.d., p. 4-30.

20

ISSUES AND CHALLENGES

The dramatic change in the international environment in the last decade—the collapse of East European communism in 1989 and of the Soviet Union two years later, the growing concern with transnational threats (particularly the proliferation of weapons of mass destruction, terrorism, and international organized crime and narcotics trafficking), and the need to reduce the U.S. national deficit—has served as a catalyst for the consideration of a variety of issues concerning the organization and activities of the U.S. intelligence community.

In addition, the mixed reviews that the U.S. intelligence community received in Desert Storm prompted virtually immediate changes in structure and operations (including the creation of the Central Imagery Office and the requirement for an interoperable imagery architecture), as well as long-term plans to improve support to military commanders. Also, recent real, grossly exaggerated, or falsely perceived failures—such as the Aldrich Ames fiasco (real), the transmission of tainted intelligence to the President (grossly exaggerated), and the "failure" to predict the Soviet collapse (false perception)—further stimulated calls for radical change in the intelligence community.[1]

One issue that received renewed attention was that of intelligence organization and structure. Proposals, produced by individual observers as well as private and government review groups, ranged from radical reorganization of the intelligence community to far less dramatic changes. A not unrelated issue—the powers of the DCI—became the subject of discussion for review groups and for Congress, as well as for the DCI himself.

As noted earlier, the post–Cold War world presents a different environment for covert action. The primary objective of such action is not helping (through words or weapons) to win a global ideological conflict but curbing or eliminating the most dangerous activities of rogue states such Iraq, Libya, North Korea, and Iran. In addition, Saddam Hussein's persistent grip on power has led some to suggest that the assassination option, presently prohibited by executive order, be considered as a means of removing the troublesome dictator.

A less visible issue is one that arises with respect to economic intelligence: the desire to counter foreign economic espionage activities and the concern that allied and friendly nations are permitting sophisticated technology to be sold to rogue states. The United States has spied to varying extents, and in varying ways, on many of its allies and friends for decades—just as those allies have spied on the United States. However, the new visibility these operations have attained, the disappearance of an overwhelming *uniting* threat, and the increased concern with the threat of WMD proliferation requires that they be examined under these new circumstances.

The challenges it faces are an integral part of any discussion of the future of the U.S. intelligence community. Beyond changes in the international *political* environment, there have been a multitude of other developments, including: the development of fiber optics technology; increasingly sophisticated encryption and denial and deception; the revolution in information acquisition, processing, and dissemination technology; and the increasing demand for nearly continuous, real-time intelligence coverage.

INTELLIGENCE STRUCTURE AND REFORM

Over the years there have been numerous reviews of intelligence structure and of proposals for reorganization of the intelligence community. In 1971, James Schlesinger, then of the Office of Management and Budget, reviewed the intelligence community and the pros and cons of a number of different options for reorganization. In 1977, in response to Presidential Review Memorandum-11, the NSC prepared a study on Intelligence Structure and Mission. The sixty-one-page, single-spaced document examined objectives and principles for U.S. foreign intelligence, problem areas, and structural options.[2]

One option for intelligence community restructuring envisioned in the PRM-11 study involved a Director of Foreign Intelligence (DFI) with line authority (that is, day-to-day control) over an intelligence analysis and production agency (consisting of the NIOs and the CIA Directorate of Intelligence), a clandestine services agency, the NSA, and the NRO (with unified Air Force and CIA programs). In addition, the option called for the DFI to direct the Navy's special reconnaissance activities. A variant of that option would have resulted in the CIA also absorbing the Army's and the Air Force's human intelligence programs.[3]

An extensive reorganization of the intelligence community was the basis of legislation that was proposed by the chairmen of the Senate and House intelligence oversight committees, Senator David Boren (D–Okla.) and Rep. David McCurdy (D–Okla.), in 1992. Their proposals (which had slight differences) would have created a Director of National Intelligence removed from the CIA; reduced the CIA to a HUMINT agency; established a new office for national intelligence analysis; created a National Imagery Agency responsible for all phases of imagery activity, from system development to tasking to operation to interpretation and processing; assigned equivalent responsibilities in the SIGINT area to the NSA; and eliminated the National Reconnaissance Office.[4]

Predictably, the legislation was opposed by both the intelligence community and Secretary of Defense and failed. Changes were made in several aspects of intelligence community management, and, as noted, a Central Imagery Office was established, but the changes were trivial relative to the drastic ones proposed in the legislation. But that was not the end of examinations of the intelligence community and of proposals for drastic restructuring.[5]

Between 1995 and 1997, two major reviews were undertaken by official groups—the Presidential-Congressional Commission on the Roles and Capabilities of the U.S. Intelligence Community (the Brown commission) and the House Permanent Select Committee on Intelligence (HPSCI). In addition, several prestigious outside bodies, including the Council on Foreign Relations and the Twentieth Century Fund, chartered groups of intelligence and foreign affairs experts to review the intelligence community and make their recommendations. Also, some former intelligence officers produced detailed studies of their own.[6]

The recent official studies came to very different conclusions with regard to intelligence reorganization. Beyond supporting creation of a National Imagery and Mapping Agency, as had been proposed by then DCI John Deutch, the Brown commission recommended no restructuring of the intelligence community.

The HPSCI study's recommendations, some of which were similar to provisions in the Boren-McCurdy legislation, included but were not limited to:

- Eliminate the NRO and give its research and development functions to a new Technology Development Office (TDO) that would perform intelligence R&D functions for space, aerial, and other technical collection systems.
- Establish a Technical Collection Agency (TCA) that would assume responsibility for tasking all technical collection systems, operating space reconnaissance systems, and managing NSA's Regional SIGINT Operations Centers. NSA would be absorbed into the new agency.
- Remove the CIA's Directorate of Operations from the CIA, rename it the Clandestine Service, and absorb into the new service the clandestine collection operations run by the Defense HUMINT Service. The new service would report directly to the DCI.
- Distribute the functions of the CIA's Directorate of Science and Technology to the Clandestine Service and TDO as appropriate.
- The CIA should become a single function agency, responsible for national intelligence analysis.
- The DCI should remain as head of the intelligence community with added authority.[7]

However, the committee's major proposals suffered the same fate as the Boren and McCurdy proposals—opposition from the intelligence community and the executive branch followed by failure to gain sufficient support within Congress, leading the HPSCI to drop its major proposals. The persistent failure of such efforts, and some lesser efforts to expand the DCI's powers (discussed in the next section), left many bemoaning yet another failed attempt at intelligence reform and searching for explanations.[8]

Certainly, there are powerful obstacles to radical intelligence reorganization. The intelligence community—supported by key players in the executive branch, particularly, the President and the Secretary of Defense—is one. One, although not the only, possible explanation for opposition is bureaucratic self-protection. Within Congress, the armed services committees have become roadblocks to significantly increasing the powers of the DCI, as they seek to prevent any reduction in military control over intelligence activities. The conflict between the intelligence and armed services committees was labeled a "turf battle par excellence."[9]

There is, however, at least one more reason that may explain, in part, why many radical reorganization proposals fail—or at least it provides a justification for why they should have failed. That reason is a simple one. Many of the proposals are simply *bad ideas*—either because they would be achieved at the cost of significant organizational disruption without commensurate benefits, or because they would actually do more harm than good.

One rationale for radical reorganization after the end of the Cold War is, as the PRM-11 study observed, that "The United States Government has an intelligence structure whose present shape and functions have been dictated more by pragmatism and historical accident than conscious design." Clearly, its organization is the reflection of staggered developments over a fifty-year span—including the creation of the CIA in 1947 and the NSA in 1952, the development of dramatic new technical capabilities (particularly space reconnaissance), and the creation of centralized Defense agencies such as the Defense Intelligence Agency.[10]

These developments were grafted on to a set of military intelligence agencies that were already involved in human and technical collection as well as in general and scientific intelligence analysis. Such a process undoubtedly means that the intelligence community is not the one that would exist if one started in 1998 from scratch—with a blank sheet of paper, some basic principles about how intelligence should be organized, no history, and the assumption of cost-free transition.

However, it is more than a tautology to observe that the United States is *not* starting from scratch—it has more than fifty years of history and experience, good and bad, in the operation of intelligence organizations. That history and experience may demonstrate that some structures that have no place in an "ideal" intelligence community have worked well and should not be tampered with, and some problems can be effectively eliminated or reduced only by violating some principle for intelligence organization that appears desirable. An ad hoc intelligence community may also be viewed as the survivor of an evolutionary process.

A proposal that has consistently found some advocates and is superficially attractive, in the sense of an idealized intelligence community, but that is a horrendously bad idea is the recurrent proposal for the establishment of a Director of National Intelligence (DNI), detached from the CIA or any other agency. The basic rationale is that the DNI would be free to focus on major intelligence issues and to serve as an impartial arbiter of key decisions concerning U.S. intelligence.

However, for a variety of reasons such a step would be a step backward for centralized direction of the intelligence community. The likely outcome of the separation would be a Director of National Intelligence with far less actual power than the present DCI—for the result would be a DNI with no resources trying to establish control over the CIA, the NSA, and the DIA, all of which, as result of their control of collection and analytical resources, would have far more influence than the DNI. As the Murphy Commission observed in 1975, "to function as the President's intelligence adviser, it is essential that the DCI have immediate access and control over the CIA facilities necessary to assemble, evaluate and reach conclusions about intelligence in all functional fields including political, economic, military and scientific subjects."[11]

Separation of the DCI from the CIA could also retard the flow of information through the intelligence community—adding the Director of the CIA to the heads of the NSA and the Navy as guardians of "their" information. In addition, by creating a position of Director of National Intelligence, the position of Director of the CIA would be sharply lowered in prestige, which would further exacerbate rivalries among the CIA, the DIA, and the NSA, as each fought to place itself at the top of the intelligence hierarchy.

Ad hoc solutions that have confronted real problems successfully include the creation of a National Reconnaissance Office and the creation of a Directorate of Science and Technology in the CIA. One proposal noted above would have eliminated the NRO in favor a Technology Development Office that would have combined the R&D and acquisition functions performed by the NRO and the now defunct Defense Airborne Reconnaissance Office. Another would have distributed NRO functions between NIMA and the NSA. One objection to such recommendations is the view expressed by NRO director Keith Hall:

> Space intelligence activities involve a set of specialties, technical challenges and requirements that make them more dissimilar than compatible with the non-space based technical collection assets. The environment of space and the unique problems associated with launch, satellite command and control, and the inability to fix or modify hardware after it is placed in orbit, all argue strongly for treating intelligence space development, acquisition, and operations in an integrated fashion.[12]

The Jeremiah Panel, appointed to consider the future of the NRO, also concluded, after considering a variety of organizational alternatives, that "no other construct satisfied the potential organizational, function or mission considerations as well as the joint venture relationship currently existing between the SECDEF and the DCI."[13]

The Directorate of Science and Technology was (as the Directorate of Research) only established fifteen years after the CIA, yet quickly grew to become the most important single component of the intelligence community, and its impact is felt today with respect to many of the collection systems in operation. Additionally, its offices work in advanced research and development areas relevant to improving the analytical, processing, and collection (human and technical) capabilities of the U.S. intelligence community. Proposals that would either distribute its functions among other agencies or simply eliminate the directorate rarely acknowledge either the diversity or importance of its activities.[14]

A separate clandestine service, recommended in the HPSCI study, would be less harmful than many other proposals.[15] However, it may also be pointless—even though one would probably create such an entity if one were starting from scratch. The major rationale the HPSCI offers—that despite the probable ability of the DDO and the DCI to meet at will, there is an intervening layer on the organization chart—is not terribly persuasive. It has also been suggested that a separate clandestine service would give the HUMINT enterprise a new start; but this suggestion leads one to ask, Exactly who would be hired to replace the present HUMINT personnel? And if the same people are to be performing the same functions why will creating a new agency improve anything?

In many cases, the structural changes needed to adapt to the changing world conditions are those that can be made *within* already existing organizations. Thus, the reorganization of the CIA's Directorate of Intelligence, the creation of a Counterproliferation Division within its Directorate of Operations, the new offices established in the Directorate of Science and Technology, and the reorganization of the NSA's Directorate of Operations—all discussed in Chapter 2—address changing world conditions and targets.

One additional intra-/cross-organizational change would represent at least a partial reversal of the most recent significant major organizational change—the creation of the National Imagery and Mapping Agency in 1996. Action should be taken to restore an independent imagery interpretation capability to the CIA, by the reestablishment either of the National Photographic Interpretation Center or of the Office of Imagery Analysis that had existed within the Directorate of Intelligence. Although it does not automatically follow that the failure to provide tactical warning of the Indian nuclear detonations of May 1998 resulted from the elimination of an independent CIA capability—it does highlight the importance of *national* intelligence as well as the need for a key element in the production of that intelligence to be placed in an agency outside of the Defense Department, in an agency for whom support to military operations is not the key mission.

The key actions needed to improve U.S. intelligence do not involve radically restructuring the intelligence community as it stands today; rather, they involve augmenting the power of the DCI with respect to key national intelligence activities and, even more importantly, confronting the challenges to intelligence collection and analysis presented by changing world conditions and technologies.

THE ROLES OF THE DCI AND DIRECTOR, DIA

From its very creation, the role of the DCI has been a subject of controversy; it has been seen as a threat to the power and independence of the other intelligence agencies—particularly the military intelligence agencies. When he took office in 1951 DCI Walter Bedell Smith was viewed, by the heads of other intelligence agencies who served on the Intelligence Advisory Committee (IAC), as acting at their direction. One of Smith's innovations was to get the IAC to act in an advisory rather than supervisory role.[16]

Since that time a number of events have served to give the DCI and the CIA a central place in the U.S. intelligence community: the production of national intelligence products under DCI/CIA direction; the placement of the National Photographic Interpretation Center within the CIA; the CIA's role in the development of space reconnaissance systems and in the analysis of the data produced by those and other technical collection systems; and the establishment of two executive committees chaired by the DCI for the direction of the National Reconnaissance and Special Navy programs. In many cases the DCI/CIA role was achieved only after major, sometimes bitter, struggles with the Defense Department and the military services.

All the developments mentioned above had taken place before 1977, when President Carter's DCI, Stansfield Turner, sought day-to-day, as well as budgetary, control of the National Reconnaissance Office (NRO) and the National Security Agency (NSA). This was an essential part of his program to give the DCI and his staff the power to fully direct the activities of the most critical parts of the intelligence community.

Turner argued that without control of the NSA and the NRO, the CIA would not be able to properly advise the president on military matters. Turner attained only a portion of his goals. After consideration of the PRM-11 study, President Carter signed Presidential Directive-17, "Reorganization of the Intelligence Community," in August 1977. Despite the title, no reorganization was involved. The directive did confirm that the DCI "[has] during peacetime full tasking responsibility and authority for translating . . . national intelligence requirements into specific intelligence collection objectives and targets and assigning these to intelligence collection organizations." It also extended the DCI's authority by its provision that the DCI would "have full and exclusive authority for approval of the National Foreign Intelligence Program (NFIP) budget prior to its presentation . . . to the President." However, the directive retained the day-to-day management responsibilities (line/budget execution authority) of the NSA and the NRO for the Secretary of Defense.[17]

The granting of line authority over the NRO and the NSA to the DCI was an option considered and rejected by the Brown commission. They concluded that "it would be unwise and undesirable to alter the fundamental relationship between the DCI and the Secretary of Defense."[18]

It can be argued, consistent with the Brown commission's conclusions, that, given the location of the NRO and the NSA within the Defense Department, the Secretary of Defense must be the person ultimately responsible for their operations and thus for day-to-day control. At the same time, however, they are *national* institutions and key elements in the production of national intelligence. At the very least, the DCI should have the formal authority and responsibility to review any and all activities of the NRO and the NSA, to inform the Secretary of Defense when he has an objection to any of those activities, and, as a last resort, to raise the issue with the president or the Assistant to the President for National Security Affairs.[19]

In addition, it is necessary for the DCI to control the key elements of national intelligence collection—to assure that they are employed in a fashion to maximize their value by addressing the most important intelligence questions for the nation, irrespective of the origin of those questions in the executive branch. In particular, the DCI should have control over the tasking for national imagery, SIGINT, and nuclear intelligence systems, as well as for HUMINT. The DCI also should have a key role in decisions with respect to the characteristics of new technical collection systems—to ensure that they are not configured largely with only one group of users in mind.

Unfortunately, a number of events in the past several years have served to undermine the DCI's control in these key areas. In April 1992 the Central Imagery Office was established as a joint DCI-DOD organization, *within* the Department of Defense. Although there was a pressing need for an organization to establish a coherent imagery dissemination architecture, the CIO was also assigned the responsibility for imagery collection and exploitation tasking—taking over the role that had been performed by the DCI's Committee on Imagery Requirements and Exploitation (COMIREX). NIMA then absorbed the CIO and the imagery tasking function. We have also seen the de facto transfer of the SIGINT Committee (now National SIGINT Committee) from the DCI to the Director of the NSA.

One means of fully restoring the DCI's authority in the area of tasking would be the creation of a central tasking organization that would report to the DCI and that would be responsible for tasking individual collection disciplines (imagery, SIGINT, HUMINT). As a means of alleviating the oft mentioned "stovepipe" problem—the tasking of collection disciplines in isolation of what others can contribute, whereby positive synergistic effects are lost or unnecessary duplication occurs—a central tasking organization also would be responsible for considering trade-offs between the tasking of different disciplines. That approach was attempted during Stansfield Turner's tenure as DCI, in the form of the National Intelligence Tasking Center, and failed due to resistance from the community's collection elements.[20] However, with appropriate support from the President and with sufficient DCI authority, a new effort might well be more successful.

Although it is important to augment the DCI's power with respect to the national intelligence effort, it is also vital not to try to turn the DCI into a governmental "intelligence czar" responsible for all intelligence—national, departmental, and tactical.

A study produced for the Brown commission found the present powers of the DCI insufficient and argued that it was necessary to "end the distinction between national and tactical intelligence program budgets . . . by combining them under the DCI's direct control." In addition, the study observed that "the National Foreign Intelligence Board needs to become a council for internal governance of the community. *This will be achieved only when those sitting around the table no longer represent independent princelings with budgets over which the DCI has no control*" (emphasis added).[21]

There are, however, a number of reasons why the DCI should not be given the authority to control all departmental and tactical activities. Senior decisionmakers in the Defense, State, Treasury, or Energy Departments, in order to operate effectively—both in making departmental decisions and in advising the President—must have their own intelligence *analytic* units. If the DCI can hire and fire the key officials or control the budget of an ostensible departmental intelligence organization, then senior departmental decisionmakers will lack the authority necessary either to direct the production of the intelligence they believe they require or to correct or punish poor performance. In addition, they may well lose, or never gain, confidence in their ostensible chief intelligence adviser. Another possible consequence of granting the DCI too much authority is the creation of alternative intelligence units, in the guise of "research" or "policy planning" units—resulting in an even greater cost of intelligence and less coordination.

Intelligence plays a role in policy formulation by being more than simply the collection and analysis of data. It requires the interaction of senior officials and their intelligence advisers. It also requires, on occasion, those senior officials to formulate the questions they want answered, to ask follow-on questions, or to reject analysis they consider irrelevant or of poor quality. The ability of senior officials to do this requires an intelligence organization that, to a significant extent, belongs to them and is not under the complete control of the DCI.

It is also important to appreciate that there are far more questions that can be asked and far more data that can analyzed than there are resources available. The choices made are a reflection of the consumer of the data. Too much central direction would result in products that do not adequately distinguish between the requirements of different consumers.

These factors have been recognized and stressed by various officials on a number of occasions. Former DCI James Woolsey has observed that the senior leadership of "agencies that are heavily involved in international matters . . . often have rather specialized intelligence needs that it is very helpful for them to be able to have their own people working on."[22]

A senior official of one of those agencies—Undersecretary of State Peter Tarnoff—remarked, "Department principals need and want an in-house intelligence bureau. The Secretary wants analysts dedicated to producing information tailored precisely for his needs. Policymakers wanted rapid turn-around . . . The Bureau of Intelligence and Research has the Secretary's needs as its first priority."[23]

In Senate testimony, General Paul Gorman, former head of the U.S. Southern Command, noted:

> From time to time . . . I dispatched one or two of my intelligence analysts, familiar with my own hypotheses and my hunches, to interact with relatively low echelon Washington based analysts, and to examine the data from which they worked from day to day. That practice yielded valuable insights for my command. My analysts discovered and reported back that unexploited information inside the Beltway Barrier was a veritable treasure trove. Basically, the folks up here looking at information simply did not recognize valuable nuggets for our purposes.[24]

As for the suggestion that the DCI should have control of both the National Foreign Intelligence Programs (NFIP) and Tactical Intelligence and Related Applications (TIARA) budgets, this would probably have several unfortunate effects—including diluting the DCI's attention from more important matters and creating unnecessary conflicts between the DCI and the DOD and military services.

In addition, aside from the fact that some of the intelligence activities involved may be of little or no relevance to the national intelligence function, many of the related activities have other important primary functions that should be under the control of the DOD or a military service. For example, Air Force TIARA assets include those devoted to areas such as Battle Management and Tactical Warning/Attack Assessment, including JSTARS, the Ballistic Missile Early Warning System, PAVE PAWS SLBM warning radars, and the Defense Support Program. Although these TW/AA assets provide intelligence of various sorts, that is not their primary function.[25]

Just as the DCI should not become czar of all U.S. intelligence, it is also important that the Director of the DIA not become the czar of military intelligence. One study suggested empowering "the Director of Defense Intelligence Agency (DIA) with the rank and resources to be the Director of Military Intelligence, in fact as well as in name. Long overdue is the consolidation of intelligence activities duplicated in each of the military services and at major military commands."[26]

However, creation of a Director of Military Intelligence (DMI) would be unwise for several reasons. It would almost certainly lead to even further decline in the power of the DCI, and a battle over control of national collection assets would certainly result. Thus, former DCI James Woolsey has observed that "it would be unfortunate if what is, I think, today a perhaps complex [system,] but nonetheless a system that lends itself to coordination under a single authority, evolved into one where you had parallel authorities."[27]

In explaining why the Brown commission chose not to recommend the creation of a DMI, Harold Brown noted "the enormous variety of intelligence functions within the Department of Defense." He went on to explain that "the services do have their own requirements . . . [N]o one but the CNO and his assistant for intelligence is going to care as much about where every ship happens to be at a certain time . . . Similarly, the unified and specified commands have to focus on their immediate area of operations, and they need their own intelligence people for that."[28]

It should also be noted with regard to the unified commands that maintaining intelligence centers is a cost of readiness. In the event of war there will need to be substantial intelligence operation in the theater—as demonstrated by Operation Desert Storm. To do that without there being a solid core of intelligence analysts and other experts would be difficult, to say the least.

None of the above comments should be taken as suggesting that the subject of reallocating analytic responsibilities between the DIA, the service intelligence components, and the unified commands should not be explored or that the Director of DIA should not review the activities of the military services and make recommendations to the Secretary of Defense with regard to reallocations of responsibility.

Indeed, that is one of the subjects that should be given careful study, with a view to rationalizing the production effort. Areas where the DIA should have the vast bulk of the responsibility include overall military doctrine, nuclear weaponry, chemical and biological weapons, proliferation, national command and control, and defense spending.

At the same time, service intelligence agencies should focus on issues such as doctrine and tactics of counterpart services, targeting support, capabilities of certain weapons systems (e.g., naval mines, anti-ship missiles), and the overall threat presented by foreign countries to that service's forces in the event of combat. It does not seem unreasonable for the Office of Naval Intelligence to produce studies such as the multivolume, *Worldwide Threat to U.S. Navy and Marine Forces* (1992).

Meanwhile, unified command intelligence centers should focus on bringing together analysis performed by CIA, DIA, and service intelligence organizations into a form directly relevant to the CINC and the rest of the command—as well as on exploiting information that may be of particular relevance to the command, but that has been ignored or overlooked by national, department, and service intelligence units.

COVERT ACTION

The end of the Cold War meant an end to worldwide ideological conflict between the United States and the Soviet Union, a conflict that involved a variety of covert operations—including subsidies to political and other kinds groups; media operations; attempts to displace governments; and, on a few occasions prior to 1975, attempted assassination. A key element of many covert actions was the intent to in some way weaken the ideological enemy's worldwide standing and power.[29]

As noted in Chapter 16, many operations became pointless after the Soviet collapse—such as the support of anticommunist publications in Europe. In addition, there is no longer a rationale for seeking to undermine a regime because of its alliance with an adversary superpower. It could be argued, however, that it makes *more* sense to try to undermine regimes such as those in Iraq, Iran, and Libya than many Cold War targets—on the grounds that those regimes, particularly because of their quest for weapons of mass destruction and their support of terrorism, represent significant dangers to the United States and its interests.

Of course, the likelihood of success in such major political covert action operations may be no greater than it proved to be in many Cold War operations. Lack of U.S. success in covert action operations directed at Libya, Iraq, and Iran (discussed in Chapter 16) may be more than the result of easily correctable mistakes. The ruthlessness of the regimes, their extensive secret police operations, the lack of a viable and united opposition, and a populace that is unwilling to fight and die to unseat its leadership (as well as the segments of the population that support that leadership) can make political operations that seek to eliminate such regimes unlikely to succeed. In addition, the United States would find it far more difficult to recruit either local allies or support from other major powers in conducting such operations than it did with respect to Afghanistan.[30]

If the regimes in question were simply detestable and no more than annoyances to the United States, it might be decided that the United States would have to deal with them on the basis of diplomatic actions and economic sanctions, unless they engaged in overt military action. However, there are at least two factors that suggest that some forms of covert action might be desirable and may be feasible.

One factor is the involvement of the regimes in the pursuit of weapons of mass destruction and terrorist activities. Here, although a desirable objective would be to bring about a complete halt in those activities, attainment of a lesser objective— retarding the development and/or acquisition of WMD and limiting terrorist activities—may be of great value. A coup that "almost" works may be of little value, but delaying the acquisition of WMD-related material or reducing the number and ferocity of terrorist attacks does have significant value. In the former case, the delay may mean that the regime collapses *prior* to acquiring a nuclear capability or a sophisticated ballistic missile system, or that it does not have such a capability when it undertakes action that calls for a U.S. military response. Israeli covert (and overt) actions directed to prevent the Iraqi acquisition of a nuclear capability may be partly responsible for the United States not having to face a nuclear armed Iraq in 1990.

Because success is possible in degrees, the feasibility of such operations should be much greater than that for political operations. A variety of potential means exists for retarding the acquisition of a WMD capability. Computer viruses in weapons laboratory computers, the shipment of faulty equipment (either through replacement or sabotage), placement of a bomb in an underground facility—all are possible means of producing severe setbacks in weapons development.[31]

Alternatively, the United States operates a variety of Army, Navy, and Air Force special operations forces, under the direction of the United States Special Operations Command (USSOCOM) and Joint Special Operations Command (JSOC). Key missions of those forces, as noted in Chapter 5, include counterproliferation, counterterrorism, and direct action. Thus, using them to target WMD or terrorist facilities would be consistent with their present focus.[32]

If it were to prove desirable and feasible to use those forces in such missions, it should, however, be done under CIA supervision. The suggestion has been made on a number of occasions to turn the responsibility for paramilitary operations over to the military. Although USSOCOM personnel are clearly better able to carry out the missions, the decision to initiate them in peacetime involves a foreign policy decision, and the CIA would be the appropriate vehicle for exercising political control.

One form of covert action that has attracted renewed attention in recent years is assassination. As a result of the political embarrassment that occurred in the mid-1970s over revelations of CIA attempts to assassinate foreign leaders, President Ford's executive order on intelligence activities forbade the CIA (or any other government agency) to engage in, or conspire to engage in, political assassination. Subsequently, President Reagan's Executive Order 12333, "United States Intelligence Activities," of December 4, 1981, extended the ban to preclude involvement in any assassination.[33]

On rare occasions that ban has been questioned. More recently, suggestions of assassination have been made, ranging from placing a bounty on Saddam Hussein to changing the executive order prohibiting assassinations in such a way that would result in "removing the comfort quotient that he currently enjoys in believing that he is personally immune from attack or the consequences of attack." Two authors have argued that "when hundreds and even thousands of innocent people are at risk, assassination of key terrorist leaders may be an option worthy of renewed debate." In the aftermath of attacks on two U.S. embassies in Africa in August 1998, two senators requested the Director of the FBI to consider the legality of assassinating the leaders of organized crime or terrorist groups. And a former CIA officer argued that "common sense dictates that in the war against terrorism—against all those who are killing Americans—the U.S. must be willing to kill terrorist chiefs."[34]

Another observer suggested eliminating the ban because it was hypocritical— given U.S. attempts to kill Muammar al-Qaddafi and Saddam Hussein in aerial attacks.[35] Several decades ago, a novelist, whose series of espionage novels featured a secret agent employed by a classified department often referred to as "Murderer's Row," made a similar point:

> It seems to be all right to plan on, and create the machines for, exterminating billions of human beings at a crack, but just to send out the guy to rub out another who's getting to be a very active menace, that's . . . considered very immoral and reprehensible.[36]

The examination of assassination involves consideration of two issues—morality and practicality. Of course, at present assassination of any sort would violate the standing executive order on intelligence activities. But that only implies that no official should sanction assassination unless that provision of the executive order (section 2-11) is changed. It does not answer the question of whether 2-11 *should* be eliminated or altered in some way.

Former DCI James Woolsey has argued that attempting to kill a foreign leader "was wrong in Cuba," and "we should not tell the world we support assassination as a tool of U.S. statecraft."[37]

Woolsey apparently did not discuss in detail why such an attempt was wrong, or discuss the issue of assassination with respect to terrorists or individuals involved in WMD programs—two prominent targets of Israeli assassination attempts.[38]

One argument that might be made against any such change is a moral one. One principle that would certainly prohibit assassination would be "thou shalt not kill." However, taken literally the commandment requires total pacifism, with no resort to violence under any circumstances. One might argue that such a commandment—by preventing innocents from defending themselves—is, in itself, immoral. Certainly, societies recognize the right to self-defense.

A more commonly accepted notion is that killing is prohibited *except* when one is in imminent danger of serious harm. That concept rules out vigilante justice and requires that individuals charged with murder or other serious crimes be brought before a judge and jury before being sentenced to prison or death— partly to ensure that the individual is actually guilty of the crime and partly in an attempt to assure appropriate punishment.

Of course, the problem in the international arena is that neither the United States nor anyone else can file a complaint, with any body that is empowered to take action, against Saddam Hussein or against terrorists protected by the Libyan regime. U.S. action to apprehend an individual and bring him to the United States may be feasible in some, but not all, cases.[39] The question then becomes—given an inability to invoke any reliable legal mechanisms to halt the activities of such individuals and groups, can assassination be morally acceptable?*

---

*Developments of interest occurred in the summer of 1998. In July of 1998, one hundred countries agreed on the fundamentals for an international court to prosecute war criminals and dictators. The United States opposed the agreements as written, for a number of reasons. Libya agreed that two suspects accused in the 1988 bombing of Pan Am Flight 103 over Scotland could be tried by a Scottish court sitting in the Netherlands. Subsequently, Libya added a number of conditions to its original proviso. (See Alessandra Stanley, "U.S. Dissents, But Accord Is Reached on War-Crime Court," *New York Times,* July 18, 1998, p. A3; John M. Goshko, "Libya Adds Conditions for Pan Am Bombing Trial," *Washington Post,* September 30, 1998, p. A20; John M. Goshko, Libyan Demand Threatens Pan Am Bombing Trial," *Washington Post,* October 27, 1998, p. A16.)

Whether such developments will have any longer practical effect in making it possible to bring such tyrants or terrorists to court remains to be seen, but skepticism is justified. Certainly, neither Saddam Hussein nor Osama bin Laden are likely to turn up anytime soon and demand their day in court. And capturing them may be far more difficult than killing them.

It is difficult to come to any answer other than "yes." Such individuals make themselves legitimate targets through repeated acts of murder—often repeated acts of mass murder—their undoubted unwillingness to subject themselves to any legal proceedings (if such a forum is successfully established), and the continuing threat they represent.[40]

It should also be noted that there are occasionally exceptions to the prohibition against preemptive action, even in countries where the law is taken seriously—for example, when a jury acquits of murder a repeated victim of parental or spousal abuse, who can convincingly demonstrate that he or she acted to prevent an inevitable fatal beating. An international equivalent, which the United States has recognized, is self-defense against a continuing or imminent threat.

One might also include key individuals involved in some WMD programs as potential targets. If, for example, the United States was unable to undermine the Iraqi biological warfare program in any way other than the elimination of some key figures, and if elimination of those individuals would have dramatically negative effects on the program, and if there was a real reason to believe that Iraq would engage in terrorist attacks employing biological agents, would it be immoral to authorize the assassination of those individuals, if there was no legal prohibition?

Of course, to say that it would not be immoral to assassinate an individual or individuals is not to say that the U.S. government should undertake assassinations. Just because it is easy to conjure up some scenarios where one may opt for such a violent option and successfully carry it out does not mean that those scenarios would actually occur. Although Tom Clancy has full control over the developments in his novels, the U.S. government lacks such powers in the real world. Thus, there are a number of practical objections that can be raised with respect to such a policy.

Feasibility is one such objection, particularly with regard to political leaders. The U.S. experience is one of profound failure—attempts or plans to assassinate foreign leaders have been unsuccessful or overtaken by events, and the political embarrassment has been significant when the details became public knowledge. Given the intense security surrounding likely targets, particularly Saddam Hussein, success is not likely.[41]

A second possible objection, particularly in the case of foreign leaders, is that it might accomplish little or even backfire. Adolf Hitler is often used as an example of a foreign leader who it would have been justifiable to assassinate. However, by the time Hitler attained that status it may already have been too late. One cannot know exactly what would have happened had Hitler met an untimely end in 1938, but it is certainly possible that events would have proceeded on the same course with a new leader. The individuals surrounding a Hitler or Saddam have attained that status by being as morally despicable as their leaders. The removal of such leaders may set off a fight for power but not necessarily a reversal of course. The survivors would have a great deal to lose in a regime they did not control. As one writer observed, "There is a good chance Saddam would be replaced by Saddam II, another Baathist general ready to continue the military dictatorship."[42]

The possibility that a successful assassination might backfire by installing a more adept enemy was at least one factor in the British decision not to attempt to kill Adolph Hitler. Possible scenarios for "Operation Foxley" included sniper attacks, aerial bombardment and paratrooper assault, destruction of Hitler's personal train, poisoning his tea, and impregnating his clothes with anthrax. The ultimate conclusion, however, was expressed in one memorandum that considered the assassination strategy—"As a strategist, Hitler has been of the greatest possible assistance to the British war effort."[43]

A third concern is retaliation, particularly with respect to U.S. leaders. Attempts to assassinate a leader, or key individuals in a weapons program, could well lead the target to attempt to return the favor. Although the evidence is persuasive that John F. Kennedy was killed by a lone assassin, it is not hard to understand the logic behind speculation that Castro would retaliate for the attempts on his life. Beyond speculation is the fact that Saddam Hussein had predelegated to Iraqi military officials the authority to fire Scuds with biological agents, should Baghdad be destroyed by a nuclear weapon. The order could just as easily have been given with respect to a successful assassination attempt. And, of course, Saddam did attempt to have former President Bush killed, presumably in retaliation for U.S. attempts to kill him.

It has been noted that because of the openness of U.S. society, American presidents are among the most vulnerable leaders. In contrast, dictators, in order to survive in power, create an elaborate protective apparatus to reduce the chances of being assassinated. Thus, Saddam has reportedly survived a number of assassination attempts.[44]

A fourth concern, is world reaction. Undoubtedly, even the suggestion that the United States was behind the demise of a foreign leader would probably produce various levels of protests from allies and adversaries as well as international condemnation. No doubt many of the protests would be hypocritical, coming from governments with their own record of assassinations or worse, but they would also represent a public relations problem of significant proportions.

A fifth potential drawback is the "oops" factor. Even Israel's Mossad, which has conducted a large number of successful assassinations over the years, is not immune to serious mistakes. The "assassination" of an Arab waiter in Norway—who the Israeli's mistook for Ali Hassan Salameh, the "Red Prince" responsible for the 1972 Munich massacre of Israeli Olympic athletes—resulted in a public relations disaster for Israel. More recently, the failed attempt to eliminate Khaled Meshal, the leader of the fundamentalist group Hamas, severely damaged relations with Jordan.[45]

There is also the danger that if covert action is often considered attractive because it appears to be a means of accomplishing a diplomatic objective cheaply, and without public debate, then assassination might come to represent a cheap alternative to political covert action. An assassination, at least in theory, could be cheaper, quicker, and far less complicated than the messy political operations that require spending hundreds of millions of dollars on squabbling political groups.

Finally, authorization for an assassination would have to be the subject of a Presidential Finding and be presented to the intelligence oversight committees. It is likely that almost any such finding will be incredibly controversial—no matter what the provocation. Leaks to prevent the plan from going ahead or an extremely divisive, even if secret, political conflict are serious possibilities.

Undoubtedly, there are additional reasons why assassination may not be a viable option, and there may be little justification for a change in the executive order. But, at the same time, it would be unwise to move beyond a prohibition in an executive order to a legislative prohibition (as had been proposed in earlier years).[46] An executive order can be changed in an instant. Legislative changes would be far more difficult, and although a U.S. president should be reluctant to change the present policy, events may leave him or her no choice. "Never say never" would be an appropriate caution to keep in mind.

FRIENDLY TARGETS

During the Cold War the United States collected intelligence on many of its allies, just as its allies spied on the United States. By mutual agreement, the United States, United Kingdom, Australia, and Canada did not attempt to recruit human sources in the other's government or society. The espionage relationship with other allied nations was less clear cut. France was a target of U.S. intelligence collection, especially with regard to its nuclear program, as well as a nation that spied on the United States, particularly to accumulate scientific and technical intelligence and industrial secrets. The Amin and Pollard cases indicate that both Israel and the United States have not been able to resist opportunities to penetrate the other's national security establishment.

Soviet espionage, including illicit acquisition of science and technology, was the key focus during the Cold War. Because of the greater concern with such espionage, and the need to maintain close alliance relationships in opposition to the Soviet Union, the activities of the intelligence services of friendly nations was generally a lesser concern—particularly when the objective was industrial espionage.

But in the aftermath of the conclusion of the Cold War, and with the growing focus on international economics by the Clinton administration, the economic espionage and/or bribery activities of nations such as France, Israel, Germany, South Korea, and other long-time allies has produced increased attention, increased criticism, and a U.S. policy of attempting to detect and neutralize such activity.

As a result of the increased focus given to the detection and neutralization of such activities, the CIA played a role in the Raytheon Corporation's defeat of a French competitor for a lucrative contract for high-tech surveillance of the

Amazon. At the same time CIA operations to penetrate the French government, not in pursuit of industrial secrets, but to gather intelligence on economic policy issues, embarrassed the U.S. government when the operation was revealed to the French press. Likewise, the disclosure that the National Security Agency was intercepting the phone calls of Japanese officials who were in the United States to negotiate a trade agreement also produced public relations problems.

Of course, the anguished reaction of a nation or public whose own government or corporations have engaged in far more extensive economic intelligence and industrial espionage activities is hard to take seriously. At the same time, it does raise the question—what should be the governing principles that guide U.S. intelligence collection with respect to allied nations?

Announced U.S. policy is that the intelligence community is not to be used to gather industrial secrets for the benefit of U.S. corporations. However, the United States has and continues to collect intelligence, through a variety of means, on both foreign economic espionage operations and foreign economic policy formulation. Detection of foreign industrial espionage and bribery is certainly a reasonable activity for the CIA and other elements of the intelligence community. Collection of intelligence on foreign economic policy and negotiating strategies, particularly if collected in the pursuit of advancing free trade, is also legitimate.

At the same time, it is necessary to weigh the potential gains that might be achieved against the possible consequences of exposure—consequences that may be a function of both the target and the means (e.g., HUMINT vs. COMINT) that are employed to collect intelligence. Thus, the threshold for engaging in such operations may need to be more carefully considered than perhaps it has been in the past—taking into account both the possibilities of obtaining much of the information through open sources (either publications or diplomatic contacts) and the potential consequences of failure.

There are, however, other situations in which it may be necessary to conduct more aggressive intelligence collection activities, even if the target is an allied government or the corporation of an allied state.

For example, Saudi Arabia proved uncooperative in the investigation of the terrorist bombing of June 1996 in Dhahran that killed nineteen members of the Air Force. The Saudis were apparently more interested in suggesting that the bombing was the result of foreign forces than addressing the possibility that it came from internal opposition (a probability they subsequently acknowledged). In 1998 disagreements with the Saudi government led the FBI to withdraw the dozens of investigators in Saudi Arabia involved in investigating the blast.[47]

A more significant problem involves the activities of governments or corporations of allies with respect to proliferation and their relations with states such as Iran or Libya. As noted in Chapter 11, according to one account a CIA officer was expelled from Germany because of his activities in collecting information about a third country, Iran, that had not been cleared with the German government.[48]

However, given the role that various European firms and governments have played in providing technology to Iraq, Iran, and other rogue states who have sought to acquire weapons of mass destruction, U.S. intelligence collection may be justified as a means of preventing or delaying the acquisition of key technologies. Former senior operations official Dewey Clarridge provided a hypothetical scenario:

> Suppose you believe that an enterprising Frenchman is getting ready to ship a load of COCOM-embargoed computers to 'Aqaba, Jordan, and on to Basra, Iraq. Because you know that the French government will not cooperate to block the shipment, your objective is to seek the clandestine assistance of an officer in the export licensing department of the appropriate French economic ministry . . . [49]

As noted in Chapter 1, Russia still presents an important intelligence target, particularly due to some of the customers for its sale of military technologies, to concern over its export control systems, and to the security of its nuclear weapons. Thus, the CIA would be derelict if it did not to try to recruit key sources in institutions such as MINATOM (Ministry of Atomic Energy) or the Russian General Staff.

Of course, the potential benefits of recruitments with respect to allied nations must be weighed against the potential damage to the relationship should such recruits be detected. And it is certainly preferable if diplomatic and cooperative measures can be used to solve a problem, such as convincing the allied nation that they should restrict the sale of key technologies to a particular country or convincing a government to improve its export control system.

The threshold for engaging in operations should certainly be higher with regard to allies than adversaries and higher for some allies than others. But with few exceptions (the United Kingdom, Australia, Canada, and New Zealand) such activity should not be automatically ruled out—not offending German, French, or Russian sensibilities is not as important as keeping weapons of mass destruction out of the hands of countries such as Iran and Iraq.

CHALLENGES

Aside from decisions on structure and the powers of the DCI, when and how to employ covert action, and the problem of friendly targets, the U.S. intelligence community faces a variety of challenges in the next several decades. Some of those have stimulated organizational changes *within* the CIA, the NSA, and the DIA, as noted in earlier chapters.

One challenge pertains to the collection, processing, and analysis of signals intelligence. A number of recent developments affect the ability to extract useful information from the data that has been intercepted. The transmission of data via fiber optic cables eliminates standard interception techniques that rely on signals being transmitted through the air or leaking out into space. Nor is it clear that it is possible to tap the communications running through a fiber optic cable in the same way that one could tap into conventional cable traffic. The growing sophistication of privately developed encryption techniques, complicated by the mobility of cell phones, also presents a problem for U.S. intelligence in monitoring international criminal activities (as well as a problem for civil libertarians, when the CIA or FBI seeks restrictions on those techniques). In addition, the growing volume of international communications has resulted in an enormous volume of data to sort through in an attempt to find the wheat among the chaff.[50]

The intelligence community also faces increasingly sophisticated denial and deception activities by key targets. These activities involve not conducting operations when it is known U.S. reconnaissance satellites are overhead, constructing underground facilities, and avoiding actions that are known to be clear signals of impending missile launches or nuclear detonations.[51] Iraq understood, partly as a result of its relationship with the Soviet Union, what aspects of Scud operations provided warning of impending launches. Likewise, India, by 1998, clearly understood that any flurry of above-ground activity at their test site would provide warning of an upcoming nuclear test. Plans for a large constellation of satellites, even with less capability on each satellite, may make denial and deception more difficult. In addition, advances in imagery and MASINT sensors, including SAR and hyperspectral sensors, and in the interpretation of the data may also prove valuable in defeating denial and deception activities.

It is critical that any cultural problems that plague the various portions of the intelligence community be reduced or eliminated. It is hard to imagine that any large government bureaucracy will be able to completely avoid such problems. The number of individuals employed, the competition from the private sector, as well as other factors ensure that a certain portion of those in both managerial and collection/analytical positions will be less than fully competent, or motivated by goals other than providing the most valuable product.

There have been a number of former intelligence community personnel who have charged that there are significant cultural problems in various components of the community—including all of the CIA's key directorates. In addition, Adm. David Jeremiah, in his review of U.S. intelligence performance with respect to India's May 1998 nuclear detonations, also pointed to a number of flaws that could be attributed to culture—such as discouraging analysis that is outside the mainstream. It is impossible, of course, to fully assess the validity of such charges from the outside. One must always allow for the possibility that critiques are wrong or overdrawn. However, it is important for those in oversight positions in the community as well as in Congress to seriously examine such charges and take corrective action if necessary.[52]

Flexibility is a third challenge facing the intelligence community. During the Cold War, there was no doubt about which countries were the key targets. In the present era, the region of the world of most concern to the United States may change dramatically from month to month. In addition, issues or nations that were very far down on the list of priorities may quickly emerge at the top of the list, requiring a substantial intelligence effort. Thus, Iraqi defiance of the Persian Gulf War cease-fire agreement may require increased reconnaissance activities one month, whereas a few months later nuclear testing in Southwest Asia may become the front-burner issue. A few months afterward North Korea may be the key concern. And areas such as the former Yugoslavian states, Rwanda, or Somalia may, as result of U.S. military involvement, experience a quick and dramatic rise on the target list. Satellites can most easily adapt to such changes, aircraft follow in flexibility, whereas ground stations' capabilities are limited by their location. Further, HUMINT, particularly in areas that have previously been of low priority, can be particularly difficult to obtain—since HUMINT capabilities are not easily surged. In addition, the mixture of language skills that is needed may shift quickly from one period to the next.

The advent of near real-time collection, sophisticated personal computers, databases, and the Internet have produced a far different information environment than existed even a decade ago. One analyst has noted a number of important trends: decentralization, tailored systems, networking, and distributed operations. One challenge for the intelligence community is to extract the maximum benefits from those changes.[53]

One specific problem for the intelligence community is to develop means that will allow analysts and policymakers quick access to information, while avoiding the problems of information overload. This process is already under way with developments such as Intelink, which allows intelligence analysts to access multimedia intelligence products, access databases, communicate with other analysts, and obtain training and educational services, all via their computers.[54]

It is also important that the intelligence community be able to balance the temptations of increasingly sophisticated collection and dissemination systems with realistic goals for the understanding of important developments and the dissemination of data. The age of information operations has arrived, and there is repeated talk of information dominance—of an ability to see and understand everything taking place underneath, particularly on the battlefield. For example, the Jeremiah report refers to "near continuous, global collection," as the twenty-first-century requirements facing the NRO, and Air Force Chief of Staff Gen. Ronald R. Fogelman often predicted that the United States would be able to "find, fix, track, target, and engage anything of military significance" on the surface of the Earth. Thus, future constellations of satellites are presented as being able to allow collection on demand (and receipt shortly after) against any target.[55]

Before the attempt is made to meet such lofty objectives it will be necessary to consider a number of issues. One might question how realistic is the ambition of being able to monitor and understand all developments, particularly during the fog of war. The question of the cost of a system that collects, processes, and analyzes such huge volumes of information is certainly relevant. Costs that need to be examined and compared to benefits include absolute costs and marginal costs of obtaining the final x percent of coverage. In addition, as is well known, much of the data collected by technical collection systems already goes unanalyzed. To prevent the problem from growing worse more sophisticated processing and analytic tools will be needed, further increasing the costs. Finally, there is the danger that focusing on the constant monitoring and reporting of activities may decrease the attention given to *detecting and understanding key developments*, whether in India, Iraq, or Russia.

Notes

1. The charge that the intelligence community, and most particularly the CIA, failed to anticipate the collapse of the Soviet Union quickly became conventional wisdom. Its most notable proponent has been Senator Daniel Patrick Moynihan (D–N.Y.). For references to a number of articles alleging such a failure and a rebuttal, see Bruce D. Berkowitz and Jeffrey T. Richelson, "The CIA Vindicated: The Soviet Collapse *Was* Predicted," *National Interest* 41, no. 3 (Fall 1995): 36–47, and Douglas J. MacEachin, "The Record Versus the Charges: CIA Assessments of the Soviet Union," *Studies in Intelligence*, Semiannual Unclassified Edition, No. 1 (1997), pp. 57–66.

2. James Schlesinger, *A Review of the Intelligence Community* (Washington, D.C.: Office of Management and Budget, 1971); National Security Council, *Report on Presidential Review Memorandum/NSC–11: Intelligence Structure and Mission*, February 22, 1977, pp. i–ii.

3. National Security Council, *Report on Presidential Review Memorandum/NSC–11: Intelligence Structure and Mission*, pp. 46–47.

4. "Statement from Senator Boren on Introduction of Boren-McCurdy Intelligence Reorganization Plan," February 5, 1992; Office of Senator David Boren, "Key Features of the Intelligence Reorganization Act of 1992," n.d.; George Lardner Jr., "Intelligence Overhaul Urged," *Washington Post*, February 6, 1992, pp. A1, A6.

5. Letter, Chester Paul Beach Jr., Acting General Counsel, to Honorable Les Aspin, Chairman, Committee on Armed Services, March 17, 1992; Dick Cheney, Secretary of Defense to Les Aspin, Chairman, Committee on Armed Services, March 17, 1992; Robert M. Gates, "Statement on Change in CIA and the Intelligence Community," April 1, 1992, statement to joint hearing of the Senate Select Committee on Intelligence and the House Permanent Select Committee on Intelligence.

6. The official studies are Commission on the Roles and Capabilities of the United States Intelligence Community, *Preparing for the 21st Century: An Appraisal of U.S. Intelligence* (Washington, D.C.: U.S. Government Printing Office, 1996) and U.S. Congress, House Permanent Select Committee on Intelligence, *IC21: Intelligence Community in the 21st Century* (Washington, D.C.: U.S. Government Printing Office, 1996). Studies produced under the auspices of the 20th Century Fund, Council on Foreign Relations and National Institute for Public Policy, are, respectively, *In from the Cold* (New York: 20th Century Fund Press, 1996), *Making Intelligence Smarter* (New York: Council on Foreign Relations, 1996), and *Modernizing Intelligence: Structure and Change for the 21st Century* (Fairfax, Va.: National Institute for Public Policy, September 1997). Significant studies produced by former intelligence officers include: John A. Gentry, *A Framework for Reform of the U.S. Intelligence Community* (Vienna, Va., June 6, 1995) and Robert David Steele, *Intelligence and Counter-*

intelligence: Proposed Program for the 21st Century, (Vienna, Va.: Open Source Solutions, April 14, 1997).

7. U.S. Congress, House Permanent Select Committee on Intelligence, *IC21: Intelligence Community in the 21st Century*, pp. 1–52.

8. It should be noted that some seem to be offended by the very existence of the CIA and the intelligence community (the *New York Times* editorial board comes to mind), and any failure, real or imagined, is taken as proof of its hopeless state and of the need for radical reform—to be achieved by budget and personnel cuts, elimination of agencies, or other inflictions of pain—without consideration of actual requirements or consequences of the proposed changes. Because any massive change is seen as reform (and reform, is by definition good) and because the community is perpetually considered to be in need of such reform, any time radical reorganization proposals, no matter how silly, fail to be implemented the conclusion is that "necessary reform" has again been blocked by sinister forces.

Thus, in response to the Brown commission's report the *New York Times* editorialized ("Spy Pablum," March 3, 1996) that the intelligence community was a "creaky and expensive relic of the Cold War" in need of a major overhaul. In their letter of response Harold Brown and Vice Chairman Warren Rudman noted that "you fail to say what overhaul should take place or how it would improve the existing system." They conclude their letter, part of which was published in the *Times* ("Spy Agencies Don't Require a Major Overhaul," March 7, 1996, p. A24), by stating:

> We urge you to bear in mind that, despite all the myths and misinformation that swirl around it, intelligence is serious business. You appear to think the Nation should satisfy its intelligence needs through news columns and CNN, and satisfy its requirements for a military capability with rolled-up copies of your newspaper. Despite all the evidence of their contributions, much of which is set out in our report, you seem bent on ignoring or disparaging what U.S. intelligence agencies are doing in the wake of the Cold War to protect U.S. lives, conserve U.S. resources, and further U.S. objectives. The performance of these agencies can be improved. They can be more effective and efficient. But the United States continues to depend on them to protect the safety and well-being of its citizens. It is not a capability to trifle with.

For the full text of the letter, see U.S. Congress, Senate Select Committee on Intelligence, *Renewal and Reform: U.S. Intelligence in a Changing World* (Washington, D.C.: U.S. Government Printing Office, 1997), pp. 116–117. For a more reasonable editorial assessment of the Brown report, see "Intelligence Fixup," *Washington Post*, March 3, 1996, p. C6.

9. Walter Pincus, "Curtain Is Falling on Another Intelligence Drama: Reform," *Washington Post*, July 8, 1996, p. A13; Walter Pincus, "Panel Rejects Intelligence Shift," *Washington Post*, July 18, 1996, p. A25; "Senate Panels Still at Odds on Intelligence Authorization," *Aerospace Daily*, June 10, 1996, pp. 403A–403B; Walter Pincus, "Intelligence Battleground: Reform Bill," *Washington Post*, May 30, 1996, p. A29.

10. National Security Council, *Report on Presidential Review Memorandum/NSC-11*, p. 31.

11. Commission on the Organization of the Government for the Conduct of Foreign Policy, *Report* (Washington, D.C.: U.S. Government Printing Office, 1975), p. 98.

12. Keith Hall, Responses to SASC Questions, Answer to #8, March 6, 1997.

13. Adm. David E. Jeremiah et al., *Defining the Future of the NRO for the 21st Century: Final Report, Executive Summary*, August 26, 1996, p. 6.

14. For a history of the DS&T, see Jeffrey T. Richelson, "The Wizards of Langley: The CIA's Directorate of Science and Technology," *Intelligence and National Security* 12, no. 1 (January 1997), pp. 82–103. Surprisingly, former DCI Robert Gates has advocated eliminating the DS&T. See Walter Pincus, "Ex-CIA Chief Backs Smaller Spy Agency," *Washington Post*, December 10, 1994, p. A4.

15. U.S. Congress, House Permanent Select Committee on Intelligence, *IC21: Intelligence Community in the 21st Century*, p. 181.

16. Ludwell Lee Montague, *General Walter Bedell Smith as Director of Central Intelligence, October 1950–February 1953* (University Park: Pennsylvania State University Press, 1992), pp. 63–74.

17. Jimmy Carter, PD/NSC–17, "Reorganization of the Intelligence Community," August 4, 1977.

18. Commission on the Roles and Capabilities of the United States Intelligence Community, *Preparing for the 21st Century: An Appraisal of U.S. Intelligence*, p. xix.

19. This augmentation of the DCI's powers would be far more important than the relatively trivial question of whether the DCI should be asked to concur in the appointments of the DNRO or DIRNSA.

20. Stansfield Turner, *Secrecy and Democracy: The CIA in Transition* (Boston, Mass.: Houghton Mifflin, 1985), pp. 260–262.

21. John Hollister Hedley, *Checklist for the Future of Intelligence* (Washington, D.C.: Institute for the Study of Diplomacy, Georgetown University, 1995), pp. 11–12.

22. U.S. Congress, Senate Select Committee on Intelligence, *Renewal and Reform*, p. 183.

23. Ibid., p. 29.

24. U.S. Congress, Senate Select Committee on Intelligence, *S.2198 and S.421 to Reorganize the United States Intelligence Community*, (Washington, D.C.: U.S. Government Printing Office, 1992), p. 267.

25. Brigadier General Frank B. Campbell, Director of Forces, *Air Force TIARA Programs: Intelligence Support to the Warfighter*, 1995.

26. Hedley, *Checklist for the Future of Intelligence*, p. 3.

27. U.S. Congress, Senate Select Committee on Intelligence, *Worldwide Intelligence Review*, (Washington, D.C.: U.S. Government Printing Office, 1995), p. 49.

28. U.S. Congress, Senate Select Committee on Intelligence, *Renewal and Reform*, p. 131. Clearly, this also is one reason why the military services should not be absorbed by the DIA, as has often been suggested. For example, see Stansfield Turner, "The Pentagon's Intelligence Mess," *Washington Post*, January 12, 1986, pp. D1–D2.

29. This was not necessarily the only factor in many operations, or even a key factor in some. One might point to Guatemala or Iran as cases where other factors were more important. However, the fundamental reason for covert action from the late 1940s until the collapse of the Soviet regime was the U.S.-Soviet conflict.

30. With respect to the difference between Afghanistan and Iraq as a target of covert action, see Milt Bearden, "Lessons from Afghanistan," *New York Times*, March 2, 1998, p. A21. Problems with the Iraqi operation are discussed in Bruce D. Berkowitz and Allan E. Goodman, "The Logic of Covert Action," *National Interest* 51 (Spring 1998): 38–46.

31. Loch K. Johnson, *Secret Agencies: U.S. Intelligence in a Hostile World* (New Haven, Conn.: Yale University Press, 1996), p. 42.

32. General Accounting Office, *Special Operations Forces: Opportunities to Preclude Overuse and Misuse*, GAO/NSIAD–97–85, (Washington, D.C.: GAO, May 1997), pp. 6–7, 22.

33. U.S. Congress, Senate Select Committee to Study Governmental Operations with Respect to Intelligence Activities, *Alleged Assassination Plots Involving Foreign Leaders* (Washington, D.C.: U.S. Government Printing Office, 1975).

34. David Newman and Bruce Bueno de Mesquita, "Repeal Order 12333, Legalize 007," *New York Times*, January 26, 1989, p. A23; Justin Blum, "Altering Assassination Ban Might Increase Pressure on Saddam Hussein, Robb Says," *Washington Post*, February 19, 1998, p. A22; Michael Romano, "Campbell Calls for Bounty on Saddam," *Rocky Mountain News*, March 7, 1998, pp. 5A, 11A; Roger Medd and Frank Goldstein, "International Terrorism on the Eve of a New Millennium," *Studies in Conflict and Terrorism* 20, no. 3 (July-September 1997): 281–316; "Senators Raise Issue of Assassinating Terrorists," *Washington Times*, September 4, 1998, p. A3; Edward G. Shirley, The Etiquette of Killing bin Laden," *Wall Street Journal*, August 27, 1998, p. A14. With respect to altering the assassination ban, Blum quotes former Assistant Secretary of Defense Lawrence J. Korb as stating, "I don't think he believes we follow our own executive orders to begin with."

35. Daniel Schorr, "Hypocrisy About Assassination," *Washington Post*, February 3, 1991, p. C7.

36. Donald Hamilton, *The Wrecking Crew* (Greenwich, Conn.: Fawcett, 1960), p. 58.

37. Ben Barber, "Security Council Endorses Annan's Baghdad Pact," *Washington Times*, March 3, 1998, p. A17.

38. Medd and Goldstein, "International Terrorism on the Eve of a New Millennium."

39. One terrorist the U.S. did apprehend overseas and bring to trial was Fawaz Yunis. See Duane R. Clarridge with Digby Diehl, *A Spy for All Seasons: My Life in the CIA* (New York: Scribner, 1997), pp. 347–359.

40. Lawrence Korb suggests that engaging in assassination would "bring us down to his [Saddam's] level" (Blum, "Altering Assassination Ban Might Increase Pressure . . . "). Such an argument, however, completely removes the proposed act from its context. It is similar to the argument that suggests executing a murderer is wrong because it involves "killing in order to demonstrate that killing is wrong." The execution is intended to demonstrate that *murder* is a grievous wrong. Thus, it is hard to think of a more appropriate response to Iranian assassinations of dissidents than the counter-assassination of those who authorize and carry out the assassinations.

41. A more optimistic view of the chance of an assassination having a positive impact and of its being feasible can be found in William Cowan, "How to Kill Saddam," *Washington Post*, February 10, 1991, p. C2.

42. Johanna McGeary, "Time to Off Saddam?" *Time*, February 16, 1998, pp. 60–61.

43. Warren Hoge, "Britain Reveals Elaborate Plots to Kill Hitler As War Neared End," *New York Times*, July 24, 1998, p. A10; T. R. Reid, "British Spies Planned Many Deaths for Hitler," *Washington Post*, July 24, 1998, p. A32.

44. Twentieth Century Fund Task Force on Covert Action and Democracy, *The Need to Know* (New York: Twentieth Century Fund, 1992), p. 14.

45. Yossi Melman, "Israel's Darkest Secrets," *New York Times*, March 25, 1998, p. A27; Ian Black and Benny Morris, *Israel's Secret Wars: A History of Israel's Intelligence Services* (New York: Grove, Weidenfeld, 1991), pp. 275–276.

46. For example, Twentieth Century Fund Task Force on Covert Action and Democracy, *The Need to Know*, pp. 13–14.

47. David Johnston, "F.B.I. Pulls out of Joint Inquiry on Fatal Blast in Saudi Arabia," *New York Times*, November 2, 1996, pp. 1, 6; David Johnston, "Reno Says Saudis Did Not

Cooperate in Bombing Inquiry," *New York Times*, January 24, 1997, pp. A1, A6; Melinda Liu, "Kept in the Dark," *Newsweek*, July 15, 1996, p. 36; Jeff Gerth, "U.S. Takes Hard Look at Saudis with Bombing and Shah in Mind," *New York Times*, December 1, 1996, pp. 1, 20; Philip Shenon and David Johnston, "U.S.-Saudi Inquiry Into 1996 Bombing Is Falling Apart," *New York Times*, June 21, 1998, pp. 1, 6.

48. William Drozdiak, "Bonn Expels U.S. Officials for Spying," *Washington Post*, March 9, 1997, pp. A1, A25; Walter Pincus, "Expelled CIA Agent Was Not Gathering Data on Germany, Sources Say," *Washington Post*, March 11, 1997, p. A11.

49. Clarridge with Diehl, *A Spy for All Seasons*, p. 305.

50. Mike Mills, "Underseas Cables Carry Growing Rivers of Data," *Washington Post*, March 9, 1998, pp. A1, A10.

51. David A. Fulghum, "DARPA Looks Anew at Hidden Targets," *Aviation Week & Space Technology*, January 6, 1997, pp. 56–57; Walter Pincus, "Buried Missile Labs Foil U.S. Satellites," *Washington Post*, July 29, 1998, pp. A1, A18.

52. The critiques include Edward G. Shirley, "Can't Anybody Here Play This Game?" *The Atlantic Monthly*, February 1998, pp. 45–62; John A. Gentry, *Lost Promise: How CIA Analysis Misserves the Nation* (Lanham, Md.: University Press of America, 1993); John A. Gentry, *A Framework for Reform of the U.S. Intelligence Community* (Vienna, Va.: June 6, 1995). On Adm. Jeremiah's findings, see Tim Weiner, "C.I.A. Study Details Failed Spy System," *New York Times*, June 3, 1998, pp. A1, A8.

53. Bruce D. Berkowitz, "Information Technology and Intelligence Reform," *Orbis* (Winter 1997): 107–118. Also see John C. Gannon, Deputy Director for Intelligence, CIA, "Advanced Information Processing and Analysis Symposium," McLean, Virginia, March 27, 1997.

54. Community Management Staff, "Intelink," April 1995.

55. Warren Ferster, "NRO Eyes Smaller Spacecraft for Eavesdropping," *Space News*, September 29–October 5, 1997, pp. 1, 19; "Cincs Want More Current Imagery, Maps," *Aerospace Daily*, July 15, 1996, p. 70; John A. Tirpak, "Complications Overhead," *Air Force Magazine*, April 1998, pp. 22–28; Adm. David E. Jeremiah et al., *Defining the Future of the NRO for the 21st Century: Final Report, Executive Summary*, p. 5.

ACRONYMS

AABL	Advanced Atmospheric Burst Locator
AARS	Advanced Airborne Reconnaissance System
ABM	Anti-Ballistic Missile
ABMA	Army Ballistic Missile Agency
ACC	Air Combat Command
ACE	Allied Command Europe
ACIS	Arms Control Intelligence Staff
ACOUSTINT	Acoustic Intelligence
ACS	Aerial Common Sensor
ADONIS	AMOS Daylight Near-Infrared Imaging System
ADSN	AFTAC Distributed Subsurface Network
AEC	Atomic Energy Commission
AEDS	Atomic Energy Detection System
AEELS	Automatic Electronic Emitter Locating System
AEOS	Advanced Electro-Optical System
AFAR	Azores Fixed Acoustic Range
AFIA	Air Force Intelligence Agency
AFIC	Air Force Intelligence Command
AFIS	Air Force Intelligence Service
AFISA	Air Force Intelligence Support Agency
AFMD	Air Force Mission Directive
AFMIC	Armed Forces Medical Intelligence Center
AFOAT-1	Air Force Office of the Assistant Deputy Chief of Staff for Atomic Energy, Section 1
AFSA	Armed Forces Security Agency
AFSAC	Air Force Special Activities Center
AFSAC/IRC	Armed Forces Security Agency Council/Intelligence Requirements Committee
AFSC	Air Force Systems Command
AFSG	Air Force Security Group
AFSS	Air Force Security Service
AFTAC	Air Force Technical Applications Center

AGER	Auxilliary General Environmental Research
AGTR	Auxilliary General Technical Research
AIA	Air Intelligence Agency
AIA	Army Intelligence Agency
AIC	Atlantic Intelligence Command
AID	Agency for International Development
ALCOR	ARPA Lincoln C-Band Observable Radar
ALTAIR	ARPA Long-Range Tracking and Instrument Radar
AMOS	Air Force Maui Optical System
AMSIC	Army Missile and Space Intelligence Center
AOMC	Army Ordnance Missile Command
AR	Army Regulation
ARIES	Airborne Reconnaissance Integrated Electronics System
ARL-M	Airborne Reconnaissance Low-Multifunction
ARPA	Advanced Research Projects Agency
ARS	Advanced Reconnaissance System
ARSA	Automated Radioxenon Sample Analyzer
ARSP	Airborne Reconnaissance Support Program
ASA	Army Security Agency
ASARS	Advanced Synthetic Aperture Radar System
ASAT	Antisatellite
ASD	Assistant Secretary of Defense
ASD (C³I)	Assistant Secretary of Defense for Command, Control, Communications, and Intelligence
ASDI	Assistant Secretary of Defense for Intelligence
ASL	Albuquerque Seismological Laboratory
ASN	AFTAC Southern Network
ASW	Antisubmarine Warfare
ATS	Advanced Telemetry System
BBC	British Broadcasting Corporation
BGPHES	Battle Group Passive Horizon Extension System
BIOT	British Indian Ocean Territory
BMEWS	Ballistic Missile Early Warning System
BND	Bundesnachrictendienst (Federal Intelligence Service, Germany)
BNE	Board of National Estimates
BRUSA	British-U.S. Communications Intelligence Agreement
C²W	Command and Control Warfare
C³I	Command, Control, Communications, and Intelligence
C⁴I	Command, Control, Communications, Computers, and Intelligence
C⁴ISR	Command, Control, Communications, Computers, Intelligence, Surveillance, and Reconnaissance

CAMS	COMIREX Automated Management System
CAOC	Combined Air Operations Center
CAPG	Covert Action Planning Group
CARIBCOM	Caribbean Command
CARS	Contingency Airborne Reconnaissance Systems
CBRS	Concept-Based Requirements System
CC&D	Counter Camouflage, Concealment, and Deception
CCD	Charge Couple Device
CCP	Consolidated Cryptologic Program
CCPC	Critical Collection Problems Committee
CCSCC	Community Counterintelligence and Security Countermeasures Committee
CENTCOM	Central Command
CERP	Combined Economic Reporting Program
CFI	Committee on Foreign Intelligence
CI	Counterintelligence
CIA	Central Intelligence Agency
CIC	Combined Intelligence Center, USSPACECOM
CIC	Counterintelligence Center, Directorate of Operations, CIA
CIG	Central Intelligence Group
CIGSS	Common Imagery Ground/Surface System
CINC	Commander in Chief
CINCPACOM	Commander in Chief, Pacific Command
CIO	Central Imagery Office
CIPC	Critical Intelligence Problems Committee
CIRL	Current Intelligence Reporting List
CIRVIS	Communications Instructions for Reporting Vital Intelligence Sightings
CIS	Commonwealth of Independent States
CISA	Counterintelligence and Security Activity
CITO	Clandestine Information Technology Office
CITS	Central Command Imagery Transmission System
CMO	Central MASINT Office, DIA
CMS	Community Management Staff
CNC	Community Nonproliferation Committee
CNC	Crime and Narcotics Center, Directorate of Intelligence, CIA
COMINT	Communications Intelligence
COMIREX	Committee on Imagery Requirements and Exploitation
COMOR	Committee on Overhead Reconnaissance
COMSEC	Communications Security
COS	Chief of Station
COSPO	Community Open Source Program Office
CPAS	Office of Current Analytic Production and Support

CPD	Counterproliferation Division
CRITIC	Critical Intelligence Communications
CSB	Collection Support Brief
CSE	Communications Security Establishment
CSS	Central Security Service
CTBT	Comprehensive Test Ban Treaty
CTC	Counterterrorist Center, Directorate of Operations, CIA
DARO	Defense Airborne Reconnaissance Office
DARP	Defense Airborne Reconnaissance Program
DARPA	Defense Advanced Research Projects Agency
DASD	Deputy Assistant Secretary of Defense
DCCC	Defense Collection Coordination Center
DCEETA	Defense Communications Electronics Evaluation and Testing Activity
DCI	Director of Central Intelligence
DCID	Director of Central Intelligence Directive
DCP	Defense Cryptologic Program
DCSI	Deputy Chief of Staff for Intelligence, U.S. Army
DDCI	Deputy Director of Central Intelligence
DDCI/CM	Deputy Director of Central Intelligence/Community Management
DDMS	Deputy Director, Military Support, NRO
DDNS	Deputy Director, National Support, NRO
DEA	Drug Enforcement Administration
DEFSMAC	Defense Special Missile and Astronautics Center
DF	Direction-Finding
DFI	Director of Foreign Intelligence
DGI	General Directorate of Intelligence (Cuba)
DGIAP	Defense General Intelligence Applications Program
DGS	Deployable Ground Station
DGSE	Directorate General of External Security (France)
DGSE	Directorate General of State Security (Nicaragua)
DHS	Defense HUMINT Service
DI	Directorate of Intelligence
DIA	Defense Intelligence Agency
DIAC	Defense Intelligence Analysis Center
DIATP	Defense Intelligence Agency's Tactical Program
DICP	Defense Intelligence Counterdrug Program
DIE	Defense Intelligence Estimate
DIEB	Daily Economic Intelligence Brief
DIMAP	Defense Imagery and Mapping Program

DIN	Defense Intelligence Network
DIRD	Defense Intelligence Reference Document
DIRNSA	Director National Security Agency
DISOB	Defense Intelligence Space Order of Battle
DISR	Directorate for Intelligence, Surveillance, and Reconnaissance
DISTP	Defense Intelligence Special Technologies Program
DITS	Digital Imagery Transmission System
DITSUM	*Defense Intelligence Terrorism Summary*
DMA	Defense Mapping Agency
DMI	Director of Military Intelligence
DMSP	Defense Meteorological Satellite Program
DMZ	Demilitarized Zone
DNI	Director of National Intelligence
DNI	Director of Naval Intelligence
DNRO	Director of the National Reconnaissance Office
DOD	Department of Defense
DODFIP	DOD Futures Intelligence Program
DRSP	Defense Reconnaissance Support Program
DS&T	Directorate of Science and Technology
DSAP	DNI's Special Access Program
DSCS	Defense Satellite Communications System
DSD	Defence Signals Directorate
DSP	Defense Support Program
DSP-A	Defense Support Program-Augmentation
DSPO	Defense Support Project Office
DSRP	Defense Space Reconnaissance Program
DST	Directorate for Territorial Surveillance (France)
DSTS	Deep Space Tracking System
DVITS	Digital Video Imagery Transmission System
EAL	Economic Alert List
EH	*NMJIC Executive Highlights*
EHF	Extremely High Frequency
EIC	Economic Intelligence Committee
EIW	*Economic Intelligence Weekly*
EL	Equipment Location
ELINT	Electronic Intelligence
EMP	Electromagnetic Pulse
EPA	Environmental Protection Agency
ERTS	Earth Resources Technology Satellite
ESC	Electronic Security Command
EUCOM	European Command

EUCOMSITS	European Command Secondary Imagery Transmission System
EUDAC	European Defense Analysis Center
EW	Electronic Warfare
FAPSI	Federal Agency for Government Communications and Information (Russia)
FASTC	Foreign Aerospace Science and Technology Center
FBI	Federal Bureau of Investigation
FBIS	Foreign Broadcast Information Service
FCC	Federal Communications Commission
FICEURLANT	Fleet Intelligence Center, Europe and Atlantic
FICPAC	Fleet Intelligence Center, Pacific
FIPC	Foreign Intelligence Priorities Committee
FIS	Front Islamique de Salvation
FISINT	Foreign Instrumentation Signals Intelligence
FISTS	Fleet Imagery Support Terminals
FLTSATCOM	Fleet Satellite Communications System
FMEP	Foreign Materiel Exploitation Program
FMPRB	Foreign Materiel Program Review Board
FOSIC	Fleet Ocean Surveillance Information Center
FRAPH	Front for the Advancement and Progress of Haiti
FRB	Foreign Resources Branch, Domestic Resources Division, Directorate of Operations, CIA
FRD	Foreign Resources Division, Directorate of Operations, CIA
FSB	Federal Security Service (Russia)
FSTC	Foreign Science and Technology Center, U.S. Army
FTC	Foreign Technology Center
FTD	Foreign Technology Division
GBS	Global Broadcast Service
GCHQ	Government Communications Headquarters (United Kingdom)
GCSB	Government Communications Security Bureau (New Zealand)
GDIAP	General Defense Intelligence and Applications Program
GDIP	General Defense Intelligence Program
GEODSS	Ground-Based Electro-Optical Deep Space Surveillance
GFU	Ground Filter Unit
GIUK	Greenland-Iceland-U.K. Gap
GMAIC	Guided Missile and Astronautics Committee
GMI	General Military Intelligence
GNAT	General Atomics
GPS	Global Positioning System
GRAB	Galactic Radiation and Background

GRSOC	Gordon Regional SIGINT Operations Center
GRU	Glavnoye Razvedyvatelnoye Upravleniye (Chief Intelligence Directorate, Russian General Staff)
GTSN	Global Telemetered Seismic Network
HF	High-Frequency
HFDF	High-Frequency Direction-Finding
HILEV	High Level
HPSCI	House Permanent Select Committee on Intelligence
HRC	Human Resources Committee
HSE	HUMINT Support Elements
HSI	Hyperspectral Imagery
HUMINT	Human Intelligence
I&W	Indications and Warning
IAC	Intelligence Advisory Committee
IAEA	International Atomic Energy Agency
IC/EXCOM	Intelligence Community Executive Committee
ICBM	Intercontinental Ballistic Missile
ICMS	Improved CRYSTAL Metric System
ICON	Image Communications and Operations Node
IDC	Interagency Defector Committee
IDC	International Data Center
IG	Intelligence Group
IHC	Information Handling Committee
IICT	Interagency Intelligence Committee on Terrorism
IIM	Interagency Intelligence Memoranda
IM	Intelligence Memorandum
IMINT	Imagery Intelligence
IMS	International Monitoring System
INA	Iraqi National Accord
INC	Iraqi National Congress
INF	Intermediate Nuclear Forces
INFOSEC	Information Security
INR	Bureau of Intelligence and Research, Department of State
INSCOM	U.S. Army Intelligence and Security Command
INTELSAT	International Telecommunications Satellite
IOSA	Integrated Overhead SIGINT Architecture
IPAC	Intelligence Center, Pacific
IPC	Information Protect Cell
IPC	Intelligence Producers Council
IR	Intelligence Report
IRBM	Intermediate Range Ballistic Missile
IRIS	Intelligence Reconnaissance Imagery System
IRSIG	*International Regulations on SIGINT*

IS	Intelligence Squadron
ISA	Intelligence Support Activity
ISS	Intelligence Systems Secretariat
ITAC	Intelligence and Threat Analysis Center, U.S. Army
ITW/AA	Integrated Tactical Warning and Attack Assessment
IW	Intelligence Wing
IWG	Interagency Working Group
J-2	Joint Staff Director for Intelligence
JAC	Joint Analysis Center
JAEIC	Joint Atomic Energy Intelligence Committee
JCS	Joint Chiefs of Staff
JIC	Joint Intelligence Center
JICCENT	Joint Intelligence Center, Central
JICPAC	Joint Intelligence Center, Pacific
JICTRANS	Joint Intelligence Center, Transportation
JMIP	Joint Military Intelligence Program
JMSDF	Japanese Maritime Self-Defense Force
JOIC	Joint Operational Intelligence Center
JPRS	Joint Publications Research Service
JRC	Joint Reconnaissance Center
JROC	Joint Requirements Oversight Council
JRS	Joint Reconnaissance Schedule
JSMB	Joint Space Management Board
JSOC	Joint Special Operations Command
KDP	Kurdish Democratic Party
KGB	Komitet Gosudastvennoy Bezopasnosti (Committee on State Security, Soviet Union)
KH	Keyhole
LANTCOM	Atlantic Command
LANTDAC	Atlantic Defense Analysis Center
LANTFAST	Atlantic Forward Area Support Team
LANTJIC	Atlantic Joint Intelligence Center
LARS	LIDAR Airborne Remote Sensing
LASS	Low Altitude Space Surveillance
LATS	Large Aperture Tracking System
LAVR	Large Area Vulnerability Reports
LIDAR	Light Detection and Ranging
MAD	Magnetic Anomaly Detector
MASINT	Measurement and Signature Intelligence
MC&G	Mapping, Charting, and Geodesy
MCCDC	Marine Corps Combat Development Command
MCG&I	Mapping, Charting, Geodetic, and Imagery
MCIA	Marine Corps Intelligence Activity

MCIC	Marine Corps Intelligence Center
MCL	McClellan Central Laboratory
MI	Military Intelligence
MIA	Military Intelligence Agency
MIB	Military Intelligence Board
MID	*Military Intelligence Digest*
MIIA	Medical Intelligence and Information Agency
MIRA	Medium-Wave Infrared Arrays
MOBSTR	Mobile Stretch
MOL	Manned Orbiting Laboratory
MOTIF	Maui Optical Tracking and Identification Facility
MRBM	Medium-Range Ballistic Missile
MRSOC	Medina Regional SIGINT Operations Center
MSI	Multispectral Imagery
MSIC	Missile and Space Intelligence Center
MSS	Multispectral Scanner
MTI	Moving Target Indicator
MUCELS	Multiple Communications Emitter Location System
NAIC	National Air Intelligence Center
NAP	NDS Augmentation Package
NAS	Naval Air Station
NASA	National Aeronautics and Space Administration
NASP	Naval Activities Support Program
NATO	North Atlantic Treaty Organization
NAVFAC	Naval Facilities
NAVMIC	Naval Maritime Intelligence Center
NAVSPASUR	Naval Space Surveillance System
NCB	National Collection Branch, Domestic Resources Division, Directorate of Operations, CIA
NCD	National Collection Division
NCIPB	National Counterintelligence Policy Board
NDS	Nuclear Detonation (NUDET) Detection System
NEIS	National Emitter Intelligence Subcommittee
NEMO	Navy Earth Map Observer
NFAC	National Foreign Assessment Center
NFIB	National Foreign Intelligence Board
NFIP	National Foreign Intelligence Program
NGIC	National Ground Intelligence Center
NHCD	National HUMINT Collection Directive
NHRTC	National HUMINT Requirements Tasking Center
NIA	National Imagery Agency
NIA	National Intelligence Authority
NIA	Naval Intelligence Activity

NIC	National Intelligence Council
NIC	Naval Intelligence Command
NICB	National Intelligence Collection Board
NICM	National Intelligence Council Memorandum
NID	*National Intelligence Daily*
NIE	National Intelligence Estimate
NIIC	Narcotics Issues Intelligence Committee
NIMA	National Imagery and Mapping Agency
NIO	National Intelligence Officer
NIPB	National Intelligence Production Board
NIST	National Intelligence Support Team
NJMIC	National Joint Military Intelligence Center
NMIC	National Maritime Intelligence Center
NMJIC	National Military Joint Intelligence Center
NOC	Non-Official Cover
NOIC	Navy Operational Intelligence Center
NPC	DCI Nonproliferation Center
NPIC	National Photographic Interpretation Center
NRD	National Resources Division
NRL	Naval Research Laboratory
NRO	National Reconnaissance Office
NROC	National Resettlement Operations Center
NRPC	Naval Regional Processing Center
NSA	National Security Agency
NSAM	National Security Action Memorandum
NSC	National Security Council
NSCIC	National Security Council Intelligence Committee
NSCID	National Security Council Intelligence Directive
NSD	National Security Directive
NSDD	National Security Decision Directive
NSDM	National Security Decision Memorandum
NSG	Naval Security Group
NSGA	Naval Security Group Activity
NSGC	Naval Security Group Command
NSOC	National SIGINT Operations Center/National Security Operations Center
NSPG	National Security Planning Group
NSPO	National Security Program Office
NSRL	National SIGINT Requirements List
NTIC	Naval Technical Intelligence Center
NTPC	National Telemetry Processing Center
NUDET	Nuclear Detonation

OAAT	Office of Advanced Analytic Tools, Directorate of Science and Technology, CIA
OACSI	Office of the Assistant Chief of Staff, Intelligence
OACSMI	Office of the Assistant Chief of Staff for Missile Intelligence
OAG	Operations Advisory Group
OBC	Optical Bar Camera
OBST	Operations Base Stuttgart
OD&E	Office of Development and Engineering
OEE	Office of Export Enforcement
OEI	Office of Energy Intelligence
OES	Office of Executive Support, Department of Commerce
OFCO	Offensive Counterintelligence Operations
OIR	Office of Information Resources
OIR	Office of Intelligence Resources
OIS	Office of Intelligence Support, Department of Treasury
OL-FR	Operating Location-France
OMA	Office of Military Affairs
OMB	Office of Management and Budget
ONE	Office of National Estimates
ONI	Office of Naval Intelligence
OPEC	Organization of Petroleum Exporting Countries
ORD	Office of Research and Development, Directorate of Science and Technology, CIA
ORTT	Office of Resources, Trade and Technology, Directorate of Intelligence, CIA
OSA	Office of System Applications, NRO
OSC	Open Source Committee
OSD	Office of the Secretary of Defense
OSI	Office of Scientific Intelligence
OSIS	Ocean Surveillance Information System
OSIS	Open Source Information System
OSO	Office of SIGINT Operations
OSS	Office of Strategic Services
OSS	Office of Support Services, Directorate of Intelligence, CIA
OTH	Over-the-Horizon
OTI	Office of Transnational Issues, Directorate of Intelligence, CIA
OTS	Office of Technical Services, Directorate of Science and Technology, CIA
OTSTI	Office of Transnational Security and Technology Issues, Directorate of Intelligence, CIA
OWI	Office of Weapons Intelligence, Directorate of Science and Technology, CIA

OWTP	Office of Weapons Technology and Proliferation, Directorate of Intelligence, CIA
PACBAR	Pacific Barrier Radar
PACFAST	Forward Area Support Team Pacific
PACOM	Pacific Command
PARCS	Perimeter Acquisition Radar Characterization System
PARPRO	Peacetime Aerial Reconnaissance Program
PASS	Passive Space Surveillance System
PAVE PAWS	Perimeter Acquisition Vehicle Entry Phased Array Warning System
PCC	Policy Coordinating Committee
PCG	Planning and Coordination Group
PD	Presidential Directive
PDB	*President's Daily Brief*
PDD	Presidential Decision Directive
PFIAB	President's Foreign Intelligence Advisory Board
PFLP-GC	Popular Front for the Liberation of Palestine—General Command
PLO	Palestine Liberation Organization
PMEL	Precision Measurement Equipment Laboratory
PNIO	Priority National Intelligence Objective
PORTS	Portable Receive and Transmit System
PRC	People's Republic of China
PRC	Policy Review Committee
PRC-I	Policy Review Committee—Intelligence
PRM	Presidential Review Memorandum
PUK	Patriotic Union of Kurdistan
QRT	Quick Reaction Team
RADEC	Radiation Detection
RAF	Royal Air Force
RASA	Radionuclide Aerosol Sampler/Analyzers
RAW	Research and Analysis Wing (India)
RDT&E	Research, Development, Test, and Evaluation
ROD	Reconnaissance Operations Division
ROFA	Remote Operations Facility, Airborne
ROSE	Rich Open Source Environment
RPV	Remote Piloted Vehicle
RRS	Remote Relay System
RS	Reconnaissance Squadron
RSOC	Regional SIGINT Operations Center
RSVC	Reconnaissance Satellite Vulnerability Computer Program
RTN	Royal Thai Navy
RTOS	Real-Time Optical System

RV	Reentry Vehicle
S&T	Science and Technology
S&TI	Scientific and Technical Intelligence
SAC	Strategic Air Command
SAR	Synthetic Aperture Radar
SATRAN	Satellite Reconnaissance Advanced Notice
SB	Sluzba Bezpeicezecstwa (Security Service, Poland)
SBI	Special Background Investigation
SBIRS	Space-Based Infrared System
SBSS	Space-Based Surveillance System
SCC	Space Control Center
SCC	Special Coordination Committee
SCE	Service Cryptologic Element
SCI	Sensitive Compartmented Information
SCOL	SIGINT Combined Operating List
SDI	Strategic Defense Initiative
SDIE	Special Defense Intelligence Estimate
SE	Special Estimate
SFS	Seismic Field Subsystem
SHF	Super High Frequency
SI	Special Intelligence
SIG	Senior Interagency Group
SIG-I	Senior Interagency Group—Intelligence
SIGINT	Signals Intelligence
SIOP	Single Integrated Operational Plan
SIPRI	Stockholm International Peace Research Institute
SIR	Special Intelligence Report
SIRVES	SIGINT Requirements Validation and Evaluation Committee
SIS	Special Intelligence Service
SISDE	Servizio per le Informazione e la Sicurezza Democratica (Democratic Security and Information Service, Italy)
SISMI	Servizio per le Informazione e la Sicurezza Militare (Military Security and Information Service, Italy)
SLBM	Submarine Launched Ballistic Missile
SMS	Special Monitoring Service (Russia)
SNCP	Special Navy Control Program
SNIE	Special National Intelligence Estimate
SOC	Space Operations Center
SOFAR	Sound Fixing and Ranging
SOI	Space Object Identification
SORS	SIGINT Overhead Reconnaissance Subcommittee
SOSUS	Sound Surveillance System
SOUTHCOM	Southern Command

SPATS   *Strategic Posture Aerospace Threat Summary*
SPIN   *Space Intelligence Notes*
SPSS   Space Surveillance Squadron
SRO   Sensitive Reconnaissance Operations
SSC   Space Surveillance Center
SSCI   Senate Select Committee on Intelligence
SSN   Space Surveillance Network
SSTS   Space Surveillance and Tracking System
STARs   Systems Threat Assessment Reports
START   Strategic Arms Reduction Talks
STIC   Scientific and Technical Intelligence Committee
STRATCOM   Strategic Command
STRATJIC   Strategic Command Joint Intelligence Center
SUSLO   Special U.S. Liaison Officer
SVR   Satellite Vulnerability Reports
SVRR   Russian Foreign Intelligence Service
SWINT   Safe Window Intelligence
SYERS   SENIOR YEAR Electro-Optical Reconnaissance System
TACDIL   Tactical Digital Information Link
TAD   Terrorism Analysis Division, DIA
TARPS   Tactical Air Reconnaissance Pod System
TCA   Technical Collection Agency
TCP   Tactical Cryptologic Program
TDF   Tactical Digital Facsimile
TDO   Technology Development Office
TDRS   Tracking and Data Relay Satellite
TELINT   Telemetry Intelligence
TGIF   Transportable Ground Intercept Facility
TIARA   Tactical Intelligence and Related Activities
TIBS   Tactical Information Broadcast Service
TID   Technical Intelligence Division
TK   Talent-Keyhole
TM   Thematic Mapper
TMO   Technology Management Office
TOS   Transportable Optical System
TRANSCOM   U.S. Transportation Command
TSD   Technical Services Division, Directorate of Operations, CIA
TTIC   Technology Transfer Intelligence Committee
TW/AA   Tactical Warning/Attack Assessment
TWD   Terrorism Warning Division, DIA
TWG   Transnational Warfare Group
UAV   Unmanned Aerial Vehicle
UCP   Unified Command Plan

UFO	UHF Follow-On
UGS	Unattended Ground Sensor
UKUSA	United Kingdom–United States Security Agreement
UMS	Unattended MASINT Sensor
UNSCOM	United Nations Special Commission
USACOM	United States Atlantic Command
USAEDS	U.S. Atomic Energy Detection System
USAREUR	United States Army Europe
USCIB	United States Communications Intelligence Board
USCIB/IC	United States Communications Intelligence Board/Intelligence Committee
USIB	United States Intelligence Board
USLANTCOM	United States Atlantic Command
USSID	United States Signals Intelligence Directive
USSOCOM	United States Special Operations Command
USSPACECOM	United States Space Command
USSS	United States SIGINT System
VRK	Very Restricted Knowledge
WMD	Weapons of Mass Destruction
WRS	Weather Reconnaissance Squadron
WSSAG	Weapons and Space Systems Advisory Group
WSSIC	Weapons and Space Systems Intelligence Committee

INDEX

DATE DUE

NOV 0 8 2003			
NOV 1 7 2004			